THE COCKTAIL BIBLE

THE COCKTAIL BIBLE

Over 3,500 recipes

STEVE QUIRK

CONTENTS

TEQUIL

BOURBON

Cognac

VODKA

ABSINTHE

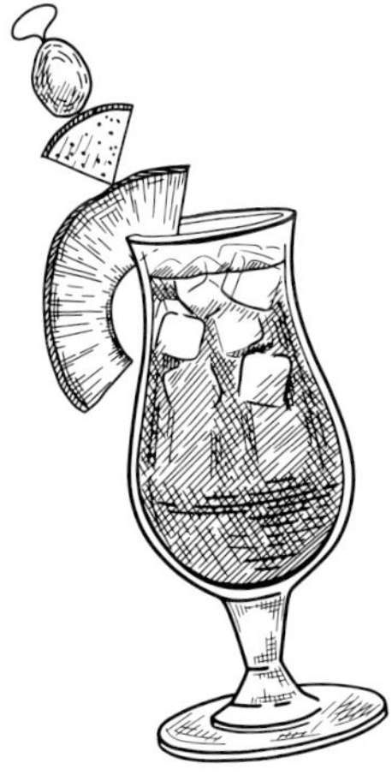

TEQUILA
HECHO
EN MEXICO
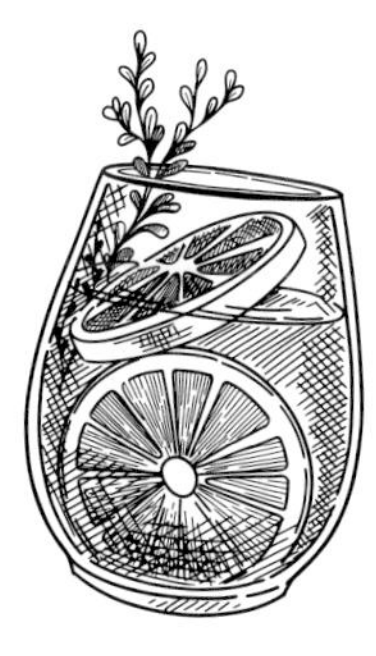

Brandy

Brandy is distilled from grapes and is produced in the majority of Wine-producing nations around the world. If Brandy is distilled from any other fruits it must be stated on the bottle's label. Brandy is distilled for a minimum of two years, although most Brandies are distilled for a longer period. The vast majority of American Brandies are produced in California where the manufactures usually complete the whole process of production from growing their own grapes through to distilling, blending and eventually marketing their final Brandy product.

Armagnac is distilled from grapes and produced in the Armagnac region of France, west of Toulouse. Armagnac is not unlike Cognac although it is only distilled the once and is aged in cask for a longer period than Cognac, leaving it with a stronger richer flavour.

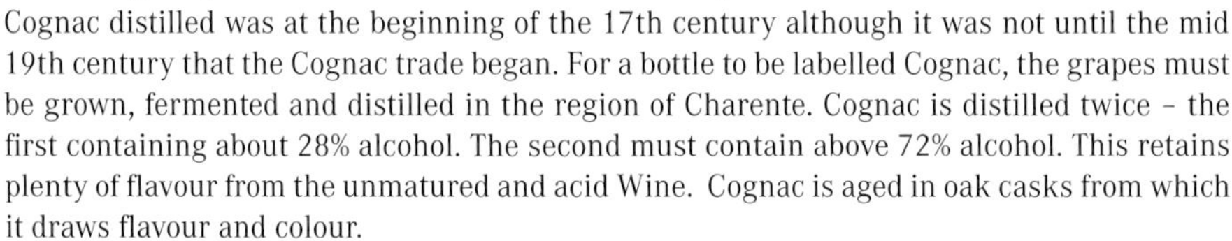

Cognac is a fine smooth Brandy produced in Charente, France and is arguably defined as the world's finest Brandy. The first Cognac distilled was at the beginning of the 17th century although it was not until the mid 19th century that the Cognac trade began. For a bottle to be labelled Cognac, the grapes must be grown, fermented and distilled in the region of Charente. Cognac is distilled twice – the first containing about 28% alcohol. The second must contain above 72% alcohol. This retains plenty of flavour from the unmatured and acid Wine. Cognac is aged in oak casks from which it draws flavour and colour.

Fruit Brandies are Brandy–based liqueurs with a wide variety available: Apple Brandies are produced from apple Cider and include Calvados which is produced in Normandy, France and Applejack which is produced in America.

Kirsch is a dry, clear and bitter cherry-flavour Brandy.

Slivovitz is Brandy produced from plums.

Poire Williams is a pear flavour Fruit Brandy distilled from william pears or bartlet pears.

Framboise is Brandy distilled from raspberries and Fraise which is a Fruit Brandy that is distilled from strawberries.

Other Fruit Brandies are produced from apricots, blackberries, cherries and peaches, just to name the more popular varieties.

The quality markings for Brandy and Cognac are as follows:

VSOP (very superior old pale)
VSO (very superior old)
VOP (very old pale)
*** (three stars)
** (two stars)
* (one star)

Brandy Crusta

36.3% ALC/VOL • 2.8 STD DRINKS

90ml (3 fl oz) Brandy
5ml (1/6 fl oz) Maraschino Liqueur
2 dashes Curaçao
Dash Angostura Bitters
Maraschino Cherry
Slice of Lemon

Prepare a champagne saucer with a sugar frosted rim – moistened with lemon juice. Pour Brandy, Liqueur, Curaçao and Bitters into a cocktail shaker over ice. Shake and strain into prepared glass. Garnish with a cherry and slice of lemon then serve.

Grenadier

27.5% ALC/VOL • 2.1 STD DRINKS

60ml (2 fl oz) Brandy
30ml (1 fl oz) Green Ginger Wine
1 teaspoon Sugar Syrup
Dash Jamaica Ginger

Pour ingredients into a mixing glass over ice and stir. Strain into a chilled cocktail glass and serve.

Pit Stop

15.5% ALC/VOL • 1.5 STD DRINKS

30ml (1 fl oz) Cherry Brandy
30ml (1 fl oz) Kirsch
5ml (1/6 fl oz) Amaretto
60ml (2 fl oz) Lemonade

Pour Brandy, Kirsch and Amaretto into an old-fashioned glass over cracked ice then stir. Add lemonade, stir gently and serve.

Golden Afternoon

9.2% ALC/VOL • 1.1 STD DRINKS

30ml (1 fl oz) Brandy
15ml (½ fl oz) Dry Vermouth
15ml (½ fl oz) Lime Syrup
90ml (3 fl oz) Dry Ginger Ale
Slice of Lime

Pour Brandy, Vermouth and syrup into a highball glass over ice then stir. Add Ginger Ale and stir gently. Garnish with a slice of lime and serve.
This drink is also known as Southerly Buster.

Bonaparte Velvet

16.3% ALC/VOL • 2 STD DRINKS

30ml (1 fl oz) Cognac
30ml (1 fl oz) Mandarine Napoleon
5ml (1/6 fl oz) Frangelico
3 scoops Vanilla Ice Cream
Maraschino Cherry
Slice of Orange

Pour Cognac, Mandarine Napoleon and Frangelico into a blender over small amount of crushed ice then add ice cream. Blend and pour into a chilled highball glass. Garnish with a cherry and slice of orange then serve with 2 straws.

Cherbourg

30.8% ALC/VOL • 1.8 STD DRINKS

30ml (1 fl oz) Brandy
15ml (½ fl oz) Applejack
15ml (½ fl oz) Cointreau
15ml (½ fl oz) Fresh Lemon Juice

Pour ingredients into a cocktail shaker over ice and shake. Strain into a chilled cocktail glass and serve.

Mandarin

16.3% ALC/VOL • 1.7 STD DRINKS

20ml (⅔ fl oz) Apricot Brandy
20ml (⅔ fl oz) Triple Sec
15ml (½ fl oz) Bénédictine
10ml (⅓ fl oz) Galliano
5ml (1/6 fl oz) Mandarine Napoleon
30ml (1 fl oz) Fresh Orange Juice
30ml (1 fl oz) Thick Cream
Cherry
Slice of Orange

Pour Brandy, Triple Sec, Bénédictine, Galliano, Mandarine Napoleon, juice and cream into a blender over crushed ice. Blend and pour into a chilled champagne saucer. Garnish with a cherry and slice of orange then serve.

Star Ruby

28.3% ALC/VOL • 1.9 STD DRINKS

45ml (1½ fl oz) Brandy
15ml (½ fl oz) Cherry Brandy
15ml (½ fl oz) Dry Vermouth
3 dashes Maraschino Liqueur
2 dashes Orange Bitters
5ml (1/6 fl oz) Fresh Lemon Juice

Pour ingredients into a mixing glass over ice and stir. Strain into a chilled cocktail glass and serve.

Steeplejack

11.2% ALC/VOL • 1.9 STD DRINKS

60ml (2 fl oz) Applejack
75ml (2½ fl oz) Apple Juice
5ml (1/6 fl oz) Lime Juice
75ml (2½ fl oz) Soda Water
Slice of Lime

Pour Applejack and juices into a collins glass over ice then stir. Add soda and stir gently. Garnish with a slice of lime and serve.

Fiord

21.4% ALC/VOL • 1.4 STD DRINKS

30ml (1 fl oz) Brandy
15ml (½ fl oz) Aquavit
5ml (1/6 fl oz) Grenadine
15ml (½ fl oz) Fresh Lime Juice

15ml (½ fl oz) Fresh
Orange Juice

Pour ingredients into a cocktail shaker over ice and shake. Strain into a chilled cocktail glass and serve.

Wallick's Special

13.3% ALC/VOL • 1.3 STD DRINKS

45ml (1½ fl oz) Brandy
2 dashes Grenadine
45ml (1½ fl oz) Fresh Cream
½ teaspoon Sugar Syrup
White of 1 Egg

Pour ingredients into a cocktail shaker over ice and shake. Strain into a chilled brandy balloon and serve.

Classic

28.4% ALC/VOL • 2.4 STD DRINKS

60ml (2 fl oz) Brandy
15ml (½ fl oz) Curaçao
15ml (½ fl oz) Maraschino
Liqueur
15ml (½ fl oz) Fresh
Lemon Juice
Slice of Lemon

Pour Brandy, Curaçao, Liqueur and juice into a cocktail shaker over ice. Shake and strain into a chilled cocktail glass. Garnish with a slice of lemon and serve.

Cherry Fizz

8.4% ALC/VOL • 1.1 STD DRINKS

60ml (2 fl oz) Cherry Brandy
15ml (½ fl oz) Fresh
Lemon Juice
90ml (3 fl oz) Soda Water
Maraschino Cherry

Pour Brandy and juice into a cocktail shaker over ice. Shake and strain into a highball glass over ice. Add soda and stir gently. Garnish with a cherry and serve.

Horse's Neck

12.5% ALC/VOL • 1.3 STD DRINKS

45ml (1½ fl oz) Brandy
Dash Angostura Bitters
90ml (3 fl oz) Dry Ginger Ale
Long Twist of Lemon Peel

Place lemon peel into a chilled highball glass with one end of peel hooked over rim of glass (thus giving the effect of a horse's neck) and the remainder of peel spiraling down inside of glass then fill glass with ice. Add Brandy and Bitters then stir. Add Ginger Ale, stir gently and serve.

Peach Sangaree

5.1% ALC/VOL • 0.6 STD DRINKS

30ml (1 fl oz) Peach Brandy
5ml (1/6 fl oz) Port
120ml (4 fl oz) Soda Water
Nutmeg

Pour Brandy into a highball glass over ice and add soda then stir gently. Layer Port on top and sprinkle nutmeg on top then serve.

Pompeii

21% ALC/VOL • 1.6 STD DRINKS

30ml (1 fl oz) Brandy
23ml (¾ fl oz) White Crème
De Cacao
15ml (½ fl oz) Amaretto
30ml (1 fl oz) Thick Cream
Almond Flakes

Pour Brandy, Cacao, Amaretto and cream into a cocktail shaker over ice. Shake and strain into a chilled champagne saucer. Sprinkle almond flakes on top and serve.

Applejack No.1

35.9% ALC/VOL • 1.5 STD DRINKS

45ml (1½ fl oz) Applejack
2 dashes Orange Bitters
Dash Angostura Bitters
1 teaspoon Sugar Syrup
Slice of Orange

Pour Applejack, Bitters and sugar into a cocktail shaker over ice. Shake and strain into a chilled cocktail glass. Garnish with a slice of orange and serve.

Ritz Royal

6.5% ALC/VOL • 0.9 STD DRINKS

30ml (1 fl oz) Peach Brandy
30ml (1 fl oz) Punt e Mes
30ml (1 fl oz) Fresh
Lemon Juice
Dash Sugar Syrup
90ml (3 fl oz) Soda Water

Pour Brandy, Punt e Mes, juice and sugar into a cocktail shaker over ice. Shake and strain into a chilled champagne flute. Add soda, stir gently and serve.

Brandied Apricot Flip

16.4% ALC/VOL • 1.4 STD DRINKS

30ml (1 fl oz) Brandy
30ml (1 fl oz) Apricot Brandy
1 teaspoon Sugar Syrup
1 Fresh Egg
Nutmeg

Pour Brandies, sugar and egg into a cocktail shaker over ice. Shake and strain into a chilled goblet. Sprinkle nutmeg on top and serve.

Foxhound

26.5% ALC/VOL • 1.5 STD DRINKS

45ml (1½ fl oz) Brandy
5ml (1/6 fl oz) Kümmel
15ml (½ fl oz) Cranberry Juice
5ml (1/6 fl oz) Fresh
Lemon Juice
Slice of Lemon

Pour Brandy, Kümmel and juices into a cocktail shaker over ice. Shake and strain into an old-fashioned glass over ice. Garnish with a slice of lemon and serve.

Seven Dials Cocktail

19% ALC/VOL • 1.6 STD DRINKS

30ml (1 fl oz) Cognac
30ml (1 fl oz) Dark Crème De Cacao
5ml (1/6 fl oz) Grand Marnier
30ml (1 fl oz) Thick Cream
Yolk of 1 Egg

Pour ingredients into a cocktail shaker over ice and shake. Strain into an old-fashioned glass over ice and serve.

Brandy Punch Cocktail

18.8% ALC/VOL • 2.2 STD DRINKS

60ml (2 fl oz) Brandy
15ml (½ fl oz) Cointreau
75ml (2½ fl oz) Dry Ginger Ale
Slice of Orange
Sprig of Fresh Mint

Pour Brandy and Cointreau into a goblet over crushed ice then stir. Add Ginger Ale and stir gently. Garnish with a slice of orange and sprig of mint then serve.

Apple Buck

12.7% ALC/VOL • 1.6 STD DRINKS

45ml (1½ fl oz) Applejack
5ml (1/6 fl oz) Ginger Brandy
90ml (3 fl oz) Dry Ginger Ale
½ Fresh Lemon

Pour Applejack and Brandy into a collins glass over ice. Twist ½ lemon above drink to release juice and add spent shell then stir. Add Ginger Ale, stir gently and serve.

Thanksgiving Special

25.7% ALC/VOL • 1.4 STD DRINKS

23ml (¾ fl oz) Apricot Brandy
23ml (¾ fl oz) Dry Gin
23ml (¾ fl oz) Dry Vermouth
Dash Fresh Lemon Juice
Maraschino Cherry

Pour Brandy, Gin, Vermouth and juice into a cocktail shaker over ice. Shake and strain into a chilled cocktail glass. Garnish with a cherry and serve.

Parson Weems

8.6% ALC/VOL • 1 STD DRINK

15ml (½ fl oz) Brandy
15ml (½ fl oz) Cherry Brandy
15ml (½ fl oz) Maraschino Liqueur
45ml (1½ fl oz) Fresh Milk (chilled)
2 scoops Chocolate Ice Cream

Pour Brandies, Liqueur and milk into a blender without ice then add ice cream. Blend until smooth and pour into a chilled brandy balloon then serve.

Calvados Cream

19.2% ALC/VOL • 1.9 STD DRINKS

60ml (2 fl oz) Calvados
30ml (1 fl oz) Thick Cream
15ml (½ fl oz) Fresh Lemon Juice
1 teaspoon Pineapple Syrup
½ Egg White

Pour ingredients into a cocktail shaker over ice and shake. Strain into a chilled cocktail glass and serve.

Saratoga Cocktail

31.9% ALC/VOL • 1.9 STD DRINKS

60ml (2 fl oz) Brandy
2 dashes Angostura Bitters
2 dashes Maraschino Liqueur
5ml (1/6 fl oz) Fresh Lemon Juice
5ml (1/6 fl oz) Pineapple Juice

Pour ingredients into a cocktail shaker over ice and shake. Strain into a chilled cocktail glass and serve.

Pink Carnation

8% ALC/VOL • 0.9 STD DRINKS

15ml (½ fl oz) Brandy
15ml (½ fl oz) Cherry Brandy
15ml (½ fl oz) Cranberry Liqueur
45ml (1½ fl oz) Fresh Milk (chilled)
2 scoops Vanilla Ice Cream

Pour Brandies, Liqueur and milk into a blender without ice then add ice cream. Blend until smooth and pour into a chilled brandy balloon then serve.

Waterbury

20.6% ALC/VOL • 1.3 STD DRINKS

45ml (1½ fl oz) Brandy
3 dashes Grenadine
15ml (½ fl oz) Fresh Lime Juice
½ teaspoon Sugar Syrup
½ Egg White

Prepare a cocktail glass with a sugar frosted rim. Pour ingredients into a cocktail shaker over ice and shake. Strain into prepared glass and serve.

Apple Blossom

19% ALC/VOL • 1.4 STD DRINKS

45ml (1½ fl oz) Applejack
30ml (1 fl oz) Apple Juice
15ml (½ fl oz) Fresh Lemon Juice
1 teaspoon Maple Syrup
Slice of Lemon

Pour Applejack, juices and syrup into a blender over crushed ice. Blend and pour into a chilled champagne saucer. Garnish with a slice of lemon and serve.

Barton Special

39.3% ALC/VOL • 2.8 STD DRINKS

45ml (1½ fl oz) Apple Brandy
23ml (¾ fl oz) Dry Gin
23ml (¾ fl oz) Scotch Whisky
Twist of Lemon Peel

Pour Brandy, Gin and Whisky into a cocktail shaker over ice. Shake and strain into a chilled cocktail glass. Garnish with lemon peel and serve.

Fancy Brandy

34.7% ALC/VOL • 1.9 STD DRINKS

60ml (2 fl oz) Brandy
5ml (1/6 fl oz) Cointreau
Dash Angostura Bitters
1 teaspoon Sugar Syrup
Wedge of Lemon

Pour Brandy, Cointreau, Bitters and sugar into a cocktail shaker over ice. Shake and strain into an old-fashioned glass over ice. Garnish with a wedge of lemon and serve.

Bitter Apple

37.2% ALC/VOL • 2 STD DRINKS

60ml (2 fl oz) Applejack
2 dashes Angostura Bitters
5ml (1/6 fl oz) Soda Water
Twist of Lemon Peel

Pour Applejack and Bitters into an old-fashioned glass over crushed ice then stir. Add soda – do not stir. Twist lemon peel above drink and place remainder of peel into drink then serve.
This drink is also known as Apple Bitter.

Gold Coaster

12.7% ALC/VOL • 1.4 STD DRINKS

30ml (1 fl oz) Brandy
30ml (1 fl oz) Dry Vermouth
5ml (1/6 fl oz) Maraschino Liqueur
60ml (2 fl oz) Pineapple Juice
15ml (½ fl oz) Fresh Lemon Juice
Slice of Pineapple

Pour Brandy, Vermouth, Liqueur and juices into a cocktail shaker over ice. Shake and strain into a collins glass over ice. Garnish with a slice of pineapple and serve.

Apollo 44

37.4% ALC/VOL • 2.2 STD DRINKS

40ml (1⅓ fl oz) Apple Brandy
20ml (⅔ fl oz) Cointreau
10ml (⅓ fl oz) Pimm's No.1
5ml (1/6 fl oz) Licor 43

Pour ingredients into a cocktail shaker over ice and shake. Strain into a chilled old-fashioned glass and serve.

Dizzy Dame

21.1% ALC/VOL • 1.5 STD DRINKS

30ml (1 fl oz) Brandy
23ml (¾ fl oz) Kahlúa
15ml (½ fl oz) Cherry Brandy
23ml (¾ fl oz) Thick Cream
Maraschino Cherry

Pour Brandies, Kahlúa and cream into a cocktail shaker over ice. Shake and strain into an old-fashioned glass over ice. Garnish with a cherry and serve.

Blackberry Flip

16.6% ALC/VOL • 1.2 STD DRINKS

45ml (1½ fl oz) Blackberry Brandy
1 teaspoon Sugar Syrup
1 Fresh Egg
Nutmeg

Pour Brandy, sugar and egg into a cocktail shaker over ice. Shake and strain into a chilled goblet. Sprinkle nutmeg on top and serve.

Puerto Apple

28.2% ALC/VOL • 1.9 STD DRINKS

38ml (1¼ fl oz) Applejack
23ml (¾ fl oz) Light Rum
8ml (¼ fl oz) Fresh Lime Juice
1½ teaspoons Sugar Syrup
Slice of Lime

Pour Applejack, Rum, juice and sugar into a cocktail shaker over ice. Shake and strain into an old-fashioned glass over ice. Garnish with a slice of lime and serve.

Sloe Brandy

32.7% ALC/VOL • 2.1 STD DRINKS

60ml (2 fl oz) Brandy
15ml (½ fl oz) Sloe Gin
5ml (1/6 fl oz) Fresh Lemon Juice
Twist of Lemon Peel

Pour Brandy, Gin and juice into a cocktail shaker over ice. Shake and strain into a chilled cocktail glass. Twist lemon peel above drink and place remainder of peel into drink then serve.

Apple River Inner Tube

15.1% ALC/VOL • 1.4 STD DRINKS

30ml (1 fl oz) Brandy
30ml (1 fl oz) Dark Crème De Cacao
2 scoops Vanilla Ice Cream
Slice of Spiced Apple

Pour Brandy and Cacao into a blender without ice then add ice cream. Blend and pour into a chilled champagne saucer. Garnish with a slice of apple and serve.

Brandy and Cassis

24.2% ALC/VOL • 1.9 STD DRINKS

60ml (2 fl oz) Brandy
10ml (⅓ fl oz) Crème De Cassis
30ml (1 fl oz) Fresh Lemon Juice
Twist of Lemon Peel

Pour Brandy, Cassis and juice into a cocktail shaker over ice. Shake and strain into a chilled cocktail glass. Garnish with lemon peel and serve.

Frozen Brandy and Port

17.6% ALC/VOL • 1.7 STD DRINKS

45ml (1½ fl oz) Brandy
30ml (1 fl oz) Port
1 teaspoon Sugar Syrup
1 Fresh Egg
Nutmeg

Pour Brandy, Port, sugar and egg into a blender over crushed ice. Blend and pour into a chilled champagne saucer. Sprinkle nutmeg on top and serve.

Cape Snow

15.6% ALC/VOL • 1.5 STD DRINKS

30ml (1 fl oz) Brandy
30ml (1 fl oz) Van Der Hum
2 scoops Vanilla Ice Cream
Slice of Orange

Pour Brandy and Van Der Hum into a blender without ice then add ice cream. Blend until smooth and pour into a chilled champagne saucer. Garnish with a slice of orange and serve.

Apricot Sour

14.8% ALC/VOL • 1.1 STD DRINKS

60ml (2 fl oz) Apricot Brandy
30ml (1 fl oz) Fresh Lemon Juice
½ teaspoon Sugar Syrup
Maraschino Cherry
Slice of Orange

Pour Brandy, juice and sugar into a cocktail shaker over ice. Shake and strain into a chilled sour glass. Garnish with a cherry and slice of orange then serve.

Brandy Alexander

20% ALC/VOL • 1.4 STD DRINKS

30ml (1 fl oz) Brandy
30ml (1 fl oz) Dark Crème De Cacao
30ml (1 fl oz) Thick Cream
Nutmeg

Pour Brandy, Cacao and cream into a cocktail shaker over ice. Shake and strain into a chilled cocktail glass. Sprinkle nutmeg on top and serve.

Indycar

9.4% ALC/VOL • 1.4 STD DRINKS

30ml (1 fl oz) Apricot Brandy
30ml (1 fl oz) Dry Vermouth
15ml (½ fl oz) Triple Sec
30ml (1 fl oz) Passion-Fruit Juice
90ml (3 fl oz) Lemonade

Pour Brandy, Vermouth, Triple Sec and juice into a highball glass over ice then stir. Add lemonade, stir gently and serve.

Tee Off

8.5% ALC/VOL • 1.1 STD DRINKS

30ml (1 fl oz) Brandy
15ml (½ fl oz) Peppermint Schnapps
60ml (2 fl oz) Fresh Orange Juice
60ml (2 fl oz) Pineapple Juice

Pour ingredients into a cocktail shaker over ice and shake. Strain into a collins glass over ice and serve.

Francine

13.4% ALC/VOL • 1.4 STD DRINKS

23ml (¾ fl oz) Cognac
23ml (¾ fl oz) Raspberry Liqueur
23ml (¾ fl oz) Sweet Vermouth
60ml (2 fl oz) Lemonade
Raspberry
Slice of Lemon

Pour Cognac, Liqueur and Vermouth into a cocktail shaker over ice. Shake and strain into an old-fashioned glass over ice. Add lemonade and stir gently. Garnish with a raspberry and slice of lemon then serve.

Cherry Sling

18.4% ALC/VOL • 1.1 STD DRINKS

60ml (2 fl oz) Cherry Brandy
15ml (½ fl oz) Fresh Lemon Juice
Twist of Lemon Peel

Pour Brandy and juice into an old-fashioned glass over ice then stir. Garnish with lemon peel and serve.

Rabbit's Foot

21.1% ALC/VOL • 1.4 STD DRINKS

23ml (¾ fl oz) Applejack
23ml (¾ fl oz) Light Rum
8ml (¼ fl oz) Grenadine
15ml (½ fl oz) Fresh Lemon Juice
15ml (½ fl oz) Fresh Orange Juice
Slice of Orange

Pour Applejack, Rum, Grenadine and juices into a cocktail shaker over ice. Shake and strain into an old-fashioned glass over ice. Garnish with a slice of orange and serve.

R.A.F. Cocktail

29.1% ALC/VOL • 2.1 STD DRINKS

53ml (1¾ fl oz) Applejack
23ml (¾ fl oz) Apricot Brandy
15ml (½ fl oz) Fresh
Lemon Juice

Pour ingredients into a cocktail shaker over ice and shake. Strain into a chilled cocktail glass and serve.

Better than Anything

23.8% ALC/VOL • 1.6 STD DRINKS

30ml (1 fl oz) Brandy
30ml (1 fl oz) Cherry Brandy
8ml (¼ fl oz) Curaçao
8ml (¼ fl oz) Grenadine
8ml (¼ fl oz) Fresh
Lemon Juice

Pour ingredients into a cocktail shaker over ice and shake. Strain into a chilled cocktail glass and serve.

Dutch Pear Frappé

25.7% ALC/VOL • 1.7 STD DRINKS

38ml (1¼ fl oz) Pear Brandy
23ml (¾ fl oz) Vandermint
15ml (½ fl oz) Thick Cream
Whipped Cream

Pour Brandy, Vandermint and thick cream into a blender over crushed ice. Blend until smooth and pour into a chilled old-fashioned glass over a few ice cubes. Float whipped cream on top and serve with 2 short straws.

Yo Ho

39% ALC/VOL • 2.8 STD DRINKS

30ml (1 fl oz) Calvados
30ml (1 fl oz) Light Rum
30ml (1 fl oz) Swedish Punsch
Twist of Lemon Peel

Pour Calvados, Rum and Punsch into a cocktail shaker over ice. Shake and strain into a chilled cocktail glass. Garnish with lemon peel and serve.

Apricot Crush

15.3% ALC/VOL • 1.3 STD DRINKS

45ml (1½ fl oz) Apricot Brandy
15ml (½ fl oz) Light Rum
30ml (1 fl oz) Fresh
Orange Juice
15ml (½ fl oz) Fresh
Lemon Juice

Pour ingredients into a cocktail shaker over ice and shake. Strain into a champagne saucer over crushed ice and serve.

Apple Grand Marnier

40% ALC/VOL • 1.9 STD DRINKS

30ml (1 fl oz) Calvados
15ml (½ fl oz) Cognac
15ml (½ fl oz) Grand Marnier
Twist of Lemon Peel
Twist of Orange Peel

Pour Calvados, Cognac and Grand Marnier into a mixing glass over ice. Stir and strain into an old-fashioned glass over ice. Twist lemon and orange peels above drink. Place remainder of peels into drink and serve.

Arch de Triumph Cocktail

22.8% ALC/VOL • 0.6 STD DRINKS

20ml (⅔ fl oz) Calvados
10ml (⅓ fl oz) Fresh
Lemon Juice
1 teaspoon Sugar Syrup

Pour ingredients into a cocktail shaker over ice and shake. Strain into a chilled cocktail glass and serve.

Missile Stopper

14% ALC/VOL • 1.2 STD DRINKS

30ml (1 fl oz) Cognac
15ml (½ fl oz) Strawberry
Liqueur
5ml (1/6 fl oz) Grenadine
30ml (1 fl oz) Grapefruit Juice
30ml (1 fl oz) Pineapple Juice

Pour ingredients into a cocktail shaker over ice and shake. Strain into an old-fashioned glass over ice and serve.

Brandy Crystal

29.9% ALC/VOL • 2.1 STD DRINKS

30ml (1 fl oz) Brandy
30ml (1 fl oz) Dry Gin
30ml (1 fl oz) Sweet Vermouth
Dash Angostura Bitters

Pour ingredients into a cocktail shaker over ice and shake. Strain into a chilled cocktail glass and serve.

Lutteur

13.1% ALC/VOL • 1.9 STD DRINKS

30ml (1 fl oz) Cognac
15ml (½ fl oz) Mandarine
Napoleon
15ml (½ fl oz) Vodka
120ml (4 fl oz) Bitter-Lemon
Soda
Maraschino Cherry
Slice of Orange

Pour Cognac, Mandarine Napoleon and Vodka into a collins glass over ice then stir. Add soda and stir gently. Garnish with a cherry and slice of orange then serve.

Sweet Talk

26.8% ALC/VOL • 1.3 STD DRINKS

30ml (1 fl oz) Blackberry Brandy
15ml (½ fl oz) Brandy
15ml (½ fl oz) Thick Cream

Pour ingredients into a cocktail shaker over ice and shake. Strain into a chilled cocktail glass and serve.

Brandy Squirt

7.7% ALC/VOL • 1.3 STD DRINKS

45ml (1½ fl oz) Brandy
5ml (1/6 fl oz) Grenadine
1 teaspoon Sugar Syrup
150ml (5 fl oz) Soda Water
Slice of Pineapple
Strawberry

Pour Brandy, Grenadine and sugar into a cocktail shaker over ice. Shake and strain into a chilled hurricane glass. Add soda and stir gently. Garnish with a slice of pineapple and a strawberry then serve.

On the Square

30.8% ALC/VOL • 1.5 STD DRINKS

30ml (1 fl oz) Apricot Brandy
15ml (½ fl oz) Calvados
15ml (½ fl oz) Dry Gin

Pour ingredients into a mixing glass over ice and stir. Strain into a chilled cocktail glass and serve.

Shoo-in

15.1% ALC/VOL • 2.5 STD DRINKS

30ml (1 fl oz) Brandy
30ml (1 fl oz) Light Rum
15ml (½ fl oz) Dark Rum
15ml (½ fl oz) Maraschino Liqueur
60ml (2 fl oz) Grapefruit Juice
60ml (2 fl oz) Pineapple Juice

Pour ingredients into a cocktail shaker over ice and shake. Strain into a collins glass over ice and serve.

Apple and Ginger

30.2% ALC/VOL • 2 STD DRINKS

45ml (1½ fl oz) Applejack
23ml (¾ fl oz) Ginger Brandy
15ml (½ fl oz) Fresh Lemon Juice
½ teaspoon Sugar Syrup

Pour ingredients into a cocktail shaker over ice and shake. Strain into a chilled cocktail glass and serve.

Brandy Melba

26.5% ALC/VOL • 1.6 STD DRINKS

45ml (1½ fl oz) Brandy
8ml (¼ fl oz) Peach Liqueur
8ml (¼ fl oz) Raspberry Liqueur
2 dashes Orange Bitters
15ml (½ fl oz) Fresh Lemon Juice
Slice of Peach

Pour Brandy, Liqueurs, Bitters and juice into a cocktail shaker over ice. Shake and strain into a chilled cocktail glass. Garnish with a slice of peach and serve.

Satin Sheets

32.8% ALC/VOL • 1.4 STD DRINKS

23ml (¾ fl oz) Brandy
23ml (¾ fl oz) Bacardi
5ml (1/6 fl oz) Triple Sec
5ml (1/6 fl oz) Fresh Lime Juice

Pour ingredients into a cocktail shaker over ice and shake. Strain into a chilled cocktail glass and serve.

Cherries from Heaven

5.5% ALC/VOL • 0.9 STD DRINKS

45ml (1½ fl oz) Cherry Brandy
Dash Angostura Bitters
30ml (1 fl oz) Fresh Lemon Juice
120ml (4 fl oz) Tonic Water
Wedge of Lime

Pour Brandy, Bitters and juice into a cocktail shaker over ice. Shake and strain into a highball glass over ice. Add tonic and stir gently. Garnish with a wedge of lime and serve.

Knickerbein

18% ALC/VOL • 1.5 STD DRINKS

30ml (1 fl oz) Brandy
30ml (1 fl oz) Maraschino Liqueur
30ml (1 fl oz) Grenadine
Yolk of 1 Egg

Pour ingredients into a cocktail shaker over ice and shake. Strain into a chilled brandy balloon and serve.

Apricot and Raspberry Sour

10.5% ALC/VOL • 0.8 STD DRINKS

30ml (1 fl oz) Apricot Brandy
15ml (½ fl oz) Framboise
30ml (1 fl oz) Fresh Orange Juice
15ml (½ fl oz) Fresh Lemon Juice
5ml (1/6 fl oz) Soda Water
Raspberry
Slice of Orange

Pour Brandy, Framboise and juices into a cocktail shaker over ice. Shake and strain into a chilled sour glass then add soda – do not stir. Garnish with a raspberry and slice of orange then serve.

A.B.C.

27.3% ALC/VOL • 1.9 STD DRINKS

45ml (1½ fl oz) Apricot Brandy
30ml (1 fl oz) Scotch Whisky
15ml (½ fl oz) Sweet Vermouth

Pour ingredients into a mixing glass over ice and stir. Strain into a chilled cocktail glass and serve.

Cognac Cream

10.7% ALC/VOL • 1.9 STD DRINKS

60ml (2 fl oz) Cognac
15ml (½ fl oz) Grenadine
90ml (3 fl oz) Fresh Milk (chilled)
60ml (2 fl oz) Fresh Cream
Nutmeg

Pour Cognac, Grenadine, milk and cream into a cocktail shaker over ice. Shake and strain into a chilled highball glass. Sprinkle nutmeg on top and serve.

Brandied Ginger

24% ALC/VOL • 1 STD DRINK

30ml (1 fl oz) Brandy
15ml (½ fl oz) Green Ginger Wine
5ml (1/6 fl oz) Fresh Lemon Juice
5ml (1/6 fl oz) Fresh Orange Juice

Pour ingredients into a cocktail shaker over ice and shake. Strain into a chilled cocktail glass and serve.

Carnival

25.5% ALC/VOL • 1.9 STD DRINKS

30ml (1 fl oz) Apricot Brandy
30ml (1 fl oz) Brandy
30ml (1 fl oz) Lillet
Dash Kirsch
Dash Fresh Orange Juice

Pour ingredients into a cocktail shaker over ice and shake. Strain into a chilled cocktail glass and serve.

King Louis

19.6% ALC/VOL • 1.7 STD DRINKS

60ml (2 fl oz) Brandy
45ml (1½ fl oz) Fresh Lemon Juice
1 teaspoon Sugar Syrup
½ teaspoon Honey

Pour ingredients into a cocktail shaker over ice and shake. Strain into a chilled cocktail glass and serve.

Brandy Cobbler

26.2% ALC/VOL • 1.8 STD DRINKS

45ml (1½ fl oz) Brandy
15ml (½ fl oz) Curaçao
5ml (1/6 fl oz) Kirsch
15ml (½ fl oz) Fresh Lemon Juice
1 teaspoon Sugar Syrup
Slice of Pineapple

Pour Brandy, Curaçao, Kirsch, juice and sugar into a highball glass over ice then stir. Garnish with a slice of pineapple and serve.

BB Cola

8.8% ALC/VOL • 1.7 STD DRINKS

60ml (2 fl oz) Blackberry Brandy
180ml (6 fl oz) Cola

Pour Brandy into a highball glass over ice and add cola, stir gently then serve.

Plum Rickey

12.6% ALC/VOL • 1.4 STD DRINKS

45ml (1½ fl oz) Plum Brandy
8ml (¼ fl oz) Fresh Lime Juice
90ml (3 fl oz) Soda Water
2 Slices of Fresh Plum

Pour Brandy and juice into a cocktail shaker over ice. Shake and strain into a collins glass over ice. Add soda and stir gently. Garnish with slices of plum and serve.

Applejack Manhattan

32.3% ALC/VOL • 2 STD DRINKS

53ml (1¾ fl oz) Applejack
23ml (¾ fl oz) Sweet Vermouth
Dash Orange Bitters
Maraschino Cherry

Pour Applejack, Vermouth and Bitters into a mixing glass over ice. Stir and strain into a chilled cocktail glass. Garnish with a cherry and serve.

Man Overboard

19.9% ALC/VOL • 2.1 STD DRINKS

30ml (1 fl oz) Cognac
23ml (¾ fl oz) Cointreau
15ml (½ fl oz) Galliano
60ml (2 fl oz) Pomegranate Juice
1 teaspoon Sugar Syrup
Maraschino Cherry

Pour Cognac, Cointreau, Galliano, juice and sugar into a cocktail shaker over ice. Shake and strain into a chilled cocktail glass. Garnish with a cherry and serve.

Emerald

27.7% ALC/VOL • 4.6 STD DRINKS

120ml (4 fl oz) Brandy
60ml (2 fl oz) Green Crème De Menthe
30ml (1 fl oz) Fresh Lemon Juice

Pour ingredients into a cocktail shaker over ice and shake. Strain into a chilled highball glass and serve.

Picasso

25.5% ALC/VOL • 1.6 STD DRINKS

45ml (1½ fl oz) Cognac
15ml (½ fl oz) Dubonnet
15ml (½ fl oz) Fresh Lime Juice
1 teaspoon Sugar Syrup
Twist of Orange Peel

Pour Cognac, Dubonnet, juice and sugar into a cocktail shaker over ice. Shake and strain into a chilled cocktail glass. Twist orange peel above drink and place remainder of peel into drink then serve.

Pernod Pit

32.5% ALC/VOL • 1.7 STD DRINKS

30ml (1 fl oz) Apple Brandy
30ml (1 fl oz) Apricot Brandy
8ml (¼ fl oz) Pernod

Pour ingredients into a cocktail shaker over ice and shake. Strain into a chilled cocktail glass and serve.

Gingerman

10.8% ALC/VOL • 1.3 STD DRINKS

30ml (1 fl oz) Ginger Brandy
15ml (½ fl oz) Light Rum
45ml (1½ fl oz) Fresh Milk (chilled)
2 scoops Chocolate Ice Cream

Pour Brandy, Rum and milk into a blender without ice. Add ice cream and blend until smooth. Pour into an old-fashioned glass over ice, stir and serve.

Polonaise

32.3% ALC/VOL • 1.9 STD DRINKS

45ml (1½ fl oz) Brandy
15ml (½ fl oz) Blackberry Brandy
15ml (½ fl oz) Dry Sherry
Dash Fresh Lemon Juice

Pour ingredients into a cocktail shaker over ice and shake. Strain into a chilled cocktail glass and serve.

Cyndi's Fun

15.3% ALC/VOL • 1.5 STD DRINKS

45ml (1½ fl oz) Cherry Brandy
23ml (¾ fl oz) Scotch Whisky
30ml (1 fl oz) Fresh Orange Juice
30ml (1 fl oz) Thick Cream
Cherry
Slice of Orange
Sprig of Fresh Mint

Pour Brandy, Whisky, juice and cream into a cocktail shaker over ice. Shake and strain into a chilled cocktail glass. Garnish with a cherry, slice of orange and sprig of mint then serve.

Alabama

24.2% ALC/VOL • 1.5 STD DRINKS

30ml (1 fl oz) Brandy
30ml (1 fl oz) Curaçao
15ml (½ fl oz) Fresh Lime Juice
½ teaspoon Sugar Syrup

Pour ingredients into a cocktail shaker over ice and shake. Strain into a chilled cocktail glass and serve.

Soother Cocktail

27% ALC/VOL • 1.4 STD DRINKS

15ml (½ fl oz) Apple Brandy
15ml (½ fl oz) Brandy
15ml (½ fl oz) Cointreau
15ml (½ fl oz) Fresh Lemon Juice
1 teaspoon Sugar Syrup

Pour ingredients into a cocktail shaker over ice and shake. Strain into a chilled cocktail glass and serve.

Brandy and Amer Picon

37% ALC/VOL • 2.2 STD DRINKS

60ml (2 fl oz) Cognac
15ml (½ fl oz) Amer Picon
Twist of Lemon Peel
Twist of Orange Peel

Pour Cognac and Amer Picon into a mixing glass over ice. Stir and strain into an old-fashioned glass over ice. Twist lemon and orange peels above drink. Place remainder of peels into drink and serve.

Brandied Peach Fizz

14.1% ALC/VOL • 2.1 STD DRINKS

60ml (2 fl oz) Brandy
15ml (½ fl oz) Peach Brandy
5ml (1/6 fl oz) Banana Liqueur
15ml (½ fl oz) Fresh Lemon Juice
1 teaspoon Caster Sugar
90ml (3 fl oz) Soda Water
Slice of Peach

Pour Brandies, Liqueur and juice into a cocktail shaker over ice then add sugar. Shake and strain into a highball glass over ice. Add soda and stir gently. Garnish with a slice of peach and serve.

Applehawk

19.2% ALC/VOL • 1.2 STD DRINKS

38ml (1¼ fl oz) Applejack
38ml (1¼ fl oz) Grapefruit Juice
½ teaspoon Sugar Syrup

Pour ingredients into a cocktail shaker over ice and shake. Strain into a chilled cocktail glass and serve.

Cognac Egg Flip

18.7% ALC/VOL • 1.8 STD DRINKS

45ml (1½ fl oz) Cognac
30ml (1 fl oz) Tawny Port

1 teaspoon Sugar Syrup
1 Fresh Egg
Nutmeg

Pour Cognac, Port, sugar and egg into a cocktail shaker over ice. Shake and strain into a chilled goblet. Sprinkle nutmeg on top and serve.

Calvados Cocktail

24.3% ALC/VOL • 1.7 STD DRINKS

30ml (1 fl oz) Calvados
15ml (½ fl oz) Cointreau
15ml (½ fl oz) Orange Bitters
30ml (1 fl oz) Fresh
Orange Juice

Pour ingredients into a cocktail shaker over ice and shake. Strain into a chilled cocktail glass and serve.

Ferocious Flip

15.8% ALC/VOL • 1.7 STD DRINKS

45ml (1½ fl oz) Brandy
30ml (1 fl oz) Port
15ml (½ fl oz) Fresh Cream
1 teaspoon Sugar Syrup
1 Fresh Egg
Nutmeg

Pour Brandy, Port, cream, sugar and egg into a cocktail shaker over ice. Shake and strain into a chilled goblet. Sprinkle nutmeg on top and serve.

Port Side

34.6% ALC/VOL • 2 STD DRINKS

45ml (1½ fl oz) Cognac
15ml (½ fl oz) Blackberry
Brandy
15ml (½ fl oz) Port

Pour ingredients into a mixing glass over ice and stir. Strain into a chilled brandy balloon and serve.

Brandy Sangaree

16.9% ALC/VOL • 2.4 STD DRINKS

75ml (2½ fl oz) Brandy
15ml (½ fl oz) Port
1 tablespoon Sugar Syrup
75ml (2½ fl oz) Soda Water
Nutmeg

Pour Brandy and sugar into an old-fashioned glass over ice then stir. Add soda and stir gently then layer Port on top. Sprinkle nutmeg on top and serve.

Button Hook Cocktail

28.3% ALC/VOL • 1.3 STD DRINKS

15ml (½ fl oz) Brandy
15ml (½ fl oz) Apricot Brandy
15ml (½ fl oz) Anisette
15ml (½ fl oz) White Crème De
Menthe

Pour ingredients into a cocktail shaker over ice and shake. Strain into a chilled cocktail glass and serve.

Frozen Apple and Banana

28.6% ALC/VOL • 1.7 STD DRINKS

45ml (1½ fl oz) Applejack
15ml (½ fl oz) Banana Liqueur
15ml (½ fl oz) Fresh
Lime Juice
Slice of Banana

Pour Applejack, Liqueur and juice into a blender over crushed ice. Blend and pour into a chilled champagne saucer. Garnish with a slice of banana and serve.

Applejack Cooler

13.3% ALC/VOL • 1.9 STD DRINKS

60ml (2 fl oz) Applejack
15ml (½ fl oz) Fresh
Lemon Juice
1 tablespoon Sugar Syrup
90ml (3 fl oz) Soda Water

Pour Applejack, juice and sugar into a cocktail shaker over ice. Shake and strain into a collins glass over ice. Add soda, stir gently and serve.

Montgomery

28.3% ALC/VOL • 1.9 STD DRINKS

60ml (2 fl oz) Brandy
5ml (1/6 fl oz) Curaçao
15ml (½ fl oz) Fresh
Lemon Juice
½ teaspoon Sugar Syrup
Twist of Orange Peel

Prepare a cocktail glass with a sugar frosted rim. Pour Brandy, Curaçao, juice and sugar into a cocktail shaker over ice. Shake and strain into prepared glass. Garnish with orange peel and serve.

Yellow Plum

24.1% ALC/VOL • 1.5 STD DRINKS

45ml (1½ fl oz) Plum Brandy
5ml (1/6 fl oz) Maraschino
Liqueur
15ml (½ fl oz) Fresh
Lemon Juice
15ml (½ fl oz) Fresh
Orange Juice

Pour ingredients into a cocktail shaker over ice and shake. Strain into a chilled cocktail glass and serve.

Almond Eye

22.9% ALC/VOL • 2.1 STD DRINKS

30ml (1 fl oz) Brandy
30ml (1 fl oz) Dry Gin
15ml (½ fl oz) Amaretto
5ml (1/6 fl oz) Grenadine
30ml (1 fl oz) Fresh
Lemon Juice
5ml (1/6 fl oz) Soda Water

Pour Brandy, Gin, Amaretto, Grenadine and juice into a cocktail shaker over ice. Shake and strain into a chilled old-fashioned glass over 2 ice cubes. Add soda – do not stir, then serve.

Princess Mary's Pride

28.4% ALC/VOL • 2 STD DRINKS

45ml (1½ fl oz) Apple Brandy
23ml (¾ fl oz) Dry Vermouth
23ml (¾ fl oz) Dubonnet

Pour ingredients into a mixing glass over ice and stir. Strain into a chilled cocktail glass and serve.

Splashdown

19.9% ALC/VOL • 1.7 STD DRINKS

45ml (1½ fl oz) Brandy
15ml (½ fl oz) Galliano
30ml (1 fl oz) Fresh Orange Juice
15ml (½ fl oz) Fresh Lime Juice
1 teaspoon Sugar Syrup
Slice of Lime

Pour Brandy, Galliano, juices and sugar into a cocktail shaker over ice. Shake and strain into an old-fashioned glass over ice. Garnish with a slice of lime and serve.

Mandarinella

33.6% ALC/VOL • 2.4 STD DRINKS

60ml (2 fl oz) Brandy
20ml (⅔ fl oz) Mandarine Napoleon
2 teaspoons Fresh Cream

Pour ingredients into a cocktail shaker over ice and shake. Strain into a chilled cocktail glass and serve.

Cherry Tree Climber

18.6% ALC/VOL • 1.3 STD DRINKS

30ml (1 fl oz) Cherry Brandy
30ml (1 fl oz) White Crème De Cacao
15ml (½ fl oz) Peppermint Schnapps
½ scoop Vanilla Ice Cream

Pour Brandy, Cacao and Schnapps into a blender over small amount of crushed ice then add ice cream. Blend and pour into a chilled cocktail glass then serve.

Janet Standard

35.2% ALC/VOL • 2.7 STD DRINKS

90ml (3 fl oz) Brandy
Dash Angostura Bitters
1 teaspoon Sugar Syrup
Twist of Lemon Peel

Pour Brandy, Bitters and sugar into a chilled cocktail glass over an ice cube then stir. Garnish with lemon peel and serve.

Goat Herder

22.6% ALC/VOL • 1.7 STD DRINKS

30ml (1 fl oz) Brandy
15ml (½ fl oz) Cherry Brandy
15ml (½ fl oz) Kirsch
5ml (⅙ fl oz) Amaretto
30ml (1 fl oz) Thick Cream
Maraschino Cherry

Pour Brandies, Kirsch, Amaretto and cream into a cocktail shaker over ice. Shake and strain into an old-fashioned glass over ice. Garnish with a cherry and serve.

Corazon

23.5% ALC/VOL • 1.7 STD DRINKS

30ml (1 fl oz) Cherry Brandy
30ml (1 fl oz) Coffee Brandy
10ml (⅓ fl oz) Brandy
20ml (⅔ fl oz) Cherry Juice

Pour ingredients into a cocktail shaker over ice and shake. Strain into a chilled cocktail glass and serve.

Goodbye Sigh

25.2% ALC/VOL • 1.5 STD DRINKS

30ml (1 fl oz) Apricot Brandy
30ml (1 fl oz) Peppermint Schnapps
15ml (½ fl oz) Cognac
Cherry

Pour Brandy, Schnapps and Cognac into a cocktail shaker over ice. Shake and strain into a champagne saucer filled with crushed ice. Add a cherry and serve with 2 short straws.

Goodness Gracious

27.1% ALC/VOL • 2 STD DRINKS

30ml (1 fl oz) Cognac
30ml (1 fl oz) Cherry Brandy
30ml (1 fl oz) White Crème De Cacao
1 teaspoon Egg White

Pour ingredients into a cocktail shaker over ice and shake. Strain into an old-fashioned glass over ice and serve.

Ambience

15.8% ALC/VOL • 1.7 STD DRINKS

30ml (1 fl oz) Cognac
30ml (1 fl oz) Vodka
8ml (¼ fl oz) Mandarine Napoleon
120ml (4 fl oz) Fresh Orange Juice
30ml (1 fl oz) Fresh Lime Juice
1½ teaspoons Sugar Syrup
Maraschino Cherry
Slice of Lime

Prepare a collins glass with a sugar frosted rim – moistened with lime juice and add ice. Pour Cognac, Vodka, Mandarine Napoleon, juices and sugar into a cocktail shaker over ice. Shake and strain into prepared glass. Garnish with a cherry and slice of lime then serve with 2 straws.

Rob Le Roy

29.9% ALC/VOL • 2.1 STD DRINKS

This drink is also known as Metropolitan, p 25.

Brandied Peach Sling

12.4% ALC/VOL • 1.8 STD DRINKS

53ml (1¾ fl oz) Brandy
15ml (½ fl oz) Peach Brandy
23ml (¾ fl oz) Fresh Lemon Juice
1 teaspoon Sugar Syrup
90ml (3 fl oz) Soda Water
Slice of Peach
Twist of Lemon Peel

Pour Brandies, juice and sugar into a cocktail shaker over ice. Shake and strain into a collins glass over ice. Add soda and stir gently. Twist lemon peel above drink and place remainder of peel into drink. Garnish with a slice of peach and serve.

Brandy Gump

17.9% ALC/VOL • 0.9 STD DRINKS

30ml (1 fl oz) Brandy
2 dashes Grenadine
30ml (1 fl oz) Fresh Lemon Juice

Pour ingredients into a cocktail shaker over ice and shake. Strain into a chilled cocktail glass and serve.

Bull's Milk

9.9% ALC/VOL • 2.2 STD DRINKS

45ml (1½ fl oz) Brandy
30ml (1 fl oz) Light Rum
200ml (6⅔ fl oz) Fresh Milk (chilled)
1 teaspoon Sugar Syrup
Cinnamon
Nutmeg

Pour Brandy, Rum, milk and sugar into a cocktail shaker over ice. Shake and strain into a chilled collins glass. Sprinkle cinnamon and nutmeg on top then serve.

Kim

25.4% ALC/VOL • 0.8 STD DRINKS

18ml (⅗ fl oz) Brandy
12ml (⅖ fl oz) Triple Sec
1 teaspoon Sugar Syrup
3 dashes Fresh Lemon Juice

Pour ingredients into a cocktail shaker over ice and shake. Strain into a chilled cocktail glass and serve.

Harvard

26.2% ALC/VOL • 1.9 STD DRINKS

45ml (1½ fl oz) Brandy
45ml (1½ fl oz) Sweet Vermouth
2 dashes Angostura Bitters
Dash Sugar Syrup
Olive
Twist of Lemon Peel

Pour Brandy, Vermouth, Bitters and sugar into a cocktail shaker over ice. Shake and strain into a chilled cocktail glass. Garnish with an olive and lemon peel then serve.

First Knight

30.2% ALC/VOL • 3 STD DRINKS

60ml (2 fl oz) Brandy
30ml (1 fl oz) Tia Maria
30ml (1 fl oz) Van Der Hum
1 teaspoon Thick Cream

Pour ingredients into a cocktail shaker over ice and shake. Strain into a chilled cocktail glass and serve.

Morning Cocktail

27.7% ALC/VOL • 1.4 STD DRINKS

30ml (1 fl oz) Brandy
30ml (1 fl oz) Dry Vermouth
2 dashes Orange Bitters
Dash Anisette
Dash Cointreau
Dash Maraschino Liqueur
Maraschino Cherry

Pour Brandy, Vermouth, Bitters, Anisette, Cointreau and Liqueur into a mixing glass over ice. Stir and strain into a chilled cocktail glass. Garnish with a cherry and serve.

Apollo 1

37.9% ALC/VOL • 2.1 STD DRINKS

40ml (1⅓ fl oz) Apple Brandy
20ml (⅔ fl oz) Cointreau
10ml (⅓ fl oz) Pimm's No.1

Pour ingredients into a cocktail shaker over cracked ice and shake. Pour into a chilled old-fashioned glass and serve.

Brandy Buck

11.4% ALC/VOL • 1.4 STD DRINKS

45ml (1½ fl oz) Brandy
5ml (1/6 fl oz) White Crème De Menthe
90ml (3 fl oz) Dry Ginger Ale
½ Fresh Lemon
3 Seedless Grapes

Pour Brandy and Crème De Menthe into a collins glass over ice. Twist ½ lemon above drink to release juice and add spent shell then stir. Add Ginger Ale and stir gently. Garnish with grapes and serve.

Billy Hamilton

28.1% ALC/VOL • 2 STD DRINKS

30ml (1 fl oz) Brandy
30ml (1 fl oz) Dark Crème De Cacao
30ml (1 fl oz) Orange Curaçao
Dash Egg White

Pour ingredients into a cocktail shaker over ice and shake. Strain into a chilled cocktail glass and serve.

Discovery Bay

12.6% ALC/VOL • 1.8 STD DRINKS

45ml (1½ fl oz) Brandy
15ml (½ fl oz) Cointreau
60ml (2 fl oz) Lemon Sherbet
60ml (2 fl oz) Dry Ginger Ale

Pour Brandy and Cointreau into a cocktail shaker over ice then add sherbet. Shake and strain into a highball glass over ice. Add Ginger Ale, stir gently and serve.

Egg Alexander

13.3% ALC/VOL • 1.4 STD DRINKS

30ml (1 fl oz) Brandy
30ml (1 fl oz) Dark Crème De Cacao
30ml (1 fl oz) Thick Cream
1 Fresh Egg

Pour ingredients into a cocktail shaker over ice and shake. Strain into a chilled champagne saucer and serve.

B & B Collins

7.6% ALC/VOL • 1.8 STD DRINKS

45ml (1½ fl oz) Brandy
15ml (½ fl oz) Bénédictine
30ml (1 fl oz) Fresh Lemon Juice
1½ tablespoons Sugar Syrup
150ml (5 fl oz) Soda Water
Maraschino Cherry
Slice of Lemon
Slice of Orange

Pour Brandy, juice and sugar into a mixing glass over ice. Stir and strain into a collins glass over ice. Add soda and stir gently then layer Bénédictine on top. Garnish with a cherry, slice of lemon and orange then serve with 2 straws.

Time Bomb

36.9% ALC/VOL • 2.7 STD DRINKS

This drink is also known as Depth Bomb, p 38.

Bitter Brandy and Sherry

12.3% ALC/VOL • 1.6 STD DRINKS

30ml (1 fl oz) Brandy
30ml (1 fl oz) Cream Sherry
15ml (½ fl oz) Cherry Liqueur
5ml (1/6 fl oz) Fresh Lemon Juice
90ml (3 fl oz) Bitter-Lemon Soda
Slice of Lemon

Pour Brandy, Sherry, Liqueur and juice into a cocktail shaker over ice. Shake and strain into a chilled old-fashioned glass over 2 ice cubes. Add soda and stir gently. Garnish with a slice of lemon and serve.

Third Rail Standard

38% ALC/VOL • 2.7 STD DRINKS

30ml (1 fl oz) Brandy
30ml (1 fl oz) Calvados
30ml (1 fl oz) Light Rum
Dash Pernod

Pour ingredients into a cocktail shaker over ice and shake. Strain into a chilled cocktail glass and serve.

Georgia Mint Julep

27.7% ALC/VOL • 1.9 STD DRINKS

45ml (1½ fl oz) Brandy
30ml (1 fl oz) Peach Brandy
5ml (1/6 fl oz) Spring Water
1 teaspoon Sugar Syrup
4 Fresh Mint Leaves

Pour water and sugar into a collins glass over ice then add 2 mint leaves. Muddle well and add Brandies then stir. Garnish with 2 mint leaves and serve.

Blue Angel

17% ALC/VOL • 1 STD DRINK

15ml (½ fl oz) Brandy
15ml (½ fl oz) Blue Curaçao
15ml (½ fl oz) Parfait Amour
15ml (½ fl oz) Fresh Lemon Juice
15ml (½ fl oz) Thick Cream

Pour ingredients into a cocktail shaker over ice and shake. Strain into a chilled cocktail glass and serve.

Apricot Fizz

7.5% ALC/VOL • 1.1 STD DRINKS

60ml (2 fl oz) Apricot Brandy
15ml (½ fl oz) Fresh Lemon Juice
15ml (½ fl oz) Fresh Lime Juice
1 teaspoon Caster Sugar
90ml (3 fl oz) Soda Water

Pour Brandy and juices into a cocktail shaker over ice then add sugar. Shake and strain into a highball glass over ice. Add soda, stir gently and serve.

Polynesian Apple

27.3% ALC/VOL • 1.6 STD DRINKS

38ml (1¼ fl oz) Applejack
15ml (½ fl oz) Brandy
23ml (¾ fl oz) Pineapple Juice
Slice of Pineapple

Pour Applejack, Brandy and juice into a cocktail shaker over ice. Shake and strain into an old-fashioned glass over ice. Garnish with a slice of pineapple and serve.

Apple Ginger Fix

27% ALC/VOL • 1.8 STD DRINKS

30ml (1 fl oz) Applejack
30ml (1 fl oz) Ginger Brandy
15ml (½ fl oz) Fresh Lemon Juice
5ml (1/6 fl oz) Spring Water
½ teaspoon Sugar Syrup
Slice of Lemon

Pour Applejack, Brandy, juice, water and sugar into an old-fashioned glass filled with crushed ice. Add more crushed ice to fill glass and stir. Garnish with a slice of lemon and serve.

Dry Cold Deck

31.7% ALC/VOL • 1.9 STD DRINKS

53ml (1¾ fl oz) Brandy
15ml (½ fl oz) Dry Vermouth
8ml (¼ fl oz) White Crème De Menthe

Pour ingredients into a cocktail shaker over ice and shake. Strain into a chilled cocktail glass and serve.

Patrician

26.9% ALC/VOL • 2 STD DRINKS

45ml (1½ fl oz) Brandy
45ml (1½ fl oz) Dubonnet
3 dashes Pernod
Slice of Orange

Pour Brandy, Dubonnet and Pernod into a cocktail shaker over ice. Shake and strain into a chilled cocktail glass. Garnish with a slice of orange and serve.

McBrandy

20.8% ALC/VOL • 1.3 STD DRINKS

45ml (1½ fl oz) Brandy
30ml (1 fl oz) Apple Juice
5ml (1/6 fl oz) Fresh Lemon Juice
Slice of Lemon

Pour Brandy and juices into a cocktail shaker over ice. Shake and strain into a chilled cocktail glass. Garnish with a slice of lemon and serve.

Strawberry Patch

19.6% ALC/VOL • 1.9 STD DRINKS

30ml (1 fl oz) Strawberry Brandy
15ml (½ fl oz) Cherry Vodka
15ml (½ fl oz) Galliano
15ml (½ fl oz) Sloe Gin
30ml (1 fl oz) Mandarin Juice
30ml (1 fl oz) Fresh Cream
Strawberry

Pour Brandy, Vodka, Galliano, Gin, juice and cream into a cocktail shaker over ice. Shake and strain into a chilled champagne saucer. Garnish with a strawberry and serve.

Javahopper

19.4% ALC/VOL • 1.1 STD DRINKS

23ml (¾ fl oz) Coffee Brandy
23ml (¾ fl oz) White Crème De Menthe
23ml (¾ fl oz) Fresh Cream

Pour ingredients into a cocktail shaker over ice and shake. Strain into an old-fashioned glass filled with ice and serve.

Apricot Cobbler

15.9% ALC/VOL • 1.7 STD DRINKS

45ml (1½ fl oz) Apricot Brandy
30ml (1 fl oz) Brandy
60ml (2 fl oz) Grapefruit Juice
Slice of Orange

Pour Brandies and juice into a cocktail shaker over ice. Shake and strain into a highball glass over ice. Garnish with a slice of orange and serve.

Brandy Blazer

35% ALC/VOL • 2.6 STD DRINKS

90ml (3 fl oz) Brandy
1 teaspoon Sugar Syrup
Slice of Orange
Twist of Lemon Peel

Pour Brandy and sugar into an old-fashioned glass then add a slice of orange. Ignite and stir until flame is extinguished. Add lemon peel and serve.

Brandy Sling

13.1% ALC/VOL • 1.8 STD DRINKS

60ml (2 fl oz) Brandy
60ml (2 fl oz) Spring Water
30ml (1 fl oz) Fresh Lemon Juice
1 tablespoon Sugar Syrup
Wedge of Lemon

Pour Brandy, water, juice and sugar into a cocktail shaker over ice. Shake and strain into a highball glass over ice. Garnish with a wedge of lemon and serve.

Thistle

30% ALC/VOL • 2.1 STD DRINKS

45ml (1½ fl oz) Brandy

45ml (1½ fl oz) Green Crème De Menthe
Red Pepper (Cayenne)

Pour Brandy and Crème De Menthe into a cocktail shaker over ice. Shake and strain into a chilled cocktail glass. Sprinkle Cayenne on top and serve.
This drink is also known as Hell.

Apricot Rickey

8.4% ALC/VOL • 1.1 STD DRINKS

60ml (2 fl oz) Apricot Brandy
15ml (½ fl oz) Fresh Lime Juice
90ml (3 fl oz) Soda Water
Twist of Lemon Peel

Pour Brandy and juice into a cocktail shaker over ice. Shake and strain into a collins glass over ice. Add soda and stir gently. Twist lemon peel above drink and place remainder of peel into drink then serve.

Apple Suissesse

25.3% ALC/VOL • 1.9 STD DRINKS

60ml (2 fl oz) Applejack
15ml (½ fl oz) Thick Cream
1 teaspoon Sugar Syrup
½ Egg White

Prepare an old-fashioned glass with a sugar frosted rim – moistened with Grenadine. Pour ingredients into a blender over crushed ice and blend. Pour into prepared glass and serve.

Brandy Milk Punch

9.9% ALC/VOL • 1.8 STD DRINKS

60ml (2 fl oz) Brandy
150ml (5 fl oz) Fresh Milk (chilled)
1 tablespoon Sugar Syrup
Maraschino Cherry
Cinnamon

Pour Brandy, milk and sugar into a cocktail shaker over ice. Shake and strain into a collins glass over ice. Sprinkle cinnamon on top and garnish with a cherry then serve.

Davis Brandy

29.9% ALC/VOL • 3.3 STD DRINKS

90ml (3 fl oz) Brandy
45ml (1½ fl oz) Dry Vermouth
Dash Angostura Bitters
4 dashes Grenadine

Pour ingredients into a mixing glass over ice and stir. Strain into a chilled cocktail glass and serve.

Gang Up

9.4% ALC/VOL • 1.4 STD DRINKS

15ml (½ fl oz) Cherry Brandy
15ml (½ fl oz) Gin
15ml (½ fl oz) Strawberry Brandy
15ml (½ fl oz) Triple Sec
135ml (4½ fl oz) Lemonade
Slice of Orange
Strawberry

Pour Brandies, Gin and Triple Sec into a highball glass over ice then stir. Add lemonade and stir gently. Garnish with a slice of orange and a strawberry then serve with 2 straws.

Dirty Mother

32.8% ALC/VOL • 1.6 STD DRINKS

45ml (1½ fl oz) Brandy
15ml (½ fl oz) Kahlúa

Pour ingredients into an old-fashioned glass filled with ice, stir and serve.

Applejack Collins

13.1% ALC/VOL • 1.9 STD DRINKS

60ml (2 fl oz) Applejack
2 dashes Orange Bitters
30ml (1 fl oz) Fresh Lemon Juice
1 teaspoon Sugar Syrup
90ml (3 fl oz) Soda Water
Slice of Lemon

Pour Applejack, Bitters, juice and sugar into a cocktail shaker over ice. Shake and strain into a collins glass over ice. Add soda and stir gently. Garnish with a slice of lemon and serve.

Fontasio Cocktail

28.1% ALC/VOL • 1.4 STD DRINKS

30ml (1 fl oz) Brandy
23ml (¾ fl oz) Dry Vermouth
5ml (1/6 fl oz) Maraschino Liqueur
5ml (1/6 fl oz) White Crème De Menthe

Pour ingredients into a mixing glass over ice and stir. Strain into a chilled cocktail glass and serve.

Bayou

21.5% ALC/VOL • 1.7 STD DRINKS

45ml (1½ fl oz) Cognac
15ml (½ fl oz) Peach Brandy
30ml (1 fl oz) Mango Juice
10ml (⅓ fl oz) Fresh Lime Juice
Slice of Peach

Pour Cognac, Brandy and juices into a cocktail shaker over cracked ice. Shake and pour into a chilled old-fashioned glass. Garnish with a slice of peach and serve.

Cuban

24.3% ALC/VOL • 2.3 STD DRINKS

60ml (2 fl oz) Brandy
30ml (1 fl oz) Apricot Brandy
30ml (1 fl oz) Fresh Lime Juice

Pour ingredients into a cocktail shaker over ice and shake. Strain into a chilled cocktail glass and serve.
This drink is also known as Bacchus.

Sharky Punch

38.2% ALC/VOL • 5.6 STD DRINKS

135ml (4½ fl oz) Apple Brandy
45ml (1½ fl oz) Rye Whiskey
1 teaspoon Sugar Syrup
Dash Soda Water

Pour Brandy, Whiskey and sugar into a cocktail shaker over ice. Shake and strain into a chilled old-fashioned glass. Add soda – do not stir, then serve.

Cherry Flash Cola

6.6% ALC/VOL • 0.9 STD DRINKS

30ml (1 fl oz) Cherry Brandy
15ml (½ fl oz) Maraschino Liqueur
120ml (4 fl oz) Cola
Maraschino Cherry

Pour Brandy and Liqueur into a highball glass over ice then stir. Add cola and stir gently. Garnish with a cherry and serve.

Orchard Orange

15.4% ALC/VOL • 2.3 STD DRINKS

60ml (2 fl oz) Apple Brandy
15ml (½ fl oz) Dry Vermouth
8ml (¼ fl oz) Amaretto
90ml (3 fl oz) Mandarin Juice
15ml (½ fl oz) Fresh Lime Juice
Slice of Lime
Slice of Mandarin

Pour Brandy, Vermouth, Amaretto and juices into a cocktail shaker over ice. Shake and strain into a highball glass over ice. Garnish with a slice of lime and mandarin then serve with 2 straws.

Roulette

39.3% ALC/VOL • 2.8 STD DRINKS

45ml (1½ fl oz) Apple Brandy
23ml (¾ fl oz) Light Rum
23ml (¾ fl oz) Swedish Punsch

Pour ingredients into a mixing glass over ice and stir. Strain into a chilled cocktail glass and serve.

Apricot Cooler

11.2% ALC/VOL • 1.1 STD DRINKS

60ml (2 fl oz) Apricot Brandy
½ teaspoon Sugar Syrup
60ml (2 fl oz) Dry Ginger Ale or Soda Water
Twist of Lemon Peel
Twist of Orange Peel

Pour sugar into a chilled collins glass and add Ginger Ale or soda as desired then stir gently. Fill glass with ice and add Brandy then stir gently. Garnish with lemon and orange peels then serve.

Tonight's the Night

28.9% ALC/VOL • 1.6 STD DRINKS

45ml (1½ fl oz) Cognac
15ml (½ fl oz) Sweet Vermouth
2 teaspoons Passion-Fruit Syrup

Pour ingredients into a cocktail shaker over crushed ice and shake. Strain into a chilled old-fashioned glass and serve.

Brandy Strega Flip

18.5% ALC/VOL • 1.8 STD DRINKS

30ml (1 fl oz) Brandy
30ml (1 fl oz) Strega
10ml (⅓ fl oz) Fresh Orange Juice
5ml (⅙ fl oz) Fresh Lemon Juice
1 teaspoon Sugar Syrup
1 Fresh Egg
Nutmeg

Pour Brandy, Strega, juices, sugar and egg into a cocktail shaker over ice. Shake and strain into a chilled goblet. Sprinkle nutmeg on top and serve.

Baltimore Bracer

24.5% ALC/VOL • 2 STD DRINKS

45ml (1½ fl oz) Brandy
30ml (1 fl oz) Anisette
White of 1 Egg

Pour ingredients into a cocktail shaker over ice and shake. Strain into a chilled cocktail glass and serve.

Calvados Fizz

12.6% ALC/VOL • 1.9 STD DRINKS

60ml (2 fl oz) Calvados
15ml (½ fl oz) Fresh Lemon Juice
1 teaspoon Thick Cream
1 teaspoon Caster Sugar
½ Egg White
90ml (3 fl oz) Soda Water
Maraschino Cherry
Slice of Lime

Pour Calvados, juice, cream and egg white into a cocktail shaker over ice then add sugar. Shake and strain into a highball glass over ice. Add soda and stir gently. Garnish with a cherry and slice of lime then serve.

Babbie's Special Cocktail

17.9% ALC/VOL • 0.9 STD DRINKS

45ml (1½ fl oz) Apricot Brandy
2 dashes Dry Gin
15ml (½ fl oz) Fresh Cream

Pour ingredients into a cocktail shaker over ice and shake. Strain into a chilled cocktail glass and serve.

Snow Apple

22.5% ALC/VOL • 1.4 STD DRINKS

45ml (1½ fl oz) Apple Brandy
15ml (½ fl oz) Fresh Lemon Juice
1 teaspoon Sugar Syrup
½ Egg White
Slice of Lemon

Pour Brandy, juice, sugar and egg white into a blender over crushed ice. Blend and pour into a cocktail glass over ice. Garnish with a slice of lemon and serve.

Ginger Brandy Cooler

10.6% ALC/VOL • 1.5 STD DRINKS

45ml (1½ fl oz) Apple Brandy
5ml (1/6 fl oz) Ginger Brandy
15ml (½ fl oz) Fresh Lemon Juice
120ml (4 fl oz) Dry Ginger Ale

Pour Brandies and juice into a collins glass over ice then stir. Add Ginger Ale, stir gently and serve.

Brandied Banana Collins

13.1% ALC/VOL • 1.9 STD DRINKS

45ml (1½ fl oz) Brandy
30ml (1 fl oz) Banana Liqueur
15ml (½ fl oz) Fresh Lemon Juice
90ml (3 fl oz) Soda Water
Slice of Banana
Slice of Lemon

Pour Brandy, Liqueur and juice into a cocktail shaker over ice. Shake and strain into a collins glass over ice. Add soda and stir gently. Garnish with a slice of banana and lemon then serve.

Betsy Ross No.2

29.2% ALC/VOL • 2.5 STD DRINKS

60ml (2 fl oz) Brandy
45ml (1½ fl oz) Tawny Port
3 dashes Cointreau

Pour ingredients into a mixing glass over ice and stir. Strain into a chilled cocktail glass and serve.

Roman Candle

19.5% ALC/VOL • 2 STD DRINKS

30ml (1 fl oz) Brandy
30ml (1 fl oz) Dark Rum
15ml (½ fl oz) Port
30ml (1 fl oz) Raspberry Syrup
23ml (¾ fl oz) Fresh Lemon Juice
Slice of Orange

Pour Brandy, Rum, Port, syrup and juice into a cocktail shaker over ice. Shake and strain into an old-fashioned glass over crushed ice. Garnish with a slice of orange and serve.

Arubian Sunset

5.3% ALC/VOL • 0.8 STD DRINKS

45ml (1½ fl oz) Cherry Brandy
150ml (5 fl oz) Fresh Orange Juice

Pour ingredients into a cocktail shaker over ice and shake. Strain into a chilled old-fashioned glass and serve.

Apple Knocker

15.9% ALC/VOL • 2.5 STD DRINKS

75ml (2½ fl oz) Applejack
15ml (½ fl oz) Sweet Vermouth
90ml (3 fl oz) Fresh Orange Juice
15ml (½ fl oz) Fresh Lemon Juice
1½ teaspoons Sugar Syrup

Pour ingredients into a blender over crushed ice and blend. Pour into a chilled old-fashioned glass and add ice to fill glass then serve.

Brandy Cocktail

32% ALC/VOL • 2.3 STD DRINKS

60ml (2 fl oz) Cognac
30ml (1 fl oz) Sweet Vermouth
2 dashes Angostura Bitters

Pour ingredients into a mixing glass over ice and stir. Strain into a chilled cocktail glass and serve.

Red Apple

32% ALC/VOL • 2 STD DRINKS

60ml (2 fl oz) Apple Brandy
5ml (1/6 fl oz) Grenadine
15ml (½ fl oz) Fresh Lemon Juice
Cherry
Slice of Apple

Pour Brandy, Grenadine and juice into a cocktail shaker over ice. Shake and strain into a chilled cocktail glass. Garnish with a cherry and slice of apple then serve.

French Bite

18.8% ALC/VOL • 1.7 STD DRINKS

30ml (1 fl oz) Cognac
23ml (¾ fl oz) Mandarine Napoleon
60ml (2 fl oz) Apple Juice Soda

Pour Cognac and Mandarine Napoleon into an old-fashioned glass over ice then stir. Add soda, stir gently and serve.

Applejack Daisy

12.3% ALC/VOL • 1.6 STD DRINKS

45ml (1½ fl oz) Applejack
5ml (1/6 fl oz) Ginger Brandy
15ml (½ fl oz) Fresh Lime Juice
1 teaspoon Raspberry Syrup
90ml (3 fl oz) Soda Water
Slice of Lime

Pour Applejack, juice and syrup into a cocktail shaker over ice. Shake and strain into a goblet over ice then add soda – do not stir. Layer Brandy on top and garnish with a slice of lime then serve.

Blackberry Cola

10.9% ALC/VOL • 1.7 STD DRINKS

45ml (1½ fl oz) Blackberry Brandy
15ml (½ fl oz) Dry Sherry
15ml (½ fl oz) Sweet Sherry
120ml (4 fl oz) Cola

Pour Brandy and Sherries into a highball glass over ice then stir. Add cola, stir gently and serve.

Last Goodbye

25.3% ALC/VOL • 1.6 STD DRINKS

30ml (1 fl oz) Cognac
23ml (¾ fl oz) Cherry Brandy
8ml (¼ fl oz) Cointreau
5ml (1/6 fl oz) Grenadine
15ml (½ fl oz) Fresh Lime Juice

Pour ingredients into an old-fashioned glass over cracked ice, stir and serve.

Apricot Flip

12.5% ALC/VOL • 1.1 STD DRINKS

60ml (2 fl oz) Apricot Brandy
1 teaspoon Sugar Syrup
1 Fresh Egg
Nutmeg

Pour Brandy, sugar and egg into a cocktail shaker over ice. Shake and strain into a chilled goblet. Sprinkle nutmeg on top and serve.

Frozen Brandy and Rum

24.6% ALC/VOL • 2.2 STD DRINKS

45ml (1½ fl oz) Brandy
30ml (1 fl oz) Golden Rum
15ml (½ fl oz) Fresh Lemon Juice
1½ teaspoons Sugar Syrup
Yolk of 1 Egg

Pour ingredients into a blender over crushed ice and blend. Pour into a chilled champagne saucer and serve.

Brandy Highball

10.6% ALC/VOL • 1.8 STD DRINKS

60ml (2 fl oz) Brandy
150ml (5 fl oz) Dry Ginger Ale or Soda Water
Twist of Lemon Peel

Pour Brandy into a highball glass over ice and add Ginger Ale or soda as desired then stir gently. Garnish with lemon peel and serve.

Calvarniac

26.7% ALC/VOL • 1.9 STD DRINKS

30ml (1 fl oz) Calvados
20ml (⅔ fl oz) Grand Marnier
10ml (⅓ fl oz) Cognac
30ml (1 fl oz) Lemonade
Wedge of Lemon

Pour Calvados, Grand Marnier and Cognac into an old-fashioned glass over cracked ice then stir. Add lemonade and stir gently. Add a wedge of lemon and serve.

Trojan Horse

22.8% ALC/VOL • 1.3 STD DRINKS

23ml (¾ fl oz) Brandy
23ml (¾ fl oz) Dubonnet
10ml (⅓ fl oz) Maraschino Liqueur
15ml (½ fl oz) Fresh Lime Juice

Pour ingredients into a cocktail shaker over ice and shake. Strain into a chilled cocktail glass and serve.

Brandied Apricot Frappé

21.4% ALC/VOL • 1.6 STD DRINKS

30ml (1 fl oz) Apricot Brandy
30ml (1 fl oz) Cognac
5ml (1/6 fl oz) Amaretto
30ml (1 fl oz) Apricot Juice
Maraschino Cherry

Pour Brandy, Cognac, Amaretto and juice into a mixing glass without ice. Stir and pour into a champagne saucer filled with crushed ice. Garnish with a cherry and serve with 2 short straws.

Brandy Buster

19.1% ALC/VOL • 2.7 STD DRINKS

60ml (2 fl oz) Brandy
30ml (1 fl oz) Advocaat
30ml (1 fl oz) Cherry Brandy
60ml (2 fl oz) Thick Cream

Pour ingredients into a blender over cracked ice and blend. Pour into a chilled champagne saucer and serve.

Topeka

26.2% ALC/VOL • 2 STD DRINKS

60ml (2 fl oz) Brandy
15ml (½ fl oz) Dry Vermouth
15ml (½ fl oz) Grapefruit Juice
5ml (1/6 fl oz) Fresh Lemon Juice

Prepare a cocktail glass with a sugar frosted rim. Pour ingredients into a cocktail shaker over ice and shake. Strain into prepared glass and serve.
This drink is also known as Santa Fe.

Tulip

23.6% ALC/VOL • 1.4 STD DRINKS

30ml (1 fl oz) Apple Brandy
15ml (½ fl oz) Apricot Brandy
15ml (½ fl oz) Sweet Vermouth
15ml (½ fl oz) Fresh Lemon Juice

Pour ingredients into a cocktail shaker over ice and shake. Strain into a chilled cocktail glass and serve.

Metropolitan

29.9% ALC/VOL • 2.1 STD DRINKS

60ml (2 fl oz) Brandy
30ml (1 fl oz) Sweet Vermouth
Dash Angostura Bitters
Maraschino Cherry

Pour Bitters into a cocktail glass and swirl around glass. Pour Brandy and Vermouth into a cocktail shaker over ice. Shake and strain into prepared glass. Garnish with a cherry and serve.
This drink is also known as Rob Le Roy.

Brandy Fizz

13.1% ALC/VOL • 1.8 STD DRINKS

60ml (2 fl oz) Brandy
15ml (½ fl oz) Fresh Lemon Juice
1 teaspoon Caster Sugar
90ml (3 fl oz) Soda Water

Pour Brandy and juice into a cocktail shaker over ice then add sugar. Shake and strain into a highball glass over ice. Add soda, stir gently and serve.

East India Cocktail

35.3% ALC/VOL • 1.6 STD DRINKS

45ml (1½ fl oz) Brandy
5ml (1/6 fl oz) Jamaica Rum
3 dashes Cointreau
Dash Angostura Bitters
3 dashes Pineapple Juice
Maraschino Cherry
Twist of Lemon Peel

Pour Brandy, Rum, Cointreau, Bitters and juice into a cocktail shaker over ice. Shake and strain into a chilled cocktail glass. Garnish with a cherry and lemon peel then serve.

Connoisseur's Treat

39% ALC/VOL • 2.3 STD DRINKS

45ml (1½ fl oz) Cognac
15ml (½ fl oz) Galliano
15ml (½ fl oz) Grand Marnier

Pour ingredients into a mixing glass over ice and stir. Strain into a chilled brandy balloon and serve.

All-in

36.9% ALC/VOL • 4.2 STD DRINKS

60ml (2 fl oz) Brandy
60ml (2 fl oz) Bourbon
10ml (⅓ fl oz) Pernod
5ml (1/6 fl oz) Curaçao
3 dashes Angostura Bitters
1 teaspoon Sugar Syrup

Pour ingredients into a cocktail shaker over ice and shake. Strain into a chilled old-fashioned glass and serve.

Warday's Cocktail

31.1% ALC/VOL • 2.3 STD DRINKS

30ml (1 fl oz) Applejack
30ml (1 fl oz) Gin
30ml (1 fl oz) Sweet Vermouth
5ml (1/6 fl oz) Yellow Chartreuse

Pour ingredients into a cocktail shaker over ice and shake. Strain into a chilled cocktail glass and serve.

Brighton Punch

21% ALC/VOL • 2.6 STD DRINKS

30ml (1 fl oz) Cognac
30ml (1 fl oz) Bourbon
23ml (¾ fl oz) Bénédictine
30ml (1 fl oz) Fresh Orange Juice
15ml (½ fl oz) Fresh Lemon Juice
30ml (1 fl oz) Soda Water
Slice of Lemon
Slice of Orange

Pour Cognac, Bourbon, Bénédictine and juices into a cocktail shaker over ice. Shake and strain into a collins glass over ice then add soda – do not stir. Garnish with a slice of lemon and orange then serve.
This drink is also known as Venetian Dream.

Venetian Dream

21% ALC/VOL • 2.6 STD DRINKS

This drink is also known as Brighton Punch, above.

Femina

30.2% ALC/VOL • 1.8 STD DRINKS

45ml (1½ fl oz) Brandy
15ml (½ fl oz) Bénédictine
15ml (½ fl oz) Fresh Orange Juice
Slice of Orange

Pour Brandy, Bénédictine and juice into a cocktail shaker over ice. Shake and strain into an old-fashioned glass over ice. Garnish with a slice of orange and serve.

Brandy Manhattan

32.8% ALC/VOL • 2 STD DRINKS

60ml (2 fl oz) Brandy
15ml (½ fl oz) Sweet Vermouth
Dash Angostura Bitters
Maraschino Cherry

Pour Brandy, Vermouth and Bitters into a mixing glass over ice. Stir and strain into a chilled cocktail glass. Garnish with a cherry and serve.

Apple Rum Rickey

12.5% ALC/VOL • 1.4 STD DRINKS

23ml (¾ fl oz) Applejack
23ml (¾ fl oz) Light Rum
8ml (¼ fl oz) Fresh Lime Juice
90ml (3 fl oz) Soda Water
Twist of Lime Peel
Twist of Orange Peel

Pour Applejack, Rum and juice into a cocktail shaker over ice. Shake and strain into a collins glass over ice. Add soda and stir gently. Twist lime and orange peels above drink. Place remainder of peels into drink and serve.

Hell

30% ALC/VOL • 2.1 STD DRINKS

This drink is also known as *Thistle, p 20.*

Cherry O

16.5% ALC/VOL • 0.6 STD DRINKS

15ml (½ fl oz) Cherry Brandy
15ml (½ fl oz) Tia Maria
15ml (½ fl oz) Fresh Cream
Cherry

Pour Brandy, Tia and cream into a cocktail shaker over ice. Shake and strain into a chilled cocktail glass. Garnish with a cherry and serve.

Cold Deck Cocktail

29.2% ALC/VOL • 1.1 STD DRINKS

30ml (1 fl oz) Brandy
15ml (½ fl oz) Sweet Vermouth
3 dashes White Crème De Menthe

Pour ingredients into a mixing glass over ice and stir. Strain into a chilled cocktail glass and serve.

Cognac Zoom

20.9% ALC/VOL • 1.9 STD DRINKS

60ml (2 fl oz) Cognac
30ml (1 fl oz) Boiling Water
20ml (⅔ fl oz) Thick Cream
1 teaspoon Honey

Pour boiling water into a mixing glass over a silver spoon (to prevent glass cracking) then add honey and stir to dissolve. Allow to cool and pour into a cocktail shaker over ice. Add Cognac and cream. Shake and strain into a chilled cocktail glass then serve.

Brandy Smash

34.2% ALC/VOL • 1.8 STD DRINKS

60ml (2 fl oz) Brandy
1 teaspoon Sugar Syrup
4 Sprigs of Fresh Mint

Place 3 sprigs of mint into a mixing glass over ice and muddle well. Add Brandy and sugar. Muddle together and pour into an old-fashioned glass half filled with ice. Add more ice to fill glass and stir. Garnish with a sprig of mint and serve.

Pear Rickey

13.5% ALC/VOL • 1.5 STD DRINKS

45ml (1½ fl oz) Dry Pear Brandy
8ml (¼ fl oz) Fresh Lime Juice
90ml (3 fl oz) Soda Water
2 Wedges of Pear

Pour Brandy and juice into a cocktail shaker over ice. Shake and strain into a collins glass over ice. Add soda and stir gently. Garnish with wedges of pear and serve.

Alexander Cocktail

20% ALC/VOL • 1.4 STD DRINKS

30ml (1 fl oz) Brandy
30ml (1 fl oz) White Crème De Cacao
30ml (1 fl oz) Fresh Cream
Nutmeg

Pour Brandy, Cacao and cream into a cocktail shaker over ice. Shake and strain into a chilled cocktail glass. Sprinkle nutmeg on top and serve.

Brandy Berry Fix

24.6% ALC/VOL • 1.8 STD DRINKS

60ml (2 fl oz) Brandy
5ml (⅙ fl oz) Strawberry Liqueur
15ml (½ fl oz) Fresh Lemon Juice
10ml (⅓ fl oz) Spring Water
1 teaspoon Sugar Syrup
Slice of Lemon
Strawberry

Pour Brandy, Liqueur, juice, water and sugar into an old-fashioned glass filled with crushed ice. Add more crushed ice to fill glass and stir. Garnish with a slice of lemon and a strawberry then serve.

Brandy Kiss

25.6% ALC/VOL • 1.8 STD DRINKS

30ml (1 fl oz) Brandy
30ml (1 fl oz) Grand Marnier
30ml (1 fl oz) Fresh
Lemon Juice

Pour ingredients into a cocktail shaker over ice and shake. Strain into a chilled cocktail glass and serve.

Blackberry Fizz

6.5% ALC/VOL • 1.2 STD DRINKS

45ml (1½ fl oz) Blackberry
Brandy
45ml (1½ fl oz) Fresh
Orange Juice
30ml (1 fl oz) Fresh
Lemon Juice
½ teaspoon Caster Sugar
120ml (4 fl oz) Lemonade
Slice of Lemon

Pour Brandy and juices into a highball glass over ice. Add sugar and stir. Add lemonade and stir gently. Garnish with a slice of lemon then serve with a swizzle stick and 2 straws.

Brandy Rickey

11.1% ALC/VOL • 1.3 STD DRINKS

This drink is also known as *Brandy, Lime and Soda, p 33.*

Berries and Cream

16.6% ALC/VOL • 1.4 STD DRINKS

30ml (1 fl oz) Blackberry
Brandy
30ml (1 fl oz) Strawberry
Liqueur
30ml (1 fl oz) Non-Dairy
Creamer
15ml (½ fl oz) Fresh
Lime Juice

Pour ingredients into a cocktail shaker over ice and shake. Strain into a chilled cocktail glass and serve.

This drink may also be served over ice if desired.

Blackjack

17.1% ALC/VOL • 1.6 STD DRINKS

30ml (1 fl oz) Cognac
15ml (½ fl oz) Kahlúa
15ml (½ fl oz) Kirsch
60ml (2 fl oz) Black Coffee
(chilled)

Pour ingredients into a cocktail shaker over cracked ice and shake. Pour into a chilled old-fashioned glass and serve.

Apple Swizzle

12.7% ALC/VOL • 2.1 STD DRINKS

45ml (1½ fl oz) Apple Brandy
23ml (¾ fl oz) Dark Rum
45ml (1½ fl oz) Fresh
Lime Juice
1 teaspoon Sugar Syrup
90ml (3 fl oz) Apple Soda

Pour Brandy, Rum, juice and sugar into a mixing glass over large amount of ice. Stir vigorously until cold and strain into a collins glass filled with crushed ice. Add soda – do not stir, then serve with a swizzle stick and 2 straws.

Bacchus

24.3% ALC/VOL • 2.3 STD DRINKS

This drink is also known as *Cuban, p 21.*

Brantini

36.7% ALC/VOL • 2.2 STD DRINKS

45ml (1½ fl oz) Brandy
30ml (1 fl oz) Dry Gin
Dash Dry Vermouth
Twist of Lemon Peel

Pour Brandy, Gin and Vermouth into a mixing glass over ice. Stir and strain into an old-fashioned glass over ice. Garnish with lemon peel and serve.

Frozen Applecart

14.4% ALC/VOL • 1.4 STD DRINKS

45ml (1½ fl oz) Applejack
15ml (½ fl oz) Fresh
Lemon Juice
1 teaspoon Sugar Syrup
¼ Cup Peeled Apple (diced)

Pour Applejack, juice and sugar into a blender over cracked ice then add diced apple. Blend and pour into a chilled champagne saucer then serve.

Apple Blow

16.4% ALC/VOL • 2.8 STD DRINKS

90ml (3 fl oz) Applejack
4 dashes Fresh Lemon Juice
1 teaspoon Sugar Syrup
White of 1 Egg
90ml (3 fl oz) Soda Water

Pour Applejack, juice, sugar and egg white into a cocktail shaker over ice. Shake and strain into a highball glass over ice. Add soda, stir gently and serve.

Grapefruit Nog

6.4% ALC/VOL • 1.3 STD DRINKS

45ml (1½ fl oz) Brandy
120ml (4 fl oz) Grapefruit Juice
30ml (1 fl oz) Fresh
Lemon Juice
1 tablespoon Honey
1 Fresh Egg

Pour ingredients into a blender over crushed ice and blend. Pour into a collins glass over ice and serve.

Brandy Mint Fizz

14% ALC/VOL • 2 STD DRINKS

60ml (2 fl oz) Brandy
10ml (⅓ fl oz) White Crème De Menthe
5ml (⅙ fl oz) White Crème De Cacao
15ml (½ fl oz) Fresh Lemon Juice
½ teaspoon Caster Sugar
90ml (3 fl oz) Soda Water
2 Fresh Mint Leaves

Pour Brandy, Crème De Menthe, Cacao and juice into a cocktail shaker over ice then add sugar. Shake and strain into a highball glass over ice. Add soda and stir gently. Garnish with mint leaves and serve.

Bonnie Prince Charlie

28.5% ALC/VOL • 1.3 STD DRINKS

30ml (1 fl oz) Brandy
15ml (½ fl oz) Drambuie
15ml (½ fl oz) Fresh Lemon Juice

Pour ingredients into a cocktail shaker over ice and shake. Strain into a chilled cocktail glass and serve.

Gamble

12.8% ALC/VOL • 1.4 STD DRINKS

30ml (1 fl oz) Apricot Brandy
23ml (¾ fl oz) Mandarine Napoleon
15ml (½ fl oz) Sweet Sherry
30ml (1 fl oz) Mango Juice
1½ scoops Vanilla Ice Cream

Pour Brandy, Mandarine Napoleon, Sherry and juice into a blender over small amount of crushed ice then add ice cream. Blend until smooth and pour into a chilled goblet then serve.

Barney Barnato

26.7% ALC/VOL • 1.9 STD DRINKS

45ml (1½ fl oz) Brandy
45ml (1½ fl oz) Dubonnet
Dash Angostura Bitters
Dash Curaçao

Pour ingredients into a mixing glass over ice and stir. Strain into a chilled cocktail glass and serve.

Frozen Apple

22.5% ALC/VOL • 1.4 STD DRINKS

45ml (1½ fl oz) Applejack
15ml (½ fl oz) Fresh Lime Juice
1 teaspoon Sugar Syrup
½ Egg White

Pour ingredients into a blender over crushed ice and blend. Pour into a chilled champagne saucer and serve.

Marryat's Mint Julep

25.1% ALC/VOL • 2.2 STD DRINKS

45ml (1½ fl oz) Cognac
45ml (1½ fl oz) Peach Brandy
1½ tablespoons Sugar Syrup
12 Sprigs of Fresh Mint

Pour Cognac, Brandy and sugar into a chilled collins glass. Add sprigs of mint and muddle well. Fill with crushed ice, stir gently and serve.

Dream Cocktail

37.9% ALC/VOL • 2.1 STD DRINKS

45ml (1½ fl oz) Brandy
23ml (¾ fl oz) Cointreau
2 dashes Anisette

Pour ingredients into a cocktail shaker over ice and shake. Strain into a chilled cocktail glass and serve.

Bee Stinger

32.1% ALC/VOL • 1.5 STD DRINKS

45ml (1½ fl oz) Blackberry Brandy
15ml (½ fl oz) White Crème De Menthe

Pour ingredients into a cocktail shaker over ice and shake. Strain into a chilled cocktail glass and serve.

Santa Fe

26.2% ALC/VOL • 2 STD DRINKS

This drink is also known as Topeka, p 25.

Apple Ginger Sangaree

33.5% ALC/VOL • 1.6 STD DRINKS

45ml (1½ fl oz) Apple Brandy
15ml (½ fl oz) Green Ginger Wine
Slice of Lemon
Nutmeg

Pour Brandy and Wine into a goblet over ice then stir. Sprinkle nutmeg on top and garnish with a slice of lemon then serve.

Cranberry Cooler No.2

13.9% ALC/VOL • 1.8 STD DRINKS

30ml (1 fl oz) Brandy
30ml (1 fl oz) Cranberry Liqueur
15ml (½ fl oz) Cointreau
90ml (3 fl oz) Tonic Water

Pour Brandy, Liqueur and Cointreau into a collins glass over ice then stir. Add tonic, stir gently and serve.

Romana

28.9% ALC/VOL • 2.1 STD DRINKS

60ml (2 fl oz) Brandy
10ml (⅓ fl oz) Sambuca

10ml (⅓ fl oz) Fresh
Lemon Juice
1 teaspoon Sugar Syrup
1 teaspoon Egg White

Pour ingredients into a cocktail shaker over ice and shake. Strain into a chilled cocktail glass and serve.
This drink is also known as Via Veneto.

Apricot

11.6% ALC/VOL • 0.8 STD DRINKS

45ml (1½ fl oz) Apricot Brandy
Dash Dry Gin
23ml (¾ fl oz) Fresh
Lime Juice
23ml (¾ fl oz) Fresh
Orange Juice

Pour ingredients into a cocktail shaker over ice and shake. Strain into a chilled cocktail glass and serve.

Brace Up

8.9% ALC/VOL • 1.4 STD DRINKS

45ml (1½ fl oz) Brandy
2 dashes Anisette
2 dashes Curaçao
15ml (½ fl oz) Fresh
Lime Juice
½ teaspoon Sugar Syrup
1 Fresh Egg
90ml (3 fl oz) Soda Water
Slice of Lime
Slice of Orange

Pour Brandy, Anisette, Curaçao, juice, sugar and egg into a cocktail shaker over ice. Shake and strain into an old-fashioned glass over ice. Add soda and stir gently. Garnish with a slice of lime and orange then serve.

Froupe Cocktail

27.2% ALC/VOL • 2.1 STD DRINKS

This drink is also known as Sweet Stinger, p 29.

Apricot Tree

12.2% ALC/VOL • 1.3 STD DRINKS

30ml (1 fl oz) Apricot Brandy
30ml (1 fl oz) Rum Tree
15ml (½ fl oz) Dry Vermouth
30ml (1 fl oz) Apricot Juice
30ml (1 fl oz) Pineapple Juice

Pour ingredients into a cocktail shaker over ice and shake. Strain into a chilled cocktail glass and serve.

Moonlight

12.6% ALC/VOL • 1.4 STD DRINKS

45ml (1½ fl oz) Calvados
30ml (1 fl oz) Fresh
Lemon Juice
1½ teaspoons Sugar Syrup
60ml (2 fl oz) Soda Water

Pour Calvados, juice and sugar into a cocktail shaker over ice. Shake and strain into an old-fashioned glass over ice. Add soda, stir gently and serve.

Alexandra

24.7% ALC/VOL • 2.4 STD DRINKS

30ml (1 fl oz) Cognac
30ml (1 fl oz) Cointreau
30ml (1 fl oz) White Crème
De Cacao
30ml (1 fl oz) Thick Cream
1 teaspoon Egg White

Pour ingredients into a cocktail shaker over ice and shake. Strain into a chilled champagne saucer and serve.

Nude Ell Cocktail

37.1% ALC/VOL • 1.8 STD DRINKS

15ml (½ fl oz) Cognac
15ml (½ fl oz) Dubonnet
15ml (½ fl oz) Gin
15ml (½ fl oz) Green
Chartreuse

Pour ingredients into a cocktail shaker over ice and shake. Strain into a chilled cocktail glass and serve.

Young Man

29.8% ALC/VOL • 2.2 STD DRINKS

60ml (2 fl oz) Brandy
30ml (1 fl oz) Sweet Vermouth
2 dashes Curaçao
Dash Angostura Bitters
Twist of Lemon Peel

Pour Brandy, Vermouth, Curaçao and Bitters into a mixing glass over ice. Stir and strain into a chilled cocktail glass. Garnish with lemon peel and serve.

Sweet Stinger

27.2% ALC/VOL • 2.1 STD DRINKS

45ml (1½ fl oz) Brandy
45ml (1½ fl oz) Sweet
Vermouth
8ml (¼ fl oz) Bénédictine

Pour ingredients into a mixing glass over ice and stir. Strain into a chilled cocktail glass and serve.
This drink is also known as Froupe Cocktail.

Klondike

29.5% ALC/VOL • 1.4 STD DRINKS

30ml (1 fl oz) Applejack
30ml (1 fl oz) Dry Vermouth
2 dashes Angostura Bitters
Olive
Twist of Lemon Peel

Pour Applejack, Vermouth and Bitters into a cocktail shaker over ice. Shake and strain into a chilled cocktail glass. Garnish with an olive and lemon peel then serve.

Brandy Puff

9.3% ALC/VOL • 1.8 STD DRINKS

60ml (2 fl oz) Brandy
90ml (3 fl oz) Fresh Milk (chilled)
90ml (3 fl oz) Soda Water

Pour Brandy and milk into a cocktail shaker over ice. Shake and strain into a chilled goblet. Add soda, stir gently and serve.

Cuban Apple

32.7% ALC/VOL • 2.3 STD DRINKS

45ml (1½ fl oz) Apple Brandy
30ml (1 fl oz) Light Rum
15ml (½ fl oz) Fresh Lime Juice
Slice of Lime

Pour Brandy, Rum and juice into a cocktail shaker over ice. Shake and strain into a chilled cocktail glass. Garnish with a slice of lime and serve.

Dry Brandy Manhattan

33.3% ALC/VOL • 2 STD DRINKS

60ml (2 fl oz) Brandy
15ml (½ fl oz) Dry Vermouth
Dash Angostura Bitters
Maraschino Cherry

Pour Brandy, Vermouth and Bitters into a mixing glass over ice. Stir and strain into a chilled cocktail glass. Garnish with a cherry and serve.

T.N.T.

33.2% ALC/VOL • 2.4 STD DRINKS

60ml (2 fl oz) Brandy
30ml (1 fl oz) Orange Curaçao
Dash Angostura Bitters
Dash Pernod
Twist of Orange Peel

Pour Brandy, Curaçao, Bitters and Pernod into a mixing glass over ice. Stir and strain into a chilled cocktail glass. Garnish with orange peel and serve.

Brandy Champarelle

40.9% ALC/VOL • 2.5 STD DRINKS

23ml (¾ fl oz) Cognac
23ml (¾ fl oz) Cointreau
15ml (½ fl oz) Anisette
15ml (½ fl oz) Green Chartreuse

Pour ingredients into a mixing glass without ice and stir. Pour into a liqueur glass and serve.

Brandy Swizzle

25.9% ALC/VOL • 1.9 STD DRINKS

60ml (2 fl oz) Brandy
3 dashes Angostura Bitters
23ml (¾ fl oz) Fresh Lime Juice
1 teaspoon Sugar Syrup
75ml (2½ fl oz) Soda Water

Pour Brandy, Bitters, juice and sugar into a mixing glass over large amount of ice. Stir vigorously until cold and strain into a collins glass filled with crushed ice. Add soda – do not stir, then serve with a swizzle stick and 2 straws.

Applejack Rabbit

19% ALC/VOL • 1.4 STD DRINKS

45ml (1½ fl oz) Calvados
5ml (⅙ fl oz) Grenadine
30ml (1 fl oz) Fresh Orange Juice
15ml (½ fl oz) Fresh Lemon Juice

Pour ingredients into a cocktail shaker over ice and shake. Strain into a chilled cocktail glass and serve.

Brandy Daisy

22.6% ALC/VOL • 1.7 STD DRINKS

60ml (2 fl oz) Brandy
8ml (¼ fl oz) Grenadine
30ml (1 fl oz) Fresh Lemon Juice
Maraschino Cherry
Sprig of Fresh Mint

Pour Brandy, Grenadine and juice into a cocktail shaker over ice. Shake and strain into a goblet over ice. Top up with soda water if desired and stir gently. Garnish with a cherry and sprig of mint then serve.

Pumpa Gubben

20% ALC/VOL • 1.4 STD DRINKS

30ml (1 fl oz) Cognac
30ml (1 fl oz) Kahlúa
30ml (1 fl oz) Fresh Cream

Pour ingredients into an old-fashioned glass over ice, stir well and serve.

Fontainebleau Special

30.4% ALC/VOL • 1.8 STD DRINKS

30ml (1 fl oz) Brandy
30ml (1 fl oz) Anisette
15ml (½ fl oz) Dry Vermouth

Pour ingredients into a cocktail shaker over ice and shake. Strain into a chilled cocktail glass and serve.

Weave and Skid

37% ALC/VOL • 1.2 STD DRINKS

30ml (1 fl oz) Cognac
10ml (⅓ fl oz) Amaretto

Pour ingredients into a brandy balloon – do not stir, then serve with a swizzle stick.

Apple Bitter

37.2% ALC/VOL • 2 STD DRINKS

This drink is also known as Bitter Apple, p 10.

Nick's Own

26.3% ALC/VOL • 1.9 STD DRINKS

45ml (1½ fl oz) Brandy
45ml (1½ fl oz) Sweet Vermouth
Dash Angostura Bitters
Dash Pernod
Maraschino Cherry
Twist of Lemon Peel

Pour Brandy, Vermouth, Bitters and Pernod into a mixing glass over ice. Stir and strain into a chilled cocktail glass. Garnish with a cherry and lemon peel then serve.

Gold Card

38.3% ALC/VOL • 1.6 STD DRINKS

30ml (1 fl oz) Brandy
15ml (½ fl oz) Bénédictine
8ml (¼ fl oz) Yellow Chartreuse

Pour ingredients into a cocktail shaker over ice and shake. Strain into a chilled cocktail glass and serve.

Bengal

25.3% ALC/VOL • 2.1 STD DRINKS

45ml (1½ fl oz) Brandy
15ml (½ fl oz) Cointreau
15ml (½ fl oz) Maraschino Liqueur
2 dashes Orange Bitters
30ml (1 fl oz) Pineapple Juice

Pour ingredients into a cocktail shaker over ice and shake. Strain into a chilled cocktail glass and serve.

Sweet William

21% ALC/VOL • 1.1 STD DRINKS

23ml (¾ fl oz) Poire Williams
23ml (¾ fl oz) Apricot Liqueur
23ml (¾ fl oz) Thick Cream
Cinnamon

Pour Poire Williams, Liqueur and cream into a cocktail shaker over ice. Shake and strain into a chilled cocktail glass. Sprinkle cinnamon on top and serve.

Egg Sour

12.9% ALC/VOL • 1.5 STD DRINKS

30ml (1 fl oz) Brandy
30ml (1 fl oz) Orange Curaçao
30ml (1 fl oz) Fresh Lemon Juice
2 teaspoons Sugar Syrup
1 Fresh Egg

Pour ingredients into a cocktail shaker over ice and shake. Strain into a chilled sour glass and serve.

Flying Fortress

38.7% ALC/VOL • 2.5 STD DRINKS

30ml (1 fl oz) Brandy
23ml (¾ fl oz) Vodka
15ml (½ fl oz) Absinthe
15ml (½ fl oz) Triple Sec

Pour ingredients into a cocktail shaker over cracked ice and shake. Pour into a chilled wine glass and serve.

Bolero

27.8% ALC/VOL • 1.8 STD DRINKS

30ml (1 fl oz) Cognac
30ml (1 fl oz) Golden Rum
15ml (½ fl oz) Fresh Lime Juice
5ml (1/6 fl oz) Fresh Orange Juice
½ teaspoon Sugar Syrup
Slice of Orange

Pour Cognac, Rum, juices and sugar into a cocktail shaker over ice. Shake and strain into a chilled cocktail glass. Garnish with a slice of orange and serve.

Apples to Oranges

30.4% ALC/VOL • 1.8 STD DRINKS

30ml (1 fl oz) Apple Brandy
30ml (1 fl oz) Dubonnet
15ml (½ fl oz) Cointreau

Pour ingredients into a cocktail shaker over ice and shake. Strain into a chilled cocktail glass and serve.

Brandy Sour

26.1% ALC/VOL • 1.8 STD DRINKS

60ml (2 fl oz) Brandy
15ml (½ fl oz) Fresh Lemon Juice
1 teaspoon Sugar Syrup
1 teaspoon Egg White
Maraschino Cherry
Twist of Lemon Peel

Pour Brandy, juice, sugar and egg white into a cocktail shaker over ice. Shake and strain into a chilled sour glass. Garnish with a cherry and lemon peel then serve.

Paradise Cocktail

16.1% ALC/VOL • 1 STD DRINK

30ml (1 fl oz) Apricot Brandy
23ml (¾ fl oz) Gin
23ml (¾ fl oz) Fresh Orange Juice

Pour ingredients into a cocktail shaker over ice and shake. Strain into a chilled cocktail glass and serve.

Brandied Port

22.3% ALC/VOL • 1.4 STD DRINKS

30ml (1 fl oz) Brandy
30ml (1 fl oz) Tawny Port

5ml (1/6 fl oz) Maraschino Liqueur
15ml (½ fl oz) Fresh Lemon Juice
Slice of Orange

Pour Brandy, Port, Liqueur and juice into a cocktail shaker over ice. Shake and strain into an old-fashioned glass over ice. Garnish with a slice of orange and serve.

Apple Dubonnet

28% ALC/VOL • 1.3 STD DRINKS

30ml (1 fl oz) Calvados
30ml (1 fl oz) Dubonnet
Slice of Lemon

Pour Calvados and Dubonnet into a mixing glass over ice. Stir and strain into an old-fashioned glass over ice. Garnish with a slice of lemon and serve.

Brandy Fix

21.2% ALC/VOL • 1.4 STD DRINKS

30ml (1 fl oz) Brandy
30ml (1 fl oz) Cherry Brandy
15ml (½ fl oz) Fresh Lemon Juice
5ml (1/6 fl oz) Spring Water
1 teaspoon Sugar Syrup
Slice of Lemon

Pour Brandies, juice, water and sugar into an old-fashioned glass filled with crushed ice. Add more crushed ice to fill glass and stir. Garnish with a slice of lemon and serve.

Sidecar Cocktail

28.5% ALC/VOL • 1.3 STD DRINKS

30ml (1 fl oz) Brandy
15ml (½ fl oz) Cointreau
15ml (½ fl oz) Fresh Lemon Juice

Pour ingredients into a cocktail shaker over ice and shake. Strain into a chilled cocktail glass and serve.

Breakfast Egg Nog

12.4% ALC/VOL • 1.6 STD DRINKS

45ml (1½ fl oz) Brandy
15ml (½ fl oz) Orange Curaçao
60ml (2 fl oz) Fresh Milk (chilled)
1 Fresh Egg
Nutmeg

Pour Brandy, Curaçao, milk and egg into a cocktail shaker over ice. Shake and strain into a chilled brandy balloon. Sprinkle nutmeg on top and serve.

Pierre Sour

27.9% ALC/VOL • 1.9 STD DRINKS

60ml (2 fl oz) Cognac
23ml (¾ fl oz) Fresh Lemon Juice
½ teaspoon Caster Sugar

Pour Cognac and juice into a cocktail shaker over ice then add sugar. Shake and strain into a chilled sour glass then serve.

Golden Dawn

24.7% ALC/VOL • 1.8 STD DRINKS

23ml (¾ fl oz) Apricot Brandy
23ml (¾ fl oz) Applejack
23ml (¾ fl oz) Dry Gin
Dash Grenadine
23ml (¾ fl oz) Fresh Orange Juice
Slice of Orange

Pour Brandy, Applejack, Gin, Grenadine and juice into a cocktail shaker over ice. Shake and strain into a chilled cocktail glass. Garnish with a slice of orange and serve.

Stinger

32.4% ALC/VOL • 2.3 STD DRINKS

60ml (2 fl oz) Brandy
30ml (1 fl oz) White Crème De Menthe

Pour ingredients into a mixing glass over ice and stir. Strain into a chilled cocktail glass and serve.

Brandy Fino

35.6% ALC/VOL • 2.1 STD DRINKS

45ml (1½ fl oz) Brandy or Cognac
15ml (½ fl oz) Drambuie
15ml (½ fl oz) Dry Sherry
Slice of Orange
Twist of Lemon Peel

Pour Brandy or Cognac, Drambuie and Sherry into a cocktail shaker over ice. Shake and strain into an old-fashioned glass over ice. Garnish with a slice of orange and lemon peel then serve.

Presto Cocktail

25.3% ALC/VOL • 1.6 STD DRINKS

45ml (1½ fl oz) Brandy
15ml (½ fl oz) Sweet Vermouth
Dash Anisette
15ml (½ fl oz) Fresh Orange Juice

Pour ingredients into a cocktail shaker over ice and shake. Strain into a chilled cocktail glass and serve.

Vanderbilt Cocktail

30.5% ALC/VOL • 1.6 STD DRINKS

30ml (1 fl oz) Cognac
30ml (1 fl oz) Cherry Brandy
2 dashes Angostura Bitters
½ teaspoon Sugar Syrup
Maraschino Cherry
Twist of Lemon Peel

Pour Cognac, Brandy, Bitters and sugar into a cocktail shaker over ice. Shake and strain into a chilled cocktail glass. Twist lemon peel above drink and discard remainder of peel. Garnish with a cherry and serve.

Hari Kari

12.9% ALC/VOL • 0.9 STD DRINKS

15ml (½ fl oz) Brandy
15ml (½ fl oz) Cointreau
60ml (2 fl oz) Fresh Orange Juice

Pour ingredients into a cocktail shaker over ice and shake. Strain into a chilled highball glass and serve.

Brandy, Lime and Soda

11.1% ALC/VOL • 1.3 STD DRINKS

45ml (1½ fl oz) Brandy
15ml (½ fl oz) Fresh Lime Juice
90ml (3 fl oz) Soda Water
Slice of Lemon

Pour Brandy and juice into an old-fashioned glass over ice then stir. Add soda and stir gently. Garnish with a slice of lemon and serve.
This drink is also known as Brandy Rickey.

Brandy Scaffa

33.4% ALC/VOL • 1.8 STD DRINKS

45ml (1½ fl oz) Brandy
23ml (¾ fl oz) Maraschino Liqueur
Dash Angostura Bitters

Pour ingredients into a cocktail glass, stir and serve.

Comforting Tiger

35.6% ALC/VOL • 2.4 STD DRINKS

60ml (2 fl oz) Brandy
15ml (½ fl oz) Southern Comfort
15ml (½ fl oz) Sweet Vermouth
Twist of Lemon Peel

Pour Brandy, Southern Comfort and Vermouth into a cocktail shaker over ice. Shake and strain into a chilled cocktail glass. Garnish with lemon peel and serve.

Newton's Special

37.8% ALC/VOL • 2.4 STD DRINKS

60ml (2 fl oz) Brandy
20ml (⅔ fl oz) Cointreau
Dash Angostura Bitters
Slice of Orange

Pour Brandy, Cointreau and Bitters into a cocktail shaker over ice. Shake and strain into a chilled cocktail glass. Garnish with a slice of orange and serve.

Apricot Cooler No.2

16.6% ALC/VOL • 1 STD DRINK

30ml (1 fl oz) Apricot Brandy
15ml (½ fl oz) Dry Gin
15ml (½ fl oz) Fresh Lemon Juice
15ml (½ fl oz) Fresh Orange Juice
Slice of Lemon
Slice of Orange

Pour Brandy, Gin and juices into a cocktail shaker over ice. Shake and strain into a chilled collins glass. Garnish with a slice of lemon and orange then serve.

Montana

27.5% ALC/VOL • 2 STD DRINKS

45ml (1½ fl oz) Brandy
30ml (1 fl oz) Port
15ml (½ fl oz) Dry Vermouth

Pour ingredients into an old-fashioned glass over ice, stir and serve.

Booster

25.3% ALC/VOL • 1.9 STD DRINKS

60ml (2 fl oz) Brandy
4 dashes Cointreau
White of 1 Egg
Nutmeg

Pour Brandy, Cointreau and egg white into a cocktail shaker over ice. Shake and strain into a chilled cocktail glass. Sprinkle nutmeg on top and serve.
This drink is also known as Yes and No.

Coronation No.2

32.8% ALC/VOL • 3.5 STD DRINKS

90ml (3 fl oz) Brandy
45ml (1½ fl oz) Curaçao
Dash Peach Bitters
Dash White Crème De Menthe

Pour ingredients into a mixing glass over ice and stir. Strain into a chilled cocktail glass and serve.

Butt Munch

20.2% ALC/VOL • 2.6 STD DRINKS

60ml (2 fl oz) Brandy
30ml (1 fl oz) Dark Rum
30ml (1 fl oz) Black Coffee (chilled)
30ml (1 fl oz) Cocoa (chilled)
15ml (½ fl oz) Honey

Pour ingredients into a blender over small amount of crushed ice and blend until smooth. Pour into a chilled coffee glass and serve.

Bloody Lip

30.8% ALC/VOL • 1.5 STD DRINKS

30ml (1 fl oz) Cherry Brandy
15ml (½ fl oz) Maraschino Liqueur
15ml (½ fl oz) Vodka
Maraschino Cherry

Pour Brandy, Liqueur and Vodka into a cocktail shaker over ice. Shake and strain into a chilled cocktail glass. Garnish with a cherry and serve.

Applejack Sour

30% ALC/VOL • 1.9 STD DRINKS

60ml (2 fl oz) Applejack
15ml (½ fl oz) Fresh Lemon Juice
1 teaspoon Sugar Syrup
Slice of Lemon

Pour Applejack, juice and sugar into a cocktail shaker over ice. Shake and strain into a chilled sour glass. Garnish with a slice of lemon and serve.

Separator

22.8% ALC/VOL • 1.3 STD DRINKS

30ml (1 fl oz) Brandy
30ml (1 fl oz) Kahlúa
15ml (½ fl oz) Fresh Cream

Pour Brandy and Kahlúa into a cocktail glass half filled with cracked ice then stir. Float cream on top and serve.

Mississippi Planters Punch

8.8% ALC/VOL • 1.8 STD DRINKS

30ml (1 fl oz) Brandy
15ml (½ fl oz) Bourbon
15ml (½ fl oz) Light Rum
15ml (½ fl oz) Fresh Lemon Juice
1 teaspoon Sugar Syrup
180ml (6 fl oz) Soda Water

Pour Brandy, Bourbon, Rum, juice and sugar into a cocktail shaker over ice. Shake and strain into a collins glass over ice. Add soda, stir gently and serve.

Liberty Cocktail

37.9% ALC/VOL • 2.1 STD DRINKS

45ml (1½ fl oz) Apple Brandy
23ml (¾ fl oz) Light Rum
2 dashes Sugar Syrup

Pour ingredients into a mixing glass over ice and stir. Strain into a chilled cocktail glass and serve.

None but the Brave

33.2% ALC/VOL • 2.7 STD DRINKS

60ml (2 fl oz) Brandy
30ml (1 fl oz) Bénédictine
8ml (¼ fl oz) Fresh Lemon Juice
1 teaspoon Sugar Syrup
Slice of Lemon

Pour Brandy, Bénédictine, juice and sugar into a cocktail shaker over ice. Shake and strain into a collins glass over ice. Top up with soda water if desired and stir gently. Garnish with a slice of lemon and serve.

Bosom Caresser

27% ALC/VOL • 2.3 STD DRINKS

60ml (2 fl oz) Brandy
30ml (1 fl oz) Orange Curaçao
5ml (⅙ fl oz) Grenadine
Yolk of 1 Egg

Pour ingredients into a cocktail shaker over ice and shake. Strain into a chilled cocktail glass and serve.

Brandy Flip

17.5% ALC/VOL • 1.3 STD DRINKS

45ml (1½ fl oz) Brandy
1 teaspoon Sugar Syrup
1 Fresh Egg
Nutmeg

Pour Brandy, sugar and egg into a cocktail shaker over ice. Shake and strain into a goblet over ice. Sprinkle nutmeg on top and serve.

Candida

20% ALC/VOL • 1.7 STD DRINKS

30ml (1 fl oz) Cognac
30ml (1 fl oz) Anisette
30ml (1 fl oz) Thick Cream
½ Egg White

Pour ingredients into a cocktail shaker over ice and shake. Strain into a champagne saucer filled with crushed ice and serve.

Laguna

34.2% ALC/VOL • 2.2 STD DRINKS

60ml (2 fl oz) Brandy
8ml (¼ fl oz) Sweet Vermouth
8ml (¼ fl oz) Vodka
5ml (⅙ fl oz) Campari
Dash Angostura Bitters
Maraschino Cherry

Pour Brandy, Vermouth, Vodka, Campari and Bitters into a cocktail shaker over ice. Shake and strain into a chilled cocktail glass. Garnish with a cherry and serve.

Jack-in-the-Box

20.4% ALC/VOL • 1 STD DRINK

30ml (1 fl oz) Apple Brandy
Dash Angostura Bitters
30ml (1 fl oz) Pineapple Juice

Pour ingredients into a cocktail shaker over ice and shake. Strain into a chilled cocktail glass and serve.

Brandy Egg Nog

10.7% ALC/VOL • 1.3 STD DRINKS

45ml (1½ fl oz) Brandy
60ml (2 fl oz) Fresh Milk (chilled)

1 teaspoon Sugar Syrup
1 Fresh Egg
Nutmeg

Pour Brandy, milk, sugar and egg into a cocktail shaker over ice. Shake and strain into a chilled collins glass. Sprinkle nutmeg on top and serve.

Three Miller

34% ALC/VOL • 2 STD DRINKS

45ml (1½ fl oz) Brandy
23ml (¾ fl oz) Light Rum
5ml (1/6 fl oz) Grenadine
Dash Fresh Lemon Juice

Pour ingredients into a mixing glass over ice and stir. Strain into a chilled cocktail glass and serve.

Disappointed Lady

23% ALC/VOL • 1.6 STD DRINKS

23ml (¾ fl oz) Brandy
23ml (¾ fl oz) Crème De Noyaux
23ml (¾ fl oz) Tia Maria
Dash Grenadine
23ml (¾ fl oz) Fresh Orange Juice
Nutmeg

Pour Brandy, Noyaux, Tia and juice into a cocktail shaker over ice. Shake and strain into a chilled cocktail glass. Add Grenadine – do not stir, then sprinkle nutmeg on top and serve.

Bull Frog

24.4% ALC/VOL • 1.8 STD DRINKS

60ml (2 fl oz) Brandy
30ml (1 fl oz) Fresh Lemon Juice
Dash Egg White

Pour ingredients into a cocktail shaker over ice and shake. Strain into a chilled cocktail glass and serve.

Baltimore Egg Nog

4.4% ALC/VOL • 1 STD DRINK

15ml (½ fl oz) Brandy
15ml (½ fl oz) Dark Rum
15ml (½ fl oz) Madeira
200ml (6⅔ fl oz) Fresh Milk (chilled)
1 teaspoon Sugar Syrup
1 Fresh Egg
Nutmeg

Pour Brandy, Rum, Madeira, milk, sugar and egg into a cocktail shaker over ice. Shake and strain into a chilled collins glass. Sprinkle nutmeg on top and serve.

Bonaparte

40% ALC/VOL • 1.7 STD DRINKS

30ml (1 fl oz) Cognac
23ml (¾ fl oz) Mandarine Napoleon

Pour ingredients into a brandy balloon, stir gently and serve.

Midnight Massacre

10.6% ALC/VOL • 2.8 STD DRINKS

30ml (1 fl oz) Brandy
30ml (1 fl oz) Bourbon
30ml (1 fl oz) Scotch Whisky
2 drops Amaretto
2 drops Chocolate Syrup
240ml (8 fl oz) Cola

Pour Brandy, Bourbon, Whisky, Amaretto and syrup into a mixing glass over ice. Stir and strain into a chilled tall glass. Add cola, stir gently and serve.

Leviathan Mix

22.3% ALC/VOL • 1.1 STD DRINKS

30ml (1 fl oz) Brandy
15ml (½ fl oz) Sweet Vermouth
15ml (½ fl oz) Fresh Orange Juice

Pour ingredients into a cocktail shaker over ice and shake. Strain into a chilled cocktail glass and serve.

Pink Whiskers

14.1% ALC/VOL • 1.2 STD DRINKS

30ml (1 fl oz) Apricot Brandy
30ml (1 fl oz) Port
15ml (½ fl oz) Dry Vermouth
3 dashes White Crème De Menthe
5ml (1/6 fl oz) Grenadine
30ml (1 fl oz) Fresh Orange Juice

Pour Brandy, Vermouth, Crème De Menthe, Grenadine and juice into a cocktail shaker over ice. Shake and strain into a highball glass filled with ice. Layer Port on top and serve.

Pisco Punch

24.7% ALC/VOL • 1.8 STD DRINKS

60ml (2 fl oz) Pisco
15ml (½ fl oz) Fresh Lemon Juice
15ml (½ fl oz) Pineapple Juice

Pour ingredients into a cocktail shaker over ice and shake. Strain into a chilled cocktail glass and serve.

Depth Charge Cocktail

30.1% ALC/VOL • 2.3 STD DRINKS

45ml (1½ fl oz) Brandy
30ml (1 fl oz) Calvados
5ml (1/6 fl oz) Grenadine
15ml (½ fl oz) Fresh Lemon Juice
Twist of Lemon Peel

Pour Brandy, Calvados, Grenadine and juice into a cocktail shaker over ice. Shake and strain into a chilled cocktail glass. Garnish with lemon peel and serve.

Roman Stinger

35.3% ALC/VOL • 1.7 STD DRINKS

30ml (1 fl oz) Cognac
15ml (½ fl oz) Green Crème De Menthe
15ml (½ fl oz) Sambuca

Pour ingredients into a cocktail shaker over ice and shake. Strain into a chilled cocktail glass and serve.

Cherry Blossom

29% ALC/VOL • 1.9 STD DRINKS

45ml (1½ fl oz) Brandy
30ml (1 fl oz) Cherry Brandy
Dash Curaçao
Dash Grenadine
5ml (1/6 fl oz) Fresh Lemon Juice

Prepare a cocktail glass with a sugar frosted rim. Pour ingredients into a cocktail shaker over ice and shake. Strain into prepared glass and serve.

Saucy Sue Cocktail

39.2% ALC/VOL • 2 STD DRINKS

60ml (2 fl oz) Apple Brandy
3 dashes Apricot Brandy
3 dashes Pernod

Pour ingredients into a mixing glass over ice and stir. Strain into a chilled cocktail glass and serve.

Bandos Wobbler

25.3% ALC/VOL • 2.4 STD DRINKS

30ml (1 fl oz) Cognac
30ml (1 fl oz) Campari
30ml (1 fl oz) Dark Rum
Dash Grenadine
30ml (1 fl oz) Fresh Orange Juice

Pour ingredients into a cocktail shaker over ice and shake. Strain into a chilled goblet and serve.

Whip

30.1% ALC/VOL • 2.2 STD DRINKS

23ml (¾ fl oz) Brandy
23ml (¾ fl oz) Curaçao
23ml (¾ fl oz) Dry Vermouth
23ml (¾ fl oz) Pernod

Pour ingredients into a cocktail shaker over ice and shake. Strain into a chilled cocktail glass and serve.

Stirrup Cup

22.5% ALC/VOL • 1.4 STD DRINKS

30ml (1 fl oz) Brandy
30ml (1 fl oz) Cherry Brandy
15ml (½ fl oz) Fresh Lemon Juice
1 teaspoon Sugar Syrup
Slice of Lemon

Pour Brandies, juice and sugar into an old-fashioned glass over crushed ice then stir. Garnish with a slice of lemon and serve.

Lady be Good

29.8% ALC/VOL • 1.8 STD DRINKS

45ml (1½ fl oz) Brandy
15ml (½ fl oz) Sweet Vermouth
15ml (½ fl oz) White Crème De Menthe

Pour ingredients into a cocktail shaker over ice and shake. Strain into a chilled cocktail glass and serve.

Kriss

9.1% ALC/VOL • 1.2 STD DRINKS

30ml (1 fl oz) Cognac
8ml (¼ fl oz) Amaretto
8ml (¼ fl oz) Dry Vermouth
1 teaspoon Sugar Syrup
120ml (4 fl oz) Tonic Water

Pour Cognac, Amaretto, Vermouth and sugar into a mixing glass over ice. Stir and strain into a highball glass over ice. Add tonic, stir gently and serve.

Bombay

30% ALC/VOL • 2.2 STD DRINKS

60ml (2 fl oz) Brandy
15ml (½ fl oz) Dry Vermouth
15ml (½ fl oz) Sweet Vermouth
2 dashes Curaçao

Pour ingredients into a cocktail shaker over ice and shake. Strain into a chilled cocktail glass and serve.

Sex in a Bubblegum Factory

12.1% ALC/VOL • 2.6 STD DRINKS

30ml (1 fl oz) Apricot Brandy
30ml (1 fl oz) Banana Liqueur
30ml (1 fl oz) Curaçao
30ml (1 fl oz) Light Rum
150ml (5 fl oz) Lemon-Lime Soda

Pour Brandy, Liqueur, Curaçao and Rum into a mixing glass over ice. Stir and strain into a chilled highball glass. Add soda, stir gently and serve.

Midnight Cocktail

21.5% ALC/VOL • 1 STD DRINK

30ml (1 fl oz) Apricot Brandy
15ml (½ fl oz) Cointreau
15ml (½ fl oz) Fresh Lemon Juice

Pour ingredients into a cocktail shaker over ice and shake. Strain into a chilled cocktail glass and serve.

Tropic Star

8.2% ALC/VOL • 1.6 STD DRINKS

30ml (1 fl oz) Cognac
15ml (½ fl oz) Apricot Brandy

15ml (½ fl oz) Banana Liqueur
3 dashes Pastis
180ml (6 fl oz) Lemonade

Pour Cognac, Brandy, Liqueur and Pastis into a highball glass over ice then stir. Add lemonade, stir gently and serve.

Yellow Parrot

34.4% ALC/VOL • 2.4 STD DRINKS

30ml (1 fl oz) Apricot Brandy
30ml (1 fl oz) Yellow Chartreuse
30ml (1 fl oz) Pernod

Pour ingredients into a cocktail shaker over ice and shake. Strain into a chilled cocktail glass and serve.

Brandy Toddy

31.7% ALC/VOL • 1.8 STD DRINKS

60ml (2 fl oz) Brandy
5ml (1/6 fl oz) Spring Water
1 teaspoon Sugar Syrup
Slice of Lemon

Pour water and sugar into a chilled old-fashioned glass then stir. Add ice and Brandy then stir. Garnish with a slice of lemon and serve.

Betsy Ross

28.2% ALC/VOL • 1.4 STD DRINKS

30ml (1 fl oz) Brandy
30ml (1 fl oz) Port
2 dashes Cointreau
Dash Angostura Bitters

Pour ingredients into a cocktail shaker over ice and shake. Strain into a chilled cocktail glass and serve.

Olympic

20.6% ALC/VOL • 1.5 STD DRINKS

30ml (1 fl oz) Brandy
30ml (1 fl oz) Curaçao
30ml (1 fl oz) Fresh Orange Juice
Slice of Orange

Pour Brandy, Curaçao and juice into a cocktail shaker over ice. Shake and strain into a chilled cocktail glass. Garnish with a slice of orange and serve.

Tulip Cocktail

23.4% ALC/VOL • 1.1 STD DRINKS

23ml (¾ fl oz) Apple Brandy
23ml (¾ fl oz) Sweet Vermouth
8ml (¼ fl oz) Apricot Brandy
8ml (¼ fl oz) Fresh Lemon Juice

Pour ingredients into a cocktail shaker over ice and shake. Strain into a chilled cocktail glass and serve.

Cherry Flip

9.4% ALC/VOL • 0.8 STD DRINKS

45ml (1½ fl oz) Cherry Brandy
2 teaspoons Fresh Cream
1 teaspoon Sugar Syrup
1 Fresh Egg
Nutmeg

Pour Brandy, cream, sugar and egg into a cocktail shaker over ice. Shake and strain into a chilled goblet. Sprinkle nutmeg on top and serve.

Special Rough Cocktail

38.3% ALC/VOL • 2.8 STD DRINKS

45ml (1½ fl oz) Apple Brandy
45ml (1½ fl oz) Brandy
3 dashes Anisette

Pour ingredients into a mixing glass over ice and stir. Strain into a chilled cocktail glass and serve.

Napoleon Cocktail

25.4% ALC/VOL • 1.8 STD DRINKS

30ml (1 fl oz) Brandy
30ml (1 fl oz) Cointreau
Dash Grenadine
30ml (1 fl oz) Pineapple Juice
Cherry
Piece of Pineapple
Slice of Orange

Pour Brandy, Cointreau, Grenadine and juice into a cocktail shaker over ice. Shake and strain into a chilled champagne saucer. Garnish with a cherry, piece of pineapple and slice of orange then serve.

Brandy Buca

37.4% ALC/VOL • 2.7 STD DRINKS

60ml (2 fl oz) Brandy
30ml (1 fl oz) Black Sambuca

Pour ingredients into a cocktail shaker over ice and shake. Strain into a chilled cocktail glass and serve.

Quaker

25.9% ALC/VOL • 1.3 STD DRINKS

30ml (1 fl oz) Brandy
15ml (½ fl oz) Light Rum
15ml (½ fl oz) Fresh Lemon Juice
1 teaspoon Raspberry Syrup
Twist of Lemon Peel

Pour Brandy, Rum, juice and syrup into a cocktail shaker over ice. Shake and strain into a chilled cocktail glass. Twist lemon peel above drink and place remainder of peel into drink then serve.

Father Sherman

21% ALC/VOL • 1.6 STD DRINKS

45ml (1½ fl oz) Brandy
15ml (½ fl oz) Apricot Brandy
36ml (1⅕ fl oz) Fresh Orange Juice

Pour ingredients into a cocktail shaker over ice and shake. Strain into a chilled cocktail glass and serve.

Far West

24.8% ALC/VOL • 0.9 STD DRINKS

15ml (½ fl oz) Brandy
15ml (½ fl oz) Advocaat
15ml (½ fl oz) Dry Vermouth
Dash Angostura Bitters
Cinnamon

Pour Brandy, Advocaat, Vermouth and Bitters into a cocktail shaker over ice. Shake and strain into a chilled cocktail glass. Sprinkle cinnamon on top and serve.

Which Way

38.3% ALC/VOL • 2.7 STD DRINKS

30ml (1 fl oz) Brandy
30ml (1 fl oz) Pernod
30ml (1 fl oz) Sambuca

Pour ingredients into a cocktail shaker over ice and shake. Strain into a chilled cocktail glass and serve.

Depth Bomb

36.9% ALC/VOL • 2.7 STD DRINKS

45ml (1½ fl oz) Applejack
45ml (1½ fl oz) Brandy
2 dashes Grenadine
2 dashes Fresh Lemon Juice

Pour ingredients into a cocktail shaker over ice and shake. Strain into a chilled cocktail glass and serve.
This drink is also known as Time Bomb.

Widow's Kiss

38.6% ALC/VOL • 1.9 STD DRINKS

30ml (1 fl oz) Brandy
15ml (½ fl oz) Bénédictine
15ml (½ fl oz) Yellow Chartreuse
Dash Angostura Bitters

Pour ingredients into a cocktail shaker over ice and shake. Strain into a chilled cocktail glass and serve.

Thunder

30.3% ALC/VOL • 2.7 STD DRINKS

90ml (3 fl oz) Brandy
1 teaspoon Sugar Syrup
Yolk of 1 Egg
Pinch of Red Pepper (Cayenne)

Pour Brandy, sugar and egg yolk into a cocktail shaker over ice then add Cayenne. Shake and strain into a chilled cocktail glass then serve.

Ray Long

30.9% ALC/VOL • 2.5 STD DRINKS

68ml (2¼ fl oz) Brandy
30ml (1 fl oz) Sweet Vermouth
4 dashes Pernod
Dash Angostura Bitters

Pour ingredients into a mixing glass over ice and stir. Strain into a chilled cocktail glass and serve.

Alabazam

30.5% ALC/VOL • 2.3 STD DRINKS

60ml (2 fl oz) Cognac
18ml (3/5 fl oz) Curaçao
2 dashes Orange Bitters
2 teaspoons Sugar Syrup
5ml (1/6 fl oz) Fresh Lemon Juice

Pour ingredients into a mixing glass over ice and stir. Strain into a chilled old-fashioned glass and serve.

Champ Elysees

30.4% ALC/VOL • 1.8 STD DRINKS

45ml (1½ fl oz) Brandy
15ml (½ fl oz) Yellow Chartreuse
Dash Angostura Bitters
15ml (½ fl oz) Fresh Lemon Juice

Pour ingredients into a cocktail shaker over ice and shake. Strain into a chilled cocktail glass and serve.

Brandy Ice

16.8% ALC/VOL • 1.6 STD DRINKS

45ml (1½ fl oz) Brandy
15ml (½ fl oz) White Crème De Cacao
2 scoops Vanilla Ice Cream
Grated Chocolate

Pour Brandy and Cacao into a blender over small amount of crushed ice then add ice cream. Blend until smooth and pour into a chilled brandy balloon. Sprinkle chocolate on top and serve.

Santini's Pousse Café

35% ALC/VOL • 1.7 STD DRINKS

15ml (½ fl oz) Brandy
15ml (½ fl oz) Maraschino Liqueur
15ml (½ fl oz) Cointreau
15ml (½ fl oz) Dark Rum

Layer ingredients in order given into a pousse café glass and serve.

Banana's Breeze

16.1% ALC/VOL • 0.7 STD DRINKS

15ml (½ fl oz) Brandy
10ml (⅓ fl oz) Banana Liqueur
5ml (1/6 fl oz) Apricot Brandy
23ml (¾ fl oz) Fresh Orange Juice
3 dashes Frothee

Pour ingredients into a cocktail shaker over ice and shake. Strain into a chilled cocktail glass and serve.

Adam and Eve

36% ALC/VOL • 2.6 STD DRINKS

30ml (1 fl oz) Brandy
30ml (1 fl oz) Forbidden Fruit
30ml (1 fl oz) Gin
Dash Fresh Lemon Juice

Pour ingredients into a cocktail shaker over ice and shake. Strain into a chilled cocktail glass and serve.

Green Winter

30.1% ALC/VOL • 2.9 STD DRINKS

60ml (2 fl oz) Brandy
60ml (2 fl oz) Green Crème De Menthe
2 dashes Angostura Bitters
2 dashes Triple Sec
Slice of Lemon
Pepper

Pour Brandy, Crème De Menthe, Bitters and Triple Sec into a cocktail shaker over ice. Shake and strain into a chilled cocktail glass. Sprinkle pepper on top and garnish with a slice of lemon then serve.

Stone Fence

22.6% ALC/VOL • 3.2 STD DRINKS

90ml (3 fl oz) Applejack
90ml (3 fl oz) Cider
3 dashes Angostura Bitters

Pour Applejack and Bitters into a collins glass over ice then stir. Add Cider, stir gently and serve.

Opera House

23.9% ALC/VOL • 2 STD DRINKS

30ml (1 fl oz) Brandy
30ml (1 fl oz) Tia Maria
15ml (½ fl oz) Cointreau
30ml (1 fl oz) Fresh Cream

Pour ingredients into a cocktail shaker over ice and shake. Strain into a chilled champagne saucer and serve.

Night Cap

26.4% ALC/VOL • 2.2 STD DRINKS

30ml (1 fl oz) Brandy
30ml (1 fl oz) Anisette
30ml (1 fl oz) Curaçao
Yolk of 1 Egg

Pour ingredients into a cocktail shaker over ice and shake. Strain into a chilled cocktail glass and serve.

Apripisco

22% ALC/VOL • 1.8 STD DRINKS

45ml (1½ fl oz) Pisco
15ml (½ fl oz) Apricot Brandy
Dash Angostura Bitters
15ml (½ fl oz) Fresh Lime Juice
White of 1 Egg
Twist of Lime Peel

Pour Pisco, Brandy, juice and egg white into a cocktail shaker over ice. Shake and strain into a chilled cocktail glass. Add Bitters – do not stir, then garnish with lime peel and serve.

Jersey Lightning

22.5% ALC/VOL • 1.6 STD DRINKS

45ml (1½ fl oz) Apple Brandy
15ml (½ fl oz) Sweet Vermouth
30ml (1 fl oz) Fresh Lime Juice

Pour ingredients into a cocktail shaker over ice and shake. Strain into a chilled cocktail glass and serve.

Greek Buck

12.3% ALC/VOL • 1.5 STD DRINKS

45ml (1½ fl oz) Brandy
5ml (⅙ fl oz) Ouzo
90ml (3 fl oz) Dry Ginger Ale
⅓ Fresh Lemon

Pour Brandy into a tall glass over ice and twist ⅓ lemon above drink to release juice then add spent shell. Add Ginger Ale and stir gently. Layer Ouzo on top and serve.

Gazette

24.9% ALC/VOL • 1.7 STD DRINKS

45ml (1½ fl oz) Brandy
30ml (1 fl oz) Sweet Vermouth
5ml (⅙ fl oz) Fresh Lemon Juice
1 teaspoon Sugar Syrup

Pour ingredients into a cocktail shaker over ice and shake. Strain into a chilled cocktail glass and serve.

Harvard No.2

23.3% ALC/VOL • 1.3 STD DRINKS

30ml (1 fl oz) Brandy
30ml (1 fl oz) Sweet Vermouth
2 dashes Angostura Bitters
8ml (¼ fl oz) Fresh Lemon Juice
Dash Sugar Syrup

Pour ingredients into a cocktail shaker over ice and shake. Strain into a chilled cocktail glass and serve.

Royal Smile Cocktail

30.3% ALC/VOL • 1.4 STD DRINKS

30ml (1 fl oz) Applejack
15ml (½ fl oz) Gin
5ml (⅙ fl oz) Grenadine
8ml (¼ fl oz) Fresh Lemon Juice

Pour ingredients into a mixing glass over ice and stir. Strain into a chilled cocktail glass and serve.

Cherry Hill

22.8% ALC/VOL • 1.9 STD DRINKS

30ml (1 fl oz) Brandy
30ml (1 fl oz) Cherry Brandy

10ml (⅓ fl oz) Triple Sec
10ml (⅓ fl oz) Grenadine
10ml (⅓ fl oz) Fresh Lemon Juice
Maraschino Cherry

Prepare a cocktail glass with a sugar frosted rim – moistened with maraschino cherry juice. Pour Brandies, Triple Sec, Grenadine and juice into a cocktail shaker over ice. Shake and strain into prepared glass. Garnish with a cherry and serve.

Gladiator's Stinger

33.1% ALC/VOL • 1.4 STD DRINKS

30ml (1 fl oz) Brandy
15ml (½ fl oz) White Crème De Menthe
8ml (¼ fl oz) Sambuca

Pour ingredients into a cocktail shaker over ice and shake. Strain into a chilled cocktail glass and serve.

Tiny Tim

25.4% ALC/VOL • 1.6 STD DRINKS

30ml (1 fl oz) Brandy
30ml (1 fl oz) Dry Vermouth
15ml (½ fl oz) Triple Sec
1 teaspoon Sugar Syrup

Pour ingredients into a cocktail shaker over ice and shake. Strain into an old-fashioned glass filled with ice and serve.

International

39.4% ALC/VOL • 2.2 STD DRINKS

45ml (1½ fl oz) Cognac
10ml (⅓ fl oz) Cointreau
10ml (⅓ fl oz) Sambuca
5ml (1/6 fl oz) Vodka

Pour ingredients into a cocktail shaker over ice and shake. Strain into a chilled cocktail glass and serve.

Brandy Julep

34.7% ALC/VOL • 2.2 STD DRINKS

75ml (2½ fl oz) Brandy
1 teaspoon Sugar Syrup
7 Sprigs of Fresh Mint
Cherry
Slice of Lemon
Slice of Pineapple

Pour Brandy and sugar into a chilled collins glass then add 6 sprigs of mint. Fill glass with crushed ice and stir well. Add more crushed ice to fill glass and stir gently. Garnish with a cherry, slice of lemon, pineapple and sprig of mint then serve.

Apricot Apple Juice

5.8% ALC/VOL • 1.1 STD DRINKS

60ml (2 fl oz) Apricot Brandy
180ml (6 fl oz) Apple Juice

Pour ingredients into a highball glass over ice, stir and serve.

Thunder Road

31.8% ALC/VOL • 2.1 STD DRINKS

45ml (1½ fl oz) Applejack
23ml (¾ fl oz) Light Rum
8ml (¼ fl oz) Fresh Lime Juice
1½ teaspoons Orgeat Syrup
Slice of Lime

Pour Applejack, Rum, juice and syrup into a cocktail shaker over cracked ice. Shake and pour into a chilled highball glass. Garnish with a slice of lime and serve.

Ginger Mist

17.1% ALC/VOL • 1.2 STD DRINKS

45ml (1½ fl oz) Ginger Brandy
2 dashes Fresh Lemon Juice
45ml (1½ fl oz) Dry Ginger Ale

Pour Brandy and juice into an old-fashioned glass over crushed ice then stir. Add Ginger Ale, stir gently and serve.

Adrienne's Dream

18.8% ALC/VOL • 2.3 STD DRINKS

60ml (2 fl oz) Brandy
15ml (½ fl oz) Peppermint Schnapps
15ml (½ fl oz) White Crème De Cacao
15ml (½ fl oz) Fresh Lemon Juice
½ teaspoon Sugar Syrup
45ml (1½ fl oz) Soda Water

Pour Brandy, Schnapps, Cacao, juice and sugar into a cocktail shaker over ice. Shake and strain into a tall glass over ice. Add soda, stir gently and serve.

Peach Bunny

15.3% ALC/VOL • 0.8 STD DRINKS

23ml (¾ fl oz) Peach Brandy
23ml (¾ fl oz) White Crème De Cacao
23ml (¾ fl oz) Fresh Cream

Pour ingredients into a cocktail shaker over ice and shake. Strain into a chilled cocktail glass and serve.

Fuzzhopper

9.8% ALC/VOL • 1.4 STD DRINKS

30ml (1 fl oz) Brandy
15ml (½ fl oz) Advocaat
15ml (½ fl oz) Peach Schnapps
3 dashes Jägermeister
60ml (2 fl oz) Lemonade
60ml (2 fl oz) Soda Water
Slice of Peach

Pour Brandy, Advocaat, Schnapps and Jägermeister into a blender without ice then add a slice of peach. Blend until smooth and pour into a highball glass over ice then add lemonade. Add soda, stir gently and serve.

Lovelight

18.5% ALC/VOL • 0.9 STD DRINKS

30ml (1 fl oz) Brandy
30ml (1 fl oz) Passion-Fruit Juice

Pour ingredients into a cocktail shaker over 2 ice cubes and shake well. Pour into a chilled cocktail glass and serve.

Bartender's Revenge

36.7% ALC/VOL • 3.6 STD DRINKS

30ml (1 fl oz) Brandy
30ml (1 fl oz) Cognac
30ml (1 fl oz) Light Rum
30ml (1 fl oz) Tequila
3 drops Tabasco Sauce
½ teaspoon Horseradish

Pour Brandy, Cognac, Rum, Tequila and sauce into an old-fashioned glass over ice. Add horseradish, stir and serve.

Golden Gate No.2

38% ALC/VOL • 1.2 STD DRINKS

20ml (⅔ fl oz) Brandy
10ml (⅓ fl oz) Bacardi
10ml (⅓ fl oz) Cointreau

Pour ingredients into a cocktail shaker over ice and shake. Strain into a chilled cocktail glass and serve.

Wet One

27.8% ALC/VOL • 1.8 STD DRINKS

60ml (2 fl oz) Brandy
10ml (⅓ fl oz) Fresh Lime Juice
2 teaspoons Orgeat Syrup
Wedge of Lime

Pour Brandy, juice and syrup into a cocktail shaker over ice. Shake and strain into a chilled cocktail glass. Garnish with a wedge of lime and serve.

Nelson Mandela

7.6% ALC/VOL • 1.3 STD DRINKS

20ml (⅔ fl oz) Apricot Brandy
20ml (⅔ fl oz) Mandarin Vodka
20ml (⅔ fl oz) Peach Schnapps
150ml (5 fl oz) Orange Soda

Pour Brandy, Vodka and Schnapps into a highball glass over ice then stir. Add soda, stir gently and serve.

Funky Monkey

11.4% ALC/VOL • 2.7 STD DRINKS

60ml (2 fl oz) Brandy
60ml (2 fl oz) Kahlúa
30ml (1 fl oz) Fresh Milk (chilled)
3 scoops Vanilla Ice Cream
1 Banana (diced)

Pour Brandy, Kahlúa and milk into a blender without ice. Add ice cream and diced banana. Blend until smooth and pour into a chilled hurricane glass then serve with a straw.

Y B Normal?

29.5% ALC/VOL • 1.3 STD DRINKS

30ml (1 fl oz) Brandy
15ml (½ fl oz) Yellow Chartreuse
8ml (¼ fl oz) Fresh Lemon Juice
1 teaspoon Sugar Syrup

Pour ingredients into a cocktail shaker over ice and shake. Strain into a chilled cocktail glass and serve.

Surreal Deal

29.1% ALC/VOL • 1.7 STD DRINKS

30ml (1 fl oz) Apple Brandy
15ml (½ fl oz) Brandy
15ml (½ fl oz) Triple Sec
8ml (¼ fl oz) Fresh Lemon Juice
1 teaspoon Sugar Syrup

Pour ingredients into a cocktail shaker over ice and shake. Strain into a chilled cocktail glass and serve.

Conquistador

31.1% ALC/VOL • 1.5 STD DRINKS

30ml (1 fl oz) Cognac
15ml (½ fl oz) Orange Curaçao
15ml (½ fl oz) White Crème De Cacao
Dash Fresh Cream
Dash Strawberry Syrup

Pour ingredients into a cocktail shaker over ice and shake. Strain into a chilled cocktail glass and serve.

Upyabum Punch

15.8% ALC/VOL • 3.2 STD DRINKS

60ml (2 fl oz) Cherry Brandy
30ml (1 fl oz) Amaretto
30ml (1 fl oz) Apricot Brandy
30ml (1 fl oz) Southern Comfort
15ml (½ fl oz) Grenadine
90ml (3 fl oz) Fresh Orange Juice

Pour ingredients into a tall glass over ice, stir well and serve.

Cherry Flower

25.2% ALC/VOL • 1.2 STD DRINKS

20ml (⅔ fl oz) Cherry Brandy
20ml (⅔ fl oz) Cognac
10ml (⅓ fl oz) Triple Sec
10ml (⅓ fl oz) Grenadine

Pour ingredients into a cocktail shaker over ice and shake. Strain into a chilled cocktail glass and serve.

Angel Paradise

8.5% ALC/VOL • 1.1 STD DRINKS

60ml (2 fl oz) Apricot Brandy
60ml (2 fl oz) Fresh Orange Juice
40ml (1⅓ fl oz) Grapefruit Juice
Dash Passion-Fruit Juice
3 drops Fresh Lemon Juice

Pour ingredients into a cocktail shaker over ice and shake. Strain into a chilled old-fashioned glass and serve.

Apricot Russian Tea

7.5% ALC/VOL • 1.4 STD DRINKS

30ml (1 fl oz) Apricot Brandy
30ml (1 fl oz) Vodka
90ml (3 fl oz) Sweet and Sour Mix
90ml (3 fl oz) Cola

Pour Brandy, Vodka and sour mix into a cocktail shaker over ice. Shake and strain into a highball glass over ice. Add cola, stir gently and serve.

Love Connection

13.9% ALC/VOL • 1.2 STD DRINKS

40ml (1⅓ fl oz) Cherry Brandy
30ml (1 fl oz) Raspberry Liqueur
2 teaspoons Cherry Soda Syrup
20ml (⅔ fl oz) Lemonade
10ml (⅓ fl oz) Mineral Water

Pour Brandy, Liqueur and syrup into a cocktail shaker over 2 ice cubes. Shake well and pour into a chilled cocktail glass then add lemonade. Add mineral water, stir gently and serve.

Ladies Sidecar

17.2% ALC/VOL • 1 STD DRINK

30ml (1 fl oz) Brandy
8ml (¼ fl oz) Triple Sec
30ml (1 fl oz) Fresh Orange Juice
8ml (¼ fl oz) Fresh Lemon Juice

Pour ingredients into a cocktail shaker over ice and shake. Strain into a chilled cocktail glass and serve.

Nicotini

13.8% ALC/VOL • 0.5 STD DRINKS

10ml (⅓ fl oz) Apricot Brandy
10ml (⅓ fl oz) Banana Liqueur
10ml (⅓ fl oz) Dark Crème De Cacao
2 teaspoons Fresh Cream
10ml (⅓ fl oz) Fresh Milk (chilled)

Pour ingredients into a cocktail shaker over ice and shake. Strain into a chilled martini glass and serve.

4-You

9.8% ALC/VOL • 1 STD DRINK

30ml (1 fl oz) Apricot Brandy
53ml (1¾ fl oz) Almond Extract
40ml (1⅓ fl oz) Passion-Fruit Juice
Kumquat Flower

Pour Brandy, extract and juice into a mixing glass over ice. Stir and strain into a chilled cocktail glass. Garnish with a flower and serve.

Coffee Kick

18.8% ALC/VOL • 5.9 STD DRINKS

100ml (3⅓ fl oz) Coffee Brandy
100ml (3⅓ fl oz) Cognac
200ml (6⅔ fl oz) Black Coffee (chilled)

Pour ingredients into a blender without ice and blend. Pour into a hurricane glass over ice and serve.

Cognac Cassis

30% ALC/VOL • 1.4 STD DRINKS

30ml (1 fl oz) Cognac
30ml (1 fl oz) Crème De Cassis

Pour ingredients into a cocktail shaker over ice and shake. Strain into a chilled cocktail glass and serve.

Dirty White Mother

28.1% ALC/VOL • 1.6 STD DRINKS

This drink is a Dirty Mother (p 21) with 2 teaspoons fresh cream floated on top.

Stinger No.2

34.2% ALC/VOL • 2 STD DRINKS

45ml (1½ fl oz) Brandy
15ml (½ fl oz) White Crème De Menthe
15ml (½ fl oz) Vodka

Pour ingredients into a cocktail shaker over ice and shake. Strain into a chilled cocktail glass and serve.

A.J.

24% ALC/VOL • 1.4 STD DRINKS

45ml (1½ fl oz) Applejack
30ml (1 fl oz) Grapefruit Juice

Pour ingredients into a mixing glass over ice and stir. Strain into a chilled cocktail glass and serve.

Via Veneto

28.9% ALC/VOL • 2.1 STD DRINKS

This drink is also known as Romana, p 28.

Paddy's Special

25.6% ALC/VOL • 1.1 STD DRINKS

30ml (1 fl oz) Cognac
8ml (¼ fl oz) Banana Liqueur
Dash Orange Curaçao
15ml (½ fl oz) Fresh Lime Juice

Dash Frothee

Pour ingredients into a cocktail shaker over ice and shake. Strain into a chilled cocktail glass and serve.

Lilac Cooler

7.4% ALC/VOL • 1.1 STD DRINKS

15ml (½ fl oz) Cognac
15ml (½ fl oz) Cointreau
15ml (½ fl oz) Sweet Vermouth
150ml (5 fl oz) Dry Ginger Ale

Pour Cognac, Cointreau and Vermouth into a cocktail shaker over ice. Shake and strain into a collins glass over ice. Add Ginger Ale, stir gently and serve.

Blowhole

12.1% ALC/VOL • 1.9 STD DRINKS

60ml (2 fl oz) Apple Brandy
8ml (¼ fl oz) Fresh Lemon Juice
1 teaspoon Sugar Syrup
White of 1 Egg
90ml (3 fl oz) Soda Water

Pour Brandy, juice, sugar and egg white into a cocktail shaker over cracked ice. Shake and pour into a chilled highball glass. Add soda, stir gently and serve.

American Sea

16.7% ALC/VOL • 1.1 STD DRINKS

20ml (⅔ fl oz) Brandy
20ml (⅔ fl oz) Dry Vermouth
10ml (⅓ fl oz) White Crème De Menthe
30ml (1 fl oz) Fresh Orange Juice

Pour ingredients into a cocktail shaker over ice and shake. Strain into a chilled cocktail glass and serve.

Long Joe

6.2% ALC/VOL • 1 STD DRINK

30ml (1 fl oz) Apricot Brandy
10ml (⅓ fl oz) Gin
10ml (⅓ fl oz) Sweet Vermouth
150ml (5 fl oz) Dry Ginger Ale

Pour Brandy, Gin and Vermouth into a mixing glass over ice. Stir and strain into a highball glass over ice. Add Ginger Ale, stir gently and serve.

Combustible Edison

24.8% ALC/VOL • 2.3 STD DRINKS

60ml (2 fl oz) Brandy
30ml (1 fl oz) Campari
30ml (1 fl oz) Fresh Lemon Juice

Pour Campari and juice into a cocktail shaker over ice. Shake and strain into a chilled cocktail glass. Pour Brandy into a ladle and ignite. Pour on top of drink – do not stir, then serve.

Oom Paul

28.8% ALC/VOL • 1.4 STD DRINKS

30ml (1 fl oz) Apple Brandy
30ml (1 fl oz) Dubonnet
3 dashes Angostura Bitters

Pour ingredients into a mixing glass over ice and stir. Strain into a cocktail glass filled with ice and serve.

Lumumba

4% ALC/VOL • 0.9 STD DRINKS

30ml (1 fl oz) Brandy
250ml (8⅓ fl oz) Chocolate Milk (chilled)

Pour ingredients into a chilled highball glass, stir and serve.

Messalina

32.3% ALC/VOL • 2.8 STD DRINKS

60ml (2 fl oz) Cognac
50ml (1⅔ fl oz) Dark Crème De Cacao
2 drops Angostura Bitters
Cherry

Prepare a cocktail glass with a sugar frosted rim. Pour Cognac, Cacao and Bitters into a cocktail shaker over ice. Shake and strain into prepared glass. Garnish with a cherry and serve.

After Dinner No.2

16% ALC/VOL • 1.1 STD DRINKS

30ml (1 fl oz) Apricot Brandy
30ml (1 fl oz) Blue Curaçao
30ml (1 fl oz) Fresh Lime Juice
Wedge of Lime

Pour Brandy, Curaçao and juice into a cocktail shaker over ice. Shake and strain into a chilled cocktail glass. Add a wedge of lime and serve.

Black Fruit Tree

25.6% ALC/VOL • 3 STD DRINKS

30ml (1 fl oz) Blackberry Brandy
30ml (1 fl oz) Amaretto
30ml (1 fl oz) Blue Curaçao
30ml (1 fl oz) Cointreau
30ml (1 fl oz) Grenadine

Pour ingredients into a mixing glass over ice and stir. Strain into a highball glass over ice and serve.

Sweet Cherry Cocktail

18.6% ALC/VOL • 0.9 STD DRINKS

15ml (½ fl oz) Cherry Brandy
15ml (½ fl oz) Scotch Whisky
15ml (½ fl oz) Sweet Vermouth
18ml (3/5 fl oz) Fresh Orange Juice

Pour ingredients into a cocktail shaker over ice and shake. Strain into a chilled cocktail glass and serve.

Just Feel

13.5% ALC/VOL • 1.7 STD DRINKS

40ml (1⅓ fl oz) Cognac
23ml (¾ fl oz) Apricot Brandy
40ml (1⅓ fl oz) Grape Juice
40ml (1⅓ fl oz) Fresh Orange Juice
15ml (½ fl oz) Strawberry Syrup

Pour ingredients into a cocktail shaker over ice and shake. Strain into a chilled tall glass over a few ice cubes and serve.

Thunder and Lightning

34% ALC/VOL • 2.8 STD DRINKS

60ml (2 fl oz) Cognac
30ml (1 fl oz) Cointreau
4 drops Hot Sauce
Yolk of 1 Egg

Pour ingredients into a cocktail shaker over ice and shake well. Strain into a chilled cocktail glass and serve.

Caledonia

17.2% ALC/VOL • 1.4 STD DRINKS

30ml (1 fl oz) Brandy
30ml (1 fl oz) Dark Crème De Cacao
30ml (1 fl oz) Fresh Milk (chilled)
Yolk of 1 Egg
Cinnamon

Pour Brandy, Cacao, milk and egg yolk into a cocktail shaker over ice. Shake well and strain into an old-fashioned glass over ice. Sprinkle cinnamon on top and serve.

Is Paris Burning?

32.2% ALC/VOL • 2.3 STD DRINKS

60ml (2 fl oz) Cognac
30ml (1 fl oz) Chambord Raspberry

Pour Cognac and Chambord into a mixing glass over ice. Stir and strain into a chilled cocktail glass. Garnish with a raspberry and serve.

Willem Van Oranje

32.4% ALC/VOL • 0.8 STD DRINKS

20ml (⅔ fl oz) Brandy
10ml (⅓ fl oz) Triple Sec
3 dashes Orange Bitters

Pour ingredients into a mixing glass over ice and stir. Strain into a chilled cocktail glass and serve.

Savoy Tango

34.4% ALC/VOL • 2 STD DRINKS

45ml (1½ fl oz) Apple Brandy
30ml (1 fl oz) Sloe Gin

Pour ingredients into a mixing glass over ice and stir. Strain into a chilled cocktail glass and serve.

Yes and No

25.3% ALC/VOL • 1.9 STD DRINKS

This drink is also known as *Booster, p33.*

Al Capone

29.7% ALC/VOL • 1.6 STD DRINKS

45ml (1½ fl oz) Brandy
23ml (¾ fl oz) Marsala
Dash Drambuie

Pour ingredients into a cocktail shaker over ice and shake. Strain into a chilled brandy balloon and serve.

Tasty One

31.5% ALC/VOL • 3 STD DRINKS

60ml (2 fl oz) Apricot Brandy
60ml (2 fl oz) Bénédictine

Pour ingredients into a tall glass over ice, stir and serve.

Polar Attraction

8.2% ALC/VOL • 1.7 STD DRINKS

60ml (2 fl oz) Brandy
210ml (7 fl oz) Tonic Water
Twist of Lemon Peel

Pour Brandy into a tall glass over ice and add tonic then stir gently. Add lemon peel and serve.

Sleepyhead

14.8% ALC/VOL • 2.6 STD DRINKS

90ml (3 fl oz) Brandy
135ml (4½ fl oz) Dry Ginger Ale

Pour Brandy into a highball glass over ice and add Ginger Ale, stir gently then serve.

Devil Cocktail

28.1% ALC/VOL • 1.1 STD DRINKS

23ml (¾ fl oz) Brandy
23ml (¾ fl oz) Dry Vermouth
3 dashes Curaçao
2 dashes Angostura Bitters
Cherry

Pour Brandy, Vermouth, Curaçao and Bitters into a mixing glass over ice. Stir and strain into a chilled cocktail glass. Garnish with a cherry and serve.

Yellow Parrot No.2

33.2% ALC/VOL • 2 STD DRINKS

30ml (1 fl oz) Apricot Brandy
30ml (1 fl oz) Pernod
15ml (½ fl oz) Yellow Chartreuse

Pour ingredients into a cocktail shaker over ice and shake. Strain into an old-fashioned glass over ice and serve.

Brandy Old-Fashioned

34.1% ALC/VOL • 2.3 STD DRINKS

75ml (2½ fl oz) Brandy
2 dashes Angostura Bitters
1 teaspoon Sugar Syrup
2 dashes Soda Water or Spring Water
Maraschino Cherry

Pour Brandy, Bitters, sugar and soda or water as desired into a chilled old-fashioned glass then stir gently. Add ice and garnish with a cherry then serve.

Dr. Stud

32.7% ALC/VOL • 2.3 STD DRINKS

30ml (1 fl oz) Applejack
30ml (1 fl oz) Ginger Brandy
30ml (1 fl oz) White Crème De Menthe

Pour ingredients into a mixing glass over ice and stir. Strain into a chilled cocktail glass and serve.

Grenada

14.2% ALC/VOL • 2 STD DRINKS

45ml (1½ fl oz) Brandy
30ml (1 fl oz) Cream Sherry
15ml (½ fl oz) White Crème De Cacao
90ml (3 fl oz) Tonic Water

Pour Brandy, Sherry and Cacao into a cocktail shaker over ice. Shake and strain into a highball glass over ice. Add tonic, stir gently and serve.

Red Palm

30.6% ALC/VOL • 1.9 STD DRINKS

45ml (1½ fl oz) Brandy
30ml (1 fl oz) Sloe Gin
1 teaspoon Sugar Syrup
Twist of Lemon Peel

Pour Brandy, Gin and sugar into a cocktail shaker over ice. Shake and strain into a chilled cocktail glass. Garnish with lemon peel and serve.

Golden Panther

26.4% ALC/VOL • 2.1 STD DRINKS

20ml (⅔ fl oz) Brandy
20ml (⅔ fl oz) Blended Whiskey
20ml (⅔ fl oz) Gin
10ml (⅓ fl oz) Dry Vermouth
30ml (1 fl oz) Fresh Orange Juice

Pour ingredients into a cocktail shaker over cracked ice and shake. Pour into a chilled highball glass and serve.

Evening Sunset

10.3% ALC/VOL • 1.5 STD DRINKS

50ml (1⅔ fl oz) Brandy
100ml (3⅓ fl oz) Fresh Orange Juice
30ml (1 fl oz) Honey

Pour ingredients into a cocktail shaker over ice and shake well. Strain into a brandy balloon over ice and serve.

Sir Knight

42.6% ALC/VOL • 3.1 STD DRINKS

60ml (2 fl oz) Cognac
15ml (½ fl oz) Cointreau
15ml (½ fl oz) Green Chartreuse
Dash Angostura Bitters
Twist of Lemon Peel

Pour Cognac, Cointreau, Chartreuse and Bitters into a cocktail shaker over ice. Shake and strain into a chilled cocktail glass. Garnish with lemon peel and serve.

Afternoon Cocktail

26.6% ALC/VOL • 1.9 STD DRINKS

30ml (1 fl oz) Cognac
30ml (1 fl oz) Fernet Branca
30ml (1 fl oz) Grenadine

Pour ingredients into a mixing glass over ice and stir. Strain into a chilled cocktail glass and serve.

Brandied Egg Sour

16.7% ALC/VOL • 2 STD DRINKS

60ml (2 fl oz) Brandy
15ml (½ fl oz) Triple Sec
30ml (1 fl oz) Fresh Lemon Juice
1 teaspoon Sugar Syrup
1 Fresh Egg

Pour ingredients into a cocktail shaker over ice and shake well. Strain into a chilled sour glass and serve.

Alabama No.2

20.6% ALC/VOL • 1.5 STD DRINKS

30ml (1 fl oz) Brandy
30ml (1 fl oz) Triple Sec
15ml (½ fl oz) Fresh Lime Juice
15ml (½ fl oz) Sugar Syrup

Pour ingredients into a cocktail shaker over ice and shake. Strain into a chilled cocktail glass and serve.

Peppermint Fizz

7.8% ALC/VOL • 1.3 STD DRINKS

38ml (1¼ fl oz) Brandy
15ml (½ fl oz) Peppermint Schnapps
60ml (2 fl oz) Fresh Lemon Juice
105ml (3½ fl oz) Soda Water
Fresh Mint Leaf

Pour Brandy, Schnapps and juice into a cocktail shaker over cracked ice. Shake and pour into a chilled highball glass. Add soda and stir gently. Garnish with a mint leaf and serve.

Alexander Special

19% ALC/VOL • 0.9 STD DRINKS

20ml (⅔ fl oz) Brandy
20ml (⅔ fl oz) Kahlúa
20ml (⅔ fl oz) Fresh Cream

Pour ingredients into a cocktail shaker over ice and shake. Strain into a chilled cocktail glass and serve.

Mikado No.2

31.5% ALC/VOL • 1.8 STD DRINKS

45ml (1½ fl oz) Brandy
15ml (½ fl oz) Triple Sec
5ml (1/6 fl oz) Crème De Noyaux
Dash Angostura Bitters
5ml (1/6 fl oz) Grenadine

Pour ingredients into an old-fashioned glass filled with ice, stir and serve.

Bermuda Cooler

12.4% ALC/VOL • 1.5 STD DRINKS

30ml (1 fl oz) Brandy
20ml (⅔ fl oz) Dry Gin
Dash Orange Bitters
100ml (3⅓ fl oz) Dry Ginger Ale

Pour Brandy, Gin and Bitters into a mixing glass over ice. Stir and strain into a collins glass over ice. Add Ginger Ale, stir gently and serve.

Night Stars

33.9% ALC/VOL • 1.4 STD DRINKS

30ml (1 fl oz) Brandy
10ml (⅓ fl oz) Blended Whiskey
10ml (⅓ fl oz) Triple Sec
3 dashes Banana Liqueur
Dash Apple Juice

Pour ingredients into a cocktail shaker over ice and shake. Strain into a chilled cocktail glass and serve.

Brandy Alexandra

19.4% ALC/VOL • 1.1 STD DRINKS

30ml (1 fl oz) Brandy
15ml (½ fl oz) Dark Crème De Cacao
1 scoop Vanilla Ice Cream
Cinnamon

Pour Brandy and Cacao into a blender without ice then add ice cream. Blend until smooth and pour into a chilled cocktail glass. Sprinkle cinnamon on top and serve.

Baked Apple

16.8% ALC/VOL • 2.8 STD DRINKS

60ml (2 fl oz) Calvados
30ml (1 fl oz) Dark Rum
Dash Crème De Cassis
120ml (4 fl oz) Apple Juice
Cinnamon Stick

Pour Calvados and Rum into a mixing glass over ice. Stir and strain into a chilled highball glass. Add Cassis and juice then stir. Garnish with a cinnamon stick and serve.

Orchidea Nera

35.5% ALC/VOL • 2.5 STD DRINKS

30ml (1 fl oz) Cognac
30ml (1 fl oz) Blended Whiskey
30ml (1 fl oz) Tia Maria

Pour ingredients into a cocktail shaker over ice and shake. Strain into a chilled cocktail glass and serve.

Cherry Vanilla

6.9% ALC/VOL • 1.1 STD DRINKS

30ml (1 fl oz) Cherry Brandy
30ml (1 fl oz) White Crème De Cacao
30ml (1 fl oz) Cherry Soda Syrup
30ml (1 fl oz) Maraschino Cherry Juice
2 scoops Vanilla Ice Cream
5 Maraschino Cherries

Pour Brandy, Cacao, syrup and juice into a blender over small amount of crushed ice. Add ice cream and 4 cherries. Blend until smooth and pour into a chilled parfait glass. Garnish with a cherry and serve.

Hineque

26.2% ALC/VOL • 1.3 STD DRINKS

40ml (1⅓ fl oz) Cognac
Dash Banana Liqueur
Dash Frothee
20ml (⅔ fl oz) Lemon Soda

Pour Cognac, Liqueur and frothee into a cocktail shaker over ice. Shake and strain into a chilled cocktail glass. Add soda, stir gently and serve.

China Doll

16% ALC/VOL • 2.7 STD DRINKS

45ml (1½ fl oz) Brandy
45ml (1½ fl oz) Tequila
120ml (4 fl oz) Fresh Milk (chilled)
Cherry

Pineapple Spear

Pour Brandy, Tequila and milk into a blender over cracked ice. Blend and pour into a chilled margarita glass. Garnish with a cherry and pineapple spear then serve.

Devil in Miss Jones

29.3% ALC/VOL • 1.8 STD DRINKS

45ml (1½ fl oz) Brandy
15ml (½ fl oz) Triple Sec
10ml (⅓ fl oz) Crème De Noyaux
10ml (⅓ fl oz) Grenadine

Pour ingredients into a cocktail shaker over ice and shake. Strain into an old-fashioned glass filled with ice and serve.

Apple Blow No.2

7.8% ALC/VOL • 1.4 STD DRINKS

45ml (1½ fl oz) Applejack
30ml (1 fl oz) Apple Juice
30ml (1 fl oz) Fresh Lemon Juice
1 teaspoon Sugar Syrup
White of 1 Egg
90ml (3 fl oz) Soda Water

Pour Applejack, juices, sugar and egg white into a cocktail shaker over ice. Shake well and strain into a highball glass over ice. Add soda, stir gently and serve.

Dalilah's Dream

30.7% ALC/VOL • 2.2 STD DRINKS

30ml (1 fl oz) Brandy
30ml (1 fl oz) Dry Vermouth
30ml (1 fl oz) Kirsch
Twist of Lemon Peel

Pour Brandy, Vermouth and Kirsch into a cocktail shaker over ice. Shake and strain into a chilled cocktail glass. Garnish with lemon peel and serve.

Lil Naue

21.6% ALC/VOL • 1.4 STD DRINKS

30ml (1 fl oz) Brandy
15ml (½ fl oz) Apricot Brandy
15ml (½ fl oz) Port
1 teaspoon Sugar Syrup
Yolk of 1 Egg
Cinnamon

Pour Brandies, Port, sugar and egg yolk into a cocktail shaker over ice. Shake well and strain into a chilled wine glass. Sprinkle cinnamon on top and serve.

Bine's Brain Blower

25.1% ALC/VOL • 2.4 STD DRINKS

30ml (1 fl oz) Brandy
30ml (1 fl oz) Amaretto
30ml (1 fl oz) Jägermeister
30ml (1 fl oz) Fresh Cream

Pour Brandy into a chilled old-fashioned glass and layer Jägermeister on top. Pour Amaretto and cream into a mixing glass over ice. Stir and strain into glass gently over Jägermeister – do not stir, then serve.

Apricot Adventure

8.9% ALC/VOL • 1 STD DRINK

40ml (1⅓ fl oz) Apricot Brandy
10ml (⅓ fl oz) Vodka
15ml (½ fl oz) Fresh Lime Juice
1 teaspoon Sugar Syrup
75ml (2½ fl oz) Soda Water
3 Sprigs of Fresh Mint

Pour sugar into a chilled old-fashioned glass and add 2 sprigs of mint. Muddle well then pour Brandy, Vodka and juice into a cocktail shaker over cracked ice. Shake and pour into glass over mint. Add soda and stir gently. Garnish with a sprig of mint and serve.

Twinkle Star

4.6% ALC/VOL • 0.8 STD DRINKS

45ml (1½ fl oz) Cherry Brandy
180ml (6 fl oz) Tonic Water

Pour Brandy into a highball glass over ice and add tonic, stir gently then serve.

Whip Cocktail

28.7% ALC/VOL • 1.8 STD DRINKS

45ml (1½ fl oz) Brandy
15ml (½ fl oz) Dry Vermouth
15ml (½ fl oz) Sweet Vermouth
5ml (⅙ fl oz) Curaçao
Dash Anise

Pour ingredients into a mixing glass over ice and stir. Strain into a chilled cocktail glass and serve.

Oak Tree

13.1% ALC/VOL • 2.2 STD DRINKS

30ml (1 fl oz) Brandy
30ml (1 fl oz) Amaretto
30ml (1 fl oz) Tia Maria
120ml (4 fl oz) Fresh Milk (chilled)

Pour ingredients into a cocktail shaker over ice and swirl well. Strain into a tall glass over ice and add more ice to fill glass then serve with 2 straws.

Sir Walter Raleigh

26.5% ALC/VOL • 1.6 STD DRINKS

45ml (1½ fl oz) Brandy
15ml (½ fl oz) Light Rum
5ml (⅙ fl oz) Blue Curaçao
5ml (⅙ fl oz) Grenadine
5ml (⅙ fl oz) Fresh Lime Juice

Pour ingredients into a cocktail shaker over ice and shake. Strain into an old-fashioned glass over ice and serve.

Anu

7.2% ALC/VOL • 1.4 STD DRINKS

30ml (1 fl oz) Apricot Brandy
20ml (⅔ fl oz) Dry Vermouth
10ml (⅓ fl oz) Triple Sec
180ml (6 fl oz) Lemonade

Pour Brandy, Vermouth and Triple Sec into a highball glass over ice then stir. Add lemonade, stir gently and serve.

Pierre Collins

15.3% ALC/VOL • 1.8 STD DRINKS

60ml (2 fl oz) Brandy
15ml (½ fl oz) Lime Syrup
2 teaspoons Sugar Syrup
60ml (2 fl oz) Soda Water

Pour Brandy, syrup and sugar into a cocktail shaker over ice. Shake and strain into a collins glass over ice. Add soda, stir gently and serve.

Primo Amore

24.7% ALC/VOL • 1 STD DRINK

20ml (⅔ fl oz) Cognac
20ml (⅔ fl oz) Apricot Brandy
Dash Grenadine
10ml (⅓ fl oz) Fresh Orange Juice

Pour ingredients into a cocktail shaker over ice and shake. Strain into a chilled cocktail glass and serve.

El Dada

10.8% ALC/VOL • 1 STD DRINK

30ml (1 fl oz) Apricot Brandy
30ml (1 fl oz) Vanilla Liqueur
30ml (1 fl oz) Black Coffee (chilled)
30ml (1 fl oz) Orgeat Syrup

Pour ingredients into a cocktail shaker over ice and shake. Strain into a chilled cocktail glass and serve.

Apricot Cocktail

15.1% ALC/VOL • 1 STD DRINK

45ml (1½ fl oz) Apricot Brandy
5ml (⅙ fl oz) Gin
23ml (¾ fl oz) Fresh Orange Juice
8ml (¼ fl oz) Fresh Lemon Juice

Pour ingredients into a cocktail shaker over ice and shake. Strain into a chilled cocktail glass and serve.

Japanese

26.3% ALC/VOL • 1.8 STD DRINKS

60ml (2 fl oz) Brandy
Dash Angostura Bitters
18ml (⅗ fl oz) Fresh Lime Juice
1½ teaspoons Orgeat Syrup
Twist of Lime Peel

Pour Brandy, Bitters, juice and syrup into a cocktail shaker over ice. Shake and strain into a chilled cocktail glass. Add lime peel and serve.

Stone Sour

7.7% ALC/VOL • 0.5 STD DRINKS

30ml (1 fl oz) Apricot Brandy
30ml (1 fl oz) Fresh Orange Juice
30ml (1 fl oz) Sweet and Sour Mix

Pour ingredients into a cocktail shaker over ice and shake. Strain into a chilled sour glass and serve.

Indy Blanket

28.6% ALC/VOL • 2.8 STD DRINKS

45ml (1½ fl oz) Cognac
30ml (1 fl oz) Light Rum
23ml (¾ fl oz) Triple Sec
15ml (½ fl oz) Fresh Lemon Juice
2 teaspoons Sugar Syrup

Pour ingredients into a cocktail shaker over ice and shake. Strain into a chilled cocktail glass and serve.

Sundown

15.1% ALC/VOL • 2.4 STD DRINKS

50ml (1⅔ fl oz) Apricot Brandy
50ml (1⅔ fl oz) Vodka
100ml (3⅓ fl oz) Pineapple Juice

Pour ingredients into a cocktail shaker over ice and shake. Strain into a chilled old-fashioned glass and serve.

Gin

Gin originated from Holland in the seventeenth century when a Dutch physician produced Gin using juniper berries and alcohol for medicinal purposes.

Today Gin is produced by distilling grain mash such as barley, corn and rye in column stills. This neutral spirit is then combined with water to reduce the strength before being redistilled with botanicals and aromatics. The botanicals and aromatics required for this procedure are primarily juniper berries and coriander. Other botanicals and aromatics that are used by distillers include bitter almonds, caraway seeds, cinnamon, fennel, ginger, lemon and orange peel, roots and other secret ingredients.

Gin is an unaged spirit with London Dry Gin being the most common type of Gin and is produced by distillers around the world. Dry Gin has become the preferred Gin consumed across the world with Dry Gin containing no sugar.

Genever or Hollands Gin is produced in pot stills containing a larger proportion of barley and other grains. This Gin is then redistilled with juniper berries.

Old Tom Gin is produced in England and is a sweet Gin.

Plymouth Gin is only produced in Plymouth, England and is a very Dry Gin.

Each distillery has their own formulas and processes for distilling and producing Gin which is the most widely required spirit for cocktails.

New Orleans Fizz

9% ALC/VOL • 1.8 STD DRINKS

60ml (2 fl oz) Dry Gin
30ml (1 fl oz) Fresh Lemon Juice
30ml (1 fl oz) Fresh Cream
2 dashes Orange Flower Water
1 teaspoon Caster Sugar
White of 1 Egg
90ml (3 fl oz) Soda Water

Pour Gin, juice, cream, flower water and egg white into a cocktail shaker over ice then add sugar. Shake and strain into a highball glass over ice. Add soda, stir gently and serve.

Piccadilly Cocktail

30.1% ALC/VOL • 1.7 STD DRINKS

45ml (1½ fl oz) Dry Gin
23ml (¾ fl oz) Dry Vermouth
Dash Anisette
Dash Grenadine

Pour ingredients into a mixing glass over ice and stir. Strain into a chilled cocktail glass and serve.

Strawberry Fizz

9.9% ALC/VOL • 1.8 STD DRINKS

60ml (2 fl oz) Gin
15ml (½ fl oz) Fresh Lemon Juice
15ml (½ fl oz) Thick Cream
1 teaspoon Caster Sugar
90ml (3 fl oz) Soda Water
4 Strawberries (crushed)
Strawberry

Pour Gin, juice and cream into a cocktail shaker over ice. Add sugar and crushed strawberries. Shake and strain into a highball glass over ice. Add soda and stir gently. Garnish with a strawberry and serve.
This drink is also known as Strawberry Blush.

Pink Gin

37.4% ALC/VOL • 1.9 STD DRINKS

60ml (2 fl oz) Gin
3 dashes Angostura Bitters

Pour Bitters into a chilled goblet and swirl around glass, then discard remaining Bitters. Add ice and Gin then serve.

Straits Sling

15.4% ALC/VOL • 2.6 STD DRINKS

60ml (2 fl oz) Gin
15ml (½ fl oz) Bénédictine
15ml (½ fl oz) Cherry Brandy
2 dashes Angostura Bitters
2 dashes Orange Bitters
30ml (1 fl oz) Fresh Orange Juice
90ml (3 fl oz) Soda Water
Slice of Lemon
Slice of Orange

Pour Gin, Bénédictine, Brandy, Bitters and juice into a highball glass over ice then stir. Add soda and stir gently. Garnish with a slice of lemon and orange then serve.

English Rose Cocktail

27% ALC/VOL • 2.1 STD DRINKS

45ml (1½ fl oz) Dry Gin
23ml (¾ fl oz) Apricot Brandy
23ml (¾ fl oz) Dry Vermouth
5ml (1/6 fl oz) Grenadine
Dash Fresh Lemon Juice
Maraschino Cherry

Prepare a cocktail glass with a sugar frosted rim – moistened with lemon juice. Pour Gin, Brandy, Vermouth, Grenadine and juice into a cocktail shaker over ice. Shake and strain into prepared glass. Garnish with a cherry and serve.

Red Gin

35.9% ALC/VOL • 1.8 STD DRINKS

60ml (2 fl oz) Gin
5ml (1/6 fl oz) Peter Heering Liqueur
Maraschino Cherry

Pour Gin and Liqueur into a mixing glass over crushed ice. Stir and strain into a chilled cocktail glass. Garnish with a cherry and serve.

Grand Royal Fizz

10% ALC/VOL • 1.8 STD DRINKS

60ml (2 fl oz) Dry Gin
2 dashes Maraschino Liqueur
45ml (1½ fl oz) Fresh Orange Juice
15ml (½ fl oz) Fresh Lemon Juice
2 teaspoons Fresh Cream
1 teaspoon Caster Sugar
90ml (3 fl oz) Soda Water

Pour Gin, Liqueur, juices and cream into a cocktail shaker over ice then add sugar. Shake and strain into a highball glass over ice. Add soda, stir gently and serve.

Opal Cocktail

26.3% ALC/VOL • 1.3 STD DRINKS

30ml (1 fl oz) Gin
15ml (½ fl oz) Cointreau
15ml (½ fl oz) Fresh Orange Juice
1 teaspoon Sugar Syrup

Pour ingredients into a cocktail shaker over ice and shake. Strain into a chilled cocktail glass and serve.

Bermuda Rose

27.5% ALC/VOL • 1.8 STD DRINKS

60ml (2 fl oz) Dry Gin
5ml (1/6 fl oz) Apricot Brandy
5ml (1/6 fl oz) Grenadine
15ml (½ fl oz) Fresh Lemon Juice
Slice of Lemon

Pour Gin, Brandy, Grenadine and juice into a cocktail shaker over ice. Shake and strain into a chilled cocktail glass. Garnish with a slice of lemon and serve.

London

34.6% ALC/VOL • 1.4 STD DRINKS

45ml (1½ fl oz) Dry Gin
2 dashes Maraschino Liqueur
2 dashes Orange Bitters
2 dashes Sugar Syrup
Twist of Lemon Peel

Pour Gin, Liqueur, Bitters and sugar into a mixing glass over ice. Stir and strain into a chilled cocktail glass. Garnish with lemon peel and serve.

Jewel Cocktail

35.6% ALC/VOL • 2 STD DRINKS

23ml (¾ fl oz) Dry Gin
23ml (¾ fl oz) Green Chartreuse
23ml (¾ fl oz) Sweet Vermouth
Dash Orange Bitters
Maraschino Cherry

Pour Gin, Chartreuse, Vermouth and Bitters into a mixing glass over ice. Stir and strain into a chilled cocktail glass. Garnish with a cherry and serve.
This drink is also known as Bijou Cocktail.

Stress Buster

25.7% ALC/VOL • 1 STD DRINK

15ml (½ fl oz) Dry Gin
15ml (½ fl oz) Dry Vermouth
8ml (¼ fl oz) Apricot Brandy
8ml (¼ fl oz) Triple Sec
5ml (⅙ fl oz) Peach Schnapps

Pour ingredients into a cocktail shaker over ice and shake. Strain into a chilled cocktail glass and serve.

Bloodhound

12.7% ALC/VOL • 0.9 STD DRINKS

15ml (½ fl oz) Dry Gin
15ml (½ fl oz) Dry Vermouth
15ml (½ fl oz) Sweet Vermouth
2 dashes Maraschino Liqueur
4 Strawberries (crushed)
Maraschino Cherry
Strawberry

Pour Gin, Vermouths and Liqueur into a blender over crushed ice then add crushed strawberries. Blend and pour into a chilled cocktail glass. Garnish with a cherry and a strawberry then serve.

Chanticleer

22.2% ALC/VOL • 2.6 STD DRINKS

90ml (3 fl oz) Dry Gin
15ml (½ fl oz) Fresh Lemon Juice
15ml (½ fl oz) Raspberry Syrup
White of 1 Egg

Pour ingredients into a cocktail shaker over ice and shake. Strain into a chilled cocktail glass and serve.

Gin Sling

12.2% ALC/VOL • 1.7 STD DRINKS

60ml (2 fl oz) Gin
Dash Grenadine
30ml (1 fl oz) Fresh Orange Juice
90ml (3 fl oz) Soda Water
Maraschino Cherry
Slice of Lemon

Pour Gin, Grenadine and juice into a highball glass over ice. Add soda and stir gently. Garnish with a cherry and slice of lemon then serve.

Wellington

27.9% ALC/VOL • 1.4 STD DRINKS

45ml (1½ fl oz) Dry Gin
2 dashes Cherry Brandy
2 dashes Swedish Punsch
15ml (½ fl oz) Fresh Lime Juice

Pour ingredients into a cocktail shaker over ice and shake. Strain into a chilled cocktail glass and serve.

Free Silver

12.6% ALC/VOL • 1.7 STD DRINKS

45ml (1½ fl oz) Dry Gin
15ml (½ fl oz) Dark Rum
15ml (½ fl oz) Fresh Milk (chilled)
8ml (¼ fl oz) Fresh Lemon Juice
½ teaspoon Sugar Syrup
90ml (3 fl oz) Soda Water

Pour Gin, Rum, milk, juice and sugar into a cocktail shaker over ice. Shake and strain into a highball glass over ice. Add soda, stir gently and serve.

Judge Jr. Cocktail

29.3% ALC/VOL • 1.3 STD DRINKS

23ml (¾ fl oz) Dry Gin
23ml (¾ fl oz) Light Rum
Dash Grenadine
8ml (¼ fl oz) Fresh Lemon Juice
½ teaspoon Sugar Syrup

Pour ingredients into a cocktail shaker over ice and shake. Strain into a chilled cocktail glass and serve.

Tom Collins

10.3% ALC/VOL • 1.7 STD DRINKS

60ml (2 fl oz) Dry Gin
60ml (2 fl oz) Fresh Lemon Juice
1 teaspoon Sugar Syrup
90ml (3 fl oz) Soda Water
Maraschino Cherry
Slice of Lemon

Pour Gin, juice and sugar into a collins glass over ice then stir. Add soda and stir gently. Garnish with a cherry and slice of lemon then serve.

Teardrop

8.2% ALC/VOL • 0.9 STD DRINKS

30ml (1 fl oz) Gin
60ml (2 fl oz) Fresh Orange Juice
30ml (1 fl oz) Fresh Cream
15ml (½ fl oz) Strawberry Syrup

Pour Gin, juice and cream into a cocktail shaker over ice. Shake and strain into an old-fashioned glass over crushed ice. Add syrup by pouring gently on top – do not stir, then serve.

Gin Fizz

12% ALC/VOL • 1.8 STD DRINKS

60ml (2 fl oz) Dry Gin
15ml (½ fl oz) Fresh Lemon Juice
15ml (½ fl oz) Fresh Lime Juice
1 teaspoon Caster Sugar
White of 1 Egg
60ml (2 fl oz) Soda Water
Slice of Lemon

Pour Gin, juices and egg white into a cocktail shaker over ice then add sugar. Shake and strain into a highball glass over ice. Add soda and stir gently. Garnish with a slice of lemon and serve with a straw. *This drink is also known as Silver Fizz.*

Third Degree

31.4% ALC/VOL • 1.2 STD DRINKS

30ml (1 fl oz) Dry Gin
15ml (½ fl oz) Dry Vermouth
4 dashes Pernod

Pour ingredients into a mixing glass over ice and stir. Strain into a chilled cocktail glass and serve.

Singapore Sling

22.9% ALC/VOL • 1.8 STD DRINKS

45ml (1½ fl oz) Gin
23ml (¾ fl oz) Cherry Brandy
Dash Angostura Bitters
Dash Bénédictine
30ml (1 fl oz) Fresh Lemon Juice
Slice of Orange
Strawberry

Pour Gin, Brandy, Bitters and juice into a cocktail shaker over ice. Shake and strain into a highball glass filled with ice then layer Bénédictine on top. Garnish with a slice of orange and a strawberry then serve with a straw.

Hula-Hula

24.7% ALC/VOL • 1.8 STD DRINKS

60ml (2 fl oz) Gin
Dash Blue Curaçao
30ml (1 fl oz) Fresh Orange Juice

Pour ingredients into a highball glass filled with ice, stir and serve.

Judgette Cocktail

23.4% ALC/VOL • 1.4 STD DRINKS

23ml (¾ fl oz) Dry Gin
23ml (¾ fl oz) Dry Vermouth
23ml (¾ fl oz) Peach Brandy
15ml (½ fl oz) Fresh Lime Juice
Maraschino Cherry

Pour Gin, Vermouth, Brandy and juice into a cocktail shaker over ice. Shake and strain into a chilled cocktail glass. Garnish with a cherry and serve.

Clover Club Cocktail

17% ALC/VOL • 1.6 STD DRINKS

45ml (1½ fl oz) Dry Gin
23ml (¾ fl oz) Sweet Vermouth
5ml (1/6 fl oz) Grenadine
15ml (½ fl oz) Fresh Lemon Juice
White of 1 Egg

Pour ingredients into a cocktail shaker over ice and shake. Strain into a chilled champagne saucer and serve.

Gin Sangaree

14.4% ALC/VOL • 2.5 STD DRINKS

60ml (2 fl oz) Dry Gin
15ml (½ fl oz) Port
5ml (1/6 fl oz) Spring Water
½ teaspoon Sugar Syrup
90ml (3 fl oz) Soda Water
Nutmeg

Pour Gin, water and sugar into a highball glass over ice. Add soda and stir gently then layer Port on top. Sprinkle nutmeg on top and serve.

Hudson Bay

27.1% ALC/VOL • 1.6 STD DRINKS

30ml (1 fl oz) Gin
15ml (½ fl oz) Cherry Brandy
8ml (¼ fl oz) 151-Proof Rum
15ml (½ fl oz) Fresh Orange Juice
8ml (¼ fl oz) Fresh Lime Juice

Pour ingredients into a cocktail shaker over ice and shake. Strain into a chilled cocktail glass and serve.

Martinez Cocktail

27% ALC/VOL • 1.4 STD DRINKS

30ml (1 fl oz) Gin
30ml (1 fl oz) Sweet Vermouth
2 dashes Angostura Bitters
2 dashes Cointreau
Maraschino Cherry
Slice of Lemon

Pour Gin, Vermouth, Bitters and Cointreau into a mixing glass over ice. Stir and strain into a chilled cocktail glass. Twist slice of lemon above drink to release juice – do not stir, then discard remainder of lemon slice. Garnish with a cherry and serve.

Harrovian

34.8% ALC/VOL • 2.9 STD DRINKS

90ml (3 fl oz) Dry Gin
Dash Angostura Bitters
5ml (1/6 fl oz) Fresh Orange Juice
Dash Fresh Lemon Juice

Pour ingredients into a cocktail shaker over ice and shake. Strain into a chilled cocktail glass and serve.

Creamy Gin Sour

8.6% ALC/VOL • 1.3 STD DRINKS

30ml (1 fl oz) Dry Gin
15ml (½ fl oz) Cointreau
30ml (1 fl oz) Fresh Lemon Juice
30ml (1 fl oz) Fresh Lime Juice
30ml (1 fl oz) Thick Cream
½ teaspoon Sugar Syrup
60ml (2 fl oz) Soda Water

Pour Gin, Cointreau, juices, cream and sugar into a blender over crushed ice. Blend and pour into a chilled sour glass. Add soda, stir gently and serve.

Jockey Club Cocktail

31.3% ALC/VOL • 1.4 STD DRINKS

45ml (1½ fl oz) Gin
2 dashes White Crème De Cacao
Dash Angostura Bitters
8ml (¼ fl oz) Fresh Lime Juice

Pour ingredients into a cocktail shaker over ice and shake. Strain into a chilled cocktail glass and serve.

Gin Toddy

30.4% ALC/VOL • 1.8 STD DRINKS

60ml (2 fl oz) Dry Gin
10ml (⅓ fl oz) Spring Water
½ teaspoon Sugar Syrup
Twist of Lemon Peel

Pour Gin, water and sugar into a chilled old-fashioned glass then stir. Add an ice cube and garnish with lemon peel then serve.

Blue Jacket

31.3% ALC/VOL • 3 STD DRINKS

60ml (2 fl oz) Gin
30ml (1 fl oz) Blue Curaçao
30ml (1 fl oz) Orange Bitters
Slice of Orange

Pour Gin, Curaçao and Bitters into a mixing glass over ice. Stir and strain into a chilled cocktail glass. Garnish with a slice of orange and serve.

Gloom Chaser

30.1% ALC/VOL • 2.2 STD DRINKS

60ml (2 fl oz) Dry Gin
30ml (1 fl oz) Dry Vermouth
2 dashes Pernod
2 dashes Grenadine
Slice of Lemon

Pour Gin, Vermouth, Pernod and Grenadine into a cocktail shaker over ice. Shake and strain into a chilled cocktail glass. Twist a slice of lemon above drink to release juice – do not stir, then place remainder of lemon slice into drink and serve.

Hoffman House Cocktail

30.6% ALC/VOL • 1.6 STD DRINKS

45ml (1½ fl oz) Dry Gin
23ml (¾ fl oz) Dry Vermouth
Olive

Pour Gin and Vermouth into a mixing glass over ice. Stir and strain into a chilled martini glass. Add an olive and serve.

Fourth Degree

24% ALC/VOL • 1.8 STD DRINKS

30ml (1 fl oz) Dry Gin
30ml (1 fl oz) Dry Vermouth
30ml (1 fl oz) Sweet Vermouth
4 dashes Pernod
Maraschino Cherry
Twist of Lemon Peel

Pour Gin, Vermouths and Pernod into a mixing glass over ice. Stir and strain into a chilled cocktail glass. Garnish with a cherry and lemon peel then serve.

Betty James

28.7% ALC/VOL • 1.2 STD DRINKS

30ml (1 fl oz) Dry Gin
15ml (½ fl oz) Maraschino Liqueur
Dash Angostura Bitters
8ml (¼ fl oz) Fresh Lemon Juice

Pour ingredients into a cocktail shaker over ice and shake. Strain into a chilled cocktail glass and serve.

Cherry Cobbler

25.8% ALC/VOL • 2.4 STD DRINKS

60ml (2 fl oz) Gin
23ml (¾ fl oz) Cherry Brandy
15ml (½ fl oz) Crème De Cassis
15ml (½ fl oz) Fresh Lemon Juice
1 teaspoon Sugar Syrup
Maraschino Cherry
Slice of Lemon

Pour Gin, Brandy, Cassis, juice and sugar into a mixing glass over ice. Stir and strain into a goblet over crushed ice. Garnish with a cherry and slice of lemon then serve.

Magnolia Blossom

18.1% ALC/VOL • 1.3 STD DRINKS

45ml (1½ fl oz) Gin
Dash Grenadine
23ml (¾ fl oz) Fresh Lemon Juice
23ml (¾ fl oz) Fresh Cream

Pour ingredients into a cocktail shaker over ice and shake. Strain into a chilled cocktail glass and serve.

Elephant Walk

27.8% ALC/VOL • 1.4 STD DRINKS

30ml (1 fl oz) Dry Gin
15ml (½ fl oz) Tequila
Dash Angostura Bitters
Dash Grenadine

15ml (½ fl oz) Fresh
Orange Juice
Slice of Lemon
Slice of Orange
Stick of Cucumber

Pour Gin, Tequila, Bitters, Grenadine and juice into an old-fashioned glass over ice then stir well. Garnish with a slice of lemon, orange and a stick of cucumber then serve with a swizzle stick.

Plead the 5th

31.7% ALC/VOL • 2.3 STD DRINKS

30ml (1 fl oz) Gin
30ml (1 fl oz) Kahlúa
30ml (1 fl oz) Sambuca

Pour ingredients into a cocktail shaker over ice and shake. Strain into a chilled cocktail glass and serve.

Fog Horn

13.5% ALC/VOL • 1.8 STD DRINKS

60ml (2 fl oz) Dry Gin
15ml (½ fl oz) Fresh
Lime Juice
90ml (3 fl oz) Dry Ginger Ale
Slice of Lime

Pour Gin and juice into a highball glass over ice. Add Ginger Ale and stir gently. Garnish with a slice of lime and serve.
This drink is also known as Gin Thing.

H.P.W. Cocktail

31.7% ALC/VOL • 1.5 STD DRINKS

45ml (1½ fl oz) Dry Gin
8ml (¼ fl oz) Dry Vermouth
8ml (¼ fl oz) Sweet Vermouth
Twist of Orange Peel

Pour Gin and Vermouths into a mixing glass over ice. Stir and strain into a chilled martini glass. Garnish with orange peel and serve.

Ramos Fizz

8% ALC/VOL • 1.8 STD DRINKS

60ml (2 fl oz) Gin
30ml (1 fl oz) Fresh
Lemon Juice
30ml (1 fl oz) Fresh Lime Juice
30ml (1 fl oz) Fresh Cream
2 dashes Fresh Orange Juice
2 dashes Orange Flower Water
1 teaspoon Caster Sugar
White of 1 Egg
90ml (3 fl oz) Soda Water

Prepare a highball glass with a sugar frosted rim. Pour Gin, juices, cream, flower water and egg white into a cocktail shaker over ice then add sugar. Shake and strain into prepared glass. Add soda, stir gently and serve.

Silver Fizz

12% ALC/VOL • 1.8 STD DRINKS

This drink is also known as Gin Fizz, p 51.

Gin Swizzle

25.9% ALC/VOL • 1.9 STD DRINKS

60ml (2 fl oz) Gin
3 dashes Angostura Bitters
23ml (¾ fl oz) Fresh
Lime Juice
1 teaspoon Sugar Syrup

Pour ingredients into a mixing glass over large amount of ice and stir vigorously until cold. Strain into a collins glass filled with crushed ice and top up with soda water if desired – do not stir. Serve with a swizzle stick and 2 straws.

Gin Buck

13.5% ALC/VOL • 1.8 STD DRINKS

60ml (2 fl oz) Gin
90ml (3 fl oz) Dry Ginger Ale
½ Fresh Lemon

Pour Gin into a highball glass over ice and twist ½ lemon above drink to release juice. Add spent shell and stir. Add Ginger Ale, stir gently and serve.

Gin Fix

27.6% ALC/VOL • 1.8 STD DRINKS

60ml (2 fl oz) Dry Gin
Dash Cointreau
8ml (¼ fl oz) Fresh
Lemon Juice
8ml (¼ fl oz) Fresh
Orange Juice
1 teaspoon Sugar Syrup
Slice of Orange
Twist of Lemon Peel

Pour Gin, Cointreau, juices and sugar into an old-fashioned glass filled with crushed ice. Add more crushed ice to fill glass and stir. Top up with soda water if desired and stir gently. Garnish with a slice of orange and lemon peel then serve.

Golden Daze

22.3% ALC/VOL • 1.6 STD DRINKS

45ml (1½ fl oz) Dry Gin
15ml (½ fl oz) Peach Brandy
30ml (1 fl oz) Fresh
Orange Juice

Pour ingredients into a cocktail shaker over ice and shake. Strain into a chilled cocktail glass and serve.

Golden Fizz

13.2% ALC/VOL • 1.7 STD DRINKS

60ml (2 fl oz) Gin
15ml (½ fl oz) Fresh
Lemon Juice
15ml (½ fl oz) Fresh
Lime Juice
½ teaspoon Caster Sugar
Yolk of 1 Egg
60ml (2 fl oz) Soda Water
Slice of Lemon

Pour Gin, juices and egg yolk into a cocktail shaker over ice then add sugar. Shake and strain into a highball glass over ice. Add soda and stir gently. Garnish with a slice of lemon and serve.

Xanthia

38.3% ALC/VOL • 2.7 STD DRINKS

30ml (1 fl oz) Dry Gin
30ml (1 fl oz) Cherry Brandy
30ml (1 fl oz) Green Chartreuse

Pour ingredients into a mixing glass without ice and stir. Pour into a cocktail glass and serve.

R.A.C. Cocktail

25.9% ALC/VOL • 2 STD DRINKS

45ml (1½ fl oz) Dry Gin
23ml (¾ fl oz) Dry Vermouth
23ml (¾ fl oz) Sweet Vermouth
3 dashes Orange Bitters
3 dashes Grenadine
Maraschino Cherry
Twist of Orange Peel

Pour Gin, Vermouths, Bitters and Grenadine into a mixing glass over ice. Stir and strain into a chilled cocktail glass. Twist orange peel above drink and discard remainder of peel. Garnish with a cherry and serve.

Union Jack

37.8% ALC/VOL • 1.8 STD DRINKS

45ml (1½ fl oz) Dry Gin
15ml (½ fl oz) Crème Yvette

Pour ingredients into a mixing glass over ice and stir. Strain into a chilled cocktail glass and serve.

Snowball

25.4% ALC/VOL • 1.5 STD DRINKS

30ml (1 fl oz) Gin
15ml (½ fl oz) Anisette
15ml (½ fl oz) White Crème De Menthe
15ml (½ fl oz) Fresh Cream
Strawberry

Pour Gin, Anisette, Crème De Menthe and cream into a cocktail shaker over ice. Shake and strain into a chilled cocktail glass. Garnish with a strawberry and serve.

Hawaii

29.2% ALC/VOL • 1.9 STD DRINKS

60ml (2 fl oz) Gin
8ml (¼ fl oz) Orange Curaçao
15ml (½ fl oz) Pineapple Juice

Pour ingredients into a cocktail shaker over ice and shake. Strain into a chilled cocktail glass and serve.

Fancy Gin

36.2% ALC/VOL • 1.8 STD DRINKS

60ml (2 fl oz) Dry Gin
Dash Cointreau
Dash Orange Bitters
Dash Sugar Syrup
Twist of Lemon Peel

Pour Gin, Cointreau, Bitters and sugar into a cocktail shaker over ice. Shake and strain into a chilled cocktail glass. Garnish with lemon peel and serve.

Sweet 16

19.5% ALC/VOL • 1.4 STD DRINKS

30ml (1 fl oz) Dry Gin
15ml (½ fl oz) Malibu
15ml (½ fl oz) White Crème De Cacao
30ml (1 fl oz) Pineapple Juice
Dash Coconut Cream

Pour ingredients into a cocktail shaker over ice and shake. Strain into a chilled cocktail glass and serve.

White Lightning

34.8% ALC/VOL • 2.1 STD DRINKS

45ml (1½ fl oz) Gin
15ml (½ fl oz) Cointreau
15ml (½ fl oz) White Crème De Menthe
Slice of Lemon
Sprig of Fresh Mint

Pour Gin, Cointreau and Crème De Menthe into a mixing glass over ice. Stir and strain into a chilled cocktail glass. Garnish with a slice of lemon and sprig of mint then serve.

Leave it to Me

22.2% ALC/VOL • 1.8 STD DRINKS

60ml (2 fl oz) Gin
30ml (1 fl oz) Fresh Lemon Juice
1 teaspoon Raspberry Syrup
5ml (1/6 fl oz) Soda Water

Pour Gin, juice and syrup into a cocktail shaker over ice. Shake and strain into a chilled wine glass. Add soda – do not stir, then serve.

Barrier Reef

23.5% ALC/VOL • 3 STD DRINKS

60ml (2 fl oz) Dry Gin
30ml (1 fl oz) Cointreau
5ml (1/6 fl oz) Blue Curaçao
5ml (1/6 fl oz) Grand Marnier
2 scoops Vanilla Ice Cream
Slice of Orange
Slice of Pineapple

Pour Gin, Cointreau, Curaçao and Grand Marnier into a blender over small amount of crushed ice then add ice cream. Blend and pour into a highball glass over ice. Garnish with a slice of orange and pineapple then serve.

Traveler's Joy

28.5% ALC/VOL • 2 STD DRINKS

30ml (1 fl oz) Gin
30ml (1 fl oz) Cherry Liqueur
30ml (1 fl oz) Fresh Lemon Juice

Pour ingredients into a mixing glass over ice and stir. Strain into a chilled cocktail glass and serve.

Fine-and-Dandy Cocktail

33.2% ALC/VOL • 1.8 STD DRINKS

45ml (1½ fl oz) Dry Gin
15ml (½ fl oz) Cointreau
Dash Orange Bitters
8ml (¼ fl oz) Fresh Lemon Juice
Maraschino Cherry

Pour Gin, Cointreau, Bitters and juice into a cocktail shaker over ice. Shake and strain into a chilled cocktail glass. Garnish with a cherry and serve.

Gin Sour

28.5% ALC/VOL • 1.8 STD DRINKS

60ml (2 fl oz) Gin
15ml (½ fl oz) Fresh Lemon Juice
½ teaspoon Sugar Syrup
Slice of Lemon

Pour Gin, juice and sugar into a cocktail shaker over ice. Shake and strain into a chilled sour glass. Garnish with a slice of lemon and serve.

Maiden's Blush

32.1% ALC/VOL • 1.4 STD DRINKS

45ml (1½ fl oz) Gin
4 dashes Orange Curaçao
4 dashes Grenadine
2 dashes Fresh Lemon Juice
Slice of Lemon

Pour Gin, Curaçao, Grenadine and juice into a mixing glass over ice. Stir and strain into a chilled cocktail glass. Garnish with a slice of lemon and serve.

Pink Lady

25.1% ALC/VOL • 1.3 STD DRINKS

30ml (1 fl oz) Gin
15ml (½ fl oz) Applejack
3 dashes Grenadine
15ml (½ fl oz) Fresh Lemon Juice
1 teaspoon Egg White

Pour ingredients into a cocktail shaker over ice and shake. Strain into a chilled champagne saucer and serve.

Red Baron

28.1% ALC/VOL • 1.8 STD DRINKS

60ml (2 fl oz) Dry Gin
Dash Grenadine
15ml (½ fl oz) Fresh Orange Juice
Dash Fresh Lemon Juice
Dash Fresh Lime Juice
Dash Sugar Syrup
Twist of Orange Peel

Pour Gin, Grenadine, juices and sugar into a cocktail shaker over ice. Shake and strain into a chilled cocktail glass. Garnish with orange peel and serve.

Dry Gibson

27.5% ALC/VOL • 2 STD DRINKS

45ml (1½ fl oz) Dry Gin
45ml (1½ fl oz) Dry Vermouth
Cocktail Onion

Pour Gin and Vermouth into a mixing glass over ice. Stir and strain into a chilled cocktail glass. Garnish with a cocktail onion and serve.

Mistress

12.4% ALC/VOL • 2 STD DRINKS

45ml (1½ fl oz) Gin
30ml (1 fl oz) White Crème De Cacao
5ml (⅙ fl oz) Campari
60ml (2 fl oz) Pineapple Juice
30ml (1 fl oz) Passion-Fruit Juice
30ml (1 fl oz) Thick Cream
Maraschino Cherry

Pour Gin, Cacao, juices and cream into a cocktail shaker over ice. Shake and strain into a highball glass over ice. Add Campari by gently pouring on top – do not stir, then garnish with a cherry and serve.

Orange Blossom

14.8% ALC/VOL • 0.9 STD DRINKS

30ml (1 fl oz) Gin
45ml (1½ fl oz) Fresh Orange Juice
Slice of Orange

Pour Gin and juice into a cocktail shaker over ice. Shake and strain into a chilled cocktail glass. Garnish with a slice of orange and serve.

Tod's Cooler

14.5% ALC/VOL • 1.5 STD DRINKS

45ml (1½ fl oz) Dry Gin
15ml (½ fl oz) Crème De Cassis
15ml (½ fl oz) Fresh Lemon Juice
60ml (2 fl oz) Soda Water
Slice of Lemon

Pour Gin, Cassis and juice into a cocktail shaker over ice. Shake and strain into a collins glass over ice. Add soda and stir gently. Garnish with a slice of lemon and serve.

Abbey

21.3% ALC/VOL • 1.8 STD DRINKS

60ml (2 fl oz) Gin
Dash Angostura Bitters
45ml (1½ fl oz) Fresh Orange Juice
Maraschino Cherry
Slice of Orange

Pour Gin, Bitters and juice into a cocktail shaker over ice. Shake and strain into a chilled cocktail glass. Garnish with a cherry and slice of orange then serve.

Long Beach Iced Tea

13.4% ALC/VOL • 2.2 STD DRINKS

15ml (½ fl oz) Gin
15ml (½ fl oz) Cointreau
15ml (½ fl oz) Gold Tequila
15ml (½ fl oz) Light Rum
15ml (½ fl oz) Vodka
90ml (3 fl oz) Cranberry Juice
30ml (1 fl oz) Fresh Lemon Juice
15ml (½ fl oz) Sugar Syrup
Slice of Lemon

Pour Gin, Cointreau, Tequila, Rum, Vodka, lemon juice and sugar into a cocktail shaker over ice. Shake and strain into a highball glass over ice. Add cranberry juice and stir. Garnish with a slice of lemon and serve.

Gin and it

26% ALC/VOL • 1.8 STD DRINKS

This drink is also known as Sweet Gibson, *p 59.*

Eton Blazer Cocktail

15.9% ALC/VOL • 2.4 STD DRINKS

60ml (2 fl oz) Dry Gin
23ml (¾ fl oz) Kirsch
15ml (½ fl oz) Fresh Lemon Juice
1 teaspoon Sugar Syrup
90ml (3 fl oz) Soda Water

Pour Gin, Kirsch, juice and sugar into a cocktail shaker over ice. Shake and strain into a highball glass over ice. Add soda, stir gently and serve.

Gin Rickey

13.5% ALC/VOL • 1.8 STD DRINKS

60ml (2 fl oz) Gin
15ml (½ fl oz) Fresh Lime Juice
90ml (3 fl oz) Soda Water
Twist of Lemon Peel

Pour Gin and juice into a collins glass over ice then stir. Add soda and stir gently. Garnish with lemon peel and serve.
This drink is also known as Billy Taylor.

Gin Crusta

36.7% ALC/VOL • 2.7 STD DRINKS

90ml (3 fl oz) Dry Gin
3 dashes Maraschino Liqueur
Dash Angostura Bitters
Maraschino Cherry
Slice of Lemon

Prepare a champagne saucer with a salt frosted rim. Pour Gin, Liqueur and Bitters into a cocktail shaker over ice. Shake and strain into prepared glass. Garnish with a cherry and slice of lemon then serve.

Gin Alexander

26.5% ALC/VOL • 2.3 STD DRINKS

60ml (2 fl oz) Dry Gin
30ml (1 fl oz) Dark Crème De Cacao
20ml (⅔ fl oz) Thick Cream
Nutmeg

Pour Gin, Cacao and cream into a cocktail shaker over ice. Shake and strain into a chilled cocktail glass. Sprinkle nutmeg on top and serve.

Around the World

20% ALC/VOL • 1.4 STD DRINKS

30ml (1 fl oz) Gin
30ml (1 fl oz) Green Crème De Menthe
30ml (1 fl oz) Pineapple Juice
Slice of Pineapple
Sprig of Fresh Mint

Pour Gin, Crème De Menthe and juice into a cocktail shaker over ice. Shake and strain into a chilled cocktail glass. Garnish with a slice of pineapple and sprig of mint then serve.

Blue Lagoon

12.4% ALC/VOL • 1.5 STD DRINKS

30ml (1 fl oz) Gin
30ml (1 fl oz) Blue Curaçao
90ml (3 fl oz) Lemonade
Sprig of Fresh Mint

Prepare a collins glass with a sugar frosted rim and add ice. Pour Gin and Curaçao into prepared glass then stir. Add lemonade and stir gently. Garnish with a sprig of mint and serve.

Charleston

26.3% ALC/VOL • 1.9 STD DRINKS

15ml (½ fl oz) Dry Gin
15ml (½ fl oz) Curaçao
15ml (½ fl oz) Dry Vermouth
15ml (½ fl oz) Kirsch
15ml (½ fl oz) Maraschino Liqueur
15ml (½ fl oz) Sweet Vermouth
Twist of Lemon Peel

Pour Gin, Curaçao, Vermouths, Kirsch and Liqueur into a mixing glass over ice. Stir and strain into a chilled cocktail glass. Twist lemon peel above drink and discard remainder of peel then serve.

Napoleon

36.5% ALC/VOL • 1.8 STD DRINKS

60ml (2 fl oz) Dry Gin
Dash Curaçao
Dash Dubonnet
Dash Fernet Branca

Pour ingredients into a cocktail shaker over ice and shake. Strain into a chilled cocktail glass and serve.

Queen's

22.2% ALC/VOL • 1.5 STD DRINKS

30ml (1 fl oz) Dry Gin
23ml (¾ fl oz) Dry Vermouth
23ml (¾ fl oz) Sweet Vermouth
8ml (¼ fl oz) Pineapple Juice
Slice of Pineapple

Pour Gin, Vermouths and juice into a cocktail shaker over ice. Shake and strain into a chilled cocktail glass. Garnish with a slice of pineapple and serve.

Sensation

27.7% ALC/VOL • 1.8 STD DRINKS

60ml (2 fl oz) Dry Gin
2 dashes Maraschino Liqueur
20ml (⅔ fl oz) Fresh Lemon Juice
3 Sprigs of Fresh Mint

Pour Gin, Liqueur and juice into a cocktail shaker over ice then add 2 sprigs of mint. Shake and strain into a chilled cocktail glass. Garnish with a sprig of mint and serve.

The Journalist

35.2% ALC/VOL • 1.5 STD DRINKS

45ml (1½ fl oz) Dry Gin
2 dashes Angostura Bitters
2 dashes Cointreau
Dash Dry Vermouth
Dash Sweet Vermouth
2 dashes Fresh Lemon Juice

Pour ingredients into a cocktail shaker over ice and shake. Strain into a chilled cocktail glass and serve.

Paradise

20% ALC/VOL • 1.4 STD DRINKS

30ml (1 fl oz) Gin
30ml (1 fl oz) Apricot Brandy
30ml (1 fl oz) Fresh Lemon Juice
Slice of Lemon

Pour Gin, Brandy and juice into a cocktail shaker over ice. Shake and strain into a chilled cocktail glass. Garnish with a slice of lemon and serve.

Star Daisy

14.7% ALC/VOL • 2.3 STD DRINKS

45ml (1½ fl oz) Dry Gin
30ml (1 fl oz) Calvados
10ml (⅓ fl oz) Grenadine
10ml (⅓ fl oz) Fresh Lemon Juice
2 teaspoons Sugar Syrup
90ml (3 fl oz) Soda Water
Slice of Lemon

Pour Gin, Calvados, Grenadine, juice and sugar into a cocktail shaker over ice. Shake and strain into a goblet over ice. Add soda and stir gently. Garnish with a slice of lemon and serve.

Tropical Dawn

19.5% ALC/VOL • 1.6 STD DRINKS

45ml (1½ fl oz) Dry Gin
15ml (½ fl oz) Campari
45ml (1½ fl oz) Fresh Orange Juice

Pour Gin and juice into a cocktail shaker over ice. Shake and strain into an old-fashioned glass over crushed ice. Add Campari by gently pouring on top – do not stir, then serve.

Gardenia

11.7% ALC/VOL • 0.9 STD DRINKS

30ml (1 fl oz) Gin
5ml (⅙ fl oz) Grenadine
30ml (1 fl oz) Pineapple Juice
30ml (1 fl oz) Thick Cream
Maraschino Cherry
Slice of Pineapple
Sprig of Fresh Mint

Pour Gin, Grenadine, juice and cream into a cocktail shaker over ice. Shake and strain into a chilled cocktail glass. Garnish with a cherry, slice of pineapple and sprig of mint then serve.

Gin and Tonic

12.3% ALC/VOL • 1.3 STD DRINKS

45ml (1½ fl oz) Gin
90ml (3 fl oz) Tonic Water
Wedge of Lime

Pour Gin into a highball glass over ice and twist wedge of lime above drink to release juice then stir. Add tonic and stir gently. Add spent lime shell and serve.

Orange Fizz

12.3% ALC/VOL • 1.7 STD DRINKS

60ml (2 fl oz) Dry Gin
15ml (½ fl oz) Fresh Lime Juice
15ml (½ fl oz) Fresh Orange Juice
90ml (3 fl oz) Soda Water
Slice of Orange

Pour Gin and juices into a cocktail shaker over ice. Shake and strain into a highball glass over ice. Add soda and stir gently. Garnish with a slice of orange and serve.

Pink Rose

14.8% ALC/VOL • 0.9 STD DRINKS

30ml (1 fl oz) Dry Gin
5ml (⅙ fl oz) Grenadine

5ml (1/6 fl oz) Fresh Lemon Juice
1 teaspoon Thick Cream
White of 1 Egg

Pour ingredients into a cocktail shaker over ice and shake. Strain into a chilled cocktail glass and serve.

Lady Lynne

28% ALC/VOL • 1.9 STD DRINKS

45ml (1½ fl oz) Gin
30ml (1 fl oz) Parfait Amour
8ml (¼ fl oz) Fresh Lemon or Lime Juice
Dash Egg White
Strawberry

Pour Gin, Parfait Amour, juice and egg white into a cocktail shaker over ice. Shake and strain into a chilled cocktail glass. Garnish with a strawberry and serve.

Sweet Gibson

26% ALC/VOL • 1.8 STD DRINKS

45ml (1½ fl oz) Gin
45ml (1½ fl oz) Sweet Vermouth
Cocktail Onion

Pour Gin and Vermouth into a mixing glass over ice. Stir and strain into a chilled cocktail glass. Add a cocktail onion and serve.
This drink is also known as Gin and it.

Strangeways to Oldham

9.9% ALC/VOL • 1.8 STD DRINKS

30ml (1 fl oz) Gin
30ml (1 fl oz) Dark Rum
60ml (2 fl oz) Mandarin Juice
30ml (1 fl oz) Passion-Fruit Juice
15ml (½ fl oz) Lime Syrup
60ml (2 fl oz) Lemonade

Pour Gin, Rum, juices and syrup into a cocktail shaker over ice. Shake and strain into a highball glass over ice. Add lemonade, stir gently and serve with a straw.

Western Rose

28.4% ALC/VOL • 2.1 STD DRINKS

45ml (1½ fl oz) Dry Gin
23ml (¾ fl oz) Apricot Brandy
23ml (¾ fl oz) Dry Vermouth
Dash Fresh Lemon Juice

Pour ingredients into a mixing glass over ice and stir. Strain into a chilled cocktail glass and serve.

Jelly Bean

10% ALC/VOL • 1.3 STD DRINKS

15ml (½ fl oz) Gin
15ml (½ fl oz) Ouzo
15ml (½ fl oz) Vodka
Dash Grenadine
120ml (4 fl oz) Fresh Orange Juice
Slice of Orange

Pour Gin, Ouzo, Vodka and juice into a mixing glass over ice. Stir and strain into a highball glass over ice. Layer Grenadine on top and garnish with a slice of orange then serve.

Alaska

37.9% ALC/VOL • 2.5 STD DRINKS

60ml (2 fl oz) Dry Gin
23ml (¾ fl oz) Yellow Chartreuse
Twist of Lemon Peel

Pour Gin and Chartreuse into a mixing glass over ice. Stir and strain into a chilled cocktail glass. Garnish with lemon peel and serve.

Bartender

22.5% ALC/VOL • 1.4 STD DRINKS

20ml (⅔ fl oz) Gin
20ml (⅔ fl oz) Dry Sherry
20ml (⅔ fl oz) Dry Vermouth
20ml (⅔ fl oz) Dubonnet
Dash Grand Marnier

Pour ingredients into a mixing glass over ice and stir. Strain into a chilled cocktail glass and serve.

Gin Smash

34.2% ALC/VOL • 1.8 STD DRINKS

60ml (2 fl oz) Gin
1 teaspoon Sugar Syrup
4 Sprigs of Fresh Mint
Slice of Lemon

Pour Gin and sugar into a mixing glass over crushed ice then add 3 sprigs of mint. Stir and pour into an old-fashioned glass half filled with ice. Add more ice to fill glass and stir. Garnish with a slice of lemon and sprig of mint then serve.

Moon River

29.5% ALC/VOL • 1.9 STD DRINKS

20ml (⅔ fl oz) Gin
20ml (⅔ fl oz) Apricot Brandy
20ml (⅔ fl oz) Cointreau
10ml (⅓ fl oz) Galliano
10ml (⅓ fl oz) Fresh Lime Juice
Maraschino Cherry

Pour Gin, Brandy, Cointreau, Galliano and juice into a mixing glass over ice. Stir and strain into a chilled cocktail glass. Garnish with a cherry and serve.

Gibson

35.6% ALC/VOL • 1.8 STD DRINKS

60ml (2 fl oz) Dry Gin
5ml (1/6 fl oz) Dry Vermouth
Slice of Lime

Pour Gin and Vermouth into a mixing glass over ice. Stir and strain into a chilled cocktail glass. Garnish with a slice of lime and serve.

Iron Bar Sling

11% ALC/VOL • 1.7 STD DRINKS

30ml (1 fl oz) Gin
30ml (1 fl oz) Cherry Brandy
10ml (⅓ fl oz) Southern Comfort
8ml (¼ fl oz) Grenadine
60ml (2 fl oz) Fresh Orange Juice
30ml (1 fl oz) Fresh Lime Juice
30ml (1 fl oz) Pineapple Juice

Pour ingredients into a cocktail shaker over ice and shake. Strain into a highball glass over ice and serve.

Bee's Knees

27.8% ALC/VOL • 1.8 STD DRINKS

60ml (2 fl oz) Gin
15ml (½ fl oz) Fresh Lemon or Lime Juice
1 teaspoon Honey
Slice of Lemon or Lime

Pour Gin, juice and honey into a cocktail shaker over ice. Shake and strain into a chilled cocktail glass. Garnish with a slice of lemon or lime as desired and serve.

Arctic Summer

11.3% ALC/VOL • 1.7 STD DRINKS

45ml (1½ fl oz) Gin
23ml (¾ fl oz) Apricot Brandy
5ml (⅙ fl oz) Grenadine
120ml (4 fl oz) Bitter-Lemon Soda
Maraschino Cherry
Slice of Lemon

Pour Gin, Brandy and Grenadine into a highball glass over ice then stir. Add soda and stir gently. Garnish with a cherry and slice of lemon then serve.

Fallen Angel

25.8% ALC/VOL • 1.8 STD DRINKS

60ml (2 fl oz) Gin
2 dashes Green Crème De Menthe
Dash Angostura Bitters
15ml (½ fl oz) Fresh Lemon Juice

Pour ingredients into a cocktail shaker over ice and shake. Strain into a chilled cocktail glass and serve.

Torrens

31.3% ALC/VOL • 1.8 STD DRINKS

60ml (2 fl oz) Gin
5ml (⅙ fl oz) Fresh Orange Juice
Dash Fresh Lemon Juice
1 teaspoon Caster Sugar
4 Fresh Mint Leaves (crushed)
Slice of Orange
Sprig of Fresh Mint

Pour Gin and juices into a cocktail shaker over ice. Add sugar and crushed mint leaves. Shake and strain into a chilled cocktail glass. Garnish with a slice of orange and sprig of mint then serve.
This drink is also known as Mr Manhattan.

Silver Streak

28% ALC/VOL • 2.7 STD DRINKS

60ml (2 fl oz) Dry Gin
30ml (1 fl oz) Kümmel
30ml (1 fl oz) Fresh Lemon Juice

Pour ingredients into a cocktail shaker over ice and shake. Strain into a chilled cocktail glass and serve.

Barbary Coast

25.1% ALC/VOL • 2.4 STD DRINKS

30ml (1 fl oz) Gin
30ml (1 fl oz) Dark Crème De Cacao
30ml (1 fl oz) Scotch Whisky
30ml (1 fl oz) Fresh Cream
Grated Chocolate

Pour Gin, Cacao, Whisky and cream into a cocktail shaker over ice. Shake and strain into a chilled cocktail glass. Sprinkle chocolate on top and serve.
This drink is also known as Whizz-Doodle.

Alexander's Sister

22.5% ALC/VOL • 1.9 STD DRINKS

45ml (1½ fl oz) Dry Gin
30ml (1 fl oz) Green Crème De Menthe
30ml (1 fl oz) Thick Cream
Nutmeg

Pour Gin, Crème De Menthe and cream into a cocktail shaker over ice. Shake and strain into a chilled cocktail glass. Sprinkle nutmeg on top and serve.

Sifi Flip

20.8% ALC/VOL • 2.7 STD DRINKS

60ml (2 fl oz) Gin
30ml (1 fl oz) Cointreau
30ml (1 fl oz) Grenadine
30ml (1 fl oz) Fresh Lemon Juice
Yolk of 1 Egg
Nutmeg

Pour Gin, Cointreau, Grenadine, juice and egg yolk into a cocktail shaker over ice. Shake and strain into a chilled goblet. Sprinkle nutmeg on top and serve.

Savoy

30.8% ALC/VOL • 1.6 STD DRINKS

45ml (1½ fl oz) Gin
20ml (⅔ fl oz) Dry Vermouth
2 dashes Dubonnet
Slice of Lemon

Pour Gin, Vermouth and Dubonnet into a mixing glass over ice. Stir and strain into a chilled cocktail glass. Garnish with a slice of lemon and serve.

Damn the Weather

31.1% ALC/VOL • 1.5 STD DRINKS

45ml (1½ fl oz) Dry Gin
15ml (½ fl oz) Sweet Vermouth
Dash Cointreau
Dash Fresh Orange Juice
Twist of Orange Peel

Pour Gin, Vermouth, Cointreau and juice into a cocktail shaker over ice. Shake and strain into a chilled cocktail glass. Garnish with orange peel and serve.

Guards

29.6% ALC/VOL • 2.1 STD DRINKS

60ml (2 fl oz) Gin
30ml (1 fl oz) Sweet Vermouth
2 dashes Curaçao
Twist of Orange Peel

Pour Gin, Vermouth and Curaçao into a cocktail shaker over ice. Shake and strain into a chilled cocktail glass. Garnish with orange peel and serve.

Red Lights

18.7% ALC/VOL • 1.8 STD DRINKS

30ml (1 fl oz) Gin
15ml (½ fl oz) Cointreau
15ml (½ fl oz) Galliano
60ml (2 fl oz) Fresh Orange Juice
Slice of Orange

Pour Gin, Cointreau, Galliano and juice into a cocktail shaker over ice. Shake and strain into a highball glass over ice. Garnish with a slice of orange and serve.

Golf

31% ALC/VOL • 2.3 STD DRINKS

60ml (2 fl oz) Dry Gin
30ml (1 fl oz) Dry Vermouth
2 dashes Angostura Bitters
Olive

Pour Gin, Vermouth and Bitters into a mixing glass over ice. Stir and strain into a chilled cocktail glass. Garnish with an olive and serve.

Jabberwock

23.6% ALC/VOL • 2.5 STD DRINKS

45ml (1½ fl oz) Dry Gin
45ml (1½ fl oz) Dry Sherry
45ml (1½ fl oz) Dubonnet
2 dashes Orange Bitters
Maraschino Cherry
Twist of Lemon Peel

Pour Gin, Sherry, Dubonnet and Bitters into a mixing glass over ice. Stir and strain into a chilled cocktail glass. Twist lemon peel above drink and discard remainder of peel. Garnish with a cherry and serve.

Bronx

17.8% ALC/VOL • 1.3 STD DRINKS

30ml (1 fl oz) Gin
15ml (½ fl oz) Dry Vermouth
15ml (½ fl oz) Sweet Vermouth
30ml (1 fl oz) Fresh Orange Juice

Pour ingredients into a cocktail shaker over ice and shake. Strain into a chilled cocktail glass and serve.

Turf

30.3% ALC/VOL • 1.2 STD DRINKS

30ml (1 fl oz) Dry Gin
15ml (½ fl oz) Dry Vermouth
2 dashes Anisette
2 dashes Maraschino Liqueur
2 dashes Orange Bitters
Olive

Pour Gin, Vermouth, Anisette, Liqueur and Bitters into a mixing glass over ice. Stir and strain into a chilled cocktail glass. Garnish with an olive and serve.

Opera

31.7% ALC/VOL • 2.3 STD DRINKS

60ml (2 fl oz) Dry Gin
15ml (½ fl oz) Dubonnet
15ml (½ fl oz) Maraschino Liqueur
Twist of Lemon Peel

Pour Gin, Dubonnet and Liqueur into a cocktail shaker over ice. Shake and strain into a chilled cocktail glass. Garnish with lemon peel and serve.

Bridesmaid Cooler

9.7% ALC/VOL • 1.8 STD DRINKS

60ml (2 fl oz) Gin
Dash Angostura Bitters
30ml (1 fl oz) Fresh Lemon Juice
23ml (¾ fl oz) Sugar Syrup
120ml (4 fl oz) Dry Ginger Ale
Twist of Lemon Peel

Pour Gin, Bitters, juice and sugar into a cocktail shaker over ice. Shake and strain into a collins glass over ice. Add Ginger Ale and stir gently. Garnish with lemon peel and serve.

Royal Fizz

9.1% ALC/VOL • 1.3 STD DRINKS

45ml (1½ fl oz) Dry Gin
2 dashes Grenadine
1 Fresh Egg
90ml (3 fl oz) Soda Water

Pour Gin, Grenadine and egg into a cocktail shaker over ice. Shake and strain into a highball glass over ice. Add soda, stir gently and serve.

Gin Lollipop

9.3% ALC/VOL • 1.8 STD DRINKS

30ml (1 fl oz) Gin
30ml (1 fl oz) Southern Comfort
150ml (5 fl oz) Fresh Orange Juice
30ml (1 fl oz) Mineral Water
Maraschino Cherry
Slice of Orange

Pour Gin, Southern Comfort and juice into a cocktail shaker over ice. Shake and strain into a highball glass over ice. Add mineral water and stir gently. Garnish with a cherry and slice of orange then serve.

Summer Time

13.9% ALC/VOL • 2.6 STD DRINKS

90ml (3 fl oz) Gin
30ml (1 fl oz) Sirop De Citron
120ml (4 fl oz) Soda Water

Pour Gin and Sirop De Citron into a mixing glass over ice. Stir and strain into a highball glass over ice. Add soda, stir gently and serve.

Hugo Rickey

13.3% ALC/VOL • 1.8 STD DRINKS

60ml (2 fl oz) Gin
3 dashes Grenadine
15ml (½ fl oz) Fresh Lime Juice
90ml (3 fl oz) Soda Water
Slice of Pineapple

Pour Gin, Grenadine and juice into a collins glass over ice. Add soda and stir gently. Garnish with a slice of pineapple and serve.

Gin Daisy

23.4% ALC/VOL • 1.8 STD DRINKS

60ml (2 fl oz) Gin
5ml (⅙ fl oz) Grenadine
30ml (1 fl oz) Fresh Lemon Juice
Slice of Lemon

Pour Gin, Grenadine and juice into a cocktail shaker over ice. Shake and strain into a goblet over ice. Top up with soda water if desired and stir gently. Garnish with a slice of lemon and serve.

Royal Gin Fizz

8.5% ALC/VOL • 1.7 STD DRINKS

60ml (2 fl oz) Gin
15ml (½ fl oz) Fresh Lemon Juice
1 teaspoon Caster Sugar
1 Fresh Egg
135ml (4½ fl oz) Soda Water

Pour Gin, juice and egg into a cocktail shaker over ice then add sugar. Shake well and strain into a chilled highball glass over 2 ice cubes. Add soda, stir gently and serve.

Princeton

32.1% ALC/VOL • 1.5 STD DRINKS

45ml (1½ fl oz) Gin
15ml (½ fl oz) Port
Dash Orange Bitters
Twist of Lemon Peel

Pour Gin, Port and Bitters into a mixing glass over ice. Stir and strain into a chilled cocktail glass. Garnish with lemon peel and serve.

Raffles Singapore Sling

16.8% ALC/VOL • 2.4 STD DRINKS

30ml (1 fl oz) Gin
30ml (1 fl oz) Cherry Brandy
15ml (½ fl oz) Bénédictine
15ml (½ fl oz) Cointreau
Dash Angostura Bitters
30ml (1 fl oz) Fresh Lime Juice
30ml (1 fl oz) Fresh Orange Juice
30ml (1 fl oz) Pineapple Juice
Slice of Orange
Sprig of Fresh Mint

Pour Gin, Brandy, Bénédictine, Cointreau, Bitters and juices into a cocktail shaker over ice. Shake and strain into a highball glass over ice. Garnish with a slice of orange and sprig of mint then serve.

Strawberry Blush

9.9% ALC/VOL • 1.8 STD DRINKS

This drink is also known as *Strawberry Fizz, p 49.*

Gilroy

23.3% ALC/VOL • 1.7 STD DRINKS

30ml (1 fl oz) Gin
30ml (1 fl oz) Cherry Brandy
15ml (½ fl oz) Dry Vermouth
Dash Angostura Bitters
15ml (½ fl oz) Fresh Lemon Juice
Maraschino Cherry
Twist of Orange Peel

Pour Gin, Brandy, Vermouth, Bitters and juice into a cocktail shaker over ice. Shake and strain into a chilled cocktail glass. Garnish with a cherry and orange peel then serve.

Blue Lady

24.4% ALC/VOL • 1.2 STD DRINKS

30ml (1 fl oz) Dry Gin
15ml (½ fl oz) Blue Curaçao
15ml (½ fl oz) Fresh
Lemon Juice
Dash Egg White

Pour ingredients into a cocktail shaker over ice and shake. Strain into a chilled cocktail glass and serve.

Cherry Gin Fizz

22.4% ALC/VOL • 1.8 STD DRINKS

45ml (1½ fl oz) Gin
15ml (½ fl oz) Cherry Brandy
8ml (¼ fl oz) Kirsch
15ml (½ fl oz) Fresh
Lemon Juice
1 teaspoon Caster Sugar
15ml (½ fl oz) Soda Water
Maraschino Cherry
Slice of Lemon

Pour Gin, Brandy, Kirsch and juice into a mixing glass over ice then add sugar. Stir and strain into a highball glass over ice then add soda - do not stir. Garnish with a cherry and slice of lemon then serve.

Colonial

24.7% ALC/VOL • 1.8 STD DRINKS

60ml (2 fl oz) Dry Gin
3 dashes Maraschino Liqueur
30ml (1 fl oz) Grapefruit Juice

Pour ingredients into a cocktail shaker over ice and shake. Strain into a chilled cocktail glass and serve.

Orange Golly

12.5% ALC/VOL • 1.6 STD DRINKS

30ml (1 fl oz) Dry Gin
15ml (½ fl oz) Dry Vermouth
15ml (½ fl oz) Malibu
15ml (½ fl oz) Orange Curaçao
90ml (3 fl oz) Fresh
Orange Juice
Strawberry

Pour Gin, Vermouth, Malibu and Curaçao into a mixing glass over ice. Stir and strain into a collins glass over ice. Add juice and stir. Garnish with a strawberry and serve.

Rolls Royce

28.3% ALC/VOL • 1.5 STD DRINKS

30ml (1 fl oz) Gin
15ml (½ fl oz) Dry Vermouth
15ml (½ fl oz) Sweet Vermouth
8ml (¼ fl oz) Bénédictine

Pour ingredients into a cocktail shaker over ice and shake. Strain into a chilled cocktail glass and serve.

Pineapple Mint Cooler

9.5% ALC/VOL • 2 STD DRINKS

60ml (2 fl oz) Dry Gin
15ml (½ fl oz) White Crème De
Menthe
90ml (3 fl oz) Pineapple Juice
30ml (1 fl oz) Fresh
Lemon Juice
75ml (2½ fl oz) Soda Water
Green Cocktail Cherry
Slice of Pineapple

Pour Gin, Crème De Menthe and juices into a cocktail shaker over ice. Shake and strain into a collins glass over ice. Add soda and stir gently. Garnish with a cherry and slice of pineapple then serve.

White Lady

28% ALC/VOL • 1.3 STD DRINKS

30ml (1 fl oz) Gin
15ml (½ fl oz) Cointreau
15ml (½ fl oz) Fresh
Lemon Juice
Dash Egg White

Pour ingredients into a cocktail shaker over ice and shake. Strain into a chilled cocktail glass and serve.

Fog Cutter

16.6% ALC/VOL • 1.6 STD DRINKS

15ml (½ fl oz) Gin
15ml (½ fl oz) Brandy
15ml (½ fl oz) Light Rum
10ml (⅓ fl oz) Sweet Sherry
5ml (1/6 fl oz) Amaretto
30ml (1 fl oz) Fresh
Orange Juice
15ml (½ fl oz) Fresh
Lemon Juice
15ml (½ fl oz) Sugar Syrup

Pour ingredients into a cocktail shaker over ice and shake. Strain into an old-fashioned glass over cracked ice and serve.

Blue Mallet

24.8% ALC/VOL • 1.2 STD DRINKS

30ml (1 fl oz) Dry Gin
15ml (½ fl oz) Blue Curaçao
15ml (½ fl oz) Fresh
Lemon Juice

Pour ingredients into a cocktail shaker over ice and shake. Strain into a chilled cocktail glass and serve.

Hong Kong

27.8% ALC/VOL • 2.2 STD DRINKS

60ml (2 fl oz) Gin
30ml (1 fl oz) Dry Vermouth
Dash Angostura Bitters
5ml (1/6 fl oz) Fresh Lime Juice
1 teaspoon Sugar Syrup
Twist of Lime Peel

Pour Gin, Vermouth, Bitters, juice and sugar into a mixing glass over ice. Stir and strain into a chilled cocktail glass. Garnish with lime peel and serve.

Caruso

26% ALC/VOL • 1.8 STD DRINKS

30ml (1 fl oz) Dry Gin
30ml (1 fl oz) Dry Vermouth
30ml (1 fl oz) Green Crème De Menthe
Sprig of Fresh Mint

Pour Gin, Vermouth and Crème De Menthe into a cocktail shaker over ice. Shake and strain into a chilled cocktail glass. Garnish with a sprig of mint and serve.

Gin Cooler

10.1% ALC/VOL • 1.8 STD DRINKS

60ml (2 fl oz) Gin
60ml (2 fl oz) Fresh Lemon Juice
2 teaspoons Sugar Syrup
90ml (3 fl oz) Ginger Beer
Slice of Lemon

Pour Gin, juice and sugar into a mixing glass over ice. Stir and strain into a collins glass over ice. Add ginger beer and stir gently. Garnish with a slice of lemon and serve. *This drink is also known as Shady Grove Cooler.*

Blue Bottle

24.8% ALC/VOL • 2.3 STD DRINKS

60ml (2 fl oz) Gin
30ml (1 fl oz) Blue Curaçao
30ml (1 fl oz) Passion-Fruit Juice
Maraschino Cherry

Pour Gin, Curaçao and juice into a mixing glass over ice. Stir and strain into a chilled cocktail glass. Garnish with a cherry and serve.

Caribbean Holiday

18.7% ALC/VOL • 1.2 STD DRINKS

30ml (1 fl oz) Gin
15ml (½ fl oz) Dry Vermouth
3 dashes Orange Bitters
30ml (1 fl oz) Grapefruit Juice
Maraschino Cherry
Slice of Orange

Pour Gin, Vermouth, Bitters and juice into a mixing glass over ice. Stir and strain into an old-fashioned glass over ice. Garnish with a cherry and slice of orange then serve.

Ideal

28% ALC/VOL • 2.2 STD DRINKS

60ml (2 fl oz) Gin
30ml (1 fl oz) Sweet Vermouth
3 dashes Maraschino Liqueur
5ml (1/6 fl oz) Grapefruit Juice

Pour ingredients into a cocktail shaker over ice and shake. Strain into a chilled cocktail glass and serve.

Ten Pin Gin

22.8% ALC/VOL • 2.9 STD DRINKS

45ml (1½ fl oz) Gin
38ml (1¼ fl oz) Mandarine Napoleon
30ml (1 fl oz) Dry Vermouth
30ml (1 fl oz) Sugar Syrup
15ml (½ fl oz) Fresh Lime Juice
1 teaspoon Egg White
Slice of Lime
Slice of Orange

Pour Gin, Mandarine Napoleon, Vermouth, sugar, juice and egg white into a cocktail shaker over ice. Shake and strain into a chilled champagne saucer. Garnish with a slice of lime and orange then serve.

Hawaiian Cocktail

24.7% ALC/VOL • 2 STD DRINKS

60ml (2 fl oz) Dry Gin
15ml (½ fl oz) Orange Curaçao
30ml (1 fl oz) Fresh Orange Juice

Pour ingredients into a cocktail shaker over ice and shake. Strain into a chilled cocktail glass and serve.

Bury Me Deep

11.6% ALC/VOL • 1.8 STD DRINKS

45ml (1½ fl oz) Gin
15ml (½ fl oz) Scotch Whisky
15ml (½ fl oz) Fresh Lime Juice
15ml (½ fl oz) Passion-Fruit Juice
15ml (½ fl oz) Raspberry Syrup
90ml (3 fl oz) Lemonade

Pour Gin, Whisky, juices and syrup into a cocktail shaker over ice. Shake and strain into a highball glass over ice. Add lemonade, stir gently and serve.

Strawberry Dawn

15.1% ALC/VOL • 1.3 STD DRINKS

45ml (1½ fl oz) Dry Gin
45ml (1½ fl oz) Coconut Cream
2 Strawberries (crushed)
Strawberry

Pour Gin and cream into a blender over cracked ice then add crushed strawberries. Blend and pour into a chilled champagne saucer. Garnish with a strawberry and serve.

Grape Vine

13.8% ALC/VOL • 1.3 STD DRINKS

30ml (1 fl oz) Dry Gin
15ml (½ fl oz) Dry Sherry
15ml (½ fl oz) Sweet Sherry
60ml (2 fl oz) Red Grape Juice
Sprig of Fresh Mint

Pour Gin, Sherries and juice into a cocktail shaker over ice. Shake and strain into an old-fashioned glass over ice. Garnish with a sprig of mint and serve.

Rose Cocktail

28.9% ALC/VOL • 2.1 STD DRINKS

30ml (1 fl oz) Dry Gin
30ml (1 fl oz) Apricot Brandy
15ml (½ fl oz) Dry Vermouth
15ml (½ fl oz) Kirsch
Dash Grenadine

Pour ingredients into a cocktail shaker over ice and shake. Strain into a chilled cocktail glass and serve.

Bougainvillea

25.8% ALC/VOL • 1.5 STD DRINKS

30ml (1 fl oz) Gin
15ml (½ fl oz) Applejack
10ml (⅓ fl oz) Sweet Vermouth
2 dashes Grenadine
15ml (½ fl oz) Fresh Lemon Juice

Pour ingredients into a cocktail shaker over ice and shake. Strain into a chilled cocktail glass and serve.
This drink is also known as Joulouville.

Beauty Spot

21.5% ALC/VOL • 1.5 STD DRINKS

45ml (1½ fl oz) Gin
10ml (⅓ fl oz) White Crème De Cacao
3 dashes Grenadine
White of 1 Egg

Pour Gin, Cacao and egg white into a cocktail shaker over ice. Shake and strain into a chilled cocktail glass. Add Grenadine by pouring into centre of drink – do not stir, then serve.

Gin and What

27.6% ALC/VOL • 2 STD DRINKS

45ml (1½ fl oz) Gin
15ml (½ fl oz) Malibu
15ml (½ fl oz) Port
15ml (½ fl oz) Sweet Vermouth
Dash Maraschino Liqueur
Maraschino Cherry

Pour Gin, Malibu, Port, Vermouth and Liqueur into a cocktail shaker over ice. Shake and strain into a chilled cocktail glass. Garnish with a cherry and serve.

Gin and Bitter-Lemon

9.1% ALC/VOL • 1.3 STD DRINKS

45ml (1½ fl oz) Gin
15ml (½ fl oz) Fresh Lemon Juice
½ teaspoon Caster Sugar
120ml (4 fl oz) Tonic Water

Pour Gin and juice into a cocktail shaker over ice then add sugar. Shake and strain into a highball glass over ice. Add tonic, stir gently and serve.

Luxury

23.1% ALC/VOL • 1.7 STD DRINKS

30ml (1 fl oz) Gin
15ml (½ fl oz) Banana Liqueur
15ml (½ fl oz) Pimm's No.1
15ml (½ fl oz) Sweet Vermouth
Dash Angostura Bitters
15ml (½ fl oz) Lime Syrup

Pour ingredients into a cocktail shaker over ice and shake. Strain into a chilled cocktail glass and serve.

Gimlet Cocktail

24.7% ALC/VOL • 1.8 STD DRINKS

60ml (2 fl oz) Dry Gin
30ml (1 fl oz) Fresh Lime Juice
Wedge of Lime

Pour Gin and juice into a cocktail shaker over ice. Shake and strain into a chilled cocktail glass. Garnish with a wedge of lime and serve.
This drink is also known as Gin and Sin.

Tropical Special

12.6% ALC/VOL • 1.8 STD DRINKS

45ml (1½ fl oz) Dry Gin
15ml (½ fl oz) Cointreau
60ml (2 fl oz) Grapefruit Juice
30ml (1 fl oz) Fresh Lime Juice
30ml (1 fl oz) Fresh Orange Juice
Maraschino Cherry
Slice of Lime
Slice of Orange

Pour Gin, Cointreau and juices into a cocktail shaker over ice. Shake and strain into a highball glass over ice. Garnish with a cherry, slice of lime and orange then serve.

Billy Taylor

13.5% ALC/VOL • 1.8 STD DRINKS

This drink is also known as Gin Rickey, p 57.

Blue Bayou

13.8% ALC/VOL • 1.8 STD DRINKS

30ml (1 fl oz) Dry Gin
15ml (½ fl oz) Blue Curaçao
15ml (½ fl oz) Dry Vermouth
15ml (½ fl oz) Galliano
90ml (3 fl oz) Lemonade
Maraschino Cherry
Slice of Lemon

Pour Gin, Curaçao, Vermouth and Galliano into a cocktail shaker over ice. Shake and strain into a highball glass over ice. Add lemonade and stir gently. Garnish with a cherry and slice of lemon then serve.

Mayfair

13.9% ALC/VOL • 1.2 STD DRINKS

30ml (1 fl oz) Dry Gin
15ml (½ fl oz) Apricot Brandy
60ml (2 fl oz) Fresh
Orange Juice

Pour ingredients into a cocktail shaker over ice and shake. Strain into a chilled cocktail glass and serve.

Golden Gin

12.8% ALC/VOL • 1.3 STD DRINKS

45ml (1½ fl oz) Gin
60ml (2 fl oz) Fresh
Orange Juice
15ml (½ fl oz) Fresh
Lemon Juice
10ml (⅓ fl oz) Dry Ginger Ale
Slice of Orange

Pour Gin and juices into a mixing glass over ice. Stir and strain into a highball glass over ice. Add Ginger Ale – do not stir, then garnish with a slice of orange and serve.

X.Y.Z.

21.1% ALC/VOL • 1.3 STD DRINKS

30ml (1 fl oz) Dry Gin
15ml (½ fl oz) Dry Vermouth
15ml (½ fl oz) Sweet Vermouth
15ml (½ fl oz) Fresh
Lemon Juice
Dash Sugar Syrup

Pour ingredients into a cocktail shaker over ice and shake. Strain into a chilled cocktail glass and serve.

K.G.B. Cocktail

36.5% ALC/VOL • 1.8 STD DRINKS

45ml (1½ fl oz) Gin
15ml (½ fl oz) Kümmel
Dash Apricot Brandy
Dash Fresh Lemon Juice
Twist of Lemon Peel

Pour Gin, Kümmel, Brandy and juice into a cocktail shaker over ice. Shake and strain into a chilled cocktail glass. Add lemon peel and serve.

Astoria

30.6% ALC/VOL • 2.2 STD DRINKS

60ml (2 fl oz) Dry Gin
30ml (1 fl oz) Dry Vermouth
Dash Orange Bitters
Slice of Lemon

Pour Gin, Vermouth and Bitters into a cocktail shaker over ice. Shake and strain into a chilled cocktail glass. Garnish with a slice of lemon and serve.

Hong Kong Fuey

17.9% ALC/VOL • 2 STD DRINKS

15ml (½ fl oz) Gin
15ml (½ fl oz) Bacardi
15ml (½ fl oz) Midori
15ml (½ fl oz) White Tequila
15ml (½ fl oz) Vodka
1½ teaspoons Lime Syrup
60ml (2 fl oz) Lemonade

Pour Gin, Bacardi, Midori, Tequila, Vodka and syrup into a cocktail shaker over ice. Shake and strain into a highball glass over ice. Add lemonade, stir gently and serve.

Elk

36.2% ALC/VOL • 1.4 STD DRINKS

23ml (¾ fl oz) Dry Gin
23ml (¾ fl oz) Prunelle Brandy
2 dashes Dry Vermouth

Pour ingredients into a cocktail shaker over ice and shake. Strain into a chilled cocktail glass and serve.

Everton Blue

20.7% ALC/VOL • 1 STD DRINK

15ml (½ fl oz) Gin
15ml (½ fl oz) Banana Liqueur
15ml (½ fl oz) Blue Curaçao
Dash Grenadine
15ml (½ fl oz) Fresh Cream
Dash Fresh Lemon Juice

Pour Gin, Liqueur, Curaçao and cream into a cocktail shaker over ice. Shake and strain into a chilled cocktail glass. Add Grenadine and juice, stir briefly then serve.

Green Dragon

29.1% ALC/VOL • 2.8 STD DRINKS

60ml (2 fl oz) Dry Gin
30ml (1 fl oz) Green Crème De
Menthe
15ml (½ fl oz) Kümmel
15ml (½ fl oz) Fresh
Lemon Juice

Pour ingredients into a cocktail shaker over ice and shake. Strain into a chilled cocktail glass and serve.

Archers Slingback

12.8% ALC/VOL • 1.7 STD DRINKS

45ml (1½ fl oz) Gin
23ml (¾ fl oz) Peach Schnapps
45ml (1½ fl oz) Apple Juice
30ml (1 fl oz) Peach Nectar
15ml (½ fl oz) Fresh
Lime Juice
1½ teaspoons Sugar Syrup

Pour ingredients into a cocktail shaker over ice and shake. Strain into a chilled champagne flute and serve.

Anniversary Cocktail

32.5% ALC/VOL • 1.9 STD DRINKS

30ml (1 fl oz) Gin
30ml (1 fl oz) Brandy
15ml (½ fl oz) Sweet Vermouth

Dash Orange Bitters

Pour ingredients into a cocktail shaker over ice and shake. Strain into a chilled cocktail glass and serve.

Minted Gin Tea

4.4% ALC/VOL • 1.8 STD DRINKS

60ml (2 fl oz) Gin
400ml (14 fl oz) Boiling Water
30ml (1 fl oz) Fresh Lemon Juice
2 teaspoons Fresh Chopped Mint
2 teaspoons Tea Leaves
4 Twists of Lemon Peel

Pour boiling water into a tea pot then add chopped mint and tea leaves. Allow to stand for five minutes to infuse then strain into a glass jug and refrigerate to chill. Add Gin and juice then stir gently. Prepare 4 collins glasses with sugar frosted rims. Pour minted tea into prepared glasses and garnish each individual serving with lemon peel.

Resolute Cocktail

24.1% ALC/VOL • 1.7 STD DRINKS

45ml (1½ fl oz) Dry Gin
23ml (¾ fl oz) Apricot Brandy
23ml (¾ fl oz) Fresh Lemon Juice

Pour ingredients into a cocktail shaker over ice and shake. Strain into a chilled cocktail glass and serve.

Pink Rose Fizz

8.2% ALC/VOL • 1.7 STD DRINKS

60ml (2 fl oz) Dry Gin
15ml (½ fl oz) Fresh Lemon Juice
10ml (⅓ fl oz) Fresh Cream
1 teaspoon Caster Sugar
White of 1 Egg
150ml (5 fl oz) Soda Water

Pour Gin, juice, cream and egg white into a cocktail shaker over ice then add sugar. Shake and strain into a chilled highball glass over 2 ice cubes. Add soda, stir gently and serve.

Fairy Belle

25% ALC/VOL • 2.5 STD DRINKS

75ml (2½ fl oz) Gin
15ml (½ fl oz) Apricot Brandy
5ml (⅙ fl oz) Grenadine
White of 1 Egg

Pour ingredients into a cocktail shaker over ice and shake. Strain into a chilled cocktail glass and serve.

Pink Goody

23.7% ALC/VOL • 1.8 STD DRINKS

30ml (1 fl oz) Gin
30ml (1 fl oz) Bacardi
Dash Maraschino Liqueur
30ml (1 fl oz) Fresh Lime Juice
5ml (⅙ fl oz) Soda Water
Slice of Pineapple

Pour Gin, Bacardi, Liqueur and juice into a cocktail shaker over cracked ice. Shake and pour into a chilled highball glass. Add soda and stir gently. Garnish with a slice of pineapple and serve.

The Rose

27.5% ALC/VOL • 2.4 STD DRINKS

45ml (1½ fl oz) Gin
45ml (1½ fl oz) Apricot Brandy
20ml (⅔ fl oz) Dry Vermouth
Dash Grenadine

Pour ingredients into a cocktail shaker over ice and shake. Strain into a chilled cocktail glass and serve.

Pink Poodle

12.9% ALC/VOL • 1.5 STD DRINKS

30ml (1 fl oz) Dry Gin
30ml (1 fl oz) Campari
45ml (1½ fl oz) Fresh Cream
4 Strawberries (diced)
Strawberry

Pour Gin, Campari and cream into a blender over crushed ice then add diced strawberries. Blend and pour into a chilled champagne saucer. Garnish with a strawberry and serve.

Gin and Sin

24.7% ALC/VOL • 1.8 STD DRINKS

This drink is also known as Gimlet Cocktail, p 65.

Mr Manhattan

31.3% ALC/VOL • 1.8 STD DRINKS

This drink is also known as Torrens, p 60.

Gold Digger

5.1% ALC/VOL • 1.1 STD DRINKS

20ml (⅔ fl oz) Dry Gin
15ml (½ fl oz) Aperol
10ml (⅓ fl oz) Kiwi Liqueur
10ml (⅓ fl oz) Midori
210ml (7 fl oz) Fresh Orange Juice

Pour Gin, Aperol, Liqueur and Midori into a cocktail shaker over ice. Shake and strain into a chilled highball glass. Add juice, stir and serve.

Silver Jubilee

24.3% ALC/VOL • 2.3 STD DRINKS

60ml (2 fl oz) Gin
30ml (1 fl oz) Banana Liqueur
30ml (1 fl oz) Thick Cream
Slice of Banana

Pour Gin, Liqueur and cream into a cocktail shaker over ice. Shake and strain into a chilled cocktail glass. Garnish with a slice of banana and serve.

Lovers

8.1% ALC/VOL • 1.6 STD DRINKS

40ml (1⅓ fl oz) Dry Gin
20ml (⅔ fl oz) Banana Liqueur
Dash Blue Curaçao
3 dashes Fresh Lemon Juice
180ml (6 fl oz) Tonic Water

Pour Gin, Liqueur, Curaçao and juice into a cocktail shaker over ice. Shake and strain into a chilled highball glass. Add tonic, stir gently and serve.

Dunk

33.8% ALC/VOL • 2 STD DRINKS

45ml (1½ fl oz) Dry Gin
15ml (½ fl oz) Blue Curaçao
15ml (½ fl oz) Galliano
Twist of Orange Peel

Pour Gin, Curaçao and Galliano into a cocktail shaker over ice. Shake and strain into a chilled cocktail glass. Garnish with orange peel and serve.

Bloomsbury Fizz

13.8% ALC/VOL • 2 STD DRINKS

60ml (2 fl oz) Gin
10ml (⅓ fl oz) Maraschino Liqueur
15ml (½ fl oz) Fresh Lemon Juice
1 teaspoon Raspberry Syrup
90ml (3 fl oz) Soda Water
Raspberry
Slice of Lemon

Pour Gin, Liqueur, juice and syrup into a mixing glass over ice. Stir and strain into a highball glass over ice. Add soda and stir gently. Garnish with a raspberry and slice of lemon then serve.
This drink is also known as Bayard Fizz.

Victor

32.6% ALC/VOL • 1.9 STD DRINKS

45ml (1½ fl oz) Dry Gin
15ml (½ fl oz) Brandy
15ml (½ fl oz) Sweet Vermouth

Pour ingredients into a cocktail shaker over ice and shake. Strain into a chilled cocktail glass and serve.

Long Beach Iced Tea No.2

34.6% ALC/VOL • 2 STD DRINKS

15ml (½ fl oz) Gin
15ml (½ fl oz) Cointreau
15ml (½ fl oz) Light Rum
15ml (½ fl oz) Midori
15ml (½ fl oz) Vodka
Wedge of Lemon

Pour Gin, Cointreau, Rum, Midori and Vodka into a cocktail shaker over ice. Shake and strain into a highball glass filled with ice. Garnish with a wedge of lemon and serve.

Perfect Lady

19.4% ALC/VOL • 2.3 STD DRINKS

60ml (2 fl oz) Gin
30ml (1 fl oz) Peach Brandy
30ml (1 fl oz) Fresh Lemon Juice
White of 1 Egg

Pour ingredients into a cocktail shaker over ice and shake. Strain into a chilled wine glass and serve.

Hippie

10.9% ALC/VOL • 1.6 STD DRINKS

30ml (1 fl oz) Gin
30ml (1 fl oz) Peach Schnapps
15ml (½ fl oz) Dry Vermouth
18ml (⅗ fl oz) Grenadine
90ml (3 fl oz) Dry Ginger Ale

Pour Gin, Schnapps, Vermouth and Grenadine into a cocktail shaker over ice. Shake and strain into an old-fashioned glass over ice. Add Ginger Ale, stir gently and serve.

Gallileo

28.1% ALC/VOL • 2 STD DRINKS

45ml (1½ fl oz) Dry Gin
15ml (½ fl oz) Banana Liqueur
15ml (½ fl oz) Galliano
15ml (½ fl oz) Grapefruit Juice

Pour ingredients into a cocktail shaker over ice and shake. Strain into a chilled cocktail glass and serve.
This drink is also known as Alcudia.

Bird of Paradise Cocktail

12.8% ALC/VOL • 1.7 STD DRINKS

60ml (2 fl oz) Gin
15ml (½ fl oz) Grenadine
1½ teaspoons Sugar Syrup
White of 1 Egg
60ml (2 fl oz) Mineral Water

Pour Gin, Grenadine, sugar and egg white into a cocktail shaker over ice. Shake and strain into a highball glass over ice. Add mineral water, stir gently and serve.

Whizz-Doodle

25.1% ALC/VOL • 2.4 STD DRINKS

This drink is also known as Barbary Coast, p 60.

Alcudia

28.1% ALC/VOL • 2 STD DRINKS

This drink is also known as Gallileo, p 68.

Voleur d Amour

3.5% ALC/VOL • 0.6 STD DRINKS

18ml (3/5 fl oz) Gin
6ml (1/5 fl oz) Banana Liqueur
Dash Grenadine
38ml (1¼ fl oz) Pineapple Juice
165ml (5½ fl oz) Bitter-Lemon Soda

Pour Gin, Liqueur, Grenadine and juice into a highball glass over ice then stir, Add soda, stir gently and serve.

White Heather

28.2% ALC/VOL • 2 STD DRINKS

45ml (1½ fl oz) Gin
15ml (½ fl oz) Cointreau
15ml (½ fl oz) Dry Vermouth
15ml (½ fl oz) Pineapple Juice

Pour ingredients into a cocktail shaker over ice and shake. Strain into a chilled cocktail glass and serve.

Orange Fizz No.2

10.6% ALC/VOL • 1.8 STD DRINKS

60ml (2 fl oz) Dry Gin
45ml (1½ fl oz) Fresh Orange Juice
15ml (½ fl oz) Fresh Lemon Juice
15ml (½ fl oz) Fresh Lime Juice
75ml (2½ fl oz) Soda Water

Pour Gin and juices into a cocktail shaker over ice. Shake and strain into a highball glass over ice. Add soda, stir gently and serve.

Lutkins Special

26.8% ALC/VOL • 2 STD DRINKS

45ml (1½ fl oz) Dry Gin
45ml (1½ fl oz) Dry Vermouth
2 dashes Apricot Brandy
2 dashes Fresh Orange Juice

Pour ingredients into a mixing glass over ice and stir. Strain into a chilled cocktail glass and serve.

Visitor

24.8% ALC/VOL • 2.4 STD DRINKS

30ml (1 fl oz) Gin
30ml (1 fl oz) Banana Liqueur
30ml (1 fl oz) Cointreau
Dash Fresh Orange Juice
White of 1 Egg

Pour ingredients into a cocktail shaker over ice and shake. Strain into a chilled goblet and serve.

Passion-Fruit Cocktail

26.4% ALC/VOL • 2.4 STD DRINKS

75ml (2½ fl oz) Gin
15ml (½ fl oz) Dry Vermouth
Pulp of 1 Passion-Fruit
1 teaspoon Passion-Fruit

Pour Gin and Vermouth into a mixing glass over ice then add pulp of 1 passion-fruit. Stir and strain into a chilled cocktail glass. Add teaspoon of passion-fruit on top and serve.

Cream Fizz

13.1% ALC/VOL • 1.8 STD DRINKS

60ml (2 fl oz) Dry Gin
15ml (½ fl oz) Fresh Lemon Juice
15ml (½ fl oz) Fresh Lime Juice
15ml (½ fl oz) Fresh Cream
1 teaspoon Caster Sugar
60ml (2 fl oz) Soda Water
Slice of Lemon

Pour Gin, juices and cream into a cocktail shaker over ice then add sugar. Shake and strain into a highball glass over ice. Add soda and stir gently. Garnish with a slice of lemon and serve with a straw.

Java Cooler

11.8% ALC/VOL • 1.4 STD DRINKS

45ml (1½ fl oz) Gin
3 dashes Angostura Bitters
15ml (½ fl oz) Fresh Lime Juice
90ml (3 fl oz) Tonic Water

Pour Gin, Bitters and juice into a collins glass over ice then stir. Add tonic, stir gently and serve.

Mint Gin

24.8% ALC/VOL • 1.8 STD DRINKS

45ml (1½ fl oz) Gin
23ml (¾ fl oz) White Crème De Menthe
5ml (1/6 fl oz) Green Crème De Menthe
5ml (1/6 fl oz) Fresh Lemon Juice
½ Egg White
Sprig of Fresh Mint

Pour Gin, Crème De Menthes, juice and egg white into a cocktail shaker over ice. Shake and strain into an old-fashioned glass over ice. Garnish with a sprig of mint and serve.

Kosciusko

22.2% ALC/VOL • 1.3 STD DRINKS

45ml (1½ fl oz) Gin
1 scoop Vanilla Ice Cream
Strawberry

Pour Gin into a blender without ice and add ice cream. Blend until smooth and pour into a chilled champagne saucer. Garnish with a strawberry and serve.

Caterpillar

34.8% ALC/VOL • 1.6 STD DRINKS

30ml (1 fl oz) Gin
15ml (½ fl oz) Blue Curaçao
15ml (½ fl oz) Yellow Chartreuse
Twist of Orange Peel

Pour Gin, Curaçao and Chartreuse into a cocktail shaker over ice. Shake and strain into a chilled cocktail glass. Garnish with orange peel and serve.

Orange Bloom

32.3% ALC/VOL • 1.5 STD DRINKS

30ml (1 fl oz) Gin
15ml (½ fl oz) Cointreau
15ml (½ fl oz) Sweet Vermouth
Maraschino Cherry

Pour Gin, Cointreau and Vermouth into a mixing glass over ice. Stir and strain into a chilled cocktail glass. Garnish with a cherry and serve.

Gin Flip

20.2% ALC/VOL • 1.8 STD DRINKS

60ml (2 fl oz) Dry Gin
1 teaspoon Sugar Syrup
1 Fresh Egg
Nutmeg

Pour Gin, sugar and egg into a cocktail shaker over ice. Shake and strain into a chilled goblet. Sprinkle nutmeg on top and serve.

Maples Cocktail

17% ALC/VOL • 1.7 STD DRINKS

45ml (1½ fl oz) Dry Gin
23ml (¾ fl oz) White Crème De Cacao
60ml (2 fl oz) Pineapple Juice
Dash Fresh Cream

Pour ingredients into a cocktail shaker over ice and shake. Strain into a chilled old-fashioned glass and serve.

Oahu Gin Sling

14.5% ALC/VOL • 2.5 STD DRINKS

60ml (2 fl oz) Gin
15ml (½ fl oz) Bénédictine
15ml (½ fl oz) Crème De Cassis
30ml (1 fl oz) Fresh Lime Juice
1 teaspoon Sugar Syrup
90ml (3 fl oz) Soda Water
Long Twist of Lime Peel

Pour Gin, Bénédictine, Cassis, juice and sugar into a cocktail shaker over ice. Shake and strain into a highball glass over ice. Add soda and stir gently. Hook one end of lime peel over rim of glass and place remainder of peel into glass then serve.

Emerald Forest

34.5% ALC/VOL • 1.5 STD DRINKS

45ml (1½ fl oz) Gin
5ml (1/6 fl oz) Green Crème De Menthe
5ml (1/6 fl oz) White Crème De Menthe

Pour ingredients into a mixing glass over ice and stir. Strain into a chilled cocktail glass and serve.

Balmain

25.7% ALC/VOL • 1.6 STD DRINKS

30ml (1 fl oz) Gin
30ml (1 fl oz) Dry Vermouth
10ml (⅓ fl oz) Pernod
10ml (⅓ fl oz) Fresh Lemon Juice
Slice of Lemon

Pour Gin, Vermouth, Pernod and juice into a mixing glass over ice. Stir and strain into a chilled cocktail glass. Garnish with a slice of lemon and serve.

Sweet Negroni

25.6% ALC/VOL • 1.8 STD DRINKS

30ml (1 fl oz) Gin
30ml (1 fl oz) Campari
30ml (1 fl oz) Sweet Vermouth
Slice of Lime

Pour Gin, Campari and Vermouth into a mixing glass over ice. Stir and strain into a chilled brandy balloon over a few ice cubes. Garnish with a slice of lime and serve.

Gin Squash

7.4% ALC/VOL • 0.9 STD DRINKS

30ml (1 fl oz) Gin
Dash Lemon Syrup
120ml (4 fl oz) Lemonade
Slice of Lemon

Pour Gin and syrup into a highball glass over ice then stir. Add lemonade and stir gently. Garnish with a slice of lemon and serve.

Concorde Cocktail

30.3% ALC/VOL • 1.3 STD DRINKS

30ml (1 fl oz) Gin
15ml (½ fl oz) Orange Curaçao
10ml (⅓ fl oz) Dry Vermouth
Twist of Orange Peel

Pour Gin, Curaçao and Vermouth into a cocktail shaker over ice. Shake and strain into a chilled cocktail glass. Garnish with orange peel and serve.

Yellow Rattler

21.4% ALC/VOL • 1.3 STD DRINKS

30ml (1 fl oz) Dry Gin

15ml (½ fl oz) Dry Vermouth
15ml (½ fl oz) Sweet Vermouth
15ml (½ fl oz) Fresh
Orange Juice
Cocktail Onion

Pour Gin, Vermouths and juice into a cocktail shaker over ice. Shake and strain into a chilled cocktail glass. Garnish with a cocktail onion and serve.

Connecticut Bullfrog

22.2% ALC/VOL • 1.3 STD DRINKS

30ml (1 fl oz) Gin
15ml (½ fl oz) Dark Rum
15ml (½ fl oz) Fresh
Lemon Juice
15ml (½ fl oz) Maple Syrup

Pour ingredients into a cocktail shaker over ice and shake. Strain into a cocktail glass over crushed ice and serve.

Cabaret

26.8% ALC/VOL • 1.9 STD DRINKS

45ml (1½ fl oz) Gin
45ml (1½ fl oz) Dubonnet
Dash Angostura Bitters
Dash Pernod
Maraschino Cherry

Pour Gin, Dubonnet, Bitters and Pernod into a mixing glass over ice. Stir and strain into a chilled cocktail glass. Garnish with a cherry and serve.

Snyder

33.8% ALC/VOL • 2 STD DRINKS

45ml (1½ fl oz) Dry Gin
15ml (½ fl oz) Cointreau
15ml (½ fl oz) Dry Vermouth
Twist of Lemon Peel

Pour Gin, Cointreau and Vermouth into a cocktail shaker over ice. Shake and strain into a chilled cocktail glass. Garnish with lemon peel and serve.

Barbarella

18.5% ALC/VOL • 1.9 STD DRINKS

30ml (1 fl oz) Plymouth Gin
23ml (¾ fl oz) Dry Vermouth
15ml (½ fl oz) Galliano
5ml (1/6 fl oz) Blue Curaçao
60ml (2 fl oz) Bitter-Lemon
Soda
Red Cherry
Slice of Lemon

Pour Gin, Vermouth, Galliano and Curaçao into a cocktail shaker over ice. Shake and strain into an old-fashioned glass over cracked ice. Add soda and stir gently. Garnish with a cherry and slice of lemon then serve.

Gin Cocktail

36.2% ALC/VOL • 1.9 STD DRINKS

60ml (2 fl oz) Dry Gin
5ml (1/6 fl oz) Orange Bitters

Pour ingredients into a cocktail shaker over ice and shake. Strain into a chilled cocktail glass and serve.

Jasmine

26% ALC/VOL • 1.7 STD DRINKS

45ml (1½ fl oz) Gin
8ml (¼ fl oz) Campari
8ml (¼ fl oz) Cointreau
23ml (¾ fl oz) Fresh
Lemon Juice
Twist of Lemon Peel

Pour Gin, Campari, Cointreau and juice into a mixing glass over ice. Stir and strain into a chilled cocktail glass. Garnish with lemon peel and serve.

Rialtococo

20.6% ALC/VOL • 1.5 STD DRINKS

30ml (1 fl oz) Dry Gin
30ml (1 fl oz) Campari
30ml (1 fl oz) Coconut Cream

Pour ingredients into a blender over crushed ice and blend until smooth. Pour into a chilled goblet and serve.

Nineteen Twenty

32.6% ALC/VOL • 3.7 STD DRINKS

90ml (3 fl oz) Dry Gin
23ml (¾ fl oz) Dry Vermouth
23ml (¾ fl oz) Kirsch
Dash Orange Bitters
1 teaspoon Groseille Syrup

Pour ingredients into a cocktail shaker over ice and shake. Strain into a chilled cocktail glass and serve.

Bulldog Highball

12.3% ALC/VOL • 0.9 STD DRINKS

30ml (1 fl oz) Gin
30ml (1 fl oz) Fresh
Orange Juice
30ml (1 fl oz) Dry Ginger Ale
Slice of Orange

Pour Gin and juice into a cocktail shaker over ice. Shake and strain into a highball glass over ice. Add Ginger Ale and stir gently. Garnish with a slice of orange and serve with a straw.

Goin' Home

15.2% ALC/VOL • 1.6 STD DRINKS

30ml (1 fl oz) Dry Gin
30ml (1 fl oz) Peach Schnapps
15ml (½ fl oz) Dry Vermouth
10ml (⅓ fl oz) Fresh
Lime Juice
45ml (1½ fl oz) Apple Juice
Soda

Pour Gin, Schnapps, Vermouth and juice into a cocktail shaker over ice. Shake and strain into an old-fashioned glass over ice. Add soda, stir gently and serve.

Bayard Fizz

13.8% ALC/VOL • 2 STD DRINKS

This drink is also known as Bloomsbury Fizz, p 68.

Shady Grove Cooler

10.1% ALC/VOL • 1.8 STD DRINKS

This drink is also known as Gin Cooler, 64.

Nana

5.7% ALC/VOL • 1.2 STD DRINKS

20ml (⅔ fl oz) Dry Gin
20ml (⅔ fl oz) Sweet Vermouth
20ml (⅔ fl oz) White Crème De Cacao
Dash Asbach Uralt Brandy
210ml (7 fl oz) Lemonade

Pour Gin, Vermouth and Cacao into a cocktail shaker over ice. Shake and strain into a chilled highball glass then add Brandy. Add lemonade, stir gently and serve with a straw.

Space

28.8% ALC/VOL • 1.9 STD DRINKS

45ml (1½ fl oz) Gin
30ml (1 fl oz) Frangelico
8ml (¼ fl oz) Fresh Lemon Juice

Pour ingredients into a cocktail shaker over ice and shake. Strain into an old-fashioned glass over ice and serve.

Final Edition

3.2% ALC/VOL • 0.7 STD DRINKS

15ml (½ fl oz) Dry Gin
15ml (½ fl oz) Banana Liqueur
Dash Grenadine
Dash Fresh Lemon Juice
250ml (8⅓ fl oz) Mineral Water
Dash Orange Soda

Pour Gin, Liqueur, Grenadine and juice into a cocktail shaker over ice. Shake and strain into a chilled highball glass. Add mineral water and soda, stir gently then serve.

Leap Frog

9.3% ALC/VOL • 1.3 STD DRINKS

45ml (1½ fl oz) Dry Gin
45ml (1½ fl oz) Fresh Lemon Juice
90ml (3 fl oz) Dry Ginger Ale

Pour Gin and juice into a collins glass over ice then stir. Add Ginger Ale, stir gently and serve.

White Rose

16% ALC/VOL • 1.1 STD DRINKS

38ml (1¼ fl oz) Gin
15ml (½ fl oz) Fresh Lime Juice
15ml (½ fl oz) Fresh Orange Juice
1 teaspoon Sugar Syrup
½ Egg White

Pour ingredients into a cocktail shaker over ice and shake. Strain into a chilled cocktail glass and serve.

Ten Quidder

37.5% ALC/VOL • 2.4 STD DRINKS

45ml (1½ fl oz) Dry Gin
30ml (1 fl oz) Cointreau
5ml (⅙ fl oz) Blue Curaçao
Dash Angostura Bitters

Pour Gin, Cointreau and Bitters into a mixing glass over ice. Stir and strain into an old-fashioned glass over ice. Add Curaçao by pouring into centre of drink – do not stir, then serve.

Slalom

19.7% ALC/VOL • 1.3 STD DRINKS

45ml (1½ fl oz) Gin
Dash Orange Bitters
30ml (1 fl oz) Fresh Lemon Juice
2 teaspoons Maple Syrup
Maraschino Cherry
Slice of Orange

Pour Gin, Bitters, juice and syrup into a mixing glass over ice. Stir and strain into a chilled cocktail glass. Garnish with a cherry and slice of orange then serve.

Marny

38% ALC/VOL • 4 STD DRINKS

90ml (3 fl oz) Dry Gin
45ml (1½ fl oz) Grand Marnier
Maraschino Cherry

Pour Gin and Grand Marnier into a mixing glass over ice. Stir and strain into a chilled cocktail glass. Garnish with a cherry and serve.

South-Side

27.8% ALC/VOL • 1.8 STD DRINKS

60ml (2 fl oz) Gin
15ml (½ fl oz) Fresh Lemon Juice
½ teaspoon Sugar Syrup
2 dashes Soda Water
2 Sprigs of Fresh Mint

Pour Gin, juice and sugar into a cocktail shaker over ice. Shake and strain into a chilled cocktail glass. Add soda – do not stir, then garnish with sprigs of mint and serve.

Mediterranean

16.5% ALC/VOL • 2.3 STD DRINKS

60ml (2 fl oz) Gin
30ml (1 fl oz) Blue Curaçao
90ml (3 fl oz) Lemonade
Sprig of Fresh Mint

Prepare a collins glass with a sugar frosted rim and add ice. Pour Gin and Curaçao into prepared glass. Add lemonade and stir gently. Garnish with a sprig of mint and serve.

Macca

8.2% ALC/VOL • 0.9 STD DRINKS

15ml (½ fl oz) Gin
5ml (1/6 fl oz) Blackberry Schnapps
15ml (½ fl oz) Dry Vermouth
15ml (½ fl oz) Sweet Vermouth
90ml (3 fl oz) Soda Water

Pour Gin, Schnapps and Vermouths into a cocktail shaker over ice. Shake and strain into a highball glass over ice. Add soda, stir gently and serve.

Captain Cook

22.8% ALC/VOL • 1.6 STD DRINKS

45ml (1½ fl oz) Gin
15ml (½ fl oz) Maraschino Liqueur
30ml (1 fl oz) Fresh Orange Juice

Pour ingredients into a cocktail shaker over ice and shake. Strain into a chilled cocktail glass and serve.

Bite of the Iguana

15.3% ALC/VOL • 1.8 STD DRINKS

60ml (2 fl oz) Gin
15ml (½ fl oz) Fresh Lemon Juice
15ml (½ fl oz) Fresh Lime Juice
1 teaspoon Fresh Cream
1 teaspoon Sugar Syrup
1 Fresh Egg

Pour ingredients into a cocktail shaker over ice and shake. Strain into a chilled champagne saucer and serve.

Jackson Standard

26.5% ALC/VOL • 2.9 STD DRINKS

68ml (2¼ fl oz) Dry Gin
68ml (2¼ fl oz) Dubonnet
2 dashes Orange Bitters

Pour ingredients into a mixing glass over ice and stir. Strain into a chilled cocktail glass and serve.

Royal Smile

25.1% ALC/VOL • 1.3 STD DRINKS

30ml (1 fl oz) Gin
15ml (½ fl oz) Applejack
3 dashes Grenadine
15ml (½ fl oz) Fresh Lemon Juice
1 teaspoon Fresh Cream

Pour ingredients into a cocktail shaker over ice and shake. Strain into a chilled champagne saucer and serve.

Bijou Cocktail

35.6% ALC/VOL • 2 STD DRINKS

This drink is also known as Jewel Cocktail, p 50.

Cloud Nine

25.8% ALC/VOL • 1.5 STD DRINKS

45ml (1½ fl oz) Gin
15ml (½ fl oz) Dry Sherry
15ml (½ fl oz) Fresh Cream
Nutmeg

Pour Gin, Sherry and cream into a cocktail shaker over ice. Shake and strain into a chilled cocktail glass. Sprinkle nutmeg on top and serve.
This drink is also known as Renaissance.

Tuxedo

30.9% ALC/VOL • 2.2 STD DRINKS

45ml (1½ fl oz) Dry Gin
30ml (1 fl oz) Dry Vermouth
2 dashes Pernod
Slice of Lemon

Pour Gin, Vermouth and Pernod into a cocktail shaker over ice. Shake and strain into a chilled cocktail glass. Twist slice of lemon above drink to release juice – do not stir, then place remainder of lemon slice into drink and serve.

Jorunder

7.5% ALC/VOL • 1.4 STD DRINKS

30ml (1 fl oz) Dry Gin
20ml (⅔ fl oz) White Crème De Cacao
10ml (⅓ fl oz) Triple Sec
2 dashes Fresh Lemon Juice
180ml (6 fl oz) Lemonade

Pour Gin, Cacao, Triple Sec and juice into a cocktail shaker over ice. Shake and strain into a chilled highball glass. Add lemonade, stir gently and serve.

Silver Bullet

37.2% ALC/VOL • 1.8 STD DRINKS

60ml (2 fl oz) Gin
15ml (½ fl oz) Scotch Whisky
Slice of Lemon

Pour Whisky into a mixing glass over ice and stir. Strain and discard Whisky. Add Gin to the mixing glass and stir. Strain into a chilled cocktail glass and garnish with a slice of lemon then serve.

Puerto Rico Rickey

13.3% ALC/VOL • 1.8 STD DRINKS

60ml (2 fl oz) Gin
15ml (½ fl oz) Fresh Lime Juice
2 dashes Raspberry Syrup
90ml (3 fl oz) Soda Water
Twist of Lime Peel

Pour Gin, juice and syrup into a collins glass over ice then stir. Add soda and stir gently. Garnish with lime peel and serve.

Belmont

21.1% ALC/VOL • 2.6 STD DRINKS

90ml (3 fl oz) Gin
45ml (1½ fl oz) Grenadine
23ml (¾ fl oz) Fresh Cream

Pour ingredients into a cocktail shaker over ice and shake. Strain into a chilled champagne saucer and serve.

Regent Star

26.8% ALC/VOL • 1.3 STD DRINKS

30ml (1 fl oz) Dry Gin
15ml (½ fl oz) Orange Curaçao
8ml (¼ fl oz) Dry Vermouth
8ml (¼ fl oz) Passion-Fruit Juice
Slice of Orange

Pour Gin, Curaçao, Vermouth and juice into a cocktail shaker over ice. Shake and strain into a chilled cocktail glass. Garnish with a slice of orange and serve.

Ruby in the Rough

32.1% ALC/VOL • 1.6 STD DRINKS

45ml (1½ fl oz) Gin
15ml (½ fl oz) Cherry Brandy
5ml (1/6 fl oz) Sweet Vermouth

Pour ingredients into a mixing glass over ice and stir. Strain into a chilled cocktail glass and serve.

Peabody

12.6% ALC/VOL • 2 STD DRINKS

60ml (2 fl oz) Gin
15ml (½ fl oz) Campari
10ml (⅓ fl oz) Grenadine
30ml (1 fl oz) Fresh Orange Juice
90ml (3 fl oz) Dry Ginger Ale
Maraschino Cherry

Pour Gin, Campari, Grenadine and juice into a cocktail shaker over cracked ice. Shake and pour into a chilled collins glass. Add Ginger Ale and stir gently. Garnish with a cherry and serve.

Greyhound

8.5% ALC/VOL • 1.3 STD DRINKS

45ml (1½ fl oz) Dry Gin
150ml (5 fl oz) Grapefruit Juice

Pour Gin into a highball glass over ice and add juice, stir then serve.

Smart Christine

20.8% ALC/VOL • 2.2 STD DRINKS

60ml (2 fl oz) Gin
15ml (½ fl oz) Bénédictine
60ml (2 fl oz) Fresh Orange Juice
Maraschino Cherry

Pour Gin, Bénédictine and juice into a cocktail shaker over ice. Shake and strain into a chilled old-fashioned glass. Garnish with a cherry and serve.
This drink is also known as Reason to Believe.

Reason to Believe

20.8% ALC/VOL • 2.2 STD DRINKS

This drink is also known as Smart Christine, above.

Joulouville

25.8% ALC/VOL • 1.5 STD DRINKS

This drink is also known as Bougainvillea, p 65.

Albemarle Fizz

11.7% ALC/VOL • 1.8 STD DRINKS

60ml (2 fl oz) Gin
30ml (1 fl oz) Fresh Lemon Juice
1 teaspoon Raspberry Syrup
90ml (3 fl oz) Soda Water

Pour Gin, juice and syrup into a cocktail shaker over ice. Shake and strain into a chilled wine glass. Add soda, stir gently and serve.

Fastlap

26.2% ALC/VOL • 2.2 STD DRINKS

60ml (2 fl oz) Gin
15ml (½ fl oz) Pernod
3 dashes Grenadine
30ml (1 fl oz) Fresh Orange Juice

Pour ingredients into a cocktail shaker over ice and shake. Strain into an old-fashioned glass over ice and serve.

Horsley's Honor

34.8% ALC/VOL • 2.5 STD DRINKS

45ml (1½ fl oz) Gin

15ml (½ fl oz) Applejack
15ml (½ fl oz) Cointreau
15ml (½ fl oz) Dry Vermouth
Slice of Orange

Pour Gin, Applejack, Cointreau and Vermouth into a mixing glass over ice. Stir and strain into an old-fashioned glass over ice. Garnish with a slice of orange and serve.

Arthur Tompkins

33.1% ALC/VOL • 2.2 STD DRINKS

60ml (2 fl oz) Gin
15ml (½ fl oz) Grand Marnier
10ml (⅓ fl oz) Fresh Lemon Juice
Slice of Lemon

Pour Gin, Grand Marnier and juice into a cocktail shaker over ice. Shake and strain into a chilled sour glass. Garnish with a slice of lemon and serve.

Danish Gin

29.8% ALC/VOL • 1.6 STD DRINKS

30ml (1 fl oz) Gin
15ml (½ fl oz) Cherry Brandy
15ml (½ fl oz) Dry Vermouth
8ml (¼ fl oz) Kirsch
Twist of Lemon Peel

Pour Gin, Brandy, Vermouth and Kirsch into a mixing glass over ice. Stir and strain into a chilled cocktail glass. Garnish with lemon peel and serve.

Seventh Heaven No.2

27.3% ALC/VOL • 1.8 STD DRINKS

45ml (1½ fl oz) Gin
23ml (¾ fl oz) Maraschino Liqueur
15ml (½ fl oz) Grapefruit Juice
Sprig of Fresh Mint

Pour Gin, Liqueur and juice into a cocktail shaker over ice. Shake and strain into a chilled cocktail glass. Garnish with a sprig of mint and serve.

Watermelon Cassis

15.4% ALC/VOL • 2 STD DRINKS

60ml (2 fl oz) Gin
15ml (½ fl oz) Crème De Cassis
23ml (¾ fl oz) Fresh Lemon Juice
5ml (1/6 fl oz) Soda Water
½ Cup Watermelon (diced)
Slice of Lemon

Pour Gin, Cassis and juice into a blender over crushed ice then add diced watermelon. Blend and pour into a highball glass over ice. Add soda – do not stir, then garnish with a slice of lemon and serve.

Loud Speaker

32.8% ALC/VOL • 4.1 STD DRINKS

60ml (2 fl oz) Dry Gin
60ml (2 fl oz) Brandy
20ml (⅔ fl oz) Cointreau
20ml (⅔ fl oz) Fresh Lemon Juice

Pour ingredients into a mixing glass over ice and stir. Strain into a chilled champagne saucer and serve.

Blue Swizzle

13.9% ALC/VOL • 2 STD DRINKS

60ml (2 fl oz) Light Rum
10ml (⅓ fl oz) Blue Curaçao
Dash Angostura Bitters
45ml (1½ fl oz) Fresh Lime Juice
1 teaspoon Sugar Syrup
60ml (2 fl oz) Soda Water

Pour Rum, Curaçao, Bitters, juice and sugar into a mixing glass over large amount of ice. Stir vigorously until cold and strain into a collins glass filled with crushed ice. Add soda – do not stir, then serve with a swizzle stick and 2 straws.

Crystal Slipper

33.8% ALC/VOL • 1.7 STD DRINKS

45ml (1½ fl oz) Dry Gin
15ml (½ fl oz) Blue Curaçao
2 dashes Orange Bitters

Pour ingredients into a mixing glass over ice and stir. Strain into a chilled cocktail glass and serve.

Berry Wall

26% ALC/VOL • 1.9 STD DRINKS

45ml (1½ fl oz) Dry Gin
45ml (1½ fl oz) Sweet Vermouth
4 dashes Curaçao
Maraschino Cherry
Twist of Lemon Peel

Pour Gin, Vermouth and Curaçao into a mixing glass over ice. Stir and strain into a chilled cocktail glass. Twist lemon peel above drink and discard remainder of peel. Garnish with a cherry and serve.

Berliner

29.4% ALC/VOL • 1.8 STD DRINKS

45ml (1½ fl oz) Gin
15ml (½ fl oz) Dry Vermouth
8ml (¼ fl oz) Kümmel
8ml (¼ fl oz) Fresh Lemon Juice

Pour ingredients into a cocktail shaker over ice and shake. Strain into a chilled cocktail glass and serve.

Roger

12.1% ALC/VOL • 0.9 STD DRINKS

30ml (1 fl oz) Dry Gin

30ml (1 fl oz) Fresh
Orange Juice
30ml (1 fl oz) Peach Juice
2 dashes Fresh Lemon Juice
Twist of Orange Peel

Pour Gin and juices into a cocktail shaker over ice. Shake and strain into a highball glass over ice. Garnish with orange peel and serve.

Gin Daiquiri

27.8% ALC/VOL • 1.8 STD DRINKS

45ml (1½ fl oz) Gin
15ml (½ fl oz) Light Rum
15ml (½ fl oz) Fresh
Lime Juice
1 teaspoon Sugar Syrup

Prepare a cocktail glass with a sugar frosted rim. Pour ingredients into a cocktail shaker over ice and shake. Strain into prepared glass and serve.

Violet Fizz

10.4% ALC/VOL • 1.3 STD DRINKS

45ml (1½ fl oz) Dry Gin
15ml (½ fl oz) Fresh
Lemon Juice
1 teaspoon Fresh Cream
1 teaspoon Raspberry Syrup
90ml (3 fl oz) Soda Water

Pour Gin, juice, cream and syrup into a cocktail shaker over ice. Shake and strain into a highball glass over ice. Add soda, stir gently and serve.

Sugar Daddy

25.1% ALC/VOL • 2 STD DRINKS

60ml (2 fl oz) Gin
10ml (⅓ fl oz) Maraschino
Liqueur
Dash Angostura Bitters
30ml (1 fl oz) Pineapple Juice

Pour ingredients into a cocktail shaker over ice and shake. Strain into a chilled cocktail glass and serve.

Have a Heart

31.8% ALC/VOL • 2.7 STD DRINKS

68ml (2¼ fl oz) Dry Gin
23ml (¾ fl oz) Swedish Punsch
2 dashes Grenadine
15ml (½ fl oz) Fresh
Lime Juice
Maraschino Cherry
Slice of Pineapple

Pour Gin, Punsch, Grenadine and juice into a cocktail shaker over ice. Shake and strain into a chilled cocktail glass. Garnish with a cherry and slice of pineapple then serve.

London Town

34% ALC/VOL • 1.7 STD DRINKS

45ml (1½ fl oz) Gin
15ml (½ fl oz) Maraschino
Liqueur
2 dashes Orange Bitters

Pour ingredients into a cocktail shaker over ice and shake. Strain into a chilled cocktail glass and serve.

Edinburgh

33.1% ALC/VOL • 1.8 STD DRINKS

30ml (1 fl oz) Gin
15ml (½ fl oz) Drambuie
15ml (½ fl oz) Scotch Whisky
15ml (½ fl oz) Fresh
Lemon Juice
Twist of Lemon Peel

Pour Gin, Drambuie, Whisky and juice into a mixing glass over ice. Stir and strain into a chilled old-fashioned glass. Garnish with lemon peel and serve.

Le Reve

28.5% ALC/VOL • 2.7 STD DRINKS

60ml (2 fl oz) Gin
30ml (1 fl oz) Mandarine
Napoleon
15ml (½ fl oz) Grenadine
15ml (½ fl oz) Fresh
Lemon Juice

Pour ingredients into a cocktail shaker over ice and shake. Strain into a chilled cocktail glass and serve.

Peach Blow Fizz

12.3% ALC/VOL • 2.6 STD DRINKS

90ml (3 fl oz) Gin
30ml (1 fl oz) Fresh Cream
15ml (½ fl oz) Fresh
Lemon Juice
15ml (½ fl oz) Fresh
Lime Juice
1 teaspoon Caster Sugar
75ml (2½ fl oz) Soda Water
4 Strawberries (crushed)

Pour Gin, cream and juices into a cocktail shaker over ice. Add sugar and diced strawberries. Shake and strain into a highball glass over ice. Add soda, stir gently and serve.

Artillery

34.1% ALC/VOL • 1.5 STD DRINKS

45ml (1½ fl oz) Gin
8ml (¼ fl oz) Sweet Vermouth
2 dashes Angostura Bitters

Pour ingredients into a mixing glass over ice and stir. Strain into a chilled cocktail glass and serve.

Bermuda Highball

13.3% ALC/VOL • 1.7 STD DRINKS

23ml (¾ fl oz) Gin
23ml (¾ fl oz) Brandy
23ml (¾ fl oz) Dry Vermouth
90ml (3 fl oz) Dry Ginger Ale
Twist of Lemon Peel

Pour Gin, Brandy and Vermouth into a highball glass over ice then stir. Add Ginger Ale and stir gently. Add lemon peel and serve.

Blue Canary

14.7% ALC/VOL • 1 STD DRINK

23ml (¾ fl oz) Gin
15ml (½ fl oz) Blue Curaçao
45ml (1½ fl oz) Grapefruit Juice
Sprig of Fresh Mint

Pour Gin, Curaçao and juice into a mixing glass over ice. Stir and strain into a cocktail glass filled with crushed ice. Garnish with a sprig of mint and serve.

Welcome Stranger

19% ALC/VOL • 2.7 STD DRINKS

30ml (1 fl oz) Dry Gin
30ml (1 fl oz) Brandy
30ml (1 fl oz) Swedish Punsch
30ml (1 fl oz) Grenadine
30ml (1 fl oz) Fresh Lemon Juice
30ml (1 fl oz) Fresh Orange Juice

Pour ingredients into a cocktail shaker over ice and shake. Strain into a chilled old-fashioned glass and serve.

Silver Bullet No.2

30% ALC/VOL • 1.8 STD DRINKS

30ml (1 fl oz) Gin
30ml (1 fl oz) Kümmel
15ml (½ fl oz) Fresh Lemon Juice

Pour ingredients into a cocktail shaker over ice and shake. Strain into a chilled cocktail glass and serve.

Supreme

23.2% ALC/VOL • 1.8 STD DRINKS

45ml (1½ fl oz) Gin
23ml (¾ fl oz) Peach Brandy
Dash Angostura Bitters
23ml (¾ fl oz) Fresh Orange Juice
1 teaspoon Egg White

Pour ingredients into a cocktail shaker over ice and shake. Strain into a cocktail glass over crushed ice and serve.

Woodstock

20.1% ALC/VOL • 1.3 STD DRINKS

45ml (1½ fl oz) Dry Gin
Dash Orange Bitters
30ml (1 fl oz) Fresh Lemon Juice
1½ teaspoons Maple Syrup

Pour ingredients into a cocktail shaker over ice and shake. Strain into a chilled cocktail glass and serve.

Morticia

26.9% ALC/VOL • 1.9 STD DRINKS

30ml (1 fl oz) Gin
15ml (½ fl oz) Dry Vermouth
15ml (½ fl oz) Pernod
15ml (½ fl oz) Sloe Gin
5ml (1/6 fl oz) Fresh Lemon Juice
1½ teaspoons Sugar Syrup

Pour ingredients into a cocktail shaker over cracked ice and shake. Pour into a chilled old-fashioned glass and serve.

Why Not?

27.2% ALC/VOL • 1.6 STD DRINKS

30ml (1 fl oz) Dry Gin
30ml (1 fl oz) Apricot Brandy
15ml (½ fl oz) Dry Vermouth
Dash Fresh Lemon Juice

Pour ingredients into a cocktail shaker over ice and shake. Strain into a chilled cocktail glass and serve.

Conca D'Ora

34.4% ALC/VOL • 1.9 STD DRINKS

45ml (1½ fl oz) Dry Gin
8ml (¼ fl oz) Cherry Brandy
8ml (¼ fl oz) Cointreau
8ml (¼ fl oz) Maraschino Liqueur
Twist of Orange Peel

Pour Gin, Brandy, Cointreau and Liqueur into a mixing glass over ice. Stir and strain into a chilled cocktail glass. Garnish with orange peel and serve.

Gasper

30% ALC/VOL • 2.1 STD DRINKS

45ml (1½ fl oz) Dry Gin
45ml (1½ fl oz) Apricot Brandy
Cocktail Onion

Pour Gin and Brandy into a mixing glass over ice. Stir and strain into a chilled cocktail glass. Garnish with a cocktail onion and serve.

Green Demon

27.1% ALC/VOL • 1.5 STD DRINKS

45ml (1½ fl oz) Gin
10ml (⅓ fl oz) Green Crème De Menthe
15ml (½ fl oz) Fresh Lime Juice
Sprig of Fresh Mint

Pour Gin, Crème De Menthe and juice into a mixing glass over ice. Stir and strain into a chilled cocktail glass. Garnish with a sprig of mint and serve. *This drink is also known as Greenback.*

Atty

33% ALC/VOL • 3 STD DRINKS

90ml (3 fl oz) Dry Gin
23ml (¾ fl oz) Dry Vermouth
3 dashes Crème De Violette
Twist of Lemon Peel

Pour Gin, Vermouth and Crème De Violette into a mixing glass over ice. Stir and strain into a chilled cocktail glass. Garnish with lemon peel and serve.

Seventh Heaven

26.4% ALC/VOL • 1 STD DRINK

23ml (¾ fl oz) Gin
23ml (¾ fl oz) Sweet Vermouth
2 dashes Maraschino Liqueur
Dash Angostura Bitters
Maraschino Cherry
Twist of Orange Peel

Pour Gin, Vermouth, Liqueur and Bitters into a mixing glass over ice. Stir and strain into a chilled cocktail glass. Garnish with a cherry and orange peel then serve.

Biffy

28.5% ALC/VOL • 4 STD DRINKS

90ml (3 fl oz) Dry Gin
45ml (1½ fl oz) Swedish Punsch
45ml (1½ fl oz) Fresh Lemon Juice

Pour ingredients into a mixing glass over ice and stir. Strain into a chilled brandy balloon and serve.

Grass Skirt

26.5% ALC/VOL • 2.3 STD DRINKS

45ml (1½ fl oz) Gin
30ml (1 fl oz) Cointreau
3 dashes Grenadine
30ml (1 fl oz) Pineapple Juice
Slice of Pineapple

Pour Gin, Cointreau, Grenadine and juice into a cocktail shaker over ice. Shake and strain into an old-fashioned glass over ice. Garnish with a slice of pineapple and serve.

London Fog

33.5% ALC/VOL • 2.4 STD DRINKS

45ml (1½ fl oz) Gin
45ml (1½ fl oz) Anisette
Slice of Lemon

Pour Gin and Anisette into a cocktail shaker over ice. Shake and strain into a cocktail glass over crushed ice. Add a slice of lemon and serve.

Everything But

14% ALC/VOL • 1.9 STD DRINKS

30ml (1 fl oz) Gin
30ml (1 fl oz) Blended Whiskey
5ml (⅙ fl oz) Apricot Brandy
30ml (1 fl oz) Fresh Lemon Juice
30ml (1 fl oz) Fresh Orange Juice
½ teaspoon Sugar Syrup
1 Fresh Egg

Pour ingredients into a cocktail shaker over ice and shake. Strain into a chilled sour glass and serve.

Granville

33.4% ALC/VOL • 1.8 STD DRINKS

45ml (1½ fl oz) Gin
8ml (¼ fl oz) Calvados
8ml (¼ fl oz) Grand Marnier
8ml (¼ fl oz) Fresh Lemon Juice

Pour ingredients into a cocktail shaker over ice and shake. Strain into a chilled cocktail glass and serve.

Silver Stallion Cocktail

9.3% ALC/VOL • 1.8 STD DRINKS

60ml (2 fl oz) Gin
15ml (½ fl oz) Fresh Lemon Juice
1 teaspoon Sugar Syrup
White of 1 Egg
1 scoop Vanilla Ice Cream
100ml (3⅓ fl oz) Soda Water

Pour Gin into a cocktail shaker without ice and add ice cream. Shake well until smooth and pour into a chilled highball glass. Pour juice, sugar and egg white into a clean cocktail shaker over ice. Shake and strain into glass over first mixture then stir well. Add soda, stir gently and serve.

Exterminator

53% ALC/VOL • 2.5 STD DRINKS

30ml (1 fl oz) Over-Proof Light Rum
30ml (1 fl oz) Green Chartreuse
Green Cherry

Pour Rum and Chartreuse into an old-fashioned glass over cracked ice then stir. Garnish with a cherry and serve.

Sorrento

22.3% ALC/VOL • 2.1 STD DRINKS

60ml (2 fl oz) Gin
30ml (1 fl oz) Sweet Vermouth
2 dashes Curaçao
30ml (1 fl oz) Fresh Orange Juice
Twist of Orange Peel

Pour Gin, Vermouth, Curaçao and juice into a cocktail shaker over ice. Shake and strain into a chilled champagne saucer. Garnish with orange peel and serve.

Gentleman's Club

23.9% ALC/VOL • 2.5 STD DRINKS

45ml (1½ fl oz) Gin
30ml (1 fl oz) Brandy
30ml (1 fl oz) Sweet Vermouth
30ml (1 fl oz) Soda Water

Pour Gin, Brandy and Vermouth into an old-fashioned glass over ice then stir. Add soda, stir gently and serve.

Gumbo Fizz

9.7% ALC/VOL • 1.9 STD DRINKS

60ml (2 fl oz) Gin
5ml (1/6 fl oz) Cointreau
30ml (1 fl oz) Fresh Lemon Juice
30ml (1 fl oz) Thick Cream
1 teaspoon Caster Sugar
White of 1 Egg
90ml (3 fl oz) Soda Water

Pour Gin, Cointreau, juice, cream and egg white into a cocktail shaker over ice then add sugar. Shake and strain into a highball glass over ice. Add soda, stir gently and serve.

Emerald Isle Cocktail

36.3% ALC/VOL • 1.9 STD DRINKS

60ml (2 fl oz) Dry Gin
5ml (1/6 fl oz) Green Crème De Menthe
3 dashes Angostura Bitters

Pour ingredients into a mixing glass over ice and stir. Strain into a chilled cocktail glass and serve.

Shanghai Gin Fizz

10.8% ALC/VOL • 1.8 STD DRINKS

20ml (⅔ fl oz) Gin
20ml (⅔ fl oz) Bénédictine
20ml (⅔ fl oz) Yellow Chartreuse
20ml (⅔ fl oz) Fresh Lemon Juice
3 teaspoons Caster Sugar
120ml (4 fl oz) Soda Water
Maraschino Cherry
Slice of Lemon

Pour Gin, Bénédictine, Chartreuse and juice into a cocktail shaker over ice then add sugar. Shake and strain into a highball glass over ice. Add soda and stir gently. Garnish with a cherry and slice of lemon then serve with a swizzle stick.

Gin Thing

13.5% ALC/VOL • 1.8 STD DRINKS

This drink is also known as *Fog Horn, p 54.*

Western Sling

11.7% ALC/VOL • 2 STD DRINKS

60ml (2 fl oz) Gin
15ml (½ fl oz) Cherry Brandy
5ml (1/6 fl oz) Grenadine
90ml (3 fl oz) Pineapple Juice
30ml (1 fl oz) Fresh Lemon Juice
20ml (⅔ fl oz) Sugar Syrup
Maraschino Cherry
Slice of Lemon
Slice of Orange

Pour Gin, Brandy, Grenadine, juices and sugar into a cocktail shaker over ice. Shake and strain into a highball glass over ice. Garnish with a cherry, slice of lemon and orange then serve with a straw.

Greenback

27.1% ALC/VOL • 1.5 STD DRINKS

This drink is also known as *Green Demon, p 77.*

Chaos Calmer

14.8% ALC/VOL • 1.5 STD DRINKS

45ml (1½ fl oz) Plymouth Gin
8ml (¼ fl oz) Triple Sec
5ml (1/6 fl oz) Grenadine
45ml (1½ fl oz) Fresh Orange Juice
23ml (¾ fl oz) Fresh Lime Juice
Slice of Orange
Strawberry

Pour Gin, Triple Sec, Grenadine and juices into a cocktail shaker over cracked ice. Shake and pour into a chilled old-fashioned glass. Garnish with a slice of orange and a strawberry then serve.

Atta Boy Cocktail

29.1% ALC/VOL • 2.2 STD DRINKS

60ml (2 fl oz) Dry Gin
30ml (1 fl oz) Dry Vermouth
5ml (1/6 fl oz) Grenadine

Pour ingredients into a mixing glass over ice and stir. Strain into a chilled cocktail glass and serve.

Widow with a Secret

29.4% ALC/VOL • 2.1 STD DRINKS

45ml (1½ fl oz) Gin
30ml (1 fl oz) Sweet Vermouth
5ml (1/6 fl oz) Bénédictine
5ml (1/6 fl oz) Campari
5ml (1/6 fl oz) Pernod
2 dashes Orange Bitters
Maraschino Cherry

Pour Gin, Vermouth, Bénédictine, Campari, Pernod and Bitters into a cocktail shaker over ice. Shake and strain into a chilled cocktail glass. Garnish with a cherry and serve.

Crow's Nest

27.5% ALC/VOL • 1.3 STD DRINKS

30ml (1 fl oz) Gin

30ml (1 fl oz) Sweet Sherry
Wedge of Lemon

Pour Gin and Sherry into an old-fashioned glass over ice then stir. Add a wedge of lemon and serve.

Green Lady

37.3% ALC/VOL • 2.4 STD DRINKS

45ml (1½ fl oz) Dry Gin
15ml (½ fl oz) Green Chartreuse
15ml (½ fl oz) Yellow Chartreuse
8ml (¼ fl oz) Fresh Lime Juice
Slice of Lime
Sprig of Fresh Mint

Pour Gin, Chartreuses and juice into a cocktail shaker over ice. Shake and strain into a chilled cocktail glass. Garnish with a slice of lime and sprig of mint then serve.

Van

30.8% ALC/VOL • 3.3 STD DRINKS

90ml (3 fl oz) Dry Gin
45ml (1½ fl oz) Dry Vermouth
2 dashes Grand Marnier

Pour ingredients into a mixing glass over ice and stir. Strain into a chilled cocktail glass and serve.

Nepean

27.1% ALC/VOL • 1.8 STD DRINKS

60ml (2 fl oz) Gin
15ml (½ fl oz) Fresh Lemon Juice
1 teaspoon Sugar Syrup
3 dashes Soda Water
3 Sprigs of Fresh Mint

Pour Gin, juice and sugar into a cocktail shaker over ice then add 2 sprigs of mint. Shake and strain into a chilled cocktail glass. Add soda – do not stir, then garnish with a sprig of mint and serve.

Deep Sea Cocktail

27.5% ALC/VOL • 1.3 STD DRINKS

30ml (1 fl oz) Dry Gin
30ml (1 fl oz) Dry Vermouth
Dash Anisette
Dash Orange Bitters

Pour ingredients into a mixing glass over ice and stir. Strain into a chilled cocktail glass and serve.

Frozen Orange Blossom

14.8% ALC/VOL • 1.6 STD DRINKS

45ml (1½ fl oz) Dry Gin
15ml (½ fl oz) Orange Curaçao
60ml (2 fl oz) Fresh Orange Juice
15ml (½ fl oz) Fresh Lemon Juice
2 dashes Orange Flower Water
Slice of Orange

Pour Gin, Curaçao, juices and flower water into a blender over cracked ice. Blend and pour into a chilled champagne saucer. Garnish with a slice of orange and serve.

Ulanda

38% ALC/VOL • 4.1 STD DRINKS

90ml (3 fl oz) Dry Gin
45ml (1½ fl oz) Cointreau
Dash Pernod

Pour ingredients into a mixing glass over ice and stir. Strain into a chilled cocktail glass and serve.

Silver

27.4% ALC/VOL • 2 STD DRINKS

45ml (1½ fl oz) Dry Gin
45ml (1½ fl oz) Dry Vermouth
2 dashes Maraschino Liqueur
2 dashes Orange Bitters
Twist of Lemon Peel

Pour Gin, Vermouth, Liqueur and Bitters into a mixing glass over ice. Stir and strain into a chilled cocktail glass. Garnish with lemon peel and serve.

Gin and Pink

10.9% ALC/VOL • 1.8 STD DRINKS

60ml (2 fl oz) Gin
3 dashes Angostura Bitters
150ml (5 fl oz) Tonic Water
Slice of Lemon

Pour Gin and Bitters into a highball glass over ice. Add tonic and stir gently. Garnish with a slice of lemon and serve.

Stratos

31.8% ALC/VOL • 1.7 STD DRINKS

30ml (1 fl oz) Dry Gin
15ml (½ fl oz) Drambuie
15ml (½ fl oz) Dry Vermouth
8ml (¼ fl oz) Banana Liqueur
Maraschino Cherry
Slice of Lemon

Pour Gin, Drambuie, Vermouth and Liqueur into a mixing glass over ice. Stir and strain into a chilled cocktail glass. Garnish with a cherry and slice of lemon then serve.

Queen Elizabeth

33.2% ALC/VOL • 1.8 STD DRINKS

45ml (1½ fl oz) Dry Gin
15ml (½ fl oz) Dry Vermouth
8ml (¼ fl oz) Bénédictine

Pour ingredients into a mixing glass over ice and stir. Strain into a chilled cocktail glass and serve.

Conca de Fuego

29.4% ALC/VOL • 2.8 STD DRINKS

30ml (1 fl oz) Gin
30ml (1 fl oz) Cognac
30ml (1 fl oz) Cointreau

30ml (1 fl oz) Thick Cream
Maraschino Cherry

Pour Gin, Cognac, Cointreau and cream into a cocktail shaker over ice. Shake and strain into a chilled cocktail glass. Garnish with a cherry and serve.

Alone

37.1% ALC/VOL • 1.3 STD DRINKS

30ml (1 fl oz) Dry Gin
15ml (½ fl oz) Grand Marnier
Dash Fresh Lemon Juice
Slice of Lemon

Pour Gin, Grand Marnier and juice into a cocktail shaker over ice. Shake and strain into a chilled cocktail glass. Garnish with a slice of lemon and serve.

Sydney Southerly

9.6% ALC/VOL • 1.9 STD DRINKS

60ml (2 fl oz) Gin
5ml (1/6 fl oz) Cherry Brandy
90ml (3 fl oz) Fresh Orange Juice
90ml (3 fl oz) Ginger Beer
Slice of Orange

Pour Gin, Brandy and juice into a mixing glass over ice. Stir and strain into a collins glass over ice. Add ginger beer and stir gently. Garnish with a slice of orange and serve.

Yale Cocktail

31.6% ALC/VOL • 1.6 STD DRINKS

45ml (1½ fl oz) Gin
15ml (½ fl oz) Dry Vermouth
5ml (1/6 fl oz) Blue Curaçao
Dash Orange Bitters

Pour ingredients into a mixing glass over ice and stir. Strain into a chilled cocktail glass and serve.

Cabaret No.2

36.3% ALC/VOL • 1.5 STD DRINKS

45ml (1½ fl oz) Gin
3 dashes Dry Vermouth
2 dashes Angostura Bitters
Dash Bénédictine
Maraschino Cherry

Pour Gin, Vermouth, Bitters and Bénédictine into a mixing glass over ice. Stir and strain into a chilled cocktail glass. Garnish with a cherry and serve.

Friar Tuck

9.6% ALC/VOL • 1.8 STD DRINKS

30ml (1 fl oz) Dry Gin
30ml (1 fl oz) Yellow Chartreuse
90ml (3 fl oz) Mandarin Juice
90ml (3 fl oz) Dry Ginger Ale

Pour Gin, Chartreuse and juice into a cocktail shaker over ice. Shake and strain into a highball glass over ice. Add Ginger Ale – do not stir, then serve with a swizzle stick.

South Pacific

14.5% ALC/VOL • 1.8 STD DRINKS

30ml (1 fl oz) Gin
20ml (⅔ fl oz) Blue Curaçao
20ml (⅔ fl oz) Galliano
90ml (3 fl oz) Lemonade
Slice of Lemon

Pour Gin and Galliano into a mixing glass over ice. Stir and strain into a highball glass over ice. Add lemonade and stir gently then add Curaçao by pouring into centre of drink – do not stir. Garnish with a slice of lemon and serve.

Lady Finger

33.4% ALC/VOL • 2.4 STD DRINKS

45ml (1½ fl oz) Gin
23ml (¾ fl oz) Cherry Brandy
23ml (¾ fl oz) Kirsch

Pour ingredients into a mixing glass over ice and stir. Strain into a chilled cocktail glass and serve.

Kup's Indispensable

28.5% ALC/VOL • 2.4 STD DRINKS

60ml (2 fl oz) Dry Gin
30ml (1 fl oz) Dry Vermouth
15ml (½ fl oz) Sweet Vermouth
Dash Angostura Bitters
Twist of Orange Peel

Pour Gin, Vermouths and Bitters into a mixing glass over ice. Stir and strain into a chilled cocktail glass. Garnish with orange peel and serve.

Emerson

23.6% ALC/VOL • 1.8 STD DRINKS

45ml (1½ fl oz) Gin
30ml (1 fl oz) Sweet Vermouth
5ml (1/6 fl oz) Maraschino Liqueur
15ml (½ fl oz) Fresh Lime Juice

Pour ingredients into a cocktail shaker over ice and shake. Strain into a chilled cocktail glass and serve.

Roselyn Cocktail

29.3% ALC/VOL • 1.6 STD DRINKS

45ml (1½ fl oz) Dry Gin
23ml (¾ fl oz) Dry Vermouth
3 dashes Grenadine
Twist of Lemon Peel

Pour Gin, Vermouth and Grenadine into a mixing glass over ice. Stir and strain into a chilled cocktail glass. Garnish with lemon peel and serve.

Orange Oasis

7.5% ALC/VOL • 1.6 STD DRINKS

45ml (1½ fl oz) Gin
15ml (½ fl oz) Cherry Brandy

120ml (4 fl oz) Fresh
Orange Juice
90ml (3 fl oz) Dry Ginger Ale

Pour Gin, Brandy and juice into a cocktail shaker over ice. Shake and strain into a highball glass over ice. Add Ginger Ale, stir gently and serve.

Sakula

10% ALC/VOL • 0.9 STD DRINKS

30ml (1 fl oz) Dry Gin
60ml (2 fl oz) Fresh
Lemon Juice
20ml (⅔ fl oz) Sugar Syrup
Dash Egg White
Maraschino Cherry

Pour Gin, juice, sugar and egg white into a cocktail shaker over ice. Shake and strain into a chilled cocktail glass. Garnish with a cherry and serve.

Bronx Terrace

30% ALC/VOL • 1.1 STD DRINKS

30ml (1 fl oz) Gin
15ml (½ fl oz) Dry Vermouth
Dash Lime Syrup
Maraschino Cherry

Pour Gin, Vermouth and syrup into a mixing glass over ice. Stir and strain into a chilled cocktail glass. Garnish with a cherry and serve.

Delmonico

28% ALC/VOL • 1.5 STD DRINKS

23ml (¾ fl oz) Dry Gin
15ml (½ fl oz) Brandy
15ml (½ fl oz) Dry Vermouth
15ml (½ fl oz) Sweet Vermouth
Twist of Lemon Peel

Pour Gin, Brandy and Vermouths into a mixing glass over ice. Stir and strain into a chilled cocktail glass. Add lemon peel and serve.

Antonio

32.8% ALC/VOL • 2.3 STD DRINKS

30ml (1 fl oz) Dry Gin
30ml (1 fl oz) Brandy
15ml (½ fl oz) Maraschino
Liqueur
15ml (½ fl oz) White Crème De
Menthe

Pour ingredients into a cocktail shaker over ice and shake. Strain into a chilled cocktail glass and serve.

Visitor's Treat

23% ALC/VOL • 2.1 STD DRINKS

30ml (1 fl oz) Dry Gin
30ml (1 fl oz) Banana Liqueur
23ml (¾ fl oz) Cointreau
30ml (1 fl oz) Mandarin Juice
1 teaspoon Egg White

Pour ingredients into a cocktail shaker over ice and shake. Strain into a chilled cocktail glass and serve.

Fleet Street

29.1% ALC/VOL • 1.7 STD DRINKS

45ml (1½ fl oz) Gin
15ml (½ fl oz) Sweet Vermouth
5ml (⅙ fl oz) Cointreau
5ml (⅙ fl oz) Dry Vermouth
5ml (⅙ fl oz) Fresh
Lemon Juice

Pour ingredients into a cocktail shaker over ice and shake. Strain into a chilled cocktail glass and serve.

Gin Mint Fix

24.6% ALC/VOL • 1.8 STD DRINKS

60ml (2 fl oz) Gin
5ml (⅙ fl oz) White Crème De
Menthe
15ml (½ fl oz) Fresh
Lemon Juice
10ml (⅓ fl oz) Spring Water
1 teaspoon Sugar Syrup
2 Fresh Mint Leaves

Pour Gin, Crème De Menthe, juice, water and sugar into an old-fashioned glass filled with crushed ice. Add more crushed ice to fill glass and stir. Float mint leaves on top and serve.

Spring Feeling Cocktail

32.3% ALC/VOL • 1.5 STD DRINKS

30ml (1 fl oz) Dry Gin
15ml (½ fl oz) Green
Chartreuse
15ml (½ fl oz) Fresh
Lemon Juice

Pour ingredients into a cocktail shaker over ice and shake. Strain into a chilled cocktail glass and serve.

Apricot Anisette Collins

13% ALC/VOL • 1.8 STD DRINKS

45ml (1½ fl oz) Gin
15ml (½ fl oz) Apricot Brandy
8ml (¼ fl oz) Anisette
15ml (½ fl oz) Fresh
Lemon Juice
90ml (3 fl oz) Soda Water
Slice of Lemon

Pour Gin, Brandy, Anisette and juice into a cocktail shaker over ice. Shake and strain into a collins glass over ice. Add soda and stir gently. Garnish with a slice of lemon and serve.

Palm Beach Cocktail

29.3% ALC/VOL • 1.4 STD DRINKS

45ml (1½ fl oz) Dry Gin
8ml (¼ fl oz) Sweet Vermouth
8ml (¼ fl oz) Grapefruit Juice

Pour ingredients into a cocktail shaker over ice and shake. Strain into a chilled cocktail glass and serve.

Bermuda Bouquet

16.6% ALC/VOL • 1.9 STD DRINKS

45ml (1½ fl oz) Gin
30ml (1 fl oz) Apricot Brandy
2 dashes Cointreau
5ml (1/6 fl oz) Grenadine
45ml (1½ fl oz) Fresh Orange Juice
15ml (½ fl oz) Fresh Lemon Juice
1 teaspoon Sugar Syrup

Pour ingredients into a cocktail shaker over ice and shake. Strain into a highball glass over ice and serve.

Cornell

22.3% ALC/VOL • 1.4 STD DRINKS

45ml (1½ fl oz) Dry Gin
3 dashes Maraschino Liqueur
White of 1 Egg

Pour ingredients into a cocktail shaker over ice and shake. Strain into a chilled cocktail glass and serve.

Lord Suffolk

32.6% ALC/VOL • 2.7 STD DRINKS

60ml (2 fl oz) Dry Gin
15ml (½ fl oz) Cointreau
15ml (½ fl oz) Maraschino Liqueur
15ml (½ fl oz) Sweet Vermouth
Twist of Lemon Peel

Pour Gin, Cointreau, Liqueur and Vermouth into a mixing glass over ice. Stir and strain into a chilled cocktail glass. Garnish with lemon peel and serve.

Absent Friend

17.1% ALC/VOL • 0.9 STD DRINKS

30ml (1 fl oz) Gin
10ml (⅓ fl oz) Grenadine
2 teaspoons Fresh Cream
½ Egg White
Nutmeg

Pour Gin, Grenadine, cream and egg white into a cocktail shaker over ice. Shake and strain into a chilled liqueur glass. Sprinkle nutmeg on top and serve.

Charlie Lindbergh

26.3% ALC/VOL • 2 STD DRINKS

45ml (1½ fl oz) English Gin
45ml (1½ fl oz) Lillet
2 dashes Apricot Brandy
2 dashes Fresh Orange Juice
Twist of Lemon Peel

Pour Gin, Lillet, Brandy and juice into a mixing glass over ice. Stir and strain into a chilled cocktail glass. Twist lemon peel above drink and discard remainder of peel then serve.

Linda

20.1% ALC/VOL • 1.3 STD DRINKS

20ml (⅔ fl oz) Dry Gin
20ml (⅔ fl oz) Banana Liqueur
20ml (⅔ fl oz) Crème De Cassis
20ml (⅔ fl oz) Fresh Lemon Juice

Pour ingredients into a cocktail shaker over ice and shake. Strain into a chilled cocktail glass and serve.

Dubarry Cocktail

30.7% ALC/VOL • 1.7 STD DRINKS

45ml (1½ fl oz) Gin
23ml (¾ fl oz) Dry Vermouth
3 dashes Anisette
Dash Angostura Bitters
Slice of Orange

Pour Gin, Vermouth, Anisette and Bitters into a mixing glass over ice. Stir and strain into a chilled cocktail glass. Garnish with a slice of orange and serve.

Forty Eight

27.5% ALC/VOL • 1.6 STD DRINKS

30ml (1 fl oz) Dry Gin
15ml (½ fl oz) Apricot Brandy
15ml (½ fl oz) Dry Vermouth
15ml (½ fl oz) Orange Curaçao
Dash Fresh Lemon Juice

Pour ingredients into a cocktail shaker over ice and shake. Strain into a chilled cocktail glass and serve.

Bombay Sunset

19.3% ALC/VOL • 1.7 STD DRINKS

53ml (1¾ fl oz) Gin
5ml (1/6 fl oz) Amaretto
20ml (⅔ fl oz) Grenadine
23ml (¾ fl oz) Pineapple Juice
1½ teaspoons Sugar Syrup

Pour Gin, Amaretto, juice and sugar into a blender over crushed ice. Blend and pour into a chilled highball glass. Layer Grenadine on top and serve.

Many Ann

20% ALC/VOL • 1.9 STD DRINKS

45ml (1½ fl oz) Dry Gin
45ml (1½ fl oz) Dubonnet
2 dashes Curaçao
30ml (1 fl oz) Fresh Lemon Juice

Pour ingredients into a cocktail shaker over ice and shake. Strain into a chilled cocktail glass and serve.

Hoffman House Fizz

16.4% ALC/VOL • 2.7 STD DRINKS

90ml (3 fl oz) Dry Gin
2 dashes Maraschino Liqueur
15ml (½ fl oz) Fresh Lemon Juice
1 teaspoon Fresh Cream
1 teaspoon Caster Sugar
90ml (3 fl oz) Soda Water

Pour Gin, Liqueur, juice and cream into a cocktail shaker over ice then add sugar. Shake and strain into a chilled highball glass. Add soda, stir gently and serve.

Polo Cocktail

18.5% ALC/VOL • 0.9 STD DRINKS

30ml (1 fl oz) Gin
15ml (½ fl oz) Fresh Lemon Juice
15ml (½ fl oz) Fresh Orange Juice

Pour ingredients into a cocktail shaker over ice and shake. Strain into a chilled cocktail glass and serve.

Slow Gin and Tonic

10.4% ALC/VOL • 1.9 STD DRINKS

45ml (1½ fl oz) Gin
30ml (1 fl oz) Sloe Gin
10ml (⅓ fl oz) Fresh Lemon Juice
150ml (5 fl oz) Tonic Water
Slice of Lemon

Pour Gins and juice into a mixing glass over ice. Stir and strain into a highball glass over ice. Add tonic and stir gently. Garnish with a slice of lemon and serve.

Dolly O'Dare

27.2% ALC/VOL • 1.4 STD DRINKS

30ml (1 fl oz) Dry Gin
30ml (1 fl oz) Dry Vermouth
5ml (1/6 fl oz) Apricot Brandy
Twist of Orange Peel

Pour Gin, Vermouth and Brandy into a mixing glass over ice. Stir and strain into a chilled cocktail glass. Twist orange peel above drink and discard remainder of peel then serve.

Major Bailey

31.7% ALC/VOL • 1.8 STD DRINKS

60ml (2 fl oz) Gin
5ml (1/6 fl oz) Fresh Lemon Juice
5ml (1/6 fl oz) Fresh Lime Juice
Maraschino Cherry
2 Sprigs of Fresh Mint

Pour Gin and juices into a cocktail glass over crushed ice. Add a sprig of mint and stir. Garnish with a cherry and sprig of mint then serve.

Webster Cocktail

23% ALC/VOL • 1.2 STD DRINKS

30ml (1 fl oz) Dry Gin
15ml (½ fl oz) Dry Vermouth
8ml (¼ fl oz) Apricot Brandy
15ml (½ fl oz) Fresh Lime Juice

Pour ingredients into a cocktail shaker over ice and shake. Strain into a chilled cocktail glass and serve.

Captain's Table

11.3% ALC/VOL • 2.1 STD DRINKS

60ml (2 fl oz) Gin
15ml (½ fl oz) Campari
5ml (1/6 fl oz) Grenadine
30ml (1 fl oz) Fresh Orange Juice
120ml (4 fl oz) Dry Ginger Ale
Maraschino Cherry

Pour Gin, Campari, Grenadine and juice into a cocktail shaker over ice. Shake and strain into a highball glass over ice. Add Ginger Ale and stir gently. Garnish with a cherry and serve.

Alexander's Big Brother

28.9% ALC/VOL • 2.1 STD DRINKS

60ml (2 fl oz) Dry Gin
15ml (½ fl oz) Blue Curaçao
15ml (½ fl oz) Thick Cream

Pour ingredients into a cocktail shaker over ice and shake. Strain into a chilled cocktail glass and serve.

Strawberry Swig

29.5% ALC/VOL • 1.6 STD DRINKS

45ml (1½ fl oz) Gin
15ml (½ fl oz) Strawberry Liqueur
Dash Orange Bitters
8ml (¼ fl oz) Fresh Lime Juice
Slice of Lime

Pour Gin, Liqueur, Bitters and juice into a cocktail shaker over ice. Shake and strain into an old-fashioned glass over ice. Garnish with a slice of lime and serve.

Tidbit

12.4% ALC/VOL • 0.9 STD DRINKS

30ml (1 fl oz) Dry Gin
Dash Dry Sherry
2 scoops Vanilla Ice Cream

Pour Gin and Sherry into a blender without ice then add ice cream. Blend until smooth and pour into a chilled highball glass then serve.

Blue Bird

37.5% ALC/VOL • 1.8 STD DRINKS

45ml (1½ fl oz) Gin
15ml (½ fl oz) Cointreau
Dash Orange Bitters
Maraschino Cherry
Twist of Lemon Peel

Pour Gin, Cointreau and Bitters into a mixing glass over ice. Stir and strain into a chilled cocktail glass. Garnish with a cherry and lemon peel then serve.

Carine

28.6% ALC/VOL • 1.5 STD DRINKS

30ml (1 fl oz) Gin
15ml (½ fl oz) Dubonnet
15ml (½ fl oz) Mandarine Napoleon
8ml (¼ fl oz) Fresh Lemon Juice

Pour ingredients into a cocktail shaker over ice and shake. Strain into a chilled cocktail glass and serve.

Gin-Cassis Fizz

11.9% ALC/VOL • 2.4 STD DRINKS

75ml (2½ fl oz) Gin
15ml (½ fl oz) Crème De Cassis
45ml (1½ fl oz) Fresh Lemon Juice
1 teaspoon Caster Sugar
120ml (4 fl oz) Soda Water

Pour Gin and juice into a cocktail shaker over ice then add sugar. Shake and strain into a highball glass over ice. Add soda and stir gently. Add Cassis by pouring into centre of drink – do not stir, then serve.

Grand Passion

21.3% ALC/VOL • 1.8 STD DRINKS

60ml (2 fl oz) Gin
Dash Angostura Bitters
30ml (1 fl oz) Passion-Fruit Juice
15ml (½ fl oz) Fresh Lemon Juice

Pour ingredients into a cocktail shaker over ice and shake. Strain into a chilled cocktail glass and serve.

Prohibition Cocktail

21.7% ALC/VOL • 2.2 STD DRINKS

60ml (2 fl oz) Plymouth Gin
60ml (2 fl oz) Lillet
3 dashes Apricot Brandy
5ml (1/6 fl oz) Fresh Orange Juice
Twist of Lemon Peel

Pour Gin, Lillet, Brandy and juice into a cocktail shaker over ice. Shake and strain into a chilled cocktail glass. Twist lemon peel above drink and discard remainder of peel then serve.

Harry's

29.8% ALC/VOL • 3.2 STD DRINKS

90ml (3 fl oz) Dry Gin
45ml (1½ fl oz) Sweet Vermouth
Dash Pernod
2 Sprigs of Fresh Mint

Pour Gin, Vermouth and Pernod into a cocktail shaker over ice then add a sprig of mint. Shake and strain into a chilled cocktail glass. Garnish with a sprig of mint and serve.

Venetian Sunset

31.4% ALC/VOL • 1.9 STD DRINKS

30ml (1 fl oz) Dry Gin
15ml (½ fl oz) Campari
15ml (½ fl oz) Dry Vermouth
15ml (½ fl oz) Grand Marnier
Maraschino Cherry

Pour Gin, Campari, Vermouth and Grand Marnier into a mixing glass over ice. Stir and strain into a chilled cocktail glass. Garnish with a cherry and serve.

Stanley Cocktail

26.1% ALC/VOL • 0.9 STD DRINKS

23ml (¾ fl oz) Dry Gin
8ml (¼ fl oz) Light Rum
5ml (1/6 fl oz) Grenadine
8ml (¼ fl oz) Fresh Lemon Juice

Pour ingredients into a cocktail shaker over ice and shake. Strain into a chilled cocktail glass and serve.

The Filby

29% ALC/VOL • 1.7 STD DRINKS

30ml (1 fl oz) Dry Gin
15ml (½ fl oz) Amaretto
15ml (½ fl oz) Campari
15ml (½ fl oz) Dry Vermouth
Slice of Orange

Pour Gin, Amaretto, Campari and Vermouth into a mixing glass over ice. Stir and strain into a chilled cocktail glass. Garnish with a slice of orange and serve.

Will Rogers

25.9% ALC/VOL • 1.6 STD DRINKS

45ml (1½ fl oz) Dry Gin
15ml (½ fl oz) Dry Vermouth
Dash Cointreau
15ml (½ fl oz) Fresh Orange Juice

Pour ingredients into a cocktail shaker over ice and shake. Strain into a chilled cocktail glass and serve.

Dundee

33.9% ALC/VOL • 1.8 STD DRINKS

30ml (1 fl oz) Gin
15ml (½ fl oz) Drambuie
15ml (½ fl oz) Scotch Whisky
8ml (¼ fl oz) Fresh Lemon Juice
Twist of Lemon Peel

Pour Gin, Drambuie, Whisky and juice into a cocktail shaker over ice. Shake and strain into an old-fashioned glass over ice. Twist lemon peel above drink and place remainder of peel into drink then serve.

Pink Pussycat

12.6% ALC/VOL • 1.8 STD DRINKS

60ml (2 fl oz) Gin
5ml (1/6 fl oz) Cherry Brandy
120ml (4 fl oz) Pineapple Juice

Pour Gin and juice into a cocktail shaker over ice. Shake and strain into an old-fashioned glass over ice. Add Brandy by pouring into centre of drink – do not stir, then serve.

Right On

27.4% ALC/VOL • 1.6 STD DRINKS

30ml (1 fl oz) Gin
15ml (½ fl oz) Apricot Brandy
15ml (½ fl oz) Cointreau
15ml (½ fl oz) Fresh Lemon Juice
Twist of Lemon Peel

Pour Gin, Brandy, Cointreau and juice into a cocktail shaker over ice. Shake and strain into a chilled cocktail glass. Twist lemon peel above drink and place remainder of peel into drink then serve.

Peter Pan Cocktail

18.5% ALC/VOL • 1 STD DRINK

23ml (¾ fl oz) Dry Gin
23ml (¾ fl oz) Dry Vermouth
2 dashes Orange Bitters
23ml (¾ fl oz) Fresh Orange Juice

Pour ingredients into a cocktail shaker over ice and shake. Strain into a chilled cocktail glass and serve.

Snake in the Grass

23.8% ALC/VOL • 1.5 STD DRINKS

20ml (⅔ fl oz) Dry Gin
20ml (⅔ fl oz) Cointreau
20ml (⅔ fl oz) Dry Vermouth
20ml (⅔ fl oz) Fresh Lemon Juice
Twist of Lemon Peel

Pour Gin, Cointreau, Vermouth and juice into a cocktail shaker over ice. Shake and strain into a chilled cocktail glass. Garnish with lemon peel and serve.

Grenadine Fizz

12.7% ALC/VOL • 1.8 STD DRINKS

60ml (2 fl oz) Gin
10ml (⅓ fl oz) Grenadine
15ml (½ fl oz) Fresh Lemon Juice
90ml (3 fl oz) Soda Water

Pour Gin, Grenadine and juice into a cocktail shaker over ice. Shake and strain into a highball glass over ice. Add soda, stir gently and serve.

Pollyanna

25.2% ALC/VOL • 1.5 STD DRINKS

45ml (1½ fl oz) Gin
15ml (½ fl oz) Sweet Vermouth
15ml (½ fl oz) Grenadine
3 Slices of Orange
3 Slices of Pineapple

Pour Gin, Vermouth and Grenadine into a cocktail shaker over ice. Add slices of orange and pineapple. Shake and strain into a chilled cocktail glass then serve.

Dempsey

37.7% ALC/VOL • 2.8 STD DRINKS

45ml (1½ fl oz) Dry Gin
45ml (1½ fl oz) Applejack
2 dashes Pernod
2 dashes Grenadine

Pour ingredients into a cocktail shaker over ice and shake. Strain into a cocktail glass over cracked ice and serve.

Gin and Ginger Cooler

10.9% ALC/VOL • 1.7 STD DRINKS

30ml (1 fl oz) Gin
30ml (1 fl oz) Ginger Brandy
15ml (½ fl oz) Fresh Lemon Juice
1 teaspoon Sugar Syrup
120ml (4 fl oz) Dry Ginger Ale
Slice of Lemon

Pour Gin, Brandy, juice and sugar into a cocktail shaker over ice. Shake and strain into a collins glass over ice. Add Ginger Ale and stir gently. Garnish with a slice of lemon and serve.

Froth Blower

20.8% ALC/VOL • 1.3 STD DRINKS

45ml (1½ fl oz) English Gin
5ml (1/6 fl oz) Grenadine
White of 1 Egg

Pour ingredients into a cocktail shaker over ice and shake. Strain into a chilled cocktail glass and serve.

Pirouetter

21.4% ALC/VOL • 1.4 STD DRINKS

30ml (1 fl oz) Gin
15ml (½ fl oz) Grand Marnier
30ml (1 fl oz) Fresh Orange Juice
5ml (1/6 fl oz) Fresh Lemon Juice
Twist of Orange Peel

Pour Gin, Grand Marnier and juices into a cocktail shaker over ice. Shake and strain into a chilled cocktail glass. Twist orange peel above drink and place remainder of peel into drink then serve.

Crimson Sunset

28.3% ALC/VOL • 2 STD DRINKS

60ml (2 fl oz) Dry Gin

15ml (½ fl oz) Tawny Port
3 dashes Grenadine
10ml (⅓ fl oz) Fresh
Lemon Juice

Pour Gin and juice into a cocktail shaker over ice. Shake and strain into a chilled cocktail glass. Add Grenadine by pouring into centre of drink - do not stir, then layer Port on top and serve.

Aviation

29.3% ALC/VOL • 1.9 STD DRINKS

60ml (2 fl oz) Gin
8ml (¼ fl oz) Maraschino
Liqueur
15ml (½ fl oz) Fresh
Lemon Juice
Maraschino Cherry
Slice of Orange

Pour Gin, Liqueur and juice into a cocktail shaker over ice. Shake and strain into a chilled cocktail glass. Garnish with a cherry and slice of orange then serve.

Beautiful Sunrise

33.5% ALC/VOL • 2.4 STD DRINKS

30ml (1 fl oz) Dry Gin
30ml (1 fl oz) Brandy
15ml (½ fl oz) Anisette
15ml (½ fl oz) White Crème
De Cacao

Pour ingredients into a cocktail shaker over ice and shake. Strain into a chilled cocktail glass and serve.

Baron Cocktail

32.7% ALC/VOL • 1.8 STD DRINKS

45ml (1½ fl oz) Gin
15ml (½ fl oz) Dry Vermouth
8ml (¼ fl oz) Cointreau
2 dashes Sweet Vermouth
Twist of Lemon Peel

Pour Gin, Vermouths and Cointreau into a mixing glass over ice. Stir and strain into a chilled cocktail glass. Garnish with lemon peel and serve.

Gin Southern

29.2% ALC/VOL • 1.8 STD DRINKS

45ml (1½ fl oz) Gin
15ml (½ fl oz) Southern
Comfort
8ml (¼ fl oz) Grapefruit Juice
8ml (¼ fl oz) Fresh
Lemon Juice

Pour ingredients into a cocktail shaker over ice and shake. Strain into a chilled cocktail glass and serve.

Nicky

8.6% ALC/VOL • 1.5 STD DRINKS

30ml (1 fl oz) Gin
30ml (1 fl oz) Apricot Brandy
Dash Light Rum
3 dashes Fresh Lemon Juice
150ml (5 fl oz) Mineral Water

Pour Gin, Brandy, Rum and juice into a cocktail shaker over ice. Shake and strain into a highball glass over ice. Add mineral water, stir gently and serve.

Leap Year

30.6% ALC/VOL • 2.3 STD DRINKS

45ml (1½ fl oz) Gin
23ml (¾ fl oz) Grand Marnier
23ml (¾ fl oz) Sweet Vermouth
5ml (1/6 fl oz) Fresh
Lemon Juice

Pour ingredients into a cocktail shaker over ice and shake. Strain into an old-fashioned glass over ice and serve.

Saint Paul

11.3% ALC/VOL • 2.7 STD DRINKS

45ml (1½ fl oz) Gin
45ml (1½ fl oz) Bacardi
Dash Angostura Bitters
210ml (7 fl oz) Bitter-Lemon
Soda

Pour Gin and Bacardi into a chilled tall glass over a few ice cubes. Add soda and stir gently. Add Bitters by pouring gently over the floating ice cubes and serve.

Greenham's Grotto

30.3% ALC/VOL • 2.6 STD DRINKS

60ml (2 fl oz) Gin
30ml (1 fl oz) Brandy
10ml (⅓ fl oz) Fresh
Lemon Juice
2 teaspoons Sugar Syrup

Pour ingredients into a cocktail shaker over ice and shake. Strain into an old-fashioned glass over ice and serve.

Royalty Fizz

9.8% ALC/VOL • 1.8 STD DRINKS

60ml (2 fl oz) Dry Gin
3 dashes Blue Curaçao
30ml (1 fl oz) Fresh
Lemon Juice
1 teaspoon Caster Sugar
1 Fresh Egg
90ml (3 fl oz) Soda Water

Pour Gin, Curaçao, juice and egg into a cocktail shaker over ice then add sugar. Shake and strain into a highball glass over ice. Add soda, stir gently and serve.

London Buck

13.7% ALC/VOL • 2.2 STD DRINKS

75ml (2½ fl oz) Gin
120ml (4 fl oz) Dry Ginger Ale
¼ Fresh Lemon

Pour Gin into a highball glass over ice and twist ¼ lemon above drink to release juice. Add spent shell and stir. Add Ginger Ale, stir gently and serve.

Pink Cream Fizz

8.9% ALC/VOL • 1.8 STD DRINKS

60ml (2 fl oz) Gin
5ml (1/6 fl oz) Grenadine
30ml (1 fl oz) Fresh Lemon Juice
30ml (1 fl oz) Fresh Cream
1 teaspoon Caster Sugar
120ml (4 fl oz) Soda Water

Pour Gin, Grenadine, juice and cream into a cocktail shaker over ice then add sugar. Shake and strain into a highball glass over ice. Add soda, stir gently and serve.

Wild Oat

36.6% ALC/VOL • 3.5 STD DRINKS

90ml (3 fl oz) Gin
30ml (1 fl oz) Kirsch
Dash Apricot Brandy
Dash Fresh Lemon Juice

Pour ingredients into a cocktail shaker over ice and shake. Strain into a chilled cocktail glass and serve.

Fairbanks

25.5% ALC/VOL • 1.9 STD DRINKS

30ml (1 fl oz) Dry Gin
30ml (1 fl oz) Apricot Brandy
30ml (1 fl oz) Dry Vermouth
Dash Grenadine
Dash Fresh Lemon Juice
Maraschino Cherry

Pour Gin, Brandy, Vermouth, Grenadine and juice into a mixing glass over ice. Stir and strain into an old-fashioned glass over ice. Garnish with a cherry and serve.

Tin Wedding

29.6% ALC/VOL • 2.1 STD DRINKS

30ml (1 fl oz) Gin
30ml (1 fl oz) Brandy
30ml (1 fl oz) Sweet Vermouth
2 dashes Orange Bitters

Pour ingredients into a cocktail shaker over ice and shake. Strain into a chilled cocktail glass and serve.

Southern Gin Cocktail

36.8% ALC/VOL • 1.9 STD DRINKS

60ml (2 fl oz) Dry Gin
3 dashes Cointreau
2 dashes Orange Bitters
Twist of Lemon Peel

Pour Gin, Cointreau and Bitters into a mixing glass over ice. Stir and strain into a chilled cocktail glass. Garnish with lemon peel and serve.

Remmsen Cooler

9.5% ALC/VOL • 1.7 STD DRINKS

60ml (2 fl oz) Gin
23ml (¾ fl oz) Sugar Syrup
150ml (5 fl oz) Soda Water
Slice of Lemon

Pour Gin and sugar into a collins glass over ice then stir. Add soda and stir gently. Garnish with a slice of lemon and serve.

Pink Fingers

27.7% ALC/VOL • 3 STD DRINKS

45ml (1½ fl oz) Gin
45ml (1½ fl oz) Blackberry Brandy
23ml (¾ fl oz) Banana Liqueur
23ml (¾ fl oz) Thick Cream
Cherry
Slice of Banana

Pour Gin, Brandy, Liqueur and cream into a cocktail shaker over ice. Shake and strain into a chilled champagne saucer. Garnish with a cherry and slice of banana then serve.

Prince's Smile

33.7% ALC/VOL • 1.6 STD DRINKS

30ml (1 fl oz) Dry Gin
15ml (½ fl oz) Applejack
15ml (½ fl oz) Apricot Brandy
Dash Fresh Lemon Juice

Pour ingredients into a cocktail shaker over ice and shake. Strain into a chilled cocktail glass and serve.

Fibber McGee

25.7% ALC/VOL • 1.6 STD DRINKS

45ml (1½ fl oz) Dry Gin
15ml (½ fl oz) Sweet Vermouth
2 dashes Angostura Bitters
15ml (½ fl oz) Grapefruit Juice
Twist of Lemon Peel

Pour Gin, Vermouth, Bitters and juice into a mixing glass over ice. Stir and strain into a chilled cocktail glass. Garnish with lemon peel and serve.

St. Lô

28.3% ALC/VOL • 1.8 STD DRINKS

45ml (1½ fl oz) Gin
15ml (½ fl oz) Calvados
15ml (½ fl oz) Fresh Lemon Juice
1 teaspoon Sugar Syrup

Pour ingredients into a cocktail shaker over ice and shake. Strain into a chilled cocktail glass and serve.

Velour Frappé

12% ALC/VOL • 1.8 STD DRINKS

45ml (1½ fl oz) Gin
30ml (1 fl oz) Green Crème De Menthe

120ml (4 fl oz) Lemonade
Green Cherry
Sprig of Fresh Mint

Pour Gin and Crème De Menthe into a highball glass filled with crushed ice. Add lemonade and stir gently. Garnish with a cherry and sprig of mint then serve with 2 straws.

Royal Romance

28% ALC/VOL • 1.3 STD DRINKS

30ml (1 fl oz) Dry Gin
15ml (½ fl oz) Grand Marnier
Dash Grenadine
15ml (½ fl oz) Passion-Fruit Juice

Pour ingredients into a cocktail shaker over ice and shake. Strain into a chilled cocktail glass and serve.

Million Dollar

19% ALC/VOL • 1.5 STD DRINKS

45ml (1½ fl oz) Dry Gin
15ml (½ fl oz) Sweet Vermouth
5ml (1/6 fl oz) Grenadine
5ml (1/6 fl oz) Pineapple Juice
White of 1 Egg

Pour ingredients into a cocktail shaker over ice and shake. Strain into a chilled cocktail glass and serve.

Coconut Gin

24.6% ALC/VOL • 1.5 STD DRINKS

45ml (1½ fl oz) Gin
8ml (¼ fl oz) Maraschino Liqueur
15ml (½ fl oz) Fresh Lemon Juice
1½ teaspoons Coconut Cream

Prepare a cocktail glass with a sugar frosted rim. Pour ingredients into a cocktail shaker over ice and shake. Strain into prepared glass and serve.

Fun and Games

23.8% ALC/VOL • 1.1 STD DRINKS

30ml (1 fl oz) Dry Gin
15ml (½ fl oz) Crème De Cassis
Dash Angostura Bitters
15ml (½ fl oz) Fresh Lemon Juice
Slice of Lemon

Pour Gin, Cassis, Bitters and juice into a cocktail shaker over ice. Shake and strain into a chilled cocktail glass. Garnish with a slice of lemon and serve.

American Fizz

30.3% ALC/VOL • 2.6 STD DRINKS

45ml (1½ fl oz) Gin
45ml (1½ fl oz) Brandy
5ml (1/6 fl oz) Grenadine
15ml (½ fl oz) Fresh Lemon Juice

Pour ingredients into a cocktail shaker over ice and shake. Strain into a chilled cocktail glass and serve.

European

25.6% ALC/VOL • 1.6 STD DRINKS

30ml (1 fl oz) Gin
15ml (½ fl oz) Cream Sherry
15ml (½ fl oz) Dry Vermouth
15ml (½ fl oz) Dubonnet
3 dashes Grand Marnier
Maraschino Cherry

Pour Gin, Sherry, Vermouth, Dubonnet and Grand Marnier into an old-fashioned glass over ice then stir. Garnish with a cherry and serve.

Hornpipe

22.3% ALC/VOL • 1.5 STD DRINKS

45ml (1½ fl oz) Gin
10ml (⅓ fl oz) Cherry Brandy
White of 1 Egg

Pour ingredients into a cocktail shaker over ice and shake. Strain into a chilled cocktail glass and serve.

Papa Yaya

10% ALC/VOL • 1.3 STD DRINKS

45ml (1½ fl oz) Gin
15ml (½ fl oz) Pineapple Juice
8ml (¼ fl oz) Fresh Lime Juice
1½ teaspoons Papaya Syrup
90ml (3 fl oz) Seltzer
Wedge of Lime

Pour Gin, juices and syrup into a cocktail shaker over cracked ice. Shake and pour into a chilled collins glass. Add seltzer and stir gently. Garnish with a wedge of lime and serve.

Army Cocktail

27.5% ALC/VOL • 1.7 STD DRINKS

45ml (1½ fl oz) Gin
30ml (1 fl oz) Sweet Vermouth
2 dashes Grenadine
Twist of Orange Peel

Pour Gin, Vermouth and Grenadine into a cocktail shaker over ice. Shake and strain into a chilled cocktail glass. Garnish with orange peel and serve.

Farmer Giles

30.4% ALC/VOL • 2.2 STD DRINKS

60ml (2 fl oz) Gin
15ml (½ fl oz) Dry Vermouth
15ml (½ fl oz) Sweet Vermouth
2 dashes Angostura Bitters
Slice of Lemon

Pour Gin, Vermouths and Bitters into a mixing glass over ice. Stir and strain into a chilled cocktail glass. Garnish with a slice of lemon and serve.

Archbishop

29.9% ALC/VOL • 2.2 STD DRINKS

60ml (2 fl oz) Gin
30ml (1 fl oz) Green Ginger Wine
5ml (1/6 fl oz) Bénédictine
Slice of Lime

Pour Gin, Wine and Bénédictine into an old-fashioned glass over ice then stir. Add a slice of lime and serve.

Pineapple Hornblower

14% ALC/VOL • 1.4 STD DRINKS

45ml (1½ fl oz) Gin
5ml (1/6 fl oz) Bailey's Irish Cream
45ml (1½ fl oz) Pineapple Juice
15ml (½ fl oz) Fresh Lemon Juice
15ml (½ fl oz) Sugar Syrup

Pour ingredients into a cocktail shaker over ice and shake. Strain into a chilled goblet and serve.

Socko

30.9% ALC/VOL • 1.7 STD DRINKS

45ml (1½ fl oz) English Gin
23ml (¾ fl oz) Dry Vermouth
2 dashes Pernod
Pickled Onion

Pour Gin, Vermouth and Pernod into a cocktail shaker over ice. Shake and strain into a chilled cocktail glass. Garnish with a pickled onion and serve.

Bernardo

33% ALC/VOL • 2.3 STD DRINKS

60ml (2 fl oz) Gin
15ml (½ fl oz) Cointreau
2 dashes Orange Bitters
10ml (⅓ fl oz) Fresh Lemon Juice
Slice of Lemon

Pour Gin, Cointreau, Bitters and juice into a cocktail shaker over ice. Shake and strain into a chilled cocktail glass. Garnish with a slice of lemon and serve.

Pall Mall

23.3% ALC/VOL • 1.4 STD DRINKS

23ml (¾ fl oz) Dry Gin
23ml (¾ fl oz) Dry Vermouth
23ml (¾ fl oz) Sweet Vermouth
5ml (1/6 fl oz) White Crème De Menthe
Dash Orange Bitters

Pour ingredients into a mixing glass over ice and stir. Strain into a chilled cocktail glass and serve.

The Jockey Club

31.8% ALC/VOL • 2.2 STD DRINKS

60ml (2 fl oz) Dry Gin
10ml (⅓ fl oz) Amaretto
5ml (1/6 fl oz) Cointreau
Dash Angostura Bitters
10ml (⅓ fl oz) Fresh Lemon Juice

Pour ingredients into a cocktail shaker over ice and shake. Strain into an old-fashioned glass over ice and serve.

Empire

34.3% ALC/VOL • 1.6 STD DRINKS

30ml (1 fl oz) Dry Gin
15ml (½ fl oz) Applejack
15ml (½ fl oz) Apricot Brandy
Maraschino Cherry

Pour Gin, Applejack and Brandy into a cocktail shaker over ice. Shake and strain into a chilled cocktail glass. Garnish with a cherry and serve.

Bird of Paradise Fizz

9.7% ALC/VOL • 1.6 STD DRINKS

53ml (1¾ fl oz) Gin
10ml (⅓ fl oz) Grenadine
10ml (⅓ fl oz) Peach Nectar
White of 1 Egg
100ml (3⅓ fl oz) Soda Water

Pour Gin, Grenadine, nectar and egg white into a cocktail shaker over ice. Shake and strain into a highball glass over ice. Add soda, stir gently and serve.

Dixie Cocktail

28% ALC/VOL • 2.2 STD DRINKS

45ml (1½ fl oz) Gin
23ml (¾ fl oz) Anisette
23ml (¾ fl oz) Dry Vermouth
23ml (¾ fl oz) Fresh Orange Juice

Pour ingredients into a cocktail shaker over ice and shake. Strain into a chilled cocktail glass and serve.

Oaxaca Jim

18.9% ALC/VOL • 1.8 STD DRINKS

60ml (2 fl oz) Gin
2 dashes Angostura Bitters
30ml (1 fl oz) Grapefruit Juice
30ml (1 fl oz) Fresh Orange Juice
Maraschino Cherry
Slice of Lemon

Pour Gin, Bitters and juices into a cocktail shaker over ice. Shake and strain into an old-fashioned glass over ice. Garnish with a cherry and slice of lemon then serve.

Loud-Hailer

15.9% ALC/VOL • 1 STD DRINK

23ml (¾ fl oz) Dry Gin
23ml (¾ fl oz) Dry Vermouth
Dash Cointreau
5ml (1/6 fl oz) Grenadine
30ml (1 fl oz) Fresh
Orange Juice

Pour ingredients into a cocktail shaker over ice and shake. Strain into a chilled cocktail glass and serve.

Mule's Hind Leg

29.8% ALC/VOL • 1.4 STD DRINKS

15ml (½ fl oz) Gin
15ml (½ fl oz) Applejack
10ml (⅓ fl oz) Apricot Brandy
10ml (⅓ fl oz) Bénédictine
2 teaspoons Maple Syrup

Pour ingredients into a cocktail shaker over ice and shake. Strain into an old-fashioned glass over ice and serve.

Weekender

24.2% ALC/VOL • 2.3 STD DRINKS

30ml (1 fl oz) Dry Gin
30ml (1 fl oz) Dry Vermouth
30ml (1 fl oz) Orange Curaçao
30ml (1 fl oz) Sweet Vermouth
3 dashes Pernod

Pour ingredients into a mixing glass over ice and stir. Strain into a chilled cocktail glass and serve.

Samuri

14.9% ALC/VOL • 1 STD DRINK

30ml (1 fl oz) Gin
8ml (¼ fl oz) Blue Curaçao
30ml (1 fl oz) Passion-
Fruit Juice
4 Cubes of Melon

Pour Gin and juice into a blender over small amount of crushed ice then add cubes of melon. Blend until smooth and pour into a chilled champagne flute. Add Curaçao by pouring over top of drink and allow to run through drink then serve.

Royal No.1

15.4% ALC/VOL • 1.3 STD DRINKS

45ml (1½ fl oz) Gin
15ml (½ fl oz) Fresh
Lemon Juice
½ teaspoon Sugar Syrup
1 Fresh Egg

Pour ingredients into a cocktail shaker over ice and shake. Strain into a chilled cocktail glass and serve.

Root Beer Fizz

30.4% ALC/VOL • 1.8 STD DRINKS

45ml (1½ fl oz) Gin
30ml (1 fl oz) Fresh
Lemon Juice
1 teaspoon Caster Sugar
120ml (4 fl oz) Root Beer
Maraschino Cherry

Pour Gin and juice into a cocktail shaker over ice then add sugar. Shake and strain into a highball glass over ice. Add root beer and stir gently. Garnish with a cherry and serve.

Bull Dog Cooler

19.5% ALC/VOL • 5.4 STD DRINKS

120ml (4 fl oz) Gin
60ml (2 fl oz) Cointreau
120ml (4 fl oz) Fresh
Orange Juice
50ml (1⅔ fl oz) Spring Water
Slice of Orange

Pour Gin, Cointreau and juice into a cocktail shaker over ice. Shake and strain into a chilled collins glass. Add water and stir. Garnish with a slice of orange and serve.

Break the Rules

8.4% ALC/VOL • 1.2 STD DRINKS

20ml (⅔ fl oz) Gin
15ml (½ fl oz) Kiwi Liqueur
15ml (½ fl oz) Midori
10ml (⅓ fl oz) Aperol
120ml (4 fl oz) Fresh
Orange Juice
Slice of Melon
Slice of Orange

Pour Gin, Liqueur, Midori and Aperol into a mixing glass over cracked ice. Stir well and pour into a chilled tall glass. Add juice and stir. Garnish with a slice of melon and orange then serve.

Colony Club

36.6% ALC/VOL • 1.5 STD DRINKS

45ml (1½ fl oz) Gin
5ml (1/6 fl oz) Anisette
2 dashes Angostura Bitters

Pour ingredients into a cocktail shaker over ice and shake. Strain into a chilled cocktail glass and serve.

Silver King

18.2% ALC/VOL • 1.3 STD DRINKS

45ml (1½ fl oz) Gin
2 dashes Orange Bitters
15ml (½ fl oz) Fresh
Lemon Juice
2 dashes Sugar Syrup
White of 1 Egg

Pour ingredients into a cocktail shaker over ice and shake. Strain into a chilled cocktail glass and serve.

V.I.P.

16.3% ALC/VOL • 2.1 STD DRINKS

45ml (1½ fl oz) Dry Gin
30ml (1 fl oz) Pimm's No.1
15ml (½ fl oz) Dry Vermouth
60ml (2 fl oz) Passion-Fruit Juice
15ml (½ fl oz) Fresh Lemon Juice

Pour ingredients into a cocktail shaker over ice and shake. Strain into a chilled goblet and serve.

Wimbledon Cup

13.8% ALC/VOL • 1.5 STD DRINKS

30ml (1 fl oz) Gin
30ml (1 fl oz) Pimm's No.1
30ml (1 fl oz) Mandarin Juice
30ml (1 fl oz) Thick Cream
15ml (½ fl oz) Strawberry Syrup

Pour ingredients into a cocktail shaker over ice and shake. Strain into a chilled champagne saucer and serve.

Palisades Cocktail

21.4% ALC/VOL • 1.6 STD DRINKS

45ml (1½ fl oz) Gin
45ml (1½ fl oz) Cider
2 dashes Angostura Bitters

Pour Gin and Bitters into a mixing glass over ice. Stir and strain into a chilled cocktail glass. Add Cider, stir gently and serve.

Green Dragon Special

29.6% ALC/VOL • 2.9 STD DRINKS

60ml (2 fl oz) Dry Gin
30ml (1 fl oz) Green Crème De Menthe
15ml (½ fl oz) Kümmel
4 dashes Peach Bitters
15ml (½ fl oz) Fresh Lemon Juice

Pour ingredients into a cocktail shaker over ice and shake. Strain into a chilled cocktail glass and serve.

San Sebastian

22.7% ALC/VOL • 1.4 STD DRINKS

30ml (1 fl oz) Dry Gin
8ml (¼ fl oz) Cointreau
8ml (¼ fl oz) Light Rum
15ml (½ fl oz) Grapefruit Juice
15ml (½ fl oz) Fresh Lemon Juice

Pour ingredients into a cocktail shaker over ice and shake. Strain into a chilled cocktail glass and serve.

Painter's Delight

9.5% ALC/VOL • 1.7 STD DRINKS

40ml (1⅓ fl oz) Gin
20ml (⅔ fl oz) Green Curaçao
5ml (⅙ fl oz) Pernod
15ml (½ fl oz) Fresh Lemon Juice
150ml (5 fl oz) Soda Water

Pour Gin, Curaçao, Pernod and juice into a highball glass over ice then stir. Add soda, stir gently and serve.

Cloister

26.1% ALC/VOL • 1.6 STD DRINKS

45ml (1½ fl oz) Gin
8ml (¼ fl oz) Yellow Chartreuse
15ml (½ fl oz) Grapefruit Juice
8ml (¼ fl oz) Fresh Lemon Juice

Pour ingredients into a cocktail shaker over ice and shake. Strain into a chilled cocktail glass and serve.

Cape May

11.2% ALC/VOL • 1.6 STD DRINKS

45ml (1½ fl oz) Gin
15ml (½ fl oz) Cherry Brandy
60ml (2 fl oz) Fresh Orange Juice
60ml (2 fl oz) Dry Ginger Ale
Wedge of Orange

Pour Gin, Brandy and juice into a cocktail shaker over cracked ice. Shake and pour into a chilled collins glass. Add Ginger Ale and stir gently. Garnish with a wedge of orange and serve.

Amsterdam

27.3% ALC/VOL • 1.8 STD DRINKS

45ml (1½ fl oz) Hollands Gin
15ml (½ fl oz) Cointreau
23ml (¾ fl oz) Mandarin Juice

Pour ingredients into a cocktail shaker over cracked ice and shake. Pour into a chilled old-fashioned glass and serve.

Cookie Dough

7.1% ALC/VOL • 1 STD DRINK

20ml (⅔ fl oz) Gin
20ml (⅔ fl oz) White Crème De Cacao
2 dashes Angostura Bitters
100ml (3⅓ fl oz) Fresh Cream
40ml (1⅓ fl oz) Coconut Cream
Grated Chocolate

Pour Gin, Cacao, Bitters and creams into a blender over crushed ice. Blend until smooth and pour into a chilled highball glass. Sprinkle chocolate on top and serve.

Up in the Air

29.4% ALC/VOL • 1.6 STD DRINKS

45ml (1½ fl oz) Dry Gin
15ml (½ fl oz) Maraschino Liqueur
10ml (⅓ fl oz) Fresh Lemon Juice

Pour ingredients into a cocktail shaker over ice and shake. Strain into a chilled cocktail glass and serve.

Boxcar

25.3% ALC/VOL • 2.3 STD DRINKS

45ml (1½ fl oz) Gin
30ml (1 fl oz) Cointreau
3 dashes Grenadine
5ml (1/6 fl oz) Fresh Lemon Juice
White of 1 Egg

Pour ingredients into a cocktail shaker over ice and shake. Strain into a chilled sour glass and serve.

Sunshine No.2

29.8% ALC/VOL • 3.2 STD DRINKS

90ml (3 fl oz) Dry Gin
45ml (1½ fl oz) Sweet Vermouth
Dash Angostura Bitters
Twist of Orange Peel

Pour Gin, Vermouth and Bitters into a mixing glass over an ice cube. Stir and strain into a chilled cocktail glass. Twist orange peel above drink and discard remainder of peel then serve.

London Fever

8.3% ALC/VOL • 1.2 STD DRINKS

20ml (⅔ fl oz) Dry Gin
20ml (⅔ fl oz) Bacardi
10ml (⅓ fl oz) Grenadine
30ml (1 fl oz) Fresh Lime Juice
100ml (3⅓ fl oz) Mineral Water

Pour Gin, Bacardi, Grenadine and juice into a cocktail shaker over ice. Shake and strain into a highball glass over ice. Add mineral water, stir gently and serve with a straw.

Last Round

28.1% ALC/VOL • 1.4 STD DRINKS

30ml (1 fl oz) Dry Gin
30ml (1 fl oz) Dry Vermouth
2 dashes Brandy
2 dashes Pernod

Pour ingredients into a mixing glass over ice and stir. Strain into a chilled cocktail glass and serve.

My Antonella

10.7% ALC/VOL • 1.3 STD DRINKS

30ml (1 fl oz) Gin
30ml (1 fl oz) Chambord
90ml (3 fl oz) Tonic Water
2 Green Olives
Wedge of Lime

Pour Gin and Chambord into a highball glass over ice then stir. Add olives and tonic then stir gently. Garnish with a wedge of lime and serve.

Yachting Club

29.8% ALC/VOL • 2.3 STD DRINKS

60ml (2 fl oz) Hollands Gin
30ml (1 fl oz) Dry Vermouth
2 dashes Peychaud's Bitters
Dash Pernod
½ teaspoon Sugar Syrup

Pour ingredients into a mixing glass over ice and stir. Strain into a chilled cocktail glass and serve.

Geisha Cup

12% ALC/VOL • 1.8 STD DRINKS

45ml (1½ fl oz) Gin
30ml (1 fl oz) Apricot Brandy
60ml (2 fl oz) Grapefruit Juice
60ml (2 fl oz) Fresh Orange Juice
Maraschino Cherry

Pour Gin, Brandy and juices into a cocktail shaker over cracked ice. Shake and pour into a chilled collins glass. Garnish with a cherry and serve.
This drink is also known as Cup of Gin.

Silver Bronx

21.8% ALC/VOL • 2.2 STD DRINKS

60ml (2 fl oz) Gin
15ml (½ fl oz) Dry Vermouth
15ml (½ fl oz) Sweet Vermouth
5ml (1/6 fl oz) Fresh Orange Juice
White of 1 Egg

Pour ingredients into a cocktail shaker over ice and shake. Strain into a chilled sour glass and serve.

Long Island Raspberry Ice Tea

12.9% ALC/VOL • 2 STD DRINKS

15ml (½ fl oz) Gin
15ml (½ fl oz) Chambord
15ml (½ fl oz) Light Rum
15ml (½ fl oz) Tequila
15ml (½ fl oz) Vodka
60ml (2 fl oz) Sweet and Sour Mix
60ml (2 fl oz) Cola
Wedge of Lemon

Pour Gin, Rum, Tequila, Vodka and sour mix into a cocktail shaker over ice. Shake and strain into a highball glass over ice. Add cola and stir gently. Layer Chambord on top and garnish with a wedge of lemon then serve.

Love-Me Tender

30.4% ALC/VOL • 2.9 STD DRINKS

60ml (2 fl oz) Gin
36ml (1 1/5 fl oz) Sherry
12ml (2/5 fl oz) Angostura Bitters

12ml (2/5 fl oz) Peach Schnapps
Drop of Apricot Brandy
Twist of Orange Peel

Pour Gin, Sherry, Bitters, Schnapps and Brandy into a mixing glass over ice. Stir and strain into a chilled cocktail glass. Add orange peel and serve.

Dr. is in

32.4% ALC/VOL • 1.9 STD DRINKS

45ml (1½ fl oz) Gin
15ml (½ fl oz) Amaretto
15ml (½ fl oz) White Crème De Cacao

Pour ingredients into a blender over cracked ice and blend. Strain into a chilled cocktail glass and serve.

Venezia

26.2% ALC/VOL • 2.1 STD DRINKS

40ml (1⅓ fl oz) Gin
30ml (1 fl oz) Dry Vermouth
30ml (1 fl oz) Peach Liqueur
Drop of Blue Curaçao
Orange Zest

Pour Gin, Vermouth, Liqueur and Curaçao into a mixing glass over ice. Stir and strain into a chilled cocktail glass. Garnish with orange zest and serve.

Diamond Head

17% ALC/VOL • 1.7 STD DRINKS

45ml (1½ fl oz) Gin
15ml (½ fl oz) Curaçao
5ml (1/6 fl oz) Dry Vermouth
60ml (2 fl oz) Pineapple Juice

Pour ingredients into a cocktail shaker over ice and shake. Strain into a chilled cocktail glass and serve.

Matinée

21% ALC/VOL • 1.3 STD DRINKS

30ml (1 fl oz) Gin
15ml (½ fl oz) Sambuca
15ml (½ fl oz) Fresh Lime Juice
1 teaspoon Thick Cream
½ Egg White

Pour ingredients into a cocktail shaker over ice and shake. Strain into a chilled cocktail glass and serve.

Tango Cocktail

22.1% ALC/VOL • 1.4 STD DRINKS

30ml (1 fl oz) Gin
15ml (½ fl oz) Dry Vermouth
15ml (½ fl oz) Sweet Vermouth
3 dashes Cointreau
15ml (½ fl oz) Fresh Orange Juice

Pour ingredients into a cocktail shaker over ice and shake. Strain into a chilled cocktail glass and serve.

Homecoming

24.3% ALC/VOL • 1.4 STD DRINKS

23ml (¾ fl oz) Gin
23ml (¾ fl oz) Apricot Brandy
23ml (¾ fl oz) Dry Vermouth
5ml (1/6 fl oz) Fresh Lemon Juice
Maraschino Cherry

Pour Gin, Brandy, Vermouth and juice into a cocktail shaker over ice. Shake and strain into a chilled cocktail glass. Garnish with a cherry and serve.

Bitch on Wheels

31.9% ALC/VOL • 2.4 STD DRINKS

60ml (2 fl oz) Gin
15ml (½ fl oz) Dry Vermouth
15ml (½ fl oz) White Crème De Menthe
5ml (1/6 fl oz) Pernod

Pour ingredients into a mixing glass over ice and stir. Strain into a chilled cocktail glass and serve.

Orange Jolie

10.2% ALC/VOL • 1.4 STD DRINKS

30ml (1 fl oz) Gin
15ml (½ fl oz) Coconut Liqueur
15ml (½ fl oz) Orange Curaçao
120ml (4 fl oz) Fresh Orange Juice
Wedge of Lime

Pour Gin, Liqueur, Curaçao and juice into a cocktail shaker over ice. Shake and strain into a highball glass over ice. Twist wedge of lime above drink to release juice – do not stir, then add spent shell and serve.

Pink Gin Tonic

10.9% ALC/VOL • 1.8 STD DRINKS

60ml (2 fl oz) Gin
5ml (1/6 fl oz) Campari
150ml (5 fl oz) Tonic Water
Wedge of Lime

Pour Gin into a highball glass over ice and add tonic then stir gently. Add Campari and stir. Garnish with a wedge of lime and serve.

Casino Royale

24.7% ALC/VOL • 1.9 STD DRINKS

60ml (2 fl oz) Gin
5ml (1/6 fl oz) Maraschino Liqueur
Dash Orange Bitters
15ml (½ fl oz) Fresh Lemon Juice
Yolk of 1 Egg

Pour ingredients into a cocktail shaker over ice and shake. Strain into a chilled sour glass and serve.

Orange Buck

9.3% ALC/VOL • 1.3 STD DRINKS

45ml (1½ fl oz) Gin
30ml (1 fl oz) Fresh
Orange Juice
90ml (3 fl oz) Dry Ginger Ale
½ Fresh Lime

Pour Gin and orange juice into a highball glass over ice. Twist ½ lime above drink to release juice and add spent shell then stir. Add Ginger Ale, stir gently and serve.

Newport Cooler

16.6% ALC/VOL • 2.4 STD DRINKS

60ml (2 fl oz) Gin
15ml (½ fl oz) Brandy
15ml (½ fl oz) Peach Schnapps
5ml (1/6 fl oz) Fresh Lime Juice
90ml (3 fl oz) Dry Ginger Ale

Pour Gin, Brandy, Schnapps and juice into a cocktail shaker over ice. Shake and strain into a collins glass over ice. Add Ginger Ale, stir gently and serve.

Adriana

17.9% ALC/VOL • 0.9 STD DRINKS

23ml (¾ fl oz) Gin
10ml (⅓ fl oz) Dry Vermouth
10ml (⅓ fl oz) Sweet Vermouth
23ml (¾ fl oz) Fresh
Orange Juice

Pour ingredients into a mixing glass over ice and stir. Strain into a chilled cocktail glass and serve.

Douglas Fairbanks

23.1% ALC/VOL • 2.4 STD DRINKS

60ml (2 fl oz) Gin
23ml (¾ fl oz) Brandy
30ml (1 fl oz) Fresh
Lemon Juice
1 teaspoon Sugar Syrup
½ Egg White

Pour ingredients into a cocktail shaker over ice and shake. Strain into a chilled cocktail glass and serve.

Petticoat Lane

31.4% ALC/VOL • 2.2 STD DRINKS

60ml (2 fl oz) Gin
15ml (½ fl oz) Campari
15ml (½ fl oz) Sweet Vermouth
Slice of Lemon

Pour Gin, Campari and Vermouth into a mixing glass over ice. Stir and strain into a chilled cocktail glass. Garnish with a slice of lemon and serve.

Lusty Lucy

8.3% ALC/VOL • 1.4 STD DRINKS

30ml (1 fl oz) Gin
30ml (1 fl oz) Midori
30ml (1 fl oz) Grapefruit Juice
1 teaspoon Egg White
113ml (3¾ fl oz) Tonic Water
3 Melon Balls (various colours)

Pour Gin, Midori, juice and egg white into a cocktail shaker over ice. Shake and strain into a chilled highball glass. Add tonic and stir gently. Garnish with melon balls and serve.

Virgin

33.4% ALC/VOL • 2 STD DRINKS

30ml (1 fl oz) Gin
30ml (1 fl oz) Forbidden Fruit
15ml (½ fl oz) White Crème De
Menthe

Pour ingredients into a cocktail shaker over ice and shake. Strain into a chilled cocktail glass and serve.

Flowerdance

17.5% ALC/VOL • 1.4 STD DRINKS

30ml (1 fl oz) Gin
30ml (1 fl oz) Lychee Liqueur
30ml (1 fl oz) Peach Nectar
15ml (½ fl oz) Fresh
Lime Juice
Kumquat Flower
Orchid

Pour Gin, Liqueur, nectar and juice into a cocktail shaker over ice. Shake and strain into a chilled cocktail glass. Garnish with a kumquat flower and orchid then serve.

Botany Bay

7.2% ALC/VOL • 1.8 STD DRINKS

60ml (2 fl oz) Gin
120ml (4 fl oz) Grapefruit Juice
120ml (4 fl oz) Fresh
Orange Juice
2 teaspoons Sugar Syrup

Pour ingredients into a cocktail shaker over ice and shake. Strain into a chilled collins glass and serve.

Shining Star

18.6% ALC/VOL • 1 STD DRINK

20ml (⅔ fl oz) Gin
20ml (⅔ fl oz) Dry Vermouth
10ml (⅓ fl oz) Passion-Fruit
Liqueur
20ml (⅔ fl oz) Grapefruit Juice
Slice of Caramole

Pour Gin, Vermouth, Liqueur and juice into a cocktail shaker over ice. Shake and strain into a chilled cocktail glass. Garnish with a slice of caramole and serve.

Ranger Cocktail

21.3% ALC/VOL • 0.6 STD DRINKS

10ml (⅓ fl oz) Gin
10ml (⅓ fl oz) Bacardi
10ml (⅓ fl oz) Fresh
Lemon Juice
1 teaspoon Sugar Syrup

Pour ingredients into a cocktail shaker over ice and shake. Strain into a chilled cocktail glass and serve.

Call Me Larsson

8.2% ALC/VOL • 1.2 STD DRINKS

40ml (1⅓ fl oz) Dry Gin
10ml (⅓ fl oz) Grenadine
20ml (⅔ fl oz) Lime Syrup
2 teaspoons Sugar Syrup
100ml (3⅓ fl oz) Soda Water
Slice of Lime

Pour Gin, Grenadine, syrup and sugar into a cocktail shaker over ice. Shake and strain into a highball glass over ice. Add soda and stir gently. Add a slice of lime and serve.

Pineapple Gimlet

13.9% ALC/VOL • 1.3 STD DRINKS

45ml (1½ fl oz) Gin
60ml (2 fl oz) Pineapple Juice
15ml (½ fl oz) Fresh Lime Juice

Pour Gin and lime juice into a highball glass filled with ice then stir well. Add pineapple juice, stir and serve.

Velvet Kiss

16% ALC/VOL • 1.1 STD DRINKS

30ml (1 fl oz) Gin
15ml (½ fl oz) Banana Liqueur
Dash Grenadine
30ml (1 fl oz) Thick Cream
15ml (½ fl oz) Pineapple Juice

Pour ingredients into a cocktail shaker over ice and shake. Strain into a chilled cocktail glass and serve.

Chain Lightning

30.5% ALC/VOL • 2 STD DRINKS

60ml (2 fl oz) Gin
15ml (½ fl oz) Triple Sec
10ml (⅓ fl oz) Fresh Lemon Juice
Twist of Lemon Peel

Pour Gin, Triple Sec and juice into a cocktail shaker over ice. Shake and strain into a chilled cocktail glass. Garnish with lemon peel and serve.

North Pole Cocktail

17.1% ALC/VOL • 1.3 STD DRINKS

30ml (1 fl oz) Gin
15ml (½ fl oz) Maraschino Liqueur
15ml (½ fl oz) Fresh Lemon Juice
White of 1 Egg
Fresh Whipped Cream

Pour Gin, Liqueur, juice and egg white into a cocktail shaker over ice. Shake and strain into a chilled cocktail glass. Float cream on top and serve.

Royal Flamingo

28.5% ALC/VOL • 0.9 STD DRINKS

20ml (⅔ fl oz) Dry Gin
20ml (⅔ fl oz) Banana Liqueur
Dash Fresh Lemon Juice
Dash Pineapple Juice

Pour ingredients into a mixing glass over ice and stir. Strain into a chilled cocktail glass and serve.

Dirty Ashtray

13.5% ALC/VOL • 2.1 STD DRINKS

15ml (½ fl oz) Gin
15ml (½ fl oz) Blue Curaçao
15ml (½ fl oz) Light Rum
15ml (½ fl oz) Tequila
15ml (½ fl oz) Vodka
15ml (½ fl oz) Grenadine
60ml (2 fl oz) Sweet and Sour Mix
45ml (1½ fl oz) Pineapple Juice
Wedge of Lemon

Pour Gin, Curaçao, Rum, Tequila, Vodka, Grenadine, sour mix and juice into a cocktail shaker over cracked ice. Shake and pour into a chilled highball glass. Garnish with a wedge of lemon and serve.

Crème De Gin Cocktail

18.2% ALC/VOL • 1.6 STD DRINKS

45ml (1½ fl oz) Gin
15ml (½ fl oz) White Crème De Menthe
10ml (⅓ fl oz) Fresh Lemon Juice
10ml (⅓ fl oz) Fresh Orange Juice
White of 1 Egg

Pour ingredients into a cocktail shaker over ice and shake. Strain into a chilled cocktail glass and serve.

Squeeze My Lemon

9.3% ALC/VOL • 1.3 STD DRINKS

45ml (1½ fl oz) Gin
15ml (½ fl oz) Fresh Lemon Juice
120ml (4 fl oz) Dry Ginger Ale
Wedge of Lemon

Pour Gin and juice into a cocktail shaker over cracked ice. Shake and pour into a chilled highball glass. Add Ginger Ale and stir gently. Garnish with a wedge of lemon and serve.

Salim

6.9% ALC/VOL • 1.3 STD DRINKS

30ml (1 fl oz) Dry Gin
10ml (⅓ fl oz) Banana Liqueur
10ml (⅓ fl oz) Southern Comfort
180ml (6 fl oz) Fresh Orange Juice
15ml (½ fl oz) Pineapple Juice

Pour Gin, Liqueur, Southern Comfort and pineapple juice into a highball glass over ice then stir. Add orange juice, stir again and serve.

Minted Gin

33.6% ALC/VOL • 1.5 STD DRINKS

50ml (1⅔ fl oz) Gin
1 teaspoon Sugar Syrup
3 Fresh Mint Leaves

Pour sugar into a chilled old-fashioned glass and add mint leaves. Muddle well and add ice. Add Gin, stir well and serve.

Manila Fizz

12% ALC/VOL • 1.8 STD DRINKS

60ml (2 fl oz) Gin
15ml (½ fl oz) Fresh
Lemon Juice
1 teaspoon Caster Sugar
1 Fresh Egg
60ml (2 fl oz) Root Beer

Pour Gin, juice and egg into a cocktail shaker over ice then add sugar. Shake well and strain into a chilled highball glass over a few ice cubes. Add root beer, stir gently and serve.

Silver Top

9.2% ALC/VOL • 1.6 STD DRINKS

40ml (1⅓ fl oz) Gin
20ml (⅔ fl oz) Triple Sec
2 dashes Fresh Lemon Juice
2 dashes Sugar Syrup
150ml (5 fl oz) Tonic Water

Pour Gin, Triple Sec, juice and sugar into a cocktail shaker over ice. Shake and strain into a highball glass over ice. Add tonic, stir gently and serve.

Nelson Special

5.8% ALC/VOL • 1.3 STD DRINKS

45ml (1½ fl oz) Gin
120ml (4 fl oz) Cranberry Juice
120ml (4 fl oz) Tonic Water
Cherry
Slice of Orange

Pour Gin and juice into a chilled highball glass then stir. Add tonic and stir gently. Add a cherry and slice of orange then serve.

Boston Cooler

8.4% ALC/VOL • 1.1 STD DRINKS

30ml (1 fl oz) Dry Gin
10ml (⅓ fl oz) Green Crème De
Menthe
120ml (4 fl oz) Mineral Water

Pour Gin and Crème De Menthe into a collins glass over ice then stir. Add mineral water, stir gently and serve.

Deedee

16.8% ALC/VOL • 1.3 STD DRINKS

45ml (1½ fl oz) Gin
30ml (1 fl oz) Cranberry Juice
8ml (¼ fl oz) Fresh
Lemon Juice
8ml (¼ fl oz) Fresh Lime Juice
8ml (¼ fl oz) Maraschino
Cherry Juice
2 Dried Cranberries
(marinated in Gin)

Pour Gin and juices into a cocktail shaker over ice. Shake and strain into a chilled cocktail glass. Garnish with cranberries and serve.

Fin n' Tonic

19% ALC/VOL • 1.3 STD DRINKS

30ml (1 fl oz) Gin
30ml (1 fl oz) Peppermint
Schnapps
30ml (1 fl oz) Tonic Water

Pour Gin and Schnapps into an old-fashioned glass over ice then stir. Add tonic, stir gently and serve.

Pendennis Club Cocktail

32.5% ALC/VOL • 2 STD DRINKS

45ml (1½ fl oz) Gin
23ml (¾ fl oz) Brandy
Dash Angostura Bitters
15ml (½ fl oz) Fresh
Lime Juice
1 teaspoon Sugar Syrup

Pour ingredients into a cocktail shaker over ice and shake. Strain into a chilled cocktail glass and serve.

Twin Six Cocktail

14.2% ALC/VOL • 1.1 STD DRINKS

30ml (1 fl oz) Gin
15ml (½ fl oz) Sweet Vermouth
Dash Grenadine
18ml (3/5 fl oz) Fresh
Orange Juice
White of 1 Egg

Pour ingredients into a cocktail shaker over ice and shake. Strain into a chilled cocktail glass and serve.

Baltimore Zoo

26.4% ALC/VOL • 4.6 STD DRINKS

45ml (1½ fl oz) Gin
45ml (1½ fl oz) Light Rum
45ml (1½ fl oz) Vodka
30ml (1 fl oz) Triple Sec
5ml (1/6 fl oz) Beer
5ml (1/6 fl oz) Grenadine
45ml (1½ fl oz) Sweet and
Sour Mix

Pour Gin, Rum, Vodka, Triple Sec and sour mix into a mixing glass over ice. Stir well and strain into a highball glass over ice. Add Beer and Grenadine, stir gently then serve.

Parisian Cocktail

29% ALC/VOL • 1.8 STD DRINKS

45ml (1½ fl oz) Dry Gin

30ml (1 fl oz) Dry Vermouth
3 dashes Crème De Cassis

Pour ingredients into a cocktail shaker over ice and shake. Strain into a chilled cocktail glass and serve.

Oueureum

27.7% ALC/VOL • 1.4 STD DRINKS

30ml (1 fl oz) Gin
30ml (1 fl oz) Apricot Brandy
Dash Orange Bitters
5ml (1/6 fl oz) Fresh Orange Juice
Maraschino Cherry
Twist of Orange Peel

Pour Gin, Brandy, Bitters and juice into a cocktail shaker over ice. Shake and strain into a chilled cocktail glass. Garnish with a cherry and orange peel then serve.

Little Red Riding Hood

13.5% ALC/VOL • 1.8 STD DRINKS

60ml (2 fl oz) Gin
15ml (½ fl oz) Loganberry Jam
90ml (3 fl oz) Lemon-Lime Soda

Pour soda into a chilled old-fashioned glass and add jam. Add Gin, stir gently and serve.

Magic Woman

14% ALC/VOL • 2.4 STD DRINKS

30ml (1 fl oz) Gin
30ml (1 fl oz) Blue Curaçao
30ml (1 fl oz) Light Rum
5ml (1/6 fl oz) Fresh Lemon Juice
120ml (4 fl oz) Lemonade

Pour Gin, Curaçao, Rum and juice into a cocktail shaker over ice. Shake and strain into a highball glass over ice. Add lemonade, stir gently and serve.

Alaska Cocktail

37% ALC/VOL • 2 STD DRINKS

45ml (1½ fl oz) Gin
23ml (¾ fl oz) Yellow Chartreuse
2 dashes Orange Bitters

Pour ingredients into a mixing glass over ice and stir. Strain into a chilled cocktail glass and serve.

Aqua Fodie

15.6% ALC/VOL • 1.5 STD DRINKS

30ml (1 fl oz) Gin
30ml (1 fl oz) Blue Curaçao
60ml (2 fl oz) Fresh Orange Juice
Cherry
Slice of Orange

Pour Gin and Curaçao into a highball glass filled with ice. Add juice and stir. Garnish with a cherry and slice of orange then serve.

Gin Breeze

8.5% ALC/VOL • 1.3 STD DRINKS

45ml (1½ fl oz) Gin
120ml (4 fl oz) Cranberry Juice
30ml (1 fl oz) Grapefruit Juice
Wedge of Lemon

Pour Gin and juices into a cocktail shaker over ice. Shake and strain into a tall glass over ice. Add a wedge of lemon and serve.

Hoya

12.3% ALC/VOL • 1.7 STD DRINKS

60ml (2 fl oz) Gin
30ml (1 fl oz) Fresh Orange Juice
90ml (3 fl oz) Dry Ginger Ale
Slice of Orange

Pour Gin and juice into a cocktail shaker over cracked ice. Shake and pour into a chilled highball glass. Add Ginger Ale and stir gently. Garnish with a slice of orange and serve.

Bloodhound No.2

26.8% ALC/VOL • 2.5 STD DRINKS

60ml (2 fl oz) Dry Gin
30ml (1 fl oz) Dry Vermouth
30ml (1 fl oz) Sweet Vermouth
2 Strawberries

Pour Gin and Vermouths into a cocktail shaker over ice. Shake and strain into a chilled cocktail glass. Garnish with strawberries and serve.

Headhunter

7.2% ALC/VOL • 1.8 STD DRINKS

50ml (1⅔ fl oz) Gin
20ml (⅔ fl oz) White Crème De Menthe
240ml (8 fl oz) Dry Ginger Ale
10 Fresh Mint Leaves

Pour Gin into a cocktail shaker without ice and add mint leaves. Muddle well then add ice and Crème De Menthe. Shake well and strain into a tall glass over ice. Add Ginger Ale – do not stir, then serve with a straw.

Gent of the Jury

14.4% ALC/VOL • 2.1 STD DRINKS

60ml (2 fl oz) Gin
15ml (½ fl oz) Cherry Brandy
Dash Angostura Bitters
90ml (3 fl oz) Pineapple Juice
15ml (½ fl oz) Fresh Lemon Juice

Pour ingredients into a cocktail shaker over ice and shake. Strain into a highball glass over ice and serve.

Rauhreif

24.2% ALC/VOL • 1.9 STD DRINKS

30ml (1 fl oz) Gin
30ml (1 fl oz) Curaçao
15ml (½ fl oz) Jamaica Rum
10ml (⅓ fl oz) Grenadine
15ml (½ fl oz) Fresh Lemon Juice

Pour ingredients into a cocktail shaker over cracked ice and shake. Pour into a chilled highball glass and serve.

Bon Voyage

36.7% ALC/VOL • 1.8 STD DRINKS

30ml (1 fl oz) Gin
30ml (1 fl oz) Tequila
Dash Blue Curaçao
Dash Fresh Lemon Juice

Pour ingredients into a cocktail glass over ice, stir and serve with a short straw.

Adam's Bomb

7.8% ALC/VOL • 2.6 STD DRINKS

60ml (2 fl oz) Gin
30ml (1 fl oz) Jägermeister
120ml (4 fl oz) Fresh Orange Juice
120ml (4 fl oz) Soda Water
90ml (3 fl oz) Gatorade

Pour Gin, Jägermeister, juice and Gatorade into a mixing glass over ice. Stir and strain into a chilled hurricane glass. Add soda, stir gently and serve.

351 Special

17.5% ALC/VOL • 1.8 STD DRINKS

60ml (2 fl oz) Dry Gin
10ml (⅓ fl oz) Knonenbourg Beer
60ml (2 fl oz) Cola

Pour Gin and Beer into a chilled coffee glass. Add cola, stir gently and serve.

Gletcher

27.3% ALC/VOL • 1.3 STD DRINKS

30ml (1 fl oz) Gin
15ml (½ fl oz) Blue Curaçao
5ml (⅙ fl oz) Anisette
10ml (⅓ fl oz) Soda Water

Prepare a brandy balloon with a sugar frosted rim and half fill with crushed ice. Pour Gin, Curaçao and Anisette into a mixing glass over cracked ice. Stir and pour into prepared glass. Add soda, stir gently and serve.

Princess Mary

20% ALC/VOL • 1.4 STD DRINKS

30ml (1 fl oz) Dry Gin
30ml (1 fl oz) White Crème De Cacao
30ml (1 fl oz) Fresh Cream

Pour ingredients into a cocktail shaker over ice and shake. Strain into a chilled cocktail glass and serve.

Green Ocean

6.4% ALC/VOL • 0.9 STD DRINKS

20ml (⅔ fl oz) Gin
20ml (⅔ fl oz) Pisang Ambon
100ml (3⅓ fl oz) Fresh Orange Juice
20ml (⅔ fl oz) Passion-Fruit Juice
20ml (⅔ fl oz) Sweet and Sour Mix

Pour ingredients into a blender over cracked ice and blend briefly. Pour into a chilled highball glass and serve.

Desert Healer

9.7% ALC/VOL • 1.5 STD DRINKS

40ml (1⅓ fl oz) Dry Gin
20ml (⅔ fl oz) Cherry Brandy
20ml (⅔ fl oz) Fresh Orange Juice
120ml (4 fl oz) Dry Ginger Ale

Pour Gin, Brandy and juice into a cocktail shaker over ice. Shake and strain into a highball glass over ice. Add Ginger Ale, stir gently and serve with a straw.

Blue Devil

26.2% ALC/VOL • 1.4 STD DRINKS

38ml (1¼ fl oz) Gin
15ml (½ fl oz) Blue Curaçao
15ml (½ fl oz) Sweet and Sour Mix
Twist of Lemon Peel

Pour Gin, Curaçao and sour mix into a blender over crushed ice. Blend and pour into a chilled cocktail glass. Garnish with lemon peel and serve.

Queen's Blossom

9.2% ALC/VOL • 1.5 STD DRINKS

40ml (1⅓ fl oz) Dry Gin
20ml (⅔ fl oz) Banana Liqueur
150ml (5 fl oz) Lemonade

Pour Gin and Liqueur into a mixing glass over ice. Stir and strain into a highball glass over ice. Add lemonade, stir gently and serve.

You and Me

32.2% ALC/VOL • 3.1 STD DRINKS

90ml (3 fl oz) Dry Gin
30ml (1 fl oz) Dry Vermouth
3 drops Bénédictine
3 drops Orange Bitters
Twist of Lemon Peel

Pour Gin, Vermouth, Bénédictine and Bitters into a mixing glass over ice. Stir and strain into a chilled cocktail glass. Garnish with lemon peel and serve.

Bachelor's Bait

21.3% ALC/VOL • 1.8 STD DRINKS

60ml (2 fl oz) Gin
3 dashes Orange Bitters
15ml (½ fl oz) Grenadine
White of 1 Egg

Pour ingredients into a cocktail shaker over ice and shake. Strain into a chilled cocktail glass and serve.

Beauty Spot Cocktail

22% ALC/VOL • 1.3 STD DRINKS

30ml (1 fl oz) Gin
15ml (½ fl oz) Dry Vermouth
15ml (½ fl oz) Sweet Vermouth
5ml (1/6 fl oz) Grenadine
8ml (¼ fl oz) Orange Flower Water

Pour ingredients into a cocktail shaker over cracked ice and shake. Pour into a chilled old-fashioned glass and serve.

Gangadine Cocktail

30.1% ALC/VOL • 1.7 STD DRINKS

20ml (⅔ fl oz) Dry Gin
20ml (⅔ fl oz) Pastis
20ml (⅔ fl oz) White Crème De Menthe
10ml (⅓ fl oz) Grenadine

Pour ingredients into a cocktail shaker over ice and shake. Strain into a chilled cocktail glass and serve.

Tuxedo Junction

22.2% ALC/VOL • 1.2 STD DRINKS

20ml (⅔ fl oz) Dry Gin
20ml (⅔ fl oz) Dry Vermouth
10ml (⅓ fl oz) Pastis
Dash Orange Bitters
20ml (⅔ fl oz) Grenadine

Pour ingredients into a cocktail shaker over ice and shake. Strain into a chilled cocktail glass and serve.

Golden Purple

34.8% ALC/VOL • 2.7 STD DRINKS

40ml (1⅓ fl oz) Gin
30ml (1 fl oz) Goldschläger
30ml (1 fl oz) Parfait Amour
2 Slices of Avocado (coated with cinnamon)

Pour Gin, Goldschläger and Parfait Amour into a cocktail shaker over ice. Shake and strain into a chilled cocktail glass. Garnish with slices of avocado and serve.

Beauty Spot No.2

17.8% ALC/VOL • 0.8 STD DRINKS

20ml (⅔ fl oz) Dry Gin
10ml (⅓ fl oz) Dry Vermouth
10ml (⅓ fl oz) Sweet Vermouth
10ml (⅓ fl oz) Grenadine
10ml (⅓ fl oz) Fresh Orange Juice

Pour Grenadine into a chilled cocktail glass and pour remaining ingredients into a cocktail shaker over ice. Shake and strain into prepared glass layering on top of Grenadine then serve.

Princetown

30.7% ALC/VOL • 3.3 STD DRINKS

90ml (3 fl oz) Gin
45ml (1½ fl oz) Port
4 drops Orange Bitters

Pour ingredients into a cocktail shaker over ice and shake. Strain into a chilled cocktail glass and serve.

Montmarte Cocktail

29.5% ALC/VOL • 1.6 STD DRINKS

38ml (1¼ fl oz) Gin
15ml (½ fl oz) Triple Sec
15ml (½ fl oz) Sweet Vermouth
4 Sprigs of Fresh Mint

Pour Gin, Triple Sec and Vermouth into a cocktail shaker without ice. Add sprigs of mint and muddle well. Add ice and shake. Strain into a chilled martini glass and serve.

Bumpy Grapefruit

4.6% ALC/VOL • 0.9 STD DRINKS

30ml (1 fl oz) Gin
210ml (7 fl oz) Grapefruit Juice
Slice of Lemon

Build ingredients into a highball glass over ice and garnish with a slice of lemon then serve with a swizzle stick.

Sunshine Avenue

26.7% ALC/VOL • 1.3 STD DRINKS

20ml (⅔ fl oz) Gin
20ml (⅔ fl oz) Apricot Brandy
20ml (⅔ fl oz) Peach Schnapps
Cherry

Pour Gin, Brandy and Schnapps into a cocktail shaker over ice. Shake and strain into a chilled cocktail glass. Garnish with a cherry and serve.

Maiden-No-More

23.5% ALC/VOL • 1.8 STD DRINKS

45ml (1½ fl oz) Gin
15ml (½ fl oz) Triple Sec
5ml (1/6 fl oz) Brandy
30ml (1 fl oz) Fresh Lemon Juice

Pour ingredients into a cocktail shaker over ice and shake. Strain into a chilled cocktail glass and serve.

White Heat

19.5% ALC/VOL • 1.4 STD DRINKS

30ml (1 fl oz) Gin
15ml (½ fl oz) Dry Vermouth

15ml (½ fl oz) Triple Sec
30ml (1 fl oz) Pineapple Juice

Pour ingredients into a cocktail shaker over ice and shake. Strain into a highball glass filled with ice and serve.

Top Hat

30.8% ALC/VOL • 1.5 STD DRINKS

40ml (1⅓ fl oz) Gin
20ml (⅔ fl oz) Apricot Brandy
2 dashes Grenadine
Dash Fresh Lemon Juice

Pour ingredients into a mixing glass over ice and stir. Strain into a chilled cocktail glass and serve.

Ramos Chill Fizz

14.2% ALC/VOL • 2.4 STD DRINKS

60ml (2 fl oz) Gin
30ml (1 fl oz) Orange Curaçao
2 scoops Vanilla Ice Cream
60ml (2 fl oz) Soda Water

Pour Gin and Curaçao into a blender over small amount of crushed ice then add ice cream. Blend until smooth and pour into a chilled highball glass. Add soda, stir gently and serve.

Normandy Cocktail

36.9% ALC/VOL • 2.5 STD DRINKS

45ml (1½ fl oz) Gin
23ml (¾ fl oz) Applejack
15ml (½ fl oz) Brandy
2 dashes Fresh Lemon Juice

Pour ingredients into a cocktail shaker over ice and shake. Strain into a chilled cocktail glass and serve.

Norwich Collins

7.3% ALC/VOL • 1.8 STD DRINKS

60ml (2 fl oz) Gin
30ml (1 fl oz) Fresh
Lemon Juice
1 teaspoon Sugar Syrup
210ml (7 fl oz) Cola
Slice of Orange

Pour Gin, juice and sugar into a cocktail shaker over ice. Shake and strain into a chilled collins glass over a few ice cubes. Add cola and stir gently. Garnish with a slice of orange and serve.

Gladiator

33.3% ALC/VOL • 1.2 STD DRINKS

23ml (¾ fl oz) Gin
15ml (½ fl oz) Campari
8ml (¼ fl oz) Sambuca

Pour ingredients into a mixing glass over ice and stir. Strain into a chilled cocktail glass and serve.

Fisher Cocktail

31.8% ALC/VOL • 1.8 STD DRINKS

60ml (2 fl oz) Dry Gin
Dash Angostura Bitters
Dash Orange Bitters
10ml (⅓ fl oz) Grenadine

Pour ingredients into a cocktail shaker over ice and shake. Strain into an old-fashioned glass over ice and serve.

Steamboat Gin

25.7% ALC/VOL • 2 STD DRINKS

45ml (1½ fl oz) Gin
23ml (¾ fl oz) Southern
Comfort
15ml (½ fl oz) Grapefruit Juice
15ml (½ fl oz) Fresh
Lemon Juice

Pour ingredients into a cocktail shaker over ice and shake. Strain into a chilled cocktail glass and serve.

Delilah

30.2% ALC/VOL • 1.8 STD DRINKS

45ml (1½ fl oz) Gin
15ml (½ fl oz) Cointreau
15ml (½ fl oz) Fresh
Lime Juice
Twist of Lemon Peel

Pour Gin, Cointreau and juice into a cocktail shaker over ice. Shake and strain into a chilled cocktail glass. Garnish with lemon peel and serve.

Green Lagoon

12% ALC/VOL • 1.4 STD DRINKS

30ml (1 fl oz) Gin
30ml (1 fl oz) Green Crème De
Menthe
90ml (3 fl oz) Pineapple Juice

Pour ingredients into a cocktail shaker over ice and shake. Strain into a chilled champagne saucer and serve.

Tropic Moon

6.3% ALC/VOL • 1.1 STD DRINKS

24ml (4/5 fl oz) Dry Gin
15ml (½ fl oz) Banana Liqueur
10ml (⅓ fl oz) Apricot Brandy
Dash Grenadine
180ml (6 fl oz) Fresh
Orange Juice

Pour ingredients into a highball glass over ice, stir and serve.

A Night at the Opera

29.6% ALC/VOL • 1.8 STD DRINKS

60ml (2 fl oz) Gin
15ml (½ fl oz) Grenadine
Twist of Lemon Peel

Pour Gin and Grenadine into a cocktail shaker over ice. Shake and strain into a chilled cocktail glass. Twist lemon peel above drink and place remainder of peel into drink then serve.

Yellow Star

14.5% ALC/VOL • 1.7 STD DRINKS

20ml (⅔ fl oz) Dry Gin
20ml (⅔ fl oz) Banana Liqueur
20ml (⅔ fl oz) Pastis
75ml (2½ fl oz) Fresh Orange Juice
2 teaspoons Maracuja Syrup

Pour ingredients into a cocktail shaker over ice and shake. Strain into a highball glass over ice and serve with a straw.

Old Etonian

24.1% ALC/VOL • 1.2 STD DRINKS

30ml (1 fl oz) Gin
30ml (1 fl oz) Lillet
2 dashes Crème De Noyaux
2 dashes Orange Bitters

Pour ingredients into a mixing glass over ice and stir. Strain into a chilled cocktail glass and serve.

Florida Rain

16.8% ALC/VOL • 0.9 STD DRINKS

15ml (½ fl oz) Gin
10ml (⅓ fl oz) Kirsch
10ml (⅓ fl oz) Triple Sec
30ml (1 fl oz) Fresh Orange Juice
5ml (⅙ fl oz) Fresh Lemon Juice

Pour ingredients into a cocktail shaker over ice and shake. Strain into a chilled cocktail glass and serve.

Fair Bank

23.8% ALC/VOL • 1.8 STD DRINKS

30ml (1 fl oz) Dry Gin
30ml (1 fl oz) Apricot Brandy
30ml (1 fl oz) Dry Vermouth
8ml (¼ fl oz) Grenadine

Pour ingredients into a cocktail shaker over ice and shake. Strain into a chilled cocktail glass and serve.

Pegu Club

30.8% ALC/VOL • 1.8 STD DRINKS

45ml (1½ fl oz) Gin
23ml (¾ fl oz) Blue Curaçao
Dash Angostura Bitters
Dash Orange Bitters
5ml (⅙ fl oz) Fresh Lime Juice

Pour ingredients into a cocktail shaker over ice and shake. Strain into a chilled cocktail glass and serve.

Park Lane

17.7% ALC/VOL • 1.5 STD DRINKS

40ml (1⅓ fl oz) Dry Gin
20ml (⅔ fl oz) Apricot Brandy
10ml (⅓ fl oz) Grenadine
40ml (1⅓ fl oz) Fresh Orange Juice

Pour ingredients into a cocktail shaker over ice and shake. Strain into a chilled cocktail glass and serve.

Woodcrest Club

17% ALC/VOL • 1.6 STD DRINKS

45ml (1½ fl oz) Gin
23ml (¾ fl oz) Sweet Vermouth
10ml (⅓ fl oz) Grenadine
10ml (⅓ fl oz) Pineapple Juice
White of 1 Egg

Pour ingredients into a cocktail shaker over ice and shake. Strain into a chilled cocktail glass and serve.

Clover Club

9% ALC/VOL • 0.9 STD DRINKS

30ml (1 fl oz) Dry Gin
4 dashes Grenadine
60ml (2 fl oz) Fresh Lemon Juice
White of 1 Egg

Pour ingredients into a cocktail shaker over ice and shake. Strain into a chilled champagne saucer and serve.

Primavera

21.1% ALC/VOL • 1 STD DRINK

18ml (⅗ fl oz) Dry Gin
12ml (⅖ fl oz) Blue Curaçao
12ml (⅖ fl oz) Orange Curaçao
18ml (⅗ fl oz) Grapefruit Juice

Pour ingredients into a mixing glass over ice and stir. Strain into a cocktail glass over crushed ice and serve.

Cousin

5% ALC/VOL • 0.9 STD DRINKS

20ml (⅔ fl oz) Dry Gin
20ml (⅔ fl oz) Apricot Brandy
20ml (⅔ fl oz) Grenadine
180ml (6 fl oz) Dry Ginger Ale

Pour Gin, Brandy and Grenadine into a highball glass over ice then stir. Add Ginger Ale, stir gently and serve.

Montreal Gin Sour

11.7% ALC/VOL • 0.9 STD DRINKS

30ml (1 fl oz) Gin
30ml (1 fl oz) Fresh Lemon Juice
1 teaspoon Sugar Syrup
White of 1 Egg
Slice of Lemon

Pour Gin, juice, sugar and egg white into a cocktail shaker over ice. Shake and strain into a chilled sour glass. Add a slice of lemon and serve.

Southern Bride

22.4% ALC/VOL • 1.3 STD DRINKS

45ml (1½ fl oz) Gin
Dash Maraschino Liqueur
30ml (1 fl oz) Grapefruit Juice

Pour ingredients into a cocktail shaker over ice and shake. Strain into a chilled cocktail glass and serve.

Yeoman's Passion

13.4% ALC/VOL • 0.6 STD DRINKS

12ml (2/5 fl oz) Gin
12ml (2/5 fl oz) Pisang Ambon
6ml (1/5 fl oz) Dry Vermouth
30ml (1 fl oz) Passion-Fruit Juice

Pour ingredients into a mixing glass over ice and stir. Strain into a cocktail glass over crushed ice and serve.

Doctor Yes

32.4% ALC/VOL • 1.9 STD DRINKS

45ml (1½ fl oz) Gin
15ml (½ fl oz) Amaretto
15ml (½ fl oz) Dark Crème De Cacao

Pour ingredients into a cocktail shaker over ice and shake. Strain into a chilled cocktail glass and serve.

Jade Lady

18.5% ALC/VOL • 1.9 STD DRINKS

30ml (1 fl oz) Gin
30ml (1 fl oz) Advocaat
30ml (1 fl oz) Blue Curaçao
40ml (1⅓ fl oz) Fresh Orange Juice

Pour ingredients into a cocktail shaker over ice and shake. Strain into a chilled cocktail glass and serve.

Sunrise Sling

18.9% ALC/VOL • 1.3 STD DRINKS

20ml (⅔ fl oz) Dry Gin
20ml (⅔ fl oz) Apricot Brandy
20ml (⅔ fl oz) Blue Curaçao
30ml (1 fl oz) Soda Water

Pour Gin, Brandy and Curaçao into a highball glass over ice then stir. Add soda, stir gently and serve.

Kyoto

29.5% ALC/VOL • 2.1 STD DRINKS

45ml (1½ fl oz) Gin
15ml (½ fl oz) Apricot Brandy
15ml (½ fl oz) Dry Vermouth
15ml (½ fl oz) Triple Sec

Pour ingredients into a cocktail shaker over ice and shake. Strain into an old-fashioned glass over ice and serve.

Mistletoe

17.1% ALC/VOL • 0.9 STD DRINKS

30ml (1 fl oz) Gin
30ml (1 fl oz) Grenadine
5ml (1/6 fl oz) Fresh Lemon Juice

Pour ingredients into a cocktail shaker over ice and shake. Strain into a chilled cocktail glass and serve.

Gin and Juice

10.6% ALC/VOL • 1.8 STD DRINKS

60ml (2 fl oz) Gin
90ml (3 fl oz) Fresh Orange Juice
60ml (2 fl oz) Grapefruit Juice
Wedge of Lemon

Pour Gin and juices into a cocktail shaker over cracked ice. Shake and pour into a chilled highball glass. Garnish with a wedge of lemon and serve.

Albermarle Fizz

13.7% ALC/VOL • 1.8 STD DRINKS

60ml (2 fl oz) Gin
5ml (1/6 fl oz) Raspberry Liqueur
15ml (½ fl oz) Raspberry Syrup
90ml (3 fl oz) Mineral Water

Pour Gin, Liqueur and syrup into a cocktail shaker over ice. Shake and strain into a highball glass over ice. Add mineral water, stir gently and serve.

Invisible Man

14.3% ALC/VOL • 2.1 STD DRINKS

60ml (2 fl oz) Gin
15ml (½ fl oz) Brandy
15ml (½ fl oz) Triple Sec
2 dashes Fresh Orange Juice
90ml (3 fl oz) Dry Ginger Ale

Pour Gin, Brandy, Triple Sec and juice into a highball glass half filled with ice then stir. Add Ginger Ale, stir gently and serve.

Casino Royal

20% ALC/VOL • 1.4 STD DRINKS

30ml (1 fl oz) Gin
30ml (1 fl oz) Apricot Brandy
30ml (1 fl oz) Pineapple Juice

Pour ingredients into a mixing glass over ice and stir. Strain into a chilled old-fashioned glass and serve.

Titano

15.4% ALC/VOL • 1.7 STD DRINKS

45ml (1½ fl oz) Dry Gin
15ml (½ fl oz) Triple Sec
3 dashes Blue Curaçao
75ml (2½ fl oz) Grapefruit Juice

Pour Gin, Triple Sec and Curaçao into a mixing glass over ice. Stir and strain into an old-fashioned glass over ice. Add juice, stir and serve.

Union League

30.6% ALC/VOL • 2.2 STD DRINKS

60ml (2 fl oz) Gin
30ml (1 fl oz) Port
2 dashes Orange Bitters

Pour ingredients into a highball glass filled with ice, stir and serve.

Boyard Fizz

11.3% ALC/VOL • 1.5 STD DRINKS

53ml (1¾ fl oz) Gin
10ml (⅓ fl oz) Grenadine
10ml (⅓ fl oz) Mango Juice
100ml (3⅓ fl oz) Soda Water

Pour Gin, Grenadine and juice into a cocktail shaker over ice. Shake and strain into a highball glass over ice. Add soda, stir gently and serve.

Perfect Cocktail

31.8% ALC/VOL • 1.6 STD DRINKS

45ml (1½ fl oz) Gin
8ml (¼ fl oz) Dry Vermouth
8ml (¼ fl oz) Sweet Vermouth
Dash Angostura Bitters

Pour ingredients into a cocktail shaker over ice and shake. Strain into a chilled cocktail glass and serve.

Zenith

16.5% ALC/VOL • 2.2 STD DRINKS

75ml (2½ fl oz) Gin
18ml (3/5 fl oz) Pineapple Juice
75ml (2½ fl oz) Soda Water
Stick of Pineapple

Pour Gin and juice into a mixing glass over ice. Stir and strain into an old-fashioned glass over ice. Add soda and stir gently. Garnish with a stick of pineapple and serve.

Once-Upon-a-Time

30.2% ALC/VOL • 1.8 STD DRINKS

45ml (1½ fl oz) Gin
15ml (½ fl oz) Apricot Brandy
15ml (½ fl oz) Lillet

Pour ingredients into a mixing glass over crushed ice and stir. Strain into a chilled cocktail glass and serve.

Skyscraper

13.3% ALC/VOL • 1.9 STD DRINKS

45ml (1½ fl oz) Gin
15ml (½ fl oz) Green Crème De Menthe
15ml (½ fl oz) Triple Sec
10ml (⅓ fl oz) Fresh Lime Juice
1 teaspoon Sugar Syrup
90ml (3 fl oz) Soda Water

Pour Gin, Crème De Menthe, Triple Sec, juice and sugar into a cocktail shaker over ice. Shake and strain into a highball glass over ice. Add soda, stir gently and serve.

White Elephant

20.2% ALC/VOL • 1.7 STD DRINKS

45ml (1½ fl oz) Gin
30ml (1 fl oz) Sweet Vermouth
White of 1 Egg

Pour ingredients into a cocktail shaker over ice and shake. Strain into a chilled cocktail glass and serve.

Blue Fizz

14% ALC/VOL • 2 STD DRINKS

60ml (2 fl oz) Dry Gin
15ml (½ fl oz) Blue Curaçao
15ml (½ fl oz) Fresh Lemon Juice
1 teaspoon Caster Sugar
90ml (3 fl oz) Soda Water
Slice of Lemon

Pour Gin, Curaçao and juice into a cocktail shaker over ice then add sugar. Shake and strain into a highball glass over ice. Add soda and stir gently. Garnish with a slice of lemon and serve.

Georgia Gin

21.8% ALC/VOL • 1.5 STD DRINKS

45ml (1½ fl oz) Gin
15ml (½ fl oz) Peach Schnapps
30ml (1 fl oz) Fresh Orange Juice

Pour ingredients into a cocktail shaker over ice and shake. Strain into a chilled cocktail glass and serve.

Bluebird

35% ALC/VOL • 2.1 STD DRINKS

45ml (1½ fl oz) Gin
15ml (½ fl oz) Blue Curaçao
15ml (½ fl oz) Cointreau
2 dashes Orange Bitters
Maraschino Cherry
Twist of Lemon Peel

Pour Gin, Curaçao, Cointreau and Bitters into a mixing glass over ice. Stir and strain into a chilled cocktail glass. Garnish with a cherry and lemon peel then serve.

Cessna

32.9% ALC/VOL • 1.8 STD DRINKS

45ml (1½ fl oz) Gin
15ml (½ fl oz) Dubonnet
10ml (⅓ fl oz) Maraschino Liqueur

Pour ingredients into a cocktail shaker over ice and shake. Strain into a chilled cocktail glass and serve.

Latino Bracing

28.1% ALC/VOL • 2 STD DRINKS

45ml (1½ fl oz) Gin

45ml (1½ fl oz) Dry Vermouth
5 drops Cherry Brandy
5 drops Triple Sec
3 Fresh Mint Leaves
2 Cherries
Slice of Lemon

Pour Gin, Vermouth, Brandy and Triple Sec into a mixing glass over ice. Stir and strain into a chilled cocktail glass. Garnish with mint leaves, cherries and a slice of lemon then serve.

Cup of Gin

12% ALC/VOL • 1.8 STD DRINKS

This drink is also known as Geisha Cup, *p 93.*

Bella, Bella

23.1% ALC/VOL • 1.8 STD DRINKS

30ml (1 fl oz) Gin
20ml (⅔ fl oz) Aperol
15ml (½ fl oz) Limoncello
15ml (½ fl oz) Mandarine Napoleon
20ml (⅔ fl oz) Fresh Orange Juice
Twist of Lemon Peel

Pour Gin, Aperol, Limoncello, Mandarine Napoleon and juice into a cocktail shaker over ice. Shake and strain into a chilled cocktail glass. Garnish with lemon peel and serve.

Grand Royal Clover Club

20.2% ALC/VOL • 2.6 STD DRINKS

90ml (3 fl oz) Dry Gin
15ml (½ fl oz) Grenadine
15ml (½ fl oz) Fresh Lemon Juice
1 Fresh Egg

Pour ingredients into a cocktail shaker over ice and shake. Strain into a chilled champagne saucer and serve.

Long Island Ice Tea – Boston Style

18.8% ALC/VOL • 3.3 STD DRINKS

30ml (1 fl oz) Gin
30ml (1 fl oz) Grand Marnier
30ml (1 fl oz) Light Rum
30ml (1 fl oz) Tia Maria
15ml (½ fl oz) Fresh Orange Juice
15ml (½ fl oz) Sweet and Sour Mix
75ml (2½ fl oz) Cola

Pour Gin, Grand Marnier, Rum, Tia, juice and sour mix into a cocktail shaker over ice. Shake and strain into a highball glass over ice. Add cola, stir gently and serve.

Allen

21.9% ALC/VOL • 1.3 STD DRINKS

45ml (1½ fl oz) Dry Gin
23ml (¾ fl oz) Grenadine
8ml (¼ fl oz) Fresh Lemon Juice

Pour ingredients into a cocktail shaker over ice and shake. Strain into a chilled cocktail glass and serve.

Green Fizz

8.9% ALC/VOL • 1.8 STD DRINKS

60ml (2 fl oz) Gin
5ml (⅙ fl oz) Green Crème De Menthe
15ml (½ fl oz) Fresh Lemon Juice
1 teaspoon Caster Sugar
White of 1 Egg
135ml (4½ fl oz) Soda Water

Pour Gin, Crème De Menthe, juice and egg white into a cocktail shaker over ice then add sugar. Shake and strain into a chilled highball glass over 2 ice cubes. Add soda, stir gently and serve.

Eagle Cocktail

22.9% ALC/VOL • 2 STD DRINKS

45ml (1½ fl oz) Gin
23ml (¾ fl oz) Crème Yvette
10ml (⅓ fl oz) Fresh Lemon Juice
1 teaspoon Sugar Syrup
White of 1 Egg

Pour ingredients into a cocktail shaker over ice and shake. Strain into a chilled wine glass and serve.

Rosette Merola

7.2% ALC/VOL • 1.4 STD DRINKS

15ml (½ fl oz) Dry Gin
15ml (½ fl oz) Aperol
15ml (½ fl oz) Goldschläger
15ml (½ fl oz) Kiwi Liqueur
180ml (6 fl oz) Fresh Orange Juice
Slice of Orange

Pour Gin, Aperol, Goldschläger and Liqueur into a mixing glass over ice. Stir and strain into a highball glass over ice. Add juice and stir. Garnish with a slice of orange and serve.

Acacia

31% ALC/VOL • 2.2 STD DRINKS

60ml (2 fl oz) Gin
15ml (½ fl oz) Bénédictine
Dash Kirsch
15ml (½ fl oz) Fresh Lemon Juice

Pour ingredients into a cocktail shaker over ice and shake. Strain into a chilled cocktail glass and serve.

Blue Hamilton

10.2% ALC/VOL • 2.8 STD DRINKS

45ml (1½ fl oz) Gin
30ml (1 fl oz) Blue Curaçao
30ml (1 fl oz) Vodka
150ml (5 fl oz) Grapefruit Juice

90ml (3 fl oz) Lemon-Lime Soda

Pour Gin, Curaçao, Vodka and juice into a tall glass over crushed ice then stir. Add soda, stir gently and serve.

Aruba

11.9% ALC/VOL • 1.2 STD DRINKS

30ml (1 fl oz) Gin
15ml (½ fl oz) Curaçao
30ml (1 fl oz) Fresh Lemon Juice
1 teaspoon Orgeat Syrup
1 Fresh Egg

Pour ingredients into a cocktail shaker over ice and shake. Strain into a chilled cocktail glass and serve.

Imperial Martini

27.7% ALC/VOL • 1.4 STD DRINKS

30ml (1 fl oz) Dry Gin
30ml (1 fl oz) Dry Vermouth
Dash Angostura Bitters
Dash Maraschino Liqueur
Olive

Pour Gin, Vermouth, Bitters and Liqueur into a mixing glass over ice. Stir and strain into a chilled martini glass. Garnish with an olive and serve.

Hawaiian Martini

31.4% ALC/VOL • 2.2 STD DRINKS

60ml (2 fl oz) Dry Gin
15ml (½ fl oz) Cointreau
15ml (½ fl oz) Pineapple Juice

Pour ingredients into a cocktail shaker over ice and shake. Strain into a chilled martini glass and serve.

Martini Exotica

26.4% ALC/VOL • 1.6 STD DRINKS

45ml (1½ fl oz) Dry Gin
15ml (½ fl oz) Midori
15ml (½ fl oz) Fresh Lime Juice
Slice of Lime

Pour Gin, Midori and juice into a mixing glass over ice. Stir and strain into a chilled martini glass. Garnish with a slice of lime and serve.

Dry Martini

33.8% ALC/VOL • 2.4 STD DRINKS

75ml (2½ fl oz) Dry Gin
15ml (½ fl oz) Dry Vermouth
Olive

Pour Gin and Vermouth into a mixing glass over ice. Stir and strain into a chilled martini glass. Add an olive and serve.

Southern Martini

33.3% ALC/VOL • 2.4 STD DRINKS

60ml (2 fl oz) Gin
15ml (½ fl oz) Southern Comfort
15ml (½ fl oz) Sweet Vermouth
Maraschino Cherry

Pour Gin, Southern Comfort and Vermouth into a mixing glass over ice. Stir and strain into a chilled martini glass. Garnish with a cherry and serve.

Smoky Martini

36.5% ALC/VOL • 1.5 STD DRINKS

50ml (1⅔ fl oz) Dry Gin
Dash Dry Vermouth
Dash Scotch Whisky

Pour ingredients into a mixing glass over ice and stir. Strain into a frosted martini glass and serve.

Perfect Martini

26.8% ALC/VOL • 1.3 STD DRINKS

30ml (1 fl oz) Dry Gin
15ml (½ fl oz) Dry Vermouth
15ml (½ fl oz) Sweet Vermouth

Pour ingredients into a mixing glass over ice and stir gently. Strain into a chilled martini glass and serve.

Harry Denton Martini

42.1% ALC/VOL • 1.8 STD DRINKS

38ml (1¼ fl oz) Gin
15ml (½ fl oz) Green Chartreuse

Pour ingredients into a cocktail shaker over ice and shake. Strain into a chilled martini glass and serve.

Cooperstown Cocktail

26.8% ALC/VOL • 1.3 STD DRINKS

This drink is a Perfect Martini that is shaken not stirred and garnished with a sprig of fresh mint.

Paisley Martini

33.7% ALC/VOL • 2.1 STD DRINKS

60ml (2 fl oz) Gin
15ml (½ fl oz) Dry Vermouth
5ml (⅙ fl oz) Scotch Whisky
Twist of Lemon Peel

Pour Gin, Vermouth and Whisky into an old-fashioned glass over ice then stir. Garnish with lemon peel and serve.

Martini on the Rocks

36.1% ALC/VOL • 1.9 STD DRINKS

60ml (2 fl oz) Dry Gin
3 dashes Dry Vermouth

Pour ingredients into an old-fashioned glass over ice, stir and serve.

Sweet Martini

29.7% ALC/VOL • 2.1 STD DRINKS

60ml (2 fl oz) Gin
30ml (1 fl oz) Sweet Vermouth
Maraschino Cherry

Pour Gin and Vermouth into a mixing glass over ice. Stir and strain into a chilled martini glass. Add a cherry and serve.

Fino Martini

34.3% ALC/VOL • 1.9 STD DRINKS

60ml (2 fl oz) Gin
10ml (⅓ fl oz) Fino Sherry
Twist of Lemon Peel

Pour Gin and Sherry into a mixing glass over ice. Stir and strain into a chilled martini glass. Add lemon peel and serve.

Saketini

33.4% ALC/VOL • 2.4 STD DRINKS

75ml (2½ fl oz) Dry Gin
15ml (½ fl oz) Sake
Twist of Lemon Peel

Pour Gin and Sake into a mixing glass over ice. Stir and strain into a chilled martini glass. Garnish with lemon peel and serve.

Pernod Martini

33.2% ALC/VOL • 2 STD DRINKS

60ml (2 fl oz) Gin
15ml (½ fl oz) Dry Vermouth
Dash Pernod

Pour ingredients into a mixing glass over ice and stir. Strain into a chilled martini glass and serve.

Sand Martini

27.5% ALC/VOL • 2.1 STD DRINKS

45ml (1½ fl oz) Dry Gin
45ml (1½ fl oz) Sweet Vermouth
5ml (1/6 fl oz) Green Chartreuse

Pour ingredients into a mixing glass over ice and stir. Strain into a chilled martini glass and serve.

Racquet Club Martini

33% ALC/VOL • 2 STD DRINKS

60ml (2 fl oz) Gin
15ml (½ fl oz) Dry Vermouth
2 dashes Orange Bitters

Pour ingredients into a mixing glass over ice and stir. Strain into a chilled martini glass and serve.

Mint Martini

32.4% ALC/VOL • 2.3 STD DRINKS

60ml (2 fl oz) Gin
30ml (1 fl oz) Green Crème De Menthe
3 Fresh Mint Leaves

Pour Gin and Crème De Menthe into a mixing glass over ice. Stir and strain into a chilled martini glass. Garnish with mint leaves and serve.

Martini Esoterica

31% ALC/VOL • 2.3 STD DRINKS

60ml (2 fl oz) Gin
30ml (1 fl oz) Dry Vermouth
3 dashes Pernod

Pour ingredients into a cocktail shaker over ice and shake. Strain into a chilled martini glass and serve.

Chambord Martini

30.2% ALC/VOL • 2.1 STD DRINKS

60ml (2 fl oz) Gin
30ml (1 fl oz) Chambord
Twist of Lemon Peel

Pour Gin and Chambord into a cocktail shaker over ice. Shake and strain into a chilled martini glass. Garnish with lemon peel and serve.

Blues Martini

36.6% ALC/VOL • 0.9 STD DRINKS

15ml (½ fl oz) Dry Gin
15ml (½ fl oz) Vodka
Dash Blue Curaçao

Pour ingredients into a mixing glass over ice and stir gently. Strain into a martini glass over ice and serve.

The Captain's Martini

32.3% ALC/VOL • 1.7 STD DRINKS

45ml (1½ fl oz) Gin
15ml (½ fl oz) White Crème De Menthe
5ml (1/6 fl oz) Dry Vermouth

Pour ingredients into a cocktail shaker over ice and shake. Strain into a chilled martini glass and serve.

Black Martini

37.4% ALC/VOL • 0.9 STD DRINKS

20ml (⅔ fl oz) Gin
10ml (⅓ fl oz) Black Sambuca

Pour ingredients into a mixing glass over ice and stir. Strain into a chilled martini glass and serve.

Homestead Cocktail

29.7% ALC/VOL • 2.1 STD DRINKS

This drink is a Sweet Martini (p 107) garnished with a slice of orange.

Rum

Rum is distilled from fermented sugarcane and is produced by most sugarcane growing countries. There are three main types of Rums: White (light), Gold and Black (dark).

Light Rums have originated from the southern Caribbean Islands and are usually only aged for approximately one year in oak casks.

Dark Rums are aged in casks for between three and fifteen years with caramel being added in some cases for the purpose of darkening the Rum's colour. Dark Rum has a richer stronger flavour than Light Rum and is traditionally produced in the tropics such as Jamaica.

151-Proof Rums are utilized in cocktails that require flaming and can also be called for in certain cooking recipes for the same purpose of flaming.

Añejo Rum is 'aged' Rum.

Christopher Columbus introduced the West Indies to sugarcane, although it was the Spanish settlers who brought the skills of distilling with them to the West Indies and so were able to produce Rum. The first distilled sugarcane was produced for medicinal purposes and then by the seventeenth century Rum had become the drink issued to slaves who worked the plantations. By the mid-seventeenth century, the Royal Navy crewmen were supplied a daily issue of Rum. This daily issue of Rum was to help battle the cold and scurvy.

In Australia, Rum became famous for the Rum Rebellion of 1808.

Cachaça is distilled from fermented and concentrated sugar cane sap. Recipes based with Cachaça have been included in this Rum section due to being similar to Light Rum, although it is a sugar cane Brandy.

Rum Cooler

12.1% ALC/VOL • 1.8 STD DRINKS

60ml (2 fl oz) Dark Rum
4 dashes Grenadine
30ml (1 fl oz) Fresh Lemon Juice
90ml (3 fl oz) Soda Water
Slice of Lemon
Slice of Orange

Pour Rum, Grenadine and juice into a collins glass over ice then stir. Add soda and stir gently. Garnish with a slice of lemon and orange then serve.

Corkscrew

31% ALC/VOL • 1.8 STD DRINKS

45ml (1½ fl oz) Light Rum
15ml (½ fl oz) Dry Vermouth
15ml (½ fl oz) Peach Brandy
Spiral of Lemon Peel

Pour Rum, Vermouth and Brandy into a cocktail shaker over ice. Shake and strain into an old-fashioned glass over cracked ice. Add lemon peel and serve.

Mai Tai

31.8% ALC/VOL • 3 STD DRINKS

60ml (2 fl oz) Light Rum
30ml (1 fl oz) Dark Rum
15ml (½ fl oz) Amaretto
15ml (½ fl oz) Fresh Lemon or Lime Juice
Maraschino Cherry
Slice of Pineapple
Sprig of Fresh Mint

Pour Rums, Amaretto and juice into a cocktail shaker over ice. Shake and strain into an old-fashioned glass over crushed ice. Garnish with a cherry, slice of pineapple and sprig of mint then serve.

Navy Rum

9.3% ALC/VOL • 0.9 STD DRINKS

30ml (1 fl oz) Dark Rum
90ml (3 fl oz) Spring Water
Slice of Lemon

Pour Rum and water into an old-fashioned glass over ice then stir. Garnish with a slice of lemon and serve.

Pineapple Fizz

12% ALC/VOL • 1.8 STD DRINKS

60ml (2 fl oz) Light Rum
30ml (1 fl oz) Pineapple Juice
1 teaspoon Caster Sugar
90ml (3 fl oz) Soda Water
Slice of Pineapple

Pour Rum and juice into a cocktail shaker over ice then add sugar. Shake and strain into a highball glass over ice. Add soda and stir gently. Garnish with a slice of pineapple and serve.

Blue Hawaiian

12.4% ALC/VOL • 2.4 STD DRINKS

60ml (2 fl oz) Light Rum
30ml (1 fl oz) Blue Curaçao
120ml (4 fl oz) Pineapple Juice
30ml (1 fl oz) Coconut Cream
Slice of Pineapple

Pour Rum, Curaçao, juice and cream into a cocktail shaker over ice. Shake and strain into a highball glass over ice. Garnish with a slice of pineapple and serve.

Planter's Punch

12.3% ALC/VOL • 1.8 STD DRINKS

60ml (2 fl oz) Dark Rum
Dash Angostura Bitters
5ml (1/6 fl oz) Grenadine
30ml (1 fl oz) Fresh Lemon or Lime Juice
90ml (3 fl oz) Soda Water
Maraschino Cherry
Slice of Lemon
Slice of Orange

Pour Rum, Bitters, Grenadine and juice into a highball glass over ice then stir. Add crushed ice and soda then stir gently. Garnish with a cherry, slice of lemon and orange then serve.

Rum Manhattan

28.4% ALC/VOL • 1.7 STD DRINKS

45ml (1½ fl oz) Dark Rum
30ml (1 fl oz) Sweet Vermouth
Dash Angostura Bitters

Pour ingredients into a mixing glass over ice and stir. Strain into a chilled cocktail glass and serve.

Rum Collins

13.1% ALC/VOL • 1.8 STD DRINKS

60ml (2 fl oz) Dark Rum
15ml (½ fl oz) Fresh Lemon or Lime Juice
1 teaspoon Sugar Syrup
90ml (3 fl oz) Soda Water
Maraschino Cherry
Slice of Orange

Pour Rum, juice and sugar into a cocktail shaker over ice. Shake and strain into a collins glass over ice. Add soda and stir gently. Garnish with a cherry and slice of orange then serve.

Cuba Libre

13.5% ALC/VOL • 1.8 STD DRINKS

60ml (2 fl oz) Dark Rum
15ml (½ fl oz) Fresh Lime Juice
90ml (3 fl oz) Cola
Slice of Lime

Pour Rum and juice into a highball glass over ice then stir. Add cola and stir gently. Garnish with a slice of lime and serve.

White Lion

25.2% ALC/VOL • 1.4 STD DRINKS

45ml (1½ fl oz) Dark Rum
3 dashes Curaçao
15ml (½ fl oz) Fresh Lemon Juice
3 dashes Raspberry Syrup
½ teaspoon Sugar Syrup
Maraschino Cherry
Slice of Orange

Pour Rum, Curaçao, juice, syrup and sugar into a cocktail shaker over ice. Shake and strain into an old-fashioned glass over crushed ice. Garnish with a cherry and slice of orange then serve.

Mary Pickford

23.9% ALC/VOL • 1.8 STD DRINKS

60ml (2 fl oz) Golden Rum
Dash Maraschino Liqueur
3 dashes Grenadine
30ml (1 fl oz) Pineapple Juice

Pour ingredients into a cocktail shaker over ice and shake. Strain into a chilled cocktail glass and serve.

Ski Lift

19.5% ALC/VOL • 2.1 STD DRINKS

45ml (1½ fl oz) Bacardi
15ml (½ fl oz) Sambuca
15ml (½ fl oz) White Crème De Cacao
30ml (1 fl oz) Coconut Milk (chilled)
30ml (1 fl oz) Fresh Cream
2 Twists of Lemon Peel

Pour Bacardi, Sambuca, Cacao, milk and cream into a cocktail shaker over ice. Shake and strain into a chilled champagne saucer. Garnish with lemon peels and serve.

A blender may also be used to prepare this drink.

Shanghai

25% ALC/VOL • 2.1 STD DRINKS

60ml (2 fl oz) Dark Rum
15ml (½ fl oz) Anisette
2 dashes Grenadine
30ml (1 fl oz) Fresh Lemon Juice

Pour ingredients into a cocktail shaker over ice and shake. Strain into a chilled cocktail glass and serve.

Strawberry Rum Flip

15.9% ALC/VOL • 1.4 STD DRINKS

30ml (1 fl oz) Light Rum
30ml (1 fl oz) Strawberry Liqueur
5ml (1/6 fl oz) Fresh Lemon Juice
1 teaspoon Sugar Syrup
1 Fresh Egg
Nutmeg

Pour Rum, Liqueur, juice, sugar and egg into a cocktail shaker over ice. Shake and strain into a chilled goblet. Sprinkle nutmeg on top and serve.

Bacardi Cocktail

24% ALC/VOL • 1.8 STD DRINKS

60ml (2 fl oz) Bacardi
5ml (1/6 fl oz) Grenadine
30ml (1 fl oz) Fresh Lemon or Lime Juice
Slice of Orange

Pour Bacardi, Grenadine and juice into a cocktail shaker over ice. Shake and strain into a chilled cocktail glass. Garnish with a slice of orange and serve.

Goldilocks

8.3% ALC/VOL • 1.4 STD DRINKS

30ml (1 fl oz) Dark Rum
30ml (1 fl oz) Malibu
90ml (3 fl oz) Pineapple Juice
60ml (2 fl oz) Fresh Orange Juice
Slice of Pineapple

Pour Rum, Malibu and juices into a cocktail shaker over ice. Shake and strain into a hurricane glass over cracked ice. Garnish with a slice of pineapple and serve.

Lazy Afternoon

34.6% ALC/VOL • 2 STD DRINKS

30ml (1 fl oz) Dark Rum
30ml (1 fl oz) Light Rum
15ml (½ fl oz) Cherry Brandy
Maraschino Cherry
Slice of Pineapple

Pour Rums and Brandy into a highball glass over crushed ice then stir. Garnish with a cherry and slice of pineapple then serve with a straw.

Antillano

18% ALC/VOL • 1.8 STD DRINKS

30ml (1 fl oz) Golden Rum
30ml (1 fl oz) Light Rum
Dash Angostura Bitters
5ml (1/6 fl oz) Grenadine
30ml (1 fl oz) Grapefruit Juice
30ml (1 fl oz) Pineapple Juice
Slice of Orange
Slice of Pineapple

Pour Rums, Bitters, Grenadine and juices into a cocktail shaker over ice. Shake and strain into a highball glass over crushed ice. Garnish with a slice of orange and pineapple then serve.

Columbia

23.3% ALC/VOL • 1.8 STD DRINKS

60ml (2 fl oz) Light Rum
30ml (1 fl oz) Fresh Lemon Juice
1½ teaspoons Raspberry Syrup

Pour ingredients into a cocktail shaker over ice and shake. Strain into a chilled cocktail glass and serve.

Mojito

14.9% ALC/VOL • 1.8 STD DRINKS

60ml (2 fl oz) Light Rum
30ml (1 fl oz) Fresh Lime Juice
½ teaspoon Sugar Syrup
60ml (2 fl oz) Soda Water
6 Sprigs of Fresh Mint

Pour sugar into a chilled collins glass and add 3 sprigs of mint. Muddle well and add juice. Add crushed ice to half fill glass and stir. Add Rum and stir. Add more crushed ice and soda then stir gently. Garnish with 3 sprigs of mint placed vertically in drink and serve.

Fox Trot

28.7% ALC/VOL • 1.5 STD DRINKS

45ml (1½ fl oz) Light Rum
5ml (1/6 fl oz) Cointreau
15ml (½ fl oz) Fresh Lime Juice
Slice of Lime

Pour Rum, Cointreau and juice into a cocktail shaker over ice. Shake and strain into a chilled cocktail glass. Garnish with a slice of lime and serve.

Apricot Lady

25.4% ALC/VOL • 1.9 STD DRINKS

45ml (1½ fl oz) Golden Rum
30ml (1 fl oz) Apricot Brandy
3 dashes Orange Curaçao
15ml (½ fl oz) Fresh Lime Juice
½ teaspoon Egg White
Slice of Orange

Pour Rum, Brandy, Curaçao, juice and egg white into a blender over crushed ice. Blend and pour into an old-fashioned glass over ice. Garnish with a slice of orange and serve.

Honey Bee

28.5% ALC/VOL • 1.8 STD DRINKS

60ml (2 fl oz) Light Rum
15ml (½ fl oz) Fresh Lime Juice
1 teaspoon Honey
Twist of Lime Peel

Pour Rum, juice and honey into a cocktail shaker over ice. Shake and strain into a chilled cocktail glass. Garnish with lime peel and serve.

Coffee Rum Cooler

11.7% ALC/VOL • 1.9 STD DRINKS

45ml (1½ fl oz) Dark Jamaica Rum
30ml (1 fl oz) Tia Maria
15ml (½ fl oz) Fresh Lime Juice
120ml (4 fl oz) Soda Water
Slice of Lime

Pour Rum, Tia and juice into a cocktail shaker over ice. Shake and strain into a collins glass over ice. Add soda and stir gently. Garnish with a slice of lime and serve.

Rum Alexander

22% ALC/VOL • 1.7 STD DRINKS

30ml (1 fl oz) Light Rum
30ml (1 fl oz) Dark Crème De Cacao
10ml (⅓ fl oz) Dark Rum
30ml (1 fl oz) Thick Cream
Nutmeg

Pour Rums, Cacao and cream into a cocktail shaker over ice. Shake and strain into a chilled cocktail glass. Sprinkle nutmeg on top and serve.

Bahama Mama

9.5% ALC/VOL • 1.4 STD DRINKS

15ml (½ fl oz) Dark Rum
15ml (½ fl oz) Coconut Liqueur
8ml (¼ fl oz) 151-Proof Dark Rum
8ml (¼ fl oz) Tia Maria
120ml (4 fl oz) Pineapple Juice
15ml (½ fl oz) Fresh Lemon Juice
Maraschino Cherry
Strawberry

Pour Rums, Liqueur, Tia and juices into a highball glass over ice then stir. Garnish with a cherry and a strawberry then serve.

Pilgrim

25.6% ALC/VOL • 1.3 STD DRINKS

45ml (1½ fl oz) New England Rum
5ml (⅙ fl oz) Grenadine
15ml (½ fl oz) Fresh Lemon Juice

Pour ingredients into a cocktail shaker over ice and shake. Strain into a chilled cocktail glass and serve.

Shark's Tooth

26.7% ALC/VOL • 1.6 STD DRINKS

45ml (1½ fl oz) Golden Rum
8ml (¼ fl oz) Sloe Gin
8ml (¼ fl oz) Sweet Vermouth
Dash Angostura Bitters
8ml (¼ fl oz) Fresh Lemon Juice
1½ teaspoons Passion-Fruit Syrup
Maraschino Cherry
Twist of Orange Peel

Prepare a cocktail glass with a sugar frosted rim. Pour Rum, Gin, Vermouth, Bitters, juice and syrup into a cocktail shaker over ice. Shake and strain into prepared glass. Twist orange peel above drink and place remainder of peel into drink. Add a cherry and serve.

Zocolo

7.4% ALC/VOL • 1.3 STD DRINKS

30ml (1 fl oz) Dark Rum
15ml (½ fl oz) Tequila
60ml (2 fl oz) Grapefruit Juice
60ml (2 fl oz) Pineapple Juice
60ml (2 fl oz) Soda Water
Maraschino Cherry
Slice of Orange
Wedge of Pineapple

Pour Rum, Tequila and juices into a cocktail shaker over ice. Shake and strain into a collins glass over ice. Add soda and stir gently. Garnish with a cherry, slice of orange and wedge of pineapple then serve.

Half Man Half Wit

12.7% ALC/VOL • 2 STD DRINKS

45ml (1½ fl oz) Light Rum
15ml (½ fl oz) Peach Schnapps

15ml (½ fl oz) Scotch Whisky
8ml (¼ fl oz) Grenadine
60ml (2 fl oz) Fresh Orange Juice
60ml (2 fl oz) Passion-Fruit Juice
Slice of Orange

Pour Rum, Schnapps, Whisky and juices into a cocktail shaker over ice. Shake and strain into a collins glass over cracked ice. Add Grenadine by pouring on top of drink – do not stir, then garnish with a slice of orange and serve with 2 straws.

Hat Trick

30% ALC/VOL • 1.1 STD DRINKS

30ml (1 fl oz) Dark Rum
30ml (1 fl oz) Light Rum
15ml (½ fl oz) Sweet Vermouth

Pour ingredients into a mixing glass over ice and stir. Strain into a chilled cocktail glass and serve.

Rum Sour

29.2% ALC/VOL • 1.8 STD DRINKS

60ml (2 fl oz) Light Rum
15ml (½ fl oz) Fresh Lemon Juice
½ teaspoon Sugar Syrup
Maraschino Cherry
Slice of Lemon

Pour Rum, juice and sugar into a cocktail shaker over ice. Shake and strain into a chilled sour glass. Garnish with a cherry and slice of lemon then serve.

Bacardi Special

32% ALC/VOL • 2.7 STD DRINKS

60ml (2 fl oz) Bacardi
30ml (1 fl oz) Dry Gin
Dash Grenadine
15ml (½ fl oz) Fresh Lime Juice
Slice of Lime

Pour Bacardi, Gin, Grenadine and juice into a cocktail shaker over ice. Shake and strain into a chilled cocktail glass. Garnish with a slice of lime and serve.

Bolo

24% ALC/VOL • 1.8 STD DRINKS

60ml (2 fl oz) Light Rum
15ml (½ fl oz) Fresh Lemon Juice
15ml (½ fl oz) Fresh Orange Juice
1 teaspoon Sugar Syrup
Slice of Lemon
Slice of Orange

Pour Rum, juices and sugar into a cocktail shaker over ice. Shake and strain into a chilled cocktail glass. Garnish with a slice of lemon and orange then serve.

Dry Rum

25.8% ALC/VOL • 1.5 STD DRINKS

45ml (1½ fl oz) Dark Rum
15ml (½ fl oz) Dry Sherry
15ml (½ fl oz) Fresh Lime Juice
Maraschino Cherry

Pour Rum, Sherry and juice into a cocktail shaker over ice. Shake and strain into a chilled cocktail glass. Garnish with a cherry and serve.

Rum Daisy

28.9% ALC/VOL • 2.1 STD DRINKS

60ml (2 fl oz) Light Rum
15ml (½ fl oz) Curaçao
2 dashes Grenadine
15ml (½ fl oz) Fresh Lemon Juice
Slice of Lemon

Pour Rum, Curaçao, Grenadine and juice into a cocktail shaker over ice. Shake and strain into an old-fashioned glass over ice. Top up with soda water if desired and stir gently. Garnish with a slice of lemon and serve.

Florida Special

19.7% ALC/VOL • 1.7 STD DRINKS

53ml (1¾ fl oz) Leilani Rum
5ml (1/6 fl oz) Dry Vermouth
5ml (1/6 fl oz) Sweet Vermouth
45ml (1½ fl oz) Grapefruit Juice

Pour ingredients into a mixing glass over crushed ice and stir. Strain into a chilled cocktail glass and serve.

Knickerbockers

33.8% ALC/VOL • 2.1 STD DRINKS

60ml (2 fl oz) Light Rum
8ml (¼ fl oz) Cointreau
5ml (1/6 fl oz) Fresh Orange Juice
2 dashes Fresh Lemon Juice
2 dashes Raspberry Syrup
Maraschino Cherry

Pour Rum, Cointreau, juices and syrup into a cocktail shaker over ice. Shake and strain into a chilled cocktail glass. Garnish with a cherry and serve.

Apple à la Mode

10.6% ALC/VOL • 0.9 STD DRINKS

30ml (1 fl oz) Dark Rum
60ml (2 fl oz) Apple Juice
½ scoop Vanilla Ice Cream
Sprig of Fresh Mint

Pour Rum and juice into a blender over small amount of crushed ice then add ice cream. Blend and pour into a chilled cocktail glass. Garnish with a sprig of mint and serve.

Rum Cow

4% ALC/VOL • 0.9 STD DRINKS

30ml (1 fl oz) Light Rum
Dash Angostura Bitters
1 teaspoon Sugar Syrup
Dash Vanilla Extract
250ml (8⅓ fl oz) Fresh Milk (chilled)
Nutmeg

Pour Rum, Bitters, sugar, extract and milk into a cocktail shaker over ice. Shake and strain into a chilled collins glass. Sprinkle nutmeg on top and serve.
This drink is also known as Rum Reviver, p 124.

Barrier Breaker

12.8% ALC/VOL • 1.9 STD DRINKS

45ml (1½ fl oz) Dark Rum
15ml (½ fl oz) Galliano
10ml (⅓ fl oz) Dark Crème De Cacao
120ml (4 fl oz) Black Coffee (chilled)

Pour ingredients into a coffee glass over crushed ice, stir and serve.

Banana Smooth

16.9% ALC/VOL • 1.8 STD DRINKS

60ml (2 fl oz) Light Rum
45ml (1½ fl oz) Thick Cream
½ Banana (diced)
2 Slices of Banana
Nutmeg

Pour Rum and cream into a blender over crushed ice then add diced banana. Blend until smooth and pour into a chilled champagne saucer. Sprinkle nutmeg on top and garnish with slices of banana then serve.

Pauline

24.7% ALC/VOL • 1.6 STD DRINKS

45ml (1½ fl oz) Light Rum
8ml (¼ fl oz) Cointreau
Dash Pernod
30ml (1 fl oz) Fresh Lemon Juice
Slice of Lemon

Pour Rum, Cointreau, Pernod and juice into a cocktail shaker over ice. Shake and strain into a chilled cocktail glass. Garnish with a slice of lemon and serve.

Envy

14.1% ALC/VOL • 1.5 STD DRINKS

30ml (1 fl oz) Light Rum
15ml (½ fl oz) Amaretto
15ml (½ fl oz) Blue Curaçao
75ml (2½ fl oz) Pineapple Juice
Slice of Lemon
Slice of Pineapple

Pour Rum, Amaretto, Curaçao and juice into a cocktail shaker over ice. Shake and strain into a chilled highball glass. Garnish with a slice of lemon and pineapple then serve.

Sonny Gets Kissed

24.8% ALC/VOL • 1.6 STD DRINKS

45ml (1½ fl oz) Light Rum
15ml (½ fl oz) Apricot Brandy
10ml (⅓ fl oz) Fresh Lemon Juice
10ml (⅓ fl oz) Fresh Lime Juice
½ teaspoon Sugar Syrup

Pour ingredients into a cocktail shaker over ice and shake. Strain into a chilled cocktail glass and serve.

Julia

14.5% ALC/VOL • 1.4 STD DRINKS

30ml (1 fl oz) Light Rum
23ml (¾ fl oz) Amaretto
30ml (1 fl oz) Thick Cream
2 teaspoons Strawberry Syrup
3 Strawberries (diced)
Strawberry

Pour Rum, Amaretto, cream and syrup into a blender over crushed ice then add diced strawberries. Blend and pour into a chilled cocktail glass. Garnish with a strawberry and serve with a short straw.

Rum Buck

9.5% ALC/VOL • 1.3 STD DRINKS

45ml (1½ fl oz) Light Rum
120ml (4 fl oz) Dry Ginger Ale
½ Fresh Lime
Slice of Lime

Pour Rum into a highball glass over ice and twist ½ lime above drink to release juice. Add spent shell and stir. Add Ginger Ale and stir gently. Garnish with a slice of lime and serve.

Hen's Night Zipper Ripper

17.5% ALC/VOL • 1.8 STD DRINKS

45ml (1½ fl oz) Light Rum
30ml (1 fl oz) Advocaat
8ml (¼ fl oz) Grenadine
23ml (¾ fl oz) Fresh Lime Juice
23ml (¾ fl oz) Mandarin Juice
Maraschino Cherry
Slice of Lime

Pour Rum, Advocaat, Grenadine and juices into a cocktail shaker over ice. Shake and strain into a chilled cocktail glass. Garnish with a cherry and slice of lime then serve.

Max the Silent

37.1% ALC/VOL • 1.9 STD DRINKS

30ml (1 fl oz) Añejo Rum
15ml (½ fl oz) Applejack
15ml (½ fl oz) Brandy
5ml (⅙ fl oz) Anisette

Pour ingredients into a mixing glass over ice and stir. Strain into a chilled cocktail glass and serve.

Fireman's Sour

14.8% ALC/VOL • 1.8 STD DRINKS

60ml (2 fl oz) Light Rum
10ml (⅓ fl oz) Grenadine
45ml (1½ fl oz) Fresh Lime Juice
1 teaspoon Sugar Syrup
30ml (1 fl oz) Soda Water
Maraschino Cherry
Slice of Orange

Pour Rum, Grenadine, juice and sugar into a cocktail shaker over ice. Shake and strain into a sour glass over ice. Add soda and stir gently. Garnish with a cherry and slice of orange then serve.

Black Maria

17.5% ALC/VOL • 3.5 STD DRINKS

60ml (2 fl oz) Light Rum
60ml (2 fl oz) Coffee Brandy
120ml (4 fl oz) Black Coffee (chilled)
2 teaspoons Sugar Syrup

Pour ingredients into a chilled brandy balloon and stir. Add cracked ice and serve.

Scorpion

15.5% ALC/VOL • 2.6 STD DRINKS

60ml (2 fl oz) Golden Rum
30ml (1 fl oz) Brandy
60ml (2 fl oz) Fresh Lemon Juice
60ml (2 fl oz) Fresh Orange Juice
1 teaspoon Sugar Syrup
Slice of Lemon

Pour Rum, Brandy, juices and sugar into a cocktail shaker over ice. Shake and strain into a highball glass over ice. Garnish with a slice of lemon and serve.

Captain's Blood

28% ALC/VOL • 1.3 STD DRINKS

45ml (1½ fl oz) Dark Rum
Dash Angostura Bitters
15ml (½ fl oz) Fresh Lime Juice
Slice of Lime

Pour Rum, Bitters and juice into a cocktail shaker over ice. Shake and strain into a chilled cocktail glass. Garnish with a slice of lime and serve.

Little Devil

31.7% ALC/VOL • 2.3 STD DRINKS

30ml (1 fl oz) Light Rum
30ml (1 fl oz) Dry Gin
15ml (½ fl oz) Cointreau
15ml (½ fl oz) Fresh Lemon Juice
Slice of Orange

Pour Rum, Gin, Cointreau and juice into a cocktail shaker over ice. Shake and strain into a chilled cocktail glass. Garnish with a slice of orange and serve.

Beachcomber

30.7% ALC/VOL • 1.9 STD DRINKS

45ml (1½ fl oz) Light Rum
15ml (½ fl oz) Cointreau
2 dashes Maraschino Liqueur
15ml (½ fl oz) Fresh Lime Juice
Slice of Lime

Pour Rum, Cointreau, Liqueur and juice into a cocktail shaker over ice. Shake and strain into a chilled cocktail glass. Garnish with a slice of lime and serve.

Polar Bear Cooler

11.3% ALC/VOL • 2.1 STD DRINKS

60ml (2 fl oz) Dark Rum
30ml (1 fl oz) Punt e Mes
30ml (1 fl oz) Fresh Lemon Juice
15ml (½ fl oz) Fresh Orange Juice
105ml (3½ fl oz) Lemonade
Maraschino Cherry
Spiral of Lemon
Wedge of Orange

Pour Rum, Punt e Mes and juices into a collins glass over crushed ice. Add a spiral of lemon and stir. Add lemonade and stir gently. Garnish with a cherry and wedge of orange then serve with 2 straws.

Havana

29.6% ALC/VOL • 1.8 STD DRINKS

45ml (1½ fl oz) Golden Rum
15ml (½ fl oz) Dry Gin
15ml (½ fl oz) Fresh Lemon Juice

Pour ingredients into a cocktail shaker over ice and shake. Strain into a chilled cocktail glass and serve.

Trinidad Punch

21.4% ALC/VOL • 1.4 STD DRINKS

45ml (1½ fl oz) Dark Rum
2 dashes Angostura Bitters
30ml (1 fl oz) Fresh Lime Juice
1 teaspoon Sugar Syrup
Twist of Lemon Peel
Nutmeg

Pour Rum, Bitters, juice and sugar into a cocktail shaker over cracked ice. Shake and pour into a goblet over ice. Add lemon peel and sprinkle nutmeg on top then serve.

Eye Opener

27.6% ALC/VOL • 1.5 STD DRINKS

45ml (1½ fl oz) Light Rum

3 dashes Curaçao
3 dashes Pernod
½ teaspoon Sugar Syrup
Yolk of 1 Egg

Pour ingredients into a cocktail shaker over ice and shake. Strain into a chilled cocktail glass and serve.

Blueberry Rumba

10.8% ALC/VOL • 1.7 STD DRINKS

30ml (1 fl oz) Light Rum
15ml (½ fl oz) Dark Rum
8ml (¼ fl oz) Blue Curaçao
8ml (¼ fl oz) Cointreau
60ml (2 fl oz) Pineapple Juice
23ml (¾ fl oz) Blueberry Syrup
60ml (2 fl oz) Lemonade

Pour Rums, Curaçao, Cointreau, juice and syrup into a cocktail shaker over ice. Shake and strain into a highball glass over ice. Add lemonade, stir gently and serve.

Purple Waters

32% ALC/VOL • 1.6 STD DRINKS

20ml (⅔ fl oz) Bacardi
15ml (½ fl oz) Parfait Amour
15ml (½ fl oz) Orange Curaçao
15ml (½ fl oz) Yellow
Chartreuse

Pour ingredients in order given into a chilled cocktail glass – do not stir, then serve.

Maraschino Cherry

14% ALC/VOL • 1.4 STD DRINKS

30ml (1 fl oz) Dark Rum
15ml (½ fl oz) Amaretto
15ml (½ fl oz) Peach Schnapps
Dash Grenadine
30ml (1 fl oz) Cranberry Juice
30ml (1 fl oz) Pineapple Juice
Fresh Whipped Cream
Maraschino Cherry

Pour Rum, Amaretto, Schnapps, Grenadine and juices into a blender over crushed ice. Blend until smooth and pour into a chilled hurricane glass. Float cream on top and garnish with a cherry then serve.

Almeria

23.5% ALC/VOL • 2.2 STD DRINKS

60ml (2 fl oz) Dark Rum
30ml (1 fl oz) Kahlúa
White of 1 Egg

Pour ingredients into a cocktail shaker over ice and shake. Strain into a chilled cocktail glass and serve.

Zombie

26.3% ALC/VOL • 3.8 STD DRINKS

30ml (1 fl oz) Dark Rum
30ml (1 fl oz) Jamaica Rum
30ml (1 fl oz) Light Rum
15ml (½ fl oz) Apricot Brandy
15ml (½ fl oz) 151-Proof Rum
30ml (1 fl oz) Fresh
Lemon Juice
15ml (½ fl oz) Papaya Juice
15ml (½ fl oz) Pineapple Juice
1 teaspoon Caster Sugar
Maraschino Cherry
Slice of Lemon
Slice of Orange
Sprig of Fresh Mint

Pour Dark, Jamaica and Light Rums into a cocktail shaker over ice. Add Brandy and juices. Shake and strain into a zombie glass over ice. Layer 151-Proof Rum on top and sprinkle sugar on top. Garnish with a cherry, slice of lemon, orange and sprig of mint then serve.

Rum and Coconut Cooler

22.8% ALC/VOL • 2.2 STD DRINKS

75ml (2½ fl oz) Light Rum
30ml (1 fl oz) Coconut Cream
15ml (½ fl oz) Fresh
Lemon Juice
5ml (⅙ fl oz) Soda Water
Maraschino Cherry
Slice of Lemon

Pour Rum, cream and juice into a cocktail shaker over ice. Shake and strain into a collins glass over ice then add soda – do not stir. Garnish with a cherry and slice of lemon then serve.

Melba

28.9% ALC/VOL • 1.5 STD DRINKS

23ml (¾ fl oz) Light Rum
23ml (¾ fl oz) Swedish Punsch
2 dashes Pernod
2 dashes Grenadine
15ml (½ fl oz) Fresh
Lemon Juice

Pour ingredients into a cocktail shaker over ice and shake. Strain into a chilled cocktail glass and serve.

The Big Chill

10.1% ALC/VOL • 1.3 STD DRINKS

45ml (1½ fl oz) Dark Rum
30ml (1 fl oz) Cranberry Juice
30ml (1 fl oz) Fresh
Orange Juice
30ml (1 fl oz) Pineapple Juice
30ml (1 fl oz) Coconut Cream
Maraschino Cherry
Wedge of Pineapple

Pour Rum, juices and cream into a blender over crushed ice. Blend until smooth and pour into a chilled pilsner glass. Garnish with a cherry and wedge of pineapple then serve.

Wedding Night

24.7% ALC/VOL • 2.6 STD DRINKS

90ml (3 fl oz) Martinique Rum
30ml (1 fl oz) Fresh Lime Juice
15ml (½ fl oz) Maple Syrup

Pour ingredients into a cocktail shaker over crushed ice and shake. Pour into a chilled champagne flute and serve.

Cherry Rum Cola

13.3% ALC/VOL • 1.7 STD DRINKS

45ml (1½ fl oz) Golden Rum
23ml (¾ fl oz) Peter Heering Liqueur
5ml (1/6 fl oz) Fresh Lemon Juice
90ml (3 fl oz) Cola
Slice of Lemon

Pour Rum, Liqueur and juice into a highball glass over ice then stir. Add cola, stir gently and garnish with a slice of lemon then serve.

Yellow Bird

14.7% ALC/VOL • 2.4 STD DRINKS

45ml (1½ fl oz) Bacardi
30ml (1 fl oz) Galliano
15ml (½ fl oz) Banana Liqueur
60ml (2 fl oz) Fresh Orange Juice
60ml (2 fl oz) Pineapple Juice

Pour ingredients into a cocktail shaker over ice and shake. Strain into a highball glass over ice and serve with a straw.

Lifetimer

12.9% ALC/VOL • 2.2 STD DRINKS

45ml (1½ fl oz) Light Rum
15ml (½ fl oz) Apricot Brandy
15ml (½ fl oz) Brandy
5ml (1/6 fl oz) Cointreau
15ml (½ fl oz) Fresh Lemon Juice
½ teaspoon Sugar Syrup
120ml (4 fl oz) Soda Water
Wedge of Lime

Pour Rum, Brandies, Cointreau, juice and sugar into a cocktail shaker over ice. Shake and strain into a highball glass over ice. Add soda and stir gently. Garnish with a wedge of lime and serve.

Little Princess

26.5% ALC/VOL • 1.3 STD DRINKS

30ml (1 fl oz) Light Rum
30ml (1 fl oz) Sweet Vermouth

Pour ingredients into a mixing glass over ice and stir. Strain into a chilled cocktail glass and serve.
This drink is also known as Poker Cocktail.

Rum Old-Fashioned

36.2% ALC/VOL • 1.7 STD DRINKS

45ml (1½ fl oz) Light Rum
5ml (1/6 fl oz) 151-Proof Rum
Dash Angostura Bitters
5ml (1/6 fl oz) Spring Water
½ teaspoon Sugar Syrup
Twist of Lemon Peel

Pour Light Rum, Bitters, water and sugar into an old-fashioned glass over ice then stir. Twist lemon peel above drink and discard remainder of peel. Layer 151-Proof Rum on top and serve.

Strawberries and Cream

14.7% ALC/VOL • 1.8 STD DRINKS

60ml (2 fl oz) Light Rum
45ml (1½ fl oz) Thick Cream
5 Strawberries (diced)
Strawberry

Pour Rum and cream into a blender over crushed ice then add diced strawberries. Blend and pour into a chilled champagne saucer. Garnish with a strawberry and serve.

Club Paradise

15.3% ALC/VOL • 1.4 STD DRINKS

30ml (1 fl oz) Light Rum
15ml (½ fl oz) Banana Liqueur
15ml (½ fl oz) White Crème De Cacao
30ml (1 fl oz) Fresh Cream
1 scoop Vanilla Ice Cream
Slice of Banana
Nutmeg

Pour Rum, Liqueur, Cacao and cream into a blender without ice then add ice cream. Blend until smooth and pour into a chilled brandy balloon. Sprinkle nutmeg on top and garnish with a slice of banana then serve.

Black Rose

10.1% ALC/VOL • 1.4 STD DRINKS

45ml (1½ fl oz) Dark Rum
120ml (4 fl oz) Black Coffee (chilled)
1 teaspoon Sugar Syrup

Pour ingredients into a mixing glass over ice and stir. Strain into a chilled champagne flute and serve.

Apricot Pie

24.7% ALC/VOL • 1.3 STD DRINKS

30ml (1 fl oz) Light Rum
30ml (1 fl oz) Sweet Vermouth
3 dashes Apricot Brandy
Dash Grenadine
3 dashes Fresh Lemon Juice
Twist of Orange Peel

Pour Rum, Vermouth, Brandy, Grenadine and juice into a cocktail shaker over ice. Shake and strain into a chilled cocktail glass. Twist orange peel above drink and place remainder of peel into drink then serve.

Columbus Cocktail

22.4% ALC/VOL • 1.7 STD DRINKS

45ml (1½ fl oz) Golden Rum
23ml (¾ fl oz) Apricot Brandy
30ml (1 fl oz) Fresh Lime Juice
Slice of Lime

Pour Rum, Brandy and juice into a cocktail shaker over crushed ice. Shake and pour into a chilled champagne saucer. Add a slice of lime and serve.

Bigger Better Blue Lagoon

17.3% ALC/VOL • 2.5 STD DRINKS

30ml (1 fl oz) Light Rum
30ml (1 fl oz) Blue Curaçao
30ml (1 fl oz) Malibu
30ml (1 fl oz) Peach Schnapps
Dash Grenadine
60ml (2 fl oz) Pineapple Juice
Cherry

Pour Rum, Curaçao, Malibu, Schnapps and juice into a cocktail shaker over ice. Shake and strain into a collins glass half filled with ice. Add Grenadine – do not stir, then add a cherry and serve.

Mallorca

32% ALC/VOL • 4.5 STD DRINKS

90ml (3 fl oz) Light Rum
30ml (1 fl oz) Banana Liqueur
30ml (1 fl oz) Drambuie
30ml (1 fl oz) Dry Vermouth

Pour ingredients into a mixing glass over ice and stir. Strain into a chilled champagne saucer and serve.

Caribbean Ice Tea

29% ALC/VOL • 4.1 STD DRINKS

30ml (1 fl oz) Golden Rum
30ml (1 fl oz) Blue Curaçao
30ml (1 fl oz) Gin
30ml (1 fl oz) Vodka
30ml (1 fl oz) White Tequila
30ml (1 fl oz) Sweet and Sour Mix
Slice of Orange

Pour Rum, Curaçao, Gin, Vodka, Tequila and sour mix into a mixing glass over ice. Stir and strain into a highball glass over ice. Garnish with a slice of orange and serve.

Boston Sidecar

32.7% ALC/VOL • 2.3 STD DRINKS

30ml (1 fl oz) Light Rum
30ml (1 fl oz) Cognac
15ml (½ fl oz) Cointreau
15ml (½ fl oz) Fresh Lemon Juice

Pour ingredients into a cocktail shaker over ice and shake. Strain into a chilled cocktail glass and serve.

Blue Haze

30.6% ALC/VOL • 1.8 STD DRINKS

30ml (1 fl oz) Bacardi
15ml (½ fl oz) Dry Vermouth
15ml (½ fl oz) Parfait Amour
10ml (⅓ fl oz) Cointreau
4 dashes Blue Curaçao

Pour Bacardi, Vermouth, Parfait Amour and Cointreau into a cocktail shaker over ice. Shake and strain into a chilled cocktail glass. Add Curaçao by pouring into centre of drink – do not stir, then serve.

Stranger-in-Town

32% ALC/VOL • 2.3 STD DRINKS

45ml (1½ fl oz) Light Rum
15ml (½ fl oz) Calvados
15ml (½ fl oz) Cherry Brandy
15ml (½ fl oz) Sweet Vermouth
Maraschino Cherry

Pour Rum, Calvados, Brandy and Vermouth into a mixing glass over ice. Stir and strain into a chilled cocktail glass. Garnish with a cherry and serve.

Sand in Your Ass

8.8% ALC/VOL • 1.5 STD DRINKS

30ml (1 fl oz) Light Rum
30ml (1 fl oz) Malibu
5ml (⅙ fl oz) Curaçao
60ml (2 fl oz) Pineapple Juice
45ml (1½ fl oz) Sweet and Sour Mix
45ml (1½ fl oz) Lemon-Lime Soda

Pour Rum, Malibu, Curaçao, juice and sour mix into a highball glass half filled with ice then stir well. Add soda, stir gently and serve.

Bahamas

24.6% ALC/VOL • 1.8 STD DRINKS

30ml (1 fl oz) Light Rum
30ml (1 fl oz) Southern Comfort
Dash Banana Liqueur
30ml (1 fl oz) Fresh Lemon Juice

Pour ingredients into a cocktail shaker over ice and shake. Strain into a chilled cocktail glass and serve.

Mostly Mal

32.5% ALC/VOL • 2 STD DRINKS

45ml (1½ fl oz) Añejo Rum
15ml (½ fl oz) Cointreau
15ml (½ fl oz) Dry Vermouth
3 dashes Grenadine
Maraschino Cherry

Pour Rum, Cointreau, Vermouth and Grenadine into a cocktail shaker over ice. Shake and strain into a chilled cocktail glass. Garnish with a cherry and serve.

El Molino

27.8% ALC/VOL • 1.3 STD DRINKS

30ml (1 fl oz) Dark Rum
6ml (1/5 fl oz) Banana Liqueur
12ml (2/5 fl oz) Vodka
Dash Grenadine
12ml (2/5 fl oz) Pineapple Juice

Pour ingredients into a cocktail shaker over ice and shake. Strain into a chilled old-fashioned glass and serve.

Vomos Latinos

18.7% ALC/VOL • 2.4 STD DRINKS

23ml (¾ fl oz) Bacardi
23ml (¾ fl oz) Cachaça
23ml (¾ fl oz) Gold Tequila
15ml (½ fl oz) Blue Curaçao
50ml (1⅔ fl oz) Pineapple Juice
23ml (¾ fl oz) Fresh Lime Juice
1 teaspoon Sugar Syrup

Pour ingredients into a blender over large amount of crushed ice and blend. Pour into a chilled highball glass and serve with a straw.

Café Trinidad

22.4% ALC/VOL • 1.9 STD DRINKS

30ml (1 fl oz) Dark Rum
23ml (¾ fl oz) Amaretto
23ml (¾ fl oz) Tia Maria
30ml (1 fl oz) Thick Cream

Pour ingredients into a cocktail shaker over ice and shake. Strain into a chilled cocktail glass and serve.

Independence Swizzle

26.7% ALC/VOL • 1.9 STD DRINKS

60ml (2 fl oz) Dark Trinidad Rum
3 dashes Angostura Bitters
15ml (½ fl oz) Fresh Lime Juice
1 teaspoon Honey
1 teaspoon Sugar Syrup
Slice of Lime

Pour Rum, Bitters, juice, honey and sugar into a mixing glass without ice. Stir well then pour into a collins glass filled with cracked and crushed ice. Add a slice of lime and serve with a swizzle stick.

Brown Cocktail

30.6% ALC/VOL • 1.7 STD DRINKS

23ml (¾ fl oz) Bacardi
23ml (¾ fl oz) Dry Vermouth
23ml (¾ fl oz) Dry Gin

Pour ingredients into a mixing glass over ice and stir. Strain into a chilled cocktail glass and serve.
This drink is also known as B.V.D.

Pink Veranda

15.9% ALC/VOL • 1.8 STD DRINKS

45ml (1½ fl oz) Golden Rum
15ml (½ fl oz) Dark Jamaica Rum
45ml (1½ fl oz) Cranberry Juice
15ml (½ fl oz) Fresh Lime Juice
1 teaspoon Sugar Syrup
½ Egg White

Pour ingredients into a cocktail shaker over ice and shake. Strain into an old-fashioned glass over ice and serve.

Moira

26.8% ALC/VOL • 1.6 STD DRINKS

30ml (1 fl oz) Dark Rum
15ml (½ fl oz) Blue Curaçao
15ml (½ fl oz) Galliano
15ml (½ fl oz) Fresh Cream

Pour ingredients into a cocktail shaker over ice and shake. Strain into a chilled liqueur glass and serve.

Navy Grog

13.5% ALC/VOL • 2.2 STD DRINKS

45ml (1½ fl oz) Golden Rum
30ml (1 fl oz) Light Rum
30ml (1 fl oz) Fresh Lime Juice
30ml (1 fl oz) Fresh Orange Juice
30ml (1 fl oz) Passion-Fruit Juice
30ml (1 fl oz) Pineapple Juice
2 teaspoons Sugar Syrup

Pour ingredients into a blender over cracked ice and blend. Pour into a chilled goblet and serve.

Unisphere

28.8% ALC/VOL • 1.5 STD DRINKS

45ml (1½ fl oz) Golden Rum
3 dashes Bénédictine

3 dashes Pernod
15ml (½ fl oz) Fresh
Lime Juice

Pour ingredients into a cocktail shaker over ice and shake. Strain into a chilled cocktail glass and serve.

Blue Hawaii

10.4% ALC/VOL • 2.2 STD DRINKS

45ml (1½ fl oz) Light Rum
45ml (1½ fl oz) Blue Curaçao
150ml (5 fl oz) Pineapple Juice
30ml (1 fl oz) Sweet and Sour
Mix
Maraschino Cherry
Wedge of Pineapple

Pour Rum, Curaçao, juice and sour mix into a cocktail shaker over cracked ice. Shake and pour into a chilled collins glass. Garnish with a cherry and wedge of pineapple then serve.

Mulata

28.2% ALC/VOL • 1.7 STD DRINKS

53ml (1¾ fl oz) Golden Rum
8ml (¼ fl oz) Dark Crème
De Cacao
15ml (½ fl oz) Fresh
Lime Juice

Pour ingredients into a cocktail shaker over crushed ice and shake. Pour into a chilled cocktail glass and serve.

Rum Rebellion

23.4% ALC/VOL • 1.8 STD DRINKS

60ml (2 fl oz) Dark Rum
30ml (1 fl oz) Fresh Lime Juice
1 teaspoon Sugar Syrup
Maraschino Cherry
Slice of Pineapple

Pour Rum, juice and sugar into a cocktail shaker over ice. Shake and strain into a chilled sour glass. Top up with pineapple juice if desired and stir. Garnish with a cherry and slice of pineapple then serve.

Archmont

28.7% ALC/VOL • 2.4 STD DRINKS

60ml (2 fl oz) Light Rum
20ml (⅔ fl oz) Grand Marnier
20ml (⅔ fl oz) Fresh Lemon or
Lime Juice
1 teaspoon Sugar Syrup

Pour ingredients into a cocktail shaker over crushed ice and shake. Strain into a frosted cocktail glass and serve.

Banana Bombshell

9.2% ALC/VOL • 1.9 STD DRINKS

45ml (1½ fl oz) Light Rum
30ml (1 fl oz) Banana Liqueur
90ml (3 fl oz) Pineapple Juice
30ml (1 fl oz) Coconut Cream
30ml (1 fl oz) Thick Cream
15ml (½ fl oz) Sugar Syrup
⅓ Banana (diced)
Maraschino Cherry
Slice of Pineapple
Twist of Lemon Peel

Pour Rum, Liqueur, juice, creams and sugar into a blender over crushed ice then add diced banana. Blend and pour into a chilled goblet. Place lemon peel into drink with one end of peel hooked over rim of glass. Garnish with a cherry and slice of pineapple then serve.

B.V.D.

30.6% ALC/VOL • 1.7 STD DRINKS

This drink is also known as Brown Cocktail, p 118.

El Presidente

31.1% ALC/VOL • 2.4 STD DRINKS

60ml (2 fl oz) Golden Rum
30ml (1 fl oz) Dry Vermouth
8ml (¼ fl oz) Cointreau
Dash Grenadine
Twist of Orange Peel

Pour Rum, Vermouth, Cointreau and Grenadine into a cocktail shaker over ice. Shake and strain into a chilled cocktail glass. Garnish with orange peel and serve.

Dean's Gate

28.5% ALC/VOL • 2.7 STD DRINKS

60ml (2 fl oz) Light Rum
30ml (1 fl oz) Drambuie
30ml (1 fl oz) Lime Juice Syrup
Twist of Orange Peel

Pour Rum, Drambuie and syrup into a mixing glass over ice. Stir and strain into a chilled cocktail glass. Twist orange peel above drink and place remainder of peel into drink then serve.

Lei Lani

12.3% ALC/VOL • 1.1 STD DRINKS

38ml (1¼ fl oz) Leilani Rum
30ml (1 fl oz) Grenadine
15ml (½ fl oz) Fresh
Lemon Juice
15ml (½ fl oz) Fresh
Orange Juice
15ml (½ fl oz) Pineapple Juice
Dash Soda Water
Wedge of Pineapple

Pour Rum, Grenadine and juices into a highball glass filled with ice then stir. Add soda – do not stir, then garnish with a wedge of pineapple and serve.

Dianne-on-the-Tower

36% ALC/VOL • 2.4 STD DRINKS

60ml (2 fl oz) Light Rum

15ml (½ fl oz) Bourbon
5ml (⅙ fl oz) Cherry Brandy
5ml (⅙ fl oz) Dark Crème De Cacao

Pour ingredients into a mixing glass over ice and stir. Strain into a chilled cocktail glass and serve.

Rum Egg Nog

10.7% ALC/VOL • 1.3 STD DRINKS

45ml (1½ fl oz) Light Rum
60ml (2 fl oz) Fresh Milk (chilled)
1 teaspoon Sugar Syrup
1 Fresh Egg
Nutmeg

Pour Rum, milk, sugar and egg into a cocktail shaker over ice. Shake and strain into a chilled old-fashioned glass. Sprinkle nutmeg on top and serve.

Amigo

17.3% ALC/VOL • 1.5 STD DRINKS

30ml (1 fl oz) Light Rum
23ml (¾ fl oz) Banana Liqueur
8ml (¼ fl oz) Apricot Brandy
Dash Grenadine
45ml (1½ fl oz) Pear Juice

Pour ingredients into a mixing glass over ice and stir. Strain into a chilled cocktail glass and serve.

Night Light

28.9% ALC/VOL • 2.4 STD DRINKS

60ml (2 fl oz) Light Rum
30ml (1 fl oz) Orange Curaçao
Yolk of 1 Egg
Nutmeg

Pour Rum, Curaçao and egg yolk into a cocktail shaker over ice. Shake and strain into a chilled champagne saucer. Sprinkle nutmeg on top and serve.

Warm milk may be added if desired.

Trinidad

26.5% ALC/VOL • 1.4 STD DRINKS

45ml (1½ fl oz) Dark Trinidad Rum
3 dashes Angostura Bitters
15ml (½ fl oz) Fresh Lime Juice
1 teaspoon Sugar Syrup

Pour ingredients into a cocktail shaker over ice and shake. Strain into a chilled cocktail glass and serve with a swizzle stick.

Mai Tai (fruity)

12% ALC/VOL • 2.6 STD DRINKS

30ml (1 fl oz) Dark Rum
15ml (½ fl oz) Amaretto
15ml (½ fl oz) Cointreau
15ml (½ fl oz) Gold Tequila
15ml (½ fl oz) Light Rum
Dash Angostura Bitters
15ml (½ fl oz) Grenadine
30ml (1 fl oz) Fresh Orange Juice
30ml (1 fl oz) Pineapple Juice
15ml (½ fl oz) Fresh Lime Juice
1½ teaspoons Almond Syrup
90ml (3 fl oz) Lemonade
Maraschino Cherry
Slice of Orange
Slice of Pineapple
Twist of Lemon Peel

Pour Rums, Amaretto, Cointreau, Tequila, Bitters, Grenadine, juices and syrup into a cocktail shaker over crushed ice. Shake and pour into a chilled hurricane glass. Add lemonade and lemon peel then stir gently. Garnish with a cherry, slice of orange and pineapple then serve with 2 straws.

Rum Cocktail

29.1% ALC/VOL • 2.1 STD DRINKS

60ml (2 fl oz) Dark Rum
15ml (½ fl oz) White Curaçao
2 dashes Angostura Bitters
15ml (½ fl oz) Grenadine
Maraschino Cherry

Pour Rum, Curaçao, Bitters and Grenadine into a cocktail shaker over ice. Shake and strain into a chilled cocktail glass. Garnish with a cherry and serve.

Palm Breeze

32.4% ALC/VOL • 2.4 STD DRINKS

45ml (1½ fl oz) Dark Rum
30ml (1 fl oz) Yellow Chartreuse
15ml (½ fl oz) White Crème De Cacao
Dash Grenadine
8ml (¼ fl oz) Fresh Lime Juice

Pour ingredients into a cocktail shaker over ice and shake. Strain into a chilled goblet and serve.

Lemon Tree

14.3% ALC/VOL • 1.5 STD DRINKS

30ml (1 fl oz) Light Rum
23ml (¾ fl oz) Rum Tree
15ml (½ fl oz) Malibu
15ml (½ fl oz) Coconut Cream
3 tablespoons Lemon Sherbet

Pour Rum, Rum Tree, Malibu and cream into a blender over 1 tablespoon crushed ice then add sherbet. Blend and pour into a chilled highball glass then serve with 2 straws.

Bacardi Fizz

8.3% ALC/VOL • 1.8 STD DRINKS

60ml (2 fl oz) Bacardi
60ml (2 fl oz) Fresh Lemon Juice
1 teaspoon Caster Sugar
150ml (5 fl oz) Soda Water

Pour Bacardi and juice into a cocktail shaker over ice then add sugar. Shake and strain into a highball glass over ice. Add soda, stir gently and serve.

Dry Hole

6.6% ALC/VOL • 1.6 STD DRINKS

30ml (1 fl oz) Light Rum
15ml (½ fl oz) Apricot Brandy
15ml (½ fl oz) Cointreau
15ml (½ fl oz) Fresh Lemon Juice
240ml (8 fl oz) Soda Water

Pour Rum, Brandy, Cointreau and juice into a cocktail shaker over ice. Shake and strain into a tall glass over crushed ice then stir. Add soda, stir gently and serve.

Beach Peach

19% ALC/VOL • 1.8 STD DRINKS

45ml (1½ fl oz) Light Rum
23ml (¾ fl oz) Peach Brandy
30ml (1 fl oz) Peach Juice
15ml (½ fl oz) Fresh Lime Juice
5ml (⅙ fl oz) Pineapple Juice

Pour ingredients into a cocktail shaker over ice and shake. Strain into an old-fashioned glass over cracked ice and serve.

Tropic Freeze

6.1% ALC/VOL • 1 STD DRINK

38ml (1¼ fl oz) Spiced Rum
15ml (½ fl oz) Grenadine
60ml (2 fl oz) Fresh Orange Juice
60ml (2 fl oz) Pineapple Juice
45ml (1½ fl oz) Coconut Cream
Slice of Orange
Slice of Pineapple

Pour Rum, Grenadine, juices and cream into a blender over crushed ice. Blend until smooth and pour into a chilled hurricane glass. Garnish with a slice of orange and pineapple then serve.

Communicator

34.6% ALC/VOL • 1.9 STD DRINKS

45ml (1½ fl oz) Dark Rum
15ml (½ fl oz) Galliano
10ml (⅓ fl oz) Dark Crème De Cacao

Pour ingredients into an old-fashioned glass over ice, stir and serve.
This drink is also known as Numbnut.

Rum Screw

12.3% ALC/VOL • 1.7 STD DRINKS

60ml (2 fl oz) Light Rum
120ml (4 fl oz) Fresh Orange Juice
Maraschino Cherry
Slice of Orange

Pour Rum into a highball glass over ice and add juice then stir. Garnish with a cherry and slice of orange then serve.
This drink is also known as Cuban Screw.

Golden Clipper

24.4% ALC/VOL • 3.5 STD DRINKS

45ml (1½ fl oz) Light Rum
45ml (1½ fl oz) Dry Gin
45ml (1½ fl oz) Peach Brandy
45ml (1½ fl oz) Fresh Orange Juice

Pour ingredients into a cocktail shaker over ice and shake. Strain into a chilled champagne saucer and serve.

Canado Saludo

16.2% ALC/VOL • 1.5 STD DRINKS

45ml (1½ fl oz) Light Rum
5ml (⅙ fl oz) Angostura Bitters
5ml (⅙ fl oz) Grenadine
30ml (1 fl oz) Fresh Orange Juice
30ml (1 fl oz) Pineapple Juice
5ml (⅙ fl oz) Fresh Lemon Juice
Maraschino Cherry
Slice of Orange
Slice of Pineapple

Pour Rum, Bitters, Grenadine and juices into an old-fashioned glass over ice then stir. Garnish with a cherry, slice of orange and pineapple then serve.

Pablo

22.4% ALC/VOL • 1.6 STD DRINKS

30ml (1 fl oz) Bacardi
15ml (½ fl oz) Advocaat
15ml (½ fl oz) Cointreau
30ml (1 fl oz) Pineapple Juice
Maraschino Cherry

Pour Bacardi, Advocaat, Cointreau and juice into a cocktail shaker over ice. Shake and strain into a chilled champagne saucer. Garnish with a cherry and serve.

Quentin

21.8% ALC/VOL • 1.5 STD DRINKS

45ml (1½ fl oz) Dark Rum
15ml (½ fl oz) Kahlúa
30ml (1 fl oz) Fresh Cream
Nutmeg

Pour Rum, Kahlúa and cream into a cocktail shaker over ice. Shake and strain into a chilled cocktail glass. Sprinkle nutmeg on top and serve.

Bacchanalian Cocktail

8.9% ALC/VOL • 1.8 STD DRINKS

30ml (1 fl oz) Light Rum
15ml (½ fl oz) Brandy
15ml (½ fl oz) Yellow Chartreuse
60ml (2 fl oz) Red Grape Juice
30ml (1 fl oz) Fresh Orange Juice
15ml (½ fl oz) Fresh Lime Juice
90ml (3 fl oz) Lemonade
Grape
Slice of Orange

Pour Rum, Brandy, Chartreuse and juices into a cocktail shaker over ice. Shake and strain into a collins glass over ice. Add lemonade and stir gently. Garnish with a grape and slice of orange then serve.

Veteran

34.2% ALC/VOL • 2 STD DRINKS

60ml (2 fl oz) Dark Rum
5ml (1/6 fl oz) Crème De Cassis

Pour ingredients into an old-fashioned glass over ice, stir and serve.

Sydney Sling

15.3% ALC/VOL • 2.8 STD DRINKS

45ml (1½ fl oz) Light Rum
30ml (1 fl oz) Cherry Brandy
15ml (½ fl oz) Cointreau
15ml (½ fl oz) Yellow Chartreuse
Dash Angostura Bitters
60ml (2 fl oz) Pineapple Juice
45ml (1½ fl oz) Fresh Orange Juice
23ml (¾ fl oz) Fresh Lime Juice
Maraschino Cherry
Slice of Lemon
Slice of Lime
Slice of Orange
Sprig of Fresh Mint

Pour Rum, Brandy, Cointreau, Chartreuse, Bitters and juices into a cocktail shaker over ice. Shake and strain into a collins glass over ice. Garnish with a cherry, slice of lemon, lime, orange and sprig of mint then serve with 2 straws.

St. Croix Cooler

16.8% ALC/VOL • 3.1 STD DRINKS

60ml (2 fl oz) Light Rum
30ml (1 fl oz) Brandy
15ml (½ fl oz) Dark Jamaica Rum
75ml (2½ fl oz) Fresh Orange Juice
45ml (1½ fl oz) Fresh Lemon Juice
Dash Orange Flower Water
1 tablespoon Brown Sugar
5ml (1/6 fl oz) Soda Water
Long Twist of Orange Peel

Place orange peel into a collins glass over ice with one end of peel hooked over rim of glass. Pour Rums, Brandy, juices and flower water into a cocktail shaker over ice then add sugar. Shake and strain into prepared glass. Add soda, stir gently and serve.

Green Swizzle

13.8% ALC/VOL • 2 STD DRINKS

This drink is a Blue Swizzle (p 75) substituting Blue Curaçao with Green Crème De Menthe.

Venus Rum

22.2% ALC/VOL • 2.4 STD DRINKS

45ml (1½ fl oz) Light Rum
30ml (1 fl oz) Apricot Brandy
15ml (½ fl oz) Cointreau
15ml (½ fl oz) Fresh Lime Juice
30ml (1 fl oz) Soda Water

Pour Rum, Brandy, Cointreau and juice into a cocktail shaker over ice. Shake and strain into an old-fashioned glass over cracked ice. Add soda – do not stir, then serve with 2 short straws.

Apple Pie

24.1% ALC/VOL • 1.1 STD DRINKS

23ml (¾ fl oz) Light Rum
23ml (¾ fl oz) Sweet Vermouth
5ml (1/6 fl oz) Apple Brandy
3 dashes Grenadine
5ml (1/6 fl oz) Fresh Lemon Juice

Pour ingredients into a cocktail shaker over ice and shake. Strain into a chilled cocktail glass and serve.

Picker's Peach

16% ALC/VOL • 2.3 STD DRINKS

45ml (1½ fl oz) Light Rum
30ml (1 fl oz) Peach Schnapps
15ml (½ fl oz) Dark Rum
5ml (1/6 fl oz) Pecher Mignon
30ml (1 fl oz) Fresh Orange Juice
23ml (¾ fl oz) Fresh Lemon Juice
½ teaspoon Sugar Syrup
⅓ Peach (diced)
Maraschino Cherry
Slice of Peach

Pour Rums, Schnapps, Mignon, juices and sugar into a blender without ice then add diced peach. Blend until smooth, add crushed ice and blend briefly then pour into a chilled collins glass. Garnish with a cherry and slice of peach then serve.

Lulu

24% ALC/VOL • 1.4 STD DRINKS

15ml (½ fl oz) Light Rum
15ml (½ fl oz) Peach Schnapps
15ml (½ fl oz) Triple Sec

15ml (½ fl oz) Vodka
15ml (½ fl oz) Sweet and Sour Mix
Maraschino Cherry

Pour Rum, Schnapps, Triple Sec, Vodka and sour mix into a cocktail shaker over ice. Shake and strain into a highball glass filled with ice. Garnish with a cherry and serve.

Cardinal

32.2% ALC/VOL • 1.8 STD DRINKS

45ml (1½ fl oz) Añejo Rum
15ml (½ fl oz) Maraschino Liqueur
5ml (1/6 fl oz) Cointreau
5ml (1/6 fl oz) Grenadine

Pour ingredients into a mixing glass over ice and stir. Strain into a chilled cocktail glass and serve.

Kansas Tornado

9.4% ALC/VOL • 2.9 STD DRINKS

45ml (1½ fl oz) Light Rum
30ml (1 fl oz) Amaretto
30ml (1 fl oz) Gin
15ml (½ fl oz) Grenadine
90ml (3 fl oz) Grapefruit Juice
90ml (3 fl oz) Fresh Orange Juice
90ml (3 fl oz) Pineapple Juice
Cherry

Pour Rum, Amaretto, Gin and juices into a hurricane glass filled with ice then stir. Layer Grenadine on top, add a cherry and serve.

Pilot Boat

17.4% ALC/VOL • 1.9 STD DRINKS

45ml (1½ fl oz) Dark Rum
30ml (1 fl oz) Banana Liqueur
60ml (2 fl oz) Fresh Lime Juice

Pour ingredients into a cocktail shaker over ice and shake. Strain into a chilled cocktail glass and serve.

Sit and Spin

13% ALC/VOL • 1.3 STD DRINKS

45ml (1½ fl oz) Dark Rum
60ml (2 fl oz) Grapefruit Juice
10ml (⅓ fl oz) Fresh Lemon Juice
8ml (¼ fl oz) Fresh Lime Juice
1 teaspoon Sugar Syrup
Wedge of Lime

Pour Rum, juices and sugar into a cocktail shaker over ice. Shake and strain into an old-fashioned glass over ice. Garnish with a wedge of lime and serve.

Jacqueline

27.9% ALC/VOL • 2.7 STD DRINKS

60ml (2 fl oz) Dark Rum
30ml (1 fl oz) Cointreau
30ml (1 fl oz) Fresh Lime Juice
½ teaspoon Sugar Syrup

Pour ingredients into a cocktail shaker over ice and shake. Strain into a chilled cocktail glass and serve.

Caribbean Mule

13.2% ALC/VOL • 2.2 STD DRINKS

45ml (1½ fl oz) Light Rum
15ml (½ fl oz) Dark Jamaica Rum
8ml (¼ fl oz) Cointreau
8ml (¼ fl oz) Maraschino Liqueur
15ml (½ fl oz) Fresh Lime Juice
120ml (4 fl oz) Dry Ginger Ale or Ginger Beer
Slice of Lime
Sprig of Fresh Mint

Pour Rums, Cointreau, Liqueur and juice into a cocktail shaker over ice. Shake and strain into a collins glass over ice. Add Ginger Ale or ginger beer as desired and stir gently. Garnish with a slice of lime and sprig of mint then serve.

Bahama Todd

14.6% ALC/VOL • 2.8 STD DRINKS

15ml (½ fl oz) Dark Rum
15ml (½ fl oz) Blue Curaçao
15ml (½ fl oz) Light Rum
15ml (½ fl oz) 151-Proof Bacardi
15ml (½ fl oz) Malibu
15ml (½ fl oz) Spiced Rum
150ml (5 fl oz) Pineapple Juice

Pour Dark, Light and Spiced Rums into a tall glass over ice. Add Curaçao, Malibu and juice then stir well. Layer Bacardi on top and serve.

Black Monday

27.7% ALC/VOL • 1.4 STD DRINKS

30ml (1 fl oz) Dark Rum
15ml (½ fl oz) Opal Nera
5ml (1/6 fl oz) Cherry Brandy
15ml (½ fl oz) Fresh Lemon Juice

Pour ingredients into a cocktail shaker over ice and shake. Strain into a chilled cocktail glass and serve.

Zulu

9.9% ALC/VOL • 1.8 STD DRINKS

30ml (1 fl oz) Dark Rum
30ml (1 fl oz) Dark Crème De Cacao
15ml (½ fl oz) Banana Liqueur
5ml (1/6 fl oz) Pernod
5ml (1/6 fl oz) Grenadine
30ml (1 fl oz) Fresh Lime Juice
120ml (4 fl oz) Cola
Maraschino Cherry
Slice of Lime

Pour Rum, Cacao, Liqueur, Pernod, Grenadine and juice into a cocktail shaker over ice. Shake and strain into a collins glass over ice. Add cola and stir gently. Garnish with a cherry and slice of lime then serve.

Rum Reviver

4% ALC/VOL • 0.9 STD DRINKS

This drink is also known as Rum Cow, p 113.

Cuban Crime of Passion

26.7% ALC/VOL • 4.7 STD DRINKS

45ml (1½ fl oz) Bacardi
45ml (1½ fl oz) Cointreau
45ml (1½ fl oz) Malibu
45ml (1½ fl oz) Spiced Rum
45ml (1½ fl oz) Pineapple Juice
Slice of Orange

Pour Bacardi, Cointreau, Malibu, Rum and juice into a cocktail shaker over ice. Shake and strain into a tall glass over ice. Garnish with a slice of orange and serve.

Costa Smeralda

16.3% ALC/VOL • 0.8 STD DRINKS

15ml (½ fl oz) Dark Rum
8ml (¼ fl oz) Apricot Brandy
8ml (¼ fl oz) Blue Curaçao
2 dashes Angostura Bitters
30ml (1 fl oz) Pineapple Juice

Pour ingredients into a cocktail shaker over ice and shake. Strain into a chilled cocktail glass and serve.

Skeet Shooter Special

12.5% ALC/VOL • 1.8 STD DRINKS

45ml (1½ fl oz) Dark Rum
15ml (½ fl oz) Light Rum
30ml (1 fl oz) Grapefruit Juice
30ml (1 fl oz) Fresh Orange Juice
30ml (1 fl oz) Pineapple Juice
30ml (1 fl oz) Lemon-Lime Soda
Pinch of Cinnamon

Pour Rums and juices into a cocktail shaker over ice then add cinnamon. Shake and strain into a highball glass over ice. Add soda, stir gently and serve.

Rummer

27.4% ALC/VOL • 1.9 STD DRINKS

45ml (1½ fl oz) Dark Rum
15ml (½ fl oz) Amaretto
15ml (½ fl oz) Triple Sec
15ml (½ fl oz) Fresh Lemon Juice

Pour ingredients into a cocktail shaker over ice and shake. Strain into a chilled cocktail glass and serve.

Sacrifice

13.2% ALC/VOL • 2.1 STD DRINKS

30ml (1 fl oz) Dark Rum
30ml (1 fl oz) Light Rum
15ml (½ fl oz) White Crème De Cacao
2 dashes Orange Bitters
60ml (2 fl oz) Pineapple Juice
30ml (1 fl oz) Cranberry Juice
30ml (1 fl oz) Fresh Orange Juice
1 teaspoon Coconut Cream
Maraschino Cherry
Slice of Orange

Pour Rums, Cacao, Bitters, juices and cream into a blender over crushed ice. Blend and pour into a chilled collins glass. Garnish with a cherry and slice of orange then serve.

Dorothy Lamour

17.5% ALC/VOL • 1.4 STD DRINKS

30ml (1 fl oz) Bacardi
30ml (1 fl oz) Banana Liqueur
15ml (½ fl oz) Fresh Lemon Juice
3 Slices of Mango
Strawberry

Pour Bacardi, Liqueur and juice into a blender over cracked ice then add slices of mango. Blend and strain into a chilled champagne saucer. Garnish with a strawberry and serve.

Carib

27.8% ALC/VOL • 1.8 STD DRINKS

30ml (1 fl oz) Light Rum
30ml (1 fl oz) Gin
15ml (½ fl oz) Fresh Lime Juice
1 teaspoon Sugar Syrup
Slice of Orange

Pour Rum, Gin, juice and sugar into a cocktail shaker over ice. Shake and strain into an old-fashioned glass over ice. Garnish with a slice of orange and serve.

Hurricane Leah

10.3% ALC/VOL • 2.1 STD DRINKS

15ml (½ fl oz) Light Rum
15ml (½ fl oz) Blue Curaçao
15ml (½ fl oz) Gin
15ml (½ fl oz) Tequila
15ml (½ fl oz) Vodka
Dash Cherry Brandy
90ml (3 fl oz) Fresh Orange Juice
90ml (3 fl oz) Sweet and Sour Mix
Slice of Orange

Pour Rum, Curaçao, Gin, Tequila, Vodka, Brandy, juice and sour mix into a hurricane glass over ice then stir. Garnish with a slice of orange and serve.

Poker Cocktail

26.5% ALC/VOL • 1.3 STD DRINKS

This drink is also known as Little Princess, p 116.

Ocha Rios

15.4% ALC/VOL • 1.3 STD DRINKS

45ml (1½ fl oz) Jamaica Rum
30ml (1 fl oz) Guava Nectar
15ml (½ fl oz) Fresh
Lime Juice
15ml (½ fl oz) Thick Cream
½ teaspoon Sugar Syrup

Pour ingredients into a blender over crushed ice and blend. Pour into a chilled champagne saucer and serve.

Howell Says So

29.8% ALC/VOL • 2.2 STD DRINKS

45ml (1½ fl oz) Dark Rum
15ml (½ fl oz) Amaretto
15ml (½ fl oz) Cointreau
2 dashes Orange Bitters
15ml (½ fl oz) Fresh
Lemon Juice

Pour ingredients into a cocktail shaker over ice and shake. Strain into an old-fashioned glass over ice and serve.

Rum Pineapple Fizz

20.5% ALC/VOL • 2.7 STD DRINKS

60ml (2 fl oz) Golden Rum
15ml (½ fl oz) 151-Proof Rum
15ml (½ fl oz) Fresh
Lemon Juice
15ml (½ fl oz) Fresh
Lime Juice
2 teaspoons Caster Sugar
½ Egg White
5ml (1/6 fl oz) Soda Water
⅓ Cup Pineapple (diced)
Slice of Lime

Pour Rums, juices and egg white into a blender over crushed ice. Add sugar and diced pineapple. Blend and pour into a highball glass over ice. Add soda – do not stir, then add a slice of lime and serve.

Tropical Itch

19.8% ALC/VOL • 3.7 STD DRINKS

45ml (1½ fl oz) Bacardi
45ml (1½ fl oz) Bourbon
30ml (1 fl oz) Dark Rum
Dash Angostura Bitters
90ml (3 fl oz) Pineapple Juice
15ml (½ fl oz) Fresh
Lime Juice
½ Fresh Passion-Fruit (pulp)
Maraschino Cherry
Pineapple Spear
Sprig of Fresh Mint

Build Bacardi, Bourbon, pineapple juice, lime juice, Bitters, passion-fruit and Dark Rum into a hurricane glass over ice. Garnish with a cherry, pineapple spear and sprig of mint. Serve with a swizzle stick and 2 straws.

Numbnut

34.6% ALC/VOL • 1.9 STD DRINKS

This drink is also known as Communicator, p 121.

Love in the Afternoon

14.4% ALC/VOL • 2 STD DRINKS

60ml (2 fl oz) Dark Rum
15ml (½ fl oz) Strawberry
Liqueur
30ml (1 fl oz) Fresh
Orange Juice
23ml (¾ fl oz) Coconut Cream
15ml (½ fl oz) Thick Cream
1 teaspoon Sugar Syrup
3 Strawberries (diced)
Strawberry

Pour Rum, Liqueur, juice, creams and sugar into a blender without ice then add diced strawberries. Blend until smooth, add crushed ice and blend briefly. Pour into a chilled hurricane glass and garnish with a strawberry then serve with 2 straws.

Tahiti Club

25.4% ALC/VOL • 1.8 STD DRINKS

60ml (2 fl oz) Light Rum
2 dashes Maraschino Liqueur
10ml (⅓ fl oz) Fresh
Lemon Juice
10ml (⅓ fl oz) Fresh
Lime Juice
10ml (⅓ fl oz) Pineapple Juice
Slice of Lemon

Pour Rum, Liqueur and juices into a cocktail shaker over ice. Shake and strain into an old-fashioned glass over ice. Add a slice of lemon and serve.

Emerald Star

17.9% ALC/VOL • 1.4 STD DRINKS

30ml (1 fl oz) Light Rum
20ml (⅔ fl oz) Midori
10ml (⅓ fl oz) Apricot Brandy
30ml (1 fl oz) Passion-
Fruit Juice
10ml (⅓ fl oz) Fresh
Lime Juice

Pour ingredients into a cocktail shaker over ice and shake. Strain into a chilled cocktail glass and serve.

Caribbean Harvest

15.1% ALC/VOL • 1.7 STD DRINKS

30ml (1 fl oz) Light Rum
30ml (1 fl oz) Malibu
15ml (½ fl oz) Banana Liqueur
5ml (1/6 fl oz) Grenadine
30ml (1 fl oz) Mango Juice
30ml (1 fl oz) Passion-
Fruit Juice

Pour ingredients into a cocktail shaker over ice and shake. Strain into a chilled cocktail glass and serve.

Trade Winds

28.7% ALC/VOL • 2.2 STD DRINKS

60ml (2 fl oz) Golden Rum
15ml (½ fl oz) Plum Brandy

15ml (½ fl oz) Fresh
Lime Juice
1½ teaspoons Sugar Syrup

Pour ingredients into a blender over crushed ice and blend. Pour into a chilled champagne saucer and serve.

Polynesian Paradise

23% ALC/VOL • 1.7 STD DRINKS

45ml (1½ fl oz) Golden Rum
15ml (½ fl oz) Sweet Vermouth
8ml (¼ fl oz) Cointreau
23ml (¾ fl oz) Fresh
Lime Juice
1 teaspoon Brown Sugar

Pour Rum, Vermouth, Cointreau and juice into a blender over crushed ice then add sugar. Blend and pour into a chilled champagne saucer then serve.

Rum Flip

20.5% ALC/VOL • 1.8 STD DRINKS

30ml (1 fl oz) Dark Rum
30ml (1 fl oz) Light Rum
1 teaspoon Sugar Syrup
1 Fresh Egg
Nutmeg

Pour Rums, sugar and egg into a cocktail shaker over ice. Shake and strain into a chilled goblet. Sprinkle nutmeg on top and serve.

Madama Rosa

7.2% ALC/VOL • 1.6 STD DRINKS

45ml (1½ fl oz) Light Rum
15ml (½ fl oz) Cherry Brandy
60ml (2 fl oz) Fresh
Orange Juice
15ml (½ fl oz) Fresh
Lime Juice
150ml (5 fl oz) Tonic Water

Pour Rum, Brandy and juices into a cocktail shaker over ice. Shake and strain into a chilled collins glass over 2 ice cubes. Add tonic, stir gently and serve.

Poppin's

23% ALC/VOL • 1.1 STD DRINKS

30ml (1 fl oz) Dark Rum
10ml (⅓ fl oz) Triple Sec
Dash Angostura Bitters
10ml (⅓ fl oz) Fresh
Orange Juice
10ml (⅓ fl oz) Pineapple Juice

Pour ingredients into a cocktail shaker over ice and shake. Strain into a cocktail glass over crushed ice and serve.

Chop Nut

17% ALC/VOL • 1.6 STD DRINKS

30ml (1 fl oz) Light Rum
23ml (¾ fl oz) Malibu
15ml (½ fl oz) White Crème
De Cacao
5ml (⅙ fl oz) Frangelico
45ml (1½ fl oz) Mandarin Juice
1 teaspoon Egg White

Pour ingredients into a cocktail shaker over ice and shake. Strain into a cocktail glass over cracked ice and serve.

Stratosphere

26.1% ALC/VOL • 1.5 STD DRINKS

30ml (1 fl oz) Rum
15ml (½ fl oz) California
Brandy
8ml (¼ fl oz) Tart Cherry
Liqueur
15ml (½ fl oz) Fresh
Lemon Juice
1 teaspoon Sugar Syrup

Pour ingredients into a cocktail shaker over ice and shake. Strain into a chilled cocktail glass and serve.

Cuban Special

21.7% ALC/VOL • 1 STD DRINK

30ml (1 fl oz) Light Rum
3 dashes Cointreau
15ml (½ fl oz) Fresh
Lime Juice
10ml (⅓ fl oz) Pineapple Juice
Maraschino Cherry
Slice of Pineapple

Pour Rum, Cointreau and juices into a cocktail shaker over ice. Shake and strain into a chilled cocktail glass. Garnish with a cherry and slice of pineapple then serve.

Jamaica Wonder

6.5% ALC/VOL • 1.3 STD DRINKS

30ml (1 fl oz) Lemon Hart
Rum
15ml (½ fl oz) Tia Maria
Dash Angostura Bitters
30ml (1 fl oz) Fresh Lime Juice

180ml (6 fl oz) Bitter-Lemon Soda

Pour Rum, Tia, Bitters and juice into a collins glass over ice then stir. Add soda, stir gently and serve.

Shiwala

20.4% ALC/VOL • 2.3 STD DRINKS

45ml (1½ fl oz) Dark Rum
45ml (1½ fl oz) Malibu
8ml (¼ fl oz) Blackberry Schnapps
8ml (¼ fl oz) Peach Schnapps
15ml (½ fl oz) Cranberry Juice
15ml (½ fl oz) Fresh Orange Juice
8ml (¼ fl oz) Pineapple Juice

Pour ingredients into a cocktail shaker over cracked ice and shake. Pour into a chilled hurricane glass and serve.

Café San Juan

8.6% ALC/VOL • 1.1 STD DRINKS

38ml (1¼ fl oz) Dark Rum
120ml (4 fl oz) Black Coffee (chilled)
1 teaspoon Sugar Syrup
Twist of Lemon Peel

Pour Rum, coffee and sugar into a highball glass over ice then stir. Garnish with lemon peel and serve.

Caribbean Punch

18.2% ALC/VOL • 2.2 STD DRINKS

60ml (2 fl oz) Dark Rum
23ml (¾ fl oz) Banana Liqueur
30ml (1 fl oz) Fresh Orange Juice
30ml (1 fl oz) Pineapple Juice
8ml (¼ fl oz) Rose's Lime Juice
Nutmeg

Pour Rum, Liqueur and juices into a cocktail shaker over ice. Shake and strain into a highball glass half filled with ice. Sprinkle nutmeg on top and serve.

Catherine of Sheridan Square

9.8% ALC/VOL • 1.6 STD DRINKS

45ml (1½ fl oz) Dark Rum
15ml (½ fl oz) Tia Maria
120ml (4 fl oz) Black Coffee (chilled)
30ml (1 fl oz) Fresh Cream

Pour ingredients into a coffee glass over crushed ice, stir and serve.

Guava Cooler

7.9% ALC/VOL • 1.6 STD DRINKS

45ml (1½ fl oz) Dark Rum
15ml (½ fl oz) Maraschino Liqueur
45ml (1½ fl oz) Guava Nectar
15ml (½ fl oz) Fresh Lemon Juice
15ml (½ fl oz) Pineapple Juice
½ teaspoon Sugar Syrup
120ml (4 fl oz) Soda Water
Guava Shell
Slice of Lemon

Pour Rum, Liqueur, nectar, juices and sugar into a cocktail shaker over ice. Shake and strain into a hurricane glass over ice. Add soda and stir gently. Garnish with a guava shell and slice of lemon then serve.

White Sands

22.4% ALC/VOL • 1.9 STD DRINKS

60ml (2 fl oz) Golden Rum
5ml (1/6 fl oz) Banana Liqueur
3 dashes Kahlúa
20ml (⅔ fl oz) Fresh Lime Juice
20ml (⅔ fl oz) Pineapple Juice
Maraschino Cherry
Slice of Pineapple

Pour Rum, Liqueur, Kahlúa and juices into a cocktail shaker over ice. Shake and strain into a chilled cocktail glass. Garnish with a cherry and slice of pineapple then serve.

Devil's Milk

16.7% ALC/VOL • 1.8 STD DRINKS

38ml (1¼ fl oz) Jamaica Rum
38ml (1¼ fl oz) White Crème De Cacao
2 scoops Vanilla Ice Cream

Pour Rum and Cacao into a cocktail shaker without ice then add ice cream. Shake until smooth and pour into a chilled champagne saucer then serve.

Rum Runner

22% ALC/VOL • 2.7 STD DRINKS

30ml (1 fl oz) Dark Rum
30ml (1 fl oz) Banana Liqueur
30ml (1 fl oz) Blackberry Brandy
15ml (½ fl oz) Light Rum
15ml (½ fl oz) Grenadine
15ml (½ fl oz) Fresh Lemon Juice
15ml (½ fl oz) Pineapple Juice
1 teaspoon Orgeat Syrup
Maraschino Cherry
Slice of Orange

Pour Rums, Liqueur, Brandy, Grenadine, juices and syrup into a blender over crushed ice. Blend and pour into a chilled goblet. Garnish with a cherry and slice of orange then serve with 2 short straws.

Maktak Special

9.9% ALC/VOL • 1.5 STD DRINKS

This drink is also known as Maestro, 141.

Battering Ram

9% ALC/VOL • 2.1 STD DRINKS

30ml (1 fl oz) Light Rum
30ml (1 fl oz) Dark Jamaica Rum
15ml (½ fl oz) Wild Turkey Liqueur
120ml (4 fl oz) Fresh Orange Juice
15ml (½ fl oz) Fresh Lime Juice
90ml (3 fl oz) Tonic Water
Slice of Lime

Pour Rums, Liqueur and juices into a cocktail shaker over ice. Shake and strain into a collins glass over ice. Add tonic and stir gently. Add a slice of lime and serve.

Cubano

18.2% ALC/VOL • 1.8 STD DRINKS

60ml (2 fl oz) Light Rum
30ml (1 fl oz) Fresh Lime Juice
30ml (1 fl oz) Pineapple Juice
1 teaspoon Sugar Syrup

Pour ingredients into a cocktail shaker over ice and shake. Strain into a chilled cocktail glass and serve.

Devil's Tail

30.9% ALC/VOL • 2.3 STD DRINKS

45ml (1½ fl oz) Light Rum
30ml (1 fl oz) Vodka
5ml (1/6 fl oz) Apricot Brandy
5ml (1/6 fl oz) Grenadine
10ml (⅓ fl oz) Fresh Lime Juice
Twist of Lime Peel

Pour Rum, Vodka, Brandy, Grenadine and juice into a blender over crushed ice. Blend and pour into a chilled champagne flute. Twist lime peel above drink and discard remainder of peel then serve.

Chump

9.8% ALC/VOL • 1.6 STD DRINKS

45ml (1½ fl oz) Dark Rum
15ml (½ fl oz) Tia Maria
120ml (4 fl oz) Black Coffee (chilled)
30ml (1 fl oz) Fresh Cream

Pour ingredients into a cocktail shaker over ice and shake. Strain into a coffee glass over crushed ice and serve.

Rum and Pineapple Cooler

19.8% ALC/VOL • 2.6 STD DRINKS

75ml (2½ fl oz) Light Rum
5ml (1/6 fl oz) 151-Proof Rum
Dash Angostura Bitters
60ml (2 fl oz) Pineapple Juice
15ml (½ fl oz) Fresh Lemon Juice
1 teaspoon Sugar Syrup
5ml (1/6 fl oz) Soda Water
Piece of Papaya
Piece of Pineapple

Pour Rums, Bitters, juices and sugar into a cocktail shaker over ice. Shake and strain into a collins glass over ice then add soda – do not stir. Garnish with a piece of papaya and pineapple then serve.

West Indian Punch Cocktail

16.6% ALC/VOL • 2.2 STD DRINKS

60ml (2 fl oz) Dark Rum
23ml (¾ fl oz) Banana Liqueur
30ml (1 fl oz) Fresh Orange Juice
30ml (1 fl oz) Pineapple Juice
23ml (¾ fl oz) Fresh Lime Juice
Slice of Banana
Slice of Orange
Slice of Pineapple
Nutmeg

Pour Rum, Liqueur and juices into a cocktail shaker over crushed ice. Shake and pour into a chilled highball glass then sprinkle nutmeg on top. Garnish with a slice of banana, orange and pineapple then serve with 2 straws.

Angel's Treat

20.3% ALC/VOL • 2 STD DRINKS

45ml (1½ fl oz) Dark Rum
30ml (1 fl oz) Amaretto
45ml (1½ fl oz) Fresh Cream
½ teaspoon Cocoa Powder
Grated Chocolate

Pour Rum, Amaretto and cream into a cocktail shaker over ice then add cocoa powder. Shake and strain into a chilled cocktail glass. Sprinkle chocolate on top and serve.

Jungle Spice

14.3% ALC/VOL • 1.4 STD DRINKS

45ml (1½ fl oz) Light Rum
30ml (1 fl oz) Guava Juice
30ml (1 fl oz) Mandarin Juice
15ml (½ fl oz) Fresh Lime Juice
Nutmeg

Pour Rum and juices into a cocktail shaker over ice. Shake and strain into a chilled cocktail glass. Sprinkle nutmeg on top and serve.

Chocolatier

9.7% ALC/VOL • 1.1 STD DRINKS

30ml (1 fl oz) Jamaica Rum
15ml (½ fl oz) Dark Crème De Cacao
45ml (1½ fl oz) Fresh Milk (chilled)
2 scoops Chocolate Ice Cream
Grated Chocolate

Pour Rum, Cacao and milk into a blender without ice then add ice cream. Blend until smooth and pour into a champagne saucer over cracked ice. Sprinkle chocolate on top and serve.

Eureka

12.8% ALC/VOL • 2.4 STD DRINKS

30ml (1 fl oz) Light Rum
30ml (1 fl oz) Lillet
15ml (½ fl oz) Apricot Brandy
90ml (3 fl oz) Fresh Orange Juice
Twist of Orange Peel

Pour Rum, Lillet, Brandy and juice into a cocktail shaker over cracked ice. Shake and strain into a chilled champagne saucer. Add orange peel and serve.

Queen's Park Swizzle

16.3% ALC/VOL • 1.8 STD DRINKS

60ml (2 fl oz) Dark Rum
2 dashes Angostura Bitters
15ml (½ fl oz) Fresh Lime Juice
1 teaspoon Sugar Syrup
60ml (2 fl oz) Soda Water
4 Fresh Mint Leaves
Sprig of Fresh Mint

Pour Rum, Bitters, juice and sugar into a mixing glass over large amount of ice then add mint leaves. Stir vigorously until cold and strain into a collins glass filled with crushed ice. Add soda – do not stir, then garnish with a sprig of mint. Serve with a swizzle stick and 2 straws.

Rum Soldier

14.3% ALC/VOL • 1.4 STD DRINKS

30ml (1 fl oz) Dark Rum
30ml (1 fl oz) Kahlúa
60ml (2 fl oz) Fresh Cream

Pour ingredients into a cocktail shaker over ice and shake. Strain into a chilled collins glass and serve.

Tall Islander

12.7% ALC/VOL • 2 STD DRINKS

60ml (2 fl oz) Light Rum
5ml (1/6 fl oz) Dark Jamaica Rum
90ml (3 fl oz) Pineapple Juice
30ml (1 fl oz) Fresh Lime Juice
1 teaspoon Sugar Syrup
5ml (1/6 fl oz) Soda Water
Slice of Lime

Pour Rums, juices and sugar into a cocktail shaker over ice. Shake and strain into a collins glass over ice. Add soda – do not stir, then add a slice of lime and serve.

Horse and Jockey

32.9% ALC/VOL • 2 STD DRINKS

30ml (1 fl oz) Añejo Rum
30ml (1 fl oz) Southern Comfort
15ml (½ fl oz) Sweet Vermouth
2 dashes Angostura Bitters

Pour ingredients into a mixing glass over ice and stir. Strain into a chilled cocktail glass and serve.

Limbo Cooler

11.3% ALC/VOL • 2.1 STD DRINKS

60ml (2 fl oz) Dark Rum
30ml (1 fl oz) Punt e Mes
15ml (½ fl oz) Grenadine
30ml (1 fl oz) Fresh Lemon Juice
105ml (3½ fl oz) Lemonade
Maraschino Cherry
Spiral of Lemon
Wedge of Orange

Pour Rum, Punt e Mes, Grenadine and juice into a collins glass over crushed ice then stir. Add spiral of lemon and lemonade then stir gently. Garnish with a cherry and wedge of orange then serve with 2 straws.

Ship's Cat

46.6% ALC/VOL • 1.3 STD DRINKS

30ml (1 fl oz) Over-Proof Dark Rum
5ml (1/6 fl oz) Crème De Cassis

Pour ingredients into a chilled shot glass over an ice cube, stir and serve.

Jamaican Iced Coffee

9.4% ALC/VOL • 1.5 STD DRINKS

30ml (1 fl oz) Dark Jamaica Rum
30ml (1 fl oz) Tia Maria
120ml (4 fl oz) Black Coffee (chilled)
23ml (¾ fl oz) Thick Cream
Sprig of Fresh Mint

Pour Rum, Tia, coffee and cream into a cocktail shaker over ice. Shake and strain into a chilled goblet. Garnish with a sprig of mint and serve with 2 short straws.

Borinquen

17.5% ALC/VOL • 1.7 STD DRINKS

45ml (1½ fl oz) Light Rum
5ml (1/6 fl oz) 151-Proof Rum
30ml (1 fl oz) Fresh Lime Juice
30ml (1 fl oz) Fresh Orange Juice
2 teaspoons Passion-Fruit Syrup

Pour ingredients into a blender over crushed ice and blend. Pour into a chilled old-fashioned glass and serve.

Million

18.1% ALC/VOL • 0.9 STD DRINKS

30ml (1 fl oz) Jamaica Rum
Dash Angostura Bitters
30ml (1 fl oz) Fresh Lime Juice
½ teaspoon Sugar Syrup
Maraschino Cherry

Pour Rum, Bitters, juice and sugar into a cocktail shaker over crushed ice. Shake and pour into a chilled cocktail glass. Garnish with a cherry and serve.

Compudreams

18.3% ALC/VOL • 3.9 STD DRINKS

45ml (1½ fl oz) Bacardi
45ml (1½ fl oz) Dark Rum
45ml (1½ fl oz) Spiced Rum
75ml (2½ fl oz) Fresh Orange Juice
60ml (2 fl oz) Pineapple Juice

Pour ingredients into a mixing glass over ice and stir. Strain into a chilled highball glass over a few ice cubes and serve.

Blueberry Rum Fizz

12.8% ALC/VOL • 2.4 STD DRINKS

75ml (2½ fl oz) Light Rum
5ml (1/6 fl oz) Cointreau
23ml (¾ fl oz) Fresh Lemon Juice
15ml (½ fl oz) Blueberry Syrup
120ml (4 fl oz) Soda Water
3 Blueberries
Slice of Lemon

Pour Rum, Cointreau, juice and syrup into a cocktail shaker over ice. Shake and strain into a highball glass over ice. Add soda and stir gently. Add blueberries and a slice of lemon then serve.

Buck Jones

10.7% ALC/VOL • 1.8 STD DRINKS

45ml (1½ fl oz) Light Rum
30ml (1 fl oz) Sweet Sherry
15ml (½ fl oz) Fresh Lime Juice
120ml (4 fl oz) Dry Ginger Ale

Pour Rum, Sherry and juice into a highball glass over ice then stir. Add Ginger Ale, stir gently and serve.

Banana Whirl

16.3% ALC/VOL • 2.1 STD DRINKS

30ml (1 fl oz) Bacardi
30ml (1 fl oz) Sambuca
15ml (½ fl oz) Amaretto
60ml (2 fl oz) Fresh Cream
½ Banana (diced)
Slice of Banana
Strawberry

Pour Bacardi, Sambuca, Amaretto and cream into a blender over cracked ice then add diced banana. Blend and pour into a chilled champagne saucer. Garnish with a slice of banana and a strawberry then serve.

Miami Cocktail

36.8% ALC/VOL • 2.5 STD DRINKS

60ml (2 fl oz) Light Rum
23ml (¾ fl oz) Cointreau
4 dashes Fresh Lemon Juice

Pour ingredients into a cocktail shaker over ice and shake. Strain into a chilled cocktail glass and serve.

Rum Do

28.6% ALC/VOL • 1.4 STD DRINKS

30ml (1 fl oz) Dark Rum
15ml (½ fl oz) Banana Liqueur
15ml (½ fl oz) Midori
Dash Fresh Lime Juice
Dash Fresh Cream
Slice of Banana
Sprig of Fresh Mint

Pour Rum, Liqueur, Midori, juice and cream into a cocktail shaker over ice. Shake and strain into a chilled cocktail glass. Garnish with a slice of banana and sprig of mint then serve.

Princess Morgan

6% ALC/VOL • 0.8 STD DRINKS

23ml (¾ fl oz) Spiced Rum
8ml (¼ fl oz) Banana Liqueur
75ml (2½ fl oz) Fresh Orange Juice
60ml (2 fl oz) Soda Water

Pour Rum, Liqueur and juice into a highball glass over ice then stir, Add soda, stir gently and serve.

Jamaican

9.3% ALC/VOL • 1.5 STD DRINKS

30ml (1 fl oz) Jamaica Rum
30ml (1 fl oz) Tia Maria
Dash Angostura Bitters
30ml (1 fl oz) Fresh Lime Juice
120ml (4 fl oz) Lemonade

Pour Rum, Tia, Bitters and juice into a cocktail shaker over cracked ice. Shake and pour into a chilled collins glass. Add lemonade, stir gently and serve.

Pomegranate Polecat

18.5% ALC/VOL • 1.8 STD DRINKS

40ml (1⅓ fl oz) Light Rum
15ml (½ fl oz) Amaretto
15ml (½ fl oz) Sweet Sherry
45ml (1½ fl oz) Pomegranate Juice
1 teaspoon Sugar Syrup

Pour ingredients into a cocktail shaker over ice and shake. Strain into an old-fashioned glass over cracked ice and serve.

Arrowhead

14.1% ALC/VOL • 1.6 STD DRINKS

30ml (1 fl oz) Dark Rum
15ml (½ fl oz) Banana Liqueur
15ml (½ fl oz) Southern Comfort
8ml (¼ fl oz) Fresh Lime Juice
75ml (2½ fl oz) Lemonade

Pour Rum, Liqueur, Southern Comfort and juice into an old-fashioned glass over cracked ice then stir. Add lemonade, stir gently and serve.

Tropica Cocktail

5.8% ALC/VOL • 1.1 STD DRINKS

38ml (1¼ fl oz) Light Rum
Dash Grenadine
150ml (5 fl oz) Pineapple Juice
60ml (2 fl oz) Grapefruit Juice
Wedge of Pineapple

Pour Rum, Grenadine and juices into a collins glass over ice then stir. Garnish with a wedge of pineapple and serve.

Port Antonio

26.5% ALC/VOL • 1.7 STD DRINKS

30ml (1 fl oz) Golden Rum
15ml (½ fl oz) Dark Jamaica Rum
15ml (½ fl oz) Tia Maria
5ml (1/6 fl oz) Falernum
15ml (½ fl oz) Fresh Lime Juice
Slice of Lime

Pour Rums, Tia, Falernum and juice into a cocktail shaker over ice. Shake and strain into an old-fashioned glass over ice. Add a slice of lime and serve.

Jamaican Crawler

11.5% ALC/VOL • 1.4 STD DRINKS

30ml (1 fl oz) Light Rum
30ml (1 fl oz) Midori
3 dashes Grenadine
90ml (3 fl oz) Pineapple Juice

Pour Rum, Midori and juice into a mixing glass over cracked ice. Stir and pour into a chilled collins glass. Layer Grenadine on top and serve.

Iced Rum Tea

11.4% ALC/VOL • 2.3 STD DRINKS

45ml (1½ fl oz) Light Rum
15ml (½ fl oz) 151-Proof Rum
5ml (1/6 fl oz) Falernum
180ml (6 fl oz) Strong Black Tea (chilled)
5ml (1/6 fl oz) Fresh Lemon Juice
1 teaspoon Sugar Syrup
2 Fresh Mint Leaves
Slice of Lemon

Pour Rums, Falernum, tea, juice and sugar into a highball glass over ice then stir gently. Garnish with mint leaves and a slice of lemon then serve.

Bee's Kiss

31.1% ALC/VOL • 1.3 STD DRINKS

45ml (1½ fl oz) Light Rum
1 teaspoon Fresh Cream
1 teaspoon Honey

Pour ingredients into a cocktail shaker over ice and shake. Strain into a chilled cocktail glass and serve.

Fern Gully Fizz

9.5% ALC/VOL • 1.8 STD DRINKS

30ml (1 fl oz) Dark Jamaica Rum
30ml (1 fl oz) Light Rum
30ml (1 fl oz) Pineapple Juice
23ml (¾ fl oz) Fresh Lime Juice
1 teaspoon Caster Sugar
120ml (4 fl oz) Soda Water
Slice of Lime
Slice of Pineapple

Pour Rums and juices into a cocktail shaker over ice then add sugar. Shake and strain into a highball glass over ice. Add soda and stir gently. Garnish with a slice of lime and pineapple then serve.

Trifecta

29.1% ALC/VOL • 1.4 STD DRINKS

45ml (1½ fl oz) Light Rum
8ml (¼ fl oz) Dubonnet
10ml (⅓ fl oz) Fresh Lemon Juice

Pour ingredients into a cocktail shaker over ice and shake. Strain into a chilled cocktail glass and serve.

Bowton Nell

15.2% ALC/VOL • 2.2 STD DRINKS

45ml (1½ fl oz) Light Rum
15ml (½ fl oz) Brandy
15ml (½ fl oz) Gin
5ml (1/6 fl oz) Grenadine
45ml (1½ fl oz) Fresh Orange Juice
30ml (1 fl oz) Fresh Lemon Juice
30ml (1 fl oz) Soda Water
Maraschino Cherry

Pour Rum, Brandy, Gin, Grenadine and juices into a cocktail shaker over ice. Shake and strain into a collins glass over ice. Add soda – do not stir, then garnish with a cherry and serve.

Rum Sidecar

29% ALC/VOL • 1.4 STD DRINKS

30ml (1 fl oz) Light Rum
15ml (½ fl oz) Cointreau
15ml (½ fl oz) Fresh Lemon Juice

Pour ingredients into a cocktail shaker over ice and shake. Strain into a chilled cocktail glass and serve.

Derby Rum Fix

19% ALC/VOL • 1.8 STD DRINKS

60ml (2 fl oz) Light Rum
30ml (1 fl oz) Fresh Orange Juice
15ml (½ fl oz) Fresh Lime Juice
10ml (⅓ fl oz) Spring Water
1 teaspoon Caster Sugar
Cocktail Orange
Maraschino Cherry

Pour water into a chilled old-fashioned glass and add sugar. Stir to dissolve sugar and add crushed ice to fill glass then add Rum. Add juices and more crushed ice to fill glass then stir gently. Garnish with a cocktail orange and cherry then serve.

Fair-and-Warmer Cocktail

30.5% ALC/VOL • 3.3 STD DRINKS

90ml (3 fl oz) Light Rum
45ml (1½ fl oz) Sweet Vermouth
2 dashes Cointreau

Pour ingredients into a mixing glass over ice and stir. Strain into a chilled cocktail glass and serve.

Rum Relaxer

8.1% ALC/VOL • 1.3 STD DRINKS

45ml (1½ fl oz) Light Rum
15ml (½ fl oz) Grenadine
30ml (1 fl oz) Pineapple Juice
120ml (4 fl oz) Lemon-Lime Soda
Maraschino Cherry
Slice of Orange

Pour Rum, Grenadine and juice into a cocktail shaker over cracked ice. Shake and pour into a chilled hurricane glass. Add soda and stir gently. Garnish with a cherry and slice of orange then serve.

Shaw Park

27.8% ALC/VOL • 1.5 STD DRINKS

30ml (1 fl oz) Golden Rum
15ml (½ fl oz) Cointreau
8ml (¼ fl oz) Apricot Liqueur
15ml (½ fl oz) Fresh Lime Juice

Pour ingredients into a cocktail shaker over ice and shake. Strain into a chilled cocktail glass and serve.

This drink may also be served in an old-fashioned glass over ice if desired.

Alla Salute!

10.2% ALC/VOL • 1.9 STD DRINKS

45ml (1½ fl oz) Light Rum
30ml (1 fl oz) Sciarada
90ml (3 fl oz) Pineapple Juice
15ml (½ fl oz) Fresh Lime Juice
60ml (2 fl oz) Soda Water
Slice of Lime

Pour Rum, Sciarada and juices into a collins glass over ice then stir. Add soda and stir gently. Add a slice of lime and serve.

Fruit Frappé

19.8% ALC/VOL • 1.3 STD DRINKS

30ml (1 fl oz) Light Rum
15ml (½ fl oz) Banana Liqueur
8ml (¼ fl oz) Crème De Cassis
30ml (1 fl oz) Mandarin Juice

Pour ingredients into a mixing glass without ice and stir. Pour into a champagne saucer filled with crushed ice and serve with 2 short straws.

Smooth Move

5.4% ALC/VOL • 0.9 STD DRINKS

30ml (1 fl oz) Light Rum
60ml (2 fl oz) Pineapple Juice
60ml (2 fl oz) Prune Juice
60ml (2 fl oz) Sweet and Sour Mix
Maraschino Cherry
Pineapple Spear

Prepare a parfait glass with a sugar frosted rim. Pour Rum, juices and sour mix into a blender over crushed ice. Blend and pour into prepared glass. Garnish with a cherry and pineapple spear then serve.

Florida Rum Runner

25.6% ALC/VOL • 2.7 STD DRINKS

45ml (1½ fl oz) Light Rum
30ml (1 fl oz) Banana Liqueur
30ml (1 fl oz) Blackberry Brandy
15ml (½ fl oz) Grenadine
15ml (½ fl oz) Fresh Lemon Juice

Pour ingredients into a blender over crushed ice and blend. Pour into a chilled highball glass and serve.

Rum Milk Punch

10.5% ALC/VOL • 1.8 STD DRINKS

30ml (1 fl oz) Dark Rum
30ml (1 fl oz) Light Rum
150ml (5 fl oz) Fresh Milk (chilled)
1 teaspoon Sugar Syrup
Maraschino Cherry
Nutmeg

Pour Rums, milk and sugar into a cocktail shaker over ice. Shake and strain into a collins glass over ice. Sprinkle nutmeg on top and garnish with a cherry then serve.

Irish Elegance

29.6% ALC/VOL • 5.4 STD DRINKS

135ml (4½ fl oz) Jamaica Rum
45ml (1½ fl oz) Brandy
5ml (⅙ fl oz) Crème De Violette

30ml (1 fl oz) Fresh Lime Juice
15ml (½ fl oz) Pineapple Juice

Pour ingredients into a blender over crushed ice and blend. Pour into a chilled collins glass and serve.

A Night in Old Mandalay

11.6% ALC/VOL • 1.8 STD DRINKS

30ml (1 fl oz) Añejo Rum
30ml (1 fl oz) Light Rum
30ml (1 fl oz) Fresh Orange Juice
15ml (½ fl oz) Fresh Lemon Juice
90ml (3 fl oz) Dry Ginger Ale
Wedge of Lemon

Pour Rums and juices into a cocktail shaker over ice. Shake and strain into a highball glass over ice. Add Ginger Ale and stir gently. Garnish with a wedge of lemon and serve.

Tangerine Dream

19.3% ALC/VOL • 1.8 STD DRINKS

45ml (1½ fl oz) Light Rum
15ml (½ fl oz) Grand Marnier
60ml (2 fl oz) Fresh Orange Juice

Pour ingredients into a cocktail shaker over ice and shake. Strain into an old-fashioned glass half filled with ice and serve.
This drink is also known as Mallelieu.

Tamarind Cooler

10.5% ALC/VOL • 2.2 STD DRINKS

45ml (1½ fl oz) Light Rum
15ml (½ fl oz) 151-Proof Rum
90ml (3 fl oz) Tamarind Nectar
60ml (2 fl oz) Mango Nectar
30ml (1 fl oz) Fresh Orange Juice
30ml (1 fl oz) Pineapple Juice
Slice of Lemon
2 Sprigs of Fresh Mint

Pour Rums, nectars and juices into a collins glass over ice then stir. Add a slice of lemon and sprigs of mint then serve.

Quarter Deck Cocktail

27% ALC/VOL • 1.5 STD DRINKS

45ml (1½ fl oz) Light Rum
10ml (⅓ fl oz) Cream Sherry
15ml (½ fl oz) Fresh Lime Juice

Pour ingredients into a mixing glass over ice and stir. Strain into a chilled cocktail glass and serve.

Leilani Tiki Standard

11% ALC/VOL • 1.3 STD DRINKS

45ml (1½ fl oz) Leilani Rum
2 dashes Grenadine
15ml (½ fl oz) Fresh Lemon Juice
90ml (3 fl oz) Soda Water
Slice of Orange
Strawberry

Pour Rum, Grenadine and juice into a cocktail shaker over cracked ice. Shake and pour into a chilled collins glass. Add soda and stir gently. Garnish with a slice of orange and a strawberry then serve.

Running Hot

24% ALC/VOL • 2.3 STD DRINKS

45ml (1½ fl oz) Bacardi
30ml (1 fl oz) Cointreau
Dash Grenadine
45ml (1½ fl oz) Pineapple Juice

Pour ingredients into a cocktail shaker over cracked ice and shake. Pour into an old-fashioned glass over ice and serve.

Haitian Gold

13.2% ALC/VOL • 2.1 STD DRINKS

30ml (1 fl oz) Light Rum
15ml (½ fl oz) Banana Liqueur
15ml (½ fl oz) Gold Tequila
15ml (½ fl oz) Mandarine Napoleon
60ml (2 fl oz) Guava Nectar
30ml (1 fl oz) Fresh Orange Juice
30ml (1 fl oz) Pineapple Juice
1 teaspoon Strawberry Syrup
Slice of Orange
Slice of Pineapple
Strawberry

Pour Rum, Liqueur, Tequila, Mandarine Napoleon, nectar, juices and syrup into a blender over crushed ice. Blend and pour into a chilled goblet. Garnish with a slice of orange, pineapple and a strawberry then serve with 2 short straws.

Rum and Coconut

19.8% ALC/VOL • 3 STD DRINKS

60ml (2 fl oz) Dark Rum
45ml (1½ fl oz) Malibu
30ml (1 fl oz) Banana Liqueur
30ml (1 fl oz) Coconut Cream
30ml (1 fl oz) Fresh Cream
Slice of Banana
Strawberry

Pour Rum, Malibu, Liqueur and creams into a blender over cracked ice. Blend and strain into a chilled highball glass. Garnish with a slice of banana and a strawberry then serve.

Georgia Rum Cooler

26.4% ALC/VOL • 2.3 STD DRINKS

75ml (2½ fl oz) Light Rum
5ml (⅙ fl oz) Falernum
5ml (⅙ fl oz) Grenadine
15ml (½ fl oz) Fresh Lemon Juice
5ml (⅙ fl oz) Soda Water
1 teaspoon Salted Peanuts (crushed)

Cinnamon

Pour Rum, Falernum, Grenadine and juice into a blender over crushed ice then add crushed peanuts. Blend and pour into a chilled collins glass over 2 ice cubes. Add soda – do not stir, then sprinkle cinnamon on top and serve.

Rum Zoom

28.5% ALC/VOL • 1.3 STD DRINKS

45ml (1½ fl oz) Light Rum
2 teaspoons Fresh Cream
1 teaspoon Honey

Pour ingredients into a cocktail shaker over ice and shake. Strain into a chilled cocktail glass and serve.

Cuban Cherry

23.1% ALC/VOL • 2.1 STD DRINKS

30ml (1 fl oz) Light Rum
23ml (¾ fl oz) Cherry Brandy
15ml (½ fl oz) Bourbon
15ml (½ fl oz) Dark Crème De Cacao
30ml (1 fl oz) Thick Cream
Maraschino Cherry
Grated Chocolate

Pour Rum, Brandy, Bourbon, Cacao and cream into a cocktail shaker over ice. Shake and strain into a chilled cocktail glass. Sprinkle chocolate on top and garnish with a cherry then serve.

Suffragette City

29.6% ALC/VOL • 1.8 STD DRINKS

45ml (1½ fl oz) Light Rum
15ml (½ fl oz) Grand Marnier
3 dashes Grenadine
15ml (½ fl oz) Fresh Lime Juice

Pour ingredients into a cocktail shaker over ice and shake. Strain into a chilled cocktail glass and serve.

Cat Walk

17.4% ALC/VOL • 1.8 STD DRINKS

30ml (1 fl oz) Bacardi
20ml (⅔ fl oz) Cointreau
15ml (½ fl oz) Malibu
15ml (½ fl oz) Fresh Lemon Juice
4 Strawberries (diced)
Strawberry

Pour Bacardi, Cointreau, Malibu and juice into a blender over crushed ice then add diced strawberries. Blend and pour into a chilled cocktail glass. Garnish with a strawberry and serve.

Bushranger

27.5% ALC/VOL • 1.3 STD DRINKS

30ml (1 fl oz) Light Rum
30ml (1 fl oz) Dubonnet
2 dashes Angostura Bitters
Twist of Lemon Peel

Pour Rum, Dubonnet and Bitters into a cocktail shaker over ice. Shake and strain into a chilled cocktail glass. Twist lemon peel above drink and place remainder of peel into drink then serve.

Caribbean Breeze

9.3% ALC/VOL • 1.6 STD DRINKS

45ml (1½ fl oz) Dark Rum
15ml (½ fl oz) Banana Liqueur
90ml (3 fl oz) Pineapple Juice
60ml (2 fl oz) Cranberry Juice
1 teaspoon Lime Syrup
Slice of Banana
Wedge of Pineapple

Pour Rum, Liqueur, juices and syrup into a cocktail shaker over crushed ice. Shake and pour into a chilled goblet. Garnish with a slice of banana and wedge of pineapple then serve with 2 short straws.

Concilium

31.4% ALC/VOL • 1.4 STD DRINKS

40ml (1⅓ fl oz) Dark Rum
12ml (⅖ fl oz) Dry Vermouth
5ml (⅙ fl oz) Blue Curaçao
Dash Fresh Orange Juice

Pour ingredients into a mixing glass over ice and stir. Strain into a chilled cocktail glass and serve.

Fortune Teller

24.9% ALC/VOL • 1.8 STD DRINKS

30ml (1 fl oz) Bacardi
15ml (½ fl oz) Cointreau
15ml (½ fl oz) Galliano
30ml (1 fl oz) Fresh Lemon Juice
Dash Sugar Syrup

Pour ingredients into a cocktail shaker over ice and shake. Strain into a chilled champagne saucer and serve.

Punta Gorda

10.3% ALC/VOL • 1.6 STD DRINKS

45ml (1½ fl oz) Jamaica Rum
15ml (½ fl oz) Sloe Gin
5ml (⅙ fl oz) Grenadine
120ml (4 fl oz) Pineapple Juice
15ml (½ fl oz) Fresh Lime Juice

Pour ingredients into a cocktail shaker over cracked ice and shake. Pour into a highball glass over ice and serve.

The Green-Tailed Dragon of the Maroon Morning

18.6% ALC/VOL • 1.7 STD DRINKS

45ml (1½ fl oz) Light Rum
15ml (½ fl oz) Midori
5ml (1/6 fl oz) Cherry Brandy
30ml (1 fl oz) Pineapple Juice
15ml (½ fl oz) Fresh Lime Juice
1 teaspoon Orgeat Syrup

Pour Rum, Midori, juices and syrup into a blender over crushed ice. Blend and pour into a chilled old-fashioned glass. Add Brandy by pouring into centre of drink – do not stir, then serve.

Mumsicle

37.6% ALC/VOL • 1.8 STD DRINKS

45ml (1½ fl oz) Dark Rum
15ml (½ fl oz) Bourbon
Dash Angostura Bitters
Maraschino Cherry

Pour Rum, Bourbon and Bitters into a mixing glass over ice. Stir and strain into a chilled cocktail glass. Garnish with a cherry and serve.

Egril

15.6% ALC/VOL • 1.4 STD DRINKS

15ml (½ fl oz) Dark Rum
15ml (½ fl oz) Irish Mist
15ml (½ fl oz) Light Rum
45ml (1½ fl oz) Pineapple Juice
1 teaspoon Sugar Syrup
½ Fresh Lime
Maraschino Cherry
Slice of Lime

Slice ½ lime into eight segments and place into a chilled old-fashioned glass. Add sugar and muddle well to release lime juice. Add Rums and Irish Mist. Add juice and stir then fill glass with cracked ice. Garnish with a cherry and slice of lime then serve with a short straw.

Jade

28.6% ALC/VOL • 1.4 STD DRINKS

45ml (1½ fl oz) Light Rum
2 dashes Cointreau
2 dashes Green Crème De Menthe
10ml (⅓ fl oz) Fresh Lime Juice
1 teaspoon Sugar Syrup
Slice of Lime

Pour Rum, Cointreau, Crème De Menthe, juice and sugar into a cocktail shaker over ice. Shake and strain into a chilled cocktail glass. Add a slice of lime and serve.

Presidente Seco (dry)

29.1% ALC/VOL • 2.2 STD DRINKS

60ml (2 fl oz) Golden Rum
30ml (1 fl oz) Dry Vermouth
5ml (1/6 fl oz) Grenadine
Twist of Orange Peel

Pour Rum, Vermouth and Grenadine into a mixing glass over ice. Stir and strain into a chilled cocktail glass. Twist orange peel above drink and discard remainder of peel then serve.

Rum Citrus Cooler

11.7% ALC/VOL • 2.3 STD DRINKS

60ml (2 fl oz) Light Rum
15ml (½ fl oz) Cointreau
30ml (1 fl oz) Fresh Orange Juice
15ml (½ fl oz) Fresh Lime Juice
1 teaspoon Sugar Syrup
120ml (4 fl oz) Lemonade
Slice of Lemon
Slice of Lime

Pour Rum, Cointreau, juices and sugar into a cocktail shaker over ice. Shake and strain into a hurricane glass over ice. Add lemonade and stir gently. Garnish with a slice of lemon and lime then serve.

Over the Rainbow

17.8% ALC/VOL • 2.2 STD DRINKS

60ml (2 fl oz) Spiced Rum
30ml (1 fl oz) Orange Curaçao
2 scoops Rainbow Sherbet
3 Slices of Peach (diced)
1 Strawberry (diced)
Slice of Peach
Strawberry

Pour Rum and Curaçao into a blender over crushed ice. Add sherbet, diced peach and diced strawberry. Blend until smooth and pour into a chilled hurricane glass. Garnish with a slice of peach and a strawberry then serve.

Plantation Coffee

10.2% ALC/VOL • 1.6 STD DRINKS

30ml (1 fl oz) Golden Rum
15ml (½ fl oz) Dark Crème De Cacao
15ml (½ fl oz) Grand Marnier
120ml (4 fl oz) Black Coffee (chilled)
23ml (¾ fl oz) Thick Cream
Grated Chocolate

Pour Rum, Cacao, Grand Marnier, coffee and cream into a cocktail shaker over ice. Shake and strain into a goblet over crushed ice. Sprinkle chocolate on top and serve with 2 short straws.

Morgan's Mountain

22.4% ALC/VOL • 1.7 STD DRINKS

45ml (1½ fl oz) Light Rum
15ml (½ fl oz) White Crème De Cacao

5ml (1/6 fl oz) Kahlúa
30ml (1 fl oz) Thick Cream

Pour Rum, Cacao and cream into a cocktail shaker over ice. Shake and strain into a chilled cocktail glass. Add Kahlúa by pouring into centre of drink - do not stir, then serve.

Cool Carlos

12.2% ALC/VOL • 1.9 STD DRINKS

45ml (1½ fl oz) Dark Rum
30ml (1 fl oz) Orange Curaçao
60ml (2 fl oz) Cranberry Juice
60ml (2 fl oz) Pineapple Juice
3 dashes Sweet and Sour Mix
Maraschino Cherry
Slice of Orange
Slice of Pineapple

Pour Rum, juices and sour mix into a cocktail shaker over cracked ice. Shake and pour into a chilled collins glass then layer Curaçao on top. Garnish with a cherry, slice of orange and pineapple then serve.

New Orleans Buck

10.6% ALC/VOL • 1.4 STD DRINKS

45ml (1½ fl oz) Light Rum
2 dashes Peychaud's Bitters
15ml (½ fl oz) Fresh Orange Juice
90ml (3 fl oz) Dry Ginger Ale
½ Fresh Lime

Pour Rum, Bitters and orange juice into a cocktail shaker over ice. Shake and strain into a highball glass over ice. Twist ½ lime above drink to release juice and add spent shell then stir. Add Ginger Ale, stir gently and serve.

Fruit Rum Frappé

24.6% ALC/VOL • 1.2 STD DRINKS

30ml (1 fl oz) Light Rum
15ml (½ fl oz) Banana Liqueur
3 dashes Crème De Cassis
15ml (½ fl oz) Fresh Orange Juice

Pour ingredients into a mixing glass without ice and stir. Pour into a champagne saucer filled with crushed ice and serve with 2 short straws.

Worried Monk

22.8% ALC/VOL • 1.7 STD DRINKS

30ml (1 fl oz) Light Rum
15ml (½ fl oz) Malibu
8ml (¼ fl oz) Cointreau
8ml (¼ fl oz) Yellow Chartreuse
23ml (¾ fl oz) Fresh Lime Juice
1½ teaspoons Orgeat Syrup

Pour ingredients into a cocktail shaker over ice and shake. Strain into an old-fashioned glass over cracked ice and serve.

Rummple

10.4% ALC/VOL • 1.1 STD DRINKS

15ml (½ fl oz) Bacardi Limon
15ml (½ fl oz) Light Rum
15ml (½ fl oz) Malibu
90ml (3 fl oz) Fresh Orange Juice

Pour ingredients into a cocktail shaker over cracked ice and shake. Pour into a chilled highball glass and serve.

Latin Manhattan

24% ALC/VOL • 2.6 STD DRINKS

45ml (1½ fl oz) Light Rum
45ml (1½ fl oz) Dry Vermouth
45ml (1½ fl oz) Sweet Vermouth
2 dashes Angostura Bitters
Twist of Lemon Peel

Pour Rum, Vermouths and Bitters into a mixing glass over ice. Stir and strain into a chilled cocktail glass. Twist lemon peel above drink and place remainder of peel into drink then serve.

Listen to the Drums of Feynman

18.3% ALC/VOL • 1.9 STD DRINKS

30ml (1 fl oz) Dark Rum
30ml (1 fl oz) Tia Maria
15ml (½ fl oz) Light Rum
60ml (2 fl oz) Fresh Cream
Nutmeg

Pour Rums, Tia and cream into a cocktail shaker over ice. Shake and strain into an old-fashioned glass over crushed ice. Sprinkle nutmeg on top and serve.

Bali Punch

8.8% ALC/VOL • 1.6 STD DRINKS

45ml (1½ fl oz) Light Rum
15ml (½ fl oz) Malibu
60ml (2 fl oz) Passion-Fruit Juice
30ml (1 fl oz) Fresh Lime Juice
15ml (½ fl oz) Pineapple Syrup
60ml (2 fl oz) Orange Soda
Wedge of Pineapple

Pour Rum, Malibu, juices and syrup into a cocktail shaker over ice. Shake and strain into a collins glass over ice. Add soda and stir gently. Garnish with a wedge of pineapple and serve with 2 straws.

Chicago Style

24.6% ALC/VOL • 1 STD DRINK

23ml (¾ fl oz) Light Rum
8ml (¼ fl oz) Anisette
8ml (¼ fl oz) Triple Sec
15ml (½ fl oz) Rose's Lime Juice

Pour ingredients into a cocktail shaker over ice and shake. Strain into a chilled cocktail glass and serve.

Blighter Bob

13.5% ALC/VOL • 1.6 STD DRINKS

30ml (1 fl oz) Light Rum
15ml (½ fl oz) Crème De Cassis
15ml (½ fl oz) Dark Rum
2 dashes Orange Bitters
30ml (1 fl oz) Fresh Orange Juice
60ml (2 fl oz) Dry Ginger Ale
Wedge of Lemon

Pour Rums, Cassis, Bitters and juice into a highball glass over ice then stir. Add Ginger Ale and stir gently. Garnish with a wedge of lemon and serve.

Honeysuckle

24.4% ALC/VOL • 1.3 STD DRINKS

45ml (1½ fl oz) Light Rum
15ml (½ fl oz) Fresh Lemon Juice
2 teaspoons Honey

Pour ingredients into a cocktail shaker over ice and shake. Strain into a chilled cocktail glass and serve.

If desired hot – Add hot water and serve in a coffee glass.

Cherry Rum Cobbler

25.8% ALC/VOL • 1.9 STD DRINKS

45ml (1½ fl oz) Light Rum
30ml (1 fl oz) Cherry Brandy
15ml (½ fl oz) Fresh Lemon Juice
½ teaspoon Sugar Syrup
Maraschino Cherry
Slice of Lemon

Pour Rum, Brandy, juice and sugar into a highball glass filled with cracked ice then stir. Add more ice to fill glass, garnish with a cherry and slice of lemon then serve.

Garath Glowworm

22.9% ALC/VOL • 1.7 STD DRINKS

45ml (1½ fl oz) Light Rum
15ml (½ fl oz) White Crème De Cacao
5ml (1/6 fl oz) Cherry Brandy
30ml (1 fl oz) Thick Cream

Pour Rum, Cacao and cream into a cocktail shaker over ice. Shake and strain into a chilled cocktail glass. Add Brandy by pouring into centre of drink – do not stir, then serve.

Bacardi Ruth Special

18.5% ALC/VOL • 4 STD DRINKS

90ml (3 fl oz) Bacardi
45ml (1½ fl oz) English Gin
5ml (1/6 fl oz) Grenadine
15ml (½ fl oz) Fresh Lime Juice
120ml (4 fl oz) Cola

Pour Bacardi, Gin, Grenadine and juice into a cocktail shaker over ice. Shake and strain into a chilled highball glass over a few ice cubes. Add cola, stir gently and serve.

P.T.O.

20.8% ALC/VOL • 2.2 STD DRINKS

45ml (1½ fl oz) Dark Rum
15ml (½ fl oz) Cointreau
15ml (½ fl oz) Vodka
60ml (2 fl oz) Fresh Orange Juice
Slice of Orange

Pour Rum, Cointreau, Vodka and juice into a highball glass over ice then stir. Garnish with a slice of orange and serve.

Crime of Passion

5.8% ALC/VOL • 0.9 STD DRINKS

30ml (1 fl oz) Dark Rum
30ml (1 fl oz) Passion-Fruit Juice
2 teaspoons Raspberry Syrup
90ml (3 fl oz) Cream Soda
1 scoop Vanilla Ice Cream
Maraschino Cherry
Slice of Orange

Pour Rum, juice and syrup into a blender without ice then add ice cream. Blend briefly and pour into a chilled goblet. Add soda and stir gently. Garnish with a cherry and slice of orange then serve with 2 short straws.

Lemon Rum Cooler

9.2% ALC/VOL • 2.2 STD DRINKS

60ml (2 fl oz) Light Rum
15ml (½ fl oz) Falernum
5ml (1/6 fl oz) 151-Proof Rum
60ml (2 fl oz) Pineapple Juice
15ml (½ fl oz) Fresh Lemon Juice
150ml (5 fl oz) Bitter-Lemon Soda
Slice of Lemon

Pour Rums, Falernum and juices into a cocktail shaker over ice. Shake and strain into a chilled collins glass over 2 ice cubes. Add soda and stir gently. Add a slice of lemon and serve.

Bermuda Triangle

17.6% ALC/VOL • 1.9 STD DRINKS

30ml (1 fl oz) Bacardi
30ml (1 fl oz) Blue Curaçao
20ml (⅔ fl oz) Amaretto
60ml (2 fl oz) Pineapple Juice

Pour ingredients into a cocktail shaker over ice and shake. Strain into a chilled cocktail glass and serve.

Cardinal No.2

22.9% ALC/VOL • 2 STD DRINKS

60ml (2 fl oz) Light Rum
8ml (¼ fl oz) Cointreau
5ml (1/6 fl oz) Grenadine
30ml (1 fl oz) Fresh Lime Juice
1½ teaspoons Orzata
Slice of Lime

Pour Rum, Cointreau, Grenadine, juice and Orzata into a cocktail shaker over ice. Shake and strain into an old-fashioned glass over ice. Garnish with a slice of lime and serve.

Leeward

33.8% ALC/VOL • 2 STD DRINKS

45ml (1½ fl oz) Light Rum
15ml (½ fl oz) Calvados
15ml (½ fl oz) Sweet Vermouth
Twist of Lemon Peel

Pour Rum, Calvados and Vermouth into a cocktail shaker over ice. Shake and strain into an old-fashioned glass over ice. Twist lemon peel above drink and place remainder of peel into drink then serve.

Barkis is Willing

8.4% ALC/VOL • 1.3 STD DRINKS

45ml (1½ fl oz) Light Rum
5ml (1/6 fl oz) Grenadine
30ml (1 fl oz) Fresh Lemon Juice
½ teaspoon Sugar Syrup
60ml (2 fl oz) Dry Ginger Ale
60ml (2 fl oz) Soda Water
Slice of Orange

Pour Rum, Grenadine, juice and sugar into a cocktail shaker over ice. Shake and strain into a collins glass over ice. Add Ginger Ale and soda then stir gently. Garnish with a slice of orange and serve.

Big Band Charlie

28.7% ALC/VOL • 2 STD DRINKS

45ml (1½ fl oz) Dark Rum
15ml (½ fl oz) Cointreau
15ml (½ fl oz) Midori
15ml (½ fl oz) Fresh Lime Juice

Pour ingredients into a cocktail shaker over ice and shake. Strain into a chilled sour glass and serve.

Banana Foster

10.7% ALC/VOL • 1.5 STD DRINKS

45ml (1½ fl oz) Spiced Rum
15ml (½ fl oz) Banana Liqueur
2 scoops Vanilla Ice Cream
1 Banana (diced)
Cinnamon

Pour Rum and Liqueur into a blender over crushed ice. Add ice cream and diced banana. Blend until smooth and pour into a chilled brandy balloon. Sprinkle cinnamon on top and serve.

Rose Hall

18.2% ALC/VOL • 1.1 STD DRINKS

30ml (1 fl oz) Jamaica Rum
15ml (½ fl oz) Banana Liqueur
30ml (1 fl oz) Fresh Orange Juice
5ml (1/6 fl oz) Fresh Lime Juice
Slice of Lime

Pour Rum, Liqueur and juices into a cocktail shaker over ice. Shake and strain into an old-fashioned glass over ice. Add a slice of lime and serve.

Banana Mango

22.8% ALC/VOL • 1.5 STD DRINKS

45ml (1½ fl oz) Light Rum
8ml (¼ fl oz) Banana Liqueur
15ml (½ fl oz) Fresh Lime Juice
15ml (½ fl oz) Mango Nectar
Slice of Mango

Pour Rum, Liqueur, juice and nectar into a cocktail shaker over ice. Shake and strain into an old-fashioned glass over ice. Garnish with a slice of mango and serve.

Palmera

18.9% ALC/VOL • 1.8 STD DRINKS

45ml (1½ fl oz) Light Rum
45ml (1½ fl oz) Medium White Wine
3 dashes Grenadine
23ml (¾ fl oz) Pineapple Juice
3 dashes Fresh Lime Juice

Pour ingredients into a cocktail shaker over ice and shake. Strain into a chilled wine glass over a large ice cube and serve.

Camp Lawless

9.6% ALC/VOL • 1.6 STD DRINKS

30ml (1 fl oz) Light Rum
15ml (½ fl oz) Campari
15ml (½ fl oz) Galliano
150ml (5 fl oz) Mandarin Juice
Maraschino Cherry
Slice of Orange

Pour Rum and juice into a highball glass over cracked ice then stir. Layer Campari and Galliano on top. Garnish with a cherry and slice of orange then serve with 2 straws.

Rum Fizz

10.3% ALC/VOL • 1.7 STD DRINKS

60ml (2 fl oz) Light Rum
30ml (1 fl oz) Fresh Lemon Juice
1 teaspoon Caster Sugar
120ml (4 fl oz) Soda Water

Pour Rum and juice into a cocktail shaker over ice then add sugar. Shake and strain into a highball glass over ice. Add soda, stir gently and serve with 2 straws.

Yum-Yum

15.5% ALC/VOL • 1.6 STD DRINKS

45ml (1½ fl oz) Light Rum
15ml (½ fl oz) Malibu
30ml (1 fl oz) Mango Juice
30ml (1 fl oz) Peach Juice
10ml (⅓ fl oz) Fresh
Lime Juice
Slice of Lime

Pour Rum, Malibu and juices into a cocktail shaker over ice. Shake and strain into a cocktail glass over crushed ice. Garnish with a slice of lime and serve.

Jamaica Sunday

15.9% ALC/VOL • 1.8 STD DRINKS

60ml (2 fl oz) Jamaica Rum
15ml (½ fl oz) Fresh
Lime Juice
1 teaspoon Honey
60ml (2 fl oz) Lemonade

Pour Rum and honey into a mixing glass over crushed ice. Stir and pour into an old-fashioned glass over cracked ice. Add juice and stir. Add lemonade, stir gently and serve.

Elephant's Eye

10.2% ALC/VOL • 1.7 STD DRINKS

30ml (1 fl oz) Jamaica Rum
30ml (1 fl oz) Sweet Vermouth
15ml (½ fl oz) Cointreau
15ml (½ fl oz) Fresh
Lime Juice
120ml (4 fl oz) Tonic Water
Slice of Lime

Pour Rum, Vermouth, Cointreau and juice into a cocktail shaker over ice. Shake and strain into a highball glass over ice. Add tonic and stir gently. Garnish with a slice of lime and serve.

Jamaica Ginger

24.8% ALC/VOL • 2.8 STD DRINKS

90ml (3 fl oz) Jamaica Rum
3 dashes Curaçao
3 dashes Maraschino Liqueur
Dash Angostura Bitters
45ml (1½ fl oz) Grenadine

Pour ingredients into a cocktail shaker over ice and shake. Strain into a chilled cocktail glass and serve.

Casablanca

10.7% ALC/VOL • 2 STD DRINKS

60ml (2 fl oz) Light Rum
15ml (½ fl oz) Malibu
10ml (⅓ fl oz) Grenadine
120ml (4 fl oz) Pineapple Juice
30ml (1 fl oz) Coconut Cream
Maraschino Cherry
Slice of Pineapple

Pour Rum, Malibu, juice and cream into a cocktail shaker over crushed ice. Shake and pour into a chilled collins glass then add Grenadine – do not stir. Garnish with a cherry and slice of pineapple then serve.

San Juan Cooler

10.2% ALC/VOL • 1.8 STD DRINKS

60ml (2 fl oz) Puerto Rican
Rum
60ml (2 fl oz) Pineapple Juice
8ml (¼ fl oz) Fresh
Lemon Juice
90ml (3 fl oz) Tonic Water

Pour Rum and juices into a collins glass over ice then stir. Add tonic, stir gently and serve.

Mary's Dream

14.9% ALC/VOL • 2.3 STD DRINKS

60ml (2 fl oz) Light Rum
15ml (½ fl oz) Cointreau
2 dashes Orange Bitters
120ml (4 fl oz) Fresh
Orange Juice
Slice of Orange

Pour Rum, Cointreau, Bitters and juice into a highball glass over ice then stir. Garnish with a slice of orange and serve.

Chocolate Rum

29.5% ALC/VOL • 1.7 STD DRINKS

30ml (1 fl oz) Light Rum
15ml (½ fl oz) Dark Crème
De Cacao
15ml (½ fl oz) White Crème De
Menthe
5ml (⅙ fl oz) 151-Proof Rum
2 teaspoons Fresh Cream

Pour ingredients into a cocktail shaker over ice and shake. Strain into an old-fashioned glass over ice and serve.

Frozen Key Lime

12.5% ALC/VOL • 1.3 STD DRINKS

30ml (1 fl oz) Light Rum
15ml (½ fl oz) Dark Rum
45ml (1½ fl oz) Fresh
Lime Juice
1½ scoops Vanilla Ice Cream
Maraschino Cherry

Slice of Lime

Pour Rums and juice into a blender over small amount of crushed ice then add ice cream. Blend and pour into a chilled goblet. Garnish with a cherry and slice of lime then serve with 2 short straws.

R.G.B.

19.5% ALC/VOL • 1.6 STD DRINKS

45ml (1½ fl oz) Light Rum
15ml (½ fl oz) Cherry Brandy
8ml (¼ fl oz) Grenadine
8ml (¼ fl oz) Fresh Lime Juice
White of 1 Egg

Pour ingredients into a cocktail shaker over ice and shake. Strain into a chilled cocktail glass and serve.

Dingo

9.2% ALC/VOL • 1.2 STD DRINKS

15ml (½ fl oz) Light Rum
15ml (½ fl oz) Amaretto
15ml (½ fl oz) Southern Comfort
3 dashes Grenadine
60ml (2 fl oz) Fresh Orange Juice
60ml (2 fl oz) Sweet and Sour Mix
Slice of Orange

Pour Rum, Amaretto, Southern Comfort, Grenadine, juice and sour mix into a cocktail shaker over cracked ice. Shake and pour into a chilled highball glass. Garnish with a slice of orange and serve.

That's Life

17.3% ALC/VOL • 1.1 STD DRINKS

30ml (1 fl oz) Bacardi
8ml (¼ fl oz) Poire Williams
15ml (½ fl oz) Passion-Fruit Juice
White of 1 Egg

Pour ingredients into a cocktail shaker over ice and shake. Strain into a chilled cocktail glass and serve.

Agent Provocateur

28.9% ALC/VOL • 2 STD DRINKS

30ml (1 fl oz) Light Rum
15ml (½ fl oz) Mandarine Napoleon
15ml (½ fl oz) Orange Curaçao
8ml (¼ fl oz) Malibu
8ml (¼ fl oz) Midori
5ml (⅙ fl oz) Parfait Amour
8ml (¼ fl oz) Fresh Lime Juice
Maraschino Cherry
Slice of Lime

Pour Rum, Mandarine Napoleon, Curaçao, Malibu, Midori, Parfait Amour and juice into a cocktail shaker over crushed ice. Shake and pour into a chilled old-fashioned glass. Garnish with a cherry and slice of lime then serve.

Cuban Screw

12.3% ALC/VOL • 1.7 STD DRINKS

This drink is also known as Rum Screw, p 121.

Hawaiian Daisy

12.7% ALC/VOL • 1.7 STD DRINKS

45ml (1½ fl oz) Light Rum
5ml (⅙ fl oz) 151-Proof Rum
5ml (⅙ fl oz) Grenadine
15ml (½ fl oz) Pineapple Juice
5ml (⅙ fl oz) Fresh Lime Juice
90ml (3 fl oz) Soda Water
Piece of Papaya

Pour Light Rum, Grenadine and juices into a cocktail shaker over ice. Shake and strain into a goblet over ice. Add soda and stir gently then layer 151-Proof Rum on top. Add a piece of papaya and serve.

Rum Flare

27.6% ALC/VOL • 1.6 STD DRINKS

30ml (1 fl oz) Light Rum
15ml (½ fl oz) Brandy
15ml (½ fl oz) Triple Sec
15ml (½ fl oz) Fresh Lemon Juice

Pour ingredients into a cocktail shaker over ice and shake. Strain into a chilled cocktail glass and serve.

Kis-Kesay

22% ALC/VOL • 1.6 STD DRINKS

40ml (1⅓ fl oz) Light Rum
20ml (⅔ fl oz) White Crème De Cacao
10ml (⅓ fl oz) Blackcurrant Juice
10ml (⅓ fl oz) Fresh Lime Juice
Fresh Whipped Cream
Slice of Orange

Pour Rum, Cacao and juices into a cocktail shaker over ice. Shake and strain into a chilled champagne saucer. Float cream on top and garnish with a slice of orange then serve.

Bacardi Buck

13.4% ALC/VOL • 2.1 STD DRINKS

53ml (1¾ fl oz) Bacardi
15ml (½ fl oz) Cointreau
120ml (4 fl oz) Dry Ginger Ale
¼ Fresh Lemon

Pour Bacardi and Cointreau into a highball glass over ice. Twist ¼ lemon above drink to release juice and add spent shell then stir. Add Ginger Ale, stir gently and serve.

Bitter Planter's Punch

10.8% ALC/VOL • 1.7 STD DRINKS

60ml (2 fl oz) Golden Rum
5ml (⅙ fl oz) Grenadine

15ml (½ fl oz) Fresh
Lemon Juice
1 teaspoon Sugar Syrup
120ml (4 fl oz) Bitter-Lemon
Soda
Slice of Lemon

Pour Rum, Grenadine, juice and sugar into a cocktail shaker over ice. Shake and strain into a collins glass over ice. Add soda and stir gently. Add a slice of lemon and serve.

Pensacola

19% ALC/VOL • 1.3 STD DRINKS

45ml (1½ fl oz) Light Rum
15ml (½ fl oz) Fresh
Lemon Juice
15ml (½ fl oz) Guava Nectar
15ml (½ fl oz) Fresh
Orange Juice

Pour ingredients into a blender over crushed ice and blend. Pour into a chilled champagne saucer and serve.

Maestro

9.9% ALC/VOL • 1.5 STD DRINKS

45ml (1½ fl oz) Añejo Rum
15ml (½ fl oz) Cream Sherry
15ml (½ fl oz) Fresh
Lime Juice
120ml (4 fl oz) Dry Ginger Ale
Wedge of Lemon

Pour Rum, Sherry and juice into a cocktail shaker over ice. Shake and strain into a collins glass over crushed ice. Add Ginger Ale and stir gently. Garnish with a wedge of lemon and serve.
This drink is also known as Maktak Special.

Cream Puff

9.4% ALC/VOL • 1.8 STD DRINKS

60ml (2 fl oz) Light Rum
30ml (1 fl oz) Fresh Cream
½ teaspoon Sugar Syrup
150ml (5 fl oz) Soda Water

Pour Rum, cream and sugar into a cocktail shaker over ice. Shake and strain into a chilled highball glass over 2 ice cubes. Add soda, stir gently and serve.

Rum Cobbler

19.4% ALC/VOL • 2.1 STD DRINKS

30ml (1 fl oz) Dark Rum
30ml (1 fl oz) Light Rum
10ml (⅓ fl oz) Cointreau
1 teaspoon Sugar Syrup
60ml (2 fl oz) Soda Water
Slice of Orange

Pour Rums, Cointreau and sugar into a cocktail shaker over cracked ice. Shake and pour into a goblet over cracked ice. Add soda and stir gently. Garnish with a slice of orange and serve.

Pago Pago

23.5% ALC/VOL • 1.5 STD DRINKS

45ml (1½ fl oz) Golden Rum
3 dashes Green Chartreuse
Dash White Crème De Cacao
15ml (½ fl oz) Fresh
Lime Juice
15ml (½ fl oz) Pineapple Juice

Pour ingredients into a cocktail shaker over ice and shake. Strain into a chilled cocktail glass and serve.

Sunshine State

32.4% ALC/VOL • 1.2 STD DRINKS

30ml (1 fl oz) Golden Rum
15ml (½ fl oz) Banana Liqueur
Dash Amaretto
Dash Angostura Bitters
Slice of Orange
Slice of Pineapple

Pour Rum, Liqueur, Amaretto and Bitters into a blender over crushed ice. Blend and pour into a chilled brandy balloon. Garnish with a slice of orange and pineapple then serve.

Rum Rickey

13.5% ALC/VOL • 1.8 STD DRINKS

60ml (2 fl oz) Light Rum
15ml (½ fl oz) Fresh
Lime Juice
90ml (3 fl oz) Soda Water
Twist of Lime Peel

Pour Rum and juice into a collins glass over ice then stir. Add soda and stir gently. Garnish with lime peel and serve.

Cherie

23.2% ALC/VOL • 1.6 STD DRINKS

30ml (1 fl oz) Light Rum
15ml (½ fl oz) Cherry Brandy
15ml (½ fl oz) Cointreau
30ml (1 fl oz) Fresh Lime Juice
Maraschino Cherry

Pour Rum, Brandy, Cointreau and juice into a cocktail shaker over ice. Shake and strain into a chilled cocktail glass. Garnish with a cherry and serve.

Frozen Coconut

19.5% ALC/VOL • 1.8 STD DRINKS

45ml (1½ fl oz) Light Rum
30ml (1 fl oz) Malibu
1½ scoops Coconut Ice Cream
Maraschino Cherry

Prepare a goblet with a grated coconut frosted rim – moistened with egg white. Pour Rum and Malibu into a blender over small amount of crushed ice then add ice cream. Blend and pour into prepared glass. Garnish with a cherry and serve.

Fern Gully

21.5% ALC/VOL • 1.8 STD DRINKS

30ml (1 fl oz) Jamaica Rum
30ml (1 fl oz) Light Rum
15ml (½ fl oz) Coconut Cream
15ml (½ fl oz) Fresh Lime Juice
10ml (⅓ fl oz) Fresh Orange Juice
1 teaspoon Orzata

Pour ingredients into a blender over crushed ice and blend. Pour into a chilled champagne saucer and serve.

Broadside

27.8% ALC/VOL • 1.9 STD DRINKS

30ml (1 fl oz) Dark Rum
15ml (½ fl oz) Cherry Brandy
15ml (½ fl oz) Frangelico
15ml (½ fl oz) Vodka
10ml (⅓ fl oz) Grenadine

Pour ingredients into a cocktail shaker over ice and shake. Strain into a chilled cocktail glass and serve.

Flamingo

10.7% ALC/VOL • 1.7 STD DRINKS

38ml (1¼ fl oz) Light Rum
30ml (1 fl oz) Sloe Gin
90ml (3 fl oz) Pineapple Juice
40ml (1⅓ fl oz) Coconut Cream
1 teaspoon Thick Cream
Maraschino Cherry
Slice of Pineapple

Pour Rum, Gin, juice and creams into a blender over crushed ice. Blend and pour into a chilled hurricane glass. Garnish with a cherry and slice of pineapple then serve.

Bacardi Martini

34.7% ALC/VOL • 2.5 STD DRINKS

75ml (2½ fl oz) Bacardi
15ml (½ fl oz) Dry Vermouth
Green Olive

Pour Bacardi and Vermouth into a mixing glass over ice. Stir and strain into a chilled martini glass. Garnish with an olive and serve.

Waikiki Beach

11% ALC/VOL • 1.7 STD DRINKS

45ml (1½ fl oz) Light Rum
15ml (½ fl oz) Amaretto
60ml (2 fl oz) Pineapple Juice
30ml (1 fl oz) Passion-Fruit Juice
30ml (1 fl oz) Fresh Cream
15ml (½ fl oz) Coconut Cream

Prepare a goblet with a grated coconut frosted rim – moistened with egg white and add ice. Pour ingredients into a cocktail shaker over ice and shake. Strain into prepared glass and serve.

Appled Rum Cooler

17.4% ALC/VOL • 1.8 STD DRINKS

45ml (1½ fl oz) Añejo Rum
15ml (½ fl oz) Applejack
10ml (⅓ fl oz) Fresh Lime Juice
60ml (2 fl oz) Soda Water

Pour Rum, Applejack and juice into a cocktail shaker over ice. Shake and strain into a collins glass over ice. Add soda, stir gently and serve.

Caribbean Sling

12.5% ALC/VOL • 2.3 STD DRINKS

60ml (2 fl oz) Light Rum
15ml (½ fl oz) Cointreau
15ml (½ fl oz) Fresh Lemon Juice
15ml (½ fl oz) Fresh Lime Juice
1 teaspoon Sugar Syrup
120ml (4 fl oz) Soda Water
Twist of Cucumber Rind

Pour Rum, Cointreau, juices and sugar into a cocktail shaker over ice. Shake and strain into a collins glass over ice. Add soda and stir gently. Add cucumber rind and serve.

Buccaneer

10.8% ALC/VOL • 1.5 STD DRINKS

45ml (1½ fl oz) Golden Rum
15ml (½ fl oz) Advocaat
120ml (4 fl oz) Dry Ginger Ale

Pour Rum and Advocaat into a cocktail shaker over ice. Shake and strain into a highball glass over ice. Add Ginger Ale, stir gently and serve.

Fell Juice

10.6% ALC/VOL • 1.3 STD DRINKS

30ml (1 fl oz) Light Rum
15ml (½ fl oz) Dark Rum
60ml (2 fl oz) Cranberry Juice
10ml (⅓ fl oz) Fresh Lemon Juice
10ml (⅓ fl oz) Fresh Lime Juice
1 teaspoon Sugar Syrup
White of 1 Egg

Pour ingredients into a cocktail shaker over ice and shake. Strain into an old-fashioned glass over crushed ice and serve.

Beachcomber's Gold

28.8% ALC/VOL • 1.7 STD DRINKS

45ml (1½ fl oz) Light Rum
15ml (½ fl oz) Dry Vermouth
15ml (½ fl oz) Sweet Vermouth

Pour ingredients into a mixing glass over ice and stir. Strain into a champagne saucer filled with cracked ice and serve.

Volcano

5.3% ALC/VOL • 1.2 STD DRINKS

15ml (½ fl oz) Bacardi

15ml (½ fl oz) Blue Curaçao
15ml (½ fl oz) Golden Rum
120ml (4 fl oz) Fresh Orange Juice
120ml (4 fl oz) Pineapple Juice
½ Fresh Lime (marinated in Green Chartreuse)

Pour Bacardi, Curaçao, Rum and juices into a cocktail shaker over ice. Shake and strain into a chilled hurricane glass. Float ½ marinated lime on top and ignite then serve.

Under the Sea

29% ALC/VOL • 3.8 STD DRINKS

68ml (2¼ fl oz) Bacardi
60ml (2 fl oz) Banana Liqueur
38ml (1¼ fl oz) Blue Curaçao
Dash Sugar Syrup
3 drops Fresh Lemon Juice

Pour ingredients into a cocktail shaker over ice and shake. Strain into a highball glass over ice and serve.

Mai Tai Swizzle

23.8% ALC/VOL • 2.7 STD DRINKS

45ml (1½ fl oz) Dark Rum
30ml (1 fl oz) Light Rum
15ml (½ fl oz) Cointreau
Dash Angostura Bitters
Dash Pernod
30ml (1 fl oz) Grapefruit Juice
15ml (½ fl oz) Fresh Lime Juice
1½ teaspoons Orgeat Syrup
Slice of Pineapple
Sprig of Fresh Mint

Pour Rums, Cointreau, Bitters, Pernod, juices and syrup into a mixing glass over large amount of ice. Stir vigorously until cold and strain into a collins glass filled with crushed ice. Garnish with a slice of pineapple and sprig of mint. Serve with a swizzle stick and 2 straws.

Easy Money

14.3% ALC/VOL • 1.6 STD DRINKS

30ml (1 fl oz) Light Rum
15ml (½ fl oz) Dark Rum
15ml (½ fl oz) Malibu
5ml (1/6 fl oz) Grenadine
30ml (1 fl oz) Fresh Orange Juice
8ml (¼ fl oz) Fresh Lime Juice
2 tablespoons Mango Sherbet
Slice of Orange

Pour Rums, Malibu and juices into a blender over crushed ice then add sherbet. Blend and pour into a chilled goblet then add Grenadine by pouring on top – do not stir. Garnish with a slice of orange and serve.

Bitter Banana Cooler

7.3% ALC/VOL • 1.4 STD DRINKS

45ml (1½ fl oz) Light Rum
2 dashes Peychaud's Bitters
60ml (2 fl oz) Pineapple Juice
15ml (½ fl oz) Fresh Lime Juice
½ Banana (diced)
90ml (3 fl oz) Bitter-Lemon Soda

Pour Rum, Bitters and juices into a blender over crushed ice then add diced banana. Blend and pour into a chilled collins glass over 2 ice cubes. Add soda, stir gently and serve.

Passion Punch

15.1% ALC/VOL • 1.3 STD DRINKS

45ml (1½ fl oz) Golden Rum
30ml (1 fl oz) Passion-Fruit Juice
30ml (1 fl oz) Red Grape Juice
1 teaspoon Pineapple Syrup

Pour ingredients into a cocktail shaker over cracked ice and shake. Pour into a chilled old-fashioned glass and serve.

Muskmelon

15% ALC/VOL • 1.3 STD DRINKS

45ml (1½ fl oz) Light Rum
15ml (½ fl oz) Fresh Lime Juice
15ml (½ fl oz) Fresh Orange Juice
½ teaspoon Sugar Syrup
¼ Cup Cantaloupe Meat (diced)
Cube of Cantaloupe Meat on Spear

Pour Rum, juices and sugar into a blender over crushed ice then add diced cantaloupe. Blend and pour into a chilled old-fashioned glass then add ice. Garnish with a cube of cantaloupe and serve.

Mariposa

25.7% ALC/VOL • 1.3 STD DRINKS

30ml (1 fl oz) Light Rum
15ml (½ fl oz) Brandy
Dash Grenadine
10ml (⅓ fl oz) Fresh Lemon Juice
10ml (⅓ fl oz) Fresh Orange Juice

Pour ingredients into a cocktail shaker over ice and shake. Strain into a chilled cocktail glass and serve.

Rum Cassis

25.7% ALC/VOL • 1.5 STD DRINKS

30ml (1 fl oz) Light Rum
30ml (1 fl oz) Dry Vermouth
10ml (⅓ fl oz) Crème De Cassis
3 dashes Soda Water
Slice of Lime

Pour Rum, Vermouth and Cassis into an old-fashioned glass over ice then stir. Add soda – do not stir, then add a slice of lime and serve.

St. Augustine

23.9% ALC/VOL • 1.5 STD DRINKS

45ml (1½ fl oz) Light Rum
5ml (1/6 fl oz) Cointreau
30ml (1 fl oz) Grapefruit Juice
Twist of Lemon Peel

Prepare a cocktail glass with a sugar frosted rim. Pour Rum, Cointreau and juice into a cocktail shaker over ice. Shake and strain into prepared glass. Twist lemon peel above drink and place remainder of peel into drink then serve.

Creole

18.2% ALC/VOL • 1.3 STD DRINKS

45ml (1½ fl oz) Light Rum
45ml (1½ fl oz) Beef Bouillon
3 dashes Fresh Lemon Juice
Dash Tabasco Sauce
Pinch of Pepper
Pinch of Salt

Pour Rum, bouillon, juice and sauce into a cocktail shaker over ice. Add pepper and salt. Shake and strain into an old-fashioned glass over ice then serve.

Bahama Mama Sunrise

8.5% ALC/VOL • 1.7 STD DRINKS

30ml (1 fl oz) Dark Rum
30ml (1 fl oz) Spiced Rum
15ml (½ fl oz) Grenadine
120ml (4 fl oz) Fresh Orange Juice
60ml (2 fl oz) Pineapple Juice

Pour ingredients into a cocktail shaker over ice and shake. Strain into a tall glass over ice and serve.

Continental

29.9% ALC/VOL • 1.7 STD DRINKS

53ml (1¾ fl oz) Light Rum
5ml (1/6 fl oz) Green Crème De Menthe
10ml (⅓ fl oz) Fresh Lime Juice
½ teaspoon Sugar Syrup
Twist of Lemon Peel

Pour Rum, Crème De Menthe, juice and sugar into a cocktail shaker over ice. Shake and strain into a chilled cocktail glass. Twist lemon peel above drink and discard remainder of peel then serve.

Star Gazer

13.8% ALC/VOL • 1.9 STD DRINKS

45ml (1½ fl oz) Dark Rum
15ml (½ fl oz) Blue Curaçao
15ml (½ fl oz) Triple Sec
2 teaspoons Sugar Syrup
90ml (3 fl oz) Soda Water

Pour Rum, Curaçao, Triple Sec and sugar into a cocktail shaker over ice. Shake and strain into a highball glass over ice. Add soda, stir gently and serve.

Biscay

21.9% ALC/VOL • 1.6 STD DRINKS

30ml (1 fl oz) Light Rum
15ml (½ fl oz) Mandarine Napoleon
15ml (½ fl oz) Rum Tree
5ml (1/6 fl oz) Fresh Lime Juice
30ml (1 fl oz) Lemonade
Maraschino Cherry
Slice of Orange

Pour Rum, Mandarine Napoleon, Rum Tree and juice into an old-fashioned glass over cracked ice then stir. Add lemonade and stir gently. Garnish with a cherry and slice of orange then serve.

Chocolate Coco

12.8% ALC/VOL • 1.4 STD DRINKS

30ml (1 fl oz) Dark Rum
30ml (1 fl oz) Coconut Liqueur
60ml (2 fl oz) Pineapple Juice
20ml (⅔ fl oz) Chocolate Syrup

Pour ingredients into a cocktail shaker over ice and shake. Strain into a chilled highball glass and serve.

Five Hundred Proof

22.1% ALC/VOL • 2.9 STD DRINKS

15ml (½ fl oz) Over-Proof Light Rum
15ml (½ fl oz) 100-Proof Bourbon
15ml (½ fl oz) Green Chartreuse
15ml (½ fl oz) Southern Comfort
15ml (½ fl oz) Vodka
15ml (½ fl oz) Grenadine
30ml (1 fl oz) Fresh Lemon Juice
30ml (1 fl oz) Fresh Orange Juice
15ml (½ fl oz) Sugar Syrup
Maraschino Cherry

Pour Rum, Bourbon, Chartreuse, Southern Comfort, Vodka, Grenadine, juices and sugar into a cocktail shaker over ice. Shake and strain into a highball glass over cracked ice. Garnish with a cherry and serve.

On the Deck

11.5% ALC/VOL • 2.2 STD DRINKS

This drink is also known as Electric Lemonade, p 172.

Quilt Lifter

13% ALC/VOL • 1.4 STD DRINKS

30ml (1 fl oz) Light Rum
15ml (½ fl oz) Banana Liqueur
15ml (½ fl oz) Dry Sherry
30ml (1 fl oz) Fresh Orange Juice
30ml (1 fl oz) Pineapple Juice
15ml (½ fl oz) Passion-Fruit Juice

Maraschino Cherry
Slice of Orange
Slice of Pineapple

Pour Rum, Liqueur, Sherry and juices into a cocktail shaker over crushed ice. Shake and pour into a chilled cocktail glass. Garnish with a cherry, slice of orange and pineapple then serve.

Havana Club

30.6% ALC/VOL • 1.6 STD DRINKS

45ml (1½ fl oz) Golden Rum
23ml (¾ fl oz) Dry Vermouth

Pour ingredients into a mixing glass over ice and stir. Strain into a chilled cocktail glass and serve.

French Colonial

12.1% ALC/VOL • 2 STD DRINKS

45ml (1½ fl oz) Golden Rum
15ml (½ fl oz) Cointreau
15ml (½ fl oz) Crème De Cassis
15ml (½ fl oz) Fresh Lemon Juice
120ml (4 fl oz) Tonic Water
Slice of Lemon

Pour Rum, Cointreau, Cassis and juice into a cocktail shaker over ice. Shake and strain into a highball glass over ice. Add tonic and stir gently. Garnish with a slice of lemon and serve.

Sloppy Joe's Cocktail

17% ALC/VOL • 1 STD DRINK

23ml (¾ fl oz) Light Rum
23ml (¾ fl oz) Dry Vermouth
Dash Cointreau
Dash Grenadine
30ml (1 fl oz) Fresh Lemon Juice

Pour ingredients into a cocktail shaker over ice and shake. Strain into a chilled cocktail glass and serve.

Rum Sunday

16.4% ALC/VOL • 1.5 STD DRINKS

30ml (1 fl oz) Dark Rum
15ml (½ fl oz) Sweet Sherry
10ml (⅓ fl oz) Over-Proof Dark Rum
15ml (½ fl oz) Grenadine
1½ scoops Vanilla Ice Cream
Grated Chocolate

Pour Dark Rum, Sherry and Grenadine into a blender over small amount of crushed ice then add ice cream. Blend and pour into a chilled collins glass then layer Over-Proof Rum on top. Sprinkle chocolate on top and serve.

Cosmos

24% ALC/VOL • 1.8 STD DRINKS

60ml (2 fl oz) Light Rum
30ml (1 fl oz) Fresh Lime Juice
1 teaspoon Sugar Syrup

Pour ingredients into a cocktail shaker over crushed ice and shake. Pour into a chilled cocktail glass and serve.

Castro Cooler

15.5% ALC/VOL • 2 STD DRINKS

45ml (1½ fl oz) Golden Rum
23ml (¾ fl oz) Apple Brandy
60ml (2 fl oz) Fresh Orange Juice
23ml (¾ fl oz) Lime Syrup
15ml (½ fl oz) Fresh Lemon Juice
Slice of Lemon

Pour Rum, Brandy, juices and syrup into a collins glass over ice then stir. Garnish with a slice of lemon and serve.

Kingston

25.9% ALC/VOL • 3.1 STD DRINKS

60ml (2 fl oz) Jamaica Rum
45ml (1½ fl oz) Gin
30ml (1 fl oz) Fresh Lime Juice
1 tablespoon Sugar Syrup

Pour ingredients into a cocktail shaker over cracked ice and shake. Pour into a chilled old-fashioned glass and serve.

Krazee Keith

11.3% ALC/VOL • 1.8 STD DRINKS

45ml (1½ fl oz) Light Rum
10ml (⅓ fl oz) Anisette
10ml (⅓ fl oz) Cherry Brandy
15ml (½ fl oz) Fresh Lemon Juice
120ml (4 fl oz) Cola
Wedge of Lemon

Pour Rum, Anisette, Brandy and juice into a highball glass over ice then stir. Add cola and stir gently. Garnish with a wedge of lemon and serve.

Surrey Slider

11% ALC/VOL • 1.6 STD DRINKS

45ml (1½ fl oz) Añejo Rum
15ml (½ fl oz) Peach Schnapps
120ml (4 fl oz) Fresh Orange Juice
Slice of Orange

Pour Rum, Schnapps and juice into a highball glass over ice then stir. Garnish with a slice of orange and serve.

Aloha

23% ALC/VOL • 1.4 STD DRINKS

30ml (1 fl oz) Light Rum
15ml (½ fl oz) Dry Vermouth
15ml (½ fl oz) Midori
15ml (½ fl oz) Fresh Lime Juice
Cube of Papaya

Pour Rum, Vermouth, Midori and juice into a cocktail shaker over ice. Shake and strain into an old-fashioned glass over ice. Garnish with a cube of papaya and serve.

Triad

7.3% ALC/VOL • 1 STD DRINK

15ml (½ fl oz) Añejo Rum
15ml (½ fl oz) Amaretto
15ml (½ fl oz) Sweet Vermouth
120ml (4 fl oz) Dry Ginger Ale
Wedge of Lemon

Pour Rum, Amaretto and Vermouth into a highball glass over ice then stir. Add Ginger Ale and stir gently. Garnish with a wedge of lemon and serve.

Cornwall-Nash

21.3% ALC/VOL • 2.4 STD DRINKS

45ml (1½ fl oz) Light Rum
15ml (½ fl oz) Cointreau
15ml (½ fl oz) Gin
5ml (1/6 fl oz) Cherry Brandy
60ml (2 fl oz) Grapefruit Juice
Maraschino Cherry

Pour Rum, Cointreau, Gin and juice into a highball glass over ice then stir. Add Brandy by pouring into centre of drink – do not stir, then garnish with a cherry and serve.

Cape of Good Will

19.7% ALC/VOL • 1.7 STD DRINKS

45ml (1½ fl oz) Light Rum
15ml (½ fl oz) Apricot Brandy
2 dashes Orange Bitters
30ml (1 fl oz) Fresh Orange Juice
15ml (½ fl oz) Fresh Lemon Juice

Pour ingredients into a cocktail shaker over ice and shake. Strain into a chilled cocktail glass and serve.

Tobago

21.5% ALC/VOL • 1.8 STD DRINKS

30ml (1 fl oz) Light Rum
30ml (1 fl oz) Gin
30ml (1 fl oz) Fresh Lime Juice
15ml (½ fl oz) Guava Syrup
Twist of Lime Peel

Pour Rum, Gin, juice and syrup into a blender over crushed ice. Blend and pour into a chilled cocktail glass. Twist lime peel above drink and discard remainder of peel then serve.

Fort Lauderdale

22% ALC/VOL • 1.5 STD DRINKS

45ml (1½ fl oz) Light Rum
15ml (½ fl oz) Sweet Vermouth
20ml (⅔ fl oz) Fresh Orange Juice
8ml (¼ fl oz) Fresh Lime Juice
Slice of Orange

Pour Rum, Vermouth and juices into a cocktail shaker over ice. Shake and strain into an old-fashioned glass over ice. Add a slice of orange and serve.

Cool Guanabana

11.6% ALC/VOL • 1.8 STD DRINKS

45ml (1½ fl oz) Light Rum
15ml (½ fl oz) Jamaica Rum
120ml (4 fl oz) Iced Guanabana Nectar
15ml (½ fl oz) Fresh Lime Juice
Slice of Lime

Prepare a collins glass with a sugar frosted rim – moistened with Grenadine. Pour Rums, nectar and juice into a cocktail shaker over ice. Shake and strain into prepared glass. Garnish with a slice of lime and serve.

Lounge Lizard

9.2% ALC/VOL • 1.2 STD DRINKS

30ml (1 fl oz) Dark Rum
15ml (½ fl oz) Amaretto
120ml (4 fl oz) Cola
Slice of Lime

Pour Rum and Amaretto into a collins glass over ice then stir. Add cola and stir gently. Garnish with a slice of lime and serve.

Costa del Sol

13.7% ALC/VOL • 2.1 STD DRINKS

60ml (2 fl oz) Light Rum
30ml (1 fl oz) Sweet Vermouth
15ml (½ fl oz) Fresh Lemon Juice
15ml (½ fl oz) Sugar Syrup
75ml (2½ fl oz) Soda Water
Maraschino Cherry
Slice of Orange

Pour Rum, Vermouth, juice and sugar into a highball glass over ice then stir. Add soda and stir gently. Garnish with a cherry and slice of orange then serve with 2 straws.

Tropical Spiced Tea

7% ALC/VOL • 1.1 STD DRINKS

38ml (1¼ fl oz) Spiced Rum
150ml (5 fl oz) Iced Tea
3 dashes Fresh Lemon Juice
Wedge of Lemon

Pour Rum, tea and juice into a highball glass over ice then stir. Garnish with a wedge of lemon and serve.

Cranberry Rum Punch

8.9% ALC/VOL • 1.8 STD DRINKS

30ml (1 fl oz) Jamaica Rum
30ml (1 fl oz) Light Rum
120ml (4 fl oz) Cranberry Juice
60ml (2 fl oz) Fresh Orange Juice

15ml (½ fl oz) Fresh
Lemon Juice
Slice of Lemon

Pour Rums and juices into a cocktail shaker over ice. Shake and strain into a collins glass over ice. Add more ice to fill glass and stir. Garnish with a slice of lemon and serve.

Son of Adam

24.8% ALC/VOL • 1.6 STD DRINKS

45ml (1½ fl oz) Light Rum
15ml (½ fl oz) Apricot Brandy
5ml (⅙ fl oz) Grenadine
15ml (½ fl oz) Fresh
Lemon Juice
½ teaspoon Sugar Syrup

Pour ingredients into a cocktail shaker over ice and shake. Strain into a chilled cocktail glass and serve.

Serpentine

23% ALC/VOL • 1.4 STD DRINKS

30ml (1 fl oz) Light Rum
15ml (½ fl oz) Brandy
15ml (½ fl oz) Sweet Vermouth
15ml (½ fl oz) Fresh
Lemon Juice
½ teaspoon Sugar Syrup
Wedge of Lemon

Pour Rum, Brandy, Vermouth, juice and sugar into a cocktail shaker over ice. Shake and strain into a chilled cocktail glass. Garnish with a wedge of lemon and serve.

Wedding March

32.9% ALC/VOL • 2.8 STD DRINKS

90ml (3 fl oz) Light Rum
2 dashes Angostura Bitters
15ml (½ fl oz) Fresh
Lime Juice
White of 2 Eggs

Pour ingredients into a cocktail shaker over ice and shake. Strain into a chilled champagne saucer and serve.

Caribbean Romance

15.2% ALC/VOL • 2 STD DRINKS

45ml (1½ fl oz) Light Rum
30ml (1 fl oz) Amaretto
3 dashes Grenadine
45ml (1½ fl oz) Fresh
Orange Juice
45ml (1½ fl oz) Pineapple Juice
Slice of Orange

Pour Rum, Amaretto and juices into a cocktail shaker over cracked ice. Shake and pour into a chilled highball glass then layer Grenadine on top. Garnish with a slice of orange and serve.

Rum Dubonnet

28.4% ALC/VOL • 1.6 STD DRINKS

45ml (1½ fl oz) Light Rum
23ml (¾ fl oz) Dubonnet
5ml (⅙ fl oz) Fresh Lime Juice
Twist of Lime Peel

Pour Rum, Dubonnet and juice into a cocktail shaker over ice. Shake and strain into a chilled cocktail glass. Twist lime peel above drink and place remainder of peel into drink then serve.

Jamaica Elegance

20.2% ALC/VOL • 1.8 STD DRINKS

45ml (1½ fl oz) Golden
Jamaica Rum
15ml (½ fl oz) Brandy
30ml (1 fl oz) Fresh Lime Juice
15ml (½ fl oz) Pineapple Juice
1 teaspoon Sugar Syrup
Slice of Lime

Pour Rum, Brandy, juices and sugar into a cocktail shaker over ice. Shake and strain into a collins glass over ice. Add a slice of lime and serve.

Midnight Express

26.4% ALC/VOL • 1.8 STD DRINKS

45ml (1½ fl oz) Dark Rum
15ml (½ fl oz) Cointreau
23ml (¾ fl oz) Fresh
Lime Juice
3 dashes Sweet and Sour Mix

Pour ingredients into a cocktail shaker over cracked ice and shake. Pour into an old-fashioned glass over ice and serve.

Sleepy Lemon Clegg

14.9% ALC/VOL • 1.6 STD DRINKS

45ml (1½ fl oz) Dark Rum
15ml (½ fl oz) Banana Liqueur
30ml (1 fl oz) Fresh
Orange Juice
30ml (1 fl oz) Pineapple Juice
15ml (½ fl oz) Fresh
Lemon Juice
Wedge of Lemon

Pour Rum, Liqueur and juices into a cocktail shaker over ice. Shake and strain into an old-fashioned glass filled with crushed ice. Garnish with a wedge of lemon and serve.

Nevada Cocktail

15.1% ALC/VOL • 1.4 STD DRINKS

45ml (1½ fl oz) Light Rum
Dash Angostura Bitters

30ml (1 fl oz) Grapefruit Juice
30ml (1 fl oz) Fresh Lime Juice
2 teaspoons Sugar Syrup

Pour ingredients into a cocktail shaker over ice and shake. Strain into a chilled cocktail glass and serve.

Grocery Boy

12.9% ALC/VOL • 1.9 STD DRINKS

30ml (1 fl oz) Light Rum
23ml (¾ fl oz) Southern Comfort
10ml (⅓ fl oz) Cointreau
120ml (4 fl oz) Bitter-Lemon Soda
Slice of Lemon
Slice of Orange

Pour Rum, Southern Comfort and Cointreau into a highball glass over ice then stir. Add soda and stir gently. Garnish with a slice of lemon and orange then serve.

Rum Toddy

30.4% ALC/VOL • 1.8 STD DRINKS

60ml (2 fl oz) Dark Rum
10ml (⅓ fl oz) Spring Water
½ teaspoon Sugar Syrup
Twist of Lemon Peel

Pour Rum, water and sugar into a chilled old-fashioned glass over an ice cube then stir. Twist lemon peel above drink and discard remainder of peel then serve.

Cracklin' Rosie

18.2% ALC/VOL • 1.6 STD DRINKS

45ml (1½ fl oz) Light Rum
15ml (½ fl oz) Banana Liqueur
23ml (¾ fl oz) Passion-Fruit Juice
15ml (½ fl oz) Fresh Lime Juice
15ml (½ fl oz) Pineapple Juice
Maraschino Cherry

Pour Rum, Liqueur and juices into a cocktail shaker over ice. Shake and strain into a chilled cocktail glass. Garnish with a cherry and serve.

Culross

29% ALC/VOL • 1.6 STD DRINKS

45ml (1½ fl oz) Golden Rum
15ml (½ fl oz) Lillet
5ml (⅙ fl oz) Apricot Brandy
5ml (⅙ fl oz) Fresh Lime Juice

Pour ingredients into a cocktail shaker over ice and shake. Strain into a chilled cocktail glass and serve.

This drink may also be served in an old-fashioned glass over ice if desired.

Mozart

32.1% ALC/VOL • 1.7 STD DRINKS

45ml (1½ fl oz) Añejo Rum
15ml (½ fl oz) Sweet Vermouth
5ml (⅙ fl oz) Cointreau
2 dashes Orange Bitters
Wedge of Lemon

Pour Rum, Vermouth, Cointreau and Bitters into a mixing glass over ice. Stir and strain into a chilled cocktail glass. Garnish with a wedge of lemon and serve.

Port Maria

20% ALC/VOL • 1.4 STD DRINKS

45ml (1½ fl oz) Light Rum
5ml (⅙ fl oz) Falernum
23ml (¾ fl oz) Pineapple Juice
15ml (½ fl oz) Fresh Lemon Juice
Nutmeg

Pour Rum, Falernum and juices into a cocktail shaker over ice. Shake and strain into a chilled cocktail glass. Sprinkle nutmeg on top and serve.

Earls Court

16.5% ALC/VOL • 1.7 STD DRINKS

40ml (1⅓ fl oz) Dark Rum
23ml (¾ fl oz) Peach Schnapps
10ml (⅓ fl oz) Pimm's No.1
30ml (1 fl oz) Mandarin Juice
30ml (1 fl oz) Lemonade
Maraschino Cherry
Slice of Orange

Pour Rum, Schnapps, Pimm's and juice into a cocktail shaker over ice. Shake and strain into an old-fashioned glass over cracked ice. Add lemonade and stir gently. Garnish with a cherry and slice of orange then serve.

Show Tune

6.5% ALC/VOL • 1 STD DRINK

30ml (1 fl oz) Spiced Rum
8ml (¼ fl oz) Amaretto
5ml (⅙ fl oz) Grenadine
90ml (3 fl oz) Grapefruit Juice
60ml (2 fl oz) Soda Water

Pour Rum, Amaretto, Grenadine and juice into a highball glass over ice then stir. Add soda, stir gently and serve.

Blue Mountain

23.8% ALC/VOL • 2.1 STD DRINKS

45ml (1½ fl oz) Añejo Rum
15ml (½ fl oz) Tia Maria
15ml (½ fl oz) Vodka
30ml (1 fl oz) Fresh Orange Juice
5ml (⅙ fl oz) Fresh Lemon Juice

Pour ingredients into a cocktail shaker over ice and shake. Strain into an old-fashioned glass over ice and serve.

Hurricane

13.2% ALC/VOL • 2.2 STD DRINKS

45ml (1½ fl oz) Dark Rum

30ml (1 fl oz) Light Rum
60ml (2 fl oz) Passion-
Fruit Juice
30ml (1 fl oz) Fresh
Orange Juice
30ml (1 fl oz) Pineapple Juice
15ml (½ fl oz) Blackcurrant
Syrup
Maraschino Cherry
Slice of Pineapple

Pour Rums, juices and syrup into a cocktail shaker over ice. Shake and strain into a hurricane glass over cracked ice. Garnish with a cherry and slice of pineapple then serve with 2 straws.

Olaffson's Punch

11.4% ALC/VOL • 1.8 STD DRINKS

60ml (2 fl oz) Dark Rum
5ml (1/6 fl oz) Maraschino
Liqueur
90ml (3 fl oz) Fresh
Orange Juice
45ml (1½ fl oz) Fresh
Lime Juice
1 teaspoon Sugar Syrup
Twist of Lime Peel
Twist of Orange Peel

Pour Rum, Liqueur, juices and sugar into a cocktail shaker over crushed ice. Shake and pour into a chilled goblet. Twist lime and orange peels above drink. Discard remainder of peels and serve with 2 short straws.

Mickey's Fin

12.2% ALC/VOL • 1.6 STD DRINKS

30ml (1 fl oz) Dark Rum
30ml (1 fl oz) Malibu
15ml (½ fl oz) Banana Liqueur
5ml (1/6 fl oz) Grenadine
30ml (1 fl oz) Fresh
Orange Juice
30ml (1 fl oz) Grapefruit Juice
30ml (1 fl oz) Pineapple Juice

Pour ingredients into a cocktail shaker over ice and shake. Strain into a collins glass over ice and serve.

Redcoat

27.4% ALC/VOL • 2.1 STD DRINKS

45ml (1½ fl oz) Light Rum
15ml (½ fl oz) Apricot Brandy
15ml (½ fl oz) Vodka
5ml (1/6 fl oz) Grenadine
15ml (½ fl oz) Fresh
Lime Juice

Pour ingredients into a cocktail shaker over ice and shake. Strain into a chilled cocktail glass and serve.

Garden Fresh

12.8% ALC/VOL • 1.2 STD DRINKS

30ml (1 fl oz) Golden Rum
15ml (½ fl oz) Midori
5ml (1/6 fl oz) Pear Liqueur
45ml (1½ fl oz)
Grapefruit Juice
23ml (¾ fl oz) Pineapple Juice
1 teaspoon Kiwi Syrup
Maraschino Cherry

Pour Rum, Midori, Liqueur, juices and syrup into a cocktail shaker over ice. Shake and strain into a chilled cocktail glass. Garnish with a cherry and serve.

Swiss Yodeler

20.3% ALC/VOL • 1.3 STD DRINKS

45ml (1½ fl oz) Bacardi
30ml (1 fl oz) Fresh Lime Juice
1 teaspoon Molasses
½ teaspoon Sugar Syrup

Pour ingredients into a cocktail shaker over ice and shake. Strain into a chilled cocktail glass and serve.

Oyster Bay

5.9% ALC/VOL • 1 STD DRINK

30ml (1 fl oz) Dark Rum
5ml (1/6 fl oz) Anisette
60ml (2 fl oz) Mango Juice
30ml (1 fl oz) Grapefruit Juice
30ml (1 fl oz) Papaya Juice
30ml (1 fl oz) Pineapple Juice
23ml (¾ fl oz) Fresh
Lime Juice
1 teaspoon Sugar Syrup
Slice of Mango
Slice of Pineapple

Pour Rum, Anisette, juices and sugar into a cocktail shaker over ice. Shake and strain into a collins glass over ice. Garnish with a slice of mango and pineapple then serve with 2 straws.

Cocomacoque

10.1% ALC/VOL • 1.9 STD DRINKS

45ml (1½ fl oz) Light Rum
60ml (2 fl oz) Claret
60ml (2 fl oz) Fresh
Orange Juice
60ml (2 fl oz) Pineapple Juice
15ml (½ fl oz) Fresh
Lemon Juice
Slice of Pineapple

Pour Rum and juices into a collins glass over ice then stir. Add Claret and stir gently. Garnish with a slice of pineapple and serve.

Silent Broadsider

30.9% ALC/VOL • 2 STD DRINKS

45ml (1½ fl oz) Light Rum
10ml (⅓ fl oz) Brandy
10ml (⅓ fl oz) Frangelico
10ml (⅓ fl oz) Sweet Vermouth
5ml (1/6 fl oz) Grenadine

Pour ingredients into a cocktail shaker over ice and shake. Strain into a chilled cocktail glass and serve.

Guanabana Cooler

8.4% ALC/VOL • 1.8 STD DRINKS

60ml (2 fl oz) Light Rum
120ml (4 fl oz) Guanabana Nectar (chilled)
30ml (1 fl oz) Fresh Orange Juice
60ml (2 fl oz) Soda Water
Slice of Lime
Slice of Orange

Pour Rum, nectar and juice into a hurricane glass over ice then stir. Add soda and stir gently. Garnish with a slice of lime and orange then serve.

Florida Freeze

9.4% ALC/VOL • 0.9 STD DRINKS

38ml (1¼ fl oz) Dark Rum
60ml (2 fl oz) Pineapple Juice
38ml (1¼ fl oz) Coconut Cream
30ml (1 fl oz) Fresh Orange Juice

Pour ingredients into a blender over large amount of crushed ice and blend. Pour into a chilled tall glass and serve.

Old-Fashioned Rum and Muscari

24.2% ALC/VOL • 1.3 STD DRINKS

30ml (1 fl oz) Light Rum
30ml (1 fl oz) Muscari
2 dashes Angostura Bitters
5ml (1/6 fl oz) Soda Water
Twist of Lemon Peel

Pour Rum, Muscari and Bitters into an old-fashioned glass over ice then stir. Add soda – do not stir, then twist lemon peel above drink. Place remainder of peel into drink and serve.

Parisian Blonde

24.3% ALC/VOL • 1.8 STD DRINKS

30ml (1 fl oz) Dark Rum
30ml (1 fl oz) Cointreau
30ml (1 fl oz) Thick Cream
1 teaspoon Sugar Syrup
Slice of Orange

Pour Rum, Cointreau, cream and sugar into a cocktail shaker over ice. Shake and strain into a chilled cocktail glass. Garnish with a slice of orange and serve.

Molokai Mike

15.3% ALC/VOL • 1.8 STD DRINKS

30ml (1 fl oz) Light Rum
15ml (½ fl oz) Brandy
15ml (½ fl oz) Dark Rum
30ml (1 fl oz) Fresh Lemon Juice
30ml (1 fl oz) Fresh Orange Juice
10ml (⅓ fl oz) Grenadine
15ml (½ fl oz) Orgeat Syrup
Slice of Lemon
Slice of Orange
Strawberry

Pour Light Rum, Brandy, juices and syrup into a cocktail shaker over ice. Shake and strain into a highball glass over crushed ice then stir. Pour Dark Rum and Grenadine into a mixing glass over large amount of crushed ice. Stir well to create a sorbet and add gently into glass to layer on top of drink. Garnish with a slice of lemon, orange and a strawberry then serve with 2 straws.

Mallelieu

19.3% ALC/VOL • 1.8 STD DRINKS

This drink is also known as Tangerine Dream, p 133.

Hollywood Nuts

20.6% ALC/VOL • 1.8 STD DRINKS

30ml (1 fl oz) Light Rum
15ml (½ fl oz) Amaretto
15ml (½ fl oz) Dark Crème De Cacao
15ml (½ fl oz) Frangelico
1 teaspoon Egg White
30ml (1 fl oz) Lemonade

Pour Rum, Amaretto, Cacao, Frangelico and egg white into a cocktail shaker over ice. Shake and strain into an old-fashioned glass over ice. Add lemonade, stir gently and serve.

Sir Walter Cocktail

31.5% ALC/VOL • 1.5 STD DRINKS

23ml (¾ fl oz) Light Rum
23ml (¾ fl oz) Brandy
5ml (1/6 fl oz) Cointreau
5ml (1/6 fl oz) Grenadine
5ml (1/6 fl oz) Fresh Lemon Juice

Pour ingredients into a cocktail shaker over ice and shake. Strain into a chilled cocktail glass and serve.

Hobart

12% ALC/VOL • 1.8 STD DRINKS

30ml (1 fl oz) Light Rum
30ml (1 fl oz) Mango Liqueur
15ml (½ fl oz) Dark Rum
60ml (2 fl oz) Mandarin Juice
30ml (1 fl oz) Pineapple Juice
30ml (1 fl oz) White Grape Juice

Pour ingredients into a cocktail shaker over ice and shake. Strain into a highball glass over ice and serve with 2 straws.

Torridora Cocktail

33.9% ALC/VOL • 2 STD DRINKS

45ml (1½ fl oz) Light Rum
15ml (½ fl oz) Tia Maria
5ml (1/6 fl oz) 151-Proof Rum
1½ teaspoons Fresh Cream

Pour Light Rum, Tia and cream into a cocktail shaker over ice. Shake and strain into a chilled cocktail glass. Layer 151-Proof Rum on top and serve.

Strain the Rein

22.1% ALC/VOL • 1.7 STD DRINKS

45ml (1½ fl oz) Light Rum
15ml (½ fl oz) Raspberry Liqueur
5ml (1/6 fl oz) Cointreau
30ml (1 fl oz) Fresh Lemon Juice
1 teaspoon Sugar Syrup

Prepare a cocktail glass with a sugar frosted rim – moistened with lime juice. Pour ingredients into a cocktail shaker over ice and shake. Strain into prepared glass and serve.

San Juan

24.7% ALC/VOL • 1.9 STD DRINKS

45ml (1½ fl oz) Light Rum
10ml (⅓ fl oz) 151-Proof Rum
30ml (1 fl oz) Grapefruit Juice
10ml (⅓ fl oz) Fresh Lime Juice
1 teaspoon Coconut Cream

Pour Light Rum, juices and cream into a blender over crushed ice. Blend and pour into a chilled champagne saucer. Layer 151-Proof Rum on top and serve.

Yellow Bird No.2

31.5% ALC/VOL • 2.2 STD DRINKS

45ml (1½ fl oz) Light Rum
15ml (½ fl oz) Cointreau
15ml (½ fl oz) Galliano
15ml (½ fl oz) Fresh Lime Juice
Slice of Lime
Slice of Orange

Pour Rum, Cointreau, Galliano and juice into a cocktail shaker over ice. Shake and strain into a chilled cocktail glass. Garnish with a slice of lime and orange then serve.

Chocolate Mountain

19.7% ALC/VOL • 1.9 STD DRINKS

45ml (1½ fl oz) Light Rum
15ml (½ fl oz) Kahlúa
15ml (½ fl oz) White Crème De Cacao
45ml (1½ fl oz) Fresh Cream

Pour Rum, Cacao and cream into a cocktail shaker over ice. Shake and strain into a chilled cocktail glass. Add Kahlúa by pouring into centre of drink – do not stir, then serve.

Pink Rum and Tonic

13.3% ALC/VOL • 2.3 STD DRINKS

75ml (2½ fl oz) Light Rum
5ml (1/6 fl oz) Grenadine
15ml (½ fl oz) Fresh Lime Juice
120ml (4 fl oz) Tonic Water
Slice of Lime

Pour Rum, Grenadine and juice into a cocktail shaker over ice. Shake and strain into a collins glass over ice. Add tonic and stir gently. Garnish with a slice of lime and serve.

Reunion

27.4% ALC/VOL • 1.5 STD DRINKS

30ml (1 fl oz) Light Rum
15ml (½ fl oz) Cherry Brandy
15ml (½ fl oz) Triple Sec
8ml (¼ fl oz) Fresh Lime Juice
Maraschino Cherry

Pour Rum, Brandy, Triple Sec and juice into a cocktail shaker over ice. Shake and strain into a chilled cocktail glass. Garnish with a cherry and serve.

Gorilla Milk

20.4% ALC/VOL • 1.7 STD DRINKS

30ml (1 fl oz) Light Rum
15ml (½ fl oz) Bailey's Irish Cream
15ml (½ fl oz) Banana Liqueur
15ml (½ fl oz) Tia Maria
30ml (1 fl oz) Fresh Cream
Slice of Banana

Pour Rum, Bailey's, Liqueur, Tia and cream into a cocktail shaker over ice. Shake and strain into a hurricane glass over ice. Garnish with a slice of banana and serve.

Big Blue Sky

9% ALC/VOL • 0.7 STD DRINKS

15ml (½ fl oz) Light Rum
15ml (½ fl oz) Blue Curaçao
60ml (2 fl oz) Pineapple Juice
15ml (½ fl oz) Coconut Cream

Pour ingredients into a blender over crushed ice and blend until smooth. Pour into a chilled goblet and serve.

Hustler

18% ALC/VOL • 1.8 STD DRINKS

30ml (1 fl oz) Golden Rum
30ml (1 fl oz) Light Rum
30ml (1 fl oz) Fresh Lime Juice
30ml (1 fl oz) Passion-Fruit Juice
1 teaspoon Sugar Syrup
Sprig of Fresh Mint

Pour Rums, juices and sugar into a cocktail shaker over ice. Shake and strain into an old-fashioned glass over cracked ice. Garnish with a sprig of mint and serve.

Immaculata

25.7% ALC/VOL • 1.7 STD DRINKS

45ml (1½ fl oz) Light Rum
15ml (½ fl oz) Amaretto
15ml (½ fl oz) Fresh Lime Juice

5ml (1/6 fl oz) Fresh
Lemon Juice
½ teaspoon Sugar Syrup

Pour ingredients into a cocktail shaker over ice and shake. Strain into a chilled cocktail glass and serve.

Rum Coconut Fizz

11.9% ALC/VOL • 2 STD DRINKS

68ml (2¼ fl oz) Light Rum
15ml (½ fl oz) Fresh
Lime Juice
15ml (½ fl oz) Coconut Cream
120ml (4 fl oz) Soda Water
Slice of Lime

Pour Rum, juice and cream into a cocktail shaker over ice. Shake and strain into a highball glass over ice. Add soda and stir gently. Add a slice of lime and serve.

Mocha Cooler

7% ALC/VOL • 1.3 STD DRINKS

30ml (1 fl oz) Light Rum
15ml (½ fl oz) Galliano
180ml (6 fl oz) Black Coffee
(chilled)
2 teaspoons Thick Cream
1 teaspoon Sugar Syrup

Pour Rum, Galliano, coffee and sugar into a mixing glass over ice. Stir and strain into a collins glass over ice. Float cream on top and serve.

Mofuco

21% ALC/VOL • 1.8 STD DRINKS

60ml (2 fl oz) Light Rum
Dash Angostura Bitters
1 teaspoon Sugar Syrup
1 Fresh Egg
Twist of Lemon Peel

Pour Rum, Bitters, sugar and egg into a cocktail shaker over ice. Shake and strain into a chilled cocktail glass. Garnish with lemon peel and serve.

Swimming Ashore for the Songs of Sunrise

13.5% ALC/VOL • 1.8 STD DRINKS

45ml (1½ fl oz) Light Rum
15ml (½ fl oz) Cointreau
10ml (⅓ fl oz) Grenadine
90ml (3 fl oz) Grapefruit Juice
15ml (½ fl oz) Fresh
Orange Juice

Pour ingredients into a cocktail shaker over ice and shake. Strain into a highball glass half filled with crushed ice and serve with a straw.

Hyatt Club

13.7% ALC/VOL • 2.2 STD DRINKS

40ml (1⅓ fl oz) Light Rum
20ml (⅔ fl oz) Cherry Brandy
20ml (⅔ fl oz) Mandarine
Napoleon
120ml (4 fl oz) Bitter-Lemon
Soda
Maraschino Cherry
Slice of Lemon

Pour Rum, Brandy and Mandarine Napoleon into a highball glass over ice then stir. Add soda and stir gently. Garnish with a cherry and slice of lemon then serve.

DeRosier

22.5% ALC/VOL • 1.9 STD DRINKS

30ml (1 fl oz) Añejo Rum
15ml (½ fl oz) Bourbon
15ml (½ fl oz) Cherry Brandy
15ml (½ fl oz) Dark Crème
De Cacao
30ml (1 fl oz) Thick Cream

Pour ingredients into a cocktail shaker over ice and shake. Strain into a chilled cocktail glass and serve.

Soho Twist

13% ALC/VOL • 2.1 STD DRINKS

45ml (1½ fl oz) Light Rum
15ml (½ fl oz) Sweet Sherry
8ml (¼ fl oz) Port
5ml (1/6 fl oz) Drambuie
15ml (½ fl oz) Fresh
Lime Juice
120ml (4 fl oz) Dry Ginger Ale
Twist of Lemon Peel

Pour Rum, Sherry, Port, Drambuie and juice into a goblet over ice then stir. Add Ginger Ale and stir gently. Garnish with lemon peel and serve.

Tropical Rainstorm

27.6% ALC/VOL • 1.7 STD DRINKS

45ml (1½ fl oz) Dark Rum
15ml (½ fl oz) Cherry Brandy
5ml (1/6 fl oz) Cointreau
15ml (½ fl oz) Fresh
Lemon Juice

Pour ingredients into a cocktail shaker over ice and shake. Strain into a chilled cocktail glass and serve.

Mandeville

29.4% ALC/VOL • 2.3 STD DRINKS

45ml (1½ fl oz) Light Rum
30ml (1 fl oz) Dark Rum
3 dashes Anisette
Dash Grenadine
10ml (⅓ fl oz) Fresh
Lemon Juice
10ml (⅓ fl oz) Cola

Pour Rums, Anisette, Grenadine and juice into a cocktail shaker over ice. Shake and strain into an old-fashioned glass over ice. Add cola – do not stir, then serve.

Margaret in the Marketplace

22.2% ALC/VOL • 1.8 STD DRINKS

60ml (2 fl oz) Añejo Rum
5ml (1/6 fl oz) Grenadine
15ml (½ fl oz) Fresh Lemon Juice
15ml (½ fl oz) Fresh Lime Juice
15ml (½ fl oz) Fresh Cream

Pour ingredients into a cocktail shaker over ice and shake. Strain into a chilled cocktail glass and serve.

Rum Fix

28.5% ALC/VOL • 2.2 STD DRINKS

75ml (2½ fl oz) Light Rum
15ml (½ fl oz) Fresh Lemon Juice
5ml (1/6 fl oz) Spring Water
1 teaspoon Sugar Syrup
Slice of Lemon

Pour juice, water and sugar into an old-fashioned glass filled with crushed ice. Add more crushed ice to fill glass and stir. Add Rum and stir gently. Add a slice of lemon and serve with a straw.

Orlando Quencher

9.8% ALC/VOL • 1.1 STD DRINKS

38ml (1¼ fl oz) Light Rum
30ml (1 fl oz) Fresh Orange Juice
15ml (½ fl oz) Fresh Lime Juice
1 teaspoon Sugar Syrup
60ml (2 fl oz) Lemonade

Pour Rum, juices and sugar into a cocktail shaker over ice. Shake and strain into a chilled old-fashioned glass over a few ice cubes. Add lemonade, stir gently and serve.

Sun City

9.5% ALC/VOL • 2 STD DRINKS

30ml (1 fl oz) Light Rum
15ml (½ fl oz) Apricot Brandy
15ml (½ fl oz) Dark Rum
15ml (½ fl oz) Galliano
60ml (2 fl oz) Pineapple Juice
8ml (¼ fl oz) Fresh Lime Juice
120ml (4 fl oz) Lemonade
Twist of Lemon Peel

Pour Rums, Brandy, Galliano and juices into a cocktail shaker over ice. Shake and strain into a hurricane glass over ice. Add lemonade and stir gently. Garnish with lemon peel and serve with 2 straws.

Miss Belle

35.7% ALC/VOL • 2 STD DRINKS

45ml (1½ fl oz) Dark Rum
15ml (½ fl oz) Grand Marnier
10ml (⅓ fl oz) Dark Crème De Cacao

Pour ingredients into a mixing glass over ice and stir. Strain into a chilled cocktail glass and serve.

Tall Dutch Egg Nog

11.4% ALC/VOL • 2.9 STD DRINKS

45ml (1½ fl oz) Light Rum
45ml (1½ fl oz) Advocaat
15ml (½ fl oz) 151-Proof Rum
180ml (6 fl oz) Fresh Milk (chilled)
30ml (1 fl oz) Fresh Orange Juice
1 teaspoon Sugar Syrup
Cinnamon

Pour Rums, Advocaat, milk, juice and sugar into a blender over cracked ice. Blend and pour into a chilled tall glass. Sprinkle cinnamon on top and serve.

Caribbean Chat

7.2% ALC/VOL • 1 STD DRINK

30ml (1 fl oz) Spiced Rum
8ml (¼ fl oz) White Crème De Cacao
90ml (3 fl oz) Fresh Orange Juice
45ml (1½ fl oz) Soda Water

Pour Rum, Cacao and juice into a highball glass over ice then stir well. Add soda, stir gently and serve.

Playboy Cooler

11.2% ALC/VOL • 1.8 STD DRINKS

38ml (1¼ fl oz) Golden Jamaica Rum
38ml (1¼ fl oz) Tia Maria
90ml (3 fl oz) Pineapple Juice
10ml (⅓ fl oz) Fresh Lemon Juice
30ml (1 fl oz) Cola
Slice of Pineapple

Pour Rum, Tia and juices into a cocktail shaker over ice. Shake and strain into a collins glass over ice. Add cola and stir gently. Garnish with a slice of pineapple and serve.

Perigrine's Peril

28.6% ALC/VOL • 1.6 STD DRINKS

30ml (1 fl oz) Dark Rum
15ml (½ fl oz) Banana Liqueur
15ml (½ fl oz) Southern Comfort
5ml (1/6 fl oz) Fresh Lemon Juice
5ml (1/6 fl oz) Fresh Lime Juice

Pour ingredients into a cocktail shaker over ice and shake. Strain into a chilled cocktail glass and serve.

Northside Special

9.4% ALC/VOL • 1.7 STD DRINKS

60ml (2 fl oz) Dark Jamaica Rum

90ml (3 fl oz) Fresh Orange Juice
15ml (½ fl oz) Fresh Lemon Juice
2 teaspoons Sugar Syrup
60ml (2 fl oz) Soda Water
Maraschino Cherry
Slice of Lemon
Slice of Orange

Pour Rum, juices and sugar into a cocktail shaker over ice. Shake and strain into a collins glass over crushed ice. Add soda and stir gently. Garnish with a cherry, slice of lemon and orange then serve with 2 straws.

Texas Sunset

11.1% ALC/VOL • 1.5 STD DRINKS

23ml (¾ fl oz) Light Rum
15ml (½ fl oz) Apricot Brandy
15ml (½ fl oz) Over-Proof Light Rum
23ml (¾ fl oz) Grenadine
60ml (2 fl oz) Fresh Orange Juice
30ml (1 fl oz) Fresh Lemon Juice
1 teaspoon Sugar Syrup
1 teaspoon Egg White

Pour Rums, Brandy, juices, sugar and egg white into a cocktail shaker over cracked ice. Shake and pour into a chilled collins glass. Add Grenadine by pouring into centre of drink – do not stir, then serve.

Waking to the Call of the Mockingbird

15.7% ALC/VOL • 1.7 STD DRINKS

45ml (1½ fl oz) Light Rum
15ml (½ fl oz) Sweet Vermouth
15ml (½ fl oz) Tawny Port
30ml (1 fl oz) Fresh Lemon Juice
1 teaspoon Sugar Syrup
White of 1 Egg

Pour ingredients into a cocktail shaker over ice and shake. Strain into an old-fashioned glass over ice and serve.

Sandra Buys a Dog

12.5% ALC/VOL • 1.8 STD DRINKS

30ml (1 fl oz) Añejo Rum
30ml (1 fl oz) Dark Rum
Dash Angostura Bitters
90ml (3 fl oz) Cranberry Juice
30ml (1 fl oz) Fresh Orange Juice

Pour ingredients into a mixing glass over ice and stir. Strain into a highball glass over ice and serve.

Marrakech Express

11.8% ALC/VOL • 1.9 STD DRINKS

30ml (1 fl oz) Light Rum
30ml (1 fl oz) Dry Vermouth
30ml (1 fl oz) White Crème De Cacao
60ml (2 fl oz) Grapefruit Juice
30ml (1 fl oz) Mandarin Juice
15ml (½ fl oz) Fresh Lime Juice
1 teaspoon Sugar Syrup

Pour ingredients into a cocktail shaker over ice and shake. Strain into a chilled goblet and serve.

Rolling Thunder

28.7% ALC/VOL • 2.1 STD DRINKS

45ml (1½ fl oz) Light Rum
15ml (½ fl oz) Apricot Brandy
15ml (½ fl oz) Vodka
8ml (¼ fl oz) Grenadine
8ml (¼ fl oz) Fresh Lime Juice

Pour ingredients into a cocktail shaker over ice and shake. Strain into a chilled cocktail glass and serve.

Solitaire

14.6% ALC/VOL • 1.4 STD DRINKS

30ml (1 fl oz) Golden Rum
15ml (½ fl oz) Cointreau
5ml (⅙ fl oz) Apricot Brandy
15ml (½ fl oz) Fresh Lime Juice
60ml (2 fl oz) Cherry Soda
Maraschino Cherry
Slice of Orange

Pour Rum, Cointreau, Brandy and juice into a goblet over cracked ice then stir. Add soda and stir gently. Garnish with a cherry and slice of orange then serve with a short straw.

Alexander

6.4% ALC/VOL • 0.9 STD DRINKS

30ml (1 fl oz) Spiced Rum
8ml (¼ fl oz) Midori
120ml (4 fl oz) Pineapple Juice
30ml (1 fl oz) Soda Water

Pour Rum, Midori and juice into a highball glass over ice then stir. Add soda, stir gently and serve.

Passion-Fruit Cooler

11.7% ALC/VOL • 2.2 STD DRINKS

45ml (1½ fl oz) Light Rum
30ml (1 fl oz) Gin
120ml (4 fl oz) Passion-Fruit Nectar
30ml (1 fl oz) Fresh Orange Juice
15ml (½ fl oz) Fresh Lemon Juice
2 Sprigs of Fresh Mint

Pour Rum, Gin, nectar and juices into a cocktail shaker over ice. Shake and strain into a collins glass over cracked ice. Garnish with sprigs of mint and serve.

Good Time Charlie

7.6% ALC/VOL • 0.9 STD DRINKS

30ml (1 fl oz) Light Rum

30ml (1 fl oz) Cranberry Juice
30ml (1 fl oz) Pineapple Juice
30ml (1 fl oz) Pink Grapefruit Juice
30ml (1 fl oz) Sweet and Sour Mix

Pour ingredients into a highball glass half filled with ice, stir well and serve.

Rum Ramsay

30.4% ALC/VOL • 1.5 STD DRINKS

45ml (1½ fl oz) Light Rum
5ml (1/6 fl oz) Bourbon
Dash Peychaud's Bitters
1 teaspoon Sugar Syrup
¼ Fresh Lime

Pour Rum, Bourbon, Bitters and sugar into an old-fashioned glass over cracked ice then stir. Twist ¼ lime above drink to release juice and add spent shell, stir then serve.

Pink Creole

28% ALC/VOL • 1.3 STD DRINKS

45ml (1½ fl oz) Light Rum
3 dashes Grenadine
10ml (⅓ fl oz) Fresh Lime Juice
½ teaspoon Fresh Cream
Black Cherry (marinated in Rum)

Pour Rum, Grenadine, juice and cream into a cocktail shaker over ice. Shake and strain into a chilled cocktail glass. Add cherry and serve.

La Paz

15.7% ALC/VOL • 1.5 STD DRINKS

30ml (1 fl oz) Light Rum
15ml (½ fl oz) Grand Marnier
15ml (½ fl oz) Sweet Vermouth
5ml (1/6 fl oz) Fresh Lime Juice
60ml (2 fl oz) Cola
Slice of Lime

Pour Rum, Grand Marnier, Vermouth and juice into an old-fashioned glass over cracked ice then stir. Add cola and stir gently. Add a slice of lime and serve.

Broken Parachute

22% ALC/VOL • 1.3 STD DRINKS

30ml (1 fl oz) Bacardi Limon
30ml (1 fl oz) Raspberry Liqueur
10ml (⅓ fl oz) Kiwi Liqueur
1 teaspoon Sugar Syrup

Pour Bacardi, Raspberry Liqueur and sugar into a cocktail shaker over ice. Shake and strain into a chilled cocktail glass. Layer Kiwi Liqueur on top and serve.

Rum Curaçao Cooler

9.6% ALC/VOL • 1.5 STD DRINKS

30ml (1 fl oz) Jamaica Rum
30ml (1 fl oz) Curaçao
15ml (½ fl oz) Fresh Lime Juice
120ml (4 fl oz) Soda Water
Slice of Lime
Slice of Orange

Pour Rum, Curaçao and juice into a cocktail shaker over ice. Shake and strain into a collins glass over ice. Add soda and stir gently. Garnish with a slice of lime and orange then serve.

Derby Special

22% ALC/VOL • 1.8 STD DRINKS

45ml (1½ fl oz) Light Rum
15ml (½ fl oz) Cointreau
30ml (1 fl oz) Fresh Orange Juice
15ml (½ fl oz) Fresh Lime Juice

Pour ingredients into a blender over crushed ice and blend until smooth. Pour into a chilled highball glass and serve.

Santiago

24.8% ALC/VOL • 1.8 STD DRINKS

45ml (1½ fl oz) Light Rum
15ml (½ fl oz) Cointreau
5ml (1/6 fl oz) Grenadine
23ml (¾ fl oz) Fresh Lime Juice
1 teaspoon Sugar Syrup
Maraschino Cherry

Pour Rum, Cointreau, Grenadine, juice and sugar into a cocktail shaker over ice. Shake and strain into an old-fashioned glass over cracked ice. Garnish with a cherry and serve.

Chocolate Coconut Smash

9.5% ALC/VOL • 0.9 STD DRINKS

30ml (1 fl oz) Light Rum
30ml (1 fl oz) Chocolate Syrup
30ml (1 fl oz) Coconut Cream
1 scoop Vanilla Ice Cream

Pour Rum, syrup and cream into a blender over small amount of crushed ice then add ice cream. Blend until smooth and pour into a chilled highball glass then serve.

Presidente

27.7% ALC/VOL • 2.3 STD DRINKS

60ml (2 fl oz) Light Rum
30ml (1 fl oz) Sweet Vermouth
10ml (⅓ fl oz) Dry Vermouth
5ml (1/6 fl oz) Grenadine
Maraschino Cherry
Slice of Orange

Pour Rum, Vermouths and Grenadine into a mixing glass over ice. Stir and strain into an old-fashioned glass over crushed ice. Garnish with a cherry and slice of orange then serve.

Jamaican Mule

11.1% ALC/VOL • 1.8 STD DRINKS

60ml (2 fl oz) Jamaica Rum
15ml (½ fl oz) Lime Syrup
1 teaspoon Sugar Syrup
120ml (4 fl oz) Ginger Beer

Pour Rum, syrup and sugar into a cocktail shaker over ice. Shake and strain into a chilled highball glass over a few ice cubes. Add ginger beer, stir gently and serve.

Nirvana

12% ALC/VOL • 1.8 STD DRINKS

60ml (2 fl oz) Dark Rum
15ml (½ fl oz) Grenadine
90ml (3 fl oz) Grapefruit Juice
15ml (½ fl oz) Orgeat Syrup
1 teaspoon Sugar Syrup

Pour Rum, Grenadine, syrup and sugar into a cocktail shaker over ice. Shake and strain into a highball glass over ice. Add juice, stir and serve.

Starseeker

10.6% ALC/VOL • 1.8 STD DRINKS

60ml (2 fl oz) Light Rum
5ml (1/6 fl oz) Grenadine
30ml (1 fl oz) Fresh Orange Juice
120ml (4 fl oz) Tonic Water
Wedge of Orange

Pour Rum, Grenadine and juice into a highball glass over ice then stir. Add tonic and stir gently. Garnish with a wedge of orange and serve.

Dracula

9.1% ALC/VOL • 1.4 STD DRINKS

45ml (1½ fl oz) Light Rum
2 dashes Angostura Bitters
3 dashes Grenadine
120ml (4 fl oz) Cranberry Juice
30ml (1 fl oz) Fresh Lemon Juice

Pour ingredients into a cocktail shaker over ice and shake. Strain into a collins glass over ice then add more ice to fill glass, stir well and serve.

Sly Goes to Havana

21.1% ALC/VOL • 1.7 STD DRINKS

45ml (1½ fl oz) Light Rum
5ml (1/6 fl oz) Green Chartreuse
5ml (1/6 fl oz) White Crème De Cacao
30ml (1 fl oz) Pineapple Juice
15ml (½ fl oz) Fresh Lime Juice

Pour ingredients into a cocktail shaker over ice and shake. Strain into an old-fashioned glass filled with crushed ice and serve.

San Juan Sling

11.4% ALC/VOL • 1.8 STD DRINKS

23ml (¾ fl oz) Light Rum
23ml (¾ fl oz) Bénédictine
23ml (¾ fl oz) Cherry Liqueur
15ml (½ fl oz) Fresh Lime Juice
120ml (4 fl oz) Soda Water
Twist of Lime Peel

Pour Rum, Bénédictine, Liqueur and juice into a cocktail shaker over ice. Shake and strain into a highball glass over cracked ice. Add soda and stir gently. Twist lime peel above drink and place remainder of peel into drink then serve.

Pino Frio

19.9% ALC/VOL • 1.4 STD DRINKS

45ml (1½ fl oz) Light Rum
1 teaspoon Sugar Syrup
2 tablespoons Pieces of Pineapple

Pour Rum and sugar into a blender without ice then add pieces of pineapple. Blend until smooth and add crushed ice then blend briefly. Pour into a chilled old-fashioned glass and serve.

Uyapar Ponche

33.2% ALC/VOL • 1.7 STD DRINKS

30ml (1 fl oz) Dark Rum
15ml (½ fl oz) Mandarine Napoleon
8ml (¼ fl oz) Cherry Brandy
8ml (¼ fl oz) Dry Gin
5ml (1/6 fl oz) Fresh Lemon Juice

Pour ingredients into a cocktail shaker over ice and shake. Strain into an old-fashioned glass over crushed ice and serve.

Rum Smash

35.1% ALC/VOL • 1.8 STD DRINKS

60ml (2 fl oz) Light Rum
1 teaspoon Sugar Syrup
4 Sprigs of Fresh Mint
Slice of Lemon

Pour Rum and sugar into a mixing glass over cracked ice. Add 3 sprigs of mint and stir well then pour into an old-fashioned glass half filled with ice. Add more ice to fill glass and stir. Garnish with a slice of lemon and sprig of mint then serve.

Maragato Special

15.9% ALC/VOL • 1.6 STD DRINKS

30ml (1 fl oz) Light Rum
23ml (¾ fl oz) Dry Vermouth

23ml (¾ fl oz) Sweet Vermouth
3 dashes Maraschino Liqueur
30ml (1 fl oz) Fresh
Orange Juice
15ml (½ fl oz) Fresh
Lime Juice
Slice of Lime
Slice of Orange

Pour Rum, Vermouths, Liqueur and juices into a cocktail shaker over ice. Shake and strain into a cocktail glass over crushed ice. Garnish with a slice of lime and orange then serve.

Stratocaster

13.7% ALC/VOL • 1.4 STD DRINKS

30ml (1 fl oz) Dark Rum
30ml (1 fl oz) Crème De Cassis
5ml (1/6 fl oz) Fresh
Lemon Juice
30ml (1 fl oz) Lemonade
30ml (1 fl oz) Soda Water
Maraschino Cherry
Slice of Lemon

Pour Rum, Cassis and juice into a goblet over cracked ice then stir. Add lemonade and soda then stir gently. Garnish with a cherry and slice of lemon then serve with a short straw.

Blue Sunrise

22.7% ALC/VOL • 2 STD DRINKS

40ml (1⅓ fl oz) Light Rum
30ml (1 fl oz) Blue Curaçao
10ml (⅓ fl oz) Parfait Amour
30ml (1 fl oz) Pineapple Juice

Pour ingredients into a cocktail shaker over ice and shake. Strain into a chilled cocktail glass and serve.

Sewer Water

14.4% ALC/VOL • 2.6 STD DRINKS

30ml (1 fl oz) 151-Proof Rum
23ml (¾ fl oz) Midori
15ml (½ fl oz) Gin
3 dashes Grenadine
150ml (5 fl oz) Pineapple Juice
8ml (¼ fl oz) Fresh Lime Juice

Pour Grenadine into a chilled hurricane glass and swirl around glass then add ice. Add Rum, Midori, Gin and pineapple juice then stir. Layer lime juice on top and serve.

Son of Sam

24.8% ALC/VOL • 1.6 STD DRINKS

45ml (1½ fl oz) Light Rum
15ml (½ fl oz) Apricot Brandy
10ml (⅓ fl oz) Grenadine
8ml (¼ fl oz) Fresh
Lemon Juice
1 teaspoon Sugar Syrup

Pour ingredients into a cocktail shaker over ice and shake. Strain into a chilled cocktail glass and serve.

Rum Swizzle

13.3% ALC/VOL • 1.8 STD DRINKS

30ml (1 fl oz) Dark Rum
30ml (1 fl oz) Light Rum
Dash Angostura Bitters
45ml (1½ fl oz) Fresh
Lime Juice
1 teaspoon Sugar Syrup
60ml (2 fl oz) Soda Water

Pour Rums, Bitters, juice and sugar into a mixing glass over large amount of ice. Stir vigorously until cold and strain into a collins glass filled with crushed ice then add soda – do not stir. Serve with a swizzle stick and 2 straws.

Flying Saucer

33.1% ALC/VOL • 2.4 STD DRINKS

45ml (1½ fl oz) Light Rum
23ml (¾ fl oz) Dry Vermouth
23ml (¾ fl oz) Swedish Punsch
Dash Grenadine

Pour ingredients into a cocktail shaker over ice and shake. Strain into a chilled cocktail glass and serve.

Calypso Cool-Aid

6.1% ALC/VOL • 1.1 STD DRINKS

38ml (1¼ fl oz) Light Rum
30ml (1 fl oz) Pineapple Juice
15ml (½ fl oz) Fresh
Lemon Juice
½ teaspoon Sugar Syrup
150ml (5 fl oz) Soda Water
Pineapple Spear
Slice of Lime

Pour Rum, juices and sugar into a blender over cracked ice. Blend and pour into a chilled tall glass. Add soda and stir gently. Garnish with a pineapple spear and slice of lime then serve.

Mobile Mule

11.7% ALC/VOL • 1.8 STD DRINKS

60ml (2 fl oz) Light Rum
120ml (4 fl oz) Ginger Beer
½ Fresh Lime

Pour Rum into a collins glass over cracked ice and twist ½ lime above drink to release juice then add spent shell. Add ginger beer, stir gently and serve.

Brian's Belief

9.8% ALC/VOL • 1.6 STD DRINKS

45ml (1½ fl oz) Añejo Rum
15ml (½ fl oz) Dark Crème
De Cacao
120ml (4 fl oz) Strong Black
Tea (chilled)
15ml (½ fl oz) Fresh
Lemon Juice
2 teaspoons Sugar Syrup

Pour Rum, Cacao, juice and sugar into a cocktail shaker over ice. Shake and strain into a highball glass over ice. Add tea, stir and serve.

Cruise Control

19.9% ALC/VOL • 1.6 STD DRINKS

30ml (1 fl oz) Light Rum
15ml (½ fl oz) Apricot Brandy
15ml (½ fl oz) Cointreau
15ml (½ fl oz) Fresh Lemon Juice
30ml (1 fl oz) Soda Water

Pour Rum, Brandy, Cointreau and juice into a highball glass over ice then stir. Add soda, stir gently and serve.

Mister Christian

18.1% ALC/VOL • 1.8 STD DRINKS

45ml (1½ fl oz) Light Rum
15ml (½ fl oz) Brandy
5ml (1/6 fl oz) Grenadine
30ml (1 fl oz) Fresh Orange Juice
15ml (½ fl oz) Fresh Lemon Juice
15ml (½ fl oz) Fresh Lime Juice

Pour ingredients into a cocktail shaker over ice and shake. Strain into a chilled cocktail glass and serve.

Bongo Cola

13.3% ALC/VOL • 2.6 STD DRINKS

60ml (2 fl oz) Bacardi
30ml (1 fl oz) Tia Maria
5ml (1/6 fl oz) Goldschläger
60ml (2 fl oz) Pineapple Juice
90ml (3 fl oz) Cola

Pour Bacardi, Tia, Goldschläger and juice into a cocktail shaker over ice. Shake and strain into a highball glass over ice. Add cola, stir gently and serve.

Sailing By

14.1% ALC/VOL • 1.6 STD DRINKS

30ml (1 fl oz) Light Rum
30ml (1 fl oz) Blueberry Liqueur
15ml (½ fl oz) Port
8ml (¼ fl oz) Fresh Lemon Juice
60ml (2 fl oz) Dry Ginger Ale
Blue Cherry
Slice of Lemon

Pour Rum, Liqueur, Port and juice into a cocktail shaker over ice. Shake and strain into a goblet over cracked ice. Add Ginger Ale and stir gently. Garnish with a cherry and slice of lemon then serve with 2 short straws.

Mikey's Island Dream

4.3% ALC/VOL • 1 STD DRINK

15ml (½ fl oz) Light Rum
15ml (½ fl oz) Banana Liqueur
15ml (½ fl oz) Malibu
Dash Grenadine
120ml (4 fl oz) Fresh Orange Juice
120ml (4 fl oz) Pineapple Juice
Dash Fresh Cream
Cherry
Piece of Pineapple

Pour Rum, Liqueur, Malibu, Grenadine, juices and cream into a cocktail shaker over ice. Shake and strain into a tall glass over ice. Garnish with a cherry and piece of pineapple then serve.

Bitch's Brew

24.9% ALC/VOL • 3.6 STD DRINKS

30ml (1 fl oz) 151-Proof Rum
30ml (1 fl oz) Brandy
30ml (1 fl oz) Canadian Whisky
Dash Fresh Lime Juice
Dash Spring Water
60ml (2 fl oz) Dr. Pepper
30ml (1 fl oz) Dry Ginger Ale

Pour Rum into a chilled collins glass over a few ice cubes and add Dr. Pepper then stir gently. Add Brandy, Whisky, juice and water then stir. Add Ginger Ale, stir gently and serve.

Rum Martini

37.5% ALC/VOL • 2.3 STD DRINKS

75ml (2½ fl oz) Light Rum
2 dashes Dry Vermouth
Wedge of Lemon

Pour Rum and Vermouth into a mixing glass over ice. Stir and strain into a cocktail glass over ice. Add a wedge of lemon and serve.

Chicago Fizz

6.8% ALC/VOL • 1.3 STD DRINKS

30ml (1 fl oz) Light Rum
30ml (1 fl oz) Port
15ml (½ fl oz) Fresh Lemon Juice
1 teaspoon Caster Sugar
White of 1 Egg
135ml (4½ fl oz) Soda Water

Pour Rum, Port, juice and egg white into a cocktail shaker over ice then add sugar. Shake and strain into a chilled highball glass over 2 ice cubes. Add soda, stir gently and serve.

Puerto Rican Pink Lady

20.4% ALC/VOL • 1.5 STD DRINKS

53ml (1¾ fl oz) Bacardi
5ml (1/6 fl oz) Grenadine
23ml (¾ fl oz) Fresh Lemon Juice
½ Egg White

Pour ingredients into a blender over crushed ice and blend. Pour into a chilled champagne saucer and serve.

Banana Mama

14% ALC/VOL • 2.3 STD DRINKS

45ml (1½ fl oz) Light Rum
30ml (1 fl oz) Banana Liqueur
15ml (½ fl oz) Dark Rum
60ml (2 fl oz) Pineapple Juice
30ml (1 fl oz) Coconut Cream
3 Strawberries (crushed)
Slice of Banana

Pour Rums, Liqueur, juice and cream into a cocktail shaker over ice then add crushed strawberries. Shake and strain into a chilled goblet. Garnish with a slice of banana and serve.

Malmaison

23.5% ALC/VOL • 1.1 STD DRINKS

30ml (1 fl oz) Light Rum
15ml (½ fl oz) Cream Sherry
15ml (½ fl oz) Fresh Lemon Juice

Prepare a cocktail glass with an Anisette moistened rim. Pour ingredients into a cocktail shaker over ice and shake. Strain into prepared glass and serve.

Ice Palace

15.7% ALC/VOL • 1.6 STD DRINKS

30ml (1 fl oz) Light Rum
15ml (½ fl oz) Apricot Brandy
15ml (½ fl oz) Galliano
60ml (2 fl oz) Pineapple Juice
8ml (¼ fl oz) Fresh Lemon Juice
Cherry
Slice of Orange

Pour Rum, Brandy, Galliano and juices into a cocktail shaker over ice. Shake and strain into a collins glass over ice. Garnish with a cherry and slice of orange then serve.

Tanglefoot

26% ALC/VOL • 1.8 STD DRINKS

30ml (1 fl oz) Light Rum
30ml (1 fl oz) Swedish Punsch
15ml (½ fl oz) Fresh Lime Juice
15ml (½ fl oz) Fresh Orange Juice

Pour ingredients into a cocktail shaker over ice and shake. Strain into a chilled cocktail glass and serve.

Mountaineer

15.7% ALC/VOL • 1.3 STD DRINKS

45ml (1½ fl oz) Dark Rum
30ml (1 fl oz) Fresh Orange Juice
8ml (¼ fl oz) Fresh Lemon Juice
8ml (¼ fl oz) Fresh Milk (chilled)
15ml (½ fl oz) Dry Ginger Ale
Pepper (ground)

Pour Rum and orange juice into a mixing glass over ice. Stir and strain into an old-fashioned glass over ice. Add Ginger Ale and stir gently. Add milk then lemon juice – do not stir. Sprinkle pepper on top and serve.

Charger

25.7% ALC/VOL • 1.6 STD DRINKS

45ml (1½ fl oz) Dark Rum
15ml (½ fl oz) Cherry Brandy
15ml (½ fl oz) Fresh Lemon Juice
½ teaspoon Sugar Syrup

Pour ingredients into a cocktail shaker over ice and shake. Strain into a chilled cocktail glass and serve.

Orange Push-Up

8.5% ALC/VOL • 1.2 STD DRINKS

45ml (1½ fl oz) Spiced Rum
15ml (½ fl oz) Grenadine
120ml (4 fl oz) Fresh Orange Juice
5ml (1/6 fl oz) Sweet and Sour Mix
Cherry
Slice of Orange

Pour Rum, Grenadine, juice and sour mix into a blender over crushed ice. Blend and pour into a chilled hurricane glass. Garnish with a cherry and slice of orange then serve.

Mutiny

32.2% ALC/VOL • 1.6 STD DRINKS

45ml (1½ fl oz) Dark Rum
15ml (½ fl oz) Dubonnet
2 dashes Angostura Bitters
Maraschino Cherry

Pour Rum, Dubonnet and Bitters into a mixing glass over ice. Stir and strain into a chilled cocktail glass. Garnish with a cherry and serve.

Virgin's Answer

14% ALC/VOL • 2 STD DRINKS

30ml (1 fl oz) Light Rum
30ml (1 fl oz) Banana Liqueur
30ml (1 fl oz) Dark Crème De Cacao
30ml (1 fl oz) Fresh Lemon Juice
30ml (1 fl oz) Fresh Orange Juice
½ Banana (diced)
Slice of Banana

Pour Rum, Liqueur, Cacao and juices into a blender over crushed ice then add diced banana. Blend until smooth and pour into a chilled wine glass. Garnish with a slice of banana and serve.

Deep Dark Secret

27.9% ALC/VOL • 2 STD DRINKS

45ml (1½ fl oz) Dark Rum
15ml (½ fl oz) Añejo Rum
15ml (½ fl oz) Kahlúa
15ml (½ fl oz) Thick Cream

Pour ingredients into a cocktail shaker over ice and shake. Strain into a chilled cocktail glass and serve.

Bora-Bora Island

11.9% ALC/VOL • 1.8 STD DRINKS

30ml (1 fl oz) Jamaica Rum
20ml (⅔ fl oz) Tia Maria
15ml (½ fl oz) Banana Liqueur
15ml (½ fl oz) Coconut Liqueur
40ml (1⅓ fl oz) Banana Juice
40ml (1⅓ fl oz) Fresh Cream
20ml (⅔ fl oz) Coconut Cream
15ml (½ fl oz) Almond Extract
Cinnamon

Pour Rum, Tia, Liqueurs, juice, creams and extract into a blender over crushed ice. Blend and pour into a chilled hurricane glass. Sprinkle cinnamon on top and serve.

Paradise Quencher

5.7% ALC/VOL • 1 STD DRINK

30ml (1 fl oz) Spiced Rum
8ml (¼ fl oz) Apricot Liqueur
60ml (2 fl oz) Passion-Fruit Juice
60ml (2 fl oz) Pineapple Juice
30ml (1 fl oz) Cranberry Juice
30ml (1 fl oz) Fresh Orange Juice
Slice of Lime

Pour Rum, Liqueur and juices into a cocktail shaker over crushed ice. Shake and pour into a chilled tall glass. Garnish with a slice of lime and serve.

Hawaiian Screw

12.5% ALC/VOL • 1.8 STD DRINKS

30ml (1 fl oz) Light Rum
30ml (1 fl oz) Vodka
60ml (2 fl oz) Fresh Orange Juice
60ml (2 fl oz) Pineapple Juice

Pour ingredients into an old-fashioned glass over ice, stir well and serve.

Eight Bells

27.2% ALC/VOL • 2.6 STD DRINKS

60ml (2 fl oz) Lemon Hart Rum
20ml (⅔ fl oz) Dry Vermouth
20ml (⅔ fl oz) Van Der Hum
10ml (⅓ fl oz) Lemon Soda
10ml (⅓ fl oz) Orange Soda

Pour Rum, Vermouth and Van Der Hum into a cocktail shaker over ice. Shake and strain into a chilled cocktail glass. Add sodas, stir gently and serve.

Creole Scream

26.2% ALC/VOL • 1.5 STD DRINKS

40ml (1⅓ fl oz) Bacardi
20ml (⅔ fl oz) Dry Vermouth
Dash Angostura Bitters
10ml (⅓ fl oz) Grenadine
Olive

Pour Bacardi, Vermouth, Bitters and Grenadine into a cocktail shaker over ice. Shake and strain into a chilled cocktail glass. Add an olive and serve.

Coconilla Delight

3.1% ALC/VOL • 0.9 STD DRINKS

30ml (1 fl oz) Golden Rum
90ml (3 fl oz) Fresh Orange Juice
90ml (3 fl oz) Pineapple Juice
30ml (1 fl oz) Coconut Cream
2 scoops Vanilla Ice Cream
1 Banana (diced)

Pour Rum, juices and cream into a blender without ice. Add ice cream and diced banana. Blend until smooth and pour into a chilled hurricane glass then serve.

Secret Place

11.8% ALC/VOL • 1.8 STD DRINKS

45ml (1½ fl oz) Dark Rum
15ml (½ fl oz) Cherry Brandy
10ml (⅓ fl oz) Dark Crème De Cacao
120ml (4 fl oz) Black Coffee (chilled)

Pour ingredients into a coffee glass filled with crushed ice, stir and serve.

Orlando Sun

23.4% ALC/VOL • 1.8 STD DRINKS

30ml (1 fl oz) Light Rum
15ml (½ fl oz) Grand Marnier
15ml (½ fl oz) Vodka
30ml (1 fl oz) Fresh Orange Juice
8ml (¼ fl oz) Fresh Lemon Juice

Pour ingredients into a cocktail shaker over ice and shake. Strain into a highball glass over ice and add more ice to fill glass then serve.

Spiced Swizzle

22.3% ALC/VOL • 2 STD DRINKS

60ml (2 fl oz) Spiced Rum
15ml (½ fl oz) Amaretto
30ml (1 fl oz) Fresh Lime Juice
1½ teaspoons Sugar Syrup

Pour Rum, juice and sugar into a mixing glass over large amount of ice. Stir vigorously until cold and strain into a collins glass filled with crushed ice. Add Amaretto by pouring on top – do not stir, then serve with a swizzle stick and 2 straws.

An Arif

7.8% ALC/VOL • 1.6 STD DRINKS

45ml (1½ fl oz) Light Rum
15ml (½ fl oz) Peach Schnapps
75ml (2½ fl oz) Fresh Orange Juice
30ml (1 fl oz) Cranberry Juice
18ml (3/5 fl oz) Fresh Lemon Juice
75ml (2½ fl oz) Dry Ginger Ale

Pour Rum, Schnapps and juices into a collins glass over ice. Add Ginger Ale – do not stir, then serve with a swizzle stick and straw.

Casa Blanca

30.5% ALC/VOL • 1.9 STD DRINKS

45ml (1½ fl oz) Light Rum
15ml (½ fl oz) Grand Marnier
5ml (1/6 fl oz) Maraschino Liqueur
15ml (½ fl oz) Fresh Lime Juice

Pour ingredients into a cocktail shaker over ice and shake. Strain into a chilled cocktail glass and serve.

Joe Banana

11.7% ALC/VOL • 1.3 STD DRINKS

30ml (1 fl oz) Bacardi
15ml (½ fl oz) Frangelico
8ml (¼ fl oz) Banana Liqueur
2 scoops Vanilla Ice Cream
½ Banana (diced)
Cherry
Slice of Banana

Pour Bacardi, Frangelico and Liqueur into a blender over small amount of crushed ice. Add ice cream and diced banana. Blend until smooth and pour into a chilled champagne saucer. Garnish with a cherry and slice of banana then serve.

Jamaican Bahama Mama

12% ALC/VOL • 2.2 STD DRINKS

45ml (1½ fl oz) Bacardi
30ml (1 fl oz) Spiced Rum
5ml (1/6 fl oz) Grenadine
60ml (2 fl oz) Fresh Orange Juice
60ml (2 fl oz) Pineapple Juice
30ml (1 fl oz) Coconut Cream

Pour Bacardi, juices and cream into a cocktail shaker over cracked ice. Shake and pour into a chilled highball glass. Add Spiced Rum - do not stir, then layer Grenadine on top and serve.

September Morning

18.6% ALC/VOL • 1.4 STD DRINKS

45ml (1½ fl oz) Light Rum
5ml (1/6 fl oz) Cherry Brandy
3 dashes Grenadine
15ml (½ fl oz) Fresh Lime Juice
White of 1 Egg

Pour ingredients into a cocktail shaker over ice and shake. Strain into a chilled cocktail glass and serve.

California Coastline

10.7% ALC/VOL • 1.6 STD DRINKS

30ml (1 fl oz) Dark Rum
30ml (1 fl oz) Peach Schnapps
15ml (½ fl oz) Blue Curaçao
60ml (2 fl oz) Pineapple Juice
60ml (2 fl oz) Sweet and Sour Mix
Slice of Pineapple

Pour Rum, Schnapps, Curaçao, juice and sour mix into a blender without ice. Blend and pour into a highball glass over crushed ice. Garnish with a slice of pineapple and serve.

Summer Dream

21.3% ALC/VOL • 2 STD DRINKS

30ml (1 fl oz) Bacardi
30ml (1 fl oz) Red Curaçao
30ml (1 fl oz) White Crème De Cacao
1 scoop Vanilla Ice Cream

Pour Bacardi, Curaçao and Cacao into a blender over small amount of crushed ice then add ice cream. Blend until smooth and pour into a chilled highball glass then serve.

Roman Punch

13% ALC/VOL • 1 STD DRINK

15ml (½ fl oz) Dark Rum
15ml (½ fl oz) Cognac
3 dashes Port
30ml (1 fl oz) Fresh Lemon Juice
30ml (1 fl oz) Raspberry Syrup
Strawberry

Pour juice and syrup into a chilled collins glass then stir. Fill with crushed ice and add Rum. Add Cognac and stir well then layer Port on top. Garnish with a strawberry and serve with a straw.

Tropical Fruits

8.6% ALC/VOL • 0.8 STD DRINKS

10ml (⅓ fl oz) Light Rum
10ml (⅓ fl oz) Apricot Brandy
10ml (⅓ fl oz) Coconut Liqueur
10ml (⅓ fl oz) Midori
83ml (2¾ fl oz) Fresh Orange Juice

Pour ingredients into a cocktail shaker over ice and shake. Strain into a tall glass filled with ice and serve.

1234...Go!

15% ALC/VOL • 3.1 STD DRINKS

90ml (3 fl oz) Bacardi
15ml (½ fl oz) Lychee Liqueur
3 dashes Angostura Bitters
2 teaspoons Sugar Syrup
120ml (4 fl oz) Mineral Water
Cherry
Slice of Lemon
Fresh Mint Leaf

Pour Bacardi, Liqueur and sugar into a chilled highball glass. Add mineral water and stir gently then add Bitters – do not stir. Garnish with a cherry, slice of lemon and mint leaf then serve.

Florida Cocktail

16.4% ALC/VOL • 1.8 STD DRINKS

60ml (2 fl oz) Light Rum
2 dashes Green Crème De Menthe
60ml (2 fl oz) Fresh Lime Juice
15ml (½ fl oz) Pineapple Juice
1 teaspoon Sugar Syrup
2 Fresh Mint Leaves

Pour Rum, Crème De Menthe, juices and sugar into a cocktail shaker over ice. Shake and strain into a chilled collins glass. Garnish with mint leaves and serve.

Heartbreaker

9% ALC/VOL • 1.2 STD DRINKS

30ml (1 fl oz) Dark Rum
20ml (⅔ fl oz) Cherry Brandy
60ml (2 fl oz) Fresh Orange Juice
60ml (2 fl oz) Pineapple Juice

Pour ingredients into a cocktail shaker over ice and shake. Strain into a highball glass over ice and serve with a straw.

Misty You

6% ALC/VOL • 1.2 STD DRINKS

30ml (1 fl oz) Bacardi
15ml (½ fl oz) Peach Schnapps
5ml (⅙ fl oz) Blue Curaçao
1 teaspoon Sugar Syrup
1 teaspoon Natural Yoghurt
200ml (6⅔ fl oz) Mineral Water

Pour Bacardi, Schnapps, Curaçao and sugar into a cocktail shaker over ice then add yoghurt. Shake well and strain into a chilled highball glass. Add mineral water, stir gently and serve.

Great White Shark Attack

18.7% ALC/VOL • 3.1 STD DRINKS

90ml (3 fl oz) Light Rum
23ml (¾ fl oz) Raspberry Liqueur
50ml (1⅔ fl oz) Coconut Milk (chilled)
3 tablespoons Pineapple (crushed)

Pour Rum and milk into a blender over crushed ice then add crushed pineapple. Blend and pour into a chilled tall glass. Layer Liqueur on top and serve.

Ronaldo

29.2% ALC/VOL • 2.1 STD DRINKS

30ml (1 fl oz) Cachaça
30ml (1 fl oz) Golden Rum
15ml (½ fl oz) Banana Liqueur
15ml (½ fl oz) Pineapple Juice
Dash Fresh Lime Juice
Wedge of Lime

Pour Cachaça, Rum, Liqueur and juices into a cocktail shaker over ice. Shake and strain into a highball glass half filled with ice. Garnish with a wedge of lime and serve.

Bacardi Blossom

16.6% ALC/VOL • 1.1 STD DRINKS

38ml (1¼ fl oz) Bacardi
30ml (1 fl oz) Fresh Orange Juice
15ml (½ fl oz) Fresh Lemon Juice
½ teaspoon Sugar Syrup

Pour ingredients into a blender over crushed ice and blend. Pour into a chilled cocktail glass and serve.

Devil's Gun

24.4% ALC/VOL • 2.6 STD DRINKS

45ml (1½ fl oz) Golden Rum
30ml (1 fl oz) Bacardi
8ml (¼ fl oz) Apricot Brandy
8ml (¼ fl oz) Dark Rum
5ml (⅙ fl oz) Grenadine
30ml (1 fl oz) Pineapple Juice
8ml (¼ fl oz) Fresh Lime Juice
Nutmeg

Pour Golden Rum, Bacardi, Brandy, Grenadine and juices into a blender over cracked ice. Blend and strain into a chilled cocktail glass. Layer Dark Rum on top and sprinkle nutmeg on top then serve.

Colonial Rummer

30.1% ALC/VOL • 3.2 STD DRINKS

75ml (2½ fl oz) Dark Rum
30ml (1 fl oz) Apricot Brandy
30ml (1 fl oz) Peach Schnapps
Cherry
Wedge of Lime
Wedge of Orange

Pour Rum, Brandy and Schnapps into an old-fashioned glass half filled with crushed ice then stir well. Garnish with a cherry, wedge of lime and orange then serve with a swizzle stick.

Caribbean Madras

8.1% ALC/VOL • 1.1 STD DRINKS

38ml (1¼ fl oz) Dark Rum
90ml (3 fl oz) Fresh Orange Juice
45ml (1½ fl oz) Cranberry Juice
Slice of Orange

Pour Rum and juices into a blender over cracked ice. Blend and strain into a wine glass over ice. Garnish with a slice of orange and serve.

Apricot Twist

23.7% ALC/VOL • 1.5 STD DRINKS

45ml (1½ fl oz) Light Rum
5ml (⅙ fl oz) Kirsch
20ml (⅔ fl oz) Apricot Nectar
2 teaspoons Lime Syrup
Apricot Kernel
Twist of Lemon Peel

Place kernel and lemon peel into an old-fashioned glass with ice. Pour Rum, Kirsch, nectar and syrup into a cocktail shaker over ice. Shake and strain into prepared glass then serve.

Rum Sling

10.5% ALC/VOL • 1.4 STD DRINKS

45ml (1½ fl oz) Jamaica Rum
2 dashes Angostura Bitters
120ml (4 fl oz) Soda Water
Slice of Lemon

Pour Rum and Bitters into a cocktail shaker over ice. Shake and strain into a highball glass over ice. Add soda and stir gently. Garnish with a slice of lemon and serve.

Expatriated American

13.7% ALC/VOL • 1.7 STD DRINKS

60ml (2 fl oz) Spiced Rum
90ml (3 fl oz) Grapefruit Juice
½ teaspoon Caster Sugar
Pinch of Cinnamon
Pinch of Nutmeg
Pinch of Salt

Pour Rum and juice into a chilled old-fashioned glass over a few ice cubes then stir. Sprinkle sugar, cinnamon, nutmeg and salt on top then serve.

Bacardi Alexander

22.8% ALC/VOL • 1 STD DRINK

23ml (¾ fl oz) Bacardi
15ml (½ fl oz) Dark Crème De Cacao
15ml (½ fl oz) Thick Cream
Nutmeg

Pour Bacardi, Cacao and cream into a cocktail shaker over ice. Shake and strain into a chilled cocktail glass. Sprinkle nutmeg on top and serve.

Mandelbrot

19.6% ALC/VOL • 1.8 STD DRINKS

30ml (1 fl oz) Dark Rum
30ml (1 fl oz) Light Rum
10ml (⅓ fl oz) Grenadine
15ml (½ fl oz) Fresh Lemon Juice
30ml (1 fl oz) Cola
Wedge of Lemon

Pour Rums, Grenadine and juice into a cocktail shaker over ice. Shake and strain into a highball glass filled with ice. Add cola and stir gently. Garnish with a wedge of lemon and serve.

Bellacuba

9.7% ALC/VOL • 1.1 STD DRINKS

30ml (1 fl oz) Dark Rum
15ml (½ fl oz) White Crème De Menthe
15ml (½ fl oz) Grenadine
90ml (3 fl oz) Lemon-Lime Soda

Pour Rum, Crème De Menthe and Grenadine into a highball glass over ice then stir. Add soda, stir gently and serve.

Celebration

30.5% ALC/VOL • 3.2 STD DRINKS

45ml (1½ fl oz) Light Rum
30ml (1 fl oz) Cognac
30ml (1 fl oz) Cointreau
30ml (1 fl oz) Fresh Lemon Juice
Twist of Orange Peel

Pour Rum, Cognac, Cointreau and juice into a cocktail shaker over ice. Shake and strain into a chilled cocktail glass. Garnish with orange peel and serve.

Black Stripe Gold

20.2% ALC/VOL • 1.8 STD DRINKS

60ml (2 fl oz) Dark Rum
30ml (1 fl oz) Boiling Water
15ml (½ fl oz) Molasses
1 teaspoon Honey

Pour Rum, molasses and honey into a mixing glass without ice. Add boiling water and stir well then pour into a cocktail shaker over ice. Shake and strain into an old-fashioned glass filled with crushed ice then serve.

Blue Horizon

10.8% ALC/VOL • 2.4 STD DRINKS

23ml (¾ fl oz) 151-Proof Bacardi
23ml (¾ fl oz) Blue Curaçao
23ml (¾ fl oz) Spiced Rum
8ml (¼ fl oz) Grenadine
210ml (7 fl oz) Fresh Orange Juice
Cherry

Pour Bacardi, Curaçao, Rum and Grenadine into a cocktail shaker over ice. Shake and strain into a chilled collins glass over a few ice cubes. Add juice and stir. Garnish with a cherry and serve.

Pink Limon

13.1% ALC/VOL • 1.2 STD DRINKS

45ml (1½ fl oz) Bacardi Limon
60ml (2 fl oz) Sweet and Sour Mix
15ml (½ fl oz) Cranberry Juice
Slice of Lemon

Prepare a cocktail glass with a sugar frosted rim. Pour Bacardi, sour mix and juice into a cocktail shaker over ice. Shake and strain into prepared glass. Garnish with a slice of lemon and serve.

Roselin

33.5% ALC/VOL • 1.8 STD DRINKS

45ml (1½ fl oz) Dark Rum
8ml (¼ fl oz) Mandarine Napoleon
8ml (¼ fl oz) Triple Sec
3 dashes Angostura Bitters
Dash Grenadine
4 dashes Pineapple Juice

Pour ingredients into a cocktail shaker over ice and shake. Strain into a chilled cocktail glass and serve.

Monsoon

9.5% ALC/VOL • 1.8 STD DRINKS

38ml (1¼ fl oz) Light Rum
23ml (¾ fl oz) Dark Jamaica Rum
120ml (4 fl oz) Sweet and Sour Mix
30ml (1 fl oz) Passion-Fruit Juice
30ml (1 fl oz) Pineapple Juice

Pour Light Rum, sour mix and juices into a hurricane glass filled with ice then stir well. Add Dark Rum, stir briefly and serve.

Misty Pink

21.4% ALC/VOL • 3.7 STD DRINKS

60ml (2 fl oz) Bacardi
38ml (1¼ fl oz) Gin
23ml (¾ fl oz) Red Curaçao
23ml (¾ fl oz) Vanilla Liqueur
75ml (2½ fl oz) Bitter-Lemon Soda

Pour Bacardi, Gin, Curaçao and Liqueur into a cocktail shaker over ice. Shake and strain into a highball glass over ice. Add soda, stir gently and serve.

Fuzzy Charlie II

6.3% ALC/VOL • 1.4 STD DRINKS

38ml (1¼ fl oz) Dark Rum
15ml (½ fl oz) Banana Liqueur
60ml (2 fl oz) Pineapple Juice
15ml (½ fl oz) Coconut Cream
150ml (5 fl oz) Dry Ginger Ale

Pour Rum, Liqueur, juice and cream into a cocktail shaker over ice. Shake and strain into a tall glass over ice. Add Ginger Ale, stir gently and serve.

Liquid Temptation

14.7% ALC/VOL • 1.6 STD DRINKS

45ml (1½ fl oz) Light Rum
15ml (½ fl oz) Banana Liqueur
30ml (1 fl oz) Sweet and Sour Mix
5 Strawberries (diced)
Slice of Banana

Pour Rum, Liqueur and sour mix into a blender over crushed ice then add diced strawberries. Blend until smooth and pour into a chilled wine glass. Garnish with a slice of banana and serve.

Spice Whirl

12% ALC/VOL • 1.2 STD DRINKS

30ml (1 fl oz) Spiced Rum
20ml (⅔ fl oz) Triple Sec
30ml (1 fl oz) Fresh Orange Juice
30ml (1 fl oz) Papaya Juice
20ml (⅔ fl oz) Fresh Lime Juice

Pour ingredients into a cocktail shaker over ice and shake. Strain into a highball glass filled with ice and serve.

Daytona 501

19.2% ALC/VOL • 2 STD DRINKS

45ml (1½ fl oz) Dark Rum
15ml (½ fl oz) Triple Sec
15ml (½ fl oz) Vodka
60ml (2 fl oz) Fresh Orange Juice
Slice of Orange

Pour Rum, Triple Sec, Vodka and juice into a cocktail shaker over large amount of crushed ice. Shake and pour into a chilled highball glass. Garnish with a slice of orange and serve.

Tsunami

10.6% ALC/VOL • 1.5 STD DRINKS

30ml (1 fl oz) Spiced Rum
15ml (½ fl oz) Dark Rum
15ml (½ fl oz) Malibu
15ml (½ fl oz) Grenadine
105ml (3½ fl oz) Pineapple Juice

Build Spiced Rum, Malibu, juice, Grenadine and Dark Rum into a highball glass filled with ice then serve with a swizzle stick.

Rudolph the Red Nose Reindeer

6.6% ALC/VOL • 1.1 STD DRINKS

38ml (1¼ fl oz) Light Rum
15ml (½ fl oz) Grenadine
45ml (1½ fl oz) Fresh Lemon Juice
120ml (4 fl oz) Cranberry Juice
Wedge of Lemon

Pour Rum, Grenadine and juices into a mixing glass over ice. Stir and strain into a highball glass over ice. Garnish with a wedge of lemon and serve.

Tea Bag

10.3% ALC/VOL • 1.6 STD DRINKS

45ml (1½ fl oz) Dark Rum
15ml (½ fl oz) Dark Crème De Cacao
120ml (4 fl oz) Strong Black Tea (chilled)
2 teaspoons Sugar Syrup
8ml (¼ fl oz) Fresh Lemon Juice

Pour ingredients into a cocktail shaker over ice and shake. Strain into a highball glass half filled with ice and serve.

Boardwalk Breezer

10.3% ALC/VOL • 1.6 STD DRINKS

45ml (1½ fl oz) Dark Rum
15ml (½ fl oz) Banana Liqueur
Dash Grenadine
120ml (4 fl oz) Pineapple Juice
15ml (½ fl oz) Fresh Lime Juice

Pour Rum, Liqueur and juices into a cocktail shaker over ice. Shake and strain into a collins glass over ice then add more ice to fill glass. Layer Grenadine on top and serve.

Rum Jaffa

13.2% ALC/VOL • 3 STD DRINKS

60ml (2 fl oz) Bacardi
60ml (2 fl oz) Triple Sec
60ml (2 fl oz) Fresh Orange Juice
15ml (½ fl oz) Lime Syrup
90ml (3 fl oz) Lemonade

Pour Bacardi, Triple Sec, juice and syrup into a cocktail shaker over ice. Shake and strain into a chilled highball glass. Add lemonade, stir gently and serve.

Blue Harbor

6% ALC/VOL • 1.1 STD DRINKS

20ml (⅔ fl oz) Light Rum
10ml (⅓ fl oz) Blue Curaçao
10ml (⅓ fl oz) Cointreau
20ml (⅔ fl oz) Fresh Lime Juice
180ml (6 fl oz) Lemonade

Pour Rum, Curaçao, Cointreau and juice into a cocktail shaker over ice. Shake and strain into a highball glass over ice. Add lemonade, stir gently and serve.

Peaceful Treasure

6.2% ALC/VOL • 0.9 STD DRINKS

30ml (1 fl oz) Dark Rum
Dash Grenadine
120ml (4 fl oz) Fresh Orange Juice
23ml (¾ fl oz) Fresh Lemon Juice
1 teaspoon Sugar Syrup

Pour ingredients into a mixing glass over ice and stir. Strain into an old-fashioned glass over ice and serve.

Anon

12.6% ALC/VOL • 3.3 STD DRINKS

60ml (2 fl oz) Bacardi
30ml (1 fl oz) Apfelkorn
30ml (1 fl oz) Coconut Liqueur
30ml (1 fl oz) Midori
90ml (3 fl oz) Apple Juice
90ml (3 fl oz) Pineapple Juice

Pour ingredients into a cocktail shaker over ice and shake. Strain into a chilled collins glass over a few ice cubes and serve.

Big Hawaiian

7.3% ALC/VOL • 1.3 STD DRINKS

23ml (¾ fl oz) Dark Rum
23ml (¾ fl oz) Malibu
15ml (½ fl oz) Midori
15ml (½ fl oz) Grenadine
150ml (5 fl oz) Pineapple Juice

Pour ingredients into a cocktail shaker over ice and shake. Strain into a chilled highball glass and serve.

Jamaican Crow

11.3% ALC/VOL • 1.3 STD DRINKS

45ml (1½ fl oz) Bacardi
15ml (½ fl oz) Grenadine
30ml (1 fl oz) Fresh Lime Juice
60ml (2 fl oz) Soda Water
Slice of Orange

Pour Bacardi, Grenadine and juice into a cocktail shaker over ice. Shake and strain into a collins glass over ice. Add soda and stir gently. Garnish with a slice of orange and serve.

Checkmate

18.2% ALC/VOL • 2.8 STD DRINKS

60ml (2 fl oz) Light Rum
60ml (2 fl oz) White Wine
30ml (1 fl oz) Brandy
30ml (1 fl oz) Chocolate Syrup
15ml (½ fl oz) Molasses

Pour ingredients into a mixing glass without ice and stir well. Pour into a highball glass over ice, stir and serve.

Reidinger

10.4% ALC/VOL • 1.8 STD DRINKS

45ml (1½ fl oz) Light Rum
30ml (1 fl oz) Midori
30ml (1 fl oz) Fresh Lime Juice
120ml (4 fl oz) Cola
Maraschino Cherry

Pour Rum, Midori and juice into a mixing glass over ice. Stir and strain into a highball glass over crushed ice. Add cola and stir gently. Garnish with a cherry and serve with a straw.

Coco-Mocha Alexander

10.4% ALC/VOL • 1.1 STD DRINKS

23ml (¾ fl oz) Spiced Rum
15ml (½ fl oz) Coffee Brandy
30ml (1 fl oz) Black Coffee (chilled)
30ml (1 fl oz) Coconut Cream
30ml (1 fl oz) Fresh Cream

Pour ingredients into a blender over small amount of crushed ice and blend until smooth. Pour into a chilled coffee glass and serve.

Lone Wolf

34.5% ALC/VOL • 2.3 STD DRINKS

45ml (1½ fl oz) Light Rum
15ml (½ fl oz) Cointreau
15ml (½ fl oz) Southern Comfort
8ml (¼ fl oz) Fresh Lemon Juice
Maraschino Cherry

Pour Rum, Cointreau, Southern Comfort and juice into a cocktail shaker over ice. Shake and strain into a highball glass filled with ice. Garnish with a cherry and serve.

Ed's Baby

29.5% ALC/VOL • 1.5 STD DRINKS

30ml (1 fl oz) Light Rum
12ml (2/5 fl oz) Cherry Brandy
12ml (2/5 fl oz) Orange Curaçao
6ml (1/5 fl oz) Banana Liqueur
3 dashes Fresh Lemon Juice

Pour Rum, Brandy, Curaçao and Liqueur into a mixing glass over ice. Stir and strain into a chilled cocktail glass. Add juice – do not stir, then serve.

Lifeline

31.9% ALC/VOL • 2.3 STD DRINKS

30ml (1 fl oz) Light Rum
15ml (½ fl oz) Apricot Brandy
15ml (½ fl oz) Brandy
15ml (½ fl oz) Cointreau
15ml (½ fl oz) Sweet Vermouth
Wedge of Lime

Pour Rum, Brandies, Cointreau and Vermouth into a cocktail shaker over ice. Shake and strain into a chilled cocktail glass. Garnish with a wedge of lime and serve.

Beau Rivage

22.9% ALC/VOL • 1.4 STD DRINKS

20ml (⅔ fl oz) Bacardi
20ml (⅔ fl oz) Dry Gin
10ml (⅓ fl oz) Dry Vermouth
10ml (⅓ fl oz) Sweet Vermouth
10ml (⅓ fl oz) Grenadine
10ml (⅓ fl oz) Fresh Orange Juice

Pour ingredients into a cocktail shaker over ice and shake. Strain into a chilled cocktail glass and serve.

Survivor

20.8% ALC/VOL • 1.5 STD DRINKS

45ml (1½ fl oz) Light Rum
8ml (¼ fl oz) White Crème De Cacao
30ml (1 fl oz) Pineapple Juice
8ml (¼ fl oz) Fresh Lime Juice

Pour ingredients into a cocktail shaker over ice and shake. Strain into an old-fashioned glass half filled with ice and serve.

Pineapple Francine

7.6% ALC/VOL • 0.7 STD DRINKS

15ml (½ fl oz) Dark Rum
15ml (½ fl oz) Apricot Brandy
30ml (1 fl oz) Pineapple Juice
30ml (1 fl oz) Fresh Cream
4 Pieces of Pineapple (diced)

Pour Rum, Brandy, juice and cream into a blender over crushed ice then add diced pineapple. Blend and pour into a chilled champagne flute then serve.

Samba Blue

15.6% ALC/VOL • 1.9 STD DRINKS

38ml (1¼ fl oz) Cachaça
23ml (¾ fl oz) Apricot Brandy
15ml (½ fl oz) Blue Curaçao
75ml (2½ fl oz) Fresh Lime Juice
1 teaspoon Sugar Syrup

Prepare a champagne flute with a sugar frosted rim – moistened with Grenadine. Pour ingredients into a cocktail shaker over ice and shake. Strain into prepared glass and serve with 2 straws.

Cuban Cutie

8.8% ALC/VOL • 1.8 STD DRINKS

60ml (2 fl oz) Bacardi
90ml (3 fl oz) Grenadine
90ml (3 fl oz) Fresh Orange Juice
20ml (⅔ fl oz) Passion-Fruit Juice
Wedge of Lime

Pour Bacardi, Grenadine and juices into a cocktail shaker over ice. Shake and strain into a tall glass over ice. Garnish with a wedge of lime and serve.

Dominican Coco Loco

18.7% ALC/VOL • 1.7 STD DRINKS

45ml (1½ fl oz) Light Rum
15ml (½ fl oz) Amaretto
5ml (⅙ fl oz) Grenadine
30ml (1 fl oz) Coconut Cream
15ml (½ fl oz) Pineapple Juice
4 dashes Fresh Milk (chilled)

Pour ingredients into a blender over crushed ice and blend until smooth. Pour into a chilled highball glass and serve.

Blue Rinse

4.1% ALC/VOL • 0.7 STD DRINKS

10ml (⅓ fl oz) Bacardi
10ml (⅓ fl oz) Banana Liqueur
10ml (⅓ fl oz) Blue Curaçao
180ml (6 fl oz) Bitter-Lemon Soda

Pour Bacardi, Liqueur and Curaçao into a highball glass over ice then stir. Add soda, stir gently and serve.

Carnival Cooler

11.6% ALC/VOL • 1.9 STD DRINKS

60ml (2 fl oz) Light Rum
2 dashes Angostura Bitters
23ml (¾ fl oz) Fresh Lime Juice
120ml (4 fl oz) Soda Water
Slice of Lime

Pour Rum, Bitters and juice into a cocktail shaker over ice. Shake and strain into a collins glass over ice. Add soda and stir gently. Garnish with a slice of lime and serve.

Hard Hat

8% ALC/VOL • 1.1 STD DRINKS

38ml (1¼ fl oz) Bacardi
8ml (¼ fl oz) Grenadine
38ml (1¼ fl oz) Lime Syrup
1 teaspoon Sugar Syrup
90ml (3 fl oz) Soda Water

Pour Bacardi, Grenadine, syrup and sugar into a cocktail shaker over ice. Shake and strain into a highball glass over ice. Add soda, stir gently and serve.

Pink Cat

16% ALC/VOL • 1.6 STD DRINKS

20ml (⅔ fl oz) Bacardi
20ml (⅔ fl oz) Banana Liqueur
20ml (⅔ fl oz) Passion-Fruit Liqueur
20ml (⅔ fl oz) White Crème De Cacao
10ml (⅓ fl oz) Grenadine
40ml (1⅓ fl oz) Fresh Milk (chilled)

Pour ingredients into a cocktail shaker over ice and shake. Strain into a chilled cocktail glass and serve.

Recife

17.2% ALC/VOL • 1.8 STD DRINKS

30ml (1 fl oz) Cachaça
20ml (⅔ fl oz) Dark Rum
10ml (⅓ fl oz) White Tequila
Dash Orange Bitters
75ml (2½ fl oz) Pineapple Juice

Pour ingredients into a cocktail shaker over ice and shake. Strain into a highball glass over crushed ice and stir gently then serve with a straw.

Sunny Sour

28.7% ALC/VOL • 1.1 STD DRINKS

38ml (1¼ fl oz) Dark Rum
8ml (¼ fl oz) Fresh Lemon Juice
½ teaspoon Sugar Syrup
Cherry
Wedge of Lemon

Pour Rum, juice and sugar into a cocktail shaker over ice. Shake and strain into a chilled sour glass. Garnish with a cherry and wedge of lemon then serve.

Martinique

10.8% ALC/VOL • 1.3 STD DRINKS

30ml (1 fl oz) Bacardi
20ml (⅔ fl oz) Orange Curaçao
60ml (2 fl oz) Pineapple Juice
20ml (⅔ fl oz) Fresh Lime Juice
20ml (⅔ fl oz) Fresh Orange Juice

Pour ingredients into a cocktail shaker over ice and shake. Strain into a highball glass over crushed ice then serve with a swizzle stick and straw.

Hurricane Cooler

15.4% ALC/VOL • 1.5 STD DRINKS

30ml (1 fl oz) Light Rum
10ml (⅓ fl oz) Pernod
15ml (½ fl oz) Orange Bitters
30ml (1 fl oz) Fresh Lime Juice
30ml (1 fl oz) Fresh Orange Juice
2 teaspoons Sugar Syrup

Pour ingredients into a cocktail shaker over ice and shake. Strain into a collins glass over crushed ice and serve.

Rum-Dinger

5.3% ALC/VOL • 0.9 STD DRINKS

30ml (1 fl oz) Dark Rum
90ml (3 fl oz) Pineapple Juice
30ml (1 fl oz) Banana Juice
30ml (1 fl oz) Cherry Juice
30ml (1 fl oz) Fresh Cream

Pour ingredients into a cocktail shaker over ice and shake. Strain into a highball glass over ice and serve.

Lallah Rookh

28.3% ALC/VOL • 2.1 STD DRINKS

45ml (1½ fl oz) Light Rum
23ml (¾ fl oz) Cognac
2 teaspoons Vanilla Extract
1 teaspoon Sugar Syrup
Fresh Whipped Cream

Pour Rum, Cognac, extract and sugar into a cocktail shaker over cracked ice. Shake and pour into a chilled old-fashioned glass. Float cream on top and serve.

Zipper

22.3% ALC/VOL • 2.2 STD DRINKS

45ml (1½ fl oz) Cachaça
45ml (1½ fl oz) Kahlúa
5ml (⅙ fl oz) Bailey's Irish Cream
30ml (1 fl oz) Thick Cream
Grated Chocolate

Pour Cachaça, Kahlúa, Bailey's and cream into a cocktail shaker over ice. Shake and strain into a chilled cocktail glass. Sprinkle chocolate on top and serve.

Spanish Mai Tai

19.4% ALC/VOL • 3.2 STD DRINKS

40ml (1⅓ fl oz) Bacardi
40ml (1⅓ fl oz) Dark Rum
40ml (1⅓ fl oz) Orange Curaçao
23ml (¾ fl oz) Grenadine
40ml (1⅓ fl oz) Fresh Lime Juice
23ml (¾ fl oz) Orgeat Syrup
2 Cherries
Slice of Pineapple
Sprig of Fresh Mint

Pour Bacardi, Rum, Curaçao, Grenadine, juice and syrup into a cocktail shaker over ice. Shake and strain into a highball glass half filled with crushed ice. Garnish with cherries, a slice of pineapple and sprig of mint then serve.

Cool by the Pool

12.1% ALC/VOL • 1.9 STD DRINKS

30ml (1 fl oz) Bacardi
23ml (¾ fl oz) Dark Rum
10ml (⅓ fl oz) Jamaica Rum
5ml (⅙ fl oz) Grenadine
60ml (2 fl oz) Fresh Orange Juice
60ml (2 fl oz) Pineapple Juice
1½ teaspoons Lime Syrup
Wedge of Lime

Pour Bacardi, Dark Rum, juices and syrup into a cocktail shaker over cracked ice. Shake and pour into a chilled highball glass. Add Grenadine – do not stir, then layer Jamaica Rum on top. Twist wedge of lime above drink to release juice – do not stir, then add spent shell and serve.

Slow Motion

12.2% ALC/VOL • 1.8 STD DRINKS

45ml (1½ fl oz) Bacardi
30ml (1 fl oz) Passion-Fruit Liqueur
8ml (¼ fl oz) Grenadine
60ml (2 fl oz) Fresh Orange Juice
30ml (1 fl oz) Pineapple Juice
15ml (½ fl oz) Sweet and Sour Mix
Cherry
Piece of Pineapple

Pour Bacardi, Liqueur, Grenadine, juices and sour mix into a cocktail shaker over ice. Shake and strain into a collins glass half filled with ice. Add a cherry and piece of pineapple then serve with 2 straws.

Missionary Downfall

15.3% ALC/VOL • 1.1 STD DRINKS

30ml (1 fl oz) Light Rum
15ml (½ fl oz) Peach Brandy
45ml (1½ fl oz) Fresh Lime Juice
1 teaspoon Sugar Syrup
3 Sprigs of Fresh Mint
Slice of Pineapple

Pour Rum, Brandy, juice and sugar into a blender without ice. Add sprigs of mint and a slice of pineapple. Blend until smooth and pour into a chilled tall glass. Fill with crushed ice, stir and serve.

Jamaica Banana

14% ALC/VOL • 1.3 STD DRINKS

20ml (⅔ fl oz) Bacardi
20ml (⅔ fl oz) Banana Liqueur
20ml (⅔ fl oz) White Crème De Cacao
2 scoops Vanilla Ice Cream

Place ice cream into a chilled parfait glass. Pour Bacardi, Liqueur and Cacao into a cocktail shaker over ice. Shake and strain into glass over ice cream. Serve with a swizzle stick and straw.

Fascination Punch

7.3% ALC/VOL • 1.4 STD DRINKS

23ml (¾ fl oz) Dark Rum
15ml (½ fl oz) Banana Liqueur
15ml (½ fl oz) Orange Curaçao
8ml (¼ fl oz) Coconut Liqueur
180ml (6 fl oz) Fresh Orange Juice
Slice of Orange

Pour Rum, Liqueurs, Curaçao and juice into a cocktail shaker over ice. Shake and strain into a highball glass over ice. Garnish with a slice of orange and serve.

I Love You

27.4% ALC/VOL • 1.5 STD DRINKS

30ml (1 fl oz) Golden Rum
20ml (⅔ fl oz) Apricot Brandy
10ml (⅓ fl oz) Peach Schnapps
5ml (⅙ fl oz) Amaretto
5ml (⅙ fl oz) Fresh Orange Juice

Pour ingredients into a cocktail shaker over ice and shake. Strain into a chilled cocktail glass and serve.

Organ Grinder

23.1% ALC/VOL • 3.1 STD DRINKS

30ml (1 fl oz) Dark Rum
30ml (1 fl oz) Light Rum
30ml (1 fl oz) Blended Whiskey
18ml (⅗ fl oz) White Crème De Cacao
60ml (2 fl oz) Coconut Cream
Grated Coconut

Pour Rums, Whiskey, Cacao and cream into a blender without ice. Blend until smooth and pour into a parfait glass over crushed ice then stir. Sprinkle coconut on top and serve.

Chocolate Mint Rum

33.2% ALC/VOL • 2.2 STD DRINKS

30ml (1 fl oz) Dark Rum
15ml (½ fl oz) 151-Proof Rum
15ml (½ fl oz) Dark Crème De Cacao
10ml (⅓ fl oz) White Crème De Menthe
15ml (½ fl oz) Fresh Cream

Pour ingredients into a cocktail shaker over ice and shake. Strain into a chilled cocktail glass and serve.

Rockaway Beach

21.4% ALC/VOL • 2.4 STD DRINKS

45ml (1½ fl oz) Light Rum
15ml (½ fl oz) Dark Rum
15ml (½ fl oz) Tequila
5ml (⅙ fl oz) Crème De Noyaux
30ml (1 fl oz) Fresh Orange Juice
15ml (½ fl oz) Cranberry Juice
15ml (½ fl oz) Pineapple Juice

Pour ingredients into a cocktail shaker over ice and shake. Strain into a highball glass over ice and serve.

Jerry's Juice

20.4% ALC/VOL • 1.4 STD DRINKS

30ml (1 fl oz) Dark Rum
15ml (½ fl oz) Cointreau
Dash Grenadine
23ml (¾ fl oz) Cranberry Juice
15ml (½ fl oz) Passion-Fruit Juice

Pour ingredients into a cocktail shaker over ice and shake. Strain into a chilled cocktail glass and serve.

Slapstick

7.3% ALC/VOL • 0.9 STD DRINKS

23ml (¾ fl oz) Spiced Rum
15ml (½ fl oz) Strawberry Liqueur
60ml (2 fl oz) Pineapple Juice
30ml (1 fl oz) Coconut Cream
30ml (1 fl oz) Strawberry Syrup
Strawberry

Pour Rum, Liqueur, juice, cream and syrup into a blender over crushed ice. Blend and pour into a chilled highball glass. Garnish with a strawberry and serve.

Majoba

29.1% ALC/VOL • 1.5 STD DRINKS

30ml (1 fl oz) Dark Rum
15ml (½ fl oz) Orange Curaçao
8ml (¼ fl oz) Banana Liqueur
8ml (¼ fl oz) Dark Crème De Cacao
3 dashes Pineapple Juice

Pour ingredients into a cocktail shaker over ice and shake. Strain into a chilled cocktail glass and serve.

Blonde Moment

13.7% ALC/VOL • 1.1 STD DRINKS

30ml (1 fl oz) Bacardi Limon
15ml (½ fl oz) Blue Curaçao
10ml (⅓ fl oz) Grenadine
45ml (1½ fl oz) Sweet and Sour Mix
5ml (⅙ fl oz) Soda Water
Cherry

Pour Bacardi, Curaçao, Grenadine and sour mix into an old-fashioned glass over ice then stir. Add soda – do not stir, then garnish with a cherry and serve.

Isle of Pines

27.1% ALC/VOL • 1.9 STD DRINKS

60ml (2 fl oz) Spiced Rum
15ml (½ fl oz) White Crème De Menthe
15ml (½ fl oz) Fresh Lime Juice
6 Fresh Mint Leaves

Pour Rum, Crème De Menthe and juice into a blender over cracked ice then add mint leaves. Blend and strain into a chilled cocktail glass then serve.

Jamaican Banana

6.5% ALC/VOL • 1 STD DRINK

15ml (½ fl oz) Bacardi
15ml (½ fl oz) Banana Liqueur
15ml (½ fl oz) White Crème De Cacao
30ml (1 fl oz) Fresh Cream
2 scoops Vanilla Ice Cream
1 Banana (diced)
Strawberry
Nutmeg

Pour Bacardi, Liqueur, Cacao and cream into a blender over small amount of crushed ice. Add ice cream and diced banana. Blend until smooth and pour into a chilled brandy balloon. Sprinkle nutmeg on top and garnish with a strawberry then serve.

Lethal Injection

12% ALC/VOL • 1.8 STD DRINKS

60ml (2 fl oz) Light Rum
10ml (⅓ fl oz) Grenadine
60ml (2 fl oz) Grapefruit Juice
60ml (2 fl oz) Fresh Orange Juice
Wedge of Orange

Pour Rum and juices into a cocktail shaker over cracked ice. Shake and pour into a chilled collins glass then add Grenadine by pouring into centre of drink – do not stir. Garnish with a wedge of orange and serve.

Easy Bahama Mama

18% ALC/VOL • 1.8 STD DRINKS

60ml (2 fl oz) Dark Rum
Dash Amaretto
Dash Grenadine
60ml (2 fl oz) Pineapple Juice
½ teaspoon Sugar Syrup
Maraschino Cherry

Pour Rum, Amaretto, Grenadine, juice and sugar into a mixing glass over ice. Stir and strain into a margarita glass over crushed ice. Garnish with a cherry and serve.

Tropical Flower

13.2% ALC/VOL • 2.2 STD DRINKS

40ml (1⅓ fl oz) Bacardi
40ml (1⅓ fl oz) Passion-Fruit Liqueur
20ml (⅔ fl oz) Lychee Liqueur
80ml (2⅔ fl oz) Passion-Fruit Juice
½ Banana (diced)

Pour Bacardi, Liqueurs and juice into a blender over crushed ice then add diced banana. Blend until smooth and pour into a chilled hurricane glass then serve.

Boston Tea

11.2% ALC/VOL • 1.2 STD DRINKS

15ml (½ fl oz) Bacardi
15ml (½ fl oz) Tia Maria
15ml (½ fl oz) Vodka
60ml (2 fl oz) Sweet and Sour Mix
30ml (1 fl oz) Cola

Pour Bacardi, Tia, Vodka and sour mix into a mixing glass over ice. Stir and strain into a highball glass over ice. Add cola, stir gently and serve.

Baso

6% ALC/VOL • 1.3 STD DRINKS

30ml (1 fl oz) Spiced Rum
15ml (½ fl oz) Goldschläger
210ml (7 fl oz) Grapefruit Juice
23ml (¾ fl oz) Fresh Lime Juice
5ml (⅙ fl oz) Soda Water
Slice of Lime

Pour Rum, Goldschläger and juices into a cocktail shaker over ice. Shake and strain into a chilled highball glass. Add soda and stir gently. Garnish with a slice of lime and serve.

Citrus Smack

13.3% ALC/VOL • 2.2 STD DRINKS

45ml (1½ fl oz) Dark Rum
45ml (1½ fl oz) Triple Sec
90ml (3 fl oz) Grapefruit Juice
30ml (1 fl oz) Sweet and Sour Mix
2 Slices of Orange
Slice of Lemon

Pour Rum, Triple Sec, juice and sour mix into a highball glass over ice then stir well. Garnish with slices of orange and a slice of lemon then serve.

Guatacarazo

28.9% ALC/VOL • 1.5 STD DRINKS

30ml (1 fl oz) Dark Rum
15ml (½ fl oz) Vodka
8ml (¼ fl oz) Banana Liqueur
8ml (¼ fl oz) Pineapple Juice
3 dashes Fresh Lemon Juice

Pour Rum, Vodka, Liqueur and pineapple juice into a cocktail shaker over ice. Shake and strain into an old-fashioned glass over crushed ice. Add lemon juice – do not stir, then serve.

Kingston Town

11.9% ALC/VOL • 1.9 STD DRINKS

30ml (1 fl oz) Bacardi
30ml (1 fl oz) Triple Sec
10ml (⅓ fl oz) Banana Liqueur
10ml (⅓ fl oz) Blue Curaçao
120ml (4 fl oz) Pineapple Juice

Pour ingredients into a cocktail shaker over ice and shake. Strain into a highball glass over ice and serve with a straw.

Apple Core

17.4% ALC/VOL • 2.1 STD DRINKS

45ml (1½ fl oz) Light Rum
15ml (½ fl oz) Applejack
15ml (½ fl oz) Apple Schnapps
15ml (½ fl oz) Rose's Lime Juice
60ml (2 fl oz) Soda Water
Wedge of Lemon

Pour Rum, Applejack, Schnapps and juice into a cocktail shaker over cracked ice. Shake and pour into a chilled highball glass. Add soda and stir gently. Garnish with a wedge of lemon and serve.

Sunnier Sour

6.6% ALC/VOL • 1.1 STD DRINKS

38ml (1¼ fl oz) Dark Rum
45ml (1½ fl oz) Grapefruit Juice
8ml (¼ fl oz) Fresh Lemon Juice
½ teaspoon Sugar Syrup
120ml (4 fl oz) Soda Water
Wedge of Grapefruit

Pour Rum, juices and sugar into a cocktail shaker over ice. Shake and strain into a sour glass over ice. Add soda and stir gently. Garnish with a wedge of grapefruit and serve.

Caribbean Cooler

12.2% ALC/VOL • 0.9 STD DRINKS

23ml (¾ fl oz) Dark Rum
15ml (½ fl oz) Apricot Brandy
30ml (1 fl oz) Coconut Cream
30ml (1 fl oz) Thick Cream
Maraschino Cherry
Grated Coconut

Pour Rum, Brandy and creams into a blender over cracked ice. Blend and pour into a chilled collins glass. Sprinkle coconut on top and garnish with a cherry then serve.

Spice Me Up Nice

8.8% ALC/VOL • 1.5 STD DRINKS

30ml (1 fl oz) Bacardi
15ml (½ fl oz) Spiced Rum
8ml (¼ fl oz) Orange Bitters
100ml (3⅓ fl oz) Pineapple Juice
30ml (1 fl oz) Fresh Orange Juice
30ml (1 fl oz) Sweet and Sour Mix

Pour ingredients into a cocktail shaker over ice and shake. Strain into a chilled highball glass and serve.

Daytona Daydream

6.5% ALC/VOL • 1 STD DRINK

38ml (1¼ fl oz) Spiced Rum
15ml (½ fl oz) Grenadine
90ml (3 fl oz) Pink Grapefruit Juice
60ml (2 fl oz) Coconut Cream
Slice of Lime

Pour Rum, Grenadine, juice and cream into a cocktail shaker over ice. Shake and strain into a highball glass over ice. Garnish with a slice of lime and serve.

Astronaut

18.4% ALC/VOL • 2.6 STD DRINKS

45ml (1½ fl oz) Jamaica Rum
45ml (1½ fl oz) Vodka
60ml (2 fl oz) Pineapple Juice
8ml (¼ fl oz) Fresh Lemon Juice
23ml (¾ fl oz) Soda Water

Pour Rum, Vodka and juices into a cocktail shaker over ice. Shake and strain into a collins glass over ice. Add soda, stir gently and serve.

One Over Par

6.3% ALC/VOL • 1.3 STD DRINKS

45ml (1½ fl oz) Light Rum
45ml (1½ fl oz) Grapefruit Juice
45ml (1½ fl oz) Fresh Orange Juice
45ml (1½ fl oz) Pineapple Juice
90ml (3 fl oz) Soda Water

Pour Rum and juices into a mixing glass over ice. Stir and strain into a highball glass over ice. Add soda, stir gently and serve.

Nang Peng

12.5% ALC/VOL • 1.9 STD DRINKS

45ml (1½ fl oz) Spiced Rum
15ml (½ fl oz) Bacardi
8ml (¼ fl oz) Pisang Ambon
3 dashes Vanilla Liqueur
105ml (3½ fl oz) Pineapple Juice
15ml (½ fl oz) Fresh Lime Juice

Pour ingredients into a cocktail shaker over ice and shake. Strain into a collins glass over ice and serve.

Coco Loco

22.6% ALC/VOL • 2.7 STD DRINKS

30ml (1 fl oz) Light Rum
30ml (1 fl oz) Tequila
30ml (1 fl oz) Vodka
30ml (1 fl oz) Fresh Lemon Juice
30ml (1 fl oz) Coconut Cream

Pour ingredients into a blender over crushed ice and blend until smooth. Pour into a chilled highball glass and serve.

Swimming Pool

16.5% ALC/VOL • 2.2 STD DRINKS

45ml (1½ fl oz) Light Rum
23ml (¾ fl oz) Vodka
8ml (¼ fl oz) Blue Curaçao
60ml (2 fl oz) Pineapple Juice
23ml (¾ fl oz) Coconut Cream
1½ teaspoons Fresh Cream

Pour Rum, Vodka, juice and creams into a mixing glass over crushed ice. Stir well and pour into a chilled brandy balloon. Layer Curaçao on top and serve.

Fiji Fizz

14.8% ALC/VOL • 2.2 STD DRINKS

45ml (1½ fl oz) Dark Rum
15ml (½ fl oz) Bourbon
5ml (1/6 fl oz) Cherry Liqueur
3 dashes Orange Bitters
120ml (4 fl oz) Cola

Pour Rum, Bourbon, Liqueur and Bitters into a cocktail shaker over ice. Shake and strain into a highball glass over ice. Add cola, stir gently and serve.

Electric Lemonade

11.5% ALC/VOL • 2.2 STD DRINKS

38ml (1¼ fl oz) Spiced Rum
23ml (¾ fl oz) Dark Rum
15ml (½ fl oz) Cointreau
30ml (1 fl oz) Cranberry Juice
135ml (4½ fl oz) Lemonade

Pour Rums, Cointreau and juice into a frosted mug then stir. Add lemonade, stir gently and serve.
This drink is also known as On the Deck.

Matt the Rat

10.5% ALC/VOL • 1.4 STD DRINKS

38ml (1¼ fl oz) Spiced Rum
15ml (½ fl oz) Triple Sec
45ml (1½ fl oz) Fresh Orange Juice
15ml (½ fl oz) Fresh Lime Juice
1 teaspoon Sugar Syrup
45ml (1½ fl oz) Lemonade

Pour Rum, Triple Sec, orange juice and sugar into a cocktail shaker over ice. Shake and strain into a highball glass over ice. Add lemonade and lime juice – do not stir, then serve.

Plantation Punch

15.7% ALC/VOL • 2.8 STD DRINKS

60ml (2 fl oz) Dark Rum
30ml (1 fl oz) Southern Comfort
15ml (½ fl oz) Port
1 teaspoon Sugar Syrup
120ml (4 fl oz) Mineral Water

Pour Rum, Southern Comfort and sugar into a cocktail shaker over ice. Shake and strain into a chilled highball glass. Add mineral water and stir gently. Layer Port on top and serve.

Red Ball

6% ALC/VOL • 1.2 STD DRINKS

30ml (1 fl oz) Bacardi
20ml (⅔ fl oz) Passoa
60ml (2 fl oz) Iced Tea
10ml (⅓ fl oz) Fresh Lime Juice
135ml (4½ fl oz) Soda Water

Pour Bacardi, Passoa and juice into a cocktail shaker over ice. Shake and strain into a chilled highball glass. Add tea and soda, stir gently then serve.

Life Saver No.2

13.3% ALC/VOL • 0.6 STD DRINKS

10ml (⅓ fl oz) Bacardi
5ml (1/6 fl oz) Blue Curaçao
5ml (1/6 fl oz) Cointreau
20ml (⅔ fl oz) Pineapple Juice
8ml (¼ fl oz) Fresh Lime Juice
1 teaspoon Sugar Syrup

Pour ingredients into a cocktail shaker over ice and shake. Strain into a chilled cocktail glass and serve.

Blue Suede Shoes

10.5% ALC/VOL • 1.9 STD DRINKS

53ml (1¾ fl oz) Bacardi
15ml (½ fl oz) Triple Sec
1½ teaspoons Blueberry Syrup
150ml (5 fl oz) Soda Water
Twist of Lemon Peel

Build ingredients into a highball glass over ice and garnish with lemon peel. Serve with a swizzle stick and 2 straws.

Christophe

30.6% ALC/VOL • 1.1 STD DRINKS

30ml (1 fl oz) Dark Rum
8ml (¼ fl oz) Gin
5ml (1/6 fl oz) Fresh Lime Juice
½ teaspoon Sugar Syrup
Twist of Lime Peel

Pour Rum, Gin, juice and sugar into a cocktail shaker over ice. Shake and strain into a chilled cocktail glass. Garnish with lime peel and serve.

Belize Rum Punch

20% ALC/VOL • 3.8 STD DRINKS

60ml (2 fl oz) Light Rum
30ml (1 fl oz) Coconut Liqueur
30ml (1 fl oz) Dark Rum
30ml (1 fl oz) Triple Sec
2 dashes Grenadine
60ml (2 fl oz) Pineapple Juice
30ml (1 fl oz) Sweet and Sour Mix
Slice of Orange
Slice of Pineapple

Pour Rums, Liqueur, Triple Sec, juice and sour mix into a cocktail shaker over cracked ice. Shake and pour into a chilled tall glass. Add Grenadine and stir gently. Garnish with a slice of orange and pineapple then serve.

Batida Abaci

13.1% ALC/VOL • 1.9 STD DRINKS

60ml (2 fl oz) Cachaça
½ teaspoon Sugar Syrup
1 Cup Pineapple (diced)

Pour Cachaça and sugar into a blender over crushed ice then add diced pineapple. Blend and pour into a chilled wine glass then serve.

Batida Morango

21.2% ALC/VOL • 1.9 STD DRINKS

60ml (2 fl oz) Cachaça
½ teaspoon Sugar Syrup
5 Strawberries (diced)

Pour Cachaça and sugar into a blender over crushed ice then add diced strawberries. Blend and pour into a chilled wine glass then serve.

Batida Mango

15% ALC/VOL • 1.9 STD DRINKS

60ml (2 fl oz) Cachaça
2 teaspoons Sugar Syrup
1 Cup Mango (diced)

Pour Cachaça and sugar into a blender over crushed ice then add diced mango. Blend and pour into a chilled wine glass then serve.

Batida Limao

24% ALC/VOL • 1.9 STD DRINKS

60ml (2 fl oz) Cachaça
30ml (1 fl oz) Fresh Lime Juice
2 teaspoons Sugar Syrup

Pour ingredients into a blender over crushed ice and blend. Pour into a chilled wine glass and serve.

Apple Colada

10.3% ALC/VOL • 1.7 STD DRINKS

38ml (1¼ fl oz) Light Rum
38ml (1¼ fl oz) Apple Schnapps
90ml (3 fl oz) Pineapple Juice
40ml (1⅓ fl oz) Coconut Cream
1 teaspoon Thick Cream
Maraschino Cherry
Slice of Pineapple

Pour Rum, Schnapps, juice and creams into a blender over crushed ice. Blend and pour into a chilled hurricane glass. Garnish with a cherry and slice of pineapple then serve with 2 straws.

Banana Colada

9.4% ALC/VOL • 1.8 STD DRINKS

38ml (1¼ fl oz) Light Rum
38ml (1¼ fl oz) Banana Liqueur
90ml (3 fl oz) Pineapple Juice
40ml (1⅓ fl oz) Coconut Cream
1 teaspoon Thick Cream
1 Banana (diced)
Maraschino Cherry
Slice of Pineapple

Pour Rum, Liqueur, juice and creams into a blender over crushed ice then add diced banana. Blend and pour into a chilled hurricane glass. Garnish with a cherry and slice of pineapple then serve with 2 straws.

Raspberry Colada

9.8% ALC/VOL • 1.6 STD DRINKS

This drink is an Apple Colada (p. 173) substituting Apple Schnapps with Chambord.

Strawberry Colada

9.4% ALC/VOL • 1.7 STD DRINKS

38ml (1¼ fl oz) Light Rum
38ml (1¼ fl oz) Strawberry Liqueur
90ml (3 fl oz) Pineapple Juice
40ml (1⅓ fl oz) Coconut Cream
1 teaspoon Thick Cream
2 Strawberries (diced)
Maraschino Cherry
Slice of Pineapple

Pour Rum, Liqueur, juice and creams into a blender over crushed ice then add diced strawberries. Blend and pour into a chilled hurricane glass. Garnish with a cherry and slice of pineapple then serve with 2 straws.

Melon Colada

10.5% ALC/VOL • 1.7 STD DRINKS

This drink is an Apple Colada (p. 173) substituting Apple Schnapps with Midori.

Piña Colada

10.6% ALC/VOL • 1.8 STD DRINKS

60ml (2 fl oz) Jamaica Rum
60ml (2 fl oz) Pineapple Juice
60ml (2 fl oz) Thick Cream
30ml (1 fl oz) Coconut Milk (chilled)

Maraschino Cherry
Slice of Pineapple

Pour Rum, juice, cream and milk into a blender over crushed ice. Blend and pour into a chilled hurricane glass. Garnish with a cherry and slice of pineapple then serve with 2 straws.

This drink may also be prepared in a cocktail shaker.

Coffee Colada

11.6% ALC/VOL • 1.9 STD DRINKS

This drink is an Apple Colada (p. 173) substituting Apple Schnapps with Tia Maria.

Tropicolada

19.1% ALC/VOL • 1.7 STD DRINKS

38ml (1¼ fl oz) Light Rum
15ml (½ fl oz) Banana Liqueur
15ml (½ fl oz) Midori
90ml (3 fl oz) Pineapple Juice
40ml (1⅓ fl oz) Coconut Cream
1 teaspoon Thick Cream
Maraschino Cherry
Slice of Pineapple

Pour Rum, Liqueur, Midori, juice and creams into a blender over crushed ice. Blend and pour into a chilled hurricane glass. Garnish with a cherry and slice of pineapple then serve with 2 straws.

Amaretto Colada

11.8% ALC/VOL • 2 STD DRINKS

This drink is an Apple Colada (p. 173) substituting Apple Schnapps with Amaretto.

Colada Collision

4.5% ALC/VOL • 1.3 STD DRINKS

45ml (1½ fl oz) Light Rum
180ml (6 fl oz) Pineapple Juice
90ml (3 fl oz) Coconut Cream
1 Banana (diced)
Slice of Banana
Slice of Pineapple

Pour Rum, juice and cream into a blender over crushed ice then add diced banana. Blend and pour into a chilled hurricane glass. Garnish with a slice of banana and pineapple then serve with 2 straws.

Cocoa Colada

17.4% ALC/VOL • 1.8 STD DRINKS

45ml (1½ fl oz) Light Rum
15ml (½ fl oz) Coconut Liqueur
8ml (¼ fl oz) Kahlúa
45ml (1½ fl oz) Fresh Milk (chilled)
15ml (½ fl oz) Chocolate Syrup
Maraschino Cherry
Grated Chocolate

Pour Rum, Liqueur, Kahlúa, milk and syrup into a blender over crushed ice. Blend and pour into a chilled hurricane glass. Sprinkle chocolate on top and garnish with a cherry then serve with 2 straws.

Strawberry Banana Colada

6.4% ALC/VOL • 1.1 STD DRINKS

38ml (1¼ fl oz) Light Rum
60ml (2 fl oz) Coconut Cream
6 Strawberries (diced)
1 Banana (diced)
Slice of Banana
Strawberry

Pour Rum and cream into a blender over crushed ice. Add diced strawberries and diced banana. Blend and pour into a chilled hurricane glass. Garnish with a slice of banana and a strawberry then serve with 2 straws.

Blue Colada

10.8% ALC/VOL • 1.7 STD DRINKS

38ml (1¼ fl oz) Light Rum
30ml (1 fl oz) Blue Curaçao
90ml (3 fl oz) Pineapple Juice
40ml (1⅓ fl oz) Coconut Cream
1 teaspoon Thick Cream
Maraschino Cherry
Slice of Pineapple

Pour Rum, Curaçao, juice and creams into a blender over crushed ice. Blend and pour into a chilled hurricane glass. Garnish with a cherry and slice of pineapple then serve with 2 straws.

Chamborlada

14.5% ALC/VOL • 3.4 STD DRINKS

60ml (2 fl oz) Bacardi
60ml (2 fl oz) Chambord
30ml (1 fl oz) Dark Rum
90ml (3 fl oz) Pineapple Juice
60ml (2 fl oz) Coconut Cream

Pour 30ml (1 fl oz) Chambord into a chilled hurricane glass. Pour Bacardi, Rum, juice and cream into a blender over crushed ice. Blend and pour into glass over Chambord – do not stir. Layer remaining 30ml (1 fl oz) Chambord on top and serve with a straw.

Daiquiri

25.6% ALC/VOL • 1.4 STD DRINKS

45ml (1½ fl oz) Bacardi
5ml (⅙ fl oz) Grenadine
15ml (½ fl oz) Fresh Lime Juice

Pour ingredients into a cocktail shaker over ice and shake. Strain into a chilled cocktail glass and serve.

Kiwi Daiquiri

19.1% ALC/VOL • 1.6 STD DRINKS

30ml (1 fl oz) Bacardi
15ml (½ fl oz) Cointreau

15ml (½ fl oz) Midori
15ml (½ fl oz) Fresh Lime Juice
½ teaspoon Sugar Syrup
½ Kiwi Fruit (diced)
Slice of Kiwi Fruit

Pour Bacardi, Cointreau, Midori, juice and sugar into a blender over crushed ice then add diced kiwi fruit. Blend and pour into a chilled cocktail glass. Garnish with a slice of kiwi fruit and serve.

Galliano Daiquiri

26.3% ALC/VOL • 1.5 STD DRINKS

30ml (1 fl oz) Bacardi
20ml (⅔ fl oz) Galliano
15ml (½ fl oz) Fresh Lime Juice
1 teaspoon Sugar Syrup

Pour ingredients into a cocktail shaker over ice and shake. Strain into a chilled cocktail glass and serve.

Pineapple Daiquiri

21.4% ALC/VOL • 2.2 STD DRINKS

60ml (2 fl oz) Bacardi
15ml (½ fl oz) Cointreau
15ml (½ fl oz) Fresh Lemon Juice
15ml (½ fl oz) Fresh Lime Juice
6 Pieces of Pineapple (diced)
Slice of Pineapple

Pour Bacardi, Cointreau and juices into a blender over crushed ice then add diced pineapple. Blend and pour into a chilled champagne saucer. Garnish with a slice of pineapple and serve.

La Florida Daiquiri

23.5% ALC/VOL • 1.9 STD DRINKS

60ml (2 fl oz) Bacardi
5ml (⅙ fl oz) Maraschino Liqueur
30ml (1 fl oz) Fresh Lime Juice
1 teaspoon Sugar Syrup

Pour ingredients into a blender over crushed ice and blend. Pour into a chilled goblet and serve with 2 short straws.

Banana Daiquiri

14.2% ALC/VOL • 1.2 STD DRINKS

30ml (1 fl oz) Bacardi
15ml (½ fl oz) Banana Liqueur
30ml (1 fl oz) Fresh Lemon Juice
½ Banana (diced)
Slice of Banana

Pour Bacardi, Liqueur and juice into a blender over crushed ice then add diced banana. Blend and pour into a chilled champagne saucer. Garnish with a slice of banana and serve.

Bacardi Daiquiri

24.4% ALC/VOL • 1.3 STD DRINKS

45ml (1½ fl oz) Bacardi
5ml (⅙ fl oz) Grenadine
15ml (½ fl oz) Fresh Lemon or Lime Juice
1 teaspoon Egg White
Maraschino Cherry

Pour Bacardi, Grenadine, juice and egg white into a cocktail shaker over ice. Shake and strain into a chilled cocktail glass. Garnish with a cherry and serve.

Peach Daiquiri

11.4% ALC/VOL • 1.6 STD DRINKS

45ml (1½ fl oz) Bacardi
15ml (½ fl oz) Peach Liqueur
30ml (1 fl oz) Fresh Lemon Juice
1 Peach (diced)
Slice of Peach

Pour Bacardi, Liqueur and juice into a blender over crushed ice then add diced peach. Blend and pour into a chilled champagne saucer. Garnish with a slice of peach and serve.

French Daiquiri

20.8% ALC/VOL • 0.6 STD DRINKS

20ml (⅔ fl oz) Bacardi
Dash Crème De Cassis
15ml (½ fl oz) Fresh Lime Juice
Dash Sugar Syrup
Sprig of Fresh Mint

Pour Bacardi, Cassis, juice and sugar into a cocktail shaker over ice. Shake and strain into a chilled cocktail glass. Garnish with a sprig of mint and serve.

Strawberry Daiquiri

16% ALC/VOL • 1.6 STD DRINKS

30ml (1 fl oz) Bacardi
15ml (½ fl oz) Cointreau
15ml (½ fl oz) Strawberry Liqueur
30ml (1 fl oz) Fresh Lemon Juice
4 Strawberries (diced)
Strawberry

Pour Bacardi, Cointreau, Liqueur and juice into a blender over crushed ice then add diced strawberries. Blend and pour into a chilled champagne saucer. Garnish with a strawberry and serve.

Apple Daiquiri

21.1% ALC/VOL • 1.3 STD DRINKS

45ml (1½ fl oz) Bacardi
15ml (½ fl oz) Apple Juice
15ml (½ fl oz) Fresh Lime Juice
1 teaspoon Sugar Syrup

Pour ingredients into a cocktail shaker over crushed ice and shake. Strain into a chilled cocktail glass and serve.

Banana Daiquiri No.2

13.4% ALC/VOL • 1.8 STD DRINKS

45ml (1½ fl oz) Bacardi
15ml (½ fl oz) Cointreau
45ml (1½ fl oz) Fresh Lime Juice
1 teaspoon Sugar Syrup
1 Banana (diced)
Maraschino Cherry
Slice of Banana

Pour Bacardi, Cointreau, juice and sugar into a blender over crushed ice then add diced banana. Blend and pour into a chilled champagne saucer. Garnish with a cherry and slice of banana then serve.

Daiquiri Nacional

24.9% ALC/VOL • 2.2 STD DRINKS

45ml (1½ fl oz) Bacardi
45ml (1½ fl oz) Apricot Brandy
15ml (½ fl oz) Fresh Lime Juice
1 teaspoon Sugar Syrup

Pour ingredients into a blender over crushed ice and blend. Pour into a chilled cocktail glass and serve.

Cherry Daiquiri

26.8% ALC/VOL • 2.3 STD DRINKS

45ml (1½ fl oz) Bacardi
30ml (1 fl oz) Cherry Brandy
15ml (½ fl oz) Kirsch
15ml (½ fl oz) Fresh Lime Juice
1 teaspoon Sugar Syrup
Maraschino Cherry
Twist of Lime Peel

Pour Bacardi, Brandy, Kirsch, juice and sugar into a cocktail shaker over ice. Shake and strain into a chilled cocktail glass. Garnish with a cherry and lime peel then serve.

Daiquiri Blossom

18.6% ALC/VOL • 0.9 STD DRINKS

30ml (1 fl oz) Bacardi
Dash Maraschino Liqueur
30ml (1 fl oz) Fresh Orange Juice

Pour ingredients into a cocktail shaker over ice and shake. Strain into a chilled cocktail glass and serve.

Mango Daiquiri

11.5% ALC/VOL • 1.6 STD DRINKS

30ml (1 fl oz) Bacardi
15ml (½ fl oz) Cointreau
15ml (½ fl oz) Mango Liqueur
30ml (1 fl oz) Fresh Lemon Juice
1 Mango (diced)
Slice of Mango

Pour Bacardi, Cointreau, Liqueur and juice into a blender over crushed ice then add diced mango. Blend and pour into a chilled champagne saucer. Garnish with a slice of mango and serve.

Coconut Daiquiri

20.9% ALC/VOL • 1.9 STD DRINKS

45ml (1½ fl oz) Bacardi
30ml (1 fl oz) Coconut Liqueur
30ml (1 fl oz) Fresh Lime Juice
1 teaspoon Sugar Syrup
1 teaspoon Egg White

Pour ingredients into a cocktail shaker over ice and shake. Strain into a chilled cocktail glass and serve.

Rockmelon Daiquiri

11.9% ALC/VOL • 2.6 STD DRINKS

45ml (1½ fl oz) Bacardi
30ml (1 fl oz) Cointreau
20ml (⅔ fl oz) Mango Liqueur
20ml (⅔ fl oz) Fresh Lemon Juice
⅓ Rockmelon (diced)

Pour Bacardi, Countreau, Liqueur and juice into a blender over crushed ice then add diced rockmelon. Blend and pour into a chilled champagne saucer then serve.

Orange Daiquiri

16.3% ALC/VOL • 1.8 STD DRINKS

60ml (2 fl oz) Bacardi
60ml (2 fl oz) Fresh Orange Juice
15ml (½ fl oz) Fresh Lime Juice
1 teaspoon Sugar Syrup
Slice of Orange

Pour Bacardi, juices and sugar into a cocktail shaker over ice. Shake and strain into a chilled cocktail glass. Garnish with a slice of orange and serve.

Mandarin Daiquiri

29.3% ALC/VOL • 2 STD DRINKS

45ml (1½ fl oz) Bacardi
23ml (¾ fl oz) Mandarine Napoleon
15ml (½ fl oz) Fresh Lime Juice
1 teaspoon Sugar Syrup
Maraschino Cherry
Slice of Orange

Pour Bacardi, Mandarine Napoleon, juice and sugar into a blender over crushed ice. Blend and pour into a chilled cocktail glass. Garnish with a cherry and slice of orange then serve.

Passion Daiquiri

18.5% ALC/VOL • 1.8 STD DRINKS

60ml (2 fl oz) Bacardi
30ml (1 fl oz) Fresh Lime Juice
30ml (1 fl oz) Passion-Fruit Juice
½ teaspoon Sugar Syrup

Pour ingredients into a cocktail shaker over ice and shake. Strain into a chilled cocktail glass and serve. *This drink is also known as Passionate Daiquiri.*

Passionate Daiquiri

18.5% ALC/VOL • 1.8 STD DRINKS

This drink is also known as Passion Daiquiri (above).

King's Daiquiri

22.3% ALC/VOL • 1.3 STD DRINKS

15ml (½ fl oz) Bacardi
15ml (½ fl oz) Cointreau
15ml (½ fl oz) Parfait Amour
15ml (½ fl oz) Fresh Lemon Juice
½ teaspoon Sugar Syrup
1 teaspoon Egg White

Pour ingredients into a cocktail shaker over ice and shake. Strain into a chilled cocktail glass and serve.

Daiquiri Liberal

29.7% ALC/VOL • 2.1 STD DRINKS

60ml (2 fl oz) Bacardi
30ml (1 fl oz) Sweet Vermouth
Dash Amer Picon

Pour ingredients into a mixing glass over ice and stir. Strain into a chilled cocktail glass and serve.

Derby Daiquiri

18% ALC/VOL • 1.3 STD DRINKS

45ml (1½ fl oz) Bacardi
30ml (1 fl oz) Fresh Orange Juice
15ml (½ fl oz) Fresh Lime Juice
1 teaspoon Sugar Syrup

Pour ingredients into a cocktail shaker over ice and shake. Strain into a chilled cocktail glass and serve.

Lime Daiquiri

26.4% ALC/VOL • 2 STD DRINKS

45ml (1½ fl oz) Bacardi
20ml (⅔ fl oz) Cointreau
30ml (1 fl oz) Fresh Lime Juice

Pour ingredients into a cocktail shaker over ice and shake. Strain into a chilled cocktail glass and serve.

The All-American Daiquiri

9.9% ALC/VOL • 1.4 STD DRINKS

Step 1:

23ml (¾ fl oz) Bacardi
45ml (1½ fl oz) Sweet and Sour Mix
15ml (½ fl oz) Blueberry Syrup

Step 2:

23ml (¾ fl oz) Bacardi
60ml (2 fl oz) Strawberry Daiquiri Mix

Step 3:

Fresh Whipped Cream
Maraschino Cherry

Blend steps 1 and 2 separately over crushed ice until thick then layer steps in order into a chilled margarita glass. Float cream on top and garnish with a cherry then serve.

Frozen Apple Daiquiri

21.4% ALC/VOL • 1.4 STD DRINKS

45ml (1½ fl oz) Bacardi
15ml (½ fl oz) Apple Juice
15ml (½ fl oz) Fresh Lemon Juice
1 teaspoon Sugar Syrup
Wedge of Apple

Pour Bacardi, juices and sugar into a blender over crushed ice. Blend and pour into a chilled champagne saucer. Add a wedge of apple and serve.

Frozen Passion-Fruit Daiquiri

17.4% ALC/VOL • 1.3 STD DRINKS

45ml (1½ fl oz) Bacardi
15ml (½ fl oz) Fresh Lime Juice
15ml (½ fl oz) Fresh Orange Juice
15ml (½ fl oz) Passion-Fruit Syrup
8ml (¼ fl oz) Fresh Lemon Juice

Pour ingredients into a blender over crushed ice and blend. Pour into a chilled champagne saucer and serve.

Frozen Strawberry Daiquiri

14.6% ALC/VOL • 1.4 STD DRINKS

45ml (1½ fl oz) Bacardi
2 dashes Maraschino Liqueur
15ml (½ fl oz) Fresh Lime Juice
15ml (½ fl oz) Thick Cream
1 teaspoon Sugar Syrup
4 Strawberries (diced)

Pour Bacardi, Liqueur, juice, cream and sugar into a blender over crushed ice then add diced strawberries. Blend and pour into a chilled champagne saucer then serve.

Frozen Banana Daiquiri

18% ALC/VOL • 1.3 STD DRINKS

45ml (1½ fl oz) Bacardi

15ml (½ fl oz) Fresh Lime Juice
1 teaspoon Sugar Syrup
½ Banana (diced)

Pour Bacardi, juice and sugar into a blender over crushed ice then add diced banana. Blend and pour into a chilled champagne saucer then serve.

Frozen Soursop Daiquiri

16.5% ALC/VOL • 1.6 STD DRINKS

45ml (1½ fl oz) Bacardi
8ml (¼ fl oz) Jamaica Rum
30ml (1 fl oz) Guanabana Nectar
8ml (¼ fl oz) Fresh Lime Juice
½ Banana (diced)

Pour Bacardi, Rum, nectar and juice into a blender over crushed ice then add diced banana. Blend and pour into a chilled champagne saucer then serve.

Frozen Mint Daiquiri

30.4% ALC/VOL • 1.8 STD DRINKS

60ml (2 fl oz) Bacardi
10ml (⅓ fl oz) Fresh Lime Juice
1 teaspoon Sugar Syrup
6 Fresh Mint Leaves

Pour Bacardi, juice and sugar into a blender over crushed ice then add mint leaves. Blend and pour into a chilled old-fashioned glass then serve.

Frozen Sesame Daiquiri

18.9% ALC/VOL • 1.6 STD DRINKS

45ml (1½ fl oz) Bacardi
15ml (½ fl oz) Dry Vermouth
15ml (½ fl oz) Fresh Lime Juice
15ml (½ fl oz) Fresh Orange Juice
15ml (½ fl oz) Sesame-Seed Syrup

Pour ingredients into a blender over crushed ice and blend. Pour into a chilled champagne saucer and serve.

Frozen Peach Daiquiri

16.3% ALC/VOL • 1.4 STD DRINKS

45ml (1½ fl oz) Bacardi
15ml (½ fl oz) Fresh Lime Juice
15ml (½ fl oz) Peach Syrup
¼ Cup Fresh Peach (diced)

Pour Bacardi, juice and syrup into a blender over crushed ice then add diced peach. Blend and pour into a chilled champagne saucer then serve.

Frozen Pineapple Daiquiri

21.5% ALC/VOL • 1.3 STD DRINKS

45ml (1½ fl oz) Bacardi
10ml (⅓ fl oz) Fresh Lime Juice
½ teaspoon Sugar Syrup
4 Pieces of Pineapple

Pour Bacardi, juice and sugar into a blender over crushed ice then add pieces of pineapple. Blend and pour into a chilled champagne saucer then serve.

Frozen Guava-Orange Daiquiri

17.4% ALC/VOL • 1.3 STD DRINKS

45ml (1½ fl oz) Bacardi
23ml (¾ fl oz) Guava Syrup
15ml (½ fl oz) Fresh Lime Juice
15ml (½ fl oz) Fresh Orange Juice

Pour ingredients into a blender over crushed ice and blend. Pour into a chilled champagne saucer and serve.

Frozen Sherry Daiquiri

12.7% ALC/VOL • 0.9 STD DRINKS

45ml (1½ fl oz) Bacardi
60ml (2 fl oz) Medium-Dry Sherry
15ml (½ fl oz) Fresh Lime Juice
2 teaspoons Sugar Syrup

Pour ingredients into a blender over crushed ice and blend. Pour into a chilled champagne saucer and serve.

Frozen Guava Daiquiri

19.2% ALC/VOL • 1.4 STD DRINKS

45ml (1½ fl oz) Bacardi
5ml (⅙ fl oz) Banana Liqueur
30ml (1 fl oz) Guava Nectar
15ml (½ fl oz) Fresh Lime Juice

Pour ingredients into a blender over crushed ice and blend. Pour into a chilled champagne saucer and serve.

Frozen Daiquiri

26.3% ALC/VOL • 1.4 STD DRINKS

This drink is a Daiquiri (p. 174) served in a collins glass over shaved ice with 2 straws.

A dash of Maraschino Liqueur may be added if desired.

Vodka

Vodka originated from Eastern Europe around the fourteenth century, perhaps even earlier. Traditional Russian Vodka is distilled from potatoes with fruit or herbs added during the distilling process to provide a hint of flavour to the Vodka.

Traditionally in Russia, Vodka is served chilled in small glasses, these glasses are then smashed after a 'toast' is made.

Vodka translates as 'little Water'.

In the western nations, Vodka is distilled from grain to a neutral spirit and filtered through charcoal leaving a clear spirit with little or no scent or taste.

Vodkas are now being produced by distilling companies with flavours added such as: lemon, lime and other fruits as well as varieties like pepper and chilli vodkas.

Today Vodka is used extensively in cocktails for improving the 'kick' in a drink without disturbing the flavour. Vodka makes for a great addition to your favourite fruit juice.

Silver Sunset

9% ALC/VOL • 1.2 STD DRINKS

30ml (1 fl oz) Vodka
15ml (½ fl oz) Apricot Brandy
Dash Campari
90ml (3 fl oz) Fresh Orange Juice
30ml (1 fl oz) Fresh Lemon Juice
Dash Egg White

Pour ingredients into a cocktail shaker over ice and shake. Strain into a highball glass over ice and serve.

Sonic Blaster

10.9% ALC/VOL • 1.2 STD DRINKS

15ml (½ fl oz) Vodka
15ml (½ fl oz) Banana Liqueur
15ml (½ fl oz) Light Rum
30ml (1 fl oz) Cranberry Juice
30ml (1 fl oz) Fresh Orange Juice
30ml (1 fl oz) Pineapple Juice
Slice of Lime
Slice of Orange

Pour Vodka, Liqueur, Rum and juices into a cocktail shaker over ice. Shake and strain into a collins glass over ice. Garnish with a slice of lime and orange then serve.

Long Black Russian

15.6% ALC/VOL • 2.2 STD DRINKS

60ml (2 fl oz) Vodka
30ml (1 fl oz) Kahlúa
90ml (3 fl oz) Cola
Strawberry

Pour Vodka and Kahlúa into a highball glass over ice then stir. Add cola and stir gently. Garnish with a strawberry and serve.

Russian

32.4% ALC/VOL • 2.3 STD DRINKS

30ml (1 fl oz) Vodka
30ml (1 fl oz) Dry Gin
30ml (1 fl oz) White Crème De Cacao

Pour ingredients into a mixing glass over ice and stir. Strain into a chilled cocktail glass and serve.

Boca Chica

14.2% ALC/VOL • 1.6 STD DRINKS

30ml (1 fl oz) Vodka
23ml (¾ fl oz) Malibu

23ml (¾ fl oz) Pisang Ambon
60ml (2 fl oz) Guava Nectar
2 teaspoons Passion-Fruit Syrup
Maraschino Cherry
Slice of Orange

Pour Vodka, Malibu, Pisang Ambon, nectar and syrup into a cocktail shaker over ice. Shake and strain into a chilled cocktail glass. Garnish with a cherry and slice of orange then serve.

Goldberg

28.1% ALC/VOL • 2 STD DRINKS

45ml (1½ fl oz) Vodka
15ml (½ fl oz) Banana Liqueur
15ml (½ fl oz) Galliano
15ml (½ fl oz) Fresh Orange Juice

Pour ingredients into a cocktail shaker over ice and shake. Strain into a chilled cocktail glass and serve.

Black Forest

14.3% ALC/VOL • 2.1 STD DRINKS

30ml (1 fl oz) Vodka
30ml (1 fl oz) Cointreau
15ml (½ fl oz) Blackberry Liqueur
90ml (3 fl oz) Apple Juice
8 Raspberries

Pour Vodka, Cointreau, Liqueur and juice into a blender over cracked ice then add 4 raspberries. Blend and strain into a highball glass over ice. Coat 4 raspberries with sugar and float them on top then serve.

Vodka Cooler

7.9% ALC/VOL • 1.3 STD DRINKS

30ml (1 fl oz) Vodka
30ml (1 fl oz) Dry Vermouth
60ml (2 fl oz) Grapefruit Juice
90ml (3 fl oz) Tonic Water

Pour Vodka, Vermouth and juice into a cocktail shaker over ice. Shake and strain into a collins glass over ice. Add tonic, stir gently and serve. *This drink is also known as Summertime.*

Goober

11.9% ALC/VOL • 1.9 STD DRINKS

23ml (¾ fl oz) Vodka
23ml (¾ fl oz) Midori
23ml (¾ fl oz) Raspberry Liqueur
15ml (½ fl oz) Cointreau
15ml (½ fl oz) Grenadine
60ml (2 fl oz) Fresh Orange Juice
45ml (1½ fl oz) Pineapple Juice
Maraschino Cherry
Slice of Orange

Pour Vodka, Midori, Liqueur, Cointreau, Grenadine and juices into a cocktail shaker over ice. Shake and strain into a collins glass over ice. Garnish with a cherry and slice of orange then serve with a straw.

Aberfoyle

38.2% ALC/VOL • 2.3 STD DRINKS

45ml (1½ fl oz) Vodka
30ml (1 fl oz) Drambuie

Pour ingredients into an old-fashioned glass filled with ice, stir and serve.

Foggy Afternoon

31.1% ALC/VOL • 1.7 STD DRINKS

30ml (1 fl oz) Vodka
15ml (½ fl oz) Apricot Brandy
15ml (½ fl oz) Cointreau
5ml (1/6 fl oz) Banana Liqueur
5ml (1/6 fl oz) Fresh Lemon Juice
Maraschino Cherry

Pour Vodka, Brandy, Cointreau, Liqueur and juice into a cocktail shaker over ice. Shake and strain into a chilled cocktail glass. Garnish with a cherry and serve.

Black Magic

31.1% ALC/VOL • 1.8 STD DRINKS

45ml (1½ fl oz) Vodka
23ml (¾ fl oz) Tia Maria
5ml (1/6 fl oz) Fresh Lime Juice
Wedge of Lime

Pour Vodka, Tia and juice into a cocktail shaker over cracked ice. Shake and pour into a chilled old-fashioned glass. Add a wedge of lime and serve.

Hairy Coconut

19.3% ALC/VOL • 1.7 STD DRINKS

30ml (1 fl oz) Vodka
15ml (½ fl oz) Amaretto
15ml (½ fl oz) Pisang Ambon
5ml (1/6 fl oz) Green Chartreuse
30ml (1 fl oz) Thick Cream
15ml (½ fl oz) Coconut Cream
Maraschino Cherry
Slice of Lime

Prepare a champagne saucer with a grated coconut frosted rim – moistened with egg white. Pour Vodka, Amaretto, Pisang Ambon, Chartreuse and creams into a cocktail shaker over ice. Shake and strain into prepared glass. Garnish with a cherry and slice of lime then serve.

Vodka Martini Sweet

28.2% ALC/VOL • 1.7 STD DRINKS

45ml (1½ fl oz) Vodka
30ml (1 fl oz) Sweet Vermouth

Pour ingredients into a mixing glass over ice and stir. Strain into a chilled martini glass and serve.

Blue Danube

25.7% ALC/VOL • 1 STD DRINK

15ml (½ fl oz) Vodka
10ml (⅓ fl oz) Banana Liqueur
10ml (⅓ fl oz) Blue Curaçao
10ml (⅓ fl oz) Triple Sec
1 teaspoon Fresh Cream
Red Cherry
Twist of Orange Peel
Wedge of Orange

Pour Vodka, Liqueur, Curaçao and Triple Sec into a mixing glass over ice. Stir and strain into a chilled cocktail glass then float cream on top. Garnish with a cherry, orange peel and wedge of orange then serve.

Brazen Hussy

30.8% ALC/VOL • 1.8 STD DRINKS

30ml (1 fl oz) Vodka
30ml (1 fl oz) Cointreau
15ml (½ fl oz) Fresh Lemon Juice

Pour ingredients into a cocktail shaker over ice and shake. Strain into a chilled cocktail glass and serve.

Frozen Citrus Neon

19.2% ALC/VOL • 2 STD DRINKS

45ml (1½ fl oz) Citrus Vodka
30ml (1 fl oz) Midori
15ml (½ fl oz) Blue Curaçao
30ml (1 fl oz) Sweet and Sour Mix
15ml (½ fl oz) Fresh Lime Juice
Cherry
Slice of Lemon

Pour Vodka, Midori, Curaçao, sour mix and juice into a blender over crushed ice. Blend until smooth and pour into a chilled parfait glass. Garnish with a cherry and slice of lemon then serve.

Madras

12.3% ALC/VOL • 1.7 STD DRINKS

60ml (2 fl oz) Vodka
60ml (2 fl oz) Cranberry Juice
60ml (2 fl oz) Fresh Orange Juice
Slice of Orange

Pour Vodka and juices into a highball glass over ice then stir. Garnish with a slice of orange and serve.

Peach Buck

10.7% ALC/VOL • 1.3 STD DRINKS

38ml (1¼ fl oz) Vodka
10ml (⅓ fl oz) Peach Brandy
90ml (3 fl oz) Dry Ginger Ale
½ Fresh Lemon
Slice of Lemon
Slice of Peach

Pour Vodka and Brandy into a cocktail shaker over ice. Shake and strain into an old-fashioned glass over ice. Twist ½ lemon above drink to release juice and add spent shell then stir. Add Ginger Ale and stir gently. Garnish with a slice of lemon and peach then serve.

Cossack

23.4% ALC/VOL • 1.8 STD DRINKS

30ml (1 fl oz) Vodka
30ml (1 fl oz) Brandy
30ml (1 fl oz) Fresh Lime Juice
1 teaspoon Sugar Syrup

Pour ingredients into a cocktail shaker over ice and shake. Strain into a chilled cocktail glass and serve.

Bunky Punch

12.9% ALC/VOL • 2.3 STD DRINKS

45ml (1½ fl oz) Vodka
30ml (1 fl oz) Midori
30ml (1 fl oz) Peach Schnapps
60ml (2 fl oz) Fresh Orange Juice
45ml (1½ fl oz) Cranberry Juice
15ml (½ fl oz) Grape Juice
Slice of Lime

Pour Vodka, Midori, Schnapps and juices into a blender over crushed ice. Blend until smooth and pour into a chilled parfait glass. Garnish with a slice of lime and serve.

Gold Rush

36.2% ALC/VOL • 2.1 STD DRINKS

45ml (1½ fl oz) Vodka
30ml (1 fl oz) Galliano
Twist of Lime Peel

Pour Vodka and Galliano into a mixing glass over ice. Stir and strain into an old-fashioned glass over ice. Twist lime peel above drink and place remainder of peel into drink then serve.

Lost Cherry

10.8% ALC/VOL • 1 STD DRINK

30ml (1 fl oz) Cherry Vodka
15ml (½ fl oz) White Crème De Cacao
8ml (¼ fl oz) White Crème De Menthe
30ml (1 fl oz) Fresh Orange Juice
30ml (1 fl oz) Thick Cream
Cherry
Slice of Orange

Pour Vodka, Cacao, Crème De Menthe, juice and cream into a cocktail shaker over ice. Shake and strain into a chilled cocktail glass. Garnish with a cherry and slice of orange then serve.

Pine Driver

9.2% ALC/VOL • 1.4 STD DRINKS

30ml (1 fl oz) Vodka
30ml (1 fl oz) Apricot Brandy
120ml (4 fl oz) Fresh Orange Juice
15ml (½ fl oz) Fresh Lemon Juice

Pour ingredients into a cocktail shaker over ice and shake. Strain into a collins glass over ice and serve.

Vodka Collins

12% ALC/VOL • 1.8 STD DRINKS

60ml (2 fl oz) Vodka
30ml (1 fl oz) Fresh Lemon Juice
1 teaspoon Sugar Syrup
90ml (3 fl oz) Soda Water
Maraschino Cherry
Slice of Lemon

Pour Vodka, juice and sugar into a collins glass over ice then stir. Add soda and stir gently. Garnish with a cherry and slice of lemon then serve.

Vodka Dry

35.1% ALC/VOL • 1.4 STD DRINKS

45ml (1½ fl oz) Vodka
5ml (1/6 fl oz) Dry Sherry
Wedge of Lemon

Pour Sherry into a brandy balloon and swirl around glass then discard remainder of Sherry. Pour Vodka into a mixing glass over ice and stir to chill. Strain into prepared glass and garnish with a wedge of lemon then serve.

Gables Collins

11.4% ALC/VOL • 2 STD DRINKS

45ml (1½ fl oz) Vodka
30ml (1 fl oz) Crème De Noyaux
15ml (½ fl oz) Fresh Lemon Juice
15ml (½ fl oz) Pineapple Juice
120ml (4 fl oz) Soda Water
Slice of Lemon
Slice of Pineapple

Pour Vodka, Noyaux and juices into a cocktail shaker over ice. Shake and strain into a collins glass over ice. Add soda and stir gently. Garnish with a slice of lemon and pineapple then serve.

Buckeye Martini

35% ALC/VOL • 2.1 STD DRINKS

68ml (2¼ fl oz) Vodka
8ml (¼ fl oz) Dry Vermouth
Black Olive

Pour Vodka and Vermouth into a mixing glass over ice. Stir and strain into a chilled martini glass. Add an olive and serve.

Chi Chi Cocktail

12% ALC/VOL • 1.6 STD DRINKS

45ml (1½ fl oz) Vodka
15ml (½ fl oz) Malibu
60ml (2 fl oz) Pineapple Juice
30ml (1 fl oz) Coconut Milk (chilled)
15ml (½ fl oz) Fresh Lemon or Lime Juice
Maraschino Cherry
Slice of Orange
Slice of Pineapple

Pour Vodka, Malibu, juices and milk into a cocktail shaker over ice. Shake and strain into a chilled champagne saucer. Garnish with a cherry, slice of orange and pineapple then serve.

Our Stanley

37.6% ALC/VOL • 2.2 STD DRINKS

45ml (1½ fl oz) Vodka
15ml (½ fl oz) Cointreau
15ml (½ fl oz) Gin

Pour ingredients into a mixing glass over ice and stir. Strain into a chilled cocktail glass and serve.

Pink Lemonade

9.9% ALC/VOL • 1.3 STD DRINKS

45ml (1½ fl oz) Citrus Vodka
3 dashes Cointreau
60ml (2 fl oz) Cranberry Juice
60ml (2 fl oz) Sweet and Sour Mix
3 dashes Fresh Lime Juice
Slice of Lemon

Pour Vodka, Cointreau, juices and sour mix into a cocktail shaker over ice. Shake and strain into a collins glass over ice. Garnish with a slice of lemon and serve.

Danielli

30.6% ALC/VOL • 2.2 STD DRINKS

60ml (2 fl oz) Vodka
30ml (1 fl oz) Dry Vermouth
2 dashes Campari
Wedge of Lemon

Pour Vodka, Vermouth and Campari into a mixing glass over ice. Stir and strain into a chilled cocktail glass. Garnish with a wedge of lemon and serve.

Long Island Tea

13.9% ALC/VOL • 2.6 STD DRINKS

30ml (1 fl oz) Vodka
30ml (1 fl oz) Dry Gin
30ml (1 fl oz) Light Rum
60ml (2 fl oz) Strong Black Tea (chilled)
90ml (3 fl oz) Cola
Slice of Lemon
Sprig of Fresh Mint

Pour Vodka, Gin, Rum and tea into a highball glass over ice then stir. Add cola and stir gently. Garnish with a slice of lemon and sprig of mint then serve.

Golden Tang

31.4% ALC/VOL • 3 STD DRINKS

60ml (2 fl oz) Vodka
30ml (1 fl oz) Strega
15ml (½ fl oz) Banana Liqueur
15ml (½ fl oz) Fresh Orange Juice

Pour ingredients into a cocktail shaker over ice and shake. Strain into a chilled goblet and serve.

Romanov

29.2% ALC/VOL • 2.4 STD DRINKS

45ml (1½ fl oz) Vodka
30ml (1 fl oz) Galliano
15ml (½ fl oz) Banana Liqueur
15ml (½ fl oz) Thick Cream
Maraschino Cherry
Slice of Banana

Pour Vodka, Galliano, Liqueur and cream into a blender over cracked ice. Blend and strain into a chilled cocktail glass. Garnish with a cherry and slice of banana then serve.

Katinka

26.2% ALC/VOL • 1.9 STD DRINKS

45ml (1½ fl oz) Vodka
30ml (1 fl oz) Apricot Brandy
15ml (½ fl oz) Fresh Lime Juice
Sprig of Fresh Mint

Pour Vodka, Brandy and juice into a cocktail shaker over ice. Shake and strain into a chilled cocktail glass. Garnish with a sprig of mint and serve.

Après Ski

14.6% ALC/VOL • 1.8 STD DRINKS

30ml (1 fl oz) Vodka
20ml (⅔ fl oz) Pernod
15ml (½ fl oz) Green Crème De Menthe
90ml (3 fl oz) Lemonade
Slice of Lemon
Sprig of Fresh Mint

Pour Vodka, Pernod and Crème De Menthe into a cocktail shaker over ice. Shake and strain into an old-fashioned glass over crushed ice. Add lemonade and stir gently. Garnish with a slice of lemon and sprig of mint then serve.

Red Russian

30% ALC/VOL • 1.4 STD DRINKS

30ml (1 fl oz) Vodka
15ml (½ fl oz) Apricot Brandy
15ml (½ fl oz) Cherry Brandy

Pour ingredients into a cocktail shaker over ice and shake. Strain into a chilled old-fashioned glass and serve.

Surf Rider

14.6% ALC/VOL • 1.5 STD DRINKS

45ml (1½ fl oz) Vodka
15ml (½ fl oz) Sweet Vermouth
Dash Grenadine
60ml (2 fl oz) Fresh Orange Juice
8ml (¼ fl oz) Fresh Lemon Juice
Maraschino Cherry
Slice of Orange

Pour Vodka, Vermouth, Grenadine and juices into a cocktail shaker over ice. Shake and strain into a chilled cocktail glass. Garnish with a cherry and slice of orange then serve.

Creamy Screwdriver

8.5% ALC/VOL • 1.7 STD DRINKS

60ml (2 fl oz) Vodka
180ml (6 fl oz) Fresh Orange Juice
1 teaspoon Sugar Syrup
Yolk of 1 Egg

Pour ingredients into a blender over cracked ice and blend. Strain into a collins glass over ice and serve.

Pinky

16.7% ALC/VOL • 2.1 STD DRINKS

60ml (2 fl oz) Vodka
15ml (½ fl oz) Galliano
Dash Strawberry Liqueur
15ml (½ fl oz) Grenadine
1½ scoops Vanilla Ice Cream
2 Strawberries (diced)
Strawberry

Pour Vodka, Galliano, Liqueur and Grenadine into a blender over cracked ice. Add ice cream and diced strawberries. Blend and strain into a chilled goblet. Garnish with a strawberry and serve.

Hairless Duck

13.5% ALC/VOL • 1.8 STD DRINKS

30ml (1 fl oz) Vodka
30ml (1 fl oz) Advocaat
15ml (½ fl oz) Bacardi
90ml (3 fl oz) Fresh Orange Juice

Pour ingredients into a cocktail shaker over ice and shake. Strain into a chilled highball glass and serve.

L.A. Sunrise

10.1% ALC/VOL • 1.4 STD DRINKS

30ml (1 fl oz) Vodka
15ml (½ fl oz) Banana Liqueur
8ml (¼ fl oz) Golden Rum
60ml (2 fl oz) Fresh Orange Juice
60ml (2 fl oz) Pineapple Juice

Maraschino Cherry
Slice of Lime

Pour Vodka, Liqueur and juices into a cocktail shaker over ice. Shake and strain into a hurricane glass over ice then layer Rum on top. Garnish with a cherry and slice of lime then serve.

Sarah

29.5% ALC/VOL • 1.3 STD DRINKS

30ml (1 fl oz) Vodka
15ml (½ fl oz) Dry Vermouth
5ml (⅙ fl oz) Banana Liqueur
5ml (⅙ fl oz) Campari

Pour ingredients into a mixing glass over ice and stir. Strain into a chilled cocktail glass and serve.

Moscow Mule

12.3% ALC/VOL • 1.7 STD DRINKS

60ml (2 fl oz) Vodka
30ml (1 fl oz) Fresh Lemon Juice
90ml (3 fl oz) Ginger Beer
Slice of Lemon
Sprig of Fresh Mint

Pour Vodka and juice into a highball glass over ice then stir. Add ginger beer and stir gently. Garnish with a slice of lemon and sprig of mint then serve.

Tall Sardinian

7.7% ALC/VOL • 1.3 STD DRINKS

30ml (1 fl oz) Vodka
30ml (1 fl oz) Cynar
60ml (2 fl oz) Fresh Orange Juice
90ml (3 fl oz) Tonic Water
Slice of Orange

Pour Vodka, Cynar and juice into a tall glass over ice then stir. Add tonic and stir gently. Garnish with a slice of orange and serve.

Hong Kong Fizz

14.7% ALC/VOL • 2.5 STD DRINKS

15ml (½ fl oz) Vodka
15ml (½ fl oz) Bénédictine
15ml (½ fl oz) Gin
15ml (½ fl oz) Green Chartreuse
15ml (½ fl oz) Yellow Chartreuse
15ml (½ fl oz) Fresh Lemon Juice
½ teaspoon Caster Sugar
120ml (4 fl oz) Soda Water

Pour Vodka, Bénédictine, Gin, Chartreuses and juice into a cocktail shaker over ice then add sugar. Shake and strain into a highball glass over ice. Add soda – do not stir, then serve with a swizzle stick.

Alvear Palace

26% ALC/VOL • 2.5 STD DRINKS

75ml (2½ fl oz) Vodka
15ml (½ fl oz) Apricot Brandy
30ml (1 fl oz) Pineapple Juice

Pour ingredients into a cocktail shaker over ice and shake. Strain into a chilled cocktail glass and serve.

Nectarine Cooler

11.5% ALC/VOL • 1.7 STD DRINKS

60ml (2 fl oz) Vodka
90ml (3 fl oz) Fresh Orange Juice
1 teaspoon Sugar Syrup
5ml (⅙ fl oz) Soda Water
½ Cup Nectarine (diced)
Slice of Lemon
Slice of Nectarine

Pour Vodka, juice and sugar into a blender over small amount of crushed ice then add diced nectarine. Blend and pour into a collins glass over ice then add soda – do not stir. Garnish with a slice of lemon and nectarine then serve.

Windex

35.7% ALC/VOL • 3 STD DRINKS

75ml (2½ fl oz) Vodka
15ml (½ fl oz) Blue Curaçao
15ml (½ fl oz) Cointreau

Pour ingredients into a mixing glass over ice and stir. Strain into a chilled cocktail glass and serve.

Mont Blanc

14.3% ALC/VOL • 1.4 STD DRINKS

30ml (1 fl oz) Vodka
30ml (1 fl oz) Raspberry Liqueur
30ml (1 fl oz) Fresh Cream
1 scoop Vanilla Ice Cream

Pour Vodka, Liqueur and cream into a blender without ice then add ice cream. Blend until smooth and pour into a chilled wine glass then serve.

Warlock

35.8% ALC/VOL • 2.3 STD DRINKS

45ml (1½ fl oz) Vodka
30ml (1 fl oz) Strega
5ml (⅙ fl oz) Fresh Lime Juice
Slice of Lime

Pour Vodka, Strega and juice into an old-fashioned glass over ice then stir. Garnish with a slice of lime and serve.

Ready Steady

18.1% ALC/VOL • 1.5 STD DRINKS

30ml (1 fl oz) Vodka
30ml (1 fl oz) Bailey's Irish Cream
15ml (½ fl oz) Sweet Sherry
30ml (1 fl oz) Thick Cream

Pour ingredients into a cocktail shaker over ice and shake. Strain into an old-fashioned glass over ice and serve.

Quick Finnish

19.6% ALC/VOL • 1.8 STD DRINKS

30ml (1 fl oz) Finlandia Vodka
23ml (¾ fl oz) Quetsch
5ml (1/6 fl oz) Dark Rum
60ml (2 fl oz) Cola

Pour Vodka, Quetsch and Rum into an old-fashioned glass over ice then stir. Add cola, stir gently and serve.

Vodka Fizz

9.1% ALC/VOL • 1.8 STD DRINKS

60ml (2 fl oz) Vodka
60ml (2 fl oz) Fresh Orange Juice
30ml (1 fl oz) Fresh Lemon Juice
1 teaspoon Caster Sugar
90ml (3 fl oz) Lemonade

Pour Vodka and juices into a cocktail shaker over ice then add sugar. Shake and strain into a highball glass over ice. Add lemonade, stir gently and serve.

Sweet Tart

9.2% ALC/VOL • 1.7 STD DRINKS

60ml (2 fl oz) Vodka
90ml (3 fl oz) Cranberry Juice
90ml (3 fl oz) Pineapple Juice
Dash Fresh Lemon Juice
Slice of Lemon

Pour Vodka and juices into a blender over crushed ice. Blend until smooth and pour into a chilled goblet. Garnish with a slice of lemon and serve.

Snow Flake

13.1% ALC/VOL • 1.9 STD DRINKS

30ml (1 fl oz) Vodka
15ml (½ fl oz) Galliano
15ml (½ fl oz) Southern Comfort
10ml (⅓ fl oz) Advocaat
20ml (⅔ fl oz) Fresh Orange Juice
Dash Fresh Cream
90ml (3 fl oz) Lemonade

Pour Vodka, Galliano, Southern Comfort, Advocaat, juice and cream into a cocktail shaker over ice. Shake and strain into a highball glass over ice. Add lemonade, stir gently and serve.

Black Eye

36.6% ALC/VOL • 1.7 STD DRINKS

45ml (1½ fl oz) Vodka
15ml (½ fl oz) Blackberry Brandy

Pour ingredients into a mixing glass over ice and stir. Strain into a chilled cocktail glass and serve.
This drink is also known as Duke's a Champ.

Pink Elephant

20.1% ALC/VOL • 1.8 STD DRINKS

23ml (¾ fl oz) Vodka
23ml (¾ fl oz) Galliano
23ml (¾ fl oz) Crème De Noyaux
Dash Grenadine
23ml (¾ fl oz) Fresh Orange Juice
23ml (¾ fl oz) Fresh Cream
Cinnamon

Pour Vodka, Galliano, Noyaux, Grenadine, juice and cream into a cocktail shaker over ice. Shake and strain into a chilled cocktail glass. Sprinkle cinnamon on top and serve.

Pink Pussy Cat

8.5% ALC/VOL • 1.3 STD DRINKS

45ml (1½ fl oz) Vodka
Dash Grenadine
150ml (5 fl oz) Pineapple Juice

Pour ingredients into a highball glass over ice, stir and serve.

French Kiss

22% ALC/VOL • 1.8 STD DRINKS

30ml (1 fl oz) Vodka
30ml (1 fl oz) Raspberry Liqueur
15ml (½ fl oz) Grand Marnier
30ml (1 fl oz) Thick Cream
Raspberry

Pour Vodka, Liqueur, Grand Marnier and cream into a cocktail shaker over ice. Shake and strain into a chilled champagne flute. Garnish with a raspberry and serve.

Lucky Dip

19.4% ALC/VOL • 2.3 STD DRINKS

60ml (2 fl oz) Vodka
30ml (1 fl oz) Banana Liqueur
White of 1 Egg
30ml (1 fl oz) Lemon Soda

Pour Vodka, Liqueur and egg white into a cocktail shaker over ice. Shake and strain into a chilled cocktail glass. Add soda, stir gently and serve.

Long Island Lemonade

13.4% ALC/VOL • 2.2 STD DRINKS

15ml (½ fl oz) Vodka
15ml (½ fl oz) Cointreau
15ml (½ fl oz) Gin
15ml (½ fl oz) Gold Tequila
15ml (½ fl oz) Light Rum
30ml (1 fl oz) Fresh Lemon Juice
15ml (½ fl oz) Sugar Syrup
90ml (3 fl oz) Lemonade
Slice of Lemon

Pour Vodka, Cointreau, Gin, Tequila, Rum, juice and sugar into a cocktail shaker over ice. Shake and strain into a highball glass over ice. Add lemonade and stir gently. Garnish with a slice of lemon and serve.

Vodka Stinger

36.5% ALC/VOL • 1.8 STD DRINKS

60ml (2 fl oz) Vodka
2 dashes White Crème De Menthe

Pour ingredients into a cocktail shaker over ice and shake. Strain into a chilled martini glass and serve.

Vodka Orange Special

19.7% ALC/VOL • 2.6 STD DRINKS

45ml (1½ fl oz) Vodka
30ml (1 fl oz) Cointreau
15ml (½ fl oz) Orange Curaçao
75ml (2½ fl oz) Fresh Orange Juice
Maraschino Cherry
Slice of Orange

Pour Vodka, Cointreau and Curaçao into a mixing glass over ice. Stir and strain into a collins glass over ice. Add juice and stir. Garnish with a cherry and slice of orange then serve.

Vodka Gimlet

24.7% ALC/VOL • 1.8 STD DRINKS

60ml (2 fl oz) Vodka
30ml (1 fl oz) Fresh Lime Juice
Wedge of Lime

Pour Vodka and juice into a cocktail shaker over ice. Shake and strain into a chilled cocktail glass. Garnish with a wedge of lime and serve.

Harvey Wallbanger

9.9% ALC/VOL • 1.3 STD DRINKS

30ml (1 fl oz) Vodka
15ml (½ fl oz) Galliano
120ml (4 fl oz) Fresh Orange Juice
Slice of Orange

Pour Vodka and juice into a highball glass over ice then stir. Add Galliano by pouring on top – do not stir, then garnish with a slice of orange and serve.

Blushin' Russian

19.9% ALC/VOL • 1.6 STD DRINKS

30ml (1 fl oz) Vodka
30ml (1 fl oz) Kahlúa
10ml (⅓ fl oz) Amaretto
30ml (1 fl oz) Thick Cream

Pour ingredients into a cocktail shaker over ice and shake. Strain into a chilled champagne flute and serve.

Albert 2000

33% ALC/VOL • 2.8 STD DRINKS

30ml (1 fl oz) Vodka
30ml (1 fl oz) Dry Vermouth
23ml (¾ fl oz) Cointreau
23ml (¾ fl oz) Mandarine Napoleon
Maraschino Cherry

Pour Vodka, Vermouth, Cointreau and Mandarine Napoleon into a cocktail shaker over ice. Shake and strain into an old-fashioned glass over ice. Garnish with a cherry and serve.

Bolshoi Punch

12.5% ALC/VOL • 1.2 STD DRINKS

30ml (1 fl oz) Vodka
8ml (¼ fl oz) Crème De Cassis
8ml (¼ fl oz) Light Rum
75ml (2½ fl oz) Fresh Lemon Juice
1 teaspoon Sugar Syrup

Pour ingredients into a cocktail shaker over ice and shake. Strain into an old-fashioned glass over ice and serve.

Island Delight

13% ALC/VOL • 1.4 STD DRINKS

30ml (1 fl oz) Cherry Vodka
15ml (½ fl oz) Dark Rum
15ml (½ fl oz) Light Rum
5ml (1/6 fl oz) Grenadine
30ml (1 fl oz) Fresh Whipped Cream
½ scoop Vanilla Ice Cream

Pour Vodka and Rums into a blender over small amount of crushed ice then add ice cream. Blend until smooth and pour into a chilled goblet. Float cream on top and add Grenadine by pouring over cream then serve.

Laura's Theme

26.1% ALC/VOL • 2.8 STD DRINKS

68ml (2¼ fl oz) Vodka
45ml (1½ fl oz) Cherry Brandy
23ml (¾ fl oz) Passion-Fruit Nectar

Pour ingredients into a mixing glass over ice and stir. Strain into a chilled cocktail glass and serve.

Banana Punch

13.9% ALC/VOL • 1.9 STD DRINKS

60ml (2 fl oz) Vodka
8ml (¼ fl oz) Apricot Brandy
15ml (½ fl oz) Fresh Lime Juice
90ml (3 fl oz) Soda Water
3 Slices of Banana
Sprig of Fresh Mint

Pour Vodka, Brandy and juice into a collins glass filled with crushed ice then stir. Add soda and stir gently. Add slices of banana and a sprig of mint then serve.

Czarine

30.5% ALC/VOL • 1.8 STD DRINKS

45ml (1½ fl oz) Vodka
15ml (½ fl oz) Apricot Brandy
15ml (½ fl oz) Dry Vermouth
Dash Angostura Bitters

Pour ingredients into a mixing glass over ice and stir. Strain into a chilled cocktail glass and serve.

Cherry Ripe

34.2% ALC/VOL • 2 STD DRINKS

45ml (1½ fl oz) Vodka
15ml (½ fl oz) Brandy
15ml (½ fl oz) Cherry Brandy
Maraschino Cherry

Pour Vodka and Brandies into a mixing glass over ice. Stir and strain into a chilled cocktail glass. Garnish with a cherry and serve.

Martian Cherry

16.2% ALC/VOL • 1.4 STD DRINKS

30ml (1 fl oz) Cherry Vodka
30ml (1 fl oz) Dry Vermouth
23ml (¾ fl oz) Sloe Gin
30ml (1 fl oz) Pineapple Juice

Pour ingredients into a cocktail shaker over ice and shake. Strain into a cocktail glass over cracked ice and serve.

Lawnmower

25% ALC/VOL • 1.8 STD DRINKS

30ml (1 fl oz) Vodka
30ml (1 fl oz) Dry Vermouth
30ml (1 fl oz) Midori
Dash Fresh Lime Juice
Maraschino Cherry
Slice of Lime

Pour Vodka, Vermouth, Midori and juice into a cocktail shaker over ice. Shake and strain into a chilled cocktail glass. Garnish with a cherry and slice of lime then serve.

Quiet Sunday

13.1% ALC/VOL • 2.5 STD DRINKS

60ml (2 fl oz) Vodka
30ml (1 fl oz) Amaretto
3 dashes Grenadine
150ml (5 fl oz) Fresh Orange Juice

Pour ingredients into a cocktail shaker over ice and shake. Strain into an old-fashioned glass over ice and serve.

Mint Collins

10.4% ALC/VOL • 1.9 STD DRINKS

60ml (2 fl oz) Vodka
10ml (⅓ fl oz) Green Crème De Menthe
30ml (1 fl oz) Fresh Lemon Juice
1 tablespoon Sugar Syrup
120ml (4 fl oz) Soda Water
Sprig of Fresh Mint

Pour Vodka, Crème De Menthe, juice and sugar into a cocktail shaker over ice. Shake and strain into a collins glass over ice. Add soda and stir gently. Garnish with a sprig of mint and serve.

Deb's Delight

28.8% ALC/VOL • 2.7 STD DRINKS

45ml (1½ fl oz) Vodka
45ml (1½ fl oz) Apricot Brandy
23ml (¾ fl oz) Anisette
1 teaspoon Fresh Cream

Pour Vodka, Brandy and Anisette into a mixing glass over cracked ice. Stir and pour into a chilled old-fashioned glass. Float cream on top and serve.

Melba Tonic

11.5% ALC/VOL • 1.8 STD DRINKS

45ml (1½ fl oz) Vodka
15ml (½ fl oz) Peach Liqueur
15ml (½ fl oz) Raspberry Liqueur
30ml (1 fl oz) Fresh Lemon Juice
1 teaspoon Sugar Syrup
90ml (3 fl oz) Tonic Water

Pour Vodka, Liqueurs, juice and sugar into a cocktail shaker over ice. Shake and strain into a chilled collins glass. Add tonic, stir gently and serve.

Bluebeard

31.8% ALC/VOL • 2.3 STD DRINKS

45ml (1½ fl oz) Vodka
30ml (1 fl oz) Cognac
15ml (½ fl oz) Blueberry Syrup

Pour ingredients into a mixing glass over ice and stir. Strain into a chilled brandy balloon and serve.

Polynesian Cocktail

16.8% ALC/VOL • 1.6 STD DRINKS

45ml (1½ fl oz) Vodka
15ml (½ fl oz) Cherry Brandy
30ml (1 fl oz) Fresh Lemon Juice
30ml (1 fl oz) Fresh Lime Juice
Maraschino Cherry

Prepare a cocktail glass with a sugar frosted rim – moistened with lime juice. Pour Vodka, Brandy and juices into a cocktail shaker over ice. Shake and strain into prepared glass. Garnish with a cherry and serve.

Handball Cooler

8.4% ALC/VOL • 1.3 STD DRINKS

45ml (1½ fl oz) Vodka
3 dashes Fresh Orange Juice
150ml (5 fl oz) Soda Water
Wedge of Lime

Pour Vodka into a collins glass over ice and add soda then stir gently. Add juice – do not stir, then garnish with a wedge of lime and serve.

Peach Feeler

26.8% ALC/VOL • 1.6 STD DRINKS

30ml (1 fl oz) Vodka
15ml (½ fl oz) Cointreau
15ml (½ fl oz) Crème De Cassis
15ml (½ fl oz) Fresh Lemon Juice
Twist of Lemon Peel

Pour Vodka, Cointreau, Cassis and juice into a cocktail shaker over ice. Shake and strain into a chilled cocktail glass. Twist lemon peel above drink and place remainder of peel into drink then serve.

Kampari

30.3% ALC/VOL • 1.8 STD DRINKS

45ml (1½ fl oz) Vodka
15ml (½ fl oz) Campari
15ml (½ fl oz) Dry Vermouth
Dash Fresh Lemon Juice
Slice of Lemon

Pour Vodka, Campari, Vermouth and juice into a cocktail shaker over ice. Shake and strain into a chilled cocktail glass. Garnish with a slice of lemon and serve.

Bay City Bomber

17% ALC/VOL • 2.7 STD DRINKS

15ml (½ fl oz) Vodka
15ml (½ fl oz) Cointreau
15ml (½ fl oz) Dry Gin
15ml (½ fl oz) Rum
15ml (½ fl oz) Tequila
8ml (¼ fl oz) 151-Proof Rum
30ml (1 fl oz) Cranberry Juice
30ml (1 fl oz) Fresh Orange Juice
30ml (1 fl oz) Pineapple Juice
30ml (1 fl oz) Sweet and Sour Mix
Maraschino Cherry
Slice of Orange

Pour Vodka, Cointreau, Gin, Rum, Tequila, juices and sour mix into a blender over crushed ice. Blend until smooth and pour into a chilled sour glass then layer 151-Proof Rum on top. Garnish with a cherry and slice of orange then serve.

Long Island Iced Tea

17% ALC/VOL • 2.2 STD DRINKS

15ml (½ fl oz) Vodka
15ml (½ fl oz) Cointreau
15ml (½ fl oz) Gin
15ml (½ fl oz) Light Rum
15ml (½ fl oz) Tequila
Dash Fresh Lemon Juice
90ml (3 fl oz) Cola
Slice of Lemon

Pour Vodka, Cointreau, Gin, Rum, Tequila and juice into a collins glass over ice then stir. Add cola and stir gently. Garnish with a slice of lemon and serve.

Vicker's Treat

10.3% ALC/VOL • 1.4 STD DRINKS

45ml (1½ fl oz) Vodka
2 dashes Orange Bitters
120ml (4 fl oz) Lemonade

Pour Vodka and Bitters into a highball glass over ice then stir. Add lemonade, stir gently and serve.

Tropical Iced Tea

13.5% ALC/VOL • 1.8 STD DRINKS

15ml (½ fl oz) Vodka
15ml (½ fl oz) Cointreau
15ml (½ fl oz) Dry Gin
15ml (½ fl oz) Golden Rum
15ml (½ fl oz) Grenadine
30ml (1 fl oz) Cranberry Juice
30ml (1 fl oz) Pineapple Juice
30ml (1 fl oz) Sweet and Sour Mix
Pineapple Spear
Slice of Orange

Pour Vodka, Cointreau, Gin, Rum, Grenadine, juices and sour mix into a mixing glass over ice. Stir and strain into a collins glass over ice. Garnish with a pineapple spear and slice of orange then serve.

Frightleberry Murzenquest

29.7% ALC/VOL • 1.9 STD DRINKS

30ml (1 fl oz) Vodka
15ml (½ fl oz) Cointreau
15ml (½ fl oz) Galliano
5ml (1/6 fl oz) Maraschino Liqueur
Dash Angostura Bitters
15ml (½ fl oz) Fresh Lime Juice

Maraschino Cherry

Pour Vodka, Cointreau, Galliano, Liqueur, Bitters and juice into a cocktail shaker over ice. Shake and strain into a chilled cocktail glass. Garnish with a cherry and serve.
This drink is also known as Scotch Frog. *p 199.*

Boston Gold

8.8% ALC/VOL • 1.1 STD DRINKS

30ml (1 fl oz) Vodka
15ml (½ fl oz) Banana Liqueur
120ml (4 fl oz) Fresh Orange Juice

Pour Vodka and Liqueur into a highball glass over ice then stir. Add juice, stir and serve.

Dreamy Monkey

10.2% ALC/VOL • 1.4 STD DRINKS

30ml (1 fl oz) Vodka
15ml (½ fl oz) Banana Liqueur
15ml (½ fl oz) Dark Crème De Cacao
30ml (1 fl oz) Fresh Cream
2 scoops Vanilla Ice Cream
½ Banana (diced)
Fresh Whipped Cream
2 Slices of Banana

Pour Vodka, Liqueur, Cacao and fresh cream into a blender without ice. Add ice cream and diced banana. Blend until smooth and pour into a chilled parfait glass. Float whipped cream on top and garnish with slices of banana then serve.

Godmother

34.6% ALC/VOL • 2.3 STD DRINKS

60ml (2 fl oz) Vodka
23ml (¾ fl oz) Amaretto

Pour ingredients into an old-fashioned glass over ice, stir and serve.

Nathalie

11.9% ALC/VOL • 1.8 STD DRINKS

30ml (1 fl oz) Cherry Vodka
23ml (¾ fl oz) Bourbon
15ml (½ fl oz) Punt e Mes
15ml (½ fl oz) Triple Sec
15ml (½ fl oz) Fresh Lemon Juice
90ml (3 fl oz) Lemonade

Pour Vodka, Bourbon, Punt e Mes, Triple Sec and juice into a cocktail shaker over ice. Shake and strain into a goblet over ice. Add lemonade, stir gently and serve.

Opal

32.1% ALC/VOL • 1.6 STD DRINKS

45ml (1½ fl oz) Vodka
10ml (⅓ fl oz) Banana Liqueur
5ml (⅙ fl oz) Campari
Dash Grenadine
2 dashes Fresh Lemon Juice

Pour ingredients into a mixing glass over ice and stir. Strain into a chilled cocktail glass and serve.

Sputnik

8.5% ALC/VOL • 1.7 STD DRINKS

38ml (1¼ fl oz) Vodka
38ml (1¼ fl oz) Peach Schnapps
90ml (3 fl oz) Fresh Orange Juice
90ml (3 fl oz) Fresh Cream
Slice of Peach

Pour Vodka, Schnapps, juice and cream into a cocktail shaker without ice. Stir well and add cracked ice. Shake and pour into a chilled goblet. Garnish with a slice of peach and serve.

Kretchma

24% ALC/VOL • 1.4 STD DRINKS

30ml (1 fl oz) Vodka
15ml (½ fl oz) White Crème De Cacao
5ml (⅙ fl oz) Grenadine
10ml (⅓ fl oz) Fresh Lemon Juice
Slice of Lemon

Pour Vodka, Cacao, Grenadine and juice into a cocktail shaker over ice. Shake and strain into a chilled old-fashioned glass. Garnish with a slice of lemon and serve.

Sea Breeze

31.5% ALC/VOL • 2.2 STD DRINKS

45ml (1½ fl oz) Vodka
15ml (½ fl oz) Blue Curaçao
15ml (½ fl oz) Dry Vermouth
15ml (½ fl oz) Galliano
Twist of Orange Peel

Pour Vodka, Curaçao, Vermouth and Galliano into an old-fashioned glass over ice then stir. Garnish with orange peel and serve.
This drink is also known as Gale at Sea.

Major Tom

31.4% ALC/VOL • 2.2 STD DRINKS

45ml (1½ fl oz) Vodka
15ml (½ fl oz) Cointreau
15ml (½ fl oz) Kirsch
15ml (½ fl oz) Grapefruit Juice

Pour ingredients into a cocktail shaker over ice and shake. Strain into a chilled cocktail glass and serve.
This drink is also known as Fish Lips.

Caribbean Cruise

9.4% ALC/VOL • 1.3 STD DRINKS

30ml (1 fl oz) Vodka
8ml (¼ fl oz) Light Rum
8ml (¼ fl oz) Malibu
3 dashes Grenadine
120ml (4 fl oz) Pineapple Juice
Maraschino Cherry

Wedge of Pineapple

Pour Vodka, Rum, Malibu and Grenadine into a cocktail shaker over ice. Shake and strain into a collins glass over ice. Add juice and stir. Garnish with a cherry and wedge of pineapple then serve.

Vodka Mist

37% ALC/VOL • 1.3 STD DRINKS

45ml (1½ fl oz) Vodka
Twist of Lemon Peel

Pour Vodka into an old-fashioned glass over ice and twist lemon peel above drink. Place remainder of peel into drink and serve.

Long Neck

21.6% ALC/VOL • 1.8 STD DRINKS

45ml (1½ fl oz) Vodka
30ml (1 fl oz) Midori
Dash Grenadine
30ml (1 fl oz) Fresh Lemon Juice

Pour Vodka, Midori and juice into a blender over crushed ice. Blend until frozen and pour into a chilled old-fashioned glass. Add Grenadine – do not stir, then serve.

Quaalude

25.6% ALC/VOL • 1.9 STD DRINKS

30ml (1 fl oz) Vodka
30ml (1 fl oz) Frangelico
30ml (1 fl oz) Kahlúa
5ml (1/6 fl oz) Fresh Milk (chilled)

Pour ingredients into an old-fashioned glass over ice, stir and serve.

Svetlana

36.5% ALC/VOL • 2.2 STD DRINKS

45ml (1½ fl oz) 100-Proof Vodka
15ml (½ fl oz) Sweet Vermouth
8ml (¼ fl oz) Kirsch
8ml (¼ fl oz) Fresh Orange Juice
Twist of Orange Peel

Pour Vodka, Vermouth, Kirsch and juice into a cocktail shaker over ice. Shake and strain into a chilled cocktail glass. Twist orange peel above drink and place remainder of peel into drink then serve.

Thank Heaven for Small Nurses

18.8% ALC/VOL • 1.7 STD DRINKS

30ml (1 fl oz) Lemon Vodka
15ml (½ fl oz) Drambuie
8ml (¼ fl oz) Bénédictine
60ml (2 fl oz) Mandarin Juice
Cherry

Pour Vodka, Drambuie, Bénédictine and juice into a cocktail shaker over ice. Shake and strain into an old-fashioned glass over cracked ice. Garnish with a cherry and serve.

Brazilian Mule

9% ALC/VOL • 1.3 STD DRINKS

30ml (1 fl oz) Vodka
15ml (½ fl oz) Green Ginger Wine
15ml (½ fl oz) Peppermint Schnapps
30ml (1 fl oz) Black Coffee (chilled)
Dash Sugar Syrup
90ml (3 fl oz) Ginger Beer

Pour Vodka, Wine, Schnapps, coffee and sugar into a cocktail shaker over ice. Shake and strain into a highball glass over ice. Add ginger beer, stir gently and serve.

Desert Shield

11% ALC/VOL • 1.6 STD DRINKS

45ml (1½ fl oz) Vodka
15ml (½ fl oz) Cranberry Liqueur
120ml (4 fl oz) Cranberry Juice

Pour ingredients into a chilled highball glass, stir and serve.

Casco Bay Lemonade

9.2% ALC/VOL • 1.2 STD DRINKS

45ml (1½ fl oz) Citrus Vodka
120ml (4 fl oz) Sweet and Sour Mix
3 dashes Cranberry Juice
3 dashes Lemon-Lime Soda
Slice of Lemon

Pour Vodka, sour mix and juice into a cocktail shaker over ice. Shake and strain into a collins glass over ice. Add soda – do not stir, then garnish with a slice of lemon and serve.

Kiwi Martini

18.4% ALC/VOL • 1.8 STD DRINKS

60ml (2 fl oz) Vodka
Dash Sugar Syrup
1 Fresh Kiwi Fruit (crushed)
Slice of Kiwi Fruit

Pour Vodka and sugar into a cocktail shaker over ice then add crushed kiwi fruit. Shake and strain into a chilled martini glass. Garnish with a slice of kiwi fruit and serve.

Grand Master

26.4% ALC/VOL • 1.6 STD DRINKS

30ml (1 fl oz) Vodka
15ml (½ fl oz) Dry Vermouth
15ml (½ fl oz) Grand Marnier
15ml (½ fl oz) Fresh Lime Juice
Maraschino Cherry
Slice of Lime

Pour Vodka, Vermouth, Grand Marnier and juice into a mixing glass over ice. Stir and strain into a collins glass over ice. Top up with soda water if desired and stir gently. Garnish with a cherry and slice of lime then serve.

Breakfast Martini

34.2% ALC/VOL • 1.8 STD DRINKS

60ml (2 fl oz) Vodka
1 teaspoon Marmalade

Pour Vodka into a cocktail shaker over ice and add marmalade. Shake and strain into a chilled martini glass then serve.

Dulcet

27.7% ALC/VOL • 2.1 STD DRINKS

30ml (1 fl oz) Vodka
15ml (½ fl oz) Anisette
15ml (½ fl oz) Apricot Brandy
15ml (½ fl oz) Apricot Liqueur
15ml (½ fl oz) Curaçao
5ml (1/6 fl oz) Fresh Lemon Juice

Pour Vodka, Anisette, Liqueur, Curaçao and juice into a cocktail shaker over ice. Shake and strain into a chilled old-fashioned glass. Add Brandy by pouring on top – do not stir, then serve.

Vodka Martini

33.8% ALC/VOL • 2.4 STD DRINKS

75ml (2½ fl oz) Vodka
15ml (½ fl oz) Dry Vermouth
Twist of Lemon Peel

Pour Vodka and Vermouth into a mixing glass over ice. Stir and strain into a chilled martini glass. Garnish with lemon peel and serve.

Marnouchka

12.9% ALC/VOL • 1.8 STD DRINKS

30ml (1 fl oz) Vodka
30ml (1 fl oz) Grand Marnier
120ml (4 fl oz) Fresh Orange Juice
Maraschino Cherry

Pour Vodka, Grand Marnier and juice into a chilled collins glass then stir well. Garnish with a cherry and serve.

Green Slammer

22.7% ALC/VOL • 2.1 STD DRINKS

45ml (1½ fl oz) Vodka
30ml (1 fl oz) Midori
15ml (½ fl oz) Amaretto
30ml (1 fl oz) Fresh Lemon Juice

Pour ingredients into a cocktail shaker over ice and shake. Strain into a chilled old-fashioned glass and serve.

John Daly

9.7% ALC/VOL • 1.3 STD DRINKS

38ml (1¼ fl oz) Citrus Vodka
8ml (¼ fl oz) Triple Sec
60ml (2 fl oz) Strong Black Tea (chilled)
60ml (2 fl oz) Lemonade
Wedge of Lemon

Pour Vodka and Triple Sec into a collins glass half filled with ice. Add tea and stir. Add lemonade and stir gently then add more ice to fill glass. Garnish with a wedge of lemon and serve.

Kremlin Colonel

27.8% ALC/VOL • 1.8 STD DRINKS

60ml (2 fl oz) Vodka
15ml (½ fl oz) Fresh Lime Juice
1 teaspoon Sugar Syrup
2 Fresh Mint Leaves

Pour Vodka, juice and sugar into a cocktail shaker over ice. Shake and strain into a chilled cocktail glass. Float mint leaves on top and serve.

Red Finnish

21.8% ALC/VOL • 1.9 STD DRINKS

30ml (1 fl oz) Finlandia Vodka
30ml (1 fl oz) Strawberry Brandy
30ml (1 fl oz) Pomegranate Juice
15ml (½ fl oz) Fresh Lime Juice
1 teaspoon Sugar Syrup
Cherry

Pour Vodka, Brandy, juices and sugar into a cocktail shaker over ice. Shake and strain into an old-fashioned glass over ice. Garnish with a cherry and serve.

Indian Summer

14.3% ALC/VOL • 1.4 STD DRINKS

30ml (1 fl oz) Vodka
30ml (1 fl oz) Kahlúa
60ml (2 fl oz) Pineapple Juice

Pour ingredients into a cocktail shaker over ice and shake. Strain into an old-fashioned glass over ice and serve.

El Nino

10.5% ALC/VOL • 1.7 STD DRINKS

30ml (1 fl oz) Vodka
30ml (1 fl oz) Peach Schnapps
15ml (½ fl oz) Blue Curaçao
60ml (2 fl oz) Fresh Orange Juice

60ml (2 fl oz) Pineapple Juice
5ml (1/6 fl oz) Soda Water
Cherry
Wedge of Pineapple

Pour Vodka, Schnapps, Curaçao and juices into a cocktail shaker over ice. Shake well and strain into a hurricane glass over ice. Add soda and stir gently. Garnish with a cherry and wedge of pineapple then serve.

Salty Dog

12.3% ALC/VOL • 1.7 STD DRINKS

60ml (2 fl oz) Vodka
120ml (4 fl oz) Grapefruit Juice

Pour ingredients into a highball glass over ice, stir and serve.

Patriot

18.8% ALC/VOL • 3.8 STD DRINKS

30ml (1 fl oz) Vodka
30ml (1 fl oz) Gin
30ml (1 fl oz) Light Rum
15ml (½ fl oz) Everclear
30ml (1 fl oz) Grenadine
60ml (2 fl oz) Grapefruit Juice
60ml (2 fl oz) Fresh Orange Juice

Pour Vodka, Gin, Rum and Everclear into a cocktail shaker over cracked ice. Shake and pour into a chilled hurricane glass then add Grenadine. Add juices, stir well and serve.

La Cabre

34.3% ALC/VOL • 1.8 STD DRINKS

45ml (1½ fl oz) Vodka
10ml (⅓ fl oz) Dry Vermouth
10ml (⅓ fl oz) Kümmel

Pour ingredients into a mixing glass over ice and stir. Strain into a chilled cocktail glass and serve.

Tropical Orchid

9.9% ALC/VOL • 1.6 STD DRINKS

38ml (1¼ fl oz) Citrus Vodka
15ml (½ fl oz) Grand Marnier
120ml (4 fl oz) Fresh Orange Juice
15ml (½ fl oz) Grapefruit Juice
15ml (½ fl oz) Rose's Lime Juice

Pour ingredients into a cocktail shaker over cracked ice and shake. Pour into a chilled old-fashioned glass and serve.

Deanne

32.3% ALC/VOL • 1.5 STD DRINKS

30ml (1 fl oz) Vodka
15ml (½ fl oz) Cointreau
15ml (½ fl oz) Sweet Vermouth
Wedge of Lemon

Pour Vodka, Cointreau and Vermouth into a mixing glass over ice. Stir and strain into a chilled cocktail glass. Garnish with a wedge of lemon and serve.

Evergreen No.2

9.3% ALC/VOL • 1.4 STD DRINKS

30ml (1 fl oz) Vodka
20ml (⅔ fl oz) Midori
10ml (⅓ fl oz) Orange Curaçao
45ml (1½ fl oz) Pineapple Juice
30ml (1 fl oz) Fresh Lime Juice
2 teaspoons Sugar Syrup
45ml (1½ fl oz) Soda Water

Pour Vodka, Midori, Curaçao, juices and sugar into a cocktail shaker over ice. Shake and strain into a highball glass over ice. Add soda, stir gently and serve.

Black Russian

31.4% ALC/VOL • 2.2 STD DRINKS

60ml (2 fl oz) Vodka
30ml (1 fl oz) Kahlúa
Strawberry

Pour Vodka and Kahlúa into a mixing glass over ice. Stir and strain into a chilled cocktail glass. Garnish with a strawberry and serve.

Fire Island Sunrise

18.6% ALC/VOL • 1.8 STD DRINKS

30ml (1 fl oz) Vodka
30ml (1 fl oz) Light Rum
30ml (1 fl oz) Fresh Orange Juice
Dash Cranberry Juice
30ml (1 fl oz) Lemonade

Pour Vodka, Rum and orange juice into an old-fashioned glass over ice then stir. Add lemonade and stir gently. Add cranberry juice – do not stir, then serve.

Vodka Daisy

23.4% ALC/VOL • 1.8 STD DRINKS

60ml (2 fl oz) Vodka
5ml (1/6 fl oz) Grenadine
30ml (1 fl oz) Fresh Lemon Juice
Slice of Lemon

Pour Vodka, Grenadine and juice into a cocktail shaker over ice. Shake and strain into a goblet over ice. Top up with soda water if desired and stir gently. Garnish with a slice of lemon and serve.

Addison Special

12.1% ALC/VOL • 1.3 STD DRINKS

45ml (1½ fl oz) Vodka
18ml (⅗ fl oz) Grenadine
75ml (2½ fl oz) Fresh Orange Juice
Cherry
Wedge of Orange

Pour Vodka, Grenadine and juice into a cocktail shaker over ice. Shake and strain into an old-fashioned glass over ice. Garnish with a cherry and wedge of orange then serve.

Georgia Punch

10.9% ALC/VOL • 1.6 STD DRINKS

45ml (1½ fl oz) Vodka
15ml (½ fl oz) Peach Schnapps
Dash Grenadine
120ml (4 fl oz) Lemonade

Pour Vodka, Schnapps and Grenadine into a collins glass over ice then stir. Add lemonade, stir gently and serve.

Operation Recoverer

14.4% ALC/VOL • 1.4 STD DRINKS

30ml (1 fl oz) Lemon Vodka
30ml (1 fl oz) Peach Schnapps
5ml (1/6 fl oz) Grenadine
60ml (2 fl oz) Mandarin Juice
Slice of Mandarin
Slice of Peach

Pour Vodka, Schnapps, Grenadine and juice into a cocktail shaker over ice. Shake and strain into an old-fashioned glass over cracked ice. Garnish with a slice of mandarin and peach then serve with a short straw.

Vodka Blue Lagoon

12.4% ALC/VOL • 1.5 STD DRINKS

30ml (1 fl oz) Vodka
30ml (1 fl oz) Blue Curaçao
90ml (3 fl oz) Lemonade

Prepare a collins glass with a sugar frosted rim. Pour Vodka and Curaçao into a mixing glass over ice. Stir and strain into prepared glass. Add lemonade, stir gently and serve.

Italian Screwdriver

8.4% ALC/VOL • 1.3 STD DRINKS

45ml (1½ fl oz) Citrus Vodka
90ml (3 fl oz) Fresh
Orange Juice
60ml (2 fl oz) Grapefruit Juice
3 dashes Dry Ginger Ale
Slice of Lime

Pour Vodka and juices into a mixing glass over ice. Stir and strain into a chilled highball glass. Add Ginger Ale – do not stir, then garnish with a slice of lime and serve.

Russian Caramel

12.3% ALC/VOL • 0.9 STD DRINKS

30ml (1 fl oz) Vodka
30ml (1 fl oz) Caramella
30ml (1 fl oz) Thick Cream
Nutmeg

Pour Vodka, caramella and cream into a cocktail shaker over ice. Shake and strain into a chilled cocktail glass. Sprinkle nutmeg on top and serve.

Sweet Red Pepper

5.4% ALC/VOL • 1.1 STD DRINKS

38ml (1¼ fl oz) Vodka
105ml (3½ fl oz) Tomato Juice
(chilled)
90ml (3 fl oz) Fresh
Orange Juice
15ml (½ fl oz) Fresh
Lime Juice
1½ teaspoons Worcestershire
Sauce
1 teaspoon Tabasco Sauce
Large pinch of Pepper
Large pinch of Salt

Pour Vodka, juices and sauces into a cocktail shaker over ice. Add pepper and salt. Shake well and strain into a chilled highball glass then serve.

Vodka Martini Medium

28.8% ALC/VOL • 1.7 STD DRINKS

45ml (1½ fl oz) Vodka
15ml (½ fl oz) Dry Vermouth
15ml (½ fl oz) Sweet Vermouth

Pour ingredients into a mixing glass over ice and stir. Strain into a chilled martini glass and serve.

Balticsub

11.8% ALC/VOL • 2.1 STD DRINKS

60ml (2 fl oz) Vodka
30ml (1 fl oz) Chambord
60ml (2 fl oz) Raspberry Juice
30ml (1 fl oz) Fresh Lime Juice
2 teaspoons Sugar Syrup
4 Raspberries

Pour Vodka, juices and sugar into a cocktail shaker over ice. Shake and strain into a highball glass over crushed ice then stir. Layer Chambord on top and garnish with raspberries then serve.

Patricia

25.6% ALC/VOL • 1.8 STD DRINKS

30ml (1 fl oz) Vodka
30ml (1 fl oz) Orange Curaçao
30ml (1 fl oz) Sweet Vermouth
Twist of Lemon Peel

Pour Vodka, Curaçao and Vermouth into a mixing glass over ice. Stir and strain into a chilled cocktail glass. Garnish with lemon peel and serve.

Flying Kangaroo

17.5% ALC/VOL • 1.9 STD DRINKS

30ml (1 fl oz) Vodka
30ml (1 fl oz) Bacardi
10ml (⅓ fl oz) Coconut
Liqueur
40ml (1⅓ fl oz) Pineapple Juice
20ml (⅔ fl oz) Fresh
Orange Juice

2 teaspoons Fresh Cream

Pour ingredients into a cocktail shaker over ice and shake. Strain into a highball glass half filled with crushed ice and serve with a straw.

Huntsman Cocktail

27.8% ALC/VOL • 1.8 STD DRINKS

45ml (1½ fl oz) Vodka
15ml (½ fl oz) Jamaica Rum
15ml (½ fl oz) Fresh Lime Juice
1 teaspoon Sugar Syrup

Pour ingredients into a cocktail shaker over ice and shake. Strain into a chilled cocktail glass and serve.

Isabella

14.7% ALC/VOL • 1.7 STD DRINKS

30ml (1 fl oz) Vodka
23ml (¾ fl oz) Cointreau
2 dashes Angostura Bitters
90ml (3 fl oz) Fresh Orange Juice
Maraschino Cherry
Slice of Orange

Pour Vodka, Cointreau, Bitters and juice into a mixing glass over ice. Stir and strain into a highball glass over ice. Garnish with a cherry and slice of orange then serve.

Cape Codder

8.5% ALC/VOL • 1.3 STD DRINKS

45ml (1½ fl oz) Vodka
150ml (5 fl oz) Cranberry Juice
Wedge of Lime

Pour Vodka and juice into a highball glass over ice then stir. Garnish with a wedge of lime and serve.

Pompanski

20% ALC/VOL • 1.3 STD DRINKS

30ml (1 fl oz) Polish Vodka
15ml (½ fl oz) Dry Vermouth
5ml (1/6 fl oz) Triple Sec
30ml (1 fl oz) Grapefruit Juice
Slice of Orange

Pour Vodka, Vermouth, Triple Sec and juice into a cocktail shaker over cracked ice. Shake and pour into a chilled old-fashioned glass. Garnish with a slice of orange and serve with a straw.

De la Ville

18.3% ALC/VOL • 1.9 STD DRINKS

60ml (2 fl oz) Vodka
10ml (⅓ fl oz) Campari
5ml (1/6 fl oz) Grenadine
60ml (2 fl oz) Grapefruit Juice

Pour ingredients into a cocktail shaker over ice and shake. Strain into a chilled cocktail glass and serve.

Blue Nuke

25.8% ALC/VOL • 4.6 STD DRINKS

30ml (1 fl oz) Vodka
30ml (1 fl oz) 151-Proof Bacardi
30ml (1 fl oz) Blueberry Schnapps
30ml (1 fl oz) Blue Curaçao
30ml (1 fl oz) Gin
75ml (2½ fl oz) Sweet and Sour Mix

Pour Vodka, Bacardi, Schnapps, Curaçao and Gin into a collins glass over ice then stir. Add sour mix, stir well and serve.

Glacier Mint

34.8% ALC/VOL • 2.1 STD DRINKS

45ml (1½ fl oz) Vodka
15ml (½ fl oz) Green Crème De Menthe
15ml (½ fl oz) Lemon Vodka

Pour ingredients into a mixing glass over ice and stir. Strain into a chilled cocktail glass and serve.

Vodka Aba Special

29% ALC/VOL • 5.7 STD DRINKS

180ml (6 fl oz) Vodka
23ml (¾ fl oz) White Crème De Cacao
45ml (1½ fl oz) Fresh Lemon Juice

Pour ingredients into a cocktail shaker over ice and shake. Strain into a chilled brandy balloon and serve.

Blenheim

16.7% ALC/VOL • 1.2 STD DRINKS

30ml (1 fl oz) Vodka
15ml (½ fl oz) Tia Maria
45ml (1½ fl oz) Fresh Orange Juice

Pour ingredients into a cocktail shaker over ice and shake. Strain into a chilled cocktail glass and serve.

Summer Hummer

9.3% ALC/VOL • 0.9 STD DRINKS

30ml (1 fl oz) Vodka
30ml (1 fl oz) Raspberry Syrup
60ml (2 fl oz) Lemonade
3 Fresh Mint Leaves
Slice of Green Apple
Slice of Red Apple

Pour Vodka and syrup into a highball glass over ice then stir. Add lemonade and stir gently. Garnish with mint leaves and slices of apple then serve with a straw.

Ninotchka

26.5% ALC/VOL • 1.1 STD DRINKS

30ml (1 fl oz) Vodka
15ml (½ fl oz) White Crème De Cacao

10ml (⅓ fl oz) Fresh
Lemon Juice
Slice of Lemon

Pour Vodka, Cacao and juice into a cocktail shaker over cracked ice. Shake and pour into a chilled old-fashioned glass. Garnish with a slice of lemon and serve.

Strawberry Cascade

9.2% ALC/VOL • 2.2 STD DRINKS

30ml (1 fl oz) Vodka
30ml (1 fl oz) Galliano
30ml (1 fl oz) Kahlúa
150ml (5 fl oz) Strawberry Purée
60ml (2 fl oz) Thick Cream
Strawberry

Pour Vodka, Galliano and cream into a blender over cracked ice then add purée. Blend and strain into a chilled goblet. Layer Kahlúa on top and garnish with a strawberry then serve.

Firefly

12% ALC/VOL • 1.8 STD DRINKS

60ml (2 fl oz) Vodka
5ml (1/6 fl oz) Grenadine
120ml (4 fl oz) Grapefruit Juice

Pour Vodka and juice into a highball glass over ice then stir. Add Grenadine by pouring into centre of drink – do not stir, then serve.

Dusty Dog

11.1% ALC/VOL • 2 STD DRINKS

60ml (2 fl oz) Vodka
15ml (½ fl oz) Crème De Cassis
Dash Angostura Bitters
5ml (1/6 fl oz) Fresh Lemon Juice
150ml (5 fl oz) Dry Ginger Ale
Wedge of Lemon

Pour Vodka, Cassis, Bitters and juice into a cocktail shaker over ice. Shake and strain into a highball glass over ice. Add Ginger Ale and stir gently. Garnish with a wedge of lemon and serve.

Pork Chop on Toast

20% ALC/VOL • 1.9 STD DRINKS

30ml (1 fl oz) Cherry Vodka
30ml (1 fl oz) Russian Vodka
60ml (2 fl oz) Tonic Water
Cherry

Pour Vodkas into a cocktail shaker over ice and shake. Strain into an old-fashioned glass over cracked ice and add tonic then stir gently. Garnish with a cherry and serve.

Vodka Fraise

26.5% ALC/VOL • 1.7 STD DRINKS

23ml (¾ fl oz) Vodka
23ml (¾ fl oz) Light Rum
15ml (½ fl oz) Fraises De Bois
3 dashes Grenadine
15ml (½ fl oz) Fresh Lime Juice
½ Strawberry

Prepare a cocktail glass with a sugar frosted rim – moistened with Fraises De Bois.
Pour Vodka, Rum, Fraises, Grenadine and juice into a cocktail shaker over ice. Shake and strain into prepared glass. Float ½ strawberry on top and serve.

Violent Lady

32.4% ALC/VOL • 3.1 STD DRINKS

30ml (1 fl oz) Vodka
30ml (1 fl oz) Bacardi
30ml (1 fl oz) Dry Vermouth
30ml (1 fl oz) Gin

Pour ingredients into a mixing glass over ice and stir. Strain into a chilled cocktail glass and serve.

Bitter-Lemon Bracer

9.9% ALC/VOL • 1.8 STD DRINKS

60ml (2 fl oz) Vodka
60ml (2 fl oz) Fresh Orange Juice
15ml (½ fl oz) Fresh Lemon Juice
90ml (3 fl oz) Bitter-Lemon Soda
Slice of Orange
Twist of Lemon Peel
Twist of Orange Peel

Pour Vodka and juices into a collins glass over ice then stir. Add soda and stir gently. Twist lemon and orange peels above drink then place remainder of peels into drink. Garnish with a slice of orange and serve.

Raspberry Beret

19.6% ALC/VOL • 1.2 STD DRINKS

30ml (1 fl oz) Vodka
23ml (¾ fl oz) Chambord
23ml (¾ fl oz) Fresh Cream

Pour Vodka and Chambord into an old-fashioned glass over ice then stir. Float cream on top and serve.

Chiquita

18.2% ALC/VOL • 1.6 STD DRINKS

45ml (1½ fl oz) Vodka
15ml (½ fl oz) Banana Liqueur
15ml (½ fl oz) Fresh Lime Juice
1 teaspoon Sugar Syrup
½ Banana (diced)

Pour Vodka, Liqueur, juice and sugar into a blender over small amount of crushed ice then add diced banana. Blend until smooth and pour into a chilled champagne saucer then serve.

Pinko

14.4% ALC/VOL • 1.4 STD DRINKS

30ml (1 fl oz) Vodka
30ml (1 fl oz) Apricot Brandy
5ml (1/6 fl oz) Grenadine
60ml (2 fl oz) Pineapple Juice
Maraschino Cherry

Pour Vodka, Brandy, Grenadine and juice into a cocktail shaker over ice. Shake and strain into a chilled wine glass. Garnish with a cherry and serve.

Liberator

14.6% ALC/VOL • 1.6 STD DRINKS

45ml (1½ fl oz) Vodka
15ml (½ fl oz) Midori
60ml (2 fl oz) Mango Juice
15ml (½ fl oz) Fresh Lime Juice
Slice of Lime

Pour Vodka, Midori and juices into a cocktail shaker over ice. Shake and strain into a chilled cocktail glass. Garnish with a slice of lime and serve.

Holy Water

25.1% ALC/VOL • 3.6 STD DRINKS

60ml (2 fl oz) Vodka
30ml (1 fl oz) Cointreau
30ml (1 fl oz) Light Rum
Dash Grenadine
60ml (2 fl oz) Tonic Water

Pour Vodka, Cointreau and Rum into an old-fashioned glass over ice then stir. Add tonic and stir gently. Add Grenadine – do not stir, then serve.

Her Name in Lights

28.9% ALC/VOL • 1.8 STD DRINKS

30ml (1 fl oz) Vodka
15ml (½ fl oz) Yellow Chartreuse
10ml (⅓ fl oz) Blue Curaçao
10ml (⅓ fl oz) Galliano
15ml (½ fl oz) Fresh Lemon Juice
Maraschino Cherry

Pour Vodka, Chartreuse, Curaçao, Galliano and juice into a cocktail shaker over ice. Shake and strain into a chilled cocktail glass. Garnish with a cherry and serve.

Vodka Grand Marnier

30.2% ALC/VOL • 1.8 STD DRINKS

45ml (1½ fl oz) Vodka
15ml (½ fl oz) Grand Marnier
15ml (½ fl oz) Fresh Lime Juice
Slice of Orange

Pour Vodka, Grand Marnier and juice into a cocktail shaker over ice. Shake and strain into an old-fashioned glass over ice. Garnish with a slice of orange and serve.

Ménage à Trois

8.2% ALC/VOL • 0.9 STD DRINKS

30ml (1 fl oz) Vodka
45ml (1½ fl oz) Strawberry Purée
30ml (1 fl oz) Coconut Cream
1 scoop Chocolate Ice Cream
Strawberry
Grated Chocolate

Pour Vodka and cream into a blender without ice. Add purée and ice cream. Blend until smooth and pour into a chilled old-fashioned glass. Sprinkle chocolate on top and garnish with a strawberry then serve with 2 short straws.

Red Rooster

28.2% ALC/VOL • 1.7 STD DRINKS

45ml (1½ fl oz) Vodka
30ml (1 fl oz) Fraises De Bois
Twist of Lemon Peel

Pour Vodka and Fraises into an old-fashioned glass over ice then stir. Garnish with lemon peel and serve with 2 short straws.

Swedish Blue

26.6% ALC/VOL • 1.9 STD DRINKS

45ml (1½ fl oz) Vodka
15ml (½ fl oz) Armagnac
5ml (1/6 fl oz) Blue Curaçao
15ml (½ fl oz) Blueberry Syrup
10ml (⅓ fl oz) Fresh Lime Juice
Blue Cherry
Slice of Orange

Pour Vodka, Armagnac, Curaçao, syrup and juice into a cocktail shaker over cracked ice. Shake and pour into a chilled old-fashioned glass. Garnish with a cherry and slice of orange then serve.

Electric Jam

8.6% ALC/VOL • 1.6 STD DRINKS

45ml (1½ fl oz) Vodka
15ml (½ fl oz) Blue Curaçao
60ml (2 fl oz) Sweet and Sour Mix
120ml (4 fl oz) Lemon-Lime Soda

Pour Vodka, Curaçao and sour mix into a collins glass over ice then stir, Add soda, stir gently and serve.

Viking Warmer

20% ALC/VOL • 1.8 STD DRINKS

45ml (1½ fl oz) Vodka
15ml (½ fl oz) Aquavit
15ml (½ fl oz) Blueberry Syrup
8ml (¼ fl oz) Fresh Lime Juice
30ml (1 fl oz) Lemonade
Cherry

Pour Vodka, Aquavit, syrup and juice into an old-fashioned glass over cracked ice then stir. Add lemonade and stir gently. Garnish with a cherry and serve.

Screwnog

13.1% ALC/VOL • 1.8 STD DRINKS

60ml (2 fl oz) Vodka
60ml (2 fl oz) Fresh Orange Juice
5ml (1/6 fl oz) Fresh Lemon Juice
1 Fresh Egg

Pour ingredients into a blender without ice and blend. Pour into a highball glass over ice and stir gently then serve.

Joy Jumper

31% ALC/VOL • 1.6 STD DRINKS

45ml (1½ fl oz) Vodka
10ml (⅓ fl oz) Kümmel
5ml (1/6 fl oz) Fresh Lemon Juice
5ml (1/6 fl oz) Fresh Lime Juice
Dash Sugar Syrup
Wedge of Lemon

Pour Vodka, Kümmel, juices and sugar into a cocktail shaker over ice. Shake and strain into a chilled cocktail glass. Garnish with a wedge of lemon and serve.

Shalom

29% ALC/VOL • 2.1 STD DRINKS

45ml (1½ fl oz) 100-Proof Vodka
30ml (1 fl oz) Madeira
15ml (½ fl oz) Fresh Orange Juice
Slice of Orange

Pour Vodka, Madeira and juice into a cocktail shaker over ice. Shake and strain into a chilled cocktail glass. Garnish with a slice of orange and serve.

Orlando

7.5% ALC/VOL • 1.1 STD DRINKS

30ml (1 fl oz) Vodka
10ml (⅓ fl oz) Banana Liqueur
90ml (3 fl oz) Fresh Orange Juice
30ml (1 fl oz) Pineapple Juice
20ml (⅔ fl oz) Fresh Cream

Pour ingredients into a cocktail shaker over cracked ice and shake. Pour into a chilled highball glass and serve.

Hammer Horror

14.3% ALC/VOL • 1.4 STD DRINKS

30ml (1 fl oz) Vodka
30ml (1 fl oz) Kahlúa
2 scoops Vanilla Ice Cream
Grated Chocolate

Pour Vodka and Kahlúa into a blender without ice then add ice cream. Blend until smooth and pour into a chilled cocktail glass. Sprinkle chocolate on top and serve.

Coexistence Collins

11.7% ALC/VOL • 1.9 STD DRINKS

60ml (2 fl oz) Vodka
5ml (1/6 fl oz) Kümmel
15ml (½ fl oz) Fresh Lemon Juice
1 teaspoon Sugar Syrup
120ml (4 fl oz) Soda Water
Twist of Cucumber Peel
Twist of Lemon Peel

Pour Vodka, Kümmel, juice and sugar into a cocktail shaker over ice. Shake and strain into a collins glass over ice. Add soda and stir gently then add cucumber peel. Twist lemon peel above drink and place remainder of peel into drink then serve.

French Screw

13.4% ALC/VOL • 2.5 STD DRINKS

60ml (2 fl oz) Vodka
60ml (2 fl oz) Chambord
120ml (4 fl oz) Fresh Orange Juice

Pour ingredients into a highball glass over ice, stir well and serve.

Bikini

26.9% ALC/VOL • 2.7 STD DRINKS

60ml (2 fl oz) Vodka
30ml (1 fl oz) Light Rum
15ml (½ fl oz) Fresh Lemon Juice
15ml (½ fl oz) Fresh Milk (chilled)
1 teaspoon Sugar Syrup
Wedge of Lemon

Pour Vodka, Rum, juice, milk and sugar into a cocktail shaker over ice. Shake and strain into a chilled cocktail glass. Garnish with a wedge of lemon and serve.

April Rain

27.7% ALC/VOL • 2 STD DRINKS

60ml (2 fl oz) Vodka
15ml (½ fl oz) Dry Vermouth
15ml (½ fl oz) Lime Syrup
Twist of Lime Peel

Pour Vodka, Vermouth and syrup into a cocktail shaker over ice. Shake and strain into a chilled cocktail glass. Garnish with lime peel and serve.

Jericho's Breeze

12.6% ALC/VOL • 1.3 STD DRINKS

30ml (1 fl oz) Vodka
23ml (¾ fl oz) Blue Curaçao
75ml (2½ fl oz) Sweet and Sour Mix
3 dashes Fresh Orange Juice
3 dashes Lemon-Lime Soda
Maraschino Cherry
Pineapple Spear

Pour Vodka, Curaçao, sour mix and juice into a cocktail shaker over ice. Shake and strain into a chilled goblet then add soda – do not stir. Garnish with a cherry and pineapple spear then serve.

Chocolate Mint Martini

31% ALC/VOL • 2.6 STD DRINKS

60ml (2 fl oz) Vodka
30ml (1 fl oz) White Crème De Cacao
30ml (1 fl oz) White Crème De Menthe

Prepare a cocktail glass with a cocoa frosted rim – moistened with Cacao. Pour ingredients into a cocktail shaker over ice and shake. Strain into prepared glass and serve.

Vodka Swizzle

11.3% ALC/VOL • 1.8 STD DRINKS

60ml (2 fl oz) Vodka
Dash Angostura Bitters
45ml (1½ fl oz) Fresh Lime Juice
1 teaspoon Sugar Syrup
90ml (3 fl oz) Soda Water

Pour Vodka, Bitters, juice and sugar into a mixing glass over large amount of ice. Stir vigorously until cold and strain into a collins glass filled with crushed ice. Add soda – do not stir, then serve with a swizzle stick and 2 straws.

Russian Cow

10.7% ALC/VOL • 1.1 STD DRINKS

30ml (1 fl oz) Vodka
10ml (⅓ fl oz) Amaretto
60ml (2 fl oz) Fresh Milk (chilled)
30ml (1 fl oz) Coconut Cream

Pour ingredients into a blender over crushed ice and blend until smooth. Pour into a chilled highball glass and serve.

Laugh a Minute

11.5% ALC/VOL • 1.2 STD DRINKS

30ml (1 fl oz) Vodka
30ml (1 fl oz) Sweet Vermouth
15ml (½ fl oz) Amaretto
60ml (2 fl oz) Lemonade

Pour Vodka, Vermouth and Amaretto into a cocktail shaker over ice. Shake and strain into an old-fashioned glass over cracked ice. Add lemonade, stir gently and serve.

Camshaft

14.2% ALC/VOL • 1.2 STD DRINKS

30ml (1 fl oz) Vodka
15ml (½ fl oz) Campari
30ml (1 fl oz) Fresh Orange Juice
30ml (1 fl oz) Lemonade

Pour Vodka, Campari and juice into an old-fashioned glass over ice then stir. Add lemonade, stir gently and serve.

Madam I'm Adam

10.9% ALC/VOL • 0.9 STD DRINKS

30ml (1 fl oz) Vodka
Dash Cointreau
30ml (1 fl oz) Cranberry Juice
30ml (1 fl oz) Grapefruit Juice
15ml (½ fl oz) Pineapple Juice
Strawberry
Twist of Lime Peel

Pour Vodka, Cointreau and cranberry juice into a cocktail shaker over ice. Shake and strain into a chilled goblet. Add grapefruit juice and stir gently. Pour pineapple juice into a clean cocktail shaker over crushed ice and shake well then scoop out iced pineapple juice to layer on top of drink. Garnish with lime peel and a strawberry then serve.

Russian Kamikaze

35.5% ALC/VOL • 1.8 STD DRINKS

60ml (2 fl oz) Vodka
5ml (⅙ fl oz) Chambord

Pour ingredients into a mixing glass over ice and stir. Strain into a chilled cocktail glass and serve.

Frosty Amour

14.2% ALC/VOL • 2.5 STD DRINKS

30ml (1 fl oz) Vodka
30ml (1 fl oz) Apricot Brandy
30ml (1 fl oz) Southern Comfort
5ml (⅙ fl oz) Banana Liqueur
5ml (⅙ fl oz) Parfait Amour

120ml (4 fl oz) Lemonade
Green Cherry
Slice of Orange

Prepare a collins glass with a sugar frosted rim – moistened with lemonade. Pour Vodka, Brandy, Southern Comfort, Liqueur and Parfait Amour into a cocktail shaker over ice. Shake and strain into prepared glass. Add lemonade and stir gently. Garnish with a cherry and slice of orange then serve.

Duke's a Champ

36.6% ALC/VOL • 1.7 STD DRINKS

This drink is also known as *Black Eye, p 185.*

Aqueduct

25.5% ALC/VOL • 3 STD DRINKS

45ml (1½ fl oz) Vodka
45ml (1½ fl oz) Apricot Brandy
45ml (1½ fl oz) White Curaçao
15ml (½ fl oz) Fresh Lime Juice
Twist of Orange Peel

Pour Vodka, Brandy, Curaçao and juice into a cocktail shaker over ice. Shake and strain into a chilled champagne saucer. Garnish with orange peel and serve.

Golden Russian

33.9% ALC/VOL • 2.1 STD DRINKS

45ml (1½ fl oz) Vodka
30ml (1 fl oz) Galliano
5ml (1/6 fl oz) Fresh Lime Juice
Slice of Lime

Pour Vodka, Galliano and juice into an old-fashioned glass over ice then stir. Garnish with a slice of lime and serve.

Glass Tower

20.4% ALC/VOL • 3.6 STD DRINKS

30ml (1 fl oz) Vodka
30ml (1 fl oz) Cointreau
30ml (1 fl oz) Golden Rum
30ml (1 fl oz) Peach Schnapps
15ml (½ fl oz) Sambuca
90ml (3 fl oz) Lemon-Lime Soda
Maraschino Cherry
Slice of Orange

Pour Vodka, Cointreau, Rum, Schnapps and Sambuca into a collins glass over ice then stir. Add soda and stir gently. Garnish with a cherry and slice of orange then serve.

Sino-Soviet Split

14.6% ALC/VOL • 2.4 STD DRINKS

60ml (2 fl oz) Vodka
30ml (1 fl oz) Amaretto
120ml (4 fl oz) Fresh Milk (chilled)

Pour Vodka and Amaretto into an old-fashioned glass over ice then stir. Add milk, stir gently and serve.

Galway Grey

17.2% ALC/VOL • 1.6 STD DRINKS

30ml (1 fl oz) Vodka
15ml (½ fl oz) Cointreau
15ml (½ fl oz) White Crème De Cacao
30ml (1 fl oz) Fresh Lime Juice
15ml (½ fl oz) Fresh Cream

Pour ingredients into a cocktail shaker over ice and shake. Strain into a chilled old-fashioned glass over a few ice cubes and serve.

Scotch Frog

29.7% ALC/VOL • 1.9 STD DRINKS

This drink is also known as *Frightleberry Murzenquest, p 188.*

Summertime

7.9% ALC/VOL • 1.3 STD DRINKS

This drink is also known as *Vodka Cooler, p 180.*

Mazrick

21.3% ALC/VOL • 2.5 STD DRINKS

45ml (1½ fl oz) Vodka
15ml (½ fl oz) Amaretto
15ml (½ fl oz) Cointreau
10ml (⅓ fl oz) Galliano
2 dashes Angostura Bitters
30ml (1 fl oz) Fresh Orange Juice
30ml (1 fl oz) Pineapple Juice

Pour ingredients into a cocktail shaker over ice and shake. Strain into a highball glass over ice and serve.

Frisky Witch

37.5% ALC/VOL • 1.8 STD DRINKS

30ml (1 fl oz) Vodka
30ml (1 fl oz) Sambuca
Black Licorice Stick

Pour Vodka and Sambuca into an old-fashioned glass over ice then stir. Garnish with a licorice stick and serve.

Vodka Standard

24.1% ALC/VOL • 1.1 STD DRINKS

30ml (1 fl oz) Vodka
15ml (½ fl oz) Cherry Brandy
15ml (½ fl oz) Fresh Lemon or Lime Juice
Maraschino Cherry

Pour Vodka, Brandy and juice into a cocktail shaker over ice. Shake and strain into a chilled cocktail glass. Garnish with a cherry and serve.
This drink is also known as Cherry Vodka.

Watermelon Martini

31.6% ALC/VOL • 1.9 STD DRINKS

60ml (2 fl oz) Vodka
Dash Sugar Syrup
Slice of Watermelon (crushed)
Wedge of Watermelon

Pour Vodka and sugar into a cocktail shaker over ice then add crushed watermelon. Shake and strain into a chilled martini glass. Garnish with a wedge of watermelon and serve.

Marvelous

16.6% ALC/VOL • 2 STD DRINKS

40ml (1⅓ fl oz) Vodka
40ml (1⅓ fl oz) Campari
10ml (⅓ fl oz) Grenadine
40ml (1⅓ fl oz) Fresh Orange Juice
20ml (⅔ fl oz) Grapefruit Juice

Pour Vodka, Campari and juices into a cocktail shaker over ice. Shake and strain into a highball glass over ice. Add Grenadine, stir and serve.

Schnaxler

16.8% ALC/VOL • 1.6 STD DRINKS

30ml (1 fl oz) Vodka
15ml (½ fl oz) Galliano
15ml (½ fl oz) White Curaçao
30ml (1 fl oz) Fresh Orange Juice
30ml (1 fl oz) Fresh Cream

Pour ingredients into a cocktail shaker over ice and shake. Strain into a chilled cocktail glass and serve.

Vampire's Delight

5.7% ALC/VOL • 1.3 STD DRINKS

30ml (1 fl oz) Vodka
20ml (⅔ fl oz) Orange Curaçao
60ml (2 fl oz) Fresh Orange Juice
2 teaspoons Almond Extract
165ml (5½ fl oz) Bitter-Lemon Soda

Pour Vodka, Curaçao, juice and extract into a cocktail shaker over ice. Shake and strain into a chilled highball glass. Add soda – do not stir, then serve with a swizzle stick and straw.

Road Runner

25.5% ALC/VOL • 2.4 STD DRINKS

60ml (2 fl oz) Vodka
30ml (1 fl oz) Amaretto
30ml (1 fl oz) Coconut Milk (chilled)
Nutmeg

Pour Vodka, Amaretto and milk into a cocktail shaker over ice. Shake and strain into a chilled champagne saucer. Sprinkle nutmeg on top and serve.

Nijinski Blini

10.8% ALC/VOL • 0.9 STD DRINKS

30ml (1 fl oz) Vodka
3 dashes Champagne (chilled)
3 dashes Peach Schnapps
60ml (2 fl oz) Puréed Peach
15ml (½ fl oz) Fresh Lemon Juice

Pour Vodka, Champagne, Schnapps and juice into a mixing glass over ice then add puréed peach. Stir gently and strain into a chilled champagne flute then serve.

Missile Rider

27% ALC/VOL • 1.7 STD DRINKS

45ml (1½ fl oz) Vodka
10ml (⅓ fl oz) Yellow Chartreuse
3 dashes Pernod
20ml (⅔ fl oz) Fresh Lime Juice
½ teaspoon Sugar Syrup

Pour ingredients into a cocktail shaker over ice and shake. Strain into a chilled old-fashioned glass and serve.

Sweet Maria

25.5% ALC/VOL • 1.2 STD DRINKS

30ml (1 fl oz) Vodka
15ml (½ fl oz) Amaretto
15ml (½ fl oz) Fresh Cream

Pour ingredients into a cocktail shaker over ice and shake. Strain into a chilled cocktail glass and serve.

Barbara

24.3% ALC/VOL • 1.2 STD DRINKS

30ml (1 fl oz) Vodka
15ml (½ fl oz) Dark Crème De Cacao
15ml (½ fl oz) Thick Cream

Pour ingredients into a cocktail shaker over ice and shake. Strain into a chilled cocktail glass and serve.

Pecker Wrecker

7% ALC/VOL • 1.7 STD DRINKS

This drink is also known as Pink Petal, p 224.

Buzzer

7.8% ALC/VOL • 1.8 STD DRINKS

30ml (1 fl oz) Vodka
30ml (1 fl oz) Gin
110ml (3⅔ fl oz) Grapefruit Juice
110ml (3⅔ fl oz) Fresh Orange Juice
5ml (⅙ fl oz) Soda Water

Pour Vodka, Gin and juices into a mixing glass over ice. Stir and strain into a chilled highball glass. Add soda, stir gently and serve.

Justine

23.7% ALC/VOL • 1.8 STD DRINKS

30ml (1 fl oz) Vodka
15ml (½ fl oz) Crème De Noyaux
15ml (½ fl oz) Kirsch
5ml (1/6 fl oz) Amaretto
30ml (1 fl oz) Fresh Cream

Pour ingredients into a cocktail shaker over ice and shake. Strain into a chilled cocktail glass and serve.

Sam-Tini

36.8% ALC/VOL • 1.2 STD DRINKS

38ml (1¼ fl oz) Vodka
3 dashes Sambuca
Dash Blue Curaçao
Wedge of Orange

Pour Vodka, Sambuca and Curaçao into a mixing glass over ice. Stir and strain into a chilled martini glass. Garnish with a wedge of orange and serve.

Soviet

29.4% ALC/VOL • 1.7 STD DRINKS

45ml (1½ fl oz) Vodka
15ml (½ fl oz) Dry Sherry
15ml (½ fl oz) Dry Vermouth
Twist of Lemon Peel

Pour Vodka, Sherry and Vermouth into a mixing glass over ice. Stir and strain into a chilled cocktail glass. Garnish with lemon peel and serve.

Save the Planet

28.5% ALC/VOL • 1.7 STD DRINKS

30ml (1 fl oz) Vodka
30ml (1 fl oz) Midori
15ml (½ fl oz) Blue Curaçao
Dash Green Chartreuse
Maraschino Cherry

Pour Vodka, Midori and Curaçao into a cocktail shaker over ice. Shake and strain into a chilled cocktail glass then add Chartreuse – do not stir. Garnish with a cherry and serve.

Royal Passion

21.6% ALC/VOL • 1.8 STD DRINKS

45ml (1½ fl oz) Vodka
30ml (1 fl oz) Raspberry Liqueur
30ml (1 fl oz) Passion-Fruit Juice

Pour ingredients into a cocktail shaker over ice and shake. Strain into an old-fashioned glass over ice and serve.

Quiet But Quick

22.4% ALC/VOL • 1.6 STD DRINKS

45ml (1½ fl oz) Vodka
15ml (½ fl oz) Cherry Brandy
Dash Orange Bitters
30ml (1 fl oz) Fresh Orange Juice

Pour ingredients into a cocktail shaker over ice and shake. Strain into a chilled cocktail glass and serve.
This drink is also known as Seether, p 222.

Desert Sunrise

10.9% ALC/VOL • 1.1 STD DRINKS

38ml (1¼ fl oz) Vodka
Dash Grenadine
45ml (1½ fl oz) Fresh Orange Juice
45ml (1½ fl oz) Pineapple Juice

Pour Vodka and juices into a collins glass over crushed ice then stir. Add Grenadine – do not stir, then serve.

Vodka Sling

26% ALC/VOL • 1.7 STD DRINKS

60ml (2 fl oz) Vodka
15ml (½ fl oz) Fresh Lemon Juice
5ml (1/6 fl oz) Spring Water
1 teaspoon Sugar Syrup
Twist of Orange Peel

Pour Vodka, juice, water and sugar into a highball glass over ice then stir. Garnish with orange peel and serve.

Kangaroo Cocktail

28.8% ALC/VOL • 2.4 STD DRINKS

60ml (2 fl oz) Vodka
45ml (1½ fl oz) Dry Vermouth
Wedge of Lemon

Pour Vodka and Vermouth into a mixing glass over ice. Stir and strain into a chilled cocktail glass. Garnish with a wedge of lemon and serve.

She's Paying

30.7% ALC/VOL • 1.9 STD DRINKS

30ml (1 fl oz) Vodka
30ml (1 fl oz) Kahlúa
15ml (½ fl oz) Grand Marnier
5ml (1/6 fl oz) Amaretto
Maraschino Cherry

Pour Vodka, Kahlúa, Grand Marnier and Amaretto into a cocktail shaker over ice. Shake and strain into an old-fashioned glass over ice. Garnish with a cherry and serve.

Twister

11.7% ALC/VOL • 1.8 STD DRINKS

60ml (2 fl oz) Vodka
10ml (⅓ fl oz) Fresh Lime Juice
120ml (4 fl oz) Lemon Soda
Twist of Lime Peel

Pour Vodka and juice into a collins glass over ice then stir. Add soda and stir gently. Twist lime peel above drink and place remainder of peel into drink then serve.

Tangerine Cocktail

22.8% ALC/VOL • 1.7 STD DRINKS

15ml (½ fl oz) Vodka
15ml (½ fl oz) Amaretto
15ml (½ fl oz) Cointreau
15ml (½ fl oz) Mandarine Napoleon
5ml (1/6 fl oz) Grenadine
30ml (1 fl oz) Tangerine Juice
Maraschino Cherry
Slice of Orange

Pour Vodka, Amaretto, Cointreau, Mandarine Napoleon, Grenadine and juice into a cocktail shaker over ice. Shake and strain into a cocktail glass over crushed ice. Garnish with a cherry and slice of orange then serve with a short straw.

White Spider

33.6% ALC/VOL • 1.6 STD DRINKS

45ml (1½ fl oz) Vodka
15ml (½ fl oz) White Crème De Menthe

Pour ingredients into a mixing glass over ice and stir. Strain into a chilled cocktail glass and serve.

Gorky Park

22.3% ALC/VOL • 1.6 STD DRINKS

45ml (1½ fl oz) Vodka
15ml (½ fl oz) Cherry Brandy
30ml (1 fl oz) Fresh Lemon Juice
Maraschino Cherry

Pour Vodka, Brandy and juice into a cocktail shaker over ice. Shake and strain into a chilled cocktail glass. Garnish with a cherry and serve.

Perfect Love

30.8% ALC/VOL • 2.9 STD DRINKS

60ml (2 fl oz) Vodka
30ml (1 fl oz) Parfait Amour
30ml (1 fl oz) Maraschino Liqueur
Twist of Lemon Peel

Layer ingredients in order given into an old-fashioned glass over ice. Garnish with lemon peel and serve.

Alexander Nevsky

9.2% ALC/VOL • 1.4 STD DRINKS

30ml (1 fl oz) Vodka
30ml (1 fl oz) Apricot Liqueur
120ml (4 fl oz) Fresh Orange Juice
15ml (½ fl oz) Fresh Lemon Juice
Slice of Orange

Pour Vodka, Liqueur and juices into a cocktail shaker over cracked ice. Shake and pour into a chilled wine glass. Garnish with a slice of orange and serve.

This drink may also be prepared in a blender.

Russian Bear Cocktail

24.3% ALC/VOL • 1.2 STD DRINKS

30ml (1 fl oz) Vodka
15ml (½ fl oz) White Crème De Cacao
15ml (½ fl oz) Fresh Cream

Pour ingredients into a mixing glass over ice and stir. Strain into a chilled cocktail glass and serve.

Jackath

35.2% ALC/VOL • 1.4 STD DRINKS

30ml (1 fl oz) Vodka
10ml (⅓ fl oz) Brandy
5ml (1/6 fl oz) Cointreau
5ml (1/6 fl oz) Crème De Cassis
2 dashes Orange Bitters

Pour ingredients into a mixing glass over ice and stir. Strain into a chilled cocktail glass and serve.

French Horn

21.9% ALC/VOL • 1.2 STD DRINKS

30ml (1 fl oz) Vodka
23ml (¾ fl oz) Chambord
15ml (½ fl oz) Fresh Lemon Juice
Maraschino Cherry

Pour Vodka, Chambord and juice into a mixing glass over ice. Stir and strain into a chilled liqueur glass. Garnish with a cherry and serve.

Victory Collins

7.3% ALC/VOL • 1.3 STD DRINKS

45ml (1½ fl oz) Vodka
90ml (3 fl oz) Grape Juice
90ml (3 fl oz) Fresh Lemon Juice
1 teaspoon Sugar Syrup
Slice of Orange

Pour Vodka, juices and sugar into a cocktail shaker over ice. Shake and strain into a collins glass over ice. Garnish with a slice of orange and serve.

Citronella Cooler

8.7% ALC/VOL • 0.8 STD DRINKS

30ml (1 fl oz) Citrus Vodka
30ml (1 fl oz) Cranberry Juice
Dash Fresh Lime Juice
60ml (2 fl oz) Lemonade

Pour Vodka and juices into a collins glass over ice then stir. Add lemonade, stir gently and serve.

Vodka Sour

25.6% ALC/VOL • 1.3 STD DRINKS

45ml (1½ fl oz) Vodka
15ml (½ fl oz) Fresh Lemon Juice
1 teaspoon Sugar Syrup
Maraschino Cherry
Slice of Lemon

Pour Vodka, juice and sugar into a cocktail shaker over ice. Shake and strain into a chilled sour glass. Garnish with a cherry and slice of lemon then serve.

Headless Horseman

11% ALC/VOL • 1.8 STD DRINKS

60ml (2 fl oz) Vodka
3 dashes Angostura Bitters
150ml (5 fl oz) Dry Ginger Ale
Slice of Orange

Pour Vodka and Bitters into a highball glass over ice then stir. Add Ginger Ale and stir gently. Garnish with a slice of orange and serve.

Watertable

29% ALC/VOL • 1.6 STD DRINKS

45ml (1½ fl oz) Vodka
10ml (⅓ fl oz) White Curaçao
5ml (1/6 fl oz) Apricot Brandy
5ml (1/6 fl oz) Fresh Lemon Juice
5ml (1/6 fl oz) Fresh Lime Juice
Slice of Lemon

Pour Vodka, Curaçao, Brandy and juices into a cocktail shaker over ice. Shake and strain into a chilled cocktail glass. Garnish with a slice of lemon and serve.

Warsaw Cocktail

30.8% ALC/VOL • 1.9 STD DRINKS

45ml (1½ fl oz) Vodka
15ml (½ fl oz) Blackberry Brandy
15ml (½ fl oz) Dry Vermouth
5ml (1/6 fl oz) Fresh Lemon Juice

Pour ingredients into a cocktail shaker over ice and shake. Strain into a chilled cocktail glass and serve.

Siberian Sleighride

13.8% ALC/VOL • 1.8 STD DRINKS

38ml (1¼ fl oz) Vodka
23ml (¾ fl oz) White Crème De Cacao
15ml (½ fl oz) White Crème De Menthe
90ml (3 fl oz) Fresh Cream
Grated Chocolate

Pour Vodka, Cacao, Crème De Menthe and cream into a cocktail shaker over ice. Shake and strain into a chilled brandy balloon. Sprinkle chocolate on top and serve.

Vodka and Bitter Lemon

9.1% ALC/VOL • 1.3 STD DRINKS

45ml (1½ fl oz) Vodka
15ml (½ fl oz) Fresh Lemon Juice
½ teaspoon Sugar Syrup
120ml (4 fl oz) Tonic Water

Pour Vodka, juice and sugar into a cocktail shaker over ice. Shake and strain into a highball glass over ice. Add tonic, stir gently and serve.

Vodka Flip

20.2% ALC/VOL • 1.8 STD DRINKS

60ml (2 fl oz) Vodka
1 teaspoon Sugar Syrup
1 Fresh Egg
Nutmeg

Pour Vodka, sugar and egg into a cocktail shaker over ice. Shake and strain into a chilled goblet. Sprinkle nutmeg on top and serve.

Vodka Rickey

11.4% ALC/VOL • 1.8 STD DRINKS

60ml (2 fl oz) Vodka
15ml (½ fl oz) Fresh Lime Juice
120ml (4 fl oz) Soda Water
Twist of Lime Peel

Pour Vodka and juice into a collins glass over ice then stir. Add soda and stir gently. Garnish with lime peel and serve.

Cold Fusion

16.6% ALC/VOL • 1.4 STD DRINKS

30ml (1 fl oz) Vodka
20ml (⅔ fl oz) Triple Sec
10ml (⅓ fl oz) Midori
40ml (1⅓ fl oz) Sweet and Sour Mix
10ml (⅓ fl oz) Fresh Lime Juice

Pour ingredients into a cocktail shaker over ice and shake. Strain into a highball glass over ice and add more ice to fill glass then serve.

Vodka Snowball

9.2% ALC/VOL • 1.3 STD DRINKS

30ml (1 fl oz) Vodka
30ml (1 fl oz) Advocaat
30ml (1 fl oz) Thick Cream
90ml (3 fl oz) Lemonade

Pour Vodka, Advocaat and cream into a cocktail shaker over ice. Shake and strain into a highball glass over ice. Add lemonade, stir gently and serve.

Stuffy-in-a-Suit

21.9% ALC/VOL • 1.6 STD DRINKS

30ml (1 fl oz) Vodka
15ml (½ fl oz) Cointreau
15ml (½ fl oz) Lillet
Dash Orange Bitters
White of 1 Egg
Slice of Orange

Pour Vodka, Cointreau, Lillet, Bitters and egg white into a cocktail shaker over ice. Shake and strain into an old-fashioned glass over ice. Garnish with a slice of orange and serve.

Vodka Grasshopper

27.5% ALC/VOL • 1.5 STD DRINKS

23ml (¾ fl oz) Vodka
23ml (¾ fl oz) White Crème De Cacao
23ml (¾ fl oz) White Crème De Menthe

Pour ingredients into a cocktail shaker over ice and shake. Strain into a chilled cocktail glass and serve.

Reggae

18.7% ALC/VOL • 2.1 STD DRINKS

60ml (2 fl oz) Vodka
15ml (½ fl oz) Banana Liqueur
Dash Orange Bitters
3 dashes Grenadine
30ml (1 fl oz) Fresh Orange Juice
15ml (½ fl oz) Grapefruit Juice
15ml (½ fl oz) Pineapple Juice
Maraschino Cherry
Slice of Orange
Wedge of Pineapple

Pour Vodka, Liqueur, Bitters, Grenadine and juices into a cocktail shaker over ice. Shake and strain into a highball glass over ice. Garnish with a cherry, slice of orange and wedge of pineapple then serve.

Fish Lips

31.4% ALC/VOL • 2.2 STD DRINKS

This drink is also known as Major Tom, p 189.

Rubenstein's Revenge

14.8% ALC/VOL • 2.6 STD DRINKS

45ml (1½ fl oz) Vodka
45ml (1½ fl oz) Gin
45ml (1½ fl oz) Cranberry Juice
45ml (1½ fl oz) Fresh Orange Juice
45ml (1½ fl oz) Tonic Water

Pour Vodka, Gin and juices into a cocktail shaker over ice. Shake and strain into a chilled highball glass. Add tonic, stir gently and serve.

Cossack Charge

34.8% ALC/VOL • 2.1 STD DRINKS

45ml (1½ fl oz) Vodka
15ml (½ fl oz) Cherry Brandy
15ml (½ fl oz) Cognac

Pour ingredients into a cocktail shaker over cracked ice and shake. Pour into a chilled cocktail glass and serve.

Hay Fever Remedy

21.1% ALC/VOL • 0.8 STD DRINKS

15ml (½ fl oz) Vodka
8ml (¼ fl oz) Amaretto
8ml (¼ fl oz) Southern Comfort
5ml (⅙ fl oz) Grenadine
15ml (½ fl oz) Pineapple Juice

Pour ingredients into a cocktail shaker over ice and shake. Strain into 2 chilled shot glasses and serve.

Velvet Peach Hammer

30% ALC/VOL • 1.7 STD DRINKS

45ml (1½ fl oz) Vodka
23ml (¾ fl oz) Peach Schnapps
3 dashes Sweet and Sour Mix
Slice of Peach

Pour Vodka and Schnapps into an old-fashioned glass over ice then stir. Add sour mix – do not stir, then garnish with a slice of peach and serve.

Karoff

7.4% ALC/VOL • 1.3 STD DRINKS

45ml (1½ fl oz) Vodka
30ml (1 fl oz) Cranberry Juice
150ml (5 fl oz) Soda Water
Wedge of Lime

Pour Vodka and juice into a highball glass over ice then stir. Add soda and stir gently. Garnish with a wedge of lime and serve.

Spymaster

19.2% ALC/VOL • 1.6 STD DRINKS

45ml (1½ fl oz) Vodka
15ml (½ fl oz) Banana Liqueur
15ml (½ fl oz) Fresh Lemon Juice
White of 1 Egg

Pour ingredients into a cocktail shaker over ice and shake. Strain into an old-fashioned glass over ice and serve.

Silver Vodka Fizz

8.5% ALC/VOL • 1.7 STD DRINKS

60ml (2 fl oz) Vodka
60ml (2 fl oz) Fresh Orange Juice
30ml (1 fl oz) Fresh Lemon Juice
1 teaspoon Caster Sugar
½ Egg White
90ml (3 fl oz) Lemonade

Pour Vodka, juices and egg white into a cocktail shaker over ice then add sugar. Shake and strain into a highball glass over ice. Add lemonade, stir gently and serve.

Screwdriver

12.3% ALC/VOL • 1.7 STD DRINKS

60ml (2 fl oz) Vodka
120ml (4 fl oz) Fresh
Orange Juice
Maraschino Cherry
Slice of Orange

Pour Vodka and juice into a highball glass over ice then stir. Garnish with a cherry and slice of orange then serve.

Orang-a-Tang

15.3% ALC/VOL • 3.2 STD DRINKS

30ml (1 fl oz) Vodka
30ml (1 fl oz) 151-Proof Rum
15ml (½ fl oz) Cointreau
3 dashes Grenadine
180ml (6 fl oz) Fresh
Orange Juice
3 dashes Sweet and Sour Mix
Slice of Orange

Pour Vodka, Cointreau, Grenadine, juice and sour mix into a blender without ice. Blend lightly and pour into a brandy balloon over ice. Layer Rum on top and garnish with a slice of orange then serve.

Pretty Thing

23.2% ALC/VOL • 1.6 STD DRINKS

45ml (1½ fl oz) Vodka
15ml (½ fl oz) Amaretto
15ml (½ fl oz) Coconut Cream
15ml (½ fl oz) Thick Cream

Pour ingredients into a cocktail shaker over ice and shake. Strain into a chilled cocktail glass and serve.

White Russian

24% ALC/VOL • 1.4 STD DRINKS

30ml (1 fl oz) Vodka
30ml (1 fl oz) White Crème
De Cacao
15ml (½ fl oz) Thick Cream
Strawberry
Nutmeg

Pour Vodka, Cacao and cream into a cocktail shaker over ice. Shake and strain into a chilled cocktail glass. Sprinkle nutmeg on top and garnish with a strawberry then serve.

On-the-Town

11% ALC/VOL • 1.2 STD DRINKS

30ml (1 fl oz) Vodka
15ml (½ fl oz) Campari
60ml (2 fl oz) Fresh
Orange Juice
White of 1 Egg

Pour ingredients into a cocktail shaker over ice and shake. Strain into an old-fashioned glass over ice and serve.

Stupid Cupid

31.9% ALC/VOL • 2 STD DRINKS

60ml (2 fl oz) Citrus Vodka
15ml (½ fl oz) Sloe Gin
3 dashes Sweet and Sour Mix
Maraschino Cherry

Pour Vodka, Gin and sour mix into a mixing glass over ice. Stir and strain into a chilled cocktail glass. Garnish with a cherry and serve.

Purple Haze

22.8% ALC/VOL • 1.6 STD DRINKS

45ml (1½ fl oz) Lemon Vodka
15ml (½ fl oz) Chambord
30ml (1 fl oz) Bitter-Lemon
Soda

Pour Chambord into a chilled brandy balloon and pour Vodka into a mixing glass over ice then stir to chill. Strain into glass to layer over Chambord and add soda gently – do not stir, then serve with a straw – drink through straw from bottom of drink.

Russian Juice

16.6% ALC/VOL • 1.4 STD DRINKS

38ml (1¼ fl oz) Vodka
15ml (½ fl oz) Banana Liqueur
3 drops Angostura Bitters
Dash Grenadine
38ml (1¼ fl oz) Fresh
Orange Juice
15ml (½ fl oz) Pineapple Juice
2 Cherries
Slice of Lemon

Pour Vodka, Liqueur, Bitters, Grenadine and juices into a cocktail shaker over ice. Shake and strain into a chilled cocktail glass. Garnish with cherries and a slice of lemon then serve.

Pinetree Martyr

10.4% ALC/VOL • 1.1 STD DRINKS

30ml (1 fl oz) Vodka
15ml (½ fl oz) Peach Schnapps
90ml (3 fl oz) Pineapple Juice

Pour ingredients into a highball glass filled with ice, stir well and serve.

Star Legend

21.7% ALC/VOL • 1 STD DRINK

24ml (4/5 fl oz) Vodka
6ml (1/5 fl oz) Apricot Brandy
6ml (1/5 fl oz) Campari
6ml (1/5 fl oz) Raspberry
Liqueur
Dash Blue Curaçao
18ml (3/5 fl oz) Fresh
Orange Juice

Pour ingredients into a cocktail shaker over ice and shake. Strain into a chilled cocktail glass and serve.

Vilamoura Marina

32% ALC/VOL • 1.1 STD DRINKS

30ml (1 fl oz) Vodka
12ml (2/5 fl oz) Blue Curaçao
2 dashes Fresh Lemon Juice

Pour ingredients into a mixing glass over ice and stir. Strain into a chilled cocktail glass and serve.

Kape Kodder

7.3% ALC/VOL • 1.3 STD DRINKS

45ml (1½ fl oz) Citrus Vodka
180ml (6 fl oz) Cranberry Juice
5ml (1/6 fl oz) Fresh Lime Juice
Twist of Lime Peel

Pour Vodka and juices into a mixing glass over ice. Stir and strain into a chilled highball glass. Garnish with lime peel and serve.

Broken Heart

12.9% ALC/VOL • 1.3 STD DRINKS

30ml (1 fl oz) Vodka
30ml (1 fl oz) Chambord
5ml (1/6 fl oz) Grenadine
60ml (2 fl oz) Fresh Orange Juice

Pour ingredients into a cocktail shaker over cracked ice and shake. Pour into a chilled highball glass and serve.

Phantasm

12.5% ALC/VOL • 1.7 STD DRINKS

45ml (1½ fl oz) Vodka
15ml (½ fl oz) Galliano
15ml (½ fl oz) Fresh Cream
90ml (3 fl oz) Cola
Fresh Whipped Cream

Pour Vodka, Galliano and fresh cream into a cocktail shaker over ice. Shake and strain into a chilled collins glass. Add cola and stir gently. Float whipped cream on top and serve.

Love Birds

14.1% ALC/VOL • 1.3 STD DRINKS

45ml (1½ fl oz) Vodka
Dash Dark Rum
15ml (½ fl oz) Grenadine
60ml (2 fl oz) Fresh Lemon Juice
Cherry

Pour Vodka, Rum, Grenadine and juice into a blender over crushed ice. Blend and pour into a chilled old-fashioned glass. Add a cherry and serve.

Dancin'

31.2% ALC/VOL • 1.5 STD DRINKS

30ml (1 fl oz) Vodka
20ml (⅔ fl oz) Dry Vermouth
10ml (⅓ fl oz) Blended Whiskey
Dash Cherry Brandy
Dash Cointreau

Pour ingredients into a cocktail shaker over ice and shake. Strain into a chilled cocktail glass and serve.

Hop Frog

28.7% ALC/VOL • 3.4 STD DRINKS

75ml (2½ fl oz) Vodka
38ml (1¼ fl oz) Dry Vermouth
38ml (1¼ fl oz) Green Crème De Menthe
Sprig of Fresh Mint

Pour Vodka, Vermouth and Crème De Menthe into a cocktail shaker over ice. Shake and strain into an old-fashioned glass over ice. Garnish with a sprig of mint and serve.

Funky Filly

10.1% ALC/VOL • 1.9 STD DRINKS

23ml (¾ fl oz) Vodka
23ml (¾ fl oz) Cherry Liqueur
23ml (¾ fl oz) Midori
23ml (¾ fl oz) Triple Sec
60ml (2 fl oz) Cranberry Juice
30ml (1 fl oz) Fresh Lime Juice
60ml (2 fl oz) Lemon-Lime Soda

Pour Vodka, Liqueur, Midori, Triple Sec and juices into a mixing glass over ice. Stir well and strain into a collins glass over ice. Add soda, stir gently and serve.

Supper Sucker

14.3% ALC/VOL • 1.9 STD DRINKS

45ml (1½ fl oz) Vodka
30ml (1 fl oz) White Crème De Cacao
60ml (2 fl oz) Cranberry Juice
30ml (1 fl oz) Fresh Orange Juice

Pour ingredients into a highball glass over ice, stir well and serve with a straw.

Tiger Paw

9.3% ALC/VOL • 1.7 STD DRINKS

60ml (2 fl oz) Citrus Vodka
60ml (2 fl oz) Fresh Lemon Juice
1 tablespoon Sugar Syrup
100ml (3⅓ fl oz) Orange Soda

Pour Vodka, juice and sugar into a cocktail shaker over cracked ice. Shake and pour into a chilled highball glass. Add soda, stir gently and serve.

Mission Accomplished

29.7% ALC/VOL • 2.3 STD DRINKS

60ml (2 fl oz) Vodka
30ml (1 fl oz) Triple Sec

5ml (1/6 fl oz) Grenadine
5ml (1/6 fl oz) Fresh Lime Juice

Pour ingredients into a cocktail shaker over ice and shake. Strain into a chilled old-fashioned glass and serve.

Iguana

15.5% ALC/VOL • 1 STD DRINK

15ml (½ fl oz) Vodka
15ml (½ fl oz) Tequila
8ml (¼ fl oz) Kahlúa
45ml (1½ fl oz) Sweet and Sour Mix
Slice of Lime

Pour Vodka, Tequila, Kahlúa and sour mix into a cocktail shaker over ice. Shake and strain into a chilled cocktail glass. Garnish with a slice of lime and serve.

Toybox

31.9% ALC/VOL • 1.6 STD DRINKS

30ml (1 fl oz) Vodka
15ml (½ fl oz) Galliano
10ml (⅓ fl oz) Blue Curaçao
10ml (⅓ fl oz) Dry Vermouth

Pour ingredients into a cocktail shaker over ice and shake. Strain into a chilled cocktail glass and serve.

Petit Zinc

25.8% ALC/VOL • 1.5 STD DRINKS

30ml (1 fl oz) Vodka
15ml (½ fl oz) Cointreau
15ml (½ fl oz) Sweet Vermouth
15ml (½ fl oz) Fresh Orange Juice
Cherry

Pour Vodka, Cointreau, Vermouth and juice into a cocktail shaker over ice. Shake and strain into a chilled cocktail glass. Garnish with a cherry and serve.

Vladimir

21.8% ALC/VOL • 1 STD DRINK

30ml (1 fl oz) Vodka
10ml (⅓ fl oz) Crème De Cassis
10ml (⅓ fl oz) Grenadine
2 teaspoons Raspberry Syrup

Pour ingredients into a mixing glass over ice and stir. Strain into a chilled cocktail glass and serve.

Maverick

24.1% ALC/VOL • 2.2 STD DRINKS

45ml (1½ fl oz) Vodka
15ml (½ fl oz) Amaretto
15ml (½ fl oz) Triple Sec
10ml (⅓ fl oz) Galliano
30ml (1 fl oz) Pineapple Juice

Pour ingredients into a cocktail shaker over cracked ice and shake. Pour into an old-fashioned glass over ice and serve.

Baltic

8.9% ALC/VOL • 1.2 STD DRINKS

38ml (1¼ fl oz) Vodka
6ml (1/5 fl oz) Blue Curaçao
120ml (4 fl oz) Fresh Orange Juice
12ml (2/5 fl oz) Passion-Fruit Juice

Pour Vodka, Curaçao and passion-fruit juice into a mixing glass over ice. Stir and strain into a highball glass over ice. Add orange juice, stir and serve.

Nordlight Cocktail

5.8% ALC/VOL • 1.2 STD DRINKS

20ml (⅔ fl oz) Vodka
10ml (⅓ fl oz) Apricot Brandy
10ml (⅓ fl oz) Dry Vermouth
10ml (⅓ fl oz) Strega
10ml (⅓ fl oz) Fresh Lime Juice
210ml (7 fl oz) Tonic Water

Pour Vodka, Brandy, Vermouth, Strega and juice into a cocktail shaker over ice. Shake and strain into a chilled highball glass. Add tonic, stir gently and serve.

Green Tuberia

10.5% ALC/VOL • 2.2 STD DRINKS

60ml (2 fl oz) Vodka
30ml (1 fl oz) Midori
60ml (2 fl oz) Fresh Lemon Juice
120ml (4 fl oz) Lemon-Lime Soda

Pour Vodka, Midori and juice into a tall glass over ice then stir. Add soda, stir gently and serve.

Atomic Lokade

8.7% ALC/VOL • 1.5 STD DRINKS

30ml (1 fl oz) Vodka
15ml (½ fl oz) Blue Curaçao
15ml (½ fl oz) Triple Sec
1 teaspoon Sugar Syrup
150ml (5 fl oz) Lemonade

Pour Vodka, Curaçao, Triple Sec and sugar into a cocktail shaker over ice. Shake and strain into a chilled highball glass. Add lemonade, stir gently and serve.

Gabriela

8.9% ALC/VOL • 1.5 STD DRINKS

30ml (1 fl oz) Vodka
15ml (½ fl oz) Blue Curaçao
15ml (½ fl oz) Coconut Liqueur
Dash Pastis
150ml (5 fl oz) Bitter-Lemon Soda

Pour Vodka, Curaçao, Liqueur and Pastis into a cocktail shaker over ice. Shake and strain into a highball glass over ice. Add soda, stir gently and serve.

Sweet Libby

23.4% ALC/VOL • 1.8 STD DRINKS

60ml (2 fl oz) Vodka
5ml (1/6 fl oz) Maraschino Cherry Juice
30ml (1 fl oz) Soda Water
Maraschino Cherry

Pour Vodka and juice into a mixing glass over ice. Stir and strain into an old-fashioned glass over crushed ice. Add soda and stir gently. Garnish with a cherry and serve.

Twenny

27.3% ALC/VOL • 1.3 STD DRINKS

20ml (⅔ fl oz) Vodka
20ml (⅔ fl oz) Kahlúa
20ml (⅔ fl oz) Triple Sec
Dash Apricot Brandy

Pour ingredients into a mixing glass over ice and stir. Strain into a chilled cocktail glass and serve.

Phoenix Paradise

3.9% ALC/VOL • 0.7 STD DRINKS

25ml (5/6 fl oz) Vodka
50ml (1⅔ fl oz) Cranberry Juice
50ml (1⅔ fl oz) Fresh Orange Juice
50ml (1⅔ fl oz) Mango Juice
2 scoops Vanilla Ice Cream

Pour Vodka and juices into a blender over small amount of cracked ice then add ice cream. Blend and pour into a chilled highball glass then serve.

Vitamin 'C'

11% ALC/VOL • 0.9 STD DRINKS

30ml (1 fl oz) Vodka
45ml (1½ fl oz) Fresh Orange Juice
45ml (1½ fl oz) Sweet and Sour Mix
Slice of Orange

Pour Vodka, juice and sour mix into a cocktail shaker over ice. Shake and strain into an old-fashioned glass over ice. Garnish with a slice of orange and serve.

High Colonic

18.9% ALC/VOL • 4.5 STD DRINKS

60ml (2 fl oz) Vodka
60ml (2 fl oz) Tennessee Whiskey
30ml (1 fl oz) Jägermeister
150ml (5 fl oz) Cola
Cherry

Pour Vodka, Whiskey and Jägermeister into a tall glass over ice then stir. Add cola, stir gently and garnish with a cherry then serve.

Harlequin Frappé

28.3% ALC/VOL • 2 STD DRINKS

30ml (1 fl oz) Vodka
30ml (1 fl oz) Dark Crème De Cacao
30ml (1 fl oz) Orange Curaçao

Pour ingredients in order given into a champagne saucer filled with crushed ice and serve with 2 short straws.

Bleeker

19.3% ALC/VOL • 1.4 STD DRINKS

30ml (1 fl oz) Vodka
15ml (½ fl oz) Lillet
15ml (½ fl oz) Triple Sec
White of 1 Egg
Slice of Orange

Pour Vodka, Lillet, Triple Sec and egg white into a cocktail shaker over ice. Shake and strain into an old-fashioned glass over ice. Add more ice to fill glass and garnish with a slice of orange then serve.

High Fashion

38% ALC/VOL • 3.4 STD DRINKS

75ml (2½ fl oz) Vodka
20ml (⅔ fl oz) Cointreau
20ml (⅔ fl oz) Scotch Whisky
Twist of Orange Peel

Pour Vodka, Cointreau and Whisky into a cocktail shaker over ice. Shake and strain into a chilled cocktail glass. Twist orange peel above drink and garnish with remainder of peel then serve.

Done for the Night

18.6% ALC/VOL • 4.4 STD DRINKS

90ml (3 fl oz) Vodka
60ml (2 fl oz) Gin
30ml (1 fl oz) Tequila
1½ teaspoons Fresh Cream
120ml (4 fl oz) Root Beer

Pour Vodka, Gin and Tequila into a mixing glass over ice. Stir and strain into a chilled highball glass. Add root beer and stir gently. Float cream on top and serve.

Saga Special

27% ALC/VOL • 1.3 STD DRINKS

20ml (⅔ fl oz) Vodka
20ml (⅔ fl oz) Kahlúa
20ml (⅔ fl oz) Triple Sec
Dash Banana Liqueur
Dash Fresh Lemon Juice

Pour ingredients into a mixing glass over ice and stir. Strain into a chilled cocktail glass and serve.

Hit-it

14.7% ALC/VOL • 2.6 STD DRINKS

45ml (1½ fl oz) Vodka
30ml (1 fl oz) Cherry Liqueur
30ml (1 fl oz) Triple Sec
60ml (2 fl oz) Cranberry Juice
60ml (2 fl oz) Fresh Orange Juice

Pour ingredients into a cocktail shaker over ice and shake. Strain into a tall glass half filled with ice and serve.

Water Buffalo

15.1% ALC/VOL • 1.8 STD DRINKS

45ml (1½ fl oz) Vodka
15ml (½ fl oz) Grand Marnier
90ml (3 fl oz) Fresh Orange Juice
Maraschino Cherry

Pour Vodka, Grand Marnier and juice into a cocktail shaker over ice. Shake and strain into a highball glass half filled with ice. Garnish with a cherry and serve.

Nan's Special

8.2% ALC/VOL • 0.9 STD DRINKS

30ml (1 fl oz) Vodka
15ml (½ fl oz) Fresh Lime Juice
60ml (2 fl oz) Soda Water
30ml (1 fl oz) Lemon-Lime Soda
Pinch of Salt

Pour Vodka into a chilled cocktail glass and add lemon-lime soda then add soda water. Add juice and stir gently. Add salt, stir briefly and serve.

57 T-Bird

10.3% ALC/VOL • 2 STD DRINKS

30ml (1 fl oz) Vodka
20ml (⅔ fl oz) Amaretto
20ml (⅔ fl oz) Midori
20ml (⅔ fl oz) Peach Schnapps
150ml (5 fl oz) Fresh Orange Juice

Pour ingredients into a cocktail shaker over ice and shake. Strain into a highball glass over ice and serve.

Purple Crayon

6.8% ALC/VOL • 1.2 STD DRINKS

30ml (1 fl oz) Vodka
23ml (¾ fl oz) Chambord
165ml (5½ fl oz) Pineapple Juice
Purple Grape
Slice of Pineapple

Pour Vodka, Chambord and juice into a highball glass over ice then stir well. Garnish with a grape and slice of pineapple then serve.

Red Bird

9.6% ALC/VOL • 1.2 STD DRINKS

20ml (⅔ fl oz) Vodka
20ml (⅔ fl oz) Sweet Vermouth
20ml (⅔ fl oz) Triple Sec
100ml (3⅓ fl oz) Tonic Water

Pour Vodka, Vermouth and Triple Sec into a mixing glass over ice. Stir and strain into a highball glass over ice. Add tonic, stir gently and serve with a straw.

Overcast Friday

15.1% ALC/VOL • 1.3 STD DRINKS

45ml (1½ fl oz) Vodka
35ml (1⅙ fl oz) Corn Syrup
15ml (½ fl oz) Fresh Lemon Juice
15ml (½ fl oz) Fresh Lime Juice
Cherry

Pour Vodka, syrup and juices into a cocktail shaker over ice. Shake and strain into a chilled highball glass over a few ice cubes. Add a cherry and serve.

Blue Bike

26.7% ALC/VOL • 2.2 STD DRINKS

30ml (1 fl oz) Vodka
30ml (1 fl oz) Blue Curaçao
15ml (½ fl oz) Light Rum
15ml (½ fl oz) Triple Sec
15ml (½ fl oz) Sweet and Sour Mix

Pour ingredients into a highball glass filled with ice, stir well and serve.

Ferrari Testarossa

9.2% ALC/VOL • 1.6 STD DRINKS

30ml (1 fl oz) Vodka
23ml (¾ fl oz) Campari
15ml (½ fl oz) Raspberry Liqueur
150ml (5 fl oz) Tonic Water
Wedge of Orange

Build Vodka, Campari and Liqueur into a highball glass over ice. Twist wedge of orange above drink to release juice and add spent shell. Add tonic – do not stir, then serve with a swizzle stick and straw.

Flying High Cooler

4.9% ALC/VOL • 0.9 STD DRINKS

23ml (¾ fl oz) Vodka
15ml (½ fl oz) Banana Liqueur
23ml (¾ fl oz) Fresh Lime Juice
180ml (6 fl oz) Orange Soda

Pour Vodka, Liqueur and juice into a cocktail shaker over ice. Shake and strain into a collins glass over ice. Add soda, stir gently and serve.

San Francisco Modern

13.2% ALC/VOL • 2.9 STD DRINKS

60ml (2 fl oz) Vodka
30ml (1 fl oz) Banana Liqueur
30ml (1 fl oz) Triple Sec
8ml (¼ fl oz) Grenadine
75ml (2½ fl oz) Fresh Orange Juice
75ml (2½ fl oz) Pineapple Juice

Pour ingredients into a cocktail shaker over ice and shake. Strain into a chilled highball glass and serve.

Annie

10.8% ALC/VOL • 1.4 STD DRINKS

30ml (1 fl oz) Vodka
30ml (1 fl oz) Cranberry Liqueur
5ml (1/6 fl oz) Fresh Lime Juice
1 teaspoon Fresh Cream
90ml (3 fl oz) Soda Water

Pour Vodka, Liqueur, juice and cream into a highball glass over ice then stir. Add soda, stir gently and serve.

Screaming Viking

23% ALC/VOL • 2.2 STD DRINKS

60ml (2 fl oz) Vodka
30ml (1 fl oz) Dry Vermouth
30ml (1 fl oz) Fresh Lime Juice
Cucumber Spear
Stick of Celery

Pour Vodka, Vermouth and juice into a mixing glass over ice. Stir and strain into a chilled cocktail glass. Garnish with a cucumber spear and stick of celery then serve.

Groovy Bagpipe

5.8% ALC/VOL • 1.3 STD DRINKS

45ml (1½ fl oz) Vodka
Dash Grenadine
30ml (1 fl oz) Sweet and Sour Mix
210ml (7 fl oz) Lemon-Lime Soda

Pour Vodka, Grenadine and sour mix into a cocktail shaker over cracked ice. Shake and pour into a chilled tall glass. Add soda, stir gently and serve.

Beach Beauty

9.2% ALC/VOL • 1.5 STD DRINKS

40ml (1⅓ fl oz) Vodka
20ml (⅔ fl oz) Banana Liqueur
10ml (⅓ fl oz) Grenadine
40ml (1⅓ fl oz) Fresh Orange Juice
100ml (3⅓ fl oz) Tonic Water

Pour Vodka, Liqueur, Grenadine and juice into a cocktail shaker over ice. Shake and strain into a highball glass over ice. Add tonic, stir gently and serve.

Discharged Soldier

27.2% ALC/VOL • 1.1 STD DRINKS

30ml (1 fl oz) Citrus Vodka
10ml (⅓ fl oz) Triple Sec
10ml (⅓ fl oz) Apple Juice
Slice of Lemon

Pour Vodka, Triple Sec and juice into a cocktail shaker over ice. Shake and strain into a chilled cocktail glass. Garnish with a slice of lemon and serve.

Ladies Night

14.2% ALC/VOL • 2.5 STD DRINKS

20ml (⅔ fl oz) Vodka
10ml (⅓ fl oz) Peach Schnapps
10ml (⅓ fl oz) Red Curaçao
75ml (2½ fl oz) Fresh Orange Juice
10ml (⅓ fl oz) Lemonade

Pour Vodka, Schnapps and Curaçao into a mixing glass over ice. Stir and strain into a chilled cocktail glass. Add lemonade and stir gently. Add juice, stir and serve.

Scanex

14.3% ALC/VOL • 0.9 STD DRINKS

20ml (⅔ fl oz) Vodka
20ml (⅔ fl oz) Cranberry Liqueur
10ml (⅓ fl oz) Grenadine
20ml (⅔ fl oz) Fresh Lemon Juice
2 teaspoons Sugar Syrup

Pour ingredients into a cocktail shaker over ice and shake. Strain into a chilled cocktail glass and serve.

Eagle Eye

8.2% ALC/VOL • 1.4 STD DRINKS

30ml (1 fl oz) Vodka
30ml (1 fl oz) Passoa
75ml (2½ fl oz) Cranberry Juice
75ml (2½ fl oz) Fresh Orange Juice
Slice of Lime

Pour Vodka, Passoa and juices into a cocktail shaker over ice. Shake and strain into a highball glass over ice. Garnish with a slice of lime and serve.

Bridget in the Buff

13.1% ALC/VOL • 2.3 STD DRINKS

60ml (2 fl oz) Vodka
45ml (1½ fl oz) Chambord
Dash Sweet and Sour Mix
120ml (4 fl oz) Lemon-Lime Soda
Twist of Lemon Peel

Pour Vodka, Chambord and sour mix into a tall glass over ice then stir. Add soda and stir gently. Add lemon peel and serve.

Blue Poison

12.5% ALC/VOL • 1.2 STD DRINKS

15ml (½ fl oz) Vodka
15ml (½ fl oz) Blue Curaçao
15ml (½ fl oz) White Tequila
75ml (2½ fl oz) Lemonade
Twist of Lemon Peel

Pour Vodka and Tequila into a mixing glass over ice. Stir and strain into a chilled cocktail glass. Add lemonade and stir gently. Layer Curaçao on top and garnish with lemon peel then serve.

Crazy Huey

24.1% ALC/VOL • 1.6 STD DRINKS

45ml (1½ fl oz) Vodka
30ml (1 fl oz) Madeira
8ml (¼ fl oz) Fresh Orange Juice
Slice of Orange

Pour Vodka, Madeira and juice into a cocktail shaker over ice. Shake and strain into a chilled cocktail glass. Garnish with a slice of orange and serve.

Nasty

27.8% ALC/VOL • 2.7 STD DRINKS

38ml (1¼ fl oz) Vodka
23ml (¾ fl oz) Dark Crème De Cacao
23ml (¾ fl oz) Kahlúa
23ml (¾ fl oz) Wild Turkey Bourbon
15ml (½ fl oz) Fresh Cream

Pour ingredients into a cocktail shaker over ice and shake. Strain into a chilled cocktail glass over a few ice cubes and serve.

Midnight Moon

13.3% ALC/VOL • 2.7 STD DRINKS

45ml (1½ fl oz) Vodka
30ml (1 fl oz) Apricot Brandy
30ml (1 fl oz) Galliano
90ml (3 fl oz) Fresh Orange Juice
60ml (2 fl oz) Pineapple Juice

Pour ingredients into a cocktail shaker over cracked ice and shake. Pour into a chilled tall glass and serve.

Amazza Vampiri

32% ALC/VOL • 7.6 STD DRINKS

70ml (2⅓ fl oz) Vodka
70ml (2⅓ fl oz) Gin
70ml (2⅓ fl oz) Tequila
70ml (2⅓ fl oz) Triple Sec
Juice of 2 Strawberries

Pour Vodka, Gin, Tequila and Triple Sec into a mixing glass over ice. Stir and add juice. Stir gently and strain into a chilled tall glass over a few ice cubes then serve.

Charging Rhino

30.8% ALC/VOL • 1.8 STD DRINKS

45ml (1½ fl oz) Vodka
15ml (½ fl oz) Campari
15ml (½ fl oz) Dry Vermouth
Twist of Lemon Peel

Pour Vodka, Campari and Vermouth into a cocktail shaker over ice. Shake and strain into a chilled cocktail glass. Garnish with lemon peel and serve.

Rosebud

15.8% ALC/VOL • 2.1 STD DRINKS

60ml (2 fl oz) Citrus Vodka
15ml (½ fl oz) Triple Sec
60ml (2 fl oz) Grapefruit Juice
30ml (1 fl oz) Fresh Lime Juice

Pour grapefruit juice into a collins glass half filled with ice. Pour Vodka, Triple Sec and lime juice into a cocktail shaker over ice. Shake and strain into glass over grapefruit juice – do not stir, then serve with a straw.

Gekko

5.9% ALC/VOL • 1 STD DRINK

30ml (1 fl oz) Vodka
10ml (⅓ fl oz) Crème De Cassis
60ml (2 fl oz) Grapefruit Juice
120ml (4 fl oz) Dry Ginger Ale

Pour Vodka, Cassis and juice into a cocktail shaker over ice. Shake and strain into a highball glass over ice. Add Ginger Ale, stir gently and serve with a straw.

Perfect Pear

26.6% ALC/VOL • 1.8 STD DRINKS

45ml (1½ fl oz) Vodka
15ml (½ fl oz) Pear Brandy
15ml (½ fl oz) Fresh Lime Juice
5ml (⅙ fl oz) Fresh Orange Juice
1 teaspoon Sugar Syrup

Prepare a martini glass with a sugar frosted rim – moistened with lime juice. Pour ingredients into a cocktail shaker over ice and shake. Strain into prepared glass and serve.

The Legend

23.1% ALC/VOL • 1.9 STD DRINKS

60ml (2 fl oz) Vodka
8ml (¼ fl oz) Blackberry Schnapps
4 drops Orange Bitters
30ml (1 fl oz) Fresh Lime Juice
1 teaspoon Sugar Syrup

Pour ingredients into a cocktail shaker over ice and shake. Strain into a chilled cocktail glass and serve.

Blushing Bride

4.6% ALC/VOL • 0.9 STD DRINKS

30ml (1 fl oz) Vodka
90ml (3 fl oz) Fresh Orange Juice
60ml (2 fl oz) Cranberry Juice
60ml (2 fl oz) Lemon-Lime Soda
Cherry

Build Vodka, soda, orange juice and cranberry juice into a chilled highball glass over a few ice cubes. Garnish with a cherry then serve with a swizzle stick and straw.

Springtime

8.2% ALC/VOL • 1.2 STD DRINKS

40ml (1⅓ fl oz) Currant Vodka
100ml (3⅓ fl oz) Cranberry Juice
10ml (⅓ fl oz) Fresh Lime Juice
30ml (1 fl oz) Bitter-Lemon Soda
Slice of Lime

Pour Vodka and juices into a highball glass half filled with ice then stir. Add soda and stir gently. Garnish with a slice of lime and serve.

Gainer

13.1% ALC/VOL • 1.7 STD DRINKS

30ml (1 fl oz) Vodka
30ml (1 fl oz) Blue Curaçao
15ml (½ fl oz) Kahlúa
90ml (3 fl oz) Lemonade
Wedge of Lemon

Pour Vodka, Curaçao and Kahlúa into a cocktail shaker over ice. Shake and strain into a highball glass half filled with ice. Add lemonade and stir gently. Garnish with a wedge of lemon and serve.

Camurai

6.2% ALC/VOL • 1.2 STD DRINKS

30ml (1 fl oz) Vodka
15ml (½ fl oz) Blue Curaçao
15ml (½ fl oz) Coconut Cream
180ml (6 fl oz) Mineral Water

Pour Vodka, Curaçao and cream into a cocktail shaker over ice. Shake and strain into a chilled highball glass over a few ice cubes. Add mineral water, stir gently and serve.

Mr. Freeze

11.8% ALC/VOL • 2 STD DRINKS

30ml (1 fl oz) Vodka
30ml (1 fl oz) Blackberry Schnapps
30ml (1 fl oz) Blue Curaçao
90ml (3 fl oz) Sweet and Sour Mix
30ml (1 fl oz) Lemon-Lime Soda

Pour Vodka, Schnapps, Curaçao and sour mix into a tall glass over ice then stir. Add soda, stir gently and serve.

Cliffhanger

31.1% ALC/VOL • 2.7 STD DRINKS

60ml (2 fl oz) Pepper Vodka
30ml (1 fl oz) Cointreau
20ml (⅔ fl oz) Lime Syrup
Slice of Lime

Pour Vodka, Cointreau and syrup into a cocktail shaker over ice. Shake and strain into a chilled cocktail glass. Garnish with a slice of lime and serve.

Burnt Out Bitch

6% ALC/VOL • 1.6 STD DRINKS

15ml (½ fl oz) Vodka
15ml (½ fl oz) Light Rum
15ml (½ fl oz) Tequila
15ml (½ fl oz) Triple Sec
285ml (9½ fl oz) Fresh Orange Juice

Pour Vodka, Rum, Tequila and Triple Sec into a mixing glass over ice. Stir and strain into a chilled tall glass. Add juice, stir and serve.

Trang Tricot

5.6% ALC/VOL • 1.1 STD DRINKS

30ml (1 fl oz) Vodka
10ml (⅓ fl oz) Banana Liqueur
20ml (⅔ fl oz) Pineapple Juice
180ml (6 fl oz) Grape Soda

Pour Vodka, Liqueur and juice into a mixing glass over ice. Stir and strain into a highball glass over ice. Add soda, stir gently and serve.

Take the 'A' Train

7.5% ALC/VOL • 1.6 STD DRINKS

38ml (1¼ fl oz) Citrus Vodka
15ml (½ fl oz) Vodka
60ml (2 fl oz) Cranberry Juice
60ml (2 fl oz) Grapefruit Juice
90ml (3 fl oz) Soda Water
Wedge of Lemon

Pour Vodkas and juices into a cocktail shaker over cracked ice. Shake and pour into a chilled collins glass. Add soda and stir gently. Garnish with a wedge of lemon and serve.

Mike R-D

22.2% ALC/VOL • 1.4 STD DRINKS

30ml (1 fl oz) Vodka
30ml (1 fl oz) Peach Brandy
20ml (⅔ fl oz) Fresh Lemon Juice
Dash Grenadine

Pour Vodka, Brandy and juice into a cocktail shaker over ice. Shake and strain into a highball glass filled with ice. Add Grenadine – do not stir, then serve.

Cosmopolitan

19.8% ALC/VOL • 1.2 STD DRINKS

30ml (1 fl oz) Vodka
15ml (½ fl oz) Triple Sec
15ml (½ fl oz) Cranberry Juice
15ml (½ fl oz) Rose's Lime Juice
Wedge of Lime

Pour Vodka, Triple Sec and juices into a cocktail shaker over ice. Shake and strain into a chilled martini glass. Garnish with a wedge of lime and serve.

Recession Depression

26.5% ALC/VOL • 1.6 STD DRINKS

45ml (1½ fl oz) Citrus Vodka
15ml (½ fl oz) Triple Sec
15ml (½ fl oz) Fresh Lemon Juice
2 dashes Rose's Lime Juice

Pour ingredients into a cocktail shaker over ice and shake. Strain into a chilled cocktail glass and serve.

Tomahawk

18.4% ALC/VOL • 1.5 STD DRINKS

30ml (1 fl oz) Vodka
15ml (½ fl oz) Triple Sec
15ml (½ fl oz) White Crème De Cacao
30ml (1 fl oz) Fresh Cream
10ml (⅓ fl oz) Fresh Lemon Juice

Pour ingredients into a cocktail shaker over ice and shake. Strain into an old-fashioned glass half filled with ice and serve.

Belmont Stakes

27.2% ALC/VOL • 2.3 STD DRINKS

45ml (1½ fl oz) Vodka
23ml (¾ fl oz) Light Rum
15ml (½ fl oz) Strawberry Liqueur
8ml (¼ fl oz) Grenadine
15ml (½ fl oz) Fresh Lime Juice

Pour ingredients into a cocktail shaker over ice and shake. Strain into a chilled cocktail glass and serve.

Jolly Jumper

19.2% ALC/VOL • 4.2 STD DRINKS

40ml (1⅓ fl oz) Vodka
40ml (1⅓ fl oz) Blended Whiskey
40ml (1⅓ fl oz) Gin
40ml (1⅓ fl oz) Passion-Fruit Liqueur
120ml (4 fl oz) Fresh Orange Juice

Pour Vodka, Whiskey, Gin and Liqueur into a tall glass over ice then stir. Add juice, stir well and serve.

Losing Your Cherry

9.5% ALC/VOL • 1.6 STD DRINKS

45ml (1½ fl oz) Vodka
15ml (½ fl oz) Cherry Brandy
90ml (3 fl oz) Sweet and Sour Mix
60ml (2 fl oz) Lemonade

Pour Vodka, Brandy and sour mix into a mixing glass over ice. Stir and strain into a chilled old-fashioned glass. Add lemonade, stir gently and serve.

Raffy

8.3% ALC/VOL • 1.4 STD DRINKS

24ml (⅘ fl oz) Vodka
18ml (⅗ fl oz) Banana Liqueur
18ml (⅗ fl oz) Kiwi Liqueur
Dash Campari
150ml (5 fl oz) Tonic Water

Pour Vodka, Liqueurs and Campari into a cocktail shaker over ice. Shake and strain into a highball glass over ice. Add tonic, stir gently and serve.

Hi Rise

10.6% ALC/VOL • 1.1 STD DRINKS

30ml (1 fl oz) Vodka
8ml (¼ fl oz) Cointreau
8ml (¼ fl oz) Grenadine
60ml (2 fl oz) Fresh Orange Juice
30ml (1 fl oz) Sweet and Sour Mix

Pour ingredients into a mixing glass without ice and stir. Pour into a tall glass filled with crushed ice and serve with 2 straws.

Siberian Husky

9% ALC/VOL • 1.3 STD DRINKS

30ml (1 fl oz) Vodka
30ml (1 fl oz) Chambord
30ml (1 fl oz) Fresh Cream
3 scoops Vanilla Ice Cream
Cherry

Pour Vodka, Chambord and cream into a blender without ice then add ice cream. Blend until smooth and pour into a chilled old-fashioned glass. Add a cherry and serve.

Frontal Lobotomy

28.2% ALC/VOL • 5.3 STD DRINKS

60ml (2 fl oz) Vodka
60ml (2 fl oz) Tequila
30ml (1 fl oz) Jägermeister
30ml (1 fl oz) Tennessee Whiskey
60ml (2 fl oz) Soda Water

Pour Vodka, Tequila, Jägermeister and Whiskey into a cocktail shaker over ice. Shake and strain into a tall glass over ice. Add soda, stir gently and serve.

Cats 'n' Roses

15.6% ALC/VOL • 2.7 STD DRINKS

60ml (2 fl oz) Vodka
60ml (2 fl oz) Raspberry Liqueur
30ml (1 fl oz) Grenadine
60ml (2 fl oz) Fresh Lime Juice
10ml (⅓ fl oz) Orange Soda

Pour Vodka, Liqueur, Grenadine and juice into a cocktail shaker over ice. Shake and strain into a highball glass over ice. Add soda – do not stir, then serve.

Lemon Drop

36.5% ALC/VOL • 2.7 STD DRINKS

45ml (1½ fl oz) Vodka
45ml (1½ fl oz) Cointreau
5ml (1/6 fl oz) Fresh Lemon Juice
Twist of Lemon Peel

Prepare a cocktail glass with a sugar frosted rim. Pour Vodka, Cointreau and juice into a cocktail shaker over ice. Shake and strain into prepared glass. Garnish with lemon peel and serve.

Red Con

7.5% ALC/VOL • 1 STD DRINK

20ml (⅔ fl oz) Vodka
20ml (⅔ fl oz) Red Curaçao
1 teaspoon Sugar Syrup
120ml (4 fl oz) Soda Water
2 Slices of Orange

Pour Vodka, Curaçao and sugar into a cocktail shaker over ice. Shake and strain into a chilled old-fashioned glass. Add soda and stir gently. Garnish with slices of orange and serve.

High Roller

13.7% ALC/VOL • 2 STD DRINKS

45ml (1½ fl oz) Vodka
23ml (¾ fl oz) Grand Marnier
2 drops Grenadine
120ml (4 fl oz) Fresh Orange Juice

Pour Vodka, Grand Marnier and juice into a cocktail shaker over ice. Shake and strain into a highball glass over ice. Add Grenadine – do not stir, then serve.

Bridge to the Moon

12.5% ALC/VOL • 1.5 STD DRINKS

30ml (1 fl oz) Currant Vodka
20ml (⅔ fl oz) Apple Schnapps
20ml (⅔ fl oz) Passion-Fruit Liqueur
83ml (2¾ fl oz) Lemon-Lime Soda
2 Slices of Orange

Place slices of orange into a chilled highball glass and muddle to release juice. Add Vodka, Schnapps and Liqueur. Add crushed ice and stir well. Add soda, stir gently and serve.

Orange Surfboard

13.1% ALC/VOL • 2.8 STD DRINKS

60ml (2 fl oz) Orange Vodka
30ml (1 fl oz) Malibu
30ml (1 fl oz) Triple Sec
150ml (5 fl oz) Fresh Orange Juice
5ml (1/6 fl oz) Cranberry Juice

Pour ingredients into a cocktail shaker over ice and shake. Strain into a tall glass over ice and serve.

Cool Lara

14.8% ALC/VOL • 1.6 STD DRINKS

20ml (⅔ fl oz) Vodka
20ml (⅔ fl oz) Dark Crème De Cacao
20ml (⅔ fl oz) Kahlúa
20ml (⅔ fl oz) White Crème De Menthe
2 scoops Vanilla Ice Cream

Pour Vodka, Cacao, Kahlúa and Crème De Menthe into a blender over small amount of crushed ice then add ice cream. Blend until smooth and pour into a chilled parfait glass then serve.

Blue Glacier

36.3% ALC/VOL • 2.7 STD DRINKS

90ml (3 fl oz) Vodka
5ml (1/6 fl oz) Blue Curaçao
Twist of Lemon Peel
Twist of Orange Peel

Pour Vodka and Curaçao into a mixing glass over ice. Stir and strain into a frosted cocktail glass. Garnish with lemon and orange peels then serve.

Maiden's Blood

8.6% ALC/VOL • 1.1 STD DRINKS

15ml (½ fl oz) Vodka
15ml (½ fl oz) Light Rum
8ml (¼ fl oz) Cointreau
120ml (4 fl oz) Grenadine
8ml (¼ fl oz) Fresh Lime Juice

Pour Vodka, Rum and Cointreau into a cocktail shaker over cracked ice. Shake and pour into a chilled old-fashioned glass. Add Grenadine and juice – do not stir, then serve with a straw.

Hector Spezial

20.4% ALC/VOL • 1.8 STD DRINKS

40ml (1⅓ fl oz) Vodka
20ml (⅔ fl oz) White Tequila
10ml (⅓ fl oz) Grenadine
40ml (1⅓ fl oz) Fresh Orange Juice

Pour Vodka, Tequila and juice into a cocktail shaker over ice. Shake and strain into a chilled old-fashioned glass. Add Grenadine, stir gently and serve with a straw.

Vodka Flinch

13.6% ALC/VOL • 1.6 STD DRINKS

45ml (1½ fl oz) Vodka
15ml (½ fl oz) Triple Sec
36ml (1⅕ fl oz) Grenadine
36ml (1⅕ fl oz) Fresh Orange Juice
18ml (⅗ fl oz) Fresh Lemon Juice

Pour ingredients into a cocktail shaker over ice and shake. Strain into a chilled champagne saucer and serve.

Wild Wendy

10.1% ALC/VOL • 1.6 STD DRINKS

45ml (1½ fl oz) Vodka
15ml (½ fl oz) Malibu
45ml (1½ fl oz) Cranberry Juice
45ml (1½ fl oz) Fresh Orange Juice
45ml (1½ fl oz) Pineapple Juice

Pour ingredients into a cocktail shaker over ice and shake. Strain into a highball glass over ice and serve.

Guapasipati

29.5% ALC/VOL • 1.5 STD DRINKS

38ml (1¼ fl oz) Vodka
15ml (½ fl oz) Dry Vermouth
8ml (¼ fl oz) Banana Liqueur
Dash Grenadine
Dash Fresh Orange Juice

Pour ingredients into a cocktail shaker over ice and shake. Strain into a chilled cocktail glass and serve.

New York Lemonade

19% ALC/VOL • 2.7 STD DRINKS

60ml (2 fl oz) Citrus Vodka
30ml (1 fl oz) Grand Marnier
60ml (2 fl oz) Fresh Lemon Juice
30ml (1 fl oz) Soda Water

Prepare a champagne saucer with a sugar frosted rim – moistened with lemon juice. Pour ingredients into a mixing glass over ice and stir. Strain into prepared glass and serve.

Red Shark

10.5% ALC/VOL • 2.3 STD DRINKS

40ml (1⅓ fl oz) Vodka
30ml (1 fl oz) Red Curaçao
30ml (1 fl oz) Triple Sec
83ml (2¾ fl oz) Passion-Fruit Juice
40ml (1⅓ fl oz) Grape Juice
60ml (2 fl oz) Bitter-Lemon Soda

Pour Vodka, Curaçao, Triple Sec and juices into a blender over crushed ice. Blend and pour into a chilled tall glass. Add soda, stir gently and serve.

Blue Jeans

8.9% ALC/VOL • 1 STD DRINK

20ml (⅔ fl oz) Vodka
20ml (⅔ fl oz) Blue Curaçao
50ml (1⅔ fl oz) Grapefruit Juice
50ml (1⅔ fl oz) Pineapple Juice

Pour Vodka, Curaçao and grapefruit juice into a cocktail shaker over cracked ice. Shake and pour into a chilled highball glass. Add pineapple juice, stir and serve.

Black River

13.3% ALC/VOL • 1.1 STD DRINKS

20ml (⅔ fl oz) Vodka
10ml (⅓ fl oz) Aquavit
10ml (⅓ fl oz) Kahlúa
3 drops Fresh Lime Juice
30ml (1 fl oz) Lemon-Lime Soda
30ml (1 fl oz) Soda Water
Slice of Lime

Pour Vodka, Aquavit and Kahlúa into a cocktail glass over ice then stir. Add sodas by pouring into glass simultaneously then stir gently. Add juice – do not stir, then garnish with a slice of lime and serve.

Scarlet Pimp

11.1% ALC/VOL • 2.5 STD DRINKS

60ml (2 fl oz) Citrus Vodka
45ml (1½ fl oz) Midori
120ml (4 fl oz) Fresh Orange Juice
60ml (2 fl oz) Sweet and Sour Mix

Pour ingredients into a cocktail shaker over ice and shake. Strain into a tall glass over ice and serve.

Odwits

17.6% ALC/VOL • 3.6 STD DRINKS

45ml (1½ fl oz) Vodka
45ml (1½ fl oz) Tequila
30ml (1 fl oz) Southern Comfort
Dash Galliano
135ml (4½ fl oz) Fresh Orange Juice
Slice of Lemon

Pour Vodka, Tequila, Southern Comfort and juice into a mixing glass over ice. Stir and strain into a chilled highball glass over a few ice cubes. Add Galliano and stir. Add a slice of lemon and serve.

Kelsey and Dori

10.1% ALC/VOL • 1.4 STD DRINKS

30ml (1 fl oz) Vodka
15ml (½ fl oz) Amaretto
15ml (½ fl oz) Midori
120ml (4 fl oz) Pineapple Juice
Dash Cranberry Juice

Pour ingredients into a cocktail shaker over ice and shake. Strain into a chilled highball glass and serve.

Daytona Bay

6.3% ALC/VOL • 1.3 STD DRINKS

30ml (1 fl oz) Vodka
30ml (1 fl oz) Raspberry Liqueur
90ml (3 fl oz) Cranberry Juice
90ml (3 fl oz) Fresh Orange Juice
30ml (1 fl oz) Peach Nectar
Slice of Orange

Pour Vodka, Liqueur, juices and nectar into a cocktail shaker over ice. Shake and strain into a tall glass over ice. Garnish with a slice of orange and serve.

Panama Deluxe

16% ALC/VOL • 1.9 STD DRINKS

30ml (1 fl oz) Vodka
30ml (1 fl oz) Kahlúa
30ml (1 fl oz) White Crème De Cacao
60ml (2 fl oz) Fresh Cream

Pour ingredients into a cocktail shaker over ice and shake. Strain into an old-fashioned glass over ice and serve.

Province Town

5.8% ALC/VOL • 1.3 STD DRINKS

30ml (1 fl oz) Vodka
15ml (½ fl oz) Citrus Vodka
60ml (2 fl oz) Cranberry Juice
60ml (2 fl oz) Grapefruit Juice
120ml (4 fl oz) Soda Water

Pour Vodkas and juices into a collins glass over ice then stir. Add soda, stir gently and serve.

Danberry

11.1% ALC/VOL • 0.9 STD DRINKS

30ml (1 fl oz) Vodka
60ml (2 fl oz) Cranberry Juice
10ml (⅓ fl oz) Soda Water
Slice of Lime

Pour Vodka and juice into an old-fashioned glass over ice then stir. Add soda – do not stir, then float a slice of lime on top and serve.

Alaskan Suntan

12.4% ALC/VOL • 2.6 STD DRINKS

30ml (1 fl oz) Vodka
30ml (1 fl oz) Gin
30ml (1 fl oz) Light Rum
90ml (3 fl oz) Fresh Orange Juice
90ml (3 fl oz) Pineapple Juice
Slice of Orange

Pour juices into a cocktail shaker over cracked ice and shake then pour into a chilled tall glass. Add Vodka, Gin and Rum then stir well. Garnish with a slice of orange and serve.

Banana Balm

16.1% ALC/VOL • 1.6 STD DRINKS

45ml (1½ fl oz) Vodka
15ml (½ fl oz) Banana Liqueur
5ml (⅙ fl oz) Fresh Lime Juice
60ml (2 fl oz) Soda Water

Pour Vodka, Liqueur and juice into a champagne saucer over ice then stir. Add soda, stir gently and serve.

Breezy Nik

11.4% ALC/VOL • 2 STD DRINKS

30ml (1 fl oz) Vodka
30ml (1 fl oz) Pear Liqueur
15ml (½ fl oz) Gin
120ml (4 fl oz) Cranberry Juice
15ml (½ fl oz) Fresh Lemon Juice
15ml (½ fl oz) Blackberry Syrup

Pour ingredients into a cocktail shaker over ice and shake. Strain into a chilled highball glass and serve.

Swedish Blackberry

29.2% ALC/VOL • 1.7 STD DRINKS

45ml (1½ fl oz) Citrus Vodka
15ml (½ fl oz) Blackberry Brandy
15ml (½ fl oz) Fresh Lemon Juice
Slice of Lemon

Pour Vodka, Brandy and juice into a cocktail shaker over ice. Shake and strain into a chilled cocktail glass. Garnish with a slice of lemon and serve.

Oh Canada!

7.5% ALC/VOL • 1.5 STD DRINKS

23ml (¾ fl oz) Vodka
23ml (¾ fl oz) Peach Schnapps
23ml (¾ fl oz) Triple Sec
90ml (3 fl oz) Fresh Orange Juice
90ml (3 fl oz) Pineapple Juice
Cherry
Slice of Orange

Pour Vodka, Schnapps, Triple Sec and juices into a cocktail shaker over ice. Shake and strain into a tall glass over ice. Garnish with a cherry and slice of orange then serve.

Foghorn

6.2% ALC/VOL • 0.9 STD DRINKS

30ml (1 fl oz) Vodka
60ml (2 fl oz) Cranberry Juice
60ml (2 fl oz) Sweet and Sour Mix
30ml (1 fl oz) Cherry Juice

Pour ingredients into a cocktail shaker over ice and shake. Strain into a highball glass over ice and serve.

Ninty Park Lane

10.8% ALC/VOL • 1.2 STD DRINKS

30ml (1 fl oz) Vodka
15ml (½ fl oz) Green Crème De Menthe
60ml (2 fl oz) Fresh Orange Juice
White of 1 Egg

Pour Vodka, juice and egg white into a cocktail shaker over ice. Shake and strain into an old-fashioned glass over crushed ice then stir. Add Crème De Menthe by pouring on top – do not stir, then serve.

Eva

22.5% ALC/VOL • 1.2 STD DRINKS

30ml (1 fl oz) Vodka
20ml (⅔ fl oz) Green Crème De Menthe
20ml (⅔ fl oz) Sugar Syrup
Cherry

Pour Vodka, Crème De Menthe and sugar into a cocktail shaker over cracked ice. Shake and pour into a chilled cocktail glass. Add a cherry and serve.

Cassis Screwdriver

9.3% ALC/VOL • 0.8 STD DRINKS

45ml (1½ fl oz) Vodka
15ml (½ fl oz) Crème De Cassis
5ml (⅙ fl oz) Grenadine
45ml (1½ fl oz) Fresh Orange Juice
5ml (⅙ fl oz) Fresh Lemon Juice
Wedge of Lemon

Pour Vodka and juices into a cocktail shaker over ice. Shake and strain into a chilled highball glass over a few ice cubes. Add Cassis and Grenadine then stir gently. Garnish with a wedge of lemon and serve with a straw.

Blonde Bomb-Shell

35.4% ALC/VOL • 1.8 STD DRINKS

30ml (1 fl oz) Vodka
30ml (1 fl oz) Brandy
3 dashes Apple Schnapps
3 dashes Pear Schnapps

Pour ingredients into a cocktail shaker over ice and shake. Strain into a chilled cocktail glass and serve.

Walking Home

22.7% ALC/VOL • 3 STD DRINKS

30ml (1 fl oz) Vodka
30ml (1 fl oz) Light Rum
30ml (1 fl oz) Tequila
15ml (½ fl oz) Sloe Gin
60ml (2 fl oz) Fresh Lime Juice
Dash Maraschino Cherry Juice

Pour Vodka, Rum, Tequila, Gin and lime juice into a cocktail shaker over ice. Shake and strain into a chilled champagne saucer. Add cherry juice – do not stir, then serve.

Rigor Mortis

18% ALC/VOL • 1.8 STD DRINKS

45ml (1½ fl oz) Vodka
23ml (¾ fl oz) Amaretto
30ml (1 fl oz) Fresh Orange Juice
30ml (1 fl oz) Pineapple Juice

Pour ingredients into a cocktail shaker over ice and shake. Strain into a chilled old-fashioned glass and serve.

Pleasure Shiver

18.9% ALC/VOL • 1.3 STD DRINKS

15ml (½ fl oz) Vodka
15ml (½ fl oz) Amaretto
15ml (½ fl oz) Triple Sec
15ml (½ fl oz) White Crème De Cacao
30ml (1 fl oz) Fresh Cream
Cinnamon

Pour Vodka, Amaretto, Triple Sec, Cacao and cream into a cocktail shaker over ice. Shake and strain into a chilled cocktail glass. Sprinkle cinnamon on top and serve.

Gorky Park Cooler

7.7% ALC/VOL • 2 STD DRINKS

45ml (1½ fl oz) Strawberry Vodka
15ml (½ fl oz) Malibu
15ml (½ fl oz) Spiced Rum
250ml (8⅓ fl oz) Pineapple Juice

Pour Vodka, Malibu and Rum into a cocktail shaker over ice. Shake and strain into a chilled collins glass. Add juice, stir and serve.

Tina Rita

32% ALC/VOL • 1.6 STD DRINKS

38ml (1¼ fl oz) Vodka
8ml (¼ fl oz) Cointreau
8ml (¼ fl oz) Grand Marnier
5ml (⅙ fl oz) Fresh Lime Juice
5ml (⅙ fl oz) Sweet and Sour Mix
Wedge of Lime

Prepare a margarita glass with a salt and sugar frosted rim – moistened with sweet and sour mix. Pour Vodka, Cointreau, Grand Marnier, juice and sour mix into a cocktail shaker over ice. Shake and strain into prepared glass. Garnish with a wedge of lime and serve.

Down Under

32.2% ALC/VOL • 1.5 STD DRINKS

30ml (1 fl oz) Vodka
10ml (⅓ fl oz) Brandy
10ml (⅓ fl oz) Crème De Cassis
10ml (⅓ fl oz) Triple Sec

Pour ingredients into a cocktail shaker over ice and shake. Strain into a chilled cocktail glass and serve.

Bikini Wax

28.5% ALC/VOL • 2.7 STD DRINKS

60ml (2 fl oz) Vodka
30ml (1 fl oz) Light Rum
15ml (½ fl oz) Fresh Milk (chilled)
8ml (¼ fl oz) Fresh Lemon Juice
1 teaspoon Sugar Syrup
Twist of Lemon Peel

Pour Vodka, Rum, milk, juice and sugar into a cocktail shaker over ice. Shake and strain into a chilled cocktail glass. Garnish with lemon peel and serve.

Drake Cooler

7.8% ALC/VOL • 1.9 STD DRINKS

45ml (1½ fl oz) Vodka
30ml (1 fl oz) Sloe Gin
120ml (4 fl oz) Grapefruit Juice
120ml (4 fl oz) Pineapple Juice
Dash Sugar Syrup

Pour ingredients into a cocktail shaker over ice and shake. Strain into a collins glass over ice and serve.

Spring Rose

5.6% ALC/VOL • 1.2 STD DRINKS

24ml (⁴⁄₅ fl oz) Vodka
12ml (²⁄₅ fl oz) Banana Liqueur
12ml (²⁄₅ fl oz) Campari
Dash Pastis
12ml (²⁄₅ fl oz) Fresh Cream
210ml (7 fl oz) Tonic Water

Pour Vodka, Liqueur, Campari, Pastis and cream into a cocktail shaker over ice. Shake and strain into a chilled highball glass. Add tonic, stir gently and serve.

Old Dirty Surprise

26% ALC/VOL • 1.5 STD DRINKS

30ml (1 fl oz) Vodka
15ml (½ fl oz) Bacardi Limon
15ml (½ fl oz) Midori
15ml (½ fl oz) Pineapple Juice

Pour Vodka, Bacardi and Midori into a mixing glass over ice. Stir and strain into a chilled old-fashioned glass. Add juice by pouring gently on top – do not stir, then serve.

Creamy Dreamer

10.4% ALC/VOL • 1.2 STD DRINKS

30ml (1 fl oz) Vodka
15ml (½ fl oz) White Crème De Cacao
5ml (⅙ fl oz) Kahlúa
90ml (3 fl oz) Fresh Orange Juice
Fresh Whipped Cream

Pour Vodka, Cacao and juice into a blender over crushed ice. Blend and pour into a chilled hurricane glass. Float cream on top and add Kahlúa by pouring over cream then serve.

Vodka Sourball

27.2% ALC/VOL • 1.6 STD DRINKS

45ml (1½ fl oz) Lemon Vodka
15ml (½ fl oz) Triple Sec
15ml (½ fl oz) Pineapple Juice
Maraschino Cherry
Slice of Pineapple

Pour Vodka, Triple Sec and juice into a cocktail shaker over ice. Shake and strain into a chilled sour glass. Garnish with a cherry and slice of pineapple then serve.

Rob Love

9.6% ALC/VOL • 1.5 STD DRINKS

40ml (1⅓ fl oz) Vodka
10ml (⅓ fl oz) Sweet Vermouth
10ml (⅓ fl oz) White Curaçao
90ml (3 fl oz) Fresh Lemon Juice
3 drops Strawberry Syrup
45ml (1½ fl oz) Lemon-Lime Soda

Pour Vodka, Vermouth, Curaçao, juice and syrup into a highball glass over ice then stir well. Add soda, stir gently and serve.

Pink Pearl

5.3% ALC/VOL • 0.9 STD DRINKS

30ml (1 fl oz) Vodka
120ml (4 fl oz) Grapefruit Juice
30ml (1 fl oz) Fresh Lime Juice
30ml (1 fl oz) Maraschino Cherry Juice

Pour ingredients into a cocktail shaker over ice and shake. Strain into a highball glass over ice and serve.

Blue do it

19.1% ALC/VOL • 3.2 STD DRINKS

30ml (1 fl oz) Vodka
30ml (1 fl oz) Blue Curaçao
30ml (1 fl oz) Gin
30ml (1 fl oz) White Tequila
1 teaspoon Egg White
90ml (3 fl oz) Soda Water

Pour Vodka, Curaçao, Gin, Tequila and egg white into a cocktail shaker over ice. Shake and strain into a highball glass over ice. Add soda, stir gently and serve.

Blue Fashion

12.4% ALC/VOL • 1.5 STD DRINKS

30ml (1 fl oz) Vodka
30ml (1 fl oz) Blue Curaçao
60ml (2 fl oz) Fresh Milk (chilled)
1 scoop Lemon Ice Cream

Pour Vodka, Curaçao and milk into a blender without ice then add ice cream. Blend until smooth and pour into a chilled parfait glass then serve.

Love Juice

7.2% ALC/VOL • 0.8 STD DRINKS

15ml (½ fl oz) Vodka
15ml (½ fl oz) Passion-Fruit Liqueur
8ml (¼ fl oz) Pisang Ambon
15ml (½ fl oz) Grenadine
45ml (1½ fl oz) Fresh Orange Juice
45ml (1½ fl oz) Pineapple Juice

Pour Vodka, Liqueur, Pisang Ambon and juices into a cocktail shaker over ice. Shake and strain into a highball glass over ice. Add Grenadine by pouring into centre of drink - do not stir, then serve.

Pimp Cocktail

13.2% ALC/VOL • 2.8 STD DRINKS

60ml (2 fl oz) Vodka
30ml (1 fl oz) Blue Curaçao
30ml (1 fl oz) Peach Schnapps
150ml (5 fl oz) Fresh Orange Juice

Pour Vodka, Curaçao and Schnapps into a mixing glass over ice. Stir and strain into a chilled highball glass. Add juice, stir and serve.

Hawaiian Sunset

7% ALC/VOL • 1.3 STD DRINKS

45ml (1½ fl oz) Vodka
75ml (2½ fl oz) Cranberry Juice
75ml (2½ fl oz) Fresh Orange Juice
45ml (1½ fl oz) Soda Water
Cherry
Slice of Pineapple

Pour Vodka and juices into a cocktail shaker over ice. Shake and strain into a highball glass over ice then add soda - do not stir. Garnish with a cherry and slice of pineapple then serve.

Kashmir

22.5% ALC/VOL • 1.4 STD DRINKS

30ml (1 fl oz) Vodka
30ml (1 fl oz) White Crème De Cacao
10ml (⅓ fl oz) Grenadine
10ml (⅓ fl oz) Fresh Lemon Juice

Pour ingredients into a cocktail shaker over ice and shake. Strain into a chilled cocktail glass and serve.

Headlights

33.4% ALC/VOL • 1.8 STD DRINKS

30ml (1 fl oz) Vodka
15ml (½ fl oz) Yellow Chartreuse
10ml (⅓ fl oz) Blue Curaçao
10ml (⅓ fl oz) Galliano
5ml (⅙ fl oz) Fresh Lemon Juice
Maraschino Cherry

Pour Vodka, Chartreuse, Curaçao, Galliano and juice into a cocktail shaker over ice. Shake and strain into a chilled cocktail glass. Garnish with a cherry and serve.

Firehammer

30.8% ALC/VOL • 1.9 STD DRINKS

45ml (1½ fl oz) Vodka
15ml (½ fl oz) Amaretto
15ml (½ fl oz) Triple Sec
5ml (⅙ fl oz) Fresh Lemon Juice

Pour ingredients into a cocktail shaker over ice and shake. Strain into a chilled cocktail glass and serve.

Dolphin Fin

14.4% ALC/VOL • 1.1 STD DRINKS

30ml (1 fl oz) Vodka
15ml (½ fl oz) Sweet Vermouth
10ml (⅓ fl oz) Grenadine
30ml (1 fl oz) Fresh Orange Juice
8ml (¼ fl oz) Fresh Lemon Juice
Maraschino Cherry

Pour Vodka, Vermouth, Grenadine and juices into a cocktail shaker over ice. Shake and strain into a chilled cocktail glass. Garnish with a cherry and serve.

Bare Cheeks

14.8% ALC/VOL • 0.9 STD DRINKS

30ml (1 fl oz) Vodka
10ml (⅓ fl oz) Grenadine
30ml (1 fl oz) Apple Juice
5ml (⅙ fl oz) Fresh Lemon Juice

Pour ingredients into a cocktail shaker over ice and shake. Strain into a chilled cocktail glass and serve.

Tropical Sun

6% ALC/VOL • 1 STD DRINK

20ml (⅔ fl oz) Vodka
10ml (⅓ fl oz) Apricot Brandy
10ml (⅓ fl oz) Dark Rum
30ml (1 fl oz) Fresh Orange Juice
150ml (5 fl oz) Tonic Water
Slice of Orange

Pour Vodka, Brandy, Rum and juice into a highball glass over ice then stir. Add tonic and stir gently. Garnish with a slice of orange and serve.

Devil's Killer

18.8% ALC/VOL • 1.8 STD DRINKS

30ml (1 fl oz) Vodka
30ml (1 fl oz) Tequila

30ml (1 fl oz) Tomato Juice (chilled)
30ml (1 fl oz) Tabasco Sauce

Pour ingredients into a mixing glass over ice and stir. Strain into a chilled old-fashioned glass and serve.

Peace Lovin'

23.5% ALC/VOL • 2.2 STD DRINKS

60ml (2 fl oz) Vodka
30ml (1 fl oz) Peach Schnapps
30ml (1 fl oz) Fresh Orange Juice
Twist of Orange Peel

Rub orange peel around the rim of a chilled cocktail glass then place remainder of peel into glass. Pour Vodka, Schnapps and juice into a cocktail shaker over ice. Shake and strain into prepared glass then serve.

Cerise's Surprise

17.8% ALC/VOL • 1.6 STD DRINKS

45ml (1½ fl oz) Vodka
15ml (½ fl oz) Cherry Brandy
45ml (1½ fl oz) Pineapple Juice
8ml (¼ fl oz) Fresh Lime Juice

Pour ingredients into a cocktail shaker over ice and shake. Strain into an old-fashioned glass over ice and serve.

Ambijaxtrious

23.6% ALC/VOL • 4.5 STD DRINKS

60ml (2 fl oz) Vodka
60ml (2 fl oz) Kahlúa
60ml (2 fl oz) Tequila
2 dashes Grenadine
60ml (2 fl oz) Fresh Milk (chilled)

Pour ingredients into a highball glass over crushed ice, stir well and serve.

Canadian Paralyzer

9.5% ALC/VOL • 1.3 STD DRINKS

30ml (1 fl oz) Vodka
30ml (1 fl oz) Kahlúa
105ml (3½ fl oz) Fresh Milk (chilled)
15ml (½ fl oz) Cola

Pour Vodka, Kahlúa and milk into a cocktail shaker over ice. Shake and strain into a chilled old-fashioned glass. Add cola, stir gently and serve.
This drink is also known as Colorado Bulldog.

Ruffles Design

8.4% ALC/VOL • 1.4 STD DRINKS

30ml (1 fl oz) Vodka
20ml (⅔ fl oz) Kiwi Liqueur
10ml (⅓ fl oz) Pisang Ambon
5ml (1/6 fl oz) Maracuja Juice
150ml (5 fl oz) Orange Soda

Pour Vodka, Liqueur, Pisang Ambon and juice into a highball glass over ice then stir. Add soda, stir gently and serve.

Creamy Miami

25.1% ALC/VOL • 1.6 STD DRINKS

30ml (1 fl oz) Vodka
30ml (1 fl oz) Sweet Vermouth
10ml (⅓ fl oz) Triple Sec
10ml (⅓ fl oz) White Crème De Cacao

Pour ingredients into a cocktail shaker over ice and shake. Strain into a chilled cocktail glass and serve.

Pink Hest

27.5% ALC/VOL • 1.3 STD DRINKS

20ml (⅔ fl oz) Vodka
20ml (⅔ fl oz) Apricot Brandy
20ml (⅔ fl oz) Triple Sec
Dash Fresh Cream
Dash Orange Soda

Pour Vodka, Brandy, Triple Sec and cream into a cocktail shaker over ice. Shake and strain into a chilled cocktail glass. Add soda, stir gently and serve.

Fantasy

14.2% ALC/VOL • 1.5 STD DRINKS

30ml (1 fl oz) Vodka
20ml (⅔ fl oz) Southern Comfort
30ml (1 fl oz) Apple Juice
50ml (1⅔ fl oz) Cola

Pour Vodka, Southern Comfort and juice into a cocktail shaker over ice. Shake and strain into a chilled old-fashioned glass over a few ice cubes. Add cola, stir gently and serve.

A Midsummernight Dream

15.6% ALC/VOL • 2.7 STD DRINKS

60ml (2 fl oz) Vodka
30ml (1 fl oz) Kirsch
5ml (1/6 fl oz) Strawberry Liqueur
75ml (2½ fl oz) Spring Water
5 Strawberries (diced)

Place diced strawberries into a blender without ice and blend to a purée. Scoop into a cocktail shaker over cracked ice then add Vodka, Kirsch and Liqueur. Shake well and pour into a chilled highball glass. Add water, stir and serve.

Barberry Coast

9.5% ALC/VOL • 1.3 STD DRINKS

30ml (1 fl oz) Vodka
30ml (1 fl oz) Raspberry Liqueur
60ml (2 fl oz) Cranberry Juice
60ml (2 fl oz) Fresh Orange Juice

Pour ingredients into a cocktail shaker over ice and shake. Strain into a highball glass over ice and serve.

Broken Golf Cart

20% ALC/VOL • 1.3 STD DRINKS

30ml (1 fl oz) Vodka
10ml (⅓ fl oz) Amaretto
10ml (⅓ fl oz) Midori
30ml (1 fl oz) Cranberry Juice
Twist of Lemon Peel

Pour Vodka, Amaretto, Midori and juice into a cocktail shaker over ice. Shake and strain into a chilled martini glass. Twist lemon peel above drink and place remainder of peel into drink then serve.

I Love Lucy

24.5% ALC/VOL • 1.2 STD DRINKS

30ml (1 fl oz) Vodka
8ml (¼ fl oz) Parfait Amour
8ml (¼ fl oz) Triple Sec
15ml (½ fl oz) Fresh Lime Juice

Pour ingredients into a cocktail shaker over ice and shake. Strain into a chilled cocktail glass and serve.

Caramel Nut

15.1% ALC/VOL • 1.4 STD DRINKS

30ml (1 fl oz) Caramel Vodka
30ml (1 fl oz) Dark Crème De Cacao
2 scoops Vanilla Ice Cream
Fresh Whipped Cream
Crushed Nuts

Pour Vodka and Cacao into a blender without ice then add ice cream. Blend until smooth and pour into a chilled champagne flute. Float cream on top and sprinkle nuts over cream then serve.

Chocolate Twist

15.3% ALC/VOL • 1.4 STD DRINKS

30ml (1 fl oz) Vodka
15ml (½ fl oz) Dark Crème De Cacao
15ml (½ fl oz) Triple Sec
30ml (1 fl oz) Fresh Lime Juice
30ml (1 fl oz) Fresh Cream

Pour ingredients into a cocktail shaker over ice and shake. Strain into a chilled cocktail glass and serve.

Dayak Surprise

14.7% ALC/VOL • 1.9 STD DRINKS

30ml (1 fl oz) Vodka
30ml (1 fl oz) Kahlúa
30ml (1 fl oz) Pisang Ambon
2 teaspoons Fresh Cream
60ml (2 fl oz) Lemonade
Maraschino Cherry

Pour lemonade into an old-fashioned glass over ice then add Vodka, Kahlúa and Pisang Ambon – do not stir. Float cream on top and garnish with a cherry then serve.

Village

19.3% ALC/VOL • 0.9 STD DRINKS

15ml (½ fl oz) Vodka
15ml (½ fl oz) Aperol
15ml (½ fl oz) Passion-Fruit Liqueur
15ml (½ fl oz) Pineapple Juice

Pour ingredients into a cocktail shaker over ice and shake. Strain into a chilled cocktail glass and serve.

Crash Landing

23.8% ALC/VOL • 1.3 STD DRINKS

45ml (1½ fl oz) Vodka
10ml (⅓ fl oz) Grenadine
5ml (⅙ fl oz) Fresh Lemon Juice
5ml (⅙ fl oz) Fresh Lime Juice
1 teaspoon Sugar Syrup
Twist of Lemon Peel

Pour Vodka, Grenadine, juices and sugar into a cocktail shaker over ice. Shake and strain into a chilled cocktail glass. Garnish with lemon peel and serve.

Heat of the Heart

29.2% ALC/VOL • 1.6 STD DRINKS

38ml (1¼ fl oz) Vodka
15ml (½ fl oz) Crème De Cassis
15ml (½ fl oz) Dry Vermouth
Dash Cointreau

Pour Vodka, Cassis and Vermouth into a mixing glass over cracked ice. Stir and pour into a chilled old-fashioned glass. Add Cointreau – do not stir, then serve.

Crista Solar

29.1% ALC/VOL • 1.4 STD DRINKS

30ml (1 fl oz) Vodka
10ml (⅓ fl oz) Dry Vermouth
10ml (⅓ fl oz) Triple Sec
10ml (⅓ fl oz) White Port
2 dashes Angostura Bitters

Pour ingredients into a cocktail shaker over ice and shake. Strain into a chilled cocktail glass and serve.

Mountain Brook

23.5% ALC/VOL • 1.1 STD DRINKS

30ml (1 fl oz) Citrus Vodka
10ml (⅓ fl oz) Blue Curaçao
10ml (⅓ fl oz) Fresh Lime Juice
10ml (⅓ fl oz) Cider

Pour Vodka, Curaçao and juice into a blender over cracked ice. Blend and pour into a chilled old-fashioned glass. Add Cider, stir gently and serve.

South Padre Island

5.2% ALC/VOL • 0.9 STD DRINKS

30ml (1 fl oz) Vodka
5ml (1/6 fl oz) Fresh Orange Juice
5ml (1/6 fl oz) Pineapple Juice
30ml (1 fl oz) Sweet and Sour Mix
23ml (3/4 fl oz) Peach Schnapps
120ml (4 fl oz) Cranberry Juice
Wedge of Lime

Build ingredients into a hurricane glass filled with ice. Garnish with a wedge of lime and serve with a swizzle stick.

Smokecurtain

31.5% ALC/VOL • 1.6 STD DRINKS

23ml (3/4 fl oz) Vodka
23ml (3/4 fl oz) Golden Rum
15ml (1/2 fl oz) Triple Sec
5ml (1/6 fl oz) Fresh Lime Juice

Pour ingredients into a cocktail shaker over ice and shake. Strain into a chilled cocktail glass and serve.

Gangbuster Punch

20.5% ALC/VOL • 2 STD DRINKS

45ml (1½ fl oz) Vodka
45ml (1½ fl oz) Peach Schnapps
30ml (1 fl oz) Cranberry Juice
5ml (1/6 fl oz) Lemon-Lime Soda

Pour Vodka, Schnapps and juice into a cocktail shaker over ice. Shake and strain into a chilled old-fashioned glass. Add soda, stir gently and serve.

White Cap

24.8% ALC/VOL • 1.2 STD DRINKS

30ml (1 fl oz) Vodka
10ml (1/3 fl oz) Kahlúa
10ml (1/3 fl oz) Port
2 teaspoons Fresh Cream

Pour Vodka, Kahlúa and Port into a mixing glass over ice. Stir and strain into a chilled cocktail glass. Float cream on top and serve.

Moonlight Drive

14.3% ALC/VOL • 3.2 STD DRINKS

30ml (1 fl oz) Vodka
30ml (1 fl oz) Light Rum
30ml (1 fl oz) Malibu
30ml (1 fl oz) Sloe Gin
15ml (1/2 fl oz) Amaretto
90ml (3 fl oz) Pineapple Juice
60ml (2 fl oz) Fresh Orange Juice
2 Cherries
2 Slices of Lemon

Pour Vodka, Rum, Malibu, Gin, Amaretto and juices into a cocktail shaker over ice. Shake and strain into a tall glass over ice. Add cherries and slices of lemon then serve.

Seether

22.4% ALC/VOL • 1.6 STD DRINKS

This drink is also known as Quiet But Quick, p 201.

Tas Beton Beynam

16.4% ALC/VOL • 3.5 STD DRINKS

75ml (2½ fl oz) Vodka
45ml (1½ fl oz) Bailey's Irish Cream
45ml (1½ fl oz) Kahlúa
45ml (1½ fl oz) Fresh Milk (chilled)
2 scoops Vanilla Ice Cream
Cinnamon

Pour Vodka, Bailey's, Kahlúa and milk into a blender without ice then add ice cream. Blend until smooth and pour into a chilled tall glass. Sprinkle cinnamon on top and serve.

Copenhagen

37.6% ALC/VOL • 2.2 STD DRINKS

60ml (2 fl oz) Vodka
15ml (½ fl oz) Aquavit
Almond (sliced thinly)

Pour Vodka and Aquavit into a cocktail shaker over ice. Shake and strain into a chilled cocktail glass. Garnish with slices of almond and serve.

Kalimba de Luna

14.3% ALC/VOL • 1.7 STD DRINKS

45ml (1½ fl oz) Vodka
8ml (1/4 fl oz) Genever Gin
5ml (1/6 fl oz) Apricot Brandy
5ml (1/6 fl oz) Cherry Brandy
90ml (3 fl oz) Pineapple Juice

Pour ingredients into a cocktail shaker over cracked ice and shake. Pour into a chilled old-fashioned glass and serve.

Italian Screw

12.1% ALC/VOL • 2.1 STD DRINKS

45ml (1½ fl oz) Vodka
30ml (1 fl oz) Galliano
180ml (6 fl oz) Fresh Orange Juice

Pour Vodka and Galliano into a chilled highball glass over a few ice cubes then stir. Add juice, stir and serve.

Triple Pleasure

13.9% ALC/VOL • 3 STD DRINKS

30ml (1 fl oz) Vodka
30ml (1 fl oz) Tequila
30ml (1 fl oz) Yukon Jack
60ml (2 fl oz) Cranberry Juice
60ml (2 fl oz) Fresh Orange Juice
60ml (2 fl oz) Pineapple Juice

Pour ingredients into a cocktail shaker over ice and shake. Strain into a tall glass over ice and serve.

Sex on the Beach with a California Blonde

6.9% ALC/VOL • 1.3 STD DRINKS

30ml (1 fl oz) Vodka
15ml (½ fl oz) Chambord
15ml (½ fl oz) Midori
90ml (3 fl oz) Cranberry Juice
90ml (3 fl oz) Pineapple Juice

Pour ingredients into a highball glass over ice, stir well and serve.

Vodka Hurricane

4.6% ALC/VOL • 0.9 STD DRINKS

30ml (1 fl oz) Vodka
90ml (3 fl oz) Fresh Orange Juice
90ml (3 fl oz) Pineapple Juice
30ml (1 fl oz) Cherry Juice
Cherry
Slice of Orange

Pour Vodka and juices into a cocktail shaker over ice. Shake and strain into a hurricane glass over ice. Garnish with a cherry and slice of orange then serve.

White Ruskie

20% ALC/VOL • 1.4 STD DRINKS

30ml (1 fl oz) Vodka
30ml (1 fl oz) White Crème De Cacao
30ml (1 fl oz) Fresh Cream

Pour Vodka and Cacao into a mixing glass over ice. Stir and strain into a cocktail glass over cracked ice. Float cream on top and serve.

Danea

6.5% ALC/VOL • 1.3 STD DRINKS

30ml (1 fl oz) Vodka
15ml (½ fl oz) Campari
5ml (⅙ fl oz) Banana Liqueur
15ml (½ fl oz) Grapefruit Juice
180ml (6 fl oz) Tonic Water

Pour Vodka, Campari, Liqueur and juice into a highball glass over ice then stir. Add tonic, stir gently and serve.

Intimate

26% ALC/VOL • 1.9 STD DRINKS

30ml (1 fl oz) Vodka
30ml (1 fl oz) Apricot Brandy
30ml (1 fl oz) Dry Vermouth
4 drops Orange Bitters

Pour ingredients into a cocktail shaker over ice and shake. Strain into a chilled cocktail glass and serve.

Gene Splice

13.5% ALC/VOL • 1.4 STD DRINKS

30ml (1 fl oz) Vodka
15ml (½ fl oz) Chambord
15ml (½ fl oz) Triple Sec
60ml (2 fl oz) Pineapple Juice
8ml (¼ fl oz) Fresh Lime Juice
Wedge of Lime

Pour Vodka, Chambord, Triple Sec and juices into a cocktail shaker over ice. Shake and strain into a highball glass half filled with ice. Garnish with a wedge of lime and serve.

Bledsko Jezero

17.4% ALC/VOL • 0.8 STD DRINKS

20ml (⅔ fl oz) Vodka
20ml (⅔ fl oz) Sweet Vermouth
Dash Blue Curaçao
20ml (⅔ fl oz) Grenadine

Pour ingredients into a mixing glass over ice and stir. Strain into a chilled cocktail glass and serve.

Hitchhiker

20.5% ALC/VOL • 2.7 STD DRINKS

30ml (1 fl oz) Vodka
30ml (1 fl oz) Mandarine Napoleon
15ml (½ fl oz) Banana Liqueur
15ml (½ fl oz) Campari
15ml (½ fl oz) Coconut Liqueur
60ml (2 fl oz) Lemonade

Pour Vodka, Mandarine Napoleon, Liqueurs and Campari into a cocktail shaker over ice. Shake and strain into a highball glass over ice. Add lemonade, stir gently and serve.

Old Car

25.1% ALC/VOL • 1 STD DRINK

20ml (⅔ fl oz) Vodka
15ml (½ fl oz) Apricot Brandy
10ml (⅓ fl oz) Triple Sec
8ml (¼ fl oz) Grapefruit Juice

Pour ingredients into a cocktail shaker over ice and shake. Strain into a cocktail glass over cracked ice and serve.

Minkki

8.9% ALC/VOL • 1.3 STD DRINKS

20ml (⅔ fl oz) Vodka
20ml (⅔ fl oz) Blue Curaçao
20ml (⅔ fl oz) Parfait Amour
60ml (2 fl oz) Fresh Cream
10ml (⅓ fl oz) Fresh Lime Juice
60ml (2 fl oz) Lemonade

Pour Vodka, Curaçao, Parfait Amour, cream and juice into a cocktail shaker over ice. Shake and strain into a chilled old-fashioned glass. Add lemonade, stir gently and serve.

Royal Blush

18.6% ALC/VOL • 1.4 STD DRINKS

30ml (1 fl oz) Vodka
30ml (1 fl oz) Framboise
2 dashes Grenadine
30ml (1 fl oz) Thick Cream

Pour ingredients into a cocktail shaker over ice and shake. Strain into a chilled cocktail glass and serve.

Blue Motorcycle

21.2% ALC/VOL • 3.8 STD DRINKS

30ml (1 fl oz) Vodka
30ml (1 fl oz) Blue Curaçao
30ml (1 fl oz) Gin
30ml (1 fl oz) Light Rum
30ml (1 fl oz) Triple Sec
5ml (1/6 fl oz) Sweet and Sour Mix
75ml (2½ fl oz) Lemon-Lime Soda

Pour Vodka, Curaçao, Gin, Rum, Triple Sec and sour mix into a highball glass over ice then stir well. Add soda, stir gently and serve.

Russian Quaalude

26% ALC/VOL • 1.8 STD DRINKS

30ml (1 fl oz) Vodka
30ml (1 fl oz) Bailey's Irish Cream
30ml (1 fl oz) Frangelico

Pour ingredients into a cocktail shaker over ice and shake. Strain into a chilled highball glass and serve.

Moonlight Venice

19.8% ALC/VOL • 1.6 STD DRINKS

30ml (1 fl oz) Vodka
30ml (1 fl oz) Sweet Vermouth
15ml (½ fl oz) Aperol
15ml (½ fl oz) Parfait Amour
15ml (½ fl oz) Strawberry Syrup

Pour ingredients into a cocktail shaker over ice and shake. Strain into a chilled cocktail glass and serve.

Yellow Fever

22.5% ALC/VOL • 2.3 STD DRINKS

60ml (2 fl oz) Vodka
20ml (⅔ fl oz) Galliano
30ml (1 fl oz) Pineapple Juice
20ml (⅔ fl oz) Fresh Lime Juice

Pour ingredients into a cocktail shaker over ice and shake. Strain into a chilled cocktail glass and serve.

S & M

11% ALC/VOL • 0.9 STD DRINKS

15ml (½ fl oz) Vodka
15ml (½ fl oz) Malibu
8ml (¼ fl oz) Blue Curaçao
60ml (2 fl oz) Lemon-Lime Soda

Pour Vodka, Malibu and Curaçao into a cocktail shaker over ice. Shake and strain into a chilled old-fashioned glass. Add soda, stir gently and serve.

Nooner

31.4% ALC/VOL • 2.4 STD DRINKS

45ml (1½ fl oz) Vodka
30ml (1 fl oz) Coffee Brandy
15ml (½ fl oz) Cream Sherry
5ml (1/6 fl oz) Fresh Lime Juice

Pour ingredients into a cocktail shaker over ice and shake. Strain into a chilled cocktail glass and serve.

The Pavilion

18% ALC/VOL • 1.3 STD DRINKS

30ml (1 fl oz) Vodka
30ml (1 fl oz) Peach Schnapps
5ml (1/6 fl oz) Grenadine
30ml (1 fl oz) Sweet and Sour Mix

Pour ingredients into a cocktail shaker over ice and shake. Strain into an old-fashioned glass over ice and serve.

Blue Ice Land

12.4% ALC/VOL • 1.6 STD DRINKS

40ml (1⅓ fl oz) Vodka
20ml (⅔ fl oz) Blue Curaçao
60ml (2 fl oz) Banana Juice
40ml (1⅓ fl oz) Fresh Cream

Pour ingredients into a blender over crushed ice and blend. Pour into a chilled parfait glass and serve.

Pink Petal

7% ALC/VOL • 1.7 STD DRINKS

60ml (2 fl oz) Vodka
15ml (½ fl oz) Fresh Lime Juice
240ml (8 fl oz) Lemon-Lime Soda
Wedge of Lime

Pour Vodka and juice into a collins glass over ice then stir. Add soda and stir gently. Garnish with a wedge of lime and serve.
This drink is also known as Pecker Wrecker.

Russian Peach

18.8% ALC/VOL • 1.5 STD DRINKS

40ml (1⅓ fl oz) Vodka
10ml (⅓ fl oz) Crème De Cassis
10ml (⅓ fl oz) Peach Schnapps
40ml (1⅓ fl oz) Fresh Orange Juice

Pour ingredients into a cocktail shaker over ice and shake. Strain into a chilled cocktail glass and serve.

357 Magnum

10.9% ALC/VOL • 1.8 STD DRINKS

30ml (1 fl oz) Vodka
30ml (1 fl oz) Dark Rum
5ml (1/6 fl oz) Amaretto
150ml (5 fl oz) Lemonade

Pour Vodka and Rum into a highball glass over ice then stir. Add lemonade and stir gently. Add Amaretto – do not stir, then serve.

Hot Bitch

37.5% ALC/VOL • 2.2 STD DRINKS

25ml (5/6 fl oz) Vodka
25ml (5/6 fl oz) Blended Whiskey
25ml (5/6 fl oz) Gin
Dash Tabasco Sauce

Pour Vodka, Whiskey and Gin into an old-fashioned glass – do not stir. Add sauce and serve.

Arlo Bomb!

12.3% ALC/VOL • 1.3 STD DRINKS

45ml (1½ fl oz) Vodka
15ml (½ fl oz) Grenadine
75ml (2½ fl oz) Cola
2 Maraschino Cherries

Pour Vodka and Grenadine into a highball glass over ice then stir. Add cola and stir gently. Garnish with cherries and serve.

Sweet Water

30.1% ALC/VOL • 4.3 STD DRINKS

60ml (2 fl oz) Vodka
60ml (2 fl oz) Triple Sec
30ml (1 fl oz) Butterscotch Schnapps
30ml (1 fl oz) Gin

Pour ingredients into a cocktail shaker over ice and shake. Strain into a chilled highball glass and serve.

Vodka Volcano

12% ALC/VOL • 1.8 STD DRINKS

60ml (2 fl oz) Vodka
5ml (1/6 fl oz) Grenadine
60ml (2 fl oz) Grapefruit Juice
60ml (2 fl oz) Pineapple Juice

Pour Vodka and juices into a cocktail shaker over cracked ice. Shake and pour into a chilled highball glass. Add Grenadine by pouring into centre of drink – do not stir, then serve.

Burning Bitch!

26.6% ALC/VOL • 6.9 STD DRINKS

210ml (7 fl oz) Vodka
60ml (2 fl oz) Bailey's Irish Cream
60ml (2 fl oz) Fresh Lemon Juice
Dash Maraschino Cherry Juice

Pour ingredients into a cocktail shaker over ice and shake. Strain into a chilled tall glass and serve.

Velociraptor

31.4% ALC/VOL • 1.3 STD DRINKS

45ml (1½ fl oz) Vodka
1 teaspoon Chicken Broth
3 dashes Tabasco Sauce
Stick of Carrot

Pour Vodka, broth and sauce into a cocktail shaker over ice. Shake and strain into an old-fashioned glass over ice. Garnish with a stick of carrot and serve.

Perfect Poison

15% ALC/VOL • 1.4 STD DRINKS

30ml (1 fl oz) Citrus Vodka
15ml (½ fl oz) Midori
15ml (½ fl oz) Triple Sec
60ml (2 fl oz) Cranberry Juice

Pour ingredients into a cocktail shaker over ice and shake. Strain into a chilled cocktail glass and serve.

Adios

7.5% ALC/VOL • 1.7 STD DRINKS

15ml (½ fl oz) Vodka
15ml (½ fl oz) Blue Curaçao
15ml (½ fl oz) Light Rum
15ml (½ fl oz) Plymouth Gin
15ml (½ fl oz) Sweet and Sour Mix
210ml (7 fl oz) Lemonade

Pour Vodka, Curaçao, Rum, Gin and sour mix into a highball glass over ice then stir. Add lemonade, stir gently and serve.

Toxic Waste

10.8% ALC/VOL • 1.5 STD DRINKS

30ml (1 fl oz) Vodka
15ml (½ fl oz) Southern Comfort
8ml (¼ fl oz) Blue Curaçao
60ml (2 fl oz) Fresh Orange Juice
60ml (2 fl oz) Pineapple Juice

Pour ingredients into a cocktail shaker over ice and shake. Strain into a brandy balloon over ice and serve.

Sexual Trance

17.6% ALC/VOL • 1.3 STD DRINKS

30ml (1 fl oz) Citrus Vodka
15ml (½ fl oz) Chambord
15ml (½ fl oz) Midori
15ml (½ fl oz) Fresh Orange Juice
15ml (½ fl oz) Pineapple Juice
5ml (1/6 fl oz) Sweet and Sour Mix
Cherry

Pour Vodka, Chambord, Midori, juices and sour mix into a cocktail shaker over ice. Shake and strain into a highball glass over ice. Garnish with a cherry and serve.

Indianapolis

20.3% ALC/VOL • 1 STD DRINK

20ml (⅔ fl oz) Vodka
20ml (⅔ fl oz) Blue Curaçao
20ml (⅔ fl oz) Fresh Cream

Pour ingredients into a cocktail shaker over ice and shake. Strain into a chilled cocktail glass and serve.

Nuclear Fizz

5.8% ALC/VOL • 1.2 STD DRINKS

23ml (¾ fl oz) Vodka
15ml (½ fl oz) Midori
15ml (½ fl oz) Triple Sec
Dash Fresh Lime Juice
210ml (7 fl oz) Soda Water

Pour Vodka, Midori, Triple Sec and juice into a cocktail shaker over ice. Shake and strain into a collins glass over ice. Add soda, stir gently and serve.

Smethport

7.5% ALC/VOL • 1.8 STD DRINKS

45ml (1½ fl oz) Vodka
30ml (1 fl oz) Peach Schnapps
90ml (3 fl oz) Fresh Orange Juice
90ml (3 fl oz) Pineapple Juice
45ml (1½ fl oz) Cherry Juice

Pour ingredients into a mixing glass over ice and stir. Strain into a chilled tall glass over a few ice cubes and serve.

Beastly Cocktail

14.3% ALC/VOL • 2.7 STD DRINKS

60ml (2 fl oz) Vodka
30ml (1 fl oz) Cointreau
150ml (5 fl oz) Dry Ginger Ale
Slice of Lemon
Slice of Orange

Pour Vodka and Cointreau into a mixing glass over ice. Stir and strain into a highball glass over ice. Add Ginger Ale and stir gently. Garnish with a slice of lemon and orange then serve.

Bit of Russian Honey

26.2% ALC/VOL • 3.1 STD DRINKS

60ml (2 fl oz) Vodka
30ml (1 fl oz) Bailey's Irish Cream
30ml (1 fl oz) Butterscotch Schnapps
30ml (1 fl oz) Kahlúa

Pour ingredients into a cocktail shaker over ice and shake. Strain into a highball glass over ice and serve.

Beetlejuice

7.8% ALC/VOL • 1.2 STD DRINKS

15ml (½ fl oz) Vodka
15ml (½ fl oz) Blue Curaçao
15ml (½ fl oz) Midori
15ml (½ fl oz) Raspberry Liqueur
120ml (4 fl oz) Sweet and Sour Mix
15ml (½ fl oz) Cranberry Juice
Cherry
Pineapple Spear

Pour Vodka into a tall glass over ice then add sour mix, Curaçao, Midori, Liqueur and juice – do not stir. Garnish with a cherry and pineapple spear then serve with a straw.

Drink of the Gods

23.5% ALC/VOL • 2.2 STD DRINKS

60ml (2 fl oz) Vodka
30ml (1 fl oz) Blueberry Schnapps
30ml (1 fl oz) Pineapple Juice

Pour ingredients into a mixing glass over ice and stir. Strain into a chilled old-fashioned glass and serve.

Before Midnight

24.5% ALC/VOL • 0.6 STD DRINKS

10ml (⅓ fl oz) Vodka
10ml (⅓ fl oz) Gin
2 dashes Apricot Brandy
10ml (⅓ fl oz) Fresh Orange Juice
Fresh Mint Leaf
Strawberry

Pour Vodka, Gin and juice into a cocktail shaker over ice. Shake and strain into a chilled cocktail glass then add Brandy – do not stir. Garnish with a mint leaf and a strawberry then serve.

Flame of Love

32.3% ALC/VOL • 1.5 STD DRINKS

45ml (1½ fl oz) Vodka
15ml (½ fl oz) Dry Sherry
Twist of Orange Peel

Pour Sherry into a chilled cocktail glass and swirl around glass then add Vodka – do not stir. Twist orange peel above drink and add remainder of peel then serve.

Exotic Flower

9.4% ALC/VOL • 1.1 STD DRINKS

30ml (1 fl oz) Vodka
15ml (½ fl oz) Passion-Fruit Liqueur
45ml (1½ fl oz) Grape Juice
45ml (1½ fl oz) Pineapple Juice
15ml (½ fl oz) Strawberry Syrup

Pour ingredients into a cocktail shaker over cracked ice and shake. Pour into a chilled highball glass and serve.

Fairytale

18.5% ALC/VOL • 1.8 STD DRINKS

60ml (2 fl oz) Vodka
40ml (1⅓ fl oz) Chocolate Syrup
2 Strawberries (crushed)

Pour Vodka and syrup into a cocktail shaker over ice. Shake and strain into an old-fashioned glass over crushed ice. Add crushed strawberries, stir well and serve.

Blue Panther

18.6% ALC/VOL • 2.4 STD DRINKS

60ml (2 fl oz) Vodka
30ml (1 fl oz) Dry Vermouth
15ml (½ fl oz) Crème De Cassis
30ml (1 fl oz) Fresh Orange Juice
White of 1 Egg

Pour ingredients into a cocktail shaker over ice and shake. Strain into a chilled champagne saucer and serve.

Forever Yours

10.3% ALC/VOL • 1.6 STD DRINKS

40ml (1⅓ fl oz) Vodka
30ml (1 fl oz) Passion-Fruit Liqueur
113ml (3¾ fl oz) Fresh Orange Juice
20ml (⅔ fl oz) Fresh Lime Juice

Pour ingredients into a cocktail shaker over ice and shake. Strain into a tall glass half filled with crushed ice and serve with a straw.

Bittersweet Italian

10.7% ALC/VOL • 1.6 STD DRINKS

40ml (1⅓ fl oz) Vodka
20ml (⅔ fl oz) Amaretto
60ml (2 fl oz) Pineapple Juice
30ml (1 fl oz) Fresh Lemon Juice
20ml (⅔ fl oz) Grapefruit Juice
2 teaspoons Sugar Syrup
10ml (⅓ fl oz) Lemon Soda

Pour Vodka, Amaretto, juices and sugar into a cocktail shaker over ice. Shake and strain into a chilled old-fashioned glass. Add soda, stir gently and serve.

Yellow Sea

27.6% ALC/VOL • 1.1 STD DRINKS

23ml (¾ fl oz) Vodka
15ml (½ fl oz) Dark Rum
8ml (¼ fl oz) Grenadine
1 teaspoon Sugar Syrup

Pour ingredients into a cocktail shaker over ice and shake. Strain into a chilled cocktail glass and serve.

Blue Cooler

7.2% ALC/VOL • 1.5 STD DRINKS

30ml (1 fl oz) Vodka
30ml (1 fl oz) Blue Curaçao
180ml (6 fl oz) Fresh Orange Juice
10ml (⅓ fl oz) Fresh Lemon Juice
10ml (⅓ fl oz) Fresh Lime Juice

Pour ingredients into a cocktail shaker over ice and shake. Strain into a collins glass over ice and serve.

Barbie

18.4% ALC/VOL • 1.8 STD DRINKS

30ml (1 fl oz) Vodka
30ml (1 fl oz) Gin
3 drops Grenadine
60ml (2 fl oz) Lemon-Lime Soda

Pour Vodka, Gin and Grenadine into a mixing glass over ice. Stir and strain into a highball glass over ice. Add soda, stir gently and serve.

Ghostbuster

27.8% ALC/VOL • 1.3 STD DRINKS

30ml (1 fl oz) Vodka
15ml (½ fl oz) Bailey's Irish Cream
15ml (½ fl oz) Kahlúa

Pour ingredients into a cocktail shaker over ice and shake. Strain into a chilled cocktail glass and serve.

Bikini Cocktail

20% ALC/VOL • 0.9 STD DRINKS

20ml (⅔ fl oz) Vodka
20ml (⅔ fl oz) Banana Liqueur
20ml (⅔ fl oz) Fresh Cream

Pour ingredients into a cocktail shaker over ice and shake. Strain into a chilled cocktail glass and serve.

Colorado Bulldog

9.5% ALC/VOL • 1.3 STD DRINKS

Also known as Canadian Paralyzer, p 220.

Face Saver

29.3% ALC/VOL • 1.9 STD DRINKS

60ml (2 fl oz) Vodka
8ml (¼ fl oz) Tia Maria
15ml (½ fl oz) Soda Water

Build ingredients into a brandy balloon over crushed ice and serve with a swizzle stick.

Bonza Monza

13.7% ALC/VOL • 1.2 STD DRINKS

30ml (1 fl oz) Vodka
20ml (⅔ fl oz) Crème De Cassis
60ml (2 fl oz) Grapefruit Juice

Pour ingredients into an old-fashioned glass over ice, stir and serve.

Vodka Infusions

The following recipes are for Vodka infusions:

Creating an infusion will require a bottle of Vodka and around fourteen days, longer periods are required for some recipes for your desired choice to infuse. Before proceeding to create your infusion remove ¼ of bottle's contents then top up once ingredients for your selected infusion have been added.

Infusions are made from mainly fruits, although you can use lollies and chocolate if you wish even chillies.

On completion of the infusion period place the bottle in the refrigerator or freezer to serve chilled in shot glasses.

Mandarin Infusion

1 Bottle Vodka
2 Sweet Imperial Mandarins
1 tablespoon Sugar Syrup

Step 1: Peel mandarins and shave white membrane off peels then cut the peels into strips approximately 2cm long.

Step 2: Place the strips of peel into Vodka bottle and add sugar. Top up with Vodka and give a gentle shake.

Step 3: Place the bottle in sunlight for three days then place indoors and allow to stand for twenty days before chilling.

Lemon Infusion

1 Bottle Vodka
3 Fresh Lemons
1½ teaspoons Sugar Syrup

Step 1: Peel lemons and shave white membrane off peels then cut the peels into strips approximately 2cm long.

Step 2: Place the strips of peel into Vodka bottle and add sugar. Top up with Vodka and give a gentle shake.

Step 3: Place the bottle in sunlight for three days then place indoors and allow to stand for fourteen days before chilling.

Banana Infusion

1 Bottle Vodka
15ml (½ fl oz) Banana Liqueur
½ Fresh Banana (diced)
10 Banana Lollies

Step 1: Pour Liqueur into Vodka bottle and add diced banana. Add lollies and top up with Vodka.

Step 2: Shake well and allow to stand indoors for fourteen days before chilling.

Chocolate Strawberry Infusion

1 Bottle Vodka
8 Fresh Strawberries
125g (2/7lb) Milk Chocolate
60ml (2 fl oz) Fresh Cream

Step 1: Crush strawberries and place into Vodka bottle.

Step 2: Pour cream into a small saucepan then add chocolate and heat gently on low heat to melt the chocolate whilst stirring continuously.

Step 3: Pour melted chocolate into Vodka bottle and top up with Vodka then shake well to combine all ingredients.

Step 4: Allow to stand indoors for fourteen days before chilling.

Whiskey

Whiskey was invented by the Irish and not the Scots, as many people believe. Whiskey takes its name from the Irish meaning 'water of life'. Whiskey is a spirit that is distilled from a fermented mash of grain (usually barley, maize or rice) then aged in wooden barrels. There are six main categories: Irish Whiskey, Scotch Whisky, American Whiskey, Blended Whiskey, Rye Whiskey and Japanese Whisky.

Whiskey or Whisky – Only Irish and American Whiskies contain 'e' in Whiskey with the exception of Makers Mark Kentucky Straight Bourbon Whisky with the founder of the distillery being given permission to remove the 'e' due to his Scottish heritage.

Irish Whiskey

Irish Whiskey is produced from a mash of cereal grains, mainly barley with a small proportion of oats and wheat. The Whiskey is distilled in pot-stills and triple-distilled which lightens its strong flavour. They are aged in Sherry casks for seven years; though most are aged for a longer period. Traditionally Irish Whiskies were straight or single malts. Now most are blended with grain Whiskies.

Irish Whiskies are similar to Scotch Whiskies although the principle or most noticeable difference between the two is that Irish Whiskey lacks the smoky taste of Scotch Whisky. This is due to the Irish Whiskey distilleries using non-porous floors to dry their barley, wheat and grains thus the smoke from the kiln fires does not reach the grains, therefore eliminating a smoky flavour or taste to the Whiskey.

Scotch Whisky

The first record of Scotch Whisky appeared in 1494, although it is believed that Whiskey was being distilled centuries earlier by the Irish monks, who brought the art of distilling with them to Scotland.

There are two types of Scotch Whisky: grain Whisky – usually consists of unmalted barley mixed with maize or other grains and distilled using continuous patent stills.

Malt Whisky – made only with malted barley. The barley is soaked in water, removed and left to germinate for one to two weeks allowing the starch in the barley to convert into sugar. Only pot-stills are used to distil malt Whiskies.

Almost all Scotch Whiskies sold are a blend of grains and malts. Blended Whiskies usually contain a large number of different Whiskies to create a blend. Single malts have a strong peaty flavour, stronger than that of blends. Single malts are aged longer than blends so they tend to have a higher % alcohol volume (% alc/vol). Vatted malts are only pure malt Whiskies that are blended together creating a vatted malt.

American Whiskey

It is believed that in America, Whiskey was first distilled in 1640 by the Dutch. What we do know is that in 1789, Rev. Elijah Craig produced the first Bourbon Whiskey in Bourbon County Kentucky from distilled corn. Straight Bourbon must contain a minimum of fifty one percent corn and containing proportions of rye or barley. For blended Bourbon or Rye, the Whiskey must contain at least fifty one percent of those types. Bourbon Whiskey is aged for two years in new charred barrels, the very best bottled in bond for at least four years.

In 1964, Congress passed a resolution recognizing Bourbon as a distinctive product of the United States – protecting the name. The sour mash process is used for Tennessee Whiskey not unlike that of Bourbon, although the process varies from this point. After distillation, the Whiskey is filtered very gradually in vats through charcoal. The charcoal required for this process is obtained from the sugar maple tree, which grows in Tennessee. This is a time consuming practice but one which gives Tennessee Whiskey its character and distinctive taste.

Light Whiskey is distilled at a higher proof than other types of Whiskies, creating a lighter character and flavour. Distilled from a variety of grains and aged in uncharred or used casks it is a recent style of Whiskey and used mainly for blending into other blended Whiskies.

Corn Whiskey is distilled from a minimum 80% corn mash.

Blended Whiskey

Blended Whiskey contains on average twenty percent straight Whiskey by volume at 100 proof, the remainder being made up of neutral spirits and or other Whiskies that have been distilled at or above 190 proof, thus becoming a blend. The more superior blends are made with extreme care, containing many Whiskies and neutral spirits blended to perfection and in some cases, re-stored in casks for maturing.

Blended Whiskies have a consistency in flavour, whereas straight Whiskies may vary slightly due to varying conditions of crops.

Rye Whiskey

It was over two hundred years ago that the Irish and Scottish introduced Canada to the art of distilling that is commonly known as 'Rye'. Canadian Whisky is produced mainly from corn with proportions of rye, wheat and barley malt.

Rye Whiskey must contain a minimum of fifty one percent rye and can be produced as either a straight Rye Whiskey or Blended Rye Whiskey. Blended Rye Whiskey can be produced using other Whiskies that have been blended from other neutral grain spirit and not necessarily rye grain.

Japanese Whisky

Japan's first distillery started producing Whisky in 1923 by the Suntory Company. Only the finest ingredients are used for the production of their Whiskies. The barley mash is distilled twice in copper pot-stills and is then aged in white oak casks until maturity. Japanese Whiskies are blended and can even be compared to some of the finest Scotch Whiskies.

Bourbon Triple Sour

20.5% ALC/VOL • 1.5 STD DRINKS

30ml (1 fl oz) Bourbon
30ml (1 fl oz) Triple Sec
30ml (1 fl oz) Fresh
Lemon Juice
1 teaspoon Sugar Syrup
Maraschino Cherry
Slice of Orange
Wedge of Lemon

Pour Bourbon, Triple Sec, juice and sugar into a cocktail shaker over ice. Shake and strain into a sour glass filled with cracked ice then add a wedge of lemon. Garnish with a cherry and slice of orange then serve.

Bobby Burns

28.4% ALC/VOL • 1.4 STD DRINKS

30ml (1 fl oz) Scotch Whisky
15ml (½ fl oz) Dry Vermouth
15ml (½ fl oz) Sweet Vermouth
Dash Bénédictine
Maraschino Cherry
Twist of Lemon Peel

Pour Whisky, Vermouths and Bénédictine into a mixing glass over ice. Stir and strain into a chilled cocktail glass. Twist lemon peel above drink and discard remainder of peel. Garnish with a cherry and serve.

Daily Mail

21% ALC/VOL • 1.5 STD DRINKS

30ml (1 fl oz) Rye Whiskey
30ml (1 fl oz) Amer Picon
30ml (1 fl oz) Orange Soda

Pour Whiskey and Amer Picon into a cocktail shaker over ice. Shake and strain into a chilled cocktail glass. Add soda - do not stir, then serve.

Dixie Smooth

26.8% ALC/VOL • 2.2 STD DRINKS

This drink is also known as J.R.'s Godchild, p 276.

Golden Gate

31.7% ALC/VOL • 1.9 STD DRINKS

30ml (1 fl oz) Irish Whiskey
30ml (1 fl oz) Cointreau
Dash Pernod
15ml (½ fl oz) Orange Syrup
Dash Egg White
Slice of Orange

Pour Whiskey, Cointreau, Pernod, syrup and egg white into a cocktail shaker over ice. Shake and strain into a chilled cocktail glass. Garnish with a slice of orange and serve.

Perfect Rob Roy

37.3% ALC/VOL • 2.5 STD DRINKS

75ml (2½ fl oz) Scotch Whisky
5ml (1/6 fl oz) Dry Vermouth
5ml (1/6 fl oz) Sweet Vermouth
Maraschino Cherry

Pour Whisky and Vermouths into a mixing glass over ice. Stir and strain into a chilled cocktail glass. Garnish with a cherry and serve.

Bourbon Sangaree

13.8% ALC/VOL • 1.6 STD DRINKS

45ml (1½ fl oz) Bourbon
15ml (½ fl oz) Tawny Port
10ml (⅓ fl oz) Spring Water
1 teaspoon Sugar Syrup
75ml (2½ fl oz) Soda Water
Slice of Lemon
Cinnamon
Nutmeg

Pour Bourbon, water and sugar into a chilled highball glass then stir. ¾ fill with crushed ice then add soda, stir gently and layer Port on top. Sprinkle cinnamon and nutmeg on top. Garnish with a slice of lemon and serve.

Rusty Nail

40% ALC/VOL • 2.8 STD DRINKS

60ml (2 fl oz) Scotch Whisky
30ml (1 fl oz) Drambuie

Pour ingredients into an old-fashioned glass over ice, stir and serve.

Old Moorhen's Shredded Sporran

15% ALC/VOL • 2 STD DRINKS

30ml (1 fl oz) Scotch Whisky
15ml (½ fl oz) Drambuie
15ml (½ fl oz) Mandarine
Napoleon
5ml (1/6 fl oz) Parfait Amour
60ml (2 fl oz) Pineapple Juice
30ml (1 fl oz) Guava Nectar
8ml (¼ fl oz) Fresh
Lemon Juice
1 teaspoon Orgeat Syrup
Maraschino Cherry
Slice of Lemon

Pour Whisky, Drambuie, Mandarine Napoleon, Parfait Amour, juices, nectar and syrup into a cocktail shaker over crushed ice. Shake and pour into a chilled goblet. Garnish with a cherry and slice of lemon then serve.

Kentucky Blizzard

14.4% ALC/VOL • 1.4 STD DRINKS

45ml (1½ fl oz) Bourbon
15ml (½ fl oz) Grenadine
45ml (1½ fl oz)
Cranberry Juice
15ml (½ fl oz) Fresh
Lime Juice
1 teaspoon Sugar Syrup
Slice of Orange

Pour Bourbon, Grenadine, juices and sugar into a cocktail shaker over ice. Shake and strain into an old-fashioned glass over ice. Garnish with a slice of orange and serve.

Ma Bonnie Wee Hen

21.8% ALC/VOL • 1.6 STD DRINKS

45ml (1½ fl oz) Scotch Whisky
15ml (½ fl oz) Cream Sherry
5ml (1/6 fl oz) Grenadine
15ml (½ fl oz) Fresh Lemon Juice
15ml (½ fl oz) Fresh Orange Juice

Pour ingredients into a cocktail shaker over ice and shake. Strain into a chilled cocktail glass and serve.

Gold Mine

12.6% ALC/VOL • 1.1 STD DRINKS

15ml (½ fl oz) Scotch Whisky
15ml (½ fl oz) Galliano
15ml (½ fl oz) Sweet Sherry
30ml (1 fl oz) Fresh Lime Juice
1 teaspoon Egg White
30ml (1 fl oz) Lemonade
Maraschino Cherry
Slice of Orange

Pour Whisky, Galliano, Sherry, juice and egg white into a cocktail shaker over ice. Shake and strain into a highball glass over cracked ice. Add lemonade and stir gently. Garnish with a cherry and slice of orange then serve.

Kiss on the Lips

10% ALC/VOL • 1.9 STD DRINKS

60ml (2 fl oz) Bourbon
180ml (6 fl oz) Apricot Nectar

Pour ingredients into a collins glass over ice, stir and serve with a straw.

Stonybrook

31.6% ALC/VOL • 1.9 STD DRINKS

45ml (1½ fl oz) Blended Whiskey
15ml (½ fl oz) Cointreau
Dash Orzata
½ Egg White
Twist of Lemon Peel
Twist of Orange Peel

Pour Whiskey, Cointreau, Orzata and egg white into a cocktail shaker over ice. Shake and strain into a chilled cocktail glass. Twist lemon and orange peels above drink. Place remainder of peels into drink and serve.

Manhasset

27.2% ALC/VOL • 1.6 STD DRINKS

45ml (1½ fl oz) Blended Whiskey
8ml (¼ fl oz) Dry Vermouth
8ml (¼ fl oz) Sweet Vermouth
15ml (½ fl oz) Fresh Lemon Juice

Pour ingredients into a cocktail shaker over ice and shake. Strain into a chilled cocktail glass and serve.

Kerry Cooler

9.3% ALC/VOL • 2.3 STD DRINKS

60ml (2 fl oz) Irish Whiskey
45ml (1½ fl oz) Madeira
30ml (1 fl oz) Fresh Lemon Juice
30ml (1 fl oz) Orgeat Syrup
150ml (5 fl oz) Soda Water
Slice of Lemon

Pour Whiskey, Madeira, juice and syrup into a chilled collins glass over a few ice cubes then stir. Add soda and stir gently. Float a slice of lemon on top and serve.

Lord Byron

35.2% ALC/VOL • 1.4 STD DRINKS

30ml (1 fl oz) Scotch Whisky
10ml (⅓ fl oz) Cointreau
10ml (⅓ fl oz) Sweet Vermouth
Dash Angostura Bitters

Pour ingredients into a mixing glass over ice and stir. Strain into a chilled cocktail glass and serve.

Quick Decision

23.1% ALC/VOL • 1.9 STD DRINKS

30ml (1 fl oz) Bourbon
23ml (¾ fl oz) Bailey's Irish Cream
15ml (½ fl oz) Dark Rum
15ml (½ fl oz) Kahlúa
23ml (¾ fl oz) Fresh Cream
Grated Chocolate

Pour Bourbon, Bailey's, Rum, Kahlúa and cream into a cocktail shaker over ice. Shake and strain into an old-fashioned glass over ice. Sprinkle chocolate on top and serve.

Turkey Feather

41.3% ALC/VOL • 2.7 STD DRINKS

60ml (2 fl oz) Wild Turkey Bourbon
15ml (½ fl oz) Drambuie
8ml (¼ fl oz) Amaretto
Slice of Orange

Pour Bourbon, Drambuie and Amaretto into a mixing glass over ice. Stir and strain into an old-fashioned glass over ice. Garnish with a slice of orange and serve.

Maori Blackthorne

16.5% ALC/VOL • 2.3 STD DRINKS

30ml (1 fl oz) Scotch Whisky
23ml (¾ fl oz) Dry Vermouth
15ml (½ fl oz) Gin
15ml (½ fl oz) Pernod
2 dashes Angostura Bitters

45ml (1½ fl oz) Dry Ginger Ale
45ml (1½ fl oz) Lemonade
Slice of Lemon

Pour Whisky, Vermouth, Gin, Pernod and Bitters into a highball glass over cracked ice then stir. Add Ginger Ale and lemonade then stir gently. Garnish with a slice of lemon and serve.

Choker

40.2% ALC/VOL • 2.4 STD DRINKS

60ml (2 fl oz) Scotch Whisky
15ml (½ fl oz) Pernod
2 dashes Angostura Bitters

Pour ingredients into a cocktail shaker over ice and shake. Strain into a chilled cocktail glass and serve.

Old Nick

27.4% ALC/VOL • 2.3 STD DRINKS

60ml (2 fl oz) Canadian Whisky
15ml (½ fl oz) Drambuie
3 dashes Orange Bitters
15ml (½ fl oz) Fresh Lemon Juice
15ml (½ fl oz) Fresh Orange Juice
Maraschino Cherry
Wedge of Lemon

Pour Whisky, Drambuie, Bitters and juices into a cocktail shaker over ice. Shake and strain into an old-fashioned glass over ice. Garnish with a cherry and wedge of lemon then serve.

Bourbon Collins

13.1% ALC/VOL • 1.9 STD DRINKS

This drink is also known as John Collins, p 233.

Waldorf Standard

32% ALC/VOL • 3.5 STD DRINKS

45ml (1½ fl oz) Bourbon
45ml (1½ fl oz) Pernod
45ml (1½ fl oz) Sweet Vermouth
3 dashes Angostura Bitters

Pour ingredients into a mixing glass over ice and stir. Strain into a brandy balloon over ice and serve.

Geraldine

32.3% ALC/VOL • 2.1 STD DRINKS

45ml (1½ fl oz) Canadian Whisky
15ml (½ fl oz) Dubonnet
15ml (½ fl oz) Yellow Chartreuse
5ml (1/6 fl oz) Dry Vermouth
Dash Angostura Bitters
Maraschino Cherry

Pour Whisky, Dubonnet, Chartreuse, Vermouth and Bitters into a mixing glass over ice. Stir and strain into a chilled cocktail glass. Garnish with a cherry and serve.

Kentucky Kernel

22.6% ALC/VOL • 1.7 STD DRINKS

45ml (1½ fl oz) Bourbon
15ml (½ fl oz) Apricot Brandy
5ml (1/6 fl oz) Grenadine
30ml (1 fl oz) Grapefruit Juice

Pour ingredients into a cocktail shaker over cracked ice and shake. Pour into a chilled old-fashioned glass and serve.

John Collins

13.1% ALC/VOL • 1.9 STD DRINKS

60ml (2 fl oz) Bourbon
30ml (1 fl oz) Fresh Lemon Juice
½ teaspoon Sugar Syrup
90ml (3 fl oz) Soda Water
Maraschino Cherry
Slice of Lemon
Slice of Orange

Pour Bourbon, juice and sugar into a cocktail shaker over ice. Shake and strain into a collins glass over ice. Add soda and stir gently. Garnish with a cherry, slice of lemon and orange then serve.
This drink is also known as Bourbon Collins, p 233.

Palmer Cocktail

39.2% ALC/VOL • 1.5 STD DRINKS

45ml (1½ fl oz) Bourbon
Dash Angostura Bitters
Dash Fresh Lemon Juice

Pour ingredients into a mixing glass over ice and stir. Strain into a chilled cocktail glass and serve.

Gringo Cocktail

11.9% ALC/VOL • 1.7 STD DRINKS

45ml (1½ fl oz) Blended Whiskey
15ml (½ fl oz) Banana Liqueur
60ml (2 fl oz) Pineapple Juice
30ml (1 fl oz) Coconut Milk (chilled)
30ml (1 fl oz) Fresh Cream
Maraschino Cherry
Slice of Pineapple
Sprig of Fresh Mint
Strawberry

Pour Whiskey, Liqueur, juice, milk and cream into a cocktail shaker over ice. Shake and strain into a highball glass over ice. Garnish with a cherry, slice of pineapple, sprig of mint and a strawberry then serve.

Whiskey Squirt

9.2% ALC/VOL • 1.4 STD DRINKS

45ml (1½ fl oz) Blended Whiskey
15ml (½ fl oz) Grenadine
1 tablespoon Sugar Syrup
120ml (4 fl oz) Soda Water
Slice of Pineapple

Strawberry

Pour Whiskey, Grenadine and sugar into a cocktail shaker over ice. Shake and strain into a highball glass over ice. Add soda and stir gently. Garnish with a slice of pineapple and a strawberry then serve.

Fox and Hounds

22.2% ALC/VOL • 1.9 STD DRINKS

45ml (1½ fl oz) Bourbon
15ml (½ fl oz) Pernod
15ml (½ fl oz) Fresh Lemon Juice
½ teaspoon Sugar Syrup
White of 1 Egg

Pour ingredients into a cocktail shaker over ice and shake. Strain into a chilled cocktail glass and serve.

Jackson Square

17.8% ALC/VOL • 1.7 STD DRINKS

45ml (1½ fl oz) Bourbon
15ml (½ fl oz) Peppermint Schnapps
3 dashes Peychaud's Bitters
60ml (2 fl oz) Soda Water
Twist of Lemon Peel

Pour Bourbon, Schnapps and Bitters into an old-fashioned glass over ice then stir. Add soda and stir gently. Twist lemon peel above drink and place remainder of peel into drink then serve.

Hadrian's Wall

15% ALC/VOL • 1.8 STD DRINKS

30ml (1 fl oz) Scotch Whisky
30ml (1 fl oz) Galliano
90ml (3 fl oz) Fresh Orange Juice
Maraschino Cherry
Slice of Orange

Pour Whisky and juice into a collins glass filled with ice then stir. Layer Galliano on top, garnish with a cherry and slice of orange then serve.

Black Death

27.9% ALC/VOL • 1.7 STD DRINKS

30ml (1 fl oz) Bourbon
30ml (1 fl oz) Dry Vermouth
10ml (⅓ fl oz) Blackberry Brandy
5ml (⅙ fl oz) Fresh Lemon Juice
Twist of Lemon Peel

Pour Bourbon, Vermouth, Brandy and juice into a cocktail shaker over ice. Shake and strain into an old-fashioned glass over cracked ice. Add lemon peel and serve. *This drink is also known as Allegheny.*

Kentucky Sunset

38% ALC/VOL • 2.2 STD DRINKS

45ml (1½ fl oz) Bourbon
15ml (½ fl oz) Anisette
15ml (½ fl oz) Strega
Twist of Orange Peel

Pour Bourbon, Anisette and Strega into a mixing glass over ice. Stir and strain into a chilled cocktail glass. Garnish with orange peel and serve.

Dusty Bill

32% ALC/VOL • 2 STD DRINKS

45ml (1½ fl oz) Canadian Whisky
15ml (½ fl oz) Applejack
5ml (⅙ fl oz) Brandy
10ml (⅓ fl oz) Fresh Lemon Juice
½ teaspoon Sugar Syrup
Maraschino Cherry

Pour Whisky, Applejack, Brandy, juice and sugar into a cocktail shaker over ice. Shake and strain into an old-fashioned glass over ice. Garnish with a cherry and serve.

Whiskey to Go

30.2% ALC/VOL • 1.9 STD DRINKS

45ml (1½ fl oz) Blended Whiskey
15ml (½ fl oz) Gin
15ml (½ fl oz) Fresh Lemon Juice
½ teaspoon Sugar Syrup

Pour ingredients into a cocktail shaker over ice and shake. Strain into an old-fashioned glass over ice and serve.

Whiskey Smash

25.8% ALC/VOL • 1.9 STD DRINKS

60ml (2 fl oz) Blended Whiskey
1 teaspoon Sugar Syrup
30ml (1 fl oz) Soda Water
4 Sprigs of Fresh Mint
Maraschino Cherry
Slice of Orange
Twist of Lemon Peel

Pour sugar into a chilled old-fashioned glass and add sprigs of mint. Muddle well and add Whiskey. Add ice and stir. Add soda and stir gently then add lemon peel. Garnish with a cherry and slice of orange then serve.

Soul Kiss

32.4% ALC/VOL • 2.4 STD DRINKS

60ml (2 fl oz) Bourbon
30ml (1 fl oz) Dry Vermouth
2 dashes Dubonnet

Pour ingredients into a cocktail shaker over ice and shake. Strain into a chilled cocktail glass and serve.

Forester's Delight

38.3% ALC/VOL • 1.9 STD DRINKS

30ml (1 fl oz) Bourbon
30ml (1 fl oz) Cointreau
2 dashes Blue Curaçao
2 dashes Fresh Lemon Juice
Maraschino Cherry

Prepare a goblet with a sugar frosted rim. Pour Bourbon, Cointreau, Curaçao and juice into a cocktail shaker over ice. Shake and strain into prepared glass. Garnish with a cherry and serve.

Rebel Yell

22.4% ALC/VOL • 2.4 STD DRINKS

60ml (2 fl oz) Rebel Yell Bourbon
15ml (½ fl oz) Cointreau
30ml (1 fl oz) Fresh Lemon Juice
White of 1 Egg
Slice of Orange

Pour Bourbon, Cointreau, juice and egg white into a cocktail shaker over cracked ice. Shake and pour into a chilled old-fashioned glass. Garnish with a slice of orange and serve.

Federal Punch

25% ALC/VOL • 1.9 STD DRINKS

30ml (1 fl oz) Bourbon
15ml (½ fl oz) Dark Rum
8ml (¼ fl oz) Cognac
8ml (¼ fl oz) Cointreau
30ml (1 fl oz) Fresh Lemon Juice
1 teaspoon Sugar Syrup
Maraschino Cherry

Pour Bourbon, Rum, Cognac, Cointreau, juice and sugar into a cocktail shaker over ice. Shake and strain into a cocktail glass filled with crushed ice. Garnish with a cherry and serve.

Italian Heather

38% ALC/VOL • 2.2 STD DRINKS

45ml (1½ fl oz) Scotch Whisky
30ml (1 fl oz) Galliano
Wedge of Lime

Pour Whisky and Galliano into an old-fashioned glass filled with crushed ice then stir gently. Garnish with a wedge of lime and serve.

National Pride

16% ALC/VOL • 2.3 STD DRINKS

30ml (1 fl oz) Blended Whiskey
30ml (1 fl oz) Galliano
30ml (1 fl oz) Midori
90ml (3 fl oz) Mineral Water
Slice of Lemon
Slice of Lime

Pour Midori into a collins glass filled with ice. Pour Whiskey and Galliano into a cocktail shaker over ice. Shake and strain into glass to layer over Midori then add mineral water – do not stir. Garnish with a slice of lemon and lime then serve with 2 straws.

Scotch Bounty

11.2% ALC/VOL • 2 STD DRINKS

30ml (1 fl oz) Scotch Whisky
30ml (1 fl oz) Malibu
30ml (1 fl oz) White Crème De Cacao
15ml (½ fl oz) Grenadine
120ml (4 fl oz) Fresh Orange Juice
Maraschino Cherry
Wedge of Pineapple

Pour Whisky, Malibu, Cacao, Grenadine and juice into a cocktail shaker over cracked ice. Shake and pour into a chilled hurricane glass. Garnish with a cherry and wedge of pineapple then serve with a straw.

Churches

33.9% ALC/VOL • 1.6 STD DRINKS

30ml (1 fl oz) Scotch Whisky
15ml (½ fl oz) Drambuie
15ml (½ fl oz) Sweet Vermouth
Dash Angostura Bitters

Pour ingredients into a cocktail shaker over ice and shake. Strain into a chilled cocktail glass and serve.

Green and Gold Cocktail

34% ALC/VOL • 1.6 STD DRINKS

30ml (1 fl oz) Blended Whiskey
15ml (½ fl oz) Galliano
15ml (½ fl oz) Green Crème De Menthe
Dash Egg White
Green Cherry
Wedge of Lemon

Pour Whiskey, Galliano, Crème De Menthe and egg white into a cocktail shaker over ice. Shake and strain into a chilled sour glass. Garnish with a cherry and wedge of lemon then serve.

Magnolian Maiden

37.1% ALC/VOL • 2.4 STD DRINKS

38ml (1¼ fl oz) Bourbon
38ml (1¼ fl oz) Mandarine Napoleon
3 dashes Sugar Syrup
3 dashes Soda Water

Pour Bourbon, Mandarine Napoleon and sugar into a cocktail shaker over crushed ice. Shake and pour into a chilled old-fashioned glass. Add soda – do not stir, then serve.

Chilly Irishman

9.7% ALC/VOL • 1.4 STD DRINKS

30ml (1 fl oz) Irish Whiskey
15ml (½ fl oz) Bailey's Irish Cream
15ml (½ fl oz) Kahlúa
90ml (3 fl oz) Espresso (chilled)
Dash Sugar Syrup
1 scoop Vanilla Ice Cream
4 Leaf Clover

Pour Whiskey, Bailey's, Kahlúa, espresso and sugar into a blender over large amount of crushed ice then add ice cream. Blend until smooth and pour into a chilled parfait glass. Garnish with a 4 leaf clover and serve.

Commonwealth

31.4% ALC/VOL • 1.9 STD DRINKS

53ml (1¾ fl oz) Canadian Whisky
15ml (½ fl oz) Van Der Hum
8ml (¼ fl oz) Fresh Lemon Juice

Pour ingredients into a mixing glass over ice and stir. Strain into a chilled brandy balloon and serve.

Bourbon and Madeira Julep

24.9% ALC/VOL • 1.8 STD DRINKS

45ml (1½ fl oz) Bourbon
45ml (1½ fl oz) Madeira
Dash Fresh Lemon Juice
½ teaspoon Sugar Syrup
Piece of Pineapple
4 Sprigs of Fresh Mint

Pour sugar into a chilled old-fashioned glass and add 3 sprigs of mint. Muddle well and fill glass with crushed ice. Add Bourbon, Madeira and juice then stir. Garnish with a piece of pineapple and sprig of mint then serve.

Hole-in-One

32.3% ALC/VOL • 2 STD DRINKS

53ml (1¾ fl oz) Scotch Whisky
23ml (¾ fl oz) Dry Vermouth
Dash Orange Bitters
2 dashes Fresh Lemon Juice

Pour ingredients into a cocktail shaker over ice and shake. Strain into a chilled cocktail glass and serve.

Sweet Adelaide

30% ALC/VOL • 2 STD DRINKS

30ml (1 fl oz) Bourbon
30ml (1 fl oz) Light Rum
15ml (½ fl oz) Sweet Vermouth
Dash Angostura Bitters
1 teaspoon Sugar Syrup
5ml (1/6 fl oz) Soda Water
Slice of Orange

Pour Bourbon, Rum, Vermouth, Bitters and sugar into an old-fashioned glass over ice then stir. Add soda – do not stir, then garnish with a slice of orange and serve. *This drink is also known as Bourbon Rumbo.*

Hoots Mon

27.9% ALC/VOL • 2 STD DRINKS

45ml (1½ fl oz) Scotch Whisky
23ml (¾ fl oz) Lillet
23ml (¾ fl oz) Sweet Vermouth

Pour ingredients into a mixing glass over ice and stir. Strain into a chilled cocktail glass and serve.

Thoroughbred Cooler

5.7% ALC/VOL • 0.9 STD DRINKS

30ml (1 fl oz) Bourbon
Dash Grenadine
30ml (1 fl oz) Fresh Orange Juice
30ml (1 fl oz) Sweet and Sour Mix
120ml (4 fl oz) Lemon-Lime Soda
Wedge of Orange

Pour Bourbon, juice and sour mix into a collins glass over ice then stir. Add soda and stir gently. Add Grenadine – do not stir, then garnish with a wedge of orange and serve.

Mean Machine

12.7% ALC/VOL • 1.8 STD DRINKS

30ml (1 fl oz) Bourbon
15ml (½ fl oz) Blackberry Brandy
15ml (½ fl oz) Gin
120ml (4 fl oz) Lemonade

Pour Bourbon, Brandy and Gin into a highball glass over ice then stir. Add lemonade, stir gently and serve.

Trouser Rouser

12.6% ALC/VOL • 1.7 STD DRINKS

45ml (1½ fl oz) Scotch Whisky
15ml (½ fl oz) Banana Liqueur
60ml (2 fl oz) Mango Juice
30ml (1 fl oz) Pineapple Juice
15ml (½ fl oz) Fresh Lime Juice
1 teaspoon Egg White
Maraschino Cherry
Sprig of Fresh Mint

Pour Whisky, Liqueur, juices and egg white into a cocktail shaker over ice. Shake and strain into a collins glass over cracked ice. Garnish with a cherry and sprig of mint then serve.

Bourble

33.3% ALC/VOL • 2.4 STD DRINKS

60ml (2 fl oz) Bourbon
15ml (½ fl oz) Cointreau
15ml (½ fl oz) Fresh
Lemon Juice

Pour ingredients into a cocktail shaker over ice and shake. Strain into a chilled cocktail glass and serve.

Jagger's Satisfaction

11.2% ALC/VOL • 1.7 STD DRINKS

30ml (1 fl oz) Bourbon
15ml (½ fl oz) Campari
15ml (½ fl oz) Rum Tree
15ml (½ fl oz) Sweet Sherry
120ml (4 fl oz) Lemonade

Pour Bourbon, Campari, Rum Tree and Sherry into a highball glass over ice then stir. Add lemonade, stir gently and serve.

Peek in Pandora's Box

12.6% ALC/VOL • 2 STD DRINKS

53ml (1¾ fl oz) Scotch Whisky
8ml (¼ fl oz) Campari
5ml (⅙ fl oz) Strega
45ml (1½ fl oz) Mandarin Juice
90ml (3 fl oz) Dry Ginger Ale

Pour Whisky, Campari, Strega and juice into a highball glass filled with ice then stir. Add Ginger Ale, stir gently and serve.

General Wolfe

10.8% ALC/VOL • 1.4 STD DRINKS

15ml (½ fl oz) Canadian
Whisky
15ml (½ fl oz) Calvados
15ml (½ fl oz) Grand Marnier
120ml (4 fl oz) Lemonade
Maraschino Cherry
Slice of Lemon
Slice of Orange

Pour Whisky, Calvados and Grand Marnier into a cocktail shaker over ice. Shake and strain into a collins glass over ice. Add lemonade and stir gently. Garnish with a cherry, slice of lemon and orange then serve.

Liberal

26.4% ALC/VOL • 0.7 STD DRINKS

15ml (½ fl oz) Canadian
Whisky
15ml (½ fl oz) Sweet Vermouth
3 dashes Amer Picon
Dash Orange Bitters

Pour ingredients into a mixing glass over ice and stir. Strain into a chilled cocktail glass and serve.

Whiskey Orange Flip

7.3% ALC/VOL • 1.9 STD DRINKS

60ml (2 fl oz) Blended
Whiskey
120ml (4 fl oz) Fresh Cream
90ml (3 fl oz) Fresh
Orange Juice
60ml (2 fl oz) Fresh Milk
(chilled)
Nutmeg

Pour Whiskey, cream, juice and milk into a blender over cracked ice. Blend and strain into a chilled goblet. Sprinkle nutmeg on top and serve.

Plenty O'Toole

27% ALC/VOL • 1.9 STD DRINKS

30ml (1 fl oz) Irish Whiskey
30ml (1 fl oz) Bailey's Irish
Cream
30ml (1 fl oz) Frangelico

Pour ingredients into a cocktail shaker over ice and shake. Strain into an old-fashioned glass over ice and serve.

North of the Border

15% ALC/VOL • 1.2 STD DRINKS

30ml (1 fl oz) Irish Whiskey
15ml (½ fl oz) Orange Curaçao
2 scoops Vanilla Ice Cream
Slice of Orange

Pour Whiskey and Curaçao into a blender without ice then add ice cream. Blend until smooth and pour into a chilled cocktail glass. Garnish with a slice of orange and serve.

East-West Cocktail

32.5% ALC/VOL • 1.9 STD DRINKS

30ml (1 fl oz) Bourbon
30ml (1 fl oz) Vodka
8ml (¼ fl oz) Peach Schnapps
8ml (¼ fl oz) Fresh
Lemon Juice

Pour ingredients into a cocktail shaker over ice and shake. Strain into an old-fashioned glass over ice and serve.

Irish Spring

14.7% ALC/VOL • 1.2 STD DRINKS

30ml (1 fl oz) Irish Whiskey
15ml (½ fl oz) Peach Brandy
30ml (1 fl oz) Fresh
Orange Juice
30ml (1 fl oz) Sweet and Sour
Mix
Cherry
Slice of Orange

Pour Whiskey, Brandy, juice and sour mix into a collins glass over ice then stir. Add a cherry and garnish with a slice of orange then serve.

Scotch Highball

11.4% ALC/VOL • 1.9 STD DRINKS

60ml (2 fl oz) Scotch Whisky
150ml (5 fl oz) Dry Ginger Ale
or Soda Water
Twist of Lemon Peel

Pour Whisky into a highball glass over ice and add Ginger Ale or soda as desired then stir gently. Add lemon peel and serve.

Light Cooler

9.4% ALC/VOL • 1.5 STD DRINKS

40ml (1⅓ fl oz) Scotch Whisky
10ml (⅓ fl oz) Orange Curaçao
2 dashes Angostura Bitters
1 teaspoon Sugar Syrup
150ml (5 fl oz) Dry Ginger Ale

Pour Whisky, Curaçao, Bitters and sugar into a cocktail shaker over ice. Shake and strain into a collins glass over ice. Add Ginger Ale, stir gently and serve.

Miami Sunset

8% ALC/VOL • 1.7 STD DRINKS

45ml (1½ fl oz) Bourbon
15ml (½ fl oz) Triple Sec
Dash Grenadine
210ml (7 fl oz) Fresh Orange Juice

Pour Bourbon, Triple Sec and juice into a tall glass over ice then stir. Add Grenadine – do not stir, then serve.

Hustlers Breakfast

11.7% ALC/VOL • 2.1 STD DRINKS

50ml (1⅔ fl oz) Bourbon
23ml (¾ fl oz) White Crème De Cacao
3 dashes Angostura Bitters
Dash Grenadine
50ml (1⅔ fl oz) Sweet and Sour Mix
100ml (3⅓ fl oz) Lemonade
Wedge of Lemon

Pour Bourbon, Cacao, Bitters, Grenadine and sour mix into a cocktail shaker over ice. Shake and strain into a chilled old-fashioned glass. Add lemonade and stir gently. Add a wedge of lemon and serve.

Jillionaire

27.8% ALC/VOL • 2.4 STD DRINKS

60ml (2 fl oz) Bourbon
15ml (½ fl oz) Cointreau
3 dashes Grenadine
White of 1 Egg

Pour ingredients into a cocktail shaker over ice and shake. Strain into a chilled cocktail glass and serve.

Whispers-of-the-Frost Cocktail

23.6% ALC/VOL • 1.4 STD DRINKS

23ml (¾ fl oz) Blended Whiskey
23ml (¾ fl oz) Cream Sherry
23ml (¾ fl oz) Port
1 teaspoon Sugar Syrup
Slice of Lemon
Slice of Orange

Pour Whiskey, Sherry, Port and sugar into a mixing glass over ice. Stir and strain into a chilled cocktail glass. Garnish with a slice of lemon and orange then serve.

Piper at the Gates of Dawn

23.3% ALC/VOL • 2.2 STD DRINKS

45ml (1½ fl oz) Scotch Whisky
30ml (1 fl oz) Kahlúa
15ml (½ fl oz) Maraschino Liqueur
30ml (1 fl oz) Thick Cream

Pour Whisky, Kahlúa and Liqueur into a cocktail shaker over ice. Shake and strain into an old-fashioned glass over ice. Float cream on top and serve.

Jock Collins

13% ALC/VOL • 1.9 STD DRINKS

60ml (2 fl oz) Scotch Whisky
30ml (1 fl oz) Fresh Lemon Juice
1 teaspoon Sugar Syrup
90ml (3 fl oz) Soda Water
Maraschino Cherry
Slice of Orange

Pour Whisky, juice and sugar into a cocktail shaker over ice. Shake and strain into a collins glass over ice. Add soda and stir gently. Garnish with a cherry and slice of orange then serve.

Bill Leaves Town

32.8% ALC/VOL • 2.1 STD DRINKS

60ml (2 fl oz) Blended Whiskey
15ml (½ fl oz) Sweet Vermouth
5ml (⅙ fl oz) Grenadine
Maraschino Cherry

Pour Whiskey, Vermouth and Grenadine into a mixing glass over ice. Stir and strain into a chilled cocktail glass. Garnish with a cherry and serve.

High Road

33.4% ALC/VOL • 2.1 STD DRINKS

45ml (1½ fl oz) Scotch Whisky
15ml (½ fl oz) Drambuie
15ml (½ fl oz) Dry Sherry
5ml (⅙ fl oz) Fresh Lemon Juice
Wedge of Lemon

Pour Whisky, Drambuie, Sherry and juice into a cocktail shaker over cracked ice. Shake and pour into a chilled old-fashioned glass. Add a wedge of lemon and serve.

Preakness Cocktail

32.1% ALC/VOL • 1.8 STD DRINKS

45ml (1½ fl oz) Blended Whiskey
23ml (¾ fl oz) Sweet Vermouth
3 dashes Bénédictine
Dash Angostura Bitters
Twist of Lemon Peel

Pour Whiskey, Vermouth, Bénédictine and Bitters into a mixing glass over ice. Stir and strain into a chilled cocktail glass. Add lemon peel and serve.

New York Sour

24.8% ALC/VOL • 2.2 STD DRINKS

60ml (2 fl oz) Blended Whiskey
30ml (1 fl oz) Claret
15ml (½ fl oz) Fresh Lemon Juice
1 teaspoon Sugar Syrup
Maraschino Cherry
Slice of Lemon

Pour Whiskey, juice and sugar into a cocktail shaker over ice. Shake and strain into a chilled sour glass then layer Claret on top. Garnish with a cherry and slice of lemon then serve.

Rye Lane

21.3% ALC/VOL • 1.5 STD DRINKS

30ml (1 fl oz) Rye Whiskey
30ml (1 fl oz) White Curaçao
2 dashes Crème De Noyaux
30ml (1 fl oz) Fresh Orange Juice

Pour ingredients into a cocktail shaker over ice and shake. Strain into a chilled cocktail glass and serve.

Cranbourbon

12.2% ALC/VOL • 1.9 STD DRINKS

60ml (2 fl oz) Bourbon
Dash Angostura Bitters
120ml (4 fl oz) Cranberry Juice
15ml (½ fl oz) Fresh Lemon Juice
1 teaspoon Sugar Syrup
Twist of Cucumber Peel

Pour Bourbon, Bitters, juices and sugar into a cocktail shaker over ice. Shake and strain into a collins glass over ice. Add cucumber peel and serve.

Bourbon Flip

21.8% ALC/VOL • 1.9 STD DRINKS

60ml (2 fl oz) Bourbon
1 teaspoon Sugar Syrup
1 Fresh Egg
Nutmeg

Pour Bourbon, sugar and egg into a cocktail shaker over ice. Shake and strain into a chilled goblet. Sprinkle nutmeg on top and serve.

Bull and Bear

24.1% ALC/VOL • 1.6 STD DRINKS

45ml (1½ fl oz) Bourbon
8ml (¼ fl oz) Orange Curaçao
15ml (½ fl oz) Grenadine
15ml (½ fl oz) Fresh Lime Juice
Maraschino Cherry
Slice of Orange

Pour Bourbon, Curaçao, Grenadine and juice into a cocktail shaker over ice. Shake and strain into a chilled cocktail glass. Garnish with a cherry and slice of orange then serve.

To Hell with Swords and Garters

19.5% ALC/VOL • 1.8 STD DRINKS

45ml (1½ fl oz) Scotch Whisky
30ml (1 fl oz) Dry Vermouth
45ml (1½ fl oz) Pineapple Juice

Pour ingredients into a cocktail shaker over ice and shake. Strain into an old-fashioned glass over ice and serve.

Affinity

24.8% ALC/VOL • 1.8 STD DRINKS

30ml (1 fl oz) Scotch Whisky
30ml (1 fl oz) Dry Vermouth
30ml (1 fl oz) Sweet Vermouth
2 dashes Angostura Bitters
Maraschino Cherry
Twist of Lemon Peel

Pour Whisky, Vermouths and Bitters into a mixing glass over ice. Stir and strain into a chilled cocktail glass. Twist lemon peel above drink and discard remainder of peel. Garnish with a cherry and serve.

Irish Milk-and-Maple Punch

7.6% ALC/VOL • 1.9 STD DRINKS

60ml (2 fl oz) Irish Whiskey
240ml (8 fl oz) Fresh Milk (chilled)
1 tablespoon Maple Syrup
Nutmeg

Pour Whiskey, milk and syrup into a cocktail shaker over ice. Shake and strain into a chilled collins glass. Sprinkle nutmeg on top and serve.

Angers Rose

26.4% ALC/VOL • 1.9 STD DRINKS

30ml (1 fl oz) Bourbon
30ml (1 fl oz) Cointreau
Dash Campari

30ml (1 fl oz) Pineapple Juice
Dash Egg White
Maraschino Cherry
Slice of Orange

Pour Bourbon, Cointreau, Campari, juice and egg white into a cocktail shaker over ice. Shake and strain into a chilled cocktail glass. Garnish with a cherry and slice of orange then serve.

Tuna on Rye

16% ALC/VOL • 1.7 STD DRINKS

45ml (1½ fl oz) Canadian Whisky
30ml (1 fl oz) Sweet Vermouth
60ml (2 fl oz) Dry Ginger Ale

Pour Whisky and Vermouth into an old-fashioned glass over ice then stir. Add Ginger Ale, stir gently and serve.

Midnight Cowboy

33.4% ALC/VOL • 2.8 STD DRINKS

60ml (2 fl oz) Bourbon
30ml (1 fl oz) Dark Rum
15ml (½ fl oz) Thick Cream

Pour ingredients into a cocktail shaker over ice and shake. Strain into a chilled cocktail glass and serve.

Rochdale Cowboy

28.5% ALC/VOL • 1.9 STD DRINKS

45ml (1½ fl oz) Blended Whiskey
15ml (½ fl oz) Southern Comfort
Dash Angostura Bitters
15ml (½ fl oz) Fresh Orange Juice
5ml (1/6 fl oz) Fresh Lemon Juice
½ teaspoon Sugar Syrup

Pour ingredients into a cocktail shaker over ice and shake. Strain into a highball glass over ice and serve.

Manhattan Skyscraper

16.5% ALC/VOL • 2.4 STD DRINKS

60ml (2 fl oz) Bourbon
30ml (1 fl oz) Dry Vermouth
Dash Angostura Bitters
90ml (3 fl oz) Dry Ginger Ale

Pour Bourbon, Vermouth and Bitters into an old-fashioned glass over ice then stir. Add Ginger Ale, stir gently and serve.

Night Shade

27.2% ALC/VOL • 1.6 STD DRINKS

45ml (1½ fl oz) Bourbon
15ml (½ fl oz) Sweet Vermouth
Dash Yellow Chartreuse
15ml (½ fl oz) Fresh Orange Juice
Slice of Lemon
Slice of Orange

Pour Bourbon, Vermouth, Chartreuse and juice into a cocktail shaker over ice. Shake and strain into an old-fashioned glass over ice. Garnish with a slice of lemon and orange then serve.

Southern Delta

31.4% ALC/VOL • 1.9 STD DRINKS

45ml (1½ fl oz) Bourbon
15ml (½ fl oz) Southern Comfort
10ml (⅓ fl oz) Fresh Lime Juice
5ml (1/6 fl oz) Pineapple Juice

Pour ingredients into a cocktail shaker over cracked ice and shake. Pour into a chilled old-fashioned glass and serve.

Mississippi Magic

14.9% ALC/VOL • 2 STD DRINKS

30ml (1 fl oz) Bourbon
30ml (1 fl oz) Southern Comfort
15ml (½ fl oz) Dry Vermouth
30ml (1 fl oz) Mandarin Juice
30ml (1 fl oz) Peach Purée
30ml (1 fl oz) Pineapple Juice
8ml (¼ fl oz) Fresh Lime Juice

Pour Bourbon, Southern Comfort, Vermouth and juices into a blender over small amount of crushed ice then add purée. Blend and pour into a chilled goblet then serve with 2 short straws.

Alice Standard

33.3% ALC/VOL • 1.6 STD DRINKS

30ml (1 fl oz) Scotch Whisky
15ml (½ fl oz) Kümmel
15ml (½ fl oz) Sweet Vermouth

Pour ingredients into a mixing glass over ice and stir. Strain into a chilled cocktail glass and serve.

Whiskey Curaçao Fizz

13.9% ALC/VOL • 2.2 STD DRINKS

60ml (2 fl oz) Blended Whiskey
15ml (½ fl oz) Curaçao
30ml (1 fl oz) Fresh Lemon Juice
1 teaspoon Caster Sugar
90ml (3 fl oz) Soda Water
Slice of Orange

Pour Whiskey, Curaçao and juice into a cocktail shaker over ice then add sugar. Shake and strain into a highball glass over ice. Add soda and stir gently. Garnish with a slice of orange and serve.

Cranberry Cooler

16.4% ALC/VOL • 1.4 STD DRINKS

45ml (1½ fl oz) Bourbon
45ml (1½ fl oz) Cranberry Juice
15ml (½ fl oz) Fresh Lime Juice
1 teaspoon Sugar Syrup

Pour ingredients into a blender over crushed ice and blend until smooth. Pour into a chilled collins glass and serve.

Under the Kilt

27.2% ALC/VOL • 1.6 STD DRINKS

30ml (1 fl oz) Scotch Whisky
15ml (½ fl oz) Banana Liqueur
15ml (½ fl oz) Galliano
15ml (½ fl oz) Fresh Cream
Dash Fresh Lime Juice
2 Slices of Banana

Pour Whisky, Liqueur, Galliano, cream and juice into a cocktail shaker over ice. Shake and strain into a chilled cocktail glass. Garnish with slices of banana and serve.

Kentucky Colonel Cocktail

40% ALC/VOL • 1.9 STD DRINKS

45ml (1½ fl oz) Bourbon
15ml (½ fl oz) Bénédictine
Twist of Lemon Peel

Pour Bourbon and Bénédictine into a mixing glass over ice. Stir and strain into a chilled cocktail glass. Add lemon peel and serve.

J.R.'s Godfather

37.6% ALC/VOL • 2.2 STD DRINKS

60ml (2 fl oz) Bourbon
15ml (½ fl oz) Amaretto

Pour ingredients into an old-fashioned glass over ice, stir and serve.

Teacher's Pet

33.4% ALC/VOL • 1.8 STD DRINKS

45ml (1½ fl oz) Blended Whiskey
15ml (½ fl oz) Dry Vermouth
5ml (⅙ fl oz) Sweet Vermouth
2 dashes Angostura Bitters
Maraschino Cherry
Slice of Orange

Pour Whiskey, Vermouths and Bitters into an old-fashioned glass over ice then stir. Garnish with a cherry and slice of orange then serve.

Embassy Royal

33.2% ALC/VOL • 3.2 STD DRINKS

60ml (2 fl oz) Bourbon
30ml (1 fl oz) Drambuie
30ml (1 fl oz) Sweet Vermouth
2 dashes Orange Soda

Pour Bourbon, Drambuie and Vermouth into a cocktail shaker over ice. Shake and strain into a chilled cocktail glass. Add soda – do not stir, then serve.

The Boss

37% ALC/VOL • 1.8 STD DRINKS

45ml (1½ fl oz) Bourbon
15ml (½ fl oz) Amaretto
Maraschino Cherry

Pour Bourbon and Amaretto into an old-fashioned glass over ice then stir. Garnish with a cherry and serve.

Slippery Surprise

11% ALC/VOL • 1.7 STD DRINKS

45ml (1½ fl oz) Scotch Whisky
15ml (½ fl oz) Banana Liqueur
60ml (2 fl oz) Grapefruit Juice
60ml (2 fl oz) Peach Juice
15ml (½ fl oz) Passion-Fruit Juice
Slice of Orange
Strawberry

Pour Whisky, Liqueur and juices into a cocktail shaker over cracked ice. Shake and pour into a chilled goblet. Garnish with a slice of orange and a strawberry then serve.

Scotch Mist

40% ALC/VOL • 1.4 STD DRINKS

60ml (2 fl oz) Scotch Whisky
Twist of Lemon Peel

Pour Whisky into an old-fashioned glass over ice and twist lemon peel above drink. Discard remainder of peel and serve.

Grapefruit Cooler

12% ALC/VOL • 1.9 STD DRINKS

60ml (2 fl oz) Blended Whiskey
120ml (4 fl oz) Grapefruit Juice
15ml (½ fl oz) Red-Currant Syrup
5ml (⅙ fl oz) Fresh Lemon Juice
Slice of Lemon
Slice of Orange

Pour Whiskey, juices and syrup into a cocktail shaker over ice. Shake and strain into a collins glass over ice. Garnish with a slice of lemon and orange then serve.

Frisco Sour

26.7% ALC/VOL • 2.5 STD DRINKS

60ml (2 fl oz) Bourbon
20ml (⅔ fl oz) Bénédictine
20ml (⅔ fl oz) Fresh Lemon Juice
20ml (⅔ fl oz) Fresh Lime Juice
Slice of Lemon
Slice of Lime

Pour Bourbon, Bénédictine and juices into a cocktail shaker over ice. Shake and strain into a chilled sour glass. Garnish with a slice of lemon and lime then serve.

Mickey Walker

30.3% ALC/VOL • 1.1 STD DRINKS

30ml (1 fl oz) Scotch Whisky
15ml (½ fl oz) Sweet Vermouth
Dash Grenadine
Dash Fresh Lemon Juice

Pour ingredients into a cocktail shaker over ice and shake. Strain into a chilled cocktail glass and serve.

Gentleman's Cocktail

13.8% ALC/VOL • 2.1 STD DRINKS

45ml (1½ fl oz) Bourbon
15ml (½ fl oz) Brandy
15ml (½ fl oz) White Crème De Menthe
120ml (4 fl oz) Soda Water
Wedge of Lemon

Pour Bourbon, Brandy and Crème De Menthe into a highball glass over ice then stir. Add soda and stir gently. Garnish with a wedge of lemon and serve.

Cowboy Shake

38% ALC/VOL • 2.7 STD DRINKS

30ml (1 fl oz) Scotch Whisky
30ml (1 fl oz) Golden Rum
30ml (1 fl oz) Gin
Strawberry

Pour Whisky, Rum and Gin into a mixing glass over cracked ice then stir. Pour into a chilled old-fashioned glass and garnish with a strawberry then serve.

Delta

30.2% ALC/VOL • 1.9 STD DRINKS

45ml (1½ fl oz) Blended Whiskey
15ml (½ fl oz) Southern Comfort
15ml (½ fl oz) Fresh Lime Juice
½ teaspoon Sugar Syrup
Slice of Orange
Slice of Peach

Pour Whiskey, Southern Comfort, juice and sugar into a cocktail shaker over ice. Shake and strain into an old-fashioned glass over ice. Garnish with a slice of orange and peach then serve.

Fans

30% ALC/VOL • 2.8 STD DRINKS

60ml (2 fl oz) Scotch Whisky
30ml (1 fl oz) Cointreau
30ml (1 fl oz) Grapefruit Juice

Pour ingredients into a cocktail shaker over ice and shake. Strain into a chilled cocktail glass and serve.

Southern Ginger

27.4% ALC/VOL • 1.9 STD DRINKS

45ml (1½ fl oz) 100-Proof Bourbon
3 dashes Ginger Brandy
8ml (¼ fl oz) Fresh Lemon Juice
30ml (1 fl oz) Dry Ginger Ale
Twist of Lemon Peel

Pour Bourbon, Brandy and juice into a mixing glass over ice. Stir and strain into a chilled cocktail glass. Add Ginger Ale and stir gently. Twist lemon peel above drink and place remainder of peel into drink then serve.

Atlanta Belle

29.7% ALC/VOL • 1.8 STD DRINKS

30ml (1 fl oz) Bourbon
23ml (¾ fl oz) Green Crème De Menthe
23ml (¾ fl oz) White Crème De Cacao
Cherry

Pour Bourbon, Crème De Menthe and Cacao into a cocktail shaker over ice. Shake and strain into an old-fashioned glass over ice. Add a cherry and serve.

Whiskey Orange

19.3% ALC/VOL • 1.5 STD DRINKS

45ml (1½ fl oz) Blended Whiskey
3 dashes Anisette
45ml (1½ fl oz) Fresh Orange Juice
1 teaspoon Sugar Syrup
Slice of Lemon
Slice of Orange

Pour Whiskey, Anisette, juice and sugar into a cocktail shaker over ice. Shake and strain into a highball glass over ice. Garnish with a slice of lemon and orange then serve.

Skerry

25.9% ALC/VOL • 2.1 STD DRINKS

45ml (1½ fl oz) Scotch Whisky
30ml (1 fl oz) Cherry Brandy
15ml (½ fl oz) Sweet Vermouth
15ml (½ fl oz) Fresh Orange Juice

Pour ingredients into a mixing glass over ice and stir. Strain into a chilled cocktail glass and serve.

Bourbon Sloe-Gin Fix

27.4% ALC/VOL • 1.7 STD DRINKS

45ml (1½ fl oz) Bourbon
15ml (½ fl oz) Sloe Gin
15ml (½ fl oz) Fresh Lemon Juice
1 teaspoon Sugar Syrup
Slice of Lemon
Slice of Peach

Pour Bourbon, Gin, juice and sugar into a cocktail shaker over ice. Shake and strain into an old-fashioned glass filled with crushed ice. Add more crushed ice to fill glass and stir gently. Garnish with a slice of lemon and peach then serve.

Bourbon Black Hawk

35.4% ALC/VOL • 2.5 STD DRINKS

60ml (2 fl oz) Bourbon
30ml (1 fl oz) Sloe Gin
Maraschino Cherry

Pour Bourbon and Gin into a mixing glass over ice. Stir and strain into a chilled cocktail glass. Garnish with a cherry and serve.

Whiskey Daisy

28.9% ALC/VOL • 1.9 STD DRINKS

60ml (2 fl oz) Blended Whiskey
5ml (1/6 fl oz) Grenadine
15ml (½ fl oz) Fresh Lemon Juice
½ teaspoon Sugar Syrup
Maraschino Cherry
Strawberry

Pour Whiskey, Grenadine, juice and sugar into a cocktail shaker over ice. Shake and strain into a goblet over ice. Garnish with a cherry and a strawberry then serve.

Jock-in-a-Box

16.8% ALC/VOL • 1.6 STD DRINKS

45ml (1½ fl oz) Scotch Whisky
15ml (½ fl oz) Sweet Vermouth
15ml (½ fl oz) Fresh Lemon Juice
1 Fresh Egg

Pour ingredients into a cocktail shaker over ice and shake. Strain into an old-fashioned glass over ice and serve.

Lind's Titanic

20.2% ALC/VOL • 1.5 STD DRINKS

30ml (1 fl oz) Bourbon
15ml (½ fl oz) Apricot Brandy
15ml (½ fl oz) White Crème De Cacao
Dash Angostura Bitters
30ml (1 fl oz) Fresh Lemon Juice
1 teaspoon Sugar Syrup
Strawberry

Pour Bourbon, Brandy, Cacao, Bitters, juice and sugar into a cocktail shaker over ice. Shake and strain into a chilled cocktail glass. Garnish with a strawberry and serve.

Thriller

21.2% ALC/VOL • 1.8 STD DRINKS

45ml (1½ fl oz) Scotch Whisky
30ml (1 fl oz) Green Ginger Wine
30ml (1 fl oz) Fresh Orange Juice

Pour ingredients into a mixing glass over ice and stir. Strain into a chilled cocktail glass and serve.

Royal Turkey

18.5% ALC/VOL • 2.2 STD DRINKS

30ml (1 fl oz) Wild Turkey Bourbon
30ml (1 fl oz) Apricot Brandy
30ml (1 fl oz) Sloe Gin
60ml (2 fl oz) Pineapple Juice
Slice of Pineapple
Strawberry

Pour Bourbon, Brandy, Gin and juice into a cocktail shaker over ice. Shake and strain into a goblet filled with ice. Garnish with a slice of pineapple and a strawberry then serve.

Indian River

27.4% ALC/VOL • 1.6 STD DRINKS

45ml (1½ fl oz) Blended Whiskey
8ml (¼ fl oz) Raspberry Liqueur
8ml (¼ fl oz) Sweet Vermouth
15ml (½ fl oz) Grapefruit Juice

Pour ingredients into a cocktail shaker over ice and shake. Strain into an old-fashioned glass over ice and serve.

Scotch Cream

25.1% ALC/VOL • 2.4 STD DRINKS

30ml (1 fl oz) Scotch Whisky
30ml (1 fl oz) Gin
30ml (1 fl oz) White Crème De Cacao
30ml (1 fl oz) Fresh Cream
Slice of Kiwi Fruit

Pour Whisky, Gin, Cacao and cream into a cocktail shaker over ice. Shake and strain into a chilled cocktail glass. Garnish with a slice of kiwi fruit and serve.

Creamy Irish Screwdriver

11.8% ALC/VOL • 1.8 STD DRINKS

45ml (1½ fl oz) Irish Whiskey
30ml (1 fl oz) Bailey's Irish Cream
120ml (4 fl oz) Fresh Orange Juice
Nutmeg

Pour Whiskey, Bailey's and juice into a cocktail shaker over ice. Shake and strain into a collins glass over ice. Sprinkle nutmeg on top and serve.

Barbera

38.4% ALC/VOL • 1.8 STD DRINKS

30ml (1 fl oz) Bourbon
15ml (½ fl oz) Drambuie
8ml (¼ fl oz) Amaretto
5ml (⅙ fl oz) Cointreau
Slice of Orange

Pour Bourbon, Drambuie, Amaretto and Cointreau into a mixing glass over ice. Stir and strain into an old-fashioned glass over ice. Garnish with a slice of orange and serve.

Eruption

34.4% ALC/VOL • 2 STD DRINKS

60ml (2 fl oz) Canadian Whisky
15ml (½ fl oz) Crème De Cassis
Maraschino Cherry

Pour Whisky and Cassis into a mixing glass over ice. Stir and strain into a chilled cocktail glass. Garnish with a cherry and serve.

Red-Hot Passion

30.8% ALC/VOL • 1.5 STD DRINKS

15ml (½ fl oz) Bourbon
15ml (½ fl oz) Amaretto
15ml (½ fl oz) Southern Comfort
8ml (¼ fl oz) Sloe Gin
3 dashes Cointreau
3 dashes Fresh Orange Juice
3 dashes Pineapple Juice
Slice of Orange

Pour Bourbon, Amaretto, Southern Comfort, Gin, Cointreau and juices into a hurricane glass over ice then stir. Garnish with a slice of orange and serve.

Beals Cocktail

30.6% ALC/VOL • 1.8 STD DRINKS

45ml (1½ fl oz) Scotch Whisky
15ml (½ fl oz) Dry Vermouth
15ml (½ fl oz) Sweet Vermouth

Pour ingredients into a mixing glass over ice and stir. Strain into a chilled cocktail glass and serve.

Screamin' Hudson

30.8% ALC/VOL • 1.8 STD DRINKS

45ml (1½ fl oz) Canadian Whisky
15ml (½ fl oz) Drambuie
15ml (½ fl oz) Fresh Lemon Juice

Pour ingredients into a cocktail shaker over ice and shake. Strain into a chilled cocktail glass and serve.

Scotch Stinger

35.8% ALC/VOL • 1.7 STD DRINKS

45ml (1½ fl oz) Scotch Whisky
15ml (½ fl oz) White Crème De Menthe

Pour ingredients into a cocktail shaker over ice and shake. Strain into a chilled cocktail glass and serve.

Kentucky

24.1% ALC/VOL • 1.5 STD DRINKS

This drink is also known as *Deep South, p 250.*

Scotch Apple

11.4% ALC/VOL • 1.9 STD DRINKS

45ml (1½ fl oz) Scotch Whisky
15ml (½ fl oz) Applejack
120ml (4 fl oz) Apple Juice
15ml (½ fl oz) Fresh Lemon Juice
15ml (½ fl oz) Fresh Orange Juice
Twist of Lemon Peel
Twist of Orange Peel

Pour Whisky, Applejack and juices into a cocktail shaker over ice. Shake and strain into a collins glass over ice. Twist lemon and orange peels above drink. Place remainder of peels into drink and serve.

Mithering Bastard

26.7% ALC/VOL • 1.9 STD DRINKS

45ml (1½ fl oz) Scotch Whisky
15ml (½ fl oz) Cointreau
30ml (1 fl oz) Fresh Orange Juice

Pour ingredients into a cocktail shaker over ice and shake. Strain into an old-fashioned glass over ice and serve.

Auld Sod

25.7% ALC/VOL • 1.6 STD DRINKS

45ml (1½ fl oz) Irish Whiskey
15ml (½ fl oz) Lillet
15ml (½ fl oz) Fresh Lemon Juice
1 teaspoon Sugar Syrup
Twist of Orange Peel

Pour Whiskey, Lillet, juice and sugar into a cocktail shaker over ice. Shake and strain into a chilled cocktail glass. Twist orange peel above drink and place remainder of peel into drink then serve.

Legbender Cocktail

24.6% ALC/VOL • 1.8 STD DRINKS

30ml (1 fl oz) Blended Whiskey
30ml (1 fl oz) Dry Vermouth
30ml (1 fl oz) Sweet Vermouth

Dash Angostura Bitters
Maraschino Cherry

Pour Whiskey, Vermouths and Bitters into a mixing glass over ice. Stir and strain into a chilled cocktail glass. Garnish with a cherry and serve.

Crown Cocktail

26.1% ALC/VOL • 0.9 STD DRINKS

30ml (1 fl oz) Blended Whiskey
Dash Grenadine
15ml (½ fl oz) Fresh Lemon Juice

Pour ingredients into a mixing glass over ice and stir. Strain into a chilled cocktail glass and serve.

Kentucky B & B

40% ALC/VOL • 2.4 STD DRINKS

60ml (2 fl oz) Bourbon
15ml (½ fl oz) Bénédictine

Pour ingredients into a brandy balloon, stir and serve.

Bourbon Rumbo

30% ALC/VOL • 2 STD DRINKS

This drink is also known as Sweet Adelaide, p 236.

Tennessee Sour

30.8% ALC/VOL • 1.9 STD DRINKS

60ml (2 fl oz) Tennessee Whiskey
15ml (½ fl oz) Fresh Lemon Juice
½ teaspoon Sugar Syrup
Maraschino Cherry
Slice of Orange

Pour Whiskey, juice and sugar into a cocktail shaker over ice. Shake and strain into a chilled sour glass. Top up with soda water if desired and stir gently. Garnish with a cherry and slice of orange then serve.

Stiletto

29.7% ALC/VOL • 2.2 STD DRINKS

60ml (2 fl oz) Blended Whiskey
15ml (½ fl oz) Amaretto
15ml (½ fl oz) Fresh Lemon Juice
5ml (1/6 fl oz) Fresh Lime Juice

Pour ingredients into a cocktail shaker over ice and shake. Strain into an old-fashioned glass over ice and serve.

Coffee Old-Fashioned

5.6% ALC/VOL • 1 STD DRINK

30ml (1 fl oz) Bourbon
2 dashes Angostura Bitters
120ml (4 fl oz) Spring Water
2 teaspoons Sugar Syrup
1½ teaspoons Coffee Powder
60ml (2 fl oz) Soda Water

Pour spring water into a mixing glass without ice and add coffee powder. Stir well to dissolve coffee then add Bourbon, Bitters and sugar. Stir and pour into an old-fashioned glass over ice. Add soda, stir gently and serve.

Prince Rupert

37.5% ALC/VOL • 1.8 STD DRINKS

45ml (1½ fl oz) Blended Whiskey
15ml (½ fl oz) Anisette
Wedge of Lemon

Pour Whiskey and Anisette into a mixing glass over ice. Stir and strain into a chilled cocktail glass. Garnish with a wedge of lemon and serve.

Scotch Horse's Neck

34.2% ALC/VOL • 3.2 STD DRINKS

90ml (3 fl oz) Scotch Whisky
15ml (½ fl oz) Dry Vermouth
15ml (½ fl oz) Sweet Vermouth
Long Twist of Lemon Peel

Place lemon peel into a chilled highball glass with one end of peel hooked over rim of glass (thus giving the effect of a horse's neck) and the remainder of peel spiraling down inside of glass then fill glass with ice. Add remaining ingredients, stir gently and serve.

Whiskey Milk Punch

8.7% ALC/VOL • 1.9 STD DRINKS

60ml (2 fl oz) Blended Whiskey
210ml (7 fl oz) Fresh Milk (chilled)
1 teaspoon Sugar Syrup
Nutmeg

Pour Whiskey, milk and sugar into a cocktail shaker over ice. Shake and strain into a chilled highball glass. Sprinkle nutmeg on top and serve.

Strip and Yell

12.1% ALC/VOL • 1.8 STD DRINKS

38ml (1¼ fl oz) Rebel Yell Bourbon
23ml (¾ fl oz) Peach Schnapps
8ml (¼ fl oz) Strega
120ml (4 fl oz) Bitter-Lemon Soda
Slice of Lemon

Pour Bourbon, Schnapps and Strega into a highball glass over ice then stir. Add soda and stir gently. Garnish with a slice of lemon and serve.

Bourbonella

30.4% ALC/VOL • 2.2 STD DRINKS

45ml (1½ fl oz) Bourbon
23ml (¾ fl oz) Dry Vermouth
23ml (¾ fl oz) Orange Curaçao
Dash Grenadine

Pour ingredients into a mixing glass over ice and stir. Strain into a chilled cocktail glass and serve.

Meet My Makers

23.1% ALC/VOL • 3.6 STD DRINKS

90ml (3 fl oz) Maker's Mark Bourbon
45ml (1½ fl oz) Vanilla Liqueur
60ml (2 fl oz) Dry Ginger Ale
3 Fresh Mint Leaves
Long Twist of Lemon Peel

Place lemon peel into a chilled highball glass with one end of peel hooked over rim of glass and the remainder of peel spiraling down inside of glass then add ice. Pour Bourbon and Liqueur into a cocktail shaker over ice then add mint leaves. Shake and strain into prepared glass. Add Ginger Ale, stir gently and serve with a straw.

J.R.'s Revenge

39.7% ALC/VOL • 3.4 STD DRINKS

90ml (3 fl oz) Bourbon
15ml (½ fl oz) Southern Comfort
2 dashes Angostura Bitters

Pour ingredients into a mixing glass over ice and stir. Strain into a chilled cocktail glass and serve.

Scotch Solace

14.1% ALC/VOL • 2.8 STD DRINKS

75ml (2½ fl oz) Scotch Whisky
15ml (½ fl oz) Cointreau
120ml (4 fl oz) Fresh Milk (chilled)
30ml (1 fl oz) Thick Cream
1 tablespoon Honey
Orange Rind (grated)

Pour Whisky, Cointreau and honey into a chilled collins glass then stir thoroughly. Add remaining ingredients then fill glass with ice, stir well and serve.

Walters

24% ALC/VOL • 1.4 STD DRINKS

45ml (1½ fl oz) Scotch Whisky
15ml (½ fl oz) Fresh Lemon Juice
15ml (½ fl oz) Fresh Orange Juice

Pour ingredients into a cocktail shaker over ice and shake. Strain into a chilled cocktail glass and serve.

Lamoone

7.7% ALC/VOL • 1.3 STD DRINKS

20ml (⅔ fl oz) Blended Whiskey
20ml (⅔ fl oz) Banana Liqueur
20ml (⅔ fl oz) Dry Vermouth
Dash Fresh Lime Juice
150ml (5 fl oz) Mineral Water

Pour Whiskey, Liqueur, Vermouth and juice into a cocktail shaker over ice. Shake and strain into a highball glass over ice. Add mineral water, stir gently and serve.

Gator Alley

28.1% ALC/VOL • 2 STD DRINKS

45ml (1½ fl oz) Blended Whiskey
30ml (1 fl oz) Banana Liqueur
2 dashes Angostura Bitters
15ml (½ fl oz) Fresh Lemon Juice
Slice of Lemon

Pour Whiskey, Liqueur, Bitters and juice into a cocktail shaker over ice. Shake and strain into an old-fashioned glass over ice. Add a slice of lemon and serve.

Colonel Collins

11.3% ALC/VOL • 1.9 STD DRINKS

60ml (2 fl oz) Bourbon
Dash Angostura Bitters
30ml (1 fl oz) Fresh Lemon Juice
1 teaspoon Sugar Syrup
120ml (4 fl oz) Soda Water
Slice of Lemon

Pour Bourbon, Bitters, juice and sugar into a cocktail shaker over ice. Shake and strain into a collins glass over ice. Add soda and stir gently. Garnish with a slice of lemon and serve.

Plank Walker

35% ALC/VOL • 2.1 STD DRINKS

45ml (1½ fl oz) Scotch Whisky
15ml (½ fl oz) Sweet Vermouth
15ml (½ fl oz) Yellow Chartreuse

Pour ingredients into an old-fashioned glass over ice, stir and serve.

Lena Cocktail

30.3% ALC/VOL • 1.4 STD DRINKS

30ml (1 fl oz) Bourbon
15ml (½ fl oz) Sweet Vermouth
5ml (⅙ fl oz) Campari
5ml (⅙ fl oz) Dry Vermouth
5ml (⅙ fl oz) Galliano
Maraschino Cherry
Sprig of Fresh Mint

Pour Bourbon, Vermouths, Campari and Galliano into a mixing glass over ice. Stir and strain into a chilled cocktail glass. Garnish with a cherry and sprig of mint then serve.

Kentucky Cocktail

26.5% ALC/VOL • 1.4 STD DRINKS

45ml (1½ fl oz) Bourbon
23ml (¾ fl oz) Pineapple Juice

Pour ingredients into a cocktail shaker over ice and shake. Strain into a chilled cocktail glass and serve.

Sidelight

15.6% ALC/VOL • 2.1 STD DRINKS

40ml (1⅓ fl oz) Blended Whiskey
30ml (1 fl oz) Kahlúa
20ml (⅔ fl oz) Dark Crème De Cacao
40ml (1⅓ fl oz) Fresh Cream
40ml (1⅓ fl oz) Fresh Milk (chilled)
Cocoa Powder

Pour Whiskey, Kahlúa, Cacao, cream and milk into a cocktail shaker over ice. Shake and strain into a coffee glass over crushed ice. Add more crushed ice to fill glass and stir. Sprinkle cocoa powder on top and serve with a straw.

Faux Scrumpy

8% ALC/VOL • 1.4 STD DRINKS

45ml (1½ fl oz) Blended Whiskey
180ml (6 fl oz) Apple Juice

Pour ingredients into a highball glass over ice, stir and serve.

Bourbon Sling

15.5% ALC/VOL • 1.9 STD DRINKS

60ml (2 fl oz) Bourbon
60ml (2 fl oz) Spring Water
30ml (1 fl oz) Fresh Lemon Juice
1 teaspoon Sugar Syrup
Wedge of Lemon

Pour Bourbon, water, juice and sugar into a cocktail shaker over ice. Shake and strain into a highball glass over ice. Garnish with a wedge of lemon and serve.

Witch Hunt

21.6% ALC/VOL • 1.4 STD DRINKS

30ml (1 fl oz) Scotch Whisky
15ml (½ fl oz) Dry Vermouth
8ml (¼ fl oz) Strega
30ml (1 fl oz) Lemonade

Pour Whisky, Vermouth and Strega into an old-fashioned glass over ice then stir. Add lemonade, stir gently and serve.

Algonquin

22.8% ALC/VOL • 2.2 STD DRINKS

60ml (2 fl oz) Canadian Whisky
30ml (1 fl oz) Dry Vermouth
30ml (1 fl oz) Pineapple Juice
Maraschino Cherry
Slice of Orange

Pour Whisky, Vermouth and juice into a cocktail shaker over ice. Shake and strain into an old-fashioned glass over cracked ice. Garnish with a cherry and slice of orange then serve.

Louisville Cooler

19% ALC/VOL • 1.4 STD DRINKS

45ml (1½ fl oz) Bourbon
30ml (1 fl oz) Fresh Orange Juice
15ml (½ fl oz) Fresh Lime Juice
1 teaspoon Sugar Syrup
Slice of Orange

Pour Bourbon, juices and sugar into a cocktail shaker over ice. Shake and strain into a collins glass over ice. Garnish with a slice of orange and serve.

Canadian Daisy

12.7% ALC/VOL • 1.7 STD DRINKS

45ml (1½ fl oz) Canadian Whisky
10ml (⅓ fl oz) Brandy
15ml (½ fl oz) Fresh Lemon Juice
1 teaspoon Raspberry Syrup
90ml (3 fl oz) Soda Water
2 Raspberries

Pour Whisky, juice and syrup into a cocktail shaker over ice. Shake and strain into a highball glass over ice. Add soda and stir gently then layer Brandy on top. Garnish with raspberries and serve.

Churchill

29.2% ALC/VOL • 0.7 STD DRINKS

15ml (½ fl oz) Scotch Whisky
5ml (⅙ fl oz) Cointreau
5ml (⅙ fl oz) Sweet Vermouth
5ml (⅙ fl oz) Fresh Lime Juice

Pour ingredients into a cocktail shaker over ice and shake. Strain into a chilled cocktail glass and serve.

Highland Cream

22.8% ALC/VOL • 1.7 STD DRINKS

30ml (1 fl oz) Scotch Whisky
15ml (½ fl oz) White Crème De Cacao
8ml (¼ fl oz) Galliano
8ml (¼ fl oz) Peppermint Schnapps
5ml (⅙ fl oz) Glayva
30ml (1 fl oz) Fresh Cream

Pour ingredients into a cocktail shaker over ice and shake. Strain into an old-fashioned glass over ice and serve.

Swiss Family Cocktail

32.7% ALC/VOL • 1.9 STD DRINKS

45ml (1½ fl oz) Blended Whiskey
23ml (¾ fl oz) Dry Vermouth
3 dashes Anisette
2 dashes Angostura Bitters

Pour ingredients into a mixing glass over ice and stir. Strain into a chilled cocktail glass and serve.

Double Derby

13.8% ALC/VOL • 2.9 STD DRINKS

75ml (2½ fl oz) Bourbon
60ml (2 fl oz) Claret
60ml (2 fl oz) Strong Black Tea (chilled)
30ml (1 fl oz) Fresh Orange Juice
30ml (1 fl oz) Red-Currant Syrup
15ml (½ fl oz) Fresh Lemon Juice
Slice of Orange

Pour Bourbon, Claret, tea, juices and syrup into an old-fashioned glass over ice then stir. Garnish with a slice of orange and serve.

Dixie Stinger

37.5% ALC/VOL • 3.2 STD DRINKS

90ml (3 fl oz) Bourbon
15ml (½ fl oz) White Crème De Menthe
3 dashes Southern Comfort

Pour ingredients into a cocktail shaker over ice and shake. Strain into a chilled cocktail glass and serve.

Scottish Revenge

8.8% ALC/VOL • 1 STD DRINK

20ml (⅔ fl oz) Scotch Whisky
20ml (⅔ fl oz) Tia Maria
60ml (2 fl oz) Black Coffee (chilled)
40ml (1⅓ fl oz) Fresh Cream
2 teaspoons Sugar Syrup
Twist of Lemon Peel

Pour Whisky, Tia, coffee, cream and sugar into a cocktail shaker over ice. Shake and strain into an old-fashioned glass over crushed ice. Garnish with lemon peel and serve.

Poor Tim

32% ALC/VOL • 1.8 STD DRINKS

45ml (1½ fl oz) Blended Whiskey
15ml (½ fl oz) Dry Vermouth
10ml (⅓ fl oz) Chambord

Pour ingredients into a mixing glass over ice and stir. Strain into a chilled cocktail glass and serve.

Kentucky Mule

14.4% ALC/VOL • 1.4 STD DRINKS

45ml (1½ fl oz) Bourbon
5ml (⅙ fl oz) Rose's Lime Juice
75ml (2½ fl oz) Ginger Beer

Pour Bourbon into a highball glass over ice and add ginger beer. Add juice, stir gently and serve.

Affinity Perfect

31.8% ALC/VOL • 1.2 STD DRINKS

30ml (1 fl oz) Scotch Whisky
8ml (¼ fl oz) Dry Vermouth
8ml (¼ fl oz) Sweet Vermouth

Pour ingredients into a mixing glass over ice and stir. Strain into a chilled cocktail glass and serve.

Cool Colonel

15.3% ALC/VOL • 2.3 STD DRINKS

This drink is also known as American Cool Change, p 250.

Macbeth's Dream

30.2% ALC/VOL • 2.1 STD DRINKS

60ml (2 fl oz) Scotch Whisky
5ml (⅙ fl oz) Amaretto
5ml (⅙ fl oz) White Curaçao
2 dashes Orange Bitters
15ml (½ fl oz) Fresh Lemon Juice
½ teaspoon Sugar Syrup

Pour ingredients into a cocktail shaker over ice and shake. Strain into a chilled cocktail glass and serve.

Grapefruit Sidecar

33.3% ALC/VOL • 2.4 STD DRINKS

45ml (1½ fl oz) Scotch Whisky
30ml (1 fl oz) Cointreau
15ml (½ fl oz) Grapefruit Juice
Maraschino Cherry
Slice of Orange

Pour Whisky, Cointreau and juice into a cocktail shaker over ice. Shake and strain into a chilled cocktail glass. Garnish with a cherry and slice of orange then serve.

Whiskey Sangaree

30.4% ALC/VOL • 2.1 STD DRINKS

60ml (2 fl oz) Blended Whiskey
15ml (½ fl oz) Port
5ml (⅙ fl oz) Spring Water
½ teaspoon Sugar Syrup
5ml (⅙ fl oz) Soda Water
Nutmeg

Pour Whiskey, spring water and sugar into an old-fashioned glass over ice then stir. Add soda – do not stir, then layer Port on top. Sprinkle nutmeg on top and serve.

Merry K

35% ALC/VOL • 2.5 STD DRINKS

60ml (2 fl oz) Bourbon
30ml (1 fl oz) Orange Curaçao
Twist of Lemon Peel

Pour Bourbon and Curaçao into a mixing glass over ice. Stir and strain into a chilled cocktail glass. Twist lemon peel above drink and discard remainder of peel then serve.

Capetown

29% ALC/VOL • 0.8 STD DRINKS

15ml (½ fl oz) Blended Whiskey
15ml (½ fl oz) Dry Vermouth
3 dashes Curaçao
Dash Angostura Bitters
Twist of Lemon Peel

Pour Whiskey, Vermouth, Curaçao and Bitters into a mixing glass over ice. Stir and strain into a chilled cocktail glass. Garnish with lemon peel and serve.

Bourbon Black Hawk No.2

25.3% ALC/VOL • 2.2 STD DRINKS

60ml (2 fl oz) Bourbon
15ml (½ fl oz) Sloe Gin
30ml (1 fl oz) Fresh Lemon Juice
1 teaspoon Sugar Syrup
Maraschino Cherry

Pour Bourbon, Gin, juice and sugar into a mixing glass over ice. Stir and strain into a chilled cocktail glass. Garnish with a cherry and serve.

Whiskey Ouzo Fix

30.4% ALC/VOL • 2 STD DRINKS

60ml (2 fl oz) Blended Whiskey
5ml (1/6 fl oz) Ouzo
15ml (½ fl oz) Fresh Lemon Juice
1 teaspoon Sugar Syrup
Twist of Lemon Peel

Pour Whiskey, juice and sugar into a cocktail shaker over ice. Shake and strain into an old-fashioned glass filled with crushed ice. Add more crushed ice to fill glass and stir gently then layer Ouzo on top. Twist lemon peel above drink and place remainder of peel into drink then serve.

Bourbon Cream

22% ALC/VOL • 1.3 STD DRINKS

30ml (1 fl oz) Bourbon
15ml (½ fl oz) Wild Turkey Liqueur
30ml (1 fl oz) Thick Cream

Pour ingredients into a cocktail shaker over ice and shake. Strain into a chilled cocktail glass and serve.

Scotch Bishop Cocktail

24.8% ALC/VOL • 1.3 STD DRINKS

30ml (1 fl oz) Scotch Whisky
15ml (½ fl oz) Dry Vermouth
3 dashes Cointreau
15ml (½ fl oz) Fresh Orange Juice
Dash Sugar Syrup
Twist of Lemon Peel

Pour Whisky, Vermouth, Cointreau, juice and sugar into a cocktail shaker over ice. Shake and strain into a chilled cocktail glass. Add lemon peel and serve.

Empire Glory

22.1% ALC/VOL • 2.1 STD DRINKS

60ml (2 fl oz) Rye Whiskey
30ml (1 fl oz) Green Ginger Wine
2 dashes Grenadine
30ml (1 fl oz) Fresh Lemon Juice

Pour ingredients into a cocktail shaker over ice and shake. Strain into a chilled cocktail glass and serve.

Jersey Gentleman

26.7% ALC/VOL • 1.9 STD DRINKS

45ml (1½ fl oz) Blended Whiskey
15ml (½ fl oz) Pernod
30ml (1 fl oz) Pineapple Juice

Pour ingredients into a cocktail shaker over ice and shake. Strain into a chilled cocktail glass and serve.

Beadlestone Cocktail

29% ALC/VOL • 2.1 STD DRINKS

45ml (1½ fl oz) Scotch Whisky
45ml (1½ fl oz) Dry Vermouth

Pour ingredients into a mixing glass over ice and stir. Strain into a chilled cocktail glass and serve.

Scotch Bird Flyer

19.8% ALC/VOL • 1.7 STD DRINKS

This drink is also known as Blastula, p 255.

Shakin' Blue Monday

28.8% ALC/VOL • 1.9 STD DRINKS

45ml (1½ fl oz) Canadian Whisky
15ml (½ fl oz) Blueberry Brandy
5ml (1/6 fl oz) Brandy
15ml (½ fl oz) Fresh Lemon Juice
1 teaspoon Sugar Syrup
Maraschino Cherry
Slice of Orange

Pour Whisky, Brandies, juice and sugar into a cocktail shaker over ice. Shake and strain into an old-fashioned glass over ice. Garnish with a cherry and slice of orange then serve.

Hearty Susan

35.8% ALC/VOL • 1.7 STD DRINKS

45ml (1½ fl oz) Blended Whiskey
15ml (½ fl oz) Cherry Brandy
Maraschino Cherry

Pour Whiskey and Brandy into a mixing glass over ice. Stir and strain into a chilled cocktail glass. Garnish with a cherry and serve.

American Cool Change

15.3% ALC/VOL • 2.3 STD DRINKS

45ml (1½ fl oz) Bourbon
30ml (1 fl oz) Southern Comfort
90ml (3 fl oz) Strong Black Tea (chilled)
10ml (⅓ fl oz) Fresh Lemon Juice
2 teaspoons Sugar Syrup
5ml (⅙ fl oz) Soda Water
Slice of Lemon
Slice of Orange

Pour Bourbon, Southern Comfort, tea, juice and sugar into a mixing glass over ice. Stir and strain into a chilled highball glass over a few ice cubes then add soda – do not stir. Garnish with a slice of lemon and orange then serve.
This drink is also known as Cool Colonel.

Canadian Old-Fashioned

34.4% ALC/VOL • 1.9 STD DRINKS

This drink is also known as Old-Fashioned Cocktail, p 281.

Frozen Irish Coffee

10% ALC/VOL • 1.4 STD DRINKS

45ml (1½ fl oz) Irish Whiskey
120ml (4 fl oz) Black Coffee (chilled)
½ scoop Vanilla Ice Cream
Sugar to Taste
Grated Chocolate

Pour Whiskey and coffee into a cocktail shaker over crushed ice then add sugar to taste. Shake and pour into a chilled highball glass. Float ice cream on top and sprinkle chocolate over ice cream then serve.

Deep South

24.1% ALC/VOL • 1.5 STD DRINKS

45ml (1½ fl oz) Bourbon
3 dashes Maraschino Liqueur
15ml (½ fl oz) Fresh Lime Juice
15ml (½ fl oz) Pineapple Juice

Prepare a cocktail glass with a sugar frosted rim. Pour ingredients into a cocktail shaker over ice and shake. Strain into prepared glass and serve.
This drink is also known as Kentucky, p 244.

Scotch Kiss

25.6% ALC/VOL • 1.8 STD DRINKS

30ml (1 fl oz) Scotch Whisky
30ml (1 fl oz) Tia Maria
15ml (½ fl oz) Malibu
15ml (½ fl oz) Pineapple Juice
Slice of Pineapple
Strawberry

Pour Whisky, Tia, Malibu and juice into a blender over cracked ice. Blend and strain into a chilled champagne saucer. Garnish with a slice of pineapple and a strawberry then serve.

Two Turtles

38.6% ALC/VOL • 2.7 STD DRINKS

60ml (2 fl oz) Canadian Whisky
15ml (½ fl oz) B & B
15ml (½ fl oz) Cointreau
Maraschino Cherry

Pour Whisky, B & B and Cointreau into a mixing glass over ice. Stir and strain into a chilled cocktail glass. Garnish with a cherry and serve.

T-Bird

14.7% ALC/VOL • 1.9 STD DRINKS

45ml (1½ fl oz) Canadian Whisky
23ml (¾ fl oz) Amaretto
2 dashes Grenadine
60ml (2 fl oz) Pineapple Juice
30ml (1 fl oz) Fresh Orange Juice
Maraschino Cherry
Slice of Orange

Pour Whisky, Amaretto, Grenadine and juices into a cocktail shaker over ice. Shake and strain into a highball glass filled with ice. Garnish with a cherry and slice of orange then serve with a straw.

Bourbon Cooler

13.3% ALC/VOL • 1.9 STD DRINKS

60ml (2 fl oz) Bourbon
120ml (4 fl oz) Lemon-Lime Soda
Wedge of Lemon

Pour Bourbon into a collins glass over ice and add soda then stir gently. Garnish with a wedge of lemon and serve.

Habitant Cocktail

21.4% ALC/VOL • 1.4 STD DRINKS

45ml (1½ fl oz) Canadian Whisky
30ml (1 fl oz) Fresh Lemon Juice
1 teaspoon Maple Syrup
Maraschino Cherry
Slice of Orange

Pour Whisky, juice and syrup into a cocktail shaker over ice. Shake and strain into an old-fashioned glass over ice. Garnish with a cherry and slice of orange then serve.

Highland Cooler

14.5% ALC/VOL • 2 STD DRINKS

60ml (2 fl oz) Scotch Whisky
2 dashes Angostura Bitters
15ml (½ fl oz) Fresh Lemon Juice
1 teaspoon Sugar Syrup
90ml (3 fl oz) Dry Ginger Ale

Pour Whisky, Bitters, juice and sugar into a cocktail shaker over ice. Shake and strain into a collins glass over ice. Add Ginger Ale, stir gently and serve.

Irish Whiskey Cocktail

39.2% ALC/VOL • 2.1 STD DRINKS

60ml (2 fl oz) Irish Whiskey
3 dashes Anisette
3 dashes Cointreau
2 dashes Maraschino Liqueur
Dash Angostura Bitters
Olive

Pour Whiskey, Anisette, Cointreau, Liqueur and Bitters into a mixing glass over ice. Stir and strain into a chilled cocktail glass. Garnish with an olive and serve.

Tootsie

6.8% ALC/VOL • 1.4 STD DRINKS

30ml (1 fl oz) Bourbon
15ml (½ fl oz) Galliano
Dash Grenadine
210ml (7 fl oz) Fresh Orange Juice

Pour ingredients into a cocktail shaker over ice and shake. Strain into a chilled highball glass and serve.

Quebec

31.7% ALC/VOL • 2.3 STD DRINKS

30ml (1 fl oz) Canadian Whisky
30ml (1 fl oz) Gin
15ml (½ fl oz) Cointreau
Dash Pernod
15ml (½ fl oz) Fresh Lemon Juice
Twist of Lemon Peel

Pour Whisky, Gin, Cointreau, Pernod and juice into a mixing glass over ice. Stir and strain into a chilled cocktail glass. Garnish with lemon peel and serve.

Mint Julep No.2

37.9% ALC/VOL • 2.8 STD DRINKS

90ml (3 fl oz) Bourbon
1 teaspoon Sugar Syrup
6 Sprigs of Fresh Mint

Pour sugar into a chilled collins glass and add 4 sprigs of mint. Muddle well and fill glass with crushed ice. Add Bourbon and stir. Garnish with 2 sprigs of mint and serve with 2 straws.

Erin and Sherry

26.7% ALC/VOL • 1.4 STD DRINKS

30ml (1 fl oz) Irish Whiskey
30ml (1 fl oz) Medium-Dry Sherry
Dash Angostura Bitters
½ teaspoon Sugar Syrup
3 dashes Soda Water
Twist of Lemon Peel

Pour Bitters, sugar and a dash of soda into a chilled old-fashioned glass then stir. Add ice, Whiskey and Sherry. Add remaining 2 dashes of soda and stir. Twist lemon peel above drink and place remainder of peel into drink then serve.

Russell House – Down the Hatch

36.9% ALC/VOL • 2.8 STD DRINKS

90ml (3 fl oz) Rye Whiskey
3 dashes Blackberry Brandy
2 dashes Orange Bitters
2 dashes Sugar Syrup

Pour ingredients into a mixing glass over ice and stir. Strain into a chilled cocktail glass and serve.

Daisy Dueller

10.1% ALC/VOL • 1.5 STD DRINKS

45ml (1½ fl oz) Tennessee Whiskey
Dash Cointreau
8ml (¼ fl oz) Fresh Lemon Juice
1½ teaspoons Sugar Syrup
120ml (4 fl oz) Soda Water
Slice of Lemon
Slice of Orange

Pour Whiskey, Cointreau, juice and sugar into a cocktail shaker over ice. Shake and strain into a highball glass over ice. Add soda and stir gently. Garnish with a slice of lemon and orange then serve.

Cameron's Kick Cocktail

33.7% ALC/VOL • 1.5 STD DRINKS

23ml (¾ fl oz) Scotch Whisky
23ml (¾ fl oz) Irish Whiskey
2 dashes Orange Bitters
8ml (¼ fl oz) Fresh Lemon Juice

Pour ingredients into a cocktail shaker over ice and shake. Strain into a chilled cocktail glass and serve.

Orange Bomb

10.2% ALC/VOL • 1.7 STD DRINKS

45ml (1½ fl oz) Scotch Whisky
8ml (¼ fl oz) Pernod
30ml (1 fl oz) Fresh Orange Juice
1 teaspoon Sugar Syrup
120ml (4 fl oz) Soda Water

Pour Whisky, Pernod, juice and sugar into a cocktail shaker over ice. Shake and strain into a highball glass over ice. Add soda, stir gently and serve.

Dead Man's Handle

23.3% ALC/VOL • 1.7 STD DRINKS

30ml (1 fl oz) Scotch Whisky
15ml (½ fl oz) Kahlúa
15ml (½ fl oz) Mandarine Napoleon
30ml (1 fl oz) Thick Cream

Pour ingredients into a cocktail shaker over ice and shake. Strain into an old-fashioned glass over ice and serve.

Rising Sun

15.9% ALC/VOL • 3 STD DRINKS

60ml (2 fl oz) Japanese Whisky
30ml (1 fl oz) Cherry Brandy
15ml (½ fl oz) Galliano
15ml (½ fl oz) Fresh Lemon or Lime Juice
120ml (4 fl oz) Lemonade
Maraschino Cherry
Slice of Orange

Pour Whisky, Galliano and juice into a highball glass over ice then stir. Add lemonade, stir gently and layer Brandy on top. Garnish with a cherry and slice of orange then serve.

Louisville Lady

22.8% ALC/VOL • 1.4 STD DRINKS

30ml (1 fl oz) Bourbon
23ml (¾ fl oz) White Crème De Cacao
23ml (¾ fl oz) Fresh Cream

Pour ingredients into a cocktail shaker over ice and shake. Strain into a chilled cocktail glass and serve.

Rob Roy, Holiday Style

35.2% ALC/VOL • 2.2 STD DRINKS

60ml (2 fl oz) Scotch Whisky
8ml (¼ fl oz) Dry Vermouth
8ml (¼ fl oz) Sweet Vermouth
3 dashes Drambuie
Maraschino Cherry

Pour Drambuie into a chilled cocktail glass and swirl around glass. Pour Whisky and Vermouths into a mixing glass over ice. Stir and strain into prepared glass. Garnish with a cherry and serve.

Down Yonder

12.5% ALC/VOL • 1.2 STD DRINKS

30ml (1 fl oz) Bourbon
15ml (½ fl oz) Peppermint Schnapps
60ml (2 fl oz) Peach Nectar
15ml (½ fl oz) Fresh Lemon Juice
Slice of Peach

Pour Bourbon, Schnapps, nectar and juice into a cocktail shaker over ice. Shake and strain into a brandy balloon over ice. Garnish with a slice of peach and serve.

Pampelmousse

18.1% ALC/VOL • 1.8 STD DRINKS

45ml (1½ fl oz) Canadian Whisky
15ml (½ fl oz) Southern Comfort
60ml (2 fl oz) Grapefruit Juice
5ml (1/6 fl oz) Pineapple Juice
Maraschino Cherry
Slice of Grapefruit

Pour Whisky, Southern Comfort and juices into a cocktail shaker over cracked ice. Shake and pour into a chilled old-fashioned glass. Garnish with a cherry and slice of grapefruit then serve.

Narragansett

36% ALC/VOL • 2.1 STD DRINKS

60ml (2 fl oz) Bourbon
10ml (⅓ fl oz) Sweet Vermouth
5ml (1/6 fl oz) Anisette
Wedge of Lemon

Pour Bourbon, Vermouth and Anisette into an old-fashioned glass over ice then stir. Add a wedge of lemon and serve.

Irish Fix

31.1% ALC/VOL • 2.2 STD DRINKS

60ml (2 fl oz) Irish Whiskey
10ml (⅓ fl oz) Irish Mist
15ml (½ fl oz) Fresh Lemon Juice
1 teaspoon Sugar Syrup
Slice of Lemon
Slice of Orange

Pour Whiskey, juice and sugar into a cocktail shaker over ice. Shake and strain into an old-fashioned glass filled with crushed ice. Add more crushed ice to fill glass and stir gently then layer Irish Mist on top. Garnish with a slice of lemon and orange then serve.

Miami Beach Cocktail

19.3% ALC/VOL • 1.4 STD DRINKS

30ml (1 fl oz) Scotch Whisky
30ml (1 fl oz) Dry Vermouth
30ml (1 fl oz) Grapefruit Juice

Pour ingredients into a cocktail shaker over ice and shake. Strain into a chilled cocktail glass and serve.

Deshler Cocktail

27.4% ALC/VOL • 2 STD DRINKS

45ml (1½ fl oz) Canadian Whisky
45ml (1½ fl oz) Dubonnet
2 dashes Cointreau
2 dashes Peychaud's Bitters
Twist of Lemon Peel
Twist of Orange Peel

Pour Whisky, Dubonnet, Cointreau and Bitters into a cocktail shaker over ice. Shake and strain into a chilled cocktail glass. Garnish with lemon and orange peels then serve.

Red Raider

23.7% ALC/VOL • 1.4 STD DRINKS

30ml (1 fl oz) Bourbon
15ml (½ fl oz) Cointreau
Dash Grenadine
30ml (1 fl oz) Fresh Lemon Juice

Pour ingredients into a cocktail shaker over ice and shake. Strain into a chilled cocktail glass and serve.

Canadian Breeze

26.3% ALC/VOL • 1.4 STD DRINKS

45ml (1½ fl oz) Canadian Whisky
3 dashes Maraschino Liqueur
15ml (½ fl oz) Fresh Lemon Juice
5ml (1/6 fl oz) Pineapple Juice
Maraschino Cherry
Pineapple Spear

Pour Whisky, Liqueur and juices into a cocktail shaker over ice. Shake and strain into an old-fashioned glass over ice. Garnish with a cherry and pineapple spear then serve.

Wild Island

29.6% ALC/VOL • 2.3 STD DRINKS

53ml (1¾ fl oz) Wild Turkey Bourbon
30ml (1 fl oz) Tropical Fruit Schnapps
15ml (½ fl oz) Mandarin Juice
Wedge of Orange

Pour Bourbon, Schnapps and juice into a cocktail shaker over ice. Shake and strain into a champagne saucer filled with crushed ice. Garnish with a wedge of orange and serve with 2 short straws.

Canal Street Daisy

6.1% ALC/VOL • 0.9 STD DRINKS

30ml (1 fl oz) Blended Whiskey
8ml (¼ fl oz) Fresh Lemon Juice
8ml (¼ fl oz) Fresh Orange Juice
150ml (5 fl oz) Soda Water
Slice of Orange

Pour Whiskey and juices into a collins glass over ice then stir. Add soda and stir gently. Garnish with a slice of orange and serve.

Sky Highball

11.8% ALC/VOL • 2 STD DRINKS

60ml (2 fl oz) Scotch Whisky
5ml (1/6 fl oz) Blue Curaçao
150ml (5 fl oz) Pineapple Juice
Wedge of Lemon

Pour Whisky and juice into a highball glass over ice then stir. Add Curaçao by pouring on top – do not stir, then add a wedge of lemon and serve.

Canadian Cooler

10.9% ALC/VOL • 1.1 STD DRINKS

38ml (1¼ fl oz) Canadian Whisky
15ml (½ fl oz) Fresh Orange Juice
15ml (½ fl oz) Pineapple Juice
1 teaspoon Sugar Syrup
60ml (2 fl oz) Soda Water
Slice of Orange

Pour Whisky, juices and sugar into a cocktail shaker over ice. Shake and strain into a collins glass over ice. Add soda and stir gently. Garnish with a slice of orange and serve.

Mamie Gilroy

12.3% ALC/VOL • 1.9 STD DRINKS

60ml (2 fl oz) Scotch Whisky
15ml (½ fl oz) Fresh Lime Juice
120ml (4 fl oz) Dry Ginger Ale

Pour Whisky and juice into a collins glass over ice then stir. Add Ginger Ale, stir gently and serve.

Muskoka Cocktail

20.8% ALC/VOL • 1.8 STD DRINKS

45ml (1½ fl oz) Canadian Whisky
15ml (½ fl oz) Scotch Whisky
Dash Grenadine
30ml (1 fl oz) Fresh Orange Juice

15ml (½ fl oz) Fresh Lemon Juice
1 teaspoon Maple Syrup

Pour ingredients into a blender over cracked ice and blend. Strain into a chilled sour glass and serve.

Canadian Black

32.9% ALC/VOL • 1.8 STD DRINKS

45ml (1½ fl oz) Canadian Whisky
15ml (½ fl oz) Blackberry Brandy
8ml (¼ fl oz) Fresh Lemon Juice

Pour ingredients into a cocktail shaker over ice and shake. Strain into a cocktail glass over crushed ice and serve.

Milky Way Punch

11.1% ALC/VOL • 1.6 STD DRINKS

20ml (⅔ fl oz) Bourbon
20ml (⅔ fl oz) Apricot Brandy
20ml (⅔ fl oz) Dark Rum
120ml (4 fl oz) Fresh Milk (chilled)
Cinnamon

Pour Bourbon, Brandy, Rum and milk into a cocktail shaker over ice. Shake and strain into a highball glass over ice. Sprinkle cinnamon on top and serve.

Irish Kilt

37.4% ALC/VOL • 2.9 STD DRINKS

60ml (2 fl oz) Irish Whiskey
30ml (1 fl oz) Scotch Whisky
4 dashes Orange Bitters
1 teaspoon Sugar Syrup

Pour ingredients into a cocktail shaker over ice and shake. Strain into a chilled cocktail glass and serve.

Lexington Lemonade

9.6% ALC/VOL • 1.2 STD DRINKS

30ml (1 fl oz) Blended Whiskey
15ml (½ fl oz) Triple Sec
30ml (1 fl oz) Sweet and Sour Mix
90ml (3 fl oz) Lemonade
2 Maraschino Cherries

Pour Whiskey, Triple Sec and sour mix into a cocktail shaker over ice. Shake and strain into a highball glass half filled with ice. Add lemonade and stir gently. Garnish with cherries and serve.

San Francisco

26.7% ALC/VOL • 1.9 STD DRINKS

45ml (1½ fl oz) Blended Whiskey
15ml (½ fl oz) Bénédictine
30ml (1 fl oz) Fresh Lemon Juice

Pour ingredients into a cocktail shaker over ice and shake. Strain into a chilled cocktail glass and serve.

Robber Baron

35.3% ALC/VOL • 2.5 STD DRINKS

45ml (1½ fl oz) Canadian Whisky
30ml (1 fl oz) Aquavit
15ml (½ fl oz) Dry Vermouth
Twist of Lemon Peel

Pour Whisky, Aquavit and Vermouth into a mixing glass over ice. Stir and strain into an old-fashioned glass over ice. Twist lemon peel above drink and place remainder of peel into drink then serve.

Bourbon Delight

32.2% ALC/VOL • 3.4 STD DRINKS

90ml (3 fl oz) Bourbon
30ml (1 fl oz) Sweet Vermouth
15ml (½ fl oz) Crème De Cassis
Slice of Lemon

Pour Bourbon, Vermouth and Cassis into a cocktail shaker over ice. Shake and strain into an old-fashioned glass over ice. Add a slice of lemon and serve.

Rebel Charge

16.2% ALC/VOL • 1.4 STD DRINKS

30ml (1 fl oz) Rebel Yell Bourbon
15ml (½ fl oz) Cointreau
18ml (⅗ fl oz) Fresh Lemon Juice
18ml (⅗ fl oz) Fresh Orange Juice
White of 1 Egg
Slice of Orange

Pour Bourbon, Cointreau, juices and egg white into a cocktail shaker over ice. Shake and strain into an old-fashioned glass over ice. Add a slice of orange and serve.

Caleigh

33.6% ALC/VOL • 2 STD DRINKS

45ml (1½ fl oz) Scotch Whisky
15ml (½ fl oz) Blue Curaçao
15ml (½ fl oz) White Crème De Cacao

Pour ingredients into a mixing glass over ice and stir. Strain into a chilled cocktail glass and serve.

Irish Shillelagh

31.9% ALC/VOL • 2 STD DRINKS

45ml (1½ fl oz) Irish Whiskey
15ml (½ fl oz) Sloe Gin
5ml (⅙ fl oz) Over-Proof Light Rum
5ml (⅙ fl oz) Peach Schnapps
5ml (⅙ fl oz) Fresh Lemon Juice
1 teaspoon Sugar Syrup

Pour ingredients into a cocktail shaker over cracked ice and shake. Pour into a chilled old-fashioned glass and serve.

Dixie Dew

39% ALC/VOL • 1.6 STD DRINKS

45ml (1½ fl oz) Bourbon
3 dashes Cointreau
3 dashes White Crème De Menthe

Pour ingredients into a mixing glass over ice and stir. Strain into a chilled cocktail glass and serve.

Captain Cook No.2

12.3% ALC/VOL • 1.9 STD DRINKS

60ml (2 fl oz) Scotch Whisky
15ml (½ fl oz) Grenadine
30ml (1 fl oz) Fresh Lime Juice
90ml (3 fl oz) Soda Water
Slice of Lime

Pour Whisky, Grenadine and juice into a cocktail shaker over ice. Shake and strain into a collins glass over ice. Add soda and stir gently. Garnish with a slice of lime and serve.

Sour Bee

33% ALC/VOL • 2.4 STD DRINKS

60ml (2 fl oz) Blended Whiskey
15ml (½ fl oz) Bénédictine
8ml (¼ fl oz) Fresh Lemon Juice
8ml (¼ fl oz) Fresh Lime Juice

Pour ingredients into a cocktail shaker over ice and shake. Strain into a chilled sour glass and serve.

Blastula

19.8% ALC/VOL • 1.7 STD DRINKS

45ml (1½ fl oz) Scotch Whisky
15ml (½ fl oz) Triple Sec
30ml (1 fl oz) Fresh Cream
1 teaspoon Sugar Syrup
Yolk of 1 Egg

Pour ingredients into a mixing glass over ice and stir well. Strain into a chilled champagne flute and serve. *This drink is also known as Scotch Bird Flyer,* *p 249.*

Thistle Cocktail

27.9% ALC/VOL • 2 STD DRINKS

45ml (1½ fl oz) Scotch Whisky
45ml (1½ fl oz) Sweet Vermouth
2 dashes Angostura Bitters

Pour ingredients into a mixing glass over ice and stir. Strain into a chilled cocktail glass and serve.

Rocky Mountain

24.5% ALC/VOL • 1.6 STD DRINKS

30ml (1 fl oz) Bourbon
30ml (1 fl oz) Dry Vermouth
10ml (⅓ fl oz) Blackberry Liqueur
Dash Angostura Bitters
10ml (⅓ fl oz) Fresh Lemon Juice
Twist of Lemon Peel

Pour Bourbon, Vermouth, Liqueur, Bitters and juice into a cocktail shaker over ice. Shake and strain into a chilled cocktail glass. Garnish with lemon peel and serve.

Master of the Hounds

34.7% ALC/VOL • 1.3 STD DRINKS

30ml (1 fl oz) Blended Whiskey
15ml (½ fl oz) Cherry Brandy
2 dashes Angostura Bitters

Pour ingredients into a mixing glass over ice and stir. Strain into a chilled cocktail glass and serve.

Dixie Whiskey Cocktail

37.6% ALC/VOL • 2 STD DRINKS

60ml (2 fl oz) Bourbon
3 dashes White Crème De Menthe
2 dashes Cointreau
Dash Angostura Bitters
½ teaspoon Sugar Syrup

Pour ingredients into a cocktail shaker over ice and shake. Strain into a chilled cocktail glass and serve.

Bible Belt

17.2% ALC/VOL • 2.8 STD DRINKS

60ml (2 fl oz) Tennessee Whiskey
30ml (1 fl oz) Cointreau
60ml (2 fl oz) Fresh Lime Juice
60ml (2 fl oz) Sweet and Sour Mix

Prepare a highball glass with a sugar frosted rim. Pour ingredients into a cocktail shaker over ice and shake. Strain into prepared glass and serve.

T.L.C.

38.7% ALC/VOL • 2.2 STD DRINKS

45ml (1½ fl oz) Blended Whiskey
15ml (½ fl oz) Cointreau
5ml (1/6 fl oz) Dubonnet
5ml (1/6 fl oz) Ricard
Dash Angostura Bitters
Maraschino Cherry
Wedge of Lemon

Pour Whiskey, Cointreau, Dubonnet, Ricard and Bitters into a mixing glass over ice. Stir and strain into a chilled cocktail glass. Garnish with a cherry and wedge of lemon then serve.

Tiger Juice

19% ALC/VOL • 1.3 STD DRINKS

45ml (1½ fl oz) Canadian Whisky
30ml (1 fl oz) Fresh Orange Juice
15ml (½ fl oz) Fresh Lemon Juice

Pour ingredients into a cocktail shaker over ice and shake. Strain into a chilled cocktail glass and serve.

Vancouver Island

23.3% ALC/VOL • 3.6 STD DRINKS

60ml (2 fl oz) Canadian Whisky
30ml (1 fl oz) Galliano
30ml (1 fl oz) Strega
15ml (½ fl oz) Grenadine
60ml (2 fl oz) Fresh Lemon Juice

Pour Grenadine into a chilled brandy balloon and swirl around glass. Pour remaining ingredients into a cocktail shaker over ice and shake. Strain into prepared glass over Grenadine – do not stir, then serve.

Irish Canadian Sangaree

32.4% ALC/VOL • 1.6 STD DRINKS

38ml (1¼ fl oz) Canadian Whisky
15ml (½ fl oz) Irish Mist
5ml (1/6 fl oz) Fresh Lemon Juice
5ml (1/6 fl oz) Fresh Orange Juice
Nutmeg

Pour Whisky, Irish Mist and juices into an old-fashioned glass over ice then stir. Sprinkle nutmeg on top and serve.

Wild Cherry

13.2% ALC/VOL • 2 STD DRINKS

45ml (1½ fl oz) Wild Turkey Bourbon
15ml (½ fl oz) Cherry Brandy
8ml (¼ fl oz) White Crème De Cacao
120ml (4 fl oz) Cherry Soda
Maraschino Cherry
Sprig of Fresh Mint

Pour Bourbon, Brandy and Cacao into a highball glass over ice then stir. Add soda and stir gently. Garnish with a cherry and sprig of mint then serve.

Crow

26.5% ALC/VOL • 2.8 STD DRINKS

90ml (3 fl oz) Blended Whiskey
Dash Grenadine
45ml (1½ fl oz) Fresh Lemon Juice

Pour ingredients into a mixing glass over ice and stir. Strain into a chilled cocktail glass and serve.

Scotch Buck

11.5% ALC/VOL • 1.4 STD DRINKS

30ml (1 fl oz) Scotch Whisky
15ml (½ fl oz) Ginger Brandy
90ml (3 fl oz) Dry Ginger Ale
½ Fresh Lime

Pour Whisky and Brandy into a highball glass over ice then stir. Twist ½ lime above drink to release juice and add spent shell. Add Ginger Ale, stir gently and serve.

Dinah Cocktail

32.2% ALC/VOL • 1.4 STD DRINKS

45ml (1½ fl oz) Blended Whiskey
8ml (¼ fl oz) Fresh Lemon Juice
½ teaspoon Sugar Syrup
Fresh Mint Leaf

Pour Whiskey, juice and sugar into a cocktail shaker over ice. Shake and strain into a chilled cocktail glass. Garnish with a mint leaf and serve.

Saratoga Fizz

18% ALC/VOL • 1.4 STD DRINKS

45ml (1½ fl oz) Bourbon
15ml (½ fl oz) Fresh Lemon Juice
5ml (1/6 fl oz) Fresh Lime Juice
1 teaspoon Caster Sugar
White of 1 Egg
Maraschino Cherry

Pour Bourbon, juices and egg white into a cocktail shaker over ice then add sugar. Shake and strain into a highball glass over ice. Garnish with a cherry and serve.

Tower Topper

30.8% ALC/VOL • 1.8 STD DRINKS

45ml (1½ fl oz) Canadian Whisky
15ml (½ fl oz) Grand Marnier
15ml (½ fl oz) Fresh Cream

Pour ingredients into a cocktail shaker over ice and shake. Strain into a chilled cocktail glass and serve.

Bourbon Cobbler

15.5% ALC/VOL • 1.9 STD DRINKS

60ml (2 fl oz) Bourbon
1 teaspoon Sugar Syrup
90ml (3 fl oz) Soda Water
Maraschino Cherry
Slice of Lemon
Slice of Orange

Pour Bourbon and sugar into a highball glass over ice then stir. Add soda and stir gently. Garnish with a cherry, slice of lemon and orange then serve.

Barney French

39.8% ALC/VOL • 1.5 STD DRINKS

45ml (1½ fl oz) Blended Whiskey
2 dashes Peychaud's Bitters
Slice of Orange
Twist of Lemon Peel

Pour Bitters into a chilled old-fashioned glass over 2 ice cubes then add a slice of orange and lemon peel. Muddle well and add Whiskey, stir then serve.

Scotch Melon Sour

19.2% ALC/VOL • 1.4 STD DRINKS

30ml (1 fl oz) Scotch Whisky
30ml (1 fl oz) Midori
30ml (1 fl oz) Fresh Lemon Juice
1 teaspoon Sugar Syrup
Maraschino Cherry
Slice of Orange
Wedge of Lemon

Pour Whisky, Midori, juice and sugar into a cocktail shaker over ice. Shake and strain into a sour glass over ice then add a wedge of lemon. Garnish with a cherry and slice of orange then serve.

Baby's Bottom

33.2% ALC/VOL • 2 STD DRINKS

45ml (1½ fl oz) Blended Whiskey
15ml (½ fl oz) White Crème De Cacao
15ml (½ fl oz) White Crème De Menthe

Pour ingredients into a cocktail shaker over ice and shake. Strain into a chilled cocktail glass and serve.

Ritz Old-Fashioned

29.1% ALC/VOL • 2.7 STD DRINKS

60ml (2 fl oz) Bourbon
20ml (⅔ fl oz) Grand Marnier
5ml (⅙ fl oz) Maraschino Liqueur
Dash Angostura Bitters
5ml (⅙ fl oz) Fresh Lemon Juice
1 teaspoon Sugar Syrup
1 teaspoon Egg White
15ml (½ fl oz) Soda Water
Maraschino Cherry
Slice of Lemon
Slice of Orange

Prepare an old-fashioned glass with a sugar frosted rim – moistened with lemon juice. Pour Bitters and juice into prepared glass then stir. Pour Bourbon, Grand Marnier, Liqueur, sugar and egg white into a cocktail shaker over ice. Shake and strain into prepared glass then add soda – do not stir. Garnish with a cherry, slice of lemon and orange then serve.

Trois Rivières

33.4% ALC/VOL • 1.8 STD DRINKS

45ml (1½ fl oz) Canadian Whisky
15ml (½ fl oz) Dubonnet
8ml (¼ fl oz) Cointreau
Twist of Orange Peel

Pour Whisky, Dubonnet and Cointreau into a cocktail shaker over ice. Shake and strain into a chilled cocktail glass. Twist orange peel above drink and place remainder of peel into drink then serve.

Wild-Eyed Rose

15.6% ALC/VOL • 2.6 STD DRINKS

83ml (2¾ fl oz) Blended Whiskey
20ml (⅔ fl oz) Grenadine
10ml (⅓ fl oz) Fresh Lime Juice
100ml (3⅓ fl oz) Soda Water

Pour Whiskey, Grenadine and juice into a mixing glass over ice. Stir and strain into a highball glass over ice. Add soda, stir gently and serve.

Tell it to the Navy

7.1% ALC/VOL • 1.4 STD DRINKS

20ml (⅔ fl oz) Blended Whiskey
20ml (⅔ fl oz) Apricot Brandy
20ml (⅔ fl oz) Kahlúa
Dash Bacardi
180ml (6 fl oz) Lemonade

Pour Whiskey, Brandy, Kahlúa and Bacardi into a highball glass over ice then stir. Add lemonade, stir gently and serve.

Black Jack

28.5% ALC/VOL • 2.4 STD DRINKS

45ml (1½ fl oz) Scotch Whisky
30ml (1 fl oz) Kahlúa
15ml (½ fl oz) Cointreau
15ml (½ fl oz) Fresh Lemon Juice

Pour ingredients into a cocktail shaker over ice and shake. Strain into a chilled cocktail glass and serve.

Whisky Cocktail

37.3% ALC/VOL • 2.3 STD DRINKS

60ml (2 fl oz) Scotch Whisky
15ml (½ fl oz) Orange Curaçao
2 dashes Orange Bitters
Maraschino Cherry

Pour Whisky, Curaçao and Bitters into a mixing glass over ice. Stir and strain into a chilled cocktail glass. Garnish with a cherry and serve.

Scotch Rickey

14.6% ALC/VOL • 1.9 STD DRINKS

60ml (2 fl oz) Scotch Whisky
15ml (½ fl oz) Fresh Lime Juice
90ml (3 fl oz) Soda Water
Twist of Lime Peel

Pour Whisky and juice into a collins glass over ice then stir. Add soda and stir gently. Garnish with lime peel and serve.

Sexual Healing

15.5% ALC/VOL • 1.1 STD DRINKS

15ml (½ fl oz) Bourbon
15ml (½ fl oz) Amaretto
15ml (½ fl oz) Sloe Gin
23ml (¾ fl oz) Fresh Orange Juice
23ml (¾ fl oz) Pineapple Juice

Pour ingredients into a cocktail shaker over ice and shake. Strain into a chilled old-fashioned glass and serve.

Winter Garden

32.5% ALC/VOL • 2.1 STD DRINKS

60ml (2 fl oz) Canadian Whisky
15ml (½ fl oz) Peach Schnapps
8ml (¼ fl oz) Sweet Sherry

Pour ingredients into a cocktail shaker over ice and shake. Strain into a cocktail glass over crushed ice and serve.

Scotch Orange Fix

29.6% ALC/VOL • 2 STD DRINKS

60ml (2 fl oz) Scotch Whisky
5ml (⅙ fl oz) Curaçao
15ml (½ fl oz) Fresh Lemon Juice
1 teaspoon Sugar Syrup
Twist of Orange Peel

Pour Whisky, juice and sugar into a cocktail shaker over ice. Shake and strain into an old-fashioned glass filled with crushed ice. Add more crushed ice to fill glass and stir gently then layer Curaçao on top. Add orange peel and serve.

Bourbon Maple Leaf

25.3% ALC/VOL • 1.9 STD DRINKS

60ml (2 fl oz) Bourbon
30ml (1 fl oz) Fresh Lemon Juice
1 teaspoon Maple Syrup

Pour ingredients into a cocktail shaker over ice and shake. Strain into a chilled cocktail glass and serve.

Country Club

31.1% ALC/VOL • 1.5 STD DRINKS

30ml (1 fl oz) Blended Whiskey
15ml (½ fl oz) Apricot Brandy
15ml (½ fl oz) Orange Curaçao
Dash Grenadine
Dash Fresh Cream

Pour ingredients into a cocktail shaker over ice and shake. Strain into a chilled cocktail glass and serve.

New World

29% ALC/VOL • 1.7 STD DRINKS

53ml (1¾ fl oz) Blended Whiskey
5ml (⅙ fl oz) Grenadine
15ml (½ fl oz) Fresh Lime Juice
Twist of Lime Peel

Pour Whiskey, Grenadine and juice into a cocktail shaker over ice. Shake and strain into a chilled cocktail glass. Twist lime peel above drink and place remainder of peel into drink then serve.

Hawaiian Eye

21.8% ALC/VOL • 2.9 STD DRINKS

45ml (1½ fl oz) Bourbon
30ml (1 fl oz) Tia Maria
15ml (½ fl oz) Banana Liqueur
15ml (½ fl oz) Vodka
5ml (⅙ fl oz) Pernod
30ml (1 fl oz) Thick Cream
White of 1 Egg

Pour ingredients into a blender over crushed ice and blend. Pour into a chilled highball glass and serve.

Old Pal

27% ALC/VOL • 1.9 STD DRINKS

30ml (1 fl oz) Rye Whiskey
30ml (1 fl oz) Campari
30ml (1 fl oz) Dry Vermouth

Pour ingredients into a mixing glass over ice and stir. Strain into a chilled cocktail glass and serve.

Bourbon Daisy

25% ALC/VOL • 1.9 STD DRINKS

60ml (2 fl oz) Bourbon
3 dashes Grenadine
30ml (1 fl oz) Fresh Lemon Juice
½ teaspoon Sugar Syrup
Maraschino Cherry
Slice of Orange

Pour Bourbon, Grenadine, juice and sugar into a cocktail shaker over cracked ice. Shake and pour into a chilled goblet. Garnish with a cherry and slice of orange then serve.

Molehill Lounger

34.8% ALC/VOL • 1.8 STD DRINKS

45ml (1½ fl oz) Blended Whiskey
15ml (½ fl oz) Dark Crème De Cacao
5ml (1/6 fl oz) White Crème De Cacao

Pour ingredients into a mixing glass over ice and stir. Strain into a chilled cocktail glass and serve.

Misty Irish

19% ALC/VOL • 1.4 STD DRINKS

30ml (1 fl oz) Irish Whiskey
15ml (½ fl oz) Irish Mist
30ml (1 fl oz) Fresh Orange Juice
15ml (½ fl oz) Fresh Lemon Juice
1 teaspoon Sugar Syrup
Brandied Cherry

Pour Whiskey, Irish Mist, juices and sugar into a blender over crushed ice. Blend and pour into an old-fashioned glass over ice. Add cherry and serve.

Kilt

10% ALC/VOL • 1.9 STD DRINKS

60ml (2 fl oz) Scotch Whisky
150ml (5 fl oz) Fresh Milk (chilled)
½ Banana (diced)
2 Maraschino Cherries

Pour Whisky and milk into a blender over cracked ice then add diced banana. Blend and strain into a chilled highball glass. Garnish with cherries and serve.

Tilt the Kilt

33.7% ALC/VOL • 2 STD DRINKS

60ml (2 fl oz) Scotch Whisky
5ml (1/6 fl oz) Triple Sec
5ml (1/6 fl oz) Fresh Lemon Juice
1 teaspoon Sugar Syrup

Pour Whisky, juice and sugar into a mixing glass over ice. Stir and strain into a cocktail glass over ice. Layer Triple Sec on top and serve.

King Cole Cocktail

38.1% ALC/VOL • 1.9 STD DRINKS

60ml (2 fl oz) Blended Whiskey
½ teaspoon Caster Sugar
Slice of Orange
Slice of Pineapple

Place sugar, a slice of orange and pineapple into a chilled old-fashioned glass then add 2 ice cubes. Add Whiskey, stir and serve.

Perfect Day

21.6% ALC/VOL • 1.5 STD DRINKS

30ml (1 fl oz) Bourbon
30ml (1 fl oz) Triple Sec
30ml (1 fl oz) Grenadine
Cherry
Twist of Orange Peel

Pour Bourbon, Triple Sec and Grenadine into a cocktail shaker over ice. Shake and strain into a chilled cocktail glass. Garnish with a cherry and orange peel then serve.

L'Aird of Summer Isle

16% ALC/VOL • 1.9 STD DRINKS

45ml (1½ fl oz) Scotch Whisky
15ml (½ fl oz) Pernod
90ml (3 fl oz) Pineapple Juice

Pour ingredients into a cocktail shaker over ice and shake. Strain into an old-fashioned glass over ice and serve.

Tempo Setter

30.8% ALC/VOL • 1.4 STD DRINKS

30ml (1 fl oz) Canadian Whisky
8ml (¼ fl oz) Anisette
8ml (¼ fl oz) Cointreau
8ml (¼ fl oz) Sweet Vermouth
5ml (1/6 fl oz) Fresh Lemon Juice
Maraschino Cherry

Pour Whisky, Anisette, Cointreau, Vermouth and juice into a cocktail shaker over ice. Shake and strain into a chilled liqueur glass. Garnish with a cherry and serve.

Ink Street

12.7% ALC/VOL • 0.9 STD DRINKS

30ml (1 fl oz) Rye Whiskey
30ml (1 fl oz) Fresh Lemon Juice
30ml (1 fl oz) Fresh Orange Juice

Pour ingredients into a cocktail shaker over ice and shake. Strain into a chilled cocktail glass and serve.

Banff Cocktail

38.3% ALC/VOL • 2.4 STD DRINKS

45ml (1½ fl oz) Canadian Whisky
15ml (½ fl oz) Grand Marnier
15ml (½ fl oz) Kirsch
Dash Angostura Bitters
Wedge of Lemon

Pour Whisky, Grand Marnier, Kirsch and Bitters into a mixing glass over ice. Stir and strain into a chilled cocktail glass. Garnish with a wedge of lemon and serve.

Celtic Mix Cocktail

33.5% ALC/VOL • 2.4 STD DRINKS

45ml (1½ fl oz) Scotch Whisky
30ml (1 fl oz) Irish Whiskey
Dash Angostura Bitters

15ml (½ fl oz) Fresh
Lemon Juice

Pour ingredients into a cocktail shaker over ice and shake. Strain into a chilled cocktail glass and serve.

Perfect Manhattan

33.4% ALC/VOL • 2.8 STD DRINKS

75ml (2½ fl oz) Blended Whiskey
15ml (½ fl oz) Dry Vermouth
15ml (½ fl oz) Sweet Vermouth
Dash Angostura Bitters
Maraschino Cherry

Pour Whiskey, Vermouths and Bitters into a mixing glass over ice. Stir and strain into a chilled cocktail glass. Garnish with a cherry and serve.

St. Patrick's Day

39.5% ALC/VOL • 2.2 STD DRINKS

23ml (¾ fl oz) Irish Whiskey
23ml (¾ fl oz) Green Chartreuse
23ml (¾ fl oz) Green Crème De Menthe
Dash Angostura Bitters

Pour ingredients into a mixing glass over ice and stir. Strain into a chilled cocktail glass and serve.

Creole Lady

24.7% ALC/VOL • 1.9 STD DRINKS

45ml (1½ fl oz) Bourbon
45ml (1½ fl oz) Madeira
5ml (⅙ fl oz) Grenadine
Green Cherry
Red Cherry

Pour Bourbon, Madeira and Grenadine into a mixing glass over ice. Stir and strain into a chilled cocktail glass. Garnish with cherries and serve.

Canada

28.4% ALC/VOL • 1.2 STD DRINKS

30ml (1 fl oz) Canadian Whisky
10ml (⅓ fl oz) Triple Sec
2 dashes Angostura Bitters
2 teaspoons Maple Syrup

Pour ingredients into a cocktail shaker over ice and shake. Strain into a chilled cocktail glass and serve.

Irresistible Manhattan

25.9% ALC/VOL • 2 STD DRINKS

30ml (1 fl oz) Canadian Whisky
30ml (1 fl oz) Amaretto
30ml (1 fl oz) Sweet Vermouth
Dash Angostura Bitters
5ml (⅙ fl oz) Maraschino Cherry Juice
Maraschino Cherry

Pour Whisky, Amaretto, Vermouth, Bitters and juice into a mixing glass over ice. Stir and strain into a cocktail glass over crushed ice. Garnish with a cherry and serve.

Paddy Cocktail

27.7% ALC/VOL • 2 STD DRINKS

45ml (1½ fl oz) Irish Whiskey
45ml (1½ fl oz) Sweet Vermouth
Dash Angostura Bitters

Pour ingredients into a mixing glass over ice and stir. Strain into a chilled cocktail glass and serve.

Double Standard Sour

27.3% ALC/VOL • 1.4 STD DRINKS

23ml (¾ fl oz) Blended Whiskey
23ml (¾ fl oz) Dry Gin
2 dashes Grenadine
15ml (½ fl oz) Fresh Lemon Juice
2 dashes Sugar Syrup
Maraschino Cherry
Slice of Lemon

Pour Whiskey, Gin, Grenadine, juice and sugar into a cocktail shaker over ice. Shake and strain into a chilled sour glass. Garnish with a cherry and slice of lemon then serve.

Gault's Gumption

32.1% ALC/VOL • 1.6 STD DRINKS

45ml (1½ fl oz) Canadian Whisky
15ml (½ fl oz) Peach Schnapps
5ml (⅙ fl oz) Sweet Vermouth

Pour ingredients into a mixing glass over ice and stir. Strain into a chilled cocktail glass and serve.

Morning Drew

14.2% ALC/VOL • 1.7 STD DRINKS

40ml (1⅓ fl oz) Blended Whiskey
20ml (⅔ fl oz) Blue Curaçao
Dash Angostura Bitters
60ml (2 fl oz) Passion-Fruit Juice
White of 1 Egg

Pour ingredients into a cocktail shaker over ice and shake. Strain into an old-fashioned glass over ice and serve.

Bazza Dazza

11.7% ALC/VOL • 1.7 STD DRINKS

45ml (1½ fl oz) Bourbon
8ml (¼ fl oz) Cointreau
8ml (¼ fl oz) Fresh Lemon Juice
120ml (4 fl oz) Cola

Pour Bourbon, Cointreau and juice into a highball glass over ice then stir. Add cola, stir gently and serve.

Canadian Mounty

21% ALC/VOL • 1.8 STD DRINKS

45ml (1½ fl oz) Canadian Whisky
30ml (1 fl oz) Cranberry Liqueur
30ml (1 fl oz) Fresh Orange Juice
5ml (1/6 fl oz) Fresh Lemon Juice
Slice of Orange

Pour Whisky, Liqueur and juices into a blender over cracked ice. Blend and pour into a chilled old-fashioned glass. Garnish with a slice of orange and serve.

Nevins

26.4% ALC/VOL • 1.6 STD DRINKS

45ml (1½ fl oz) Bourbon
8ml (¼ fl oz) Apricot Brandy
Dash Angostura Bitters
15ml (½ fl oz) Grapefruit Juice
8ml (¼ fl oz) Fresh Lemon Juice

Pour ingredients into a cocktail shaker over ice and shake. Strain into a chilled cocktail glass and serve.

Blue Valium

34.1% ALC/VOL • 1.6 STD DRINKS

15ml (½ fl oz) Canadian Whisky
15ml (½ fl oz) 151-Proof Bacardi
15ml (½ fl oz) Blue Curaçao
8ml (¼ fl oz) Sweet and Sour Mix
8ml (¼ fl oz) Lemonade

Pour Whisky, Bacardi, Curaçao and sour mix into a mixing glass over ice. Stir and strain into a chilled old-fashioned glass. Add lemonade, stir gently and serve.

Inedible Cocktail

35.9% ALC/VOL • 1.9 STD DRINKS

45ml (1½ fl oz) Canadian Whisky
15ml (½ fl oz) Glayva
8ml (¼ fl oz) Punt e Mes

Pour ingredients into a cocktail shaker over cracked ice and shake. Pour into a chilled old-fashioned glass and serve.

Bitter Bourbon Lemonade

9% ALC/VOL • 1.9 STD DRINKS

60ml (2 fl oz) Bourbon
5ml (1/6 fl oz) Grenadine
30ml (1 fl oz) Fresh Lemon Juice
15ml (½ fl oz) Fresh Lime Juice
1 teaspoon Sugar Syrup
150ml (5 fl oz) Bitter-Lemon Soda
Slice of Lemon

Pour Bourbon, Grenadine, juices and sugar into a cocktail shaker over ice. Shake and strain into a chilled collins glass over 2 ice cubes. Add soda and stir gently. Garnish with a slice of lemon and serve.

Widow Wood's Nightcap

14.1% ALC/VOL • 2.2 STD DRINKS

60ml (2 fl oz) Scotch Whisky
15ml (½ fl oz) Dark Crème De Cacao
120ml (4 fl oz) Fresh Milk (chilled)

Pour ingredients into a cocktail shaker over ice and shake. Strain into a chilled goblet and serve.

Bourbon Fix

22.8% ALC/VOL • 1.9 STD DRINKS

60ml (2 fl oz) Bourbon
30ml (1 fl oz) Fresh Lemon Juice
10ml (⅓ fl oz) Spring Water
1 teaspoon Sugar Syrup
Maraschino Cherry
Slice of Lemon

Pour Bourbon, juice, water and sugar into a cocktail shaker over ice. Shake and strain into an old-fashioned glass filled with crushed ice. Add more crushed ice to fill glass and stir gently. Garnish with a cherry and slice of lemon then serve.

Down the Hatch

39.9% ALC/VOL • 1.6 STD DRINKS

45ml (1½ fl oz) Blended Whiskey
3 dashes Blackberry Brandy
2 dashes Orange Bitters

Pour ingredients into a cocktail shaker over ice and shake. Strain into a chilled cocktail glass and serve.

Horse's Neck (spiked)

8% ALC/VOL • 0.9 STD DRINKS

30ml (1 fl oz) Blended Whiskey
30ml (1 fl oz) Fresh Lemon Juice
90ml (3 fl oz) Dry Ginger Ale
Long Twist of Lemon Peel

Place lemon peel into a highball glass with one end of peel hooked over rim of glass (thus giving the effect of a horse's neck) and the remainder of peel spiraling down inside of glass then fill glass with ice. Add Whiskey and juice then stir. Add Ginger Ale, stir gently and serve.

Man of the Moment

27.3% ALC/VOL • 2.4 STD DRINKS

45ml (1½ fl oz) Scotch Whisky
30ml (1 fl oz) Grand Marnier
5ml (1/6 fl oz) Grenadine
30ml (1 fl oz) Fresh Lemon Juice

Pour ingredients into a cocktail shaker over ice and shake. Strain into a chilled cocktail glass and serve.

Lady's Dream

17.2% ALC/VOL • 1.9 STD DRINKS

30ml (1 fl oz) Blended Whiskey
30ml (1 fl oz) Cointreau
30ml (1 fl oz) Pineapple Juice
30ml (1 fl oz) Fresh Cream
20ml (⅔ fl oz) Strawberry Syrup

Pour ingredients into a cocktail shaker over ice and shake. Strain into a chilled champagne saucer and serve.

Park Paradise

32% ALC/VOL • 1.7 STD DRINKS

45ml (1½ fl oz) Canadian Whisky
15ml (½ fl oz) Sweet Vermouth
5ml (1/6 fl oz) Maraschino Liqueur
Dash Angostura Bitters

Pour ingredients into a mixing glass over ice and stir. Strain into a chilled cocktail glass and serve.

Whiskey Sling

28.2% ALC/VOL • 1.9 STD DRINKS

60ml (2 fl oz) Blended Whiskey
15ml (½ fl oz) Fresh Lemon Juice
5ml (1/6 fl oz) Spring Water
1 teaspoon Sugar Syrup
Twist of Lemon Peel

Pour Whiskey, juice, water and sugar into a highball glass over ice then stir. Add lemon peel and serve.

Dixie Julep

37.5% ALC/VOL • 2.4 STD DRINKS

75ml (2½ fl oz) Bourbon
1 teaspoon Sugar Syrup
2 Sprigs of Fresh Mint

Pour Bourbon and sugar into a chilled collins glass. Add crushed ice to fill glass and stir until frosted. Garnish with sprigs of mint and serve with 2 straws.

Bourbon Sour

28.2% ALC/VOL • 1.9 STD DRINKS

60ml (2 fl oz) Bourbon
15ml (½ fl oz) Fresh Lemon Juice
1 teaspoon Sugar Syrup
1 teaspoon Egg White
Maraschino Cherry
Twist of Lemon Peel

Pour Bourbon, juice, sugar and egg white into a cocktail shaker over ice. Shake and strain into a chilled sour glass. Top up with soda water if desired and stir gently. Garnish with a cherry and lemon peel then serve.

Woodward Cocktail

27.6% ALC/VOL • 1.6 STD DRINKS

45ml (1½ fl oz) Scotch Whisky
15ml (½ fl oz) Dry Vermouth
15ml (½ fl oz) Grapefruit Juice

Pour ingredients into a cocktail shaker over ice and shake. Strain into a chilled cocktail glass and serve.

Whisky Cobbler

39% ALC/VOL • 2.1 STD DRINKS

60ml (2 fl oz) Scotch Whisky
4 dashes Brandy
4 dashes Curaçao
Slice of Lemon
Sprig of Fresh Mint
Strawberry

Pour Whisky, Brandy and Curaçao into a highball glass filled with ice then stir. Garnish with a slice of lemon, sprig of mint and a strawberry then serve.

Quickie

39.1% ALC/VOL • 3.1 STD DRINKS

45ml (1½ fl oz) Bourbon
45ml (1½ fl oz) Light Rum
10ml (⅓ fl oz) Cointreau

Pour ingredients into a cocktail shaker over ice and shake. Strain into a chilled cocktail glass and serve.

Southern Lady

14.7% ALC/VOL • 3.5 STD DRINKS

60ml (2 fl oz) Bourbon
30ml (1 fl oz) Crème De Noyaux
30ml (1 fl oz) Southern Comfort
90ml (3 fl oz) Pineapple Juice
30ml (1 fl oz) Fresh Lime Juice
60ml (2 fl oz) Lemon-Lime Soda
Maraschino Cherry
Pineapple Wheel

Pour Bourbon, Noyaux, Southern Comfort and pineapple juice into a cocktail shaker over ice. Shake and strain into a hurricane glass over ice. Add soda and stir gently then add lime juice – do not stir. Garnish with a cherry and pineapple wheel then serve.

Old Groaner

36% ALC/VOL • 2.1 STD DRINKS

60ml (2 fl oz) Canadian Whisky
15ml (½ fl oz) Amaretto

Pour ingredients into an old-fashioned glass over ice, stir and serve.

Ragged Company

35.5% ALC/VOL • 2.3 STD DRINKS

60ml (2 fl oz) Bourbon
15ml (½ fl oz) Sweet Vermouth
5ml (1/6 fl oz) Bénédictine
2 dashes Angostura Bitters
Slice of Lemon

Pour Bourbon, Vermouth, Bénédictine and Bitters into a mixing glass over ice. Stir and strain into a chilled cocktail glass. Garnish with a slice of lemon and serve.

Rory O'More

31.5% ALC/VOL • 1.7 STD DRINKS

45ml (1½ fl oz) Irish Whiskey
23ml (¾ fl oz) Sweet Vermouth
Dash Orange Bitters

Pour ingredients into a mixing glass over ice and stir. Strain into a chilled cocktail glass and serve.

Bourbon Crusta

26.6% ALC/VOL • 2.1 STD DRINKS

45ml (1½ fl oz) Bourbon
15ml (½ fl oz) Cointreau
10ml (⅓ fl oz) Maraschino Liqueur
15ml (½ fl oz) Fresh Lemon Juice
1 tablespoon Sugar Syrup
Long Twist of Orange Peel

Prepare a champagne saucer with a sugar frosted rim – moistened with lemon juice. Place orange peel into prepared glass with one end of peel hooked over rim of glass and remainder of peel spiraling down inside of glass then fill with crushed ice. Pour remaining ingredients into a cocktail shaker over ice and shake. Strain into prepared glass and serve.

Blue Monday

37.6% ALC/VOL • 1.9 STD DRINKS

45ml (1½ fl oz) Canadian Whisky
15ml (½ fl oz) Blueberry Brandy
5ml (1/6 fl oz) Brandy

Pour ingredients into a mixing glass over ice and stir. Strain into a chilled cocktail glass and serve.

Fred's Special

16.8% ALC/VOL • 2.7 STD DRINKS

90ml (3 fl oz) Canadian Whisky
23ml (¾ fl oz) Fresh Lemon Juice
90ml (3 fl oz) Cola
Slice of Lemon

Pour Whisky and juice into a mixing glass over ice. Stir and strain into a chilled old-fashioned glass. Add cola and stir gently. Garnish with a slice of lemon and serve.

Cat and Fiddle

33.9% ALC/VOL • 2.1 STD DRINKS

45ml (1½ fl oz) Canadian Whisky
15ml (½ fl oz) Cointreau
5ml (1/6 fl oz) Dubonnet
5ml (1/6 fl oz) Pernod

Pour ingredients into a mixing glass over ice and stir. Strain into a chilled cocktail glass and serve.

Porterhouse Blue

30.8% ALC/VOL • 1.8 STD DRINKS

45ml (1½ fl oz) Canadian Whisky
15ml (½ fl oz) Armagnac
15ml (½ fl oz) Blueberry Syrup
Blue Cherry
Slice of Lemon

Pour Whisky, Armagnac and syrup into a cocktail shaker over ice. Shake and strain into an old-fashioned glass over ice. Garnish with a cherry and slice of lemon then serve.

Hot Deck

29.7% ALC/VOL • 2.7 STD DRINKS

68ml (2¼ fl oz) Blended Whiskey
45ml (1½ fl oz) Sweet Vermouth
Dash Jamaica Ginger

Pour ingredients into a cocktail shaker over ice and shake. Strain into a chilled cocktail glass and serve.

Jungle Wild

11.4% ALC/VOL • 2.1 STD DRINKS

30ml (1 fl oz) Wild Turkey Bourbon
30ml (1 fl oz) Light Rum
10ml (⅓ fl oz) Pisang Ambon
60ml (2 fl oz) Papaya Juice
30ml (1 fl oz) Mandarin Juice
10ml (⅓ fl oz) Fresh Lime Juice
60ml (2 fl oz) Lemonade
Slice of Orange
Strawberry

Pour Bourbon, Rum, Pisang Ambon and juices into a cocktail shaker over ice. Shake and strain into a zombie glass over cracked ice. Add lemonade and stir gently. Garnish with a slice of orange and a strawberry then serve.

F.B.I. Fizz

5.3% ALC/VOL • 1.2 STD DRINKS

This drink is also known as Parisette, p 271.

Lark

12.2% ALC/VOL • 1.9 STD DRINKS

30ml (1 fl oz) Scotch Whisky
30ml (1 fl oz) Grand Marnier
8ml (¼ fl oz) Grenadine
8ml (¼ fl oz) Fresh Lemon Juice
120ml (4 fl oz) Orange Soda
Maraschino Cherry
Slice of Lemon
Slice of Orange

Pour Whisky, Grand Marnier, Grenadine and juice into a goblet over ice then stir. Add soda and stir gently. Garnish with a cherry, slice of lemon and orange then serve.

Kilted Bastard

25.8% ALC/VOL • 4.6 STD DRINKS

120ml (4 fl oz) Scotch Whisky
60ml (2 fl oz) Bailey's Irish Cream
1 Fresh Egg

Pour ingredients into a cocktail shaker over ice and shake. Strain into a highball glass over ice and serve.

Coffee Egg Nog

8.8% ALC/VOL • 1.8 STD DRINKS

45ml (1½ fl oz) Canadian Whisky
30ml (1 fl oz) Kahlúa
120ml (4 fl oz) Fresh Milk (chilled)
15ml (½ fl oz) Thick Cream
1 teaspoon Sugar Syrup
½ teaspoon Coffee Powder
1 Fresh Egg
Coriander Seed (ground)

Pour Whisky, Kahlúa, milk, cream, sugar, and egg into a cocktail shaker over ice then add coffee powder. Shake and strain into a chilled collins glass. Sprinkle coriander on top and serve.

Oppenheim

23.3% ALC/VOL • 0.6 STD DRINKS

15ml (½ fl oz) Bourbon
8ml (¼ fl oz) Sweet Vermouth
8ml (¼ fl oz) Grenadine

Pour ingredients into a mixing glass over ice and stir. Strain into a chilled liqueur glass and serve.

Temptation

37% ALC/VOL • 1.6 STD DRINKS

45ml (1½ fl oz) Rye Whiskey
3 dashes Cointreau
3 dashes Dubonnet
3 dashes Pernod
Twist of Orange Peel

Pour Whiskey, Cointreau, Dubonnet and Pernod into a mixing glass over ice. Stir and strain into a chilled cocktail glass. Garnish with orange peel and serve.

Sand Dance

17.9% ALC/VOL • 1.7 STD DRINKS

45ml (1½ fl oz) Blended Whiskey
15ml (½ fl oz) Cherry Brandy
60ml (2 fl oz) Cranberry Juice

Pour ingredients into a highball glass over ice, stir and serve.

Noxious Weed

38.4% ALC/VOL • 2.4 STD DRINKS

60ml (2 fl oz) Blended Whiskey
15ml (½ fl oz) Blackberry Brandy
4 dashes Orange Bitters
Strawberry

Pour Whiskey, Brandy and Bitters into a cocktail shaker over ice. Shake and strain into a chilled cocktail glass. Garnish with a strawberry and serve.

Black Hawk

30.8% ALC/VOL • 1.8 STD DRINKS

30ml (1 fl oz) Blended Whiskey
30ml (1 fl oz) Dry Gin
15ml (½ fl oz) Fresh Lemon Juice
Maraschino Cherry

Pour Whiskey, Gin and juice into a cocktail shaker over ice. Shake and strain into a chilled cocktail glass. Garnish with a cherry and serve.

Assassino

20% ALC/VOL • 2.4 STD DRINKS

60ml (2 fl oz) Blended Whiskey
30ml (1 fl oz) Dry Vermouth
3 dashes Sambuca
30ml (1 fl oz) Pineapple Juice
30ml (1 fl oz) Soda Water

Pour Whiskey, Vermouth and juice into a cocktail shaker over ice. Shake and strain into a collins glass over ice. Add soda – do not stir. Add Sambuca – do not stir, then serve.

Nightie Lifter

37% ALC/VOL • 2.1 STD DRINKS

45ml (1½ fl oz) Bourbon
23ml (¾ fl oz) Blackberry Brandy
5ml (⅙ fl oz) Peach Schnapps

Pour ingredients into a cocktail shaker over cracked ice and shake. Pour into a chilled old-fashioned glass and serve.

Pendennis Toddy

35.3% ALC/VOL • 1.9 STD DRINKS

60ml (2 fl oz) Bourbon
10ml (⅓ fl oz) Spring Water
½ teaspoon Sugar Syrup
2 Slices of Lemon

Pour Bourbon, water and sugar into a chilled old-fashioned glass then stir. Add an ice cube and garnish with slices of lemon then serve.

Major Bradbury

35.4% ALC/VOL • 2 STD DRINKS

45ml (1½ fl oz) Canadian Whisky
15ml (½ fl oz) Grand Marnier
5ml (⅙ fl oz) Dry Vermouth
5ml (⅙ fl oz) Sweet Vermouth

Pour ingredients into a mixing glass over ice and stir. Strain into a chilled cocktail glass and serve.

Blended Rickey

14.6% ALC/VOL • 1.9 STD DRINKS

60ml (2 fl oz) Blended Whiskey
15ml (½ fl oz) Fresh Lime Juice
90ml (3 fl oz) Soda Water
Slice of Lime

Pour Whiskey and juice into a collins glass over ice then stir. Add soda and stir gently. Garnish with a slice of lime and serve.

Dry Rob Roy

37.9% ALC/VOL • 2.5 STD DRINKS

75ml (2½ fl oz) Scotch Whisky
8ml (¼ fl oz) Dry Vermouth
Wedge of Lemon

Pour Whisky and Vermouth into a mixing glass over ice. Stir and strain into a chilled cocktail glass. Garnish with a wedge of lemon and serve.

Bourbon Swizzle

15.7% ALC/VOL • 1.9 STD DRINKS

60ml (2 fl oz) Bourbon
Dash Angostura Bitters
30ml (1 fl oz) Fresh Lime Juice
1 teaspoon Sugar Syrup
60ml (2 fl oz) Soda Water

Pour Bourbon, Bitters, juice and sugar into a mixing glass over large amount of ice. Stir vigorously until cold and strain into a collins glass filled with crushed ice then add soda – do not stir. Serve with a swizzle stick and 2 straws.

Flying Irishman

31.7% ALC/VOL • 2.3 STD DRINKS

60ml (2 fl oz) Irish Whiskey
30ml (1 fl oz) Sweet Vermouth
Green Cherry

Pour Whiskey and Vermouth into a mixing glass over ice. Stir and strain into a chilled cocktail glass. Garnish with a cherry and serve.

Highland Sling

22.8% ALC/VOL • 1.9 STD DRINKS

60ml (2 fl oz) Scotch Whisky
30ml (1 fl oz) Fresh Lime Juice
10ml (⅓ fl oz) Spring Water
1 teaspoon Sugar Syrup
Wedge of Lemon

Pour Whisky, juice, water and sugar into a cocktail shaker over ice. Shake and strain into a highball glass over ice. Garnish with a wedge of lemon and serve.

Cold Kiss

33.3% ALC/VOL • 1.8 STD DRINKS

45ml (1½ fl oz) Blended Whiskey
15ml (½ fl oz) Peppermint Schnapps
10ml (⅓ fl oz) White Crème De Cacao

Pour ingredients into a cocktail shaker over ice and shake. Strain into a chilled old-fashioned glass and serve.

Palmetto Cooler

14.6% ALC/VOL • 2.5 STD DRINKS

60ml (2 fl oz) Bourbon
15ml (½ fl oz) Apricot Liqueur
15ml (½ fl oz) Sweet Vermouth
3 dashes Angostura Bitters
120ml (4 fl oz) Soda Water
Sprig of Fresh Mint

Pour Bourbon, Liqueur, Vermouth and Bitters into a collins glass over ice then stir. Add soda and stir gently. Garnish with a sprig of mint and serve.

Canadian Citrus Sour

13.5% ALC/VOL • 1.1 STD DRINKS

38ml (1¼ fl oz) Canadian Whisky
23ml (¾ fl oz) Fresh Lime Juice
23ml (¾ fl oz) Fresh Orange Juice
23ml (¾ fl oz) Sweet and Sour Mix

Pour ingredients into a cocktail shaker over ice and shake. Strain into a chilled sour glass and serve.

Bourbon Smash

36.9% ALC/VOL • 1.9 STD DRINKS

60ml (2 fl oz) Bourbon
1 teaspoon Sugar Syrup

4 Sprigs of Fresh Mint
Slice of Lemon

Pour Bourbon and sugar into a mixing glass without ice then add 3 sprigs of mint. Muddle well and pour into an old-fashioned glass half filled with ice. Add more ice to fill glass and stir. Garnish with a slice of lemon and sprig of mint then serve.

Black Hawk Collins

8.7% ALC/VOL • 1.1 STD DRINKS

30ml (1 fl oz) Canadian Whisky
15ml (½ fl oz) Crème De Cassis
60ml (2 fl oz) Sweet and Sour Mix
60ml (2 fl oz) Soda Water

Pour Whisky, Cassis and sour mix into a cocktail shaker over ice. Shake and strain into a collins glass over ice. Add soda, stir gently and serve.

Tennessee Tea

23.9% ALC/VOL • 3.2 STD DRINKS

23ml (¾ fl oz) Tennessee Whiskey
23ml (¾ fl oz) Gin
23ml (¾ fl oz) Light Rum
23ml (¾ fl oz) Triple Sec
23ml (¾ fl oz) Vodka
45ml (1½ fl oz) Sweet and Sour Mix
5ml (⅙ fl oz) Fresh Orange Juice
5ml (⅙ fl oz) Cola
Wedge of Lemon

Pour Whiskey, Gin, Rum, Triple Sec, Vodka, sour mix and juice into a cocktail shaker over ice. Shake and strain into a chilled highball glass. Add cola and stir gently. Garnish with a wedge of lemon and serve.

Whizz Bang

31.9% ALC/VOL • 2.4 STD DRINKS

60ml (2 fl oz) Scotch Whisky
30ml (1 fl oz) Dry Vermouth
2 dashes Orange Bitters
2 dashes Pernod
2 dashes Grenadine
Twist of Lemon Peel

Pour Whisky, Vermouth, Bitters, Pernod and Grenadine into a cocktail shaker over ice. Shake and strain into a chilled cocktail glass. Twist lemon peel above drink and place remainder of peel into drink then serve.

Hunter

33% ALC/VOL • 2.3 STD DRINKS

60ml (2 fl oz) Rye Whiskey
30ml (1 fl oz) Cherry Brandy

Pour ingredients into a mixing glass over ice and stir. Strain into a chilled cocktail glass and serve.

Fancy Japanese

39% ALC/VOL • 2 STD DRINKS

60ml (2 fl oz) Japanese Whisky
2 dashes Cointreau
Dash Angostura Bitters
½ teaspoon Sugar Syrup
Twist of Lemon Peel

Pour Whisky, Cointreau, Bitters and sugar into a cocktail shaker over ice. Shake and strain into a chilled cocktail glass. Add lemon peel and serve.

Lochy

37.3% ALC/VOL • 2 STD DRINKS

60ml (2 fl oz) Scotch Whisky
3 dashes Angostura Bitters
1 teaspoon Sugar Syrup

Pour ingredients into a cocktail shaker over ice and shake. Strain into an old-fashioned glass over ice and serve.

Southern Belle

17.7% ALC/VOL • 1.7 STD DRINKS

30ml (1 fl oz) Bourbon
15ml (½ fl oz) Southern Comfort
15ml (½ fl oz) Green Crème De Menthe
15ml (½ fl oz) White Crème De Cacao
30ml (1 fl oz) Peach Juice
30ml (1 fl oz) Fresh Cream

Pour ingredients into a cocktail shaker over ice and shake. Strain into a chilled cocktail glass and serve.

Barbican

32.8% ALC/VOL • 2.1 STD DRINKS

60ml (2 fl oz) Scotch Whisky
8ml (¼ fl oz) Drambuie
15ml (½ fl oz) Passion-Fruit Juice

Pour ingredients into a cocktail shaker over ice and shake. Strain into a chilled goblet over a few ice cubes and serve.

Bay Horse

26.1% ALC/VOL • 2.2 STD DRINKS

45ml (1½ fl oz) Blended Whiskey
15ml (½ fl oz) Dark Crème De Cacao
15ml (½ fl oz) Pernod
30ml (1 fl oz) Thick Cream
Nutmeg

Pour Whiskey, Cacao, Pernod and cream into a cocktail shaker over ice. Shake and strain into an old-fashioned glass over ice. Sprinkle nutmeg on top and serve.

Mountain

22.1% ALC/VOL • 3.3 STD DRINKS

90ml (3 fl oz) Rye Whiskey
23ml (¾ fl oz) Dry Vermouth
23ml (¾ fl oz) Sweet Vermouth
23ml (¾ fl oz) Fresh Lemon Juice
White of 1 Egg

Pour ingredients into a cocktail shaker over ice and shake. Strain into a chilled champagne saucer and serve.

Whiskey Sour

30.8% ALC/VOL • 1.9 STD DRINKS

60ml (2 fl oz) Blended Whiskey
15ml (½ fl oz) Fresh Lemon Juice
½ teaspoon Sugar Syrup
Maraschino Cherry
Slice of Lemon

Pour Whiskey, juice and sugar into a cocktail shaker over ice. Shake and strain into a chilled sour glass. Top up with soda water if desired and stir gently. Garnish with a cherry and slice of lemon then serve.

Millionaire

26.4% ALC/VOL • 1.9 STD DRINKS

45ml (1½ fl oz) Bourbon
15ml (½ fl oz) Cointreau
Dash Grenadine
White of 1 Egg

Pour ingredients into a cocktail shaker over ice and shake. Strain into a chilled cocktail glass and serve.

Hell Hole

10.5% ALC/VOL • 1.9 STD DRINKS

45ml (1½ fl oz) Scotch Whisky
15ml (½ fl oz) Dry Vermouth
15ml (½ fl oz) Peach Schnapps
60ml (2 fl oz) Pineapple Juice
90ml (3 fl oz) Bitter-Lemon Soda

Pour Whisky, Vermouth, Schnapps and juice into a highball glass over ice then stir. Add soda, stir gently and serve.

Yashmak

31.8% ALC/VOL • 3.4 STD DRINKS

45ml (1½ fl oz) Rye Whiskey
45ml (1½ fl oz) Dry Vermouth
45ml (1½ fl oz) Pernod
Dash Angostura Bitters
Dash Sugar Syrup

Pour ingredients into a mixing glass over ice and stir. Strain into a chilled cocktail glass and serve.

Whiskey Swizzle

15.9% ALC/VOL • 2 STD DRINKS

60ml (2 fl oz) Blended Whiskey
2 dashes Angostura Bitters
30ml (1 fl oz) Fresh Lime Juice
1 teaspoon Sugar Syrup
60ml (2 fl oz) Soda Water

Pour Whiskey, Bitters, juice and sugar into a mixing glass over large amount of ice. Stir vigorously until cold and strain into a collins glass filled with crushed ice. Add soda – do not stir, then serve with a swizzle stick and 2 straws.

Mint Cooler

17.2% ALC/VOL • 2.9 STD DRINKS

90ml (3 fl oz) Scotch Whisky
3 dashes White Crème De Menthe
120ml (4 fl oz) Soda Water

Pour Whisky and Crème De Menthe into a collins glass over ice then stir. Add soda, stir gently and serve.

Broker's Thought

13.4% ALC/VOL • 1.4 STD DRINKS

23ml (¾ fl oz) Bourbon
23ml (¾ fl oz) Light Rum
60ml (2 fl oz) Fresh Milk (chilled)
23ml (¾ fl oz) Fresh Lemon Juice
1 teaspoon Sugar Syrup

Pour ingredients into a cocktail shaker over ice and shake. Strain into a chilled cocktail glass and serve.

Commando Cocktail

32.8% ALC/VOL • 1.9 STD DRINKS

45ml (1½ fl oz) Bourbon
23ml (¾ fl oz) Triple Sec
2 dashes Pernod
5ml (1/6 fl oz) Fresh Lime Juice

Pour ingredients into a cocktail shaker over cracked ice and shake. Pour into a chilled highball glass and serve.

Scofflaw

20.7% ALC/VOL • 1.3 STD DRINKS

30ml (1 fl oz) Canadian Whisky
30ml (1 fl oz) Dry Vermouth
Dash Orange Bitters
2 dashes Grenadine
15ml (½ fl oz) Fresh Lemon Juice
Slice of Lemon

Pour Whisky, Vermouth, Bitters, Grenadine and juice into a cocktail shaker over ice. Shake and strain into a chilled cocktail glass. Garnish with a slice of lemon and serve.

Monte Carlo

38.9% ALC/VOL • 2.1 STD DRINKS

45ml (1½ fl oz) Rye Whiskey
23ml (¾ fl oz) Bénédictine
2 dashes Angostura Bitters

Pour ingredients into a cocktail shaker over ice and shake. Strain into a chilled cocktail glass and serve.

Trilby

26.2% ALC/VOL • 1.9 STD DRINKS

30ml (1 fl oz) Scotch Whisky
30ml (1 fl oz) Parfait Amour
30ml (1 fl oz) Sweet Vermouth
2 dashes Orange Bitters
2 dashes Pernod

Pour ingredients into a mixing glass over ice and stir. Strain into a chilled cocktail glass and serve.

Grand Master No.2

16.4% ALC/VOL • 2.1 STD DRINKS

60ml (2 fl oz) Scotch Whisky
15ml (½ fl oz) Peppermint Schnapps
90ml (3 fl oz) Soda Water
Wedge of Lemon

Pour Whisky and Schnapps into a highball glass over ice then stir. Add soda and stir gently. Garnish with a wedge of lemon and serve.

Macbeth

29.3% ALC/VOL • 2.3 STD DRINKS

60ml (2 fl oz) Scotch Whisky
10ml (⅓ fl oz) Amaretto
10ml (⅓ fl oz) Blue Curaçao
15ml (½ fl oz) Fresh Lemon Juice
1 teaspoon Sugar Syrup

Pour ingredients into a cocktail shaker over ice and shake. Strain into a chilled cocktail glass and serve.

Aquarius

23.8% ALC/VOL • 1.7 STD DRINKS

45ml (1½ fl oz) Blended Whiskey
15ml (½ fl oz) Cherry Brandy
30ml (1 fl oz) Cranberry Juice

Pour ingredients into a cocktail shaker over ice and shake. Strain into an old-fashioned glass over ice and serve.

Irish

37.9% ALC/VOL • 1.9 STD DRINKS

45ml (1½ fl oz) Irish Whiskey
8ml (¼ fl oz) Curaçao
8ml (¼ fl oz) Pernod
Dash Angostura Bitters
Dash Maraschino Liqueur
Twist of Orange Peel

Pour Whiskey, Curaçao, Pernod, Bitters and Liqueur into a cocktail shaker over ice. Shake and strain into a chilled cocktail glass. Garnish with orange peel and serve.

Oriental

27% ALC/VOL • 1.6 STD DRINKS

30ml (1 fl oz) Blended Whiskey
15ml (½ fl oz) Cointreau
15ml (½ fl oz) Sweet Vermouth
15ml (½ fl oz) Fresh Lime Juice

Pour ingredients into a cocktail shaker over ice and shake. Strain into a chilled cocktail glass and serve.

Cool Change

12.4% ALC/VOL • 1.9 STD DRINKS

45ml (1½ fl oz) Irish Whiskey
30ml (1 fl oz) Midori
120ml (4 fl oz) Soda Water
Slice of Lime

Pour Whiskey and Midori into a highball glass over ice then stir. Add soda and stir gently. Garnish with a slice of lime and serve.

Socrates

34.8% ALC/VOL • 1.8 STD DRINKS

45ml (1½ fl oz) Canadian Whisky
15ml (½ fl oz) Apricot Brandy
5ml (⅙ fl oz) Cointreau
Dash Angostura Bitters

Pour ingredients into a mixing glass over ice and stir. Strain into a chilled cocktail glass and serve.

Wild Jackalope

34% ALC/VOL • 1.7 STD DRINKS

45ml (1½ fl oz) Canadian Whisky
15ml (½ fl oz) Peppermint Schnapps
5ml (⅙ fl oz) Pernod
Wedge of Lemon

Pour Whisky, Schnapps and Pernod into a mixing glass over ice. Stir and strain into an old-fashioned glass over ice. Garnish with a wedge of lemon and serve.

Bourbon Fog

13.3% ALC/VOL • 1.9 STD DRINKS

60ml (2 fl oz) Bourbon
60ml (2 fl oz) Black Coffee (chilled)
2 scoops Vanilla Ice Cream

Pour Bourbon and coffee into a cocktail shaker over cracked ice then add ice cream. Shake well and pour into a chilled champagne saucer then serve.

Rob Roy

31.9% ALC/VOL • 2.3 STD DRINKS

60ml (2 fl oz) Scotch Whisky
30ml (1 fl oz) Sweet Vermouth
Dash Angostura Bitters
Maraschino Cherry

Pour Whisky, Vermouth and Bitters into a mixing glass over ice. Stir and strain into a chilled old-fashioned glass. Garnish with a cherry and serve.

Balmoral

31% ALC/VOL • 1.9 STD DRINKS

45ml (1½ fl oz) Scotch Whisky
15ml (½ fl oz) Dry Vermouth
15ml (½ fl oz) Sweet Vermouth
2 dashes Angostura Bitters

Pour ingredients into a mixing glass over ice and stir. Strain into a chilled cocktail glass and serve.

Dickie Ward

13.5% ALC/VOL • 1.9 STD DRINKS

60ml (2 fl oz) Scotch Whisky
Dash Angostura Bitters
120ml (4 fl oz) Dry Ginger Ale
Wedge of Lime

Pour Whisky and Bitters into a highball glass over ice then stir. Add Ginger Ale and stir gently. Garnish with a wedge of lime and serve.

Jim Collins

13.3% ALC/VOL • 1.4 STD DRINKS

45ml (1½ fl oz) Bourbon
90ml (3 fl oz) Soda Water
Slice of Lemon

Pour Bourbon into a collins glass over ice and add soda then stir gently. Garnish with a slice of lemon and serve.

Brooklyn

27.5% ALC/VOL • 1.6 STD DRINKS

45ml (1½ fl oz) Bourbon
15ml (½ fl oz) Dry Vermouth
Dash Maraschino Liqueur
15ml (½ fl oz) Fresh Lemon Juice
Slice of Lemon

Pour Bourbon, Vermouth, Liqueur and juice into a cocktail shaker over ice. Shake and strain into a chilled cocktail glass. Garnish with a slice of lemon and serve.

New York Cocktail

30% ALC/VOL • 1.8 STD DRINKS

60ml (2 fl oz) Canadian Whisky
Dash Grenadine
15ml (½ fl oz) Fresh Lemon Juice
Twist of Orange Peel

Pour Whisky, Grenadine and juice into a cocktail shaker over ice. Shake and strain into a chilled cocktail glass. Garnish with orange peel and serve.

Connolly's Irish Connection

27.8% ALC/VOL • 3.3 STD DRINKS

30ml (1 fl oz) Irish Whiskey
30ml (1 fl oz) Bailey's Irish Cream
30ml (1 fl oz) Frangelico
30ml (1 fl oz) Midori
30ml (1 fl oz) Vodka

Pour ingredients into a cocktail shaker over cracked ice and shake. Pour into a chilled collins glass and serve.

Buckaroo

11.5% ALC/VOL • 2 STD DRINKS

60ml (2 fl oz) Bourbon
4 dashes Angostura Bitters
160ml (5⅓ fl oz) Cola

Pour Bourbon and Bitters into a highball glass over ice then stir. Add cola, stir gently and serve.

Paterson's Curse

35.5% ALC/VOL • 2.2 STD DRINKS

60ml (2 fl oz) Scotch Whisky
15ml (½ fl oz) Crème De Cassis
4 dashes Orange Bitters
2 Blackberries
Sprig of Fresh Mint

Pour Whisky, Cassis and Bitters into a cocktail shaker over ice. Shake and strain into a chilled cocktail glass. Garnish with blackberries and a sprig of mint then serve.

Oh Henry

26% ALC/VOL • 1.8 STD DRINKS

30ml (1 fl oz) Canadian Whisky
30ml (1 fl oz) Bénédictine
30ml (1 fl oz) Dry Ginger Ale

Pour Whisky and Bénédictine into a mixing glass over ice. Stir and strain into a chilled cocktail glass. Add Ginger Ale, stir gently and serve.

Piza

23.4% ALC/VOL • 1.2 STD DRINKS

15ml (½ fl oz) Scotch Whisky
15ml (½ fl oz) Amaretto
15ml (½ fl oz) Dry Vermouth
10ml (⅓ fl oz) Banana Liqueur
2 teaspoons Lime Syrup
Slice of Lime

Pour Whisky, Amaretto, Vermouth, Liqueur and syrup into a cocktail shaker over ice. Shake and strain into an old-fashioned glass over ice. Garnish with a slice of lime and serve.

Old Groaner's Wife

23.7% ALC/VOL • 1.7 STD DRINKS

60ml (2 fl oz) Canadian Whisky
15ml (½ fl oz) Amaretto
30ml (1 fl oz) Thick Cream

Pour ingredients into an old-fashioned glass over ice, stir and serve.

Fox River Cocktail

34.7% ALC/VOL • 2.6 STD DRINKS

60ml (2 fl oz) Blended Whiskey
30ml (1 fl oz) Dark Crème De Cacao
4 dashes Angostura Bitters

Pour ingredients into a mixing glass over ice and stir. Strain into a chilled cocktail glass and serve.

Cowboy

26.7% ALC/VOL • 1.9 STD DRINKS

60ml (2 fl oz) Scotch Whisky
30ml (1 fl oz) Fresh Cream

Pour ingredients into a cocktail shaker over ice and shake. Strain into a chilled cocktail glass and serve.

Cup Final

19.3% ALC/VOL • 1.4 STD DRINKS

This drink is also known as Wembley, p 270.

Sherman Tank

34.3% ALC/VOL • 2.4 STD DRINKS

60ml (2 fl oz) Blended Whiskey
15ml (½ fl oz) B & B
2 dashes Angostura Bitters
5ml (⅙ fl oz) Fresh Lemon Juice
5ml (⅙ fl oz) Fresh Lime Juice
½ teaspoon Sugar Syrup

Pour ingredients into a cocktail shaker over ice and shake. Strain into a chilled cocktail glass and serve.

Piper at Arms

31.2% ALC/VOL • 1.8 STD DRINKS

45ml (1½ fl oz) Scotch Whisky
30ml (1 fl oz) Dry Vermouth
Wedge of Lemon

Pour Whisky and Vermouth into a mixing glass over ice. Stir and strain into a chilled cocktail glass. Garnish with a wedge of lemon and serve.

King Edward Cocktail

34.3% ALC/VOL • 2 STD DRINKS

60ml (2 fl oz) Canadian Whisky
10ml (⅓ fl oz) Dry Vermouth
Dash Pernod
2 dashes Soda Water
Twist of Orange Peel

Pour Whisky, Vermouth and Pernod into a mixing glass over ice. Stir and strain into an old-fashioned glass over ice then add soda – do not stir. Garnish with orange peel and serve.

Old Cobber

29% ALC/VOL • 1.4 STD DRINKS

30ml (1 fl oz) Blended Whiskey
30ml (1 fl oz) Dry Vermouth
Wedge of Lemon

Pour Whiskey and Vermouth into an old-fashioned glass over ice then stir. Garnish with a wedge of lemon and serve.

Classic Bourbon

29.4% ALC/VOL • 1.8 STD DRINKS

45ml (1½ fl oz) Bourbon
15ml (½ fl oz) White Curaçao
Dash Angostura Bitters
Dash Bénédictine
15ml (½ fl oz) Fresh Lemon Juice

Pour ingredients into a cocktail shaker over ice and shake. Strain into a chilled cocktail glass and serve.

Wembley

19.3% ALC/VOL • 1.4 STD DRINKS

30ml (1 fl oz) Scotch Whisky
30ml (1 fl oz) Dry Vermouth
30ml (1 fl oz) Pineapple Juice

Pour ingredients into a cocktail shaker over ice and shake. Strain into a chilled cocktail glass and serve. *This drink is also known as Cup Final.*

Chapel Hill

32% ALC/VOL • 1.9 STD DRINKS

45ml (1½ fl oz) Blended Whiskey
15ml (½ fl oz) Cointreau
15ml (½ fl oz) Fresh Lemon Juice
Twist of Orange Peel

Pour Whiskey, Cointreau and juice into a cocktail shaker over ice. Shake and strain into a chilled cocktail glass. Garnish with orange peel and serve.

Blinder

11.2% ALC/VOL • 1.9 STD DRINKS

60ml (2 fl oz) Scotch Whisky
5ml (⅙ fl oz) Grenadine
150ml (5 fl oz) Grapefruit Juice

Pour Whisky and juice into a highball glass over ice then stir. Add Grenadine by pouring into centre of drink – do not stir, then serve.

Japanese Fizz

17.9% ALC/VOL • 2.5 STD DRINKS

68ml (2¼ fl oz) Japanese Whisky
23ml (¾ fl oz) Port
15ml (½ fl oz) Fresh Lemon Juice
1 teaspoon Caster Sugar
75ml (2½ fl oz) Soda Water
Twist of Orange Peel

Pour Whisky, Port and juice into a cocktail shaker over ice then add sugar. Shake and strain into a highball glass over ice. Add soda and stir gently. Garnish with orange peel and serve.

Scotch Sangaree

38.1% ALC/VOL • 1.9 STD DRINKS

60ml (2 fl oz) Scotch Whisky
½ teaspoon Sugar Syrup
Nutmeg

Pour Whisky and sugar into an old-fashioned glass over ice then stir. Sprinkle nutmeg on top and serve.

Blackthorn

30.2% ALC/VOL • 1.6 STD DRINKS

30ml (1 fl oz) Irish Whiskey
30ml (1 fl oz) Dry Vermouth
3 dashes Angostura Bitters
3 dashes Pernod
Twist of Lemon Peel

Pour Whiskey, Vermouth, Bitters and Pernod into a cocktail shaker over ice. Shake and strain into a chilled cocktail glass. Garnish with lemon peel and serve.

Scotch Milk Punch

8.7% ALC/VOL • 1.9 STD DRINKS

60ml (2 fl oz) Scotch Whisky
210ml (7 fl oz) Fresh Milk (chilled)
1 teaspoon Sugar Syrup
Nutmeg

Pour Whisky, milk and sugar into a cocktail shaker over ice. Shake and strain into a chilled highball glass. Sprinkle nutmeg on top and serve.

Queen of Scots

32.5% ALC/VOL • 2.1 STD DRINKS

60ml (2 fl oz) Scotch Whisky
3 dashes Blue Curaçao
3 dashes Green Chartreuse
2 teaspoons Sugar Syrup
5ml (1/6 fl oz) Fresh Lemon Juice

Pour Whisky, sugar and juice into a mixing glass over ice. Stir and strain into a cocktail glass half filled with ice. Layer Curaçao and Chartreuse on top then serve.

Carlton Cocktail

29% ALC/VOL • 1.4 STD DRINKS

30ml (1 fl oz) Canadian Whisky
15ml (½ fl oz) Cointreau
15ml (½ fl oz) Fresh Orange Juice

Pour ingredients into a cocktail shaker over ice and shake. Strain into a chilled cocktail glass and serve.

Whiskey Flip

20.9% ALC/VOL • 1.9 STD DRINKS

60ml (2 fl oz) Blended Whiskey
1 teaspoon Fresh Cream
1 teaspoon Sugar Syrup
1 Fresh Egg
Nutmeg

Pour Whiskey, cream, sugar and egg into a cocktail shaker over ice. Shake and strain into a chilled goblet. Sprinkle nutmeg on top and serve.

Maple Leaf

27.1% ALC/VOL • 2.4 STD DRINKS

60ml (2 fl oz) Canadian Whisky
15ml (½ fl oz) Irish Mist
5ml (1/6 fl oz) Dark Crème De Cacao
30ml (1 fl oz) Thick Cream

Pour ingredients into a cocktail shaker over ice and shake. Strain into a chilled cocktail glass and serve.

Dublin Milkshake

10% ALC/VOL • 1.8 STD DRINKS

45ml (1½ fl oz) Irish Whiskey
30ml (1 fl oz) Bailey's Irish Cream
120ml (4 fl oz) Fresh Milk (chilled)
1 scoop Vanilla Ice Cream
1 teaspoon Cocoa Powder
Grated Chocolate

Pour Whiskey, Bailey's and milk into a cocktail shaker over ice. Shake and strain into a chilled highball glass. Float ice cream on top and sprinkle cocoa powder over ice cream. Sprinkle chocolate on top and serve.

Irish Alexander on the Rocks

19% ALC/VOL • 1 STD DRINK

23ml (¾ fl oz) Irish Whiskey
23ml (¾ fl oz) Bailey's Irish Cream
23ml (¾ fl oz) Thick Cream

Pour ingredients into a cocktail shaker over cracked ice and shake then pour into a chilled old-fashioned glass. Fill glass with ice, stir and serve.

Parisette

5.3% ALC/VOL • 1.2 STD DRINKS

15ml (½ fl oz) Bourbon
15ml (½ fl oz) Jamaica Rum
15ml (½ fl oz) Peter Heering Liqueur
240ml (8 fl oz) Soda Water
Twist of Orange Peel

Pour Bourbon, Rum and Liqueur into a cocktail shaker over ice. Shake and strain into a chilled highball glass. Add soda and stir gently. Garnish with orange peel and serve. *This drink is also known as F.B.I. Fizz.*

Polly's Special

28.2% ALC/VOL • 1.7 STD DRINKS

45ml (1½ fl oz) Scotch Whisky
10ml (⅓ fl oz) Cointreau
23ml (¾ fl oz) Grapefruit Juice

Pour ingredients into a cocktail shaker over ice and shake. Strain into a chilled cocktail glass and serve.

Ward Standard

27.1% ALC/VOL • 1.3 STD DRINKS

45ml (1½ fl oz) Canadian Whisky
3 dashes Grenadine
15ml (½ fl oz) Fresh Lemon Juice
Maraschino Cherry
Slice of Orange

Pour Whisky, Grenadine and juice into a cocktail shaker over ice. Shake and strain into a chilled cocktail glass. Top up with soda water if desired and stir gently. Garnish with a cherry and slice of orange then serve.

Strongarm

33.3% ALC/VOL • 2.4 STD DRINKS

60ml (2 fl oz) Blended Whiskey
15ml (½ fl oz) Cointreau
15ml (½ fl oz) Fresh Lemon Juice

Pour ingredients into a cocktail shaker over ice and shake. Strain into a chilled cocktail glass and serve.

Dead 'orse

16.4% ALC/VOL • 1.5 STD DRINKS

45ml (1½ fl oz) Blended Whiskey
2 dashes Angostura Bitters
30ml (1 fl oz) Fresh Lemon Juice
1 tablespoon Tomato Sauce (chilled)
1 tablespoon Worcestershire Sauce
2 dashes Tabasco Sauce
Slice of Lemon

Pour Whiskey, Bitters, juice and sauces into a mixing glass over ice. Stir and strain into a chilled old-fashioned glass over a few ice cubes. Garnish with a slice of lemon and serve.

Atholl Brose

17.2% ALC/VOL • 1.4 STD DRINKS

45ml (1½ fl oz) Scotch Whisky
30ml (1 fl oz) Fresh Cream
30ml (1 fl oz) Honey

Pour ingredients into a cocktail shaker over ice and shake. Strain into a chilled cocktail glass and serve.

Whiskey Fix

31.6% ALC/VOL • 2.4 STD DRINKS

75ml (2½ fl oz) Blended Whiskey
15ml (½ fl oz) Fresh Lemon Juice
1 teaspoon Sugar Syrup
Slice of Lemon

Pour Whiskey, juice and sugar into an old-fashioned glass filled with crushed ice. Add more crushed ice to fill glass and stir. Garnish with a slice of lemon and serve.

Whisky Mac

34.8% ALC/VOL • 2.1 STD DRINKS

60ml (2 fl oz) Scotch Whisky
15ml (½ fl oz) Green Ginger Wine
Slice of Lemon

Pour Whisky and Wine into an old-fashioned glass over ice then stir. Top up with Ginger Ale if desired and stir gently. Garnish with a slice of lemon and serve.

Bourbon Old-Fashioned

36.1% ALC/VOL • 2 STD DRINKS

60ml (2 fl oz) Bourbon
2 dashes Angostura Bitters
1 teaspoon Sugar Syrup
2 dashes Soda Water or Spring Water
Maraschino Cherry
Slice of Orange

Pour Bitters, sugar and soda or water as desired into an old-fashioned glass over ice then stir. Add Bourbon and add more ice to fill glass then stir. Garnish with a cherry and slice of orange then serve.

Evens

37.6% ALC/VOL • 1.8 STD DRINKS

60ml (2 fl oz) Canadian Whisky
Dash Apricot Brandy
Dash Curaçao

Pour ingredients into a mixing glass over ice and stir. Strain into a chilled cocktail glass and serve.

Southern Belle No.2

6.7% ALC/VOL • 1.9 STD DRINKS

38ml (1¼ fl oz) Tennessee Whiskey
23ml (¾ fl oz) Cointreau
3 dashes Grenadine
240ml (8 fl oz) Pineapple Juice
60ml (2 fl oz) Fresh Orange Juice

Pour Whiskey, Cointreau and juices into a collins glass over ice then stir. Add Grenadine and stir once then serve.

Japanese Cooler

11.5% ALC/VOL • 1.1 STD DRINKS

30ml (1 fl oz) Japanese Whisky
Dash Angostura Bitters
90ml (3 fl oz) Soda Water
Wedge of Lemon

Pour Whisky and Bitters into a collins glass over ice then stir. Add soda and stir gently. Garnish with a wedge of lemon and serve.

Speaker of the House

25.4% ALC/VOL • 1.6 STD DRINKS

45ml (1½ fl oz) Canadian Whisky
15ml (½ fl oz) Green Ginger Wine
5ml (1/6 fl oz) Cherry Brandy
15ml (½ fl oz) Fresh Lemon Juice
Maraschino Cherry

Pour Whisky, Wine, Brandy and juice into a cocktail shaker over ice. Shake and strain into a chilled cocktail glass. Garnish with a cherry and serve.

Twin Peaks

34.4% ALC/VOL • 1.8 STD DRINKS

45ml (1½ fl oz) Blended Whiskey
15ml (½ fl oz) Dubonnet
5ml (1/6 fl oz) Cointreau
Wedge of Lemon

Pour Whiskey, Dubonnet and Cointreau into a mixing glass over ice. Stir and strain into a chilled cocktail glass. Garnish with a wedge of lemon and serve.

Cotillion Cocktail

24.3% ALC/VOL • 1.7 STD DRINKS

45ml (1½ fl oz) Bourbon
15ml (½ fl oz) Triple Sec
Dash Light Rum
15ml (½ fl oz) Fresh Lemon Juice
15ml (½ fl oz) Fresh Orange Juice

Pour ingredients into a cocktail shaker over ice and shake. Strain into a chilled cocktail glass and serve.

Tartantula

31.7% ALC/VOL • 2.3 STD DRINKS

45ml (1½ fl oz) Scotch Whisky
30ml (1 fl oz) Sweet Vermouth
15ml (½ fl oz) Bénédictine
Wedge of Lemon

Pour Whisky, Vermouth and Bénédictine into a mixing glass over ice. Stir and strain into a chilled cocktail glass. Garnish with a wedge of lemon and serve.

Up-to-Date

28.8% ALC/VOL • 1.5 STD DRINKS

30ml (1 fl oz) Canadian Whisky
30ml (1 fl oz) Medium Sherry
2 dashes Angostura Bitters
2 dashes Cointreau
Slice of Orange

Pour Whisky, Sherry, Bitters and Cointreau into a cocktail shaker over ice. Shake and strain into a chilled cocktail glass. Garnish with a slice of orange and serve.

Lawhill

32.8% ALC/VOL • 2.4 STD DRINKS

60ml (2 fl oz) Blended Whiskey
30ml (1 fl oz) Dry Vermouth
Dash Angostura Bitters
Dash Maraschino Liqueur
Dash Pernod

Pour ingredients into a mixing glass over ice and stir. Strain into a chilled cocktail glass and serve.

Canadian Salad

23.5% ALC/VOL • 2.3 STD DRINKS

30ml (1 fl oz) Canadian Whisky
15ml (½ fl oz) Brandy
15ml (½ fl oz) Irish Mist
15ml (½ fl oz) Scotch Whisky
30ml (1 fl oz) Fresh Orange Juice
15ml (½ fl oz) Fresh Lemon Juice
½ teaspoon Sugar Syrup
Maraschino Cherry
Slice of Orange

Pour Whiskies, Brandy, Irish Mist, juices and sugar into a cocktail shaker over ice. Shake and strain into an old-fashioned glass over ice. Garnish with a cherry and slice of orange then serve.

New Orleans

38.3% ALC/VOL • 2.1 STD DRINKS

45ml (1½ fl oz) Bourbon
15ml (½ fl oz) Pernod
4 dashes Angostura Bitters
Dash Orange Bitters
Dash Sambuca
½ teaspoon Sugar Syrup

Pour ingredients into a cocktail shaker over cracked ice and shake. Pour into a chilled old-fashioned glass and serve.

Godfather

35.9% ALC/VOL • 1.9 STD DRINKS

45ml (1½ fl oz) Scotch Whisky
23ml (¾ fl oz) Amaretto
Slice of Orange

Pour Whisky and Amaretto into an old-fashioned glass over ice then stir. Garnish with a slice of orange and serve.

Scotch Cooler

13.4% ALC/VOL • 1.9 STD DRINKS

60ml (2 fl oz) Scotch Whisky
Dash Curaçao
60ml (2 fl oz) Fresh Orange Juice
60ml (2 fl oz) Soda Water
Slice of Orange

Pour Whisky, Curaçao and juice into a cocktail shaker over ice. Shake and strain into a collins glass over ice. Add soda and stir gently. Garnish with a slice of orange and serve.

Menday's Peril

23.9% ALC/VOL • 1.7 STD DRINKS

45ml (1½ fl oz) Blended Whiskey
15ml (½ fl oz) Cherry Brandy
2 dashes Orange Bitters
15ml (½ fl oz) Fresh Lemon Juice
15ml (½ fl oz) Fresh Orange Juice

Pour ingredients into a cocktail shaker over ice and shake. Strain into an old-fashioned glass over ice and serve.

Suntory Sour

32.6% ALC/VOL • 2 STD DRINKS

60ml (2 fl oz) Suntory Whisky
15ml (½ fl oz) Fresh Lemon Juice
½ teaspoon Sugar Syrup
Dash Egg White
Maraschino Cherry
Slice of Orange

Pour Whisky, juice, sugar and egg white into a cocktail shaker over ice. Shake and strain into a chilled sour glass. Top up with soda water if desired and stir gently. Garnish with a cherry and slice of orange then serve.

Tipperary Cocktail

36.6% ALC/VOL • 2.6 STD DRINKS

30ml (1 fl oz) Irish Whiskey
30ml (1 fl oz) Green Chartreuse
30ml (1 fl oz) Sweet Vermouth

Pour ingredients into a mixing glass over ice and stir. Strain into a chilled cocktail glass and serve.

Tartan Swizzle

15.7% ALC/VOL • 1.9 STD DRINKS

60ml (2 fl oz) Scotch Whisky
Dash Angostura Bitters
30ml (1 fl oz) Fresh Lime Juice
1 teaspoon Sugar Syrup
60ml (2 fl oz) Soda Water

Pour Whisky, Bitters, juice and sugar into a mixing glass over large amount of ice. Stir vigorously until cold and strain into a collins glass filled with crushed ice. Add soda – do not stir, then serve with a swizzle stick and 2 straws.

Presbyterian

11.4% ALC/VOL • 1.9 STD DRINKS

60ml (2 fl oz) Blended Whiskey
90ml (3 fl oz) Soda Water
60ml (2 fl oz) Dry Ginger Ale
Wedge of Lemon

Pour Whiskey into a highball glass over ice and add soda. Add Ginger Ale and stir gently. Garnish with a wedge of lemon and serve.

Mint Julep

29.4% ALC/VOL • 2.2 STD DRINKS

60ml (2 fl oz) Bourbon
8ml (¼ fl oz) Dark Rum
3 dashes Kirsch
15ml (½ fl oz) Spring Water
1 teaspoon Sugar Syrup
5ml (⅙ fl oz) Soda Water
7 Sprigs of Fresh Mint

Pour sugar into a chilled collins glass and add 3 sprigs of mint. Muddle well to crush mint then add Kirsch and water. Add ice to half fill glass and stir. Add Bourbon and stir. Add more ice to fill glass and place 4 sprigs of mint vertically into drink. Add soda – do not stir, then layer Rum on top and serve.

Bourbon Zoom

30% ALC/VOL • 1.4 STD DRINKS

45ml (1½ fl oz) Bourbon
2 teaspoons Fresh Cream
1 teaspoon Honey

Pour ingredients into a cocktail shaker over ice and shake. Strain into a chilled cocktail glass and serve.

Linestead

19.6% ALC/VOL • 1.5 STD DRINKS

45ml (1½ fl oz) Scotch Whisky
3 dashes Pernod
45ml (1½ fl oz) Pineapple Juice
1 teaspoon Sugar Syrup
Wedge of Lemon

Pour Whisky, Pernod, juice and sugar into a cocktail shaker over ice. Shake and strain into an old-fashioned glass over ice. Garnish with a wedge of lemon and serve.

Purgavie

10.1% ALC/VOL • 1.7 STD DRINKS

45ml (1½ fl oz) Canadian Whisky

15ml (½ fl oz) Amer Picon
2 dashes Orange Bitters
60ml (2 fl oz) Fresh Orange Juice
90ml (3 fl oz) Soda Water

Pour Whisky, Amer Picon, Bitters and juice into a highball glass over ice then stir. Add soda, stir gently and serve.

Barnstormer

26.3% ALC/VOL • 1.8 STD DRINKS

45ml (1½ fl oz) Canadian Whisky
15ml (½ fl oz) Peppermint Schnapps
5ml (1/6 fl oz) Dark Crème De Cacao
5ml (1/6 fl oz) White Crème De Cacao
15ml (½ fl oz) Fresh Lemon Juice

Pour ingredients into a cocktail shaker over ice and shake. Strain into an old-fashioned glass over ice and serve.

Red Whiskey

26.4% ALC/VOL • 1.6 STD DRINKS

30ml (1 fl oz) Blended Whiskey
30ml (1 fl oz) Sloe Gin
15ml (½ fl oz) Fresh Lemon Juice
Maraschino Cherry

Pour Whiskey, Gin and juice into a cocktail shaker over ice. Shake and strain into a chilled cocktail glass. Garnish with a cherry and serve.

Twin Hills

30.8% ALC/VOL • 2.2 STD DRINKS

60ml (2 fl oz) Blended Whiskey
10ml (⅓ fl oz) Bénédictine
8ml (¼ fl oz) Fresh Lemon Juice
8ml (¼ fl oz) Fresh Lime Juice
1 teaspoon Sugar Syrup
Slice of Lemon
Slice of Lime

Pour Whiskey, Bénédictine, juices and sugar into a cocktail shaker over ice. Shake and strain into a chilled sour glass. Garnish with a slice of lemon and lime then serve.

Green Paddy

10.5% ALC/VOL • 1.5 STD DRINKS

30ml (1 fl oz) Irish Whiskey
30ml (1 fl oz) Green Crème De Menthe
120ml (4 fl oz) Soda Water

Pour Whiskey and Crème De Menthe into a cocktail shaker over ice. Shake and strain into a chilled wine glass. Add soda, stir gently and serve.

Derby Fizz

9.7% ALC/VOL • 1.5 STD DRINKS

45ml (1½ fl oz) Blended Whiskey
3 dashes Orange Curaçao
5ml (1/6 fl oz) Fresh Lemon Juice
1 teaspoon Caster Sugar
1 Fresh Egg
90ml (3 fl oz) Soda Water
Slice of Orange

Pour Whiskey, Curaçao, juice and egg into a cocktail shaker over ice then add sugar. Shake and strain into a highball glass over ice. Add soda and stir gently. Garnish with a slice of orange and serve.

Irish Cooler

10% ALC/VOL • 0.9 STD DRINKS

30ml (1 fl oz) Irish Whiskey
90ml (3 fl oz) Soda Water
Twist of Lemon Peel

Pour Whiskey into a collins glass over ice and add soda then stir gently. Garnish with lemon peel and serve.

Canadian Cocktail No.2

35.2% ALC/VOL • 1.9 STD DRINKS

60ml (2 fl oz) Canadian Whisky
2 dashes Angostura Bitters
Dash Curaçao
1 teaspoon Sugar Syrup
Twist of Orange Peel

Pour Whisky, Bitters, Curaçao and sugar into a cocktail shaker over ice. Shake and strain into a chilled cocktail glass. Garnish with orange peel and serve.

Exotic

17.2% ALC/VOL • 2.3 STD DRINKS

60ml (2 fl oz) Blended Whiskey
15ml (½ fl oz) Triple Sec
8ml (¼ fl oz) White Crème De Cacao
60ml (2 fl oz) Pineapple Juice
30ml (1 fl oz) Apricot Nectar

Pour ingredients into a cocktail shaker over ice and shake. Strain into a highball glass over ice and serve.

Canadian Cocktail

34.9% ALC/VOL • 1.5 STD DRINKS

45ml (1½ fl oz) Canadian Whisky
2 dashes Angostura Bitters
2 dashes Cointreau
1 teaspoon Sugar Syrup
Twist of Lemon Peel
Twist of Orange Peel

Pour Whisky, Bitters, Cointreau and sugar into a cocktail shaker over ice. Shake and strain into a chilled cocktail glass. Garnish with lemon and orange peels then serve.

Bourbon Rickey

14.6% ALC/VOL • 1.9 STD DRINKS

60ml (2 fl oz) Bourbon
15ml (½ fl oz) Fresh Lime Juice
90ml (3 fl oz) Soda Water
Twist of Lime Peel

Pour Bourbon and juice into a collins glass over ice then stir. Add soda and stir gently. Garnish with lime peel and serve.

Scotch Holiday Sour

21.7% ALC/VOL • 2.1 STD DRINKS

45ml (1½ fl oz) Scotch Whisky
30ml (1 fl oz) Cherry Brandy
15ml (½ fl oz) Sweet Vermouth
30ml (1 fl oz) Fresh Lemon Juice
1 teaspoon Egg White
Slice of Lemon

Pour Whisky, Brandy, Vermouth, juice and egg white into a cocktail shaker over ice. Shake and strain into a sour glass over ice. Garnish with a slice of lemon and serve.

Dubonnet Manhattan

35.4% ALC/VOL • 2.1 STD DRINKS

60ml (2 fl oz) Blended Whiskey
15ml (½ fl oz) Dubonnet
Dash Angostura Bitters
Maraschino Cherry

Pour Whiskey, Dubonnet and Bitters into a mixing glass over ice. Stir and strain into a chilled cocktail glass. Garnish with a cherry and serve.

Cablegram

11.8% ALC/VOL • 1.4 STD DRINKS

45ml (1½ fl oz) Blended Whiskey
15ml (½ fl oz) Fresh Lemon Juice
½ teaspoon Sugar Syrup
90ml (3 fl oz) Dry Ginger Ale
Slice of Lemon

Pour Whiskey, juice and sugar into a highball glass over ice then stir. Add Ginger Ale and stir gently. Garnish with a slice of lemon and serve.

J.R.'s Godchild

26.8% ALC/VOL • 2.2 STD DRINKS

60ml (2 fl oz) Bourbon
15ml (½ fl oz) Amaretto
30ml (1 fl oz) Fresh Milk (chilled)

Pour ingredients into a cocktail shaker over cracked ice and shake. Pour into a chilled old-fashioned glass and serve.
This drink is also known as Dixie Smooth, p 231.

California Lemonade

9.8% ALC/VOL • 1.4 STD DRINKS

45ml (1½ fl oz) Blended Whiskey
Dash Grenadine
30ml (1 fl oz) Fresh Lemon Juice
30ml (1 fl oz) Fresh Lime Juice
1 tablespoon Sugar Syrup
60ml (2 fl oz) Soda Water
Slice of Lemon
Slice of Orange

Pour Whiskey, Grenadine, juices and sugar into a cocktail shaker over ice. Shake and strain into a highball glass over ice. Add soda and stir gently. Garnish with a slice of lemon and orange then serve.

Frisco

33.7% ALC/VOL • 2.5 STD DRINKS

60ml (2 fl oz) Bourbon
20ml (⅔ fl oz) Bénédictine
15ml (½ fl oz) Fresh Lemon Juice

Pour ingredients into a cocktail shaker over ice and shake. Strain into a chilled cocktail glass and serve.

Opening

26% ALC/VOL • 2.2 STD DRINKS

60ml (2 fl oz) Canadian Whisky
30ml (1 fl oz) Sweet Vermouth
15ml (½ fl oz) Grenadine

Pour ingredients into a cocktail shaker over ice and shake. Strain into a chilled cocktail glass and serve.

Sazarac

37.8% ALC/VOL • 1.5 STD DRINKS

45ml (1½ fl oz) Blended Whiskey
2 dashes Pernod
Dash Angostura Bitters
½ teaspoon Sugar Syrup
Twist of Lemon Peel

Pour Pernod into a chilled old-fashioned glass and swirl around glass. Pour Whiskey, Bitters and sugar into a mixing glass over ice. Stir and strain into prepared glass. Garnish with lemon peel and serve.

La Belle Quebec

28.1% ALC/VOL • 2.1 STD DRINKS

45ml (1½ fl oz) Canadian Whisky
15ml (½ fl oz) Brandy
15ml (½ fl oz) Cherry Brandy
15ml (½ fl oz) Fresh Lemon Juice
½ teaspoon Sugar Syrup

Pour ingredients into a cocktail shaker over ice and shake. Strain into a chilled cocktail glass and serve.

Everybody's Irish

39.7% ALC/VOL • 2.8 STD DRINKS

60ml (2 fl oz) Irish Whiskey
15ml (½ fl oz) Green Chartreuse
15ml (½ fl oz) Green Crème De Menthe
Green Olive

Pour Whiskey, Chartreuse and Crème De Menthe into a mixing glass over ice. Stir and strain into a chilled cocktail glass. Garnish with an olive and serve.

Scotch Sidecar

30% ALC/VOL • 1.4 STD DRINKS

30ml (1 fl oz) Scotch Whisky
15ml (½ fl oz) Cointreau
15ml (½ fl oz) Fresh Lemon Juice
Slice of Lemon

Pour Whisky, Cointreau and juice into a cocktail shaker over ice. Shake and strain into a chilled cocktail glass. Garnish with a slice of lemon and serve.

Pink Almond

29.2% ALC/VOL • 2.1 STD DRINKS

30ml (1 fl oz) Blended Whiskey
15ml (½ fl oz) Amaretto
15ml (½ fl oz) Crème De Noyaux
15ml (½ fl oz) Kirsch
15ml (½ fl oz) Fresh Lemon Juice
Slice of Lemon

Pour Whiskey, Amaretto, Noyaux, Kirsch and juice into a cocktail shaker over ice. Shake and strain into a chilled cocktail glass. Garnish with a slice of lemon and serve.

Modern Cocktail

36.4% ALC/VOL • 1.8 STD DRINKS

45ml (1½ fl oz) Blended Whiskey
5ml (1/6 fl oz) Golden Rum
3 dashes Cointreau
3 dashes Pernod
5ml (1/6 fl oz) Fresh Lemon Juice
Maraschino Cherry

Pour Whiskey, Rum, Cointreau, Pernod and juice into a cocktail shaker over ice. Shake and strain into a chilled cocktail glass. Garnish with a cherry and serve.

Mamie Taylor

13.3% ALC/VOL • 1.9 STD DRINKS

60ml (2 fl oz) Scotch Whisky
120ml (4 fl oz) Dry Ginger Ale
Slice of Lemon

Pour Whisky into a highball glass over ice and add Ginger Ale then stir gently. Garnish with a slice of lemon and serve.

Brainstorm

39.1% ALC/VOL • 1.5 STD DRINKS

45ml (1½ fl oz) Irish Whiskey
2 dashes Bénédictine
2 dashes Dry Vermouth
Twist of Orange Peel

Pour Whiskey, Bénédictine and Vermouth into a chilled cocktail glass then stir gently. Garnish with orange peel and serve.

Commodore

29.9% ALC/VOL • 1.9 STD DRINKS

60ml (2 fl oz) Blended Whiskey
2 dashes Orange Bitters
15ml (½ fl oz) Fresh Lemon or Lime Juice
1 teaspoon Sugar Syrup

Pour ingredients into a cocktail shaker over ice and shake. Strain into a chilled cocktail glass and serve.

Manhattan

30% ALC/VOL • 2.2 STD DRINKS

60ml (2 fl oz) Canadian Whisky
30ml (1 fl oz) Sweet Vermouth
Dash Angostura Bitters
Maraschino Cherry

Pour Whisky, Vermouth and Bitters into a mixing glass over ice. Stir and strain into a chilled cocktail glass. Garnish with a cherry and serve.

Rye Whiskey Cocktail

27.1% ALC/VOL • 1.9 STD DRINKS

60ml (2 fl oz) Rye Whiskey
Dash Angostura Bitters
1 teaspoon Sugar Syrup
Cherry

Pour Whiskey, Bitters and sugar into a cocktail shaker over ice. Shake and strain into a chilled cocktail glass. Add a cherry and serve.

Blended Collins

14.1% ALC/VOL • 1.9 STD DRINKS

60ml (2 fl oz) Blended Whiskey
15ml (½ fl oz) Fresh Lemon Juice
1 teaspoon Sugar Syrup
90ml (3 fl oz) Soda Water
Slice of Lemon
Slice of Orange

Pour Whiskey, juice and sugar into a cocktail shaker over ice. Shake and strain into a collins glass over ice. Add soda and stir gently. Garnish with a slice of lemon and orange then serve.

Liberty Bell

33.2% ALC/VOL • 2.4 STD DRINKS

60ml (2 fl oz) Bourbon
30ml (1 fl oz) Peach Schnapps
Dash Apricot Brandy
Dash Campari

Pour ingredients into a mixing glass over ice and stir. Strain into a chilled cocktail glass and serve.

Fresh Canadian

11.4% ALC/VOL • 1.3 STD DRINKS

45ml (1½ fl oz) Canadian Whisky
60ml (2 fl oz) Lemonade
45ml (1½ fl oz) Dry Ginger Ale
Slice of Lemon

Pour Whisky into a highball glass filled with ice and add lemonade. Add Ginger Ale and stir gently. Garnish with a slice of lemon and serve.

Borrowed Time

25.9% ALC/VOL • 1.6 STD DRINKS

45ml (1½ fl oz) Canadian Whisky
15ml (½ fl oz) Ruby Port
5ml (⅙ fl oz) Grenadine
Yolk of 1 Egg

Pour ingredients into a cocktail shaker over ice and shake. Strain into a chilled cocktail glass and serve.

Suntory Dry

17.6% ALC/VOL • 2.1 STD DRINKS

60ml (2 fl oz) Suntory Whisky
2 dashes Angostura Bitters
90ml (3 fl oz) Dry Ginger Ale
Twist of Lemon Peel
Wedge of Lime

Pour Whisky and Bitters into a highball glass over ice then stir. Add Ginger Ale and stir gently. Garnish with lemon peel and a wedge of lime then serve.

Boot Hill

32.3% ALC/VOL • 2.4 STD DRINKS

60ml (2 fl oz) Blended Whiskey
15ml (½ fl oz) Applejack
15ml (½ fl oz) Fresh Lemon Juice
½ teaspoon Sugar Syrup

Pour ingredients into a cocktail shaker over ice and shake. Strain into a chilled cocktail glass and serve.

Los Angeles

19.9% ALC/VOL • 1.9 STD DRINKS

60ml (2 fl oz) Scotch Whisky
Dash Sweet Vermouth
15ml (½ fl oz) Fresh Lemon Juice
1 Fresh Egg
Twist of Lemon Peel

Pour Whisky, Vermouth, juice and egg into a cocktail shaker over ice. Shake and strain into a chilled cocktail glass. Garnish with lemon peel and serve.

Artist's Cocktail

19.3% ALC/VOL • 1.4 STD DRINKS

30ml (1 fl oz) Scotch Whisky
30ml (1 fl oz) Sherry
15ml (½ fl oz) Fresh Lemon Juice
1 tablespoon Sugar Syrup

Pour ingredients into a cocktail shaker over ice and shake. Strain into a chilled cocktail glass and serve.

Dry Tennessee Manhattan

32.8% ALC/VOL • 2.4 STD DRINKS

60ml (2 fl oz) Tennessee Whiskey
30ml (1 fl oz) Dry Vermouth
Dash Angostura Bitters
Wedge of Lemon

Pour Whiskey, Vermouth and Bitters into a mixing glass over ice. Stir and strain into a chilled cocktail glass. Garnish with a wedge of lemon and serve.

Bourbon Manhattan

31.9% ALC/VOL • 2.3 STD DRINKS

60ml (2 fl oz) Bourbon
30ml (1 fl oz) Sweet Vermouth
Dash Angostura Bitters
Maraschino Cherry

Pour Bourbon, Vermouth and Bitters into a mixing glass over ice. Stir and strain into a chilled cocktail glass. Garnish with a cherry and serve.

Seaboard

28.9% ALC/VOL • 1.8 STD DRINKS

30ml (1 fl oz) Blended Whiskey
30ml (1 fl oz) Dry Gin
15ml (½ fl oz) Fresh Lemon Juice
1 teaspoon Sugar Syrup
Sprig of Fresh Mint

Pour Whiskey, Gin, juice and sugar into a cocktail shaker over ice. Shake and strain into an old-fashioned glass over ice. Garnish with a sprig of mint and serve.

Trocadero

30.7% ALC/VOL • 1.9 STD DRINKS

45ml (1½ fl oz) Bourbon
30ml (1 fl oz) Dry Vermouth
Dash Orange Bitters
Dash Grenadine

Pour ingredients into a cocktail shaker over ice and shake. Strain into a chilled cocktail glass and serve.

Blood Shot

31.5% ALC/VOL • 1.3 STD DRINKS

20ml (⅔ fl oz) Blended Whiskey
10ml (⅓ fl oz) Apricot Brandy
10ml (⅓ fl oz) Sweet Vermouth
10ml (⅓ fl oz) Vodka
2 dashes Angostura Bitters

Pour ingredients into a cocktail shaker over ice and shake. Strain into a chilled cocktail glass and serve.

Blarney Stone

27.5% ALC/VOL • 2 STD DRINKS

30ml (1 fl oz) Irish Whiskey
30ml (1 fl oz) Dry Vermouth
30ml (1 fl oz) Green Curaçao
3 dashes Orange Bitters

Pour ingredients into a cocktail shaker over ice and shake. Strain into a chilled cocktail glass and serve.

Burbank Special

11.4% ALC/VOL • 1.9 STD DRINKS

60ml (2 fl oz) Bourbon
60ml (2 fl oz) Fresh Orange Juice
30ml (1 fl oz) Maple Syrup
15ml (½ fl oz) Lemon Syrup
1 Fresh Egg
Slice of Lemon
Slice of Orange

Pour Bourbon, juice, syrups and egg into a cocktail shaker over ice. Shake and strain into a chilled goblet. Garnish with a slice of lemon and orange then serve.

Opening Night

32.2% ALC/VOL • 1.9 STD DRINKS

45ml (1½ fl oz) Blended Whiskey
15ml (½ fl oz) Dry Vermouth
15ml (½ fl oz) Strawberry Liqueur

Pour ingredients into a cocktail shaker over ice and shake. Strain into a chilled cocktail glass and serve.

The Shoot

23.8% ALC/VOL • 1.4 STD DRINKS

30ml (1 fl oz) Scotch Whisky
30ml (1 fl oz) Dry Sherry
5ml (⅙ fl oz) Fresh Lemon Juice
5ml (⅙ fl oz) Fresh Orange Juice
½ teaspoon Sugar Syrup

Pour ingredients into a cocktail shaker over ice and shake. Strain into a chilled cocktail glass and serve.

Wildflower

23.7% ALC/VOL • 1.4 STD DRINKS

45ml (1½ fl oz) Scotch Whisky
Dash Grenadine
30ml (1 fl oz) Grapefruit Juice

Pour ingredients into a mixing glass without ice and stir. Pour into a champagne saucer filled with crushed ice and serve with 2 short straws.

Dandy

28.8% ALC/VOL • 1.5 STD DRINKS

30ml (1 fl oz) Canadian Whisky
30ml (1 fl oz) Dry Vermouth
3 dashes Cointreau
Dash Angostura Bitters
Twist of Lemon Peel
Twist of Orange Peel

Pour Whisky, Vermouth, Cointreau and Bitters into a mixing glass over ice. Stir and strain into a chilled cocktail glass. Garnish with lemon and orange peels then serve.

Houston Hurricane

27.3% ALC/VOL • 3.6 STD DRINKS

45ml (1½ fl oz) Blended Whiskey
45ml (1½ fl oz) Gin
45ml (1½ fl oz) White Crème De Menthe
30ml (1 fl oz) Fresh Lemon Juice

Pour ingredients into a cocktail shaker over ice and shake. Strain into a chilled hurricane glass and serve.

Fancy Free

39.6% ALC/VOL • 2 STD DRINKS

60ml (2 fl oz) Bourbon
2 dashes Maraschino Liqueur
Dash Angostura Bitters
Dash Orange Bitters
Maraschino Cherry

Pour Bourbon, Liqueur and Bitters into a mixing glass over ice. Stir and strain into a chilled cocktail glass. Garnish with a cherry and serve.

Flying Scotsman

26.6% ALC/VOL • 2 STD DRINKS

45ml (1½ fl oz) Scotch Whisky
45ml (1½ fl oz) Sweet Vermouth
2 dashes Curaçao

½ teaspoon Sugar Syrup

Pour ingredients into a cocktail shaker over ice and shake. Strain into a chilled old-fashioned glass over a few ice cubes and serve.

Shamrock

29.9% ALC/VOL • 1.6 STD DRINKS

30ml (1 fl oz) Irish Whiskey
30ml (1 fl oz) Dry Vermouth
3 dashes Green Chartreuse
3 dashes Green Crème De Menthe
Green Olive
Sprig of Fresh Mint

Pour Whiskey, Vermouth, Chartreuse and Crème De Menthe into a mixing glass over ice. Stir and strain into a chilled cocktail glass. Garnish with an olive and sprig of mint then serve.

Kiltlifter

20% ALC/VOL • 2.4 STD DRINKS

45ml (1½ fl oz) Scotch Whisky
30ml (1 fl oz) Drambuie
75ml (2½ fl oz) Fresh Lime Juice

Pour ingredients into a cocktail shaker over ice and shake. Strain into an old-fashioned glass over ice and serve.

Rattlesnake

19.7% ALC/VOL • 1.5 STD DRINKS

45ml (1½ fl oz) Canadian Whisky
5ml (⅙ fl oz) Pernod
15ml (½ fl oz) Fresh Lemon Juice
½ teaspoon Sugar Syrup
White of 1 Egg

Pour ingredients into a cocktail shaker over ice and shake. Strain into a chilled cocktail glass and serve.

Highland Fling

34.8% ALC/VOL • 2.1 STD DRINKS

60ml (2 fl oz) Scotch Whisky
15ml (½ fl oz) Sweet Vermouth
2 dashes Orange Bitters
Maraschino Cherry

Pour Whisky, Vermouth and Bitters into a mixing glass over ice. Stir and strain into a chilled cocktail glass. Garnish with a cherry and serve.

Club Cocktail

36.7% ALC/VOL • 1.4 STD DRINKS

45ml (1½ fl oz) Canadian Whisky
2 dashes Angostura Bitters
2 dashes Grenadine
Maraschino Cherry
Twist of Lemon Peel

Pour Whisky, Bitters and Grenadine into a mixing glass over ice. Stir and strain into an old-fashioned glass over ice. Top up with soda water if desired and stir gently. Garnish with a cherry and lemon peel then serve.

Loch Ness Monster

13.5% ALC/VOL • 1.5 STD DRINKS

45ml (1½ fl oz) Scotch Whisky
5ml (⅙ fl oz) Peppermint Schnapps
90ml (3 fl oz) Soda Water

Pour Whisky and Schnapps into a cocktail shaker over ice. Shake and strain into a chilled old-fashioned glass. Add soda, stir gently and serve.

Wild Irish Rose

13.8% ALC/VOL • 1.4 STD DRINKS

45ml (1½ fl oz) Irish Whiskey
10ml (⅓ fl oz) Grenadine
15ml (½ fl oz) Fresh Lemon Juice
60ml (2 fl oz) Soda Water
Slice of Lemon

Pour Whiskey, Grenadine and juice into a cocktail shaker over ice. Shake and strain into an old-fashioned glass over ice. Add soda and stir gently. Garnish with a slice of lemon and serve.

Manhattan (dry)

28.2% ALC/VOL • 2 STD DRINKS

45ml (1½ fl oz) Canadian Whisky
45ml (1½ fl oz) Dry Vermouth
Dash Angostura Bitters
Olive

Pour Whisky, Vermouth and Bitters into a mixing glass over ice. Stir and strain into a chilled cocktail glass. Garnish with an olive and serve.

Ward Eight

21.4% ALC/VOL • 1.4 STD DRINKS

45ml (1½ fl oz) Canadian Whisky
5ml (⅙ fl oz) Grenadine
15ml (½ fl oz) Fresh Lemon Juice
15ml (½ fl oz) Fresh Orange Juice
Slice of Lemon

Pour Whisky, Grenadine and juices into a cocktail shaker over ice. Shake and strain into a chilled cocktail glass. Garnish with a slice of lemon.

Pink Panther

21.4% ALC/VOL • 2.3 STD DRINKS

45ml (1½ fl oz) Bourbon
30ml (1 fl oz) Vodka
Dash Grenadine
30ml (1 fl oz) Coconut Milk (chilled)
30ml (1 fl oz) Thick Cream

Pour ingredients into a cocktail shaker over ice and shake. Strain into a chilled cocktail glass and serve.

Zazarac

36% ALC/VOL • 1.7 STD DRINKS

45ml (1½ fl oz) Bourbon
5ml (⅙ fl oz) Anisette
5ml (⅙ fl oz) Pernod
Dash Angostura Bitters
1 teaspoon Sugar Syrup
Slice of Orange
Twist of Lemon Peel

Pour Bourbon, Anisette, Pernod, Bitters and sugar into a cocktail shaker over ice. Shake and strain into a chilled old-fashioned glass. Twist lemon peel above drink and place remainder of peel into drink. Garnish with a slice of orange and serve.

Mountie

34.8% ALC/VOL • 1.6 STD DRINKS

45ml (1½ fl oz) Canadian Whisky
15ml (½ fl oz) Campari

Pour ingredients into a mixing glass over ice and stir. Strain into a chilled cocktail glass and serve.

Old-Fashioned Cocktail

34.4% ALC/VOL • 1.9 STD DRINKS

60ml (2 fl oz) Canadian Whisky
2 dashes Angostura Bitters
1 teaspoon Sugar Syrup
2 dashes Soda Water or Spring Water
Maraschino Cherry
Slice of Orange

Pour Bitters, sugar and soda or water as desired into a chilled old-fashioned glass then stir. Add ice, Whisky and more ice to fill glass then stir. Garnish with a cherry and slice of orange then serve.
This drink is also known as Canadian Old-Fashioned.

Elephant Gun

17.2% ALC/VOL • 0.9 STD DRINKS

30ml (1 fl oz) Blended Whiskey
30ml (1 fl oz) Pineapple Juice
5ml (⅙ fl oz) Fresh Lemon Juice
1 teaspoon Sugar Syrup

Pour ingredients into a cocktail shaker over ice and shake. Strain into a chilled cocktail glass and serve.

Jocose Julep

16.7% ALC/VOL • 2.6 STD DRINKS

75ml (2½ fl oz) Bourbon
15ml (½ fl oz) Green Crème De Menthe
30ml (1 fl oz) Fresh Lime Juice
1 teaspoon Sugar Syrup
75ml (2½ fl oz) Soda Water
6 Fresh Mint Leaves (crushed)
Sprig of Fresh Mint

Pour Bourbon, Crème De Menthe, juice and sugar into a blender without ice then add crushed mint leaves. Blend until mixed and pour into a highball glass over ice. Add soda and stir gently. Garnish with a sprig of mint and serve.

Blinker

12.7% ALC/VOL • 0.9 STD DRINKS

30ml (1 fl oz) Canadian Whisky
15ml (½ fl oz) Grenadine
45ml (1½ fl oz) Grapefruit Juice

Pour ingredients into a cocktail shaker over ice and shake. Strain into a chilled cocktail glass and serve.

Cinnamon Road

10.3% ALC/VOL • 2 STD DRINKS

30ml (1 fl oz) Wild Turkey Bourbon
20ml (⅔ fl oz) Apfelkorn
20ml (⅔ fl oz) Goldschläger
180ml (6 fl oz) Dry Ginger Ale
Slice of Dried Apple

Pour Bourbon, Apfelkorn and Goldschläger into a cocktail shaker over ice. Shake and strain into a chilled highball glass over a few ice cubes. Add Ginger Ale and stir gently. Garnish with a slice of dried apple and serve.

Serpent's Tooth

19.9% ALC/VOL • 2.1 STD DRINKS

30ml (1 fl oz) Irish Whiskey
60ml (2 fl oz) Sweet Vermouth
15ml (½ fl oz) Kümmel
Dash Angostura Bitters
30ml (1 fl oz) Fresh Lemon Juice

Pour ingredients into a mixing glass over ice and stir. Strain into a chilled cocktail glass and serve.

Sand Trap

25.9% ALC/VOL • 2.1 STD DRINKS

45ml (1½ fl oz) Scotch Whisky
30ml (1 fl oz) Cherry Brandy
15ml (½ fl oz) Sweet Vermouth
15ml (½ fl oz) Fresh Lemon Juice
Slice of Lemon

Pour Whisky, Brandy, Vermouth and juice into a cocktail shaker over ice. Shake and strain into a highball glass over ice. Add more ice to fill glass and garnish with a slice of lemon then serve.

Canadian Cherry

27% ALC/VOL • 1.6 STD DRINKS

45ml (1½ fl oz) Canadian Whisky
15ml (½ fl oz) Cherry Brandy
8ml (¼ fl oz) Fresh Lemon Juice

8ml (¼ fl oz) Fresh Orange Juice

Prepare an old-fashioned glass with a Cherry Brandy moistened rim and half fill with ice. Pour ingredients into a cocktail shaker over ice and shake. Strain into prepared glass and serve.

Boomerang

34.7% ALC/VOL • 2.1 STD DRINKS

45ml (1½ fl oz) Scotch Whisky
15ml (½ fl oz) Dry Vermouth
15ml (½ fl oz) Swedish Punsch
2 dashes Fresh Lemon Juice
Twist of Lemon Peel

Pour Whisky, Vermouth, Punsch and juice into a cocktail shaker over ice. Shake and strain into a chilled cocktail glass. Garnish with lemon peel and serve.

Emerald Isle Cooler

6.3% ALC/VOL • 1.5 STD DRINKS

30ml (1 fl oz) Irish Whiskey
30ml (1 fl oz) Green Crème De Menthe
2 scoops Vanilla Ice Cream
180ml (6 fl oz) Soda Water

Place ice cream into a chilled collins glass. Add Whiskey and Crème De Menthe then stir well. Add soda, stir gently and serve.

River in Peace

20.5% ALC/VOL • 2.3 STD DRINKS

60ml (2 fl oz) Blended Whiskey
20ml (⅔ fl oz) Dark Crème De Cacao
2 scoops Vanilla Ice Cream
Sprig of Fresh Mint

Pour Whiskey and Cacao into a blender without ice then add ice cream. Blend until smooth and pour into a chilled sour glass. Garnish with a sprig of mint and serve.

Laura

28.6% ALC/VOL • 2.7 STD DRINKS

45ml (1½ fl oz) Bourbon
30ml (1 fl oz) Sweet Vermouth
15ml (½ fl oz) Campari
15ml (½ fl oz) Dry Vermouth
15ml (½ fl oz) Galliano

Pour ingredients into a mixing glass over ice and stir. Strain into a chilled cocktail glass and serve.

Sweet Scotch

13% ALC/VOL • 1.9 STD DRINKS

45ml (1½ fl oz) Scotch Whisky
15ml (½ fl oz) Bénédictine
120ml (4 fl oz) Peach Nectar
1 teaspoon Honey

Pour Whisky, Bénédictine and nectar into a cocktail shaker over crushed ice. Shake and pour into a chilled highball glass. Add honey by pouring on top – do not stir, then serve with a straw.

Nocturnal

29.4% ALC/VOL • 2.4 STD DRINKS

60ml (2 fl oz) Bourbon
30ml (1 fl oz) Dark Crème De Cacao
15ml (½ fl oz) Fresh Cream

Pour ingredients into a cocktail shaker over ice and shake. Strain into a cocktail glass over crushed ice and serve.

After Burner

19.8% ALC/VOL • 3.7 STD DRINKS

60ml (2 fl oz) Scotch Whisky
30ml (1 fl oz) Rye Whiskey
30ml (1 fl oz) Tequila
60ml (2 fl oz) Fresh Lemon Juice
60ml (2 fl oz) Tabasco Sauce

Pour ingredients into a mixing glass over ice and stir. Strain into a chilled old-fashioned glass and serve.

Marlon Brando

24.7% ALC/VOL • 1.8 STD DRINKS

45ml (1½ fl oz) Scotch Whisky
15ml (½ fl oz) Amaretto
30ml (1 fl oz) Fresh Cream

Pour Whisky and Amaretto into an old-fashioned glass filled with ice then stir. Float cream on top and serve.

Irish Mink

19.2% ALC/VOL • 2.1 STD DRINKS

40ml (1⅓ fl oz) Irish Whiskey
30ml (1 fl oz) Dark Crème De Cacao
10ml (⅓ fl oz) Cointreau
60ml (2 fl oz) Fresh Cream

Pour ingredients into a cocktail shaker over ice and shake. Strain into a chilled champagne saucer and serve.

Prince Edward

35.6% ALC/VOL • 2.2 STD DRINKS

45ml (1½ fl oz) Scotch Whisky
18ml (⅗ fl oz) Drambuie
15ml (½ fl oz) Lillet

Pour ingredients into a cocktail shaker over ice and shake. Strain into an old-fashioned glass filled with ice and serve.

Kiss Me Again

24.6% ALC/VOL • 1.5 STD DRINKS

45ml (1½ fl oz) Scotch Whisky
3 dashes Pernod
White of 1 Egg

Slice of Orange

Pour Whisky, Pernod and egg white into a cocktail shaker over ice. Shake and strain into a chilled cocktail glass. Garnish with a slice of orange and serve.

Huntress Cocktail

21.5% ALC/VOL • 1.4 STD DRINKS

23ml (¾ fl oz) Bourbon
23ml (¾ fl oz) Cherry Liqueur
5ml (1/6 fl oz) Triple Sec
30ml (1 fl oz) Fresh Cream

Pour ingredients into a cocktail shaker over ice and shake. Strain into a chilled cocktail glass and serve.

Harry Boy

15.4% ALC/VOL • 1.6 STD DRINKS

20ml (⅔ fl oz) Blended Whiskey
20ml (⅔ fl oz) Cointreau
20ml (⅔ fl oz) Kahlúa
70ml (2⅓ fl oz) Fresh Milk (chilled)

Pour ingredients into a mixing glass over ice and stir. Strain into a chilled old-fashioned glass and serve.

Prince

39.4% ALC/VOL • 1.5 STD DRINKS

45ml (1½ fl oz) Rye Whiskey
2 dashes Orange Bitters
3 drops White Crème De Menthe

Pour Whiskey and Bitters into a mixing glass over ice. Stir and strain into an old-fashioned glass filled with ice. Add Crème De Menthe – do not stir, then serve.

Basin Street

30% ALC/VOL • 2.8 STD DRINKS

60ml (2 fl oz) Bourbon
30ml (1 fl oz) Cointreau
30ml (1 fl oz) Fresh Lemon Juice

Pour ingredients into a cocktail shaker over ice and shake. Strain into a chilled cocktail glass and serve.

De Rigueur

24.6% ALC/VOL • 1.4 STD DRINKS

45ml (1½ fl oz) Blended Whiskey
23ml (¾ fl oz) Grapefruit Juice
1 teaspoon Honey

Pour ingredients into a cocktail shaker over ice and shake. Strain into a chilled cocktail glass and serve.

Harrity

38.1% ALC/VOL • 1 STD DRINK

30ml (1 fl oz) Canadian Whisky
Dash Angostura Bitters
Dash Dry Gin

Pour ingredients into a mixing glass over ice and stir. Strain into a chilled cocktail glass and serve.

Green Mist

25.2% ALC/VOL • 1.5 STD DRINKS

30ml (1 fl oz) Scotch Whisky
30ml (1 fl oz) Green Crème De Menthe
15ml (½ fl oz) Fresh Lemon Juice
Slice of Kiwi Fruit
Sprig of Fresh Mint

Pour Whisky, Crème De Menthe and juice into a cocktail shaker over ice. Shake and strain into a chilled cocktail glass. Garnish with a slice of kiwi fruit and sprig of mint then serve.

Lively Shamrock

6.1% ALC/VOL • 1.3 STD DRINKS

30ml (1 fl oz) Irish Whiskey
20ml (⅔ fl oz) Green Crème De Menthe
225ml (7½ fl oz) Fresh Milk (chilled)

Pour Whiskey and Crème De Menthe into a mixing glass over ice. Stir and strain into a chilled highball glass. Add milk, stir well and serve.

Black Dog

32.2% ALC/VOL • 3.4 STD DRINKS

90ml (3 fl oz) Bourbon
30ml (1 fl oz) Sweet Vermouth
15ml (½ fl oz) Blackberry Schnapps

Pour ingredients into a mixing glass over ice and stir. Strain into an old-fashioned glass over ice and serve.

Tequila

Tequila is a Mexican spirit, although it is believed that the Aztecs drank pulque, a version of what we know as Tequila long before Christopher Columbus.

Tequila is distilled from the blue agave plant which is also known as the century plant. This plant resembles a large pineapple with spikes similar to the cactus plant, growing in abundance in the desert. When the plant reaches maturity (about ten years) the spikes are removed and the remainder of the plant is crushed to remove the sap (mescal). Sugar and yeast are then added to the mescal which is then fermented for a few days and distilled twice in pot stills.

Tequila is distilled in only two designated regions of Mexico, one being the surrounding area of Tequila and the other in the region of Tepatitlan.

There are two varieties of Tequila; White or Silver and Gold. White Tequila is aged for a very short period of time in wax-lined vats. Gold Tequila is aged in Whisky barrels for usually between two and four years until the spirit changes to a golden colour and is then ready to be bottled.

Tequila is continuing to grow in popularity with a large array of assorted margaritas being made with various colours and flavours. Of course the ever popular Tequila Sunrise and Tequila Slammer remain in high demand across the globe in clubs, cocktail bars and restaurants.

Cactus Bite

21.7% ALC/VOL • 2.5 STD DRINKS

60ml (2 fl oz) Tequila
10ml (⅓ fl oz) Cointreau
10ml (⅓ fl oz) Drambuie
Dash Angostura Bitters
60ml (2 fl oz) Fresh Lemon Juice
½ teaspoon Sugar Syrup

Pour ingredients into a cocktail shaker over ice and shake. Strain into a chilled cocktail glass and serve.

Tequila Cocktail

28.5% ALC/VOL • 1.8 STD DRINKS

60ml (2 fl oz) Tequila
4 dashes Grenadine
15ml (½ fl oz) Fresh Lemon Juice
Dash Egg White
Wedge of Lemon

Pour Tequila, Grenadine, juice and egg white into a cocktail shaker over ice. Shake and strain into a chilled cocktail glass. Garnish with a wedge of lemon and serve.

Sombrero Spinner

17% ALC/VOL • 2.2 STD DRINKS

30ml (1 fl oz) Tequila
30ml (1 fl oz) Cointreau
20ml (⅔ fl oz) Strawberry Liqueur
45ml (1½ fl oz) Orange-Mango Juice
4 Strawberries (diced)
Slice of Orange
Strawberry

Pour Tequila, Cointreau, Liqueur and juice into a blender over crushed ice then add diced strawberries. Blend and pour into a chilled champagne flute. Garnish with a slice of orange and a strawberry then serve.

Tequila Pink

29.6% ALC/VOL • 1.8 STD DRINKS

45ml (1½ fl oz) Tequila
30ml (1 fl oz) Dry Vermouth
Dash Grenadine

Pour ingredients into a cocktail shaker over ice and shake. Strain into a chilled cocktail glass and serve.

Alleluia

10.3% ALC/VOL • 1.6 STD DRINKS

45ml (1½ fl oz) Tequila
5ml (1/6 fl oz) Curaçao
5ml (1/6 fl oz) Maraschino Liqueur
15ml (½ fl oz) Fresh Lemon Juice
½ teaspoon Sugar Syrup
120ml (4 fl oz) Tonic Water
Maraschino Cherry
Slice of Orange

Pour Tequila, Curaçao, Liqueur, juice and sugar into a cocktail shaker over ice. Shake and strain into a highball glass over ice. Add tonic and stir gently. Garnish with a cherry and slice of orange then serve.

Apricot and Tequila Sour

27% ALC/VOL • 1.8 STD DRINKS

45ml (1½ fl oz) Tequila
23ml (¾ fl oz) Apricot Liqueur
15ml (½ fl oz) Fresh Lemon Juice

Pour ingredients into a cocktail shaker over ice and shake. Strain into a sour glass over ice and serve.

Rancho Contento

11% ALC/VOL • 1.6 STD DRINKS

45ml (1½ fl oz) Tequila
8ml (¼ fl oz) Dry Vermouth
8ml (¼ fl oz) Sweet Vermouth
120ml (4 fl oz) Fresh Orange Juice
Slice of Orange

Pour Tequila, Vermouths and juice into a cocktail shaker over ice. Shake and strain into a chilled highball glass over 2 ice cubes. Add a slice of orange and serve.

Tequila Mockingbird

22.8% ALC/VOL • 1.8 STD DRINKS

45ml (1½ fl oz) Tequila
23ml (¾ fl oz) Green Crème De Menthe
30ml (1 fl oz) Fresh Lime Juice
Slice of Lime

Pour Tequila, Crème De Menthe and juice into a cocktail shaker over ice. Shake and strain into a chilled cocktail glass. Garnish with a slice of lime and serve.

Las Vegas

6.7% ALC/VOL • 1.3 STD DRINKS

45ml (1½ fl oz) Gold Tequila
60ml (2 fl oz) Coconut Cream
60ml (2 fl oz) Fresh Orange Juice
60ml (2 fl oz) Pineapple Juice
30ml (1 fl oz) Fresh Cream
Slice of Pineapple

Pour Tequila, creams and juices into a blender over crushed ice. Blend and pour into a chilled hurricane glass. Garnish with a slice of pineapple and serve with 2 straws.

House Standard

12.5% ALC/VOL • 1.4 STD DRINKS

45ml (1½ fl oz) Tequila
90ml (3 fl oz) Tomato Juice (chilled)
2 dashes Tabasco Sauce
Slice of Lemon

Pour Tequila, juice and sauce into a cocktail shaker over ice. Shake and Strain into a chilled cocktail glass. Add a slice of lemon and serve.

Mexican Milk Punch

8.5% ALC/VOL • 1.8 STD DRINKS

30ml (1 fl oz) Tequila
30ml (1 fl oz) Dark Rum
120ml (4 fl oz) Fresh Milk (chilled)
30ml (1 fl oz) Thick Cream
2 teaspoons Sugar Syrup
1 Fresh Egg
Nutmeg

Pour Tequila, Rum, milk, cream, sugar and egg into a cocktail shaker over ice. Shake and strain into a chilled collins glass. Sprinkle nutmeg on top and serve.

Compadre

33.5% ALC/VOL • 1.5 STD DRINKS

45ml (1½ fl oz) Tequila
3 dashes Maraschino Liqueur
2 dashes Orange Bitters
5ml (1/6 fl oz) Grenadine

Pour ingredients into a mixing glass over ice and stir. Strain into a chilled cocktail glass and serve.

Yucatán Tonic

10.3% ALC/VOL • 1.6 STD DRINKS

45ml (1½ fl oz) Tequila
15ml (½ fl oz) Crème De Cassis
120ml (4 fl oz) Tonic Water
½ Fresh Lime

Pour Tequila and Cassis into a highball glass over ice. Twist ½ lime above drink to release juice and add spent shell then stir. Add tonic, stir gently and serve.

Mexico Pacifico

19% ALC/VOL • 1.3 STD DRINKS

45ml (1½ fl oz) Tequila
30ml (1 fl oz) Passion-Fruit Syrup
15ml (½ fl oz) Fresh Lime Juice
Slice of Lime

Pour Tequila, syrup and juice into a blender over crushed ice. Blend and pour into a chilled champagne saucer. Add a slice of lime and serve.

Boomer

16.7% ALC/VOL • 0.9 STD DRINKS

20ml (⅔ fl oz) Gold Tequila
15ml (½ fl oz) Apricot Brandy
15ml (½ fl oz) Fresh Orange Juice
8ml (¼ fl oz) Fresh Lemon Juice
1½ teaspoons Sugar Syrup

Pour ingredients into a cocktail shaker over ice and shake. Strain into a chilled liqueur glass and serve.

Matador

10.8% ALC/VOL • 1.3 STD DRINKS

45ml (1½ fl oz) Tequila
90ml (3 fl oz) Pineapple Juice
23ml (¾ fl oz) Fresh Lime Juice

Pour ingredients into a cocktail shaker over crushed ice and shake. Strain into a chilled old-fashioned glass and serve.

Border Crossing

25.2% ALC/VOL • 1.6 STD DRINKS

45ml (1½ fl oz) Tequila
15ml (½ fl oz) Cranberry Liqueur
15ml (½ fl oz) Fresh Lime Juice
1 teaspoon Sugar Syrup
Slice of Lime

Pour Tequila, Liqueur, juice and sugar into a cocktail shaker over ice. Shake and strain into a collins glass over ice. Add a slice of lime and serve.

Mexican Connection

9% ALC/VOL • 1.5 STD DRINKS

30ml (1 fl oz) Tequila
30ml (1 fl oz) Amer Picon
150ml (5 fl oz) Fresh Orange Juice

Pour Tequila and Amer Picon into a chilled old-fashioned glass over 2 ice cubes then stir. Add juice, stir and serve.

Frozen Sunset

22.8% ALC/VOL • 1.3 STD DRINKS

45ml (1½ fl oz) Tequila
15ml (½ fl oz) Grenadine
15ml (½ fl oz) Fresh Lime Juice
Slice of Lime

Pour Tequila, Grenadine and juice into a blender over crushed ice. Blend and pour into a chilled old-fashioned glass. Add more crushed ice to fill glass and stir gently. Garnish with a slice of lime and serve.

Coconut Tequila

23% ALC/VOL • 1.5 STD DRINKS

45ml (1½ fl oz) Tequila
5ml (⅙ fl oz) Maraschino Liqueur
15ml (½ fl oz) Fresh Lemon Juice
15ml (½ fl oz) Coconut Cream

Pour ingredients into a blender over crushed ice and blend. Pour into a chilled champagne saucer and serve.

Big Red Hooter

8.8% ALC/VOL • 1.4 STD DRINKS

30ml (1 fl oz) Tequila
23ml (¾ fl oz) Amaretto
30ml (1 fl oz) Grenadine
120ml (4 fl oz) Pineapple Juice
Maraschino Cherry

Pour Tequila and Amaretto into a collins glass over ice then stir. Add juice and stir again. Add Grenadine by pouring on top of drink – do not stir, then garnish with a cherry and serve with a straw.

Shaker

11.2% ALC/VOL • 1.4 STD DRINKS

45ml (1½ fl oz) Tequila
3 dashes Grenadine
90ml (3 fl oz) Pineapple Juice
15ml (½ fl oz) Fresh Lemon Juice

Pour ingredients into a cocktail shaker over ice and shake. Strain into a chilled cocktail glass and serve.

Tequila Collins

10.7% ALC/VOL • 1.8 STD DRINKS

60ml (2 fl oz) Gold Tequila
30ml (1 fl oz) Fresh Lemon Juice
½ teaspoon Sugar Syrup
120ml (4 fl oz) Soda Water
Maraschino Cherry
Slice of Orange

Pour Tequila, juice and sugar into a cocktail shaker over ice. Shake and strain into a collins glass over ice. Add soda and stir gently. Garnish with a cherry and slice of orange then serve.

Icebreaker

18.8% ALC/VOL • 2.3 STD DRINKS

60ml (2 fl oz) Tequila
15ml (½ fl oz) Cointreau
18ml (3/5 fl oz) Grenadine
60ml (2 fl oz) Grapefruit Juice

Pour ingredients into a blender over cracked ice and blend. Strain into a chilled sour glass and serve.

Tequila Moonrise

22.5% ALC/VOL • 4.9 STD DRINKS

90ml (3 fl oz) Tequila
60ml (2 fl oz) Ale
30ml (1 fl oz) Dark Rum
30ml (1 fl oz) Light Rum
15ml (½ fl oz) Fresh Lemon Juice
15ml (½ fl oz) Rose's Lime Juice
1 teaspoon Sugar Syrup

Pour Tequila, Rums, juices and sugar into a cocktail shaker over ice. Shake and strain into a collins glass over ice. Add Ale, stir gently and serve.

Mexicana

19% ALC/VOL • 1.3 STD DRINKS

45ml (1½ fl oz) Tequila
5ml (1/6 fl oz) Grenadine
30ml (1 fl oz) Fresh Lemon Juice
10ml (⅓ fl oz) Pineapple Juice

Pour ingredients into a cocktail shaker over ice and shake. Strain into a chilled cocktail glass and serve.

Mexican Bliss

20.1% ALC/VOL • 1.9 STD DRINKS

45ml (1½ fl oz) Gold Tequila
15ml (½ fl oz) Banana Liqueur
10ml (⅓ fl oz) Galliano
30ml (1 fl oz) Fresh Cream
15ml (½ fl oz) Mandarin Juice
5ml (1/6 fl oz) Fresh Lemon Juice
Slice of Orange

Pour Tequila, Liqueur, Galliano, cream and juices into a cocktail shaker over ice. Shake and strain into a chilled champagne saucer. Garnish with a slice of orange and serve.

Mexicola

11.7% ALC/VOL • 1.8 STD DRINKS

60ml (2 fl oz) Tequila
15ml (½ fl oz) Fresh Lime Juice
120ml (4 fl oz) Cola

Pour Tequila and juice into a collins glass over ice then stir. Add cola, stir gently and serve.

Smiler

25.9% ALC/VOL • 1.5 STD DRINKS

45ml (1½ fl oz) Tequila
10ml (⅓ fl oz) Port
15ml (½ fl oz) Fresh Lemon Juice
½ teaspoon Sugar Syrup
Maraschino Cherry

Pour Tequila, Port, juice and sugar into a cocktail shaker over cracked ice. Shake and pour into a highball glass over ice. Garnish with a cherry and serve.

Firebird

15.3% ALC/VOL • 1.6 STD DRINKS

45ml (1½ fl oz) White Tequila
15ml (½ fl oz) Banana Liqueur
15ml (½ fl oz) Fresh Lime Juice
60ml (2 fl oz) Lemonade

Pour Tequila, Liqueur and juice into an old-fashioned glass over cracked ice then stir. Add lemonade, stir gently and serve.

Tequila Exotica

15.7% ALC/VOL • 1.6 STD DRINKS

45ml (1½ fl oz) Gold Tequila
8ml (¼ fl oz) White Crème De Cacao
5ml (1/6 fl oz) Cointreau
30ml (1 fl oz) Mango Juice
30ml (1 fl oz) White Grape Juice
15ml (½ fl oz) Fresh Lime Juice
Slice of Orange
Strawberry

Pour Tequila, Cacao, Cointreau and juices into a cocktail shaker over ice. Shake and strain into an old-fashioned glass over cracked ice. Garnish with a slice of orange and a strawberry then serve.

Tequila Mist

38% ALC/VOL • 1.3 STD DRINKS

45ml (1½ fl oz) Gold Tequila
Twist of Lemon Peel

Pour Tequila into an old-fashioned glass over ice and twist lemon peel above drink. Discard remainder of peel and serve.

Acapulco Gold

20.3% ALC/VOL • 2.4 STD DRINKS

30ml (1 fl oz) Tequila
30ml (1 fl oz) Dark Rum
30ml (1 fl oz) Tia Maria
30ml (1 fl oz) Pineapple Juice
30ml (1 fl oz) Coconut Cream
Wedge of Pineapple

Pour Tequila, Rum, Tia, juice and cream into a cocktail shaker over ice. Shake and strain into a chilled highball glass. Garnish with a wedge of pineapple and serve.

Executive Sunrise

10.9% ALC/VOL • 1.5 STD DRINKS

45ml (1½ fl oz) Tequila
10ml (⅓ fl oz) Crème De Cassis
120ml (4 fl oz) Fresh Orange Juice

Pour Tequila and juice into a collins glass over ice then stir. Add Cassis by pouring into centre of drink – do not stir, then serve.

Pepper Eater

20.3% ALC/VOL • 2 STD DRINKS

30ml (1 fl oz) Gold Tequila
30ml (1 fl oz) Cointreau
5ml (⅙ fl oz) Pepper Vodka
30ml (1 fl oz) Cranberry Juice
30ml (1 fl oz) Fresh Orange Juice
Red Pepper

Pour Tequila, Cointreau, Vodka and juices into a cocktail shaker over ice. Shake and strain into an old-fashioned glass over cracked ice. Add a pepper and serve.

Cactus Juice

24.8% ALC/VOL • 2 STD DRINKS

60ml (2 fl oz) Tequila
5ml (⅙ fl oz) Drambuie
30ml (1 fl oz) Fresh Lemon Juice
1 teaspoon Sugar Syrup

Pour ingredients into a cocktail shaker over cracked ice and shake. Pour into a chilled old-fashioned glass and serve.

Tequila Cooler

8.5% ALC/VOL • 2 STD DRINKS

45ml (1½ fl oz) Tequila
60ml (2 fl oz) Green Ginger Wine
60ml (2 fl oz) Fresh Orange Juice
15ml (½ fl oz) Fresh Lime Juice
120ml (4 fl oz) Tonic Water
Slice of Lime
Slice of Orange

Pour Tequila, Wine and juices into a collins glass over ice then stir. Add tonic and stir gently. Add a slice of lime and orange then serve.

Jumping Bean

38% ALC/VOL • 1.8 STD DRINKS

45ml (1½ fl oz) Tequila
15ml (½ fl oz) Sambuca
3 Coffee Beans

Pour Tequila and Sambuca into a mixing glass over ice. Stir and strain into a chilled cocktail glass. Add coffee beans and serve.

Fruits of the Desert

18.5% ALC/VOL • 1.8 STD DRINKS

45ml (1½ fl oz) Gold Tequila
15ml (½ fl oz) Cointreau
60ml (2 fl oz) Grapefruit Juice
1 teaspoon Sugar Syrup
Maraschino Cherry

Pour Tequila, Cointreau, juice and sugar into a cocktail shaker over ice. Shake and strain into an old-fashioned glass over cracked ice. Garnish with a cherry and serve.

Tornado

24.8% ALC/VOL • 2.3 STD DRINKS

60ml (2 fl oz) White Tequila
30ml (1 fl oz) White Crème De Cacao
30ml (1 fl oz) Thick Cream
Grated Chocolate

Pour Tequila, Cacao and cream into a cocktail shaker over ice. Shake and strain into a chilled champagne saucer. Sprinkle chocolate on top and serve.

Purple Pancho

10.6% ALC/VOL • 1.5 STD DRINKS

30ml (1 fl oz) Tequila
15ml (½ fl oz) Blue Curaçao
15ml (½ fl oz) Sloe Gin
60ml (2 fl oz) Fresh Lime Juice
60ml (2 fl oz) Sweet and Sour Mix
Slice of Lime

Prepare a margarita glass with a salt frosted rim. Pour Tequila, Curaçao, Gin, juice and sour mix into a cocktail shaker over cracked ice. Shake and pour into prepared glass. Garnish with a slice of lime and serve.

Tequila Gimlet

25.3% ALC/VOL • 1.8 STD DRINKS

60ml (2 fl oz) Gold Tequila
30ml (1 fl oz) Fresh Lime Juice
Wedge of Lime

Pour Tequila and juice into a cocktail shaker over ice. Shake and strain into a chilled cocktail glass. Garnish with a wedge of lime and serve.

La Bomba

15.4% ALC/VOL • 1.9 STD DRINKS

38ml (1¼ fl oz) Gold Tequila
23ml (¾ fl oz) Cointreau
2 dashes Grenadine
45ml (1½ fl oz) Fresh Orange Juice
45ml (1½ fl oz) Pineapple Juice
Slice of Lime

Prepare a champagne saucer with a sugar frosted rim. Pour Tequila, Cointreau, Grenadine and juices into a cocktail shaker over cracked ice. Shake and pour into prepared glass. Garnish with a slice of lime and serve.

Gringo

28.8% ALC/VOL • 2.3 STD DRINKS

30ml (1 fl oz) Tequila
30ml (1 fl oz) Midori
30ml (1 fl oz) Vodka
10ml (⅓ fl oz) Fresh Lemon Juice

Pour ingredients into a cocktail shaker over ice and shake. Strain into a chilled cocktail glass and serve.

Tequila Fizz

8.4% ALC/VOL • 1.9 STD DRINKS

60ml (2 fl oz) Tequila
2 dashes Angostura Bitters
45ml (1½ fl oz) Fresh Lemon Juice
2 teaspoons Caster Sugar
1 Fresh Egg
120ml (4 fl oz) Soda Water
Salt

Pour Tequila, Bitters, juice and egg into a cocktail shaker over ice then add sugar. Shake and strain into a highball glass over ice. Add soda and stir gently. Lightly sprinkle salt on top and serve.

Buenas Tardes

7.6% ALC/VOL • 1.3 STD DRINKS

45ml (1½ fl oz) Tequila
150ml (5 fl oz) Apple Juice
30ml (1 fl oz) Fresh Lemon Juice
Slice of Lemon

Pour Tequila and juices into a collins glass over ice then stir. Add a slice of lemon and serve.

Mia Vida

23.4% ALC/VOL • 1.4 STD DRINKS

30ml (1 fl oz) Tequila
15ml (½ fl oz) Dark Crème De Cacao
15ml (½ fl oz) Kahlúa
15ml (½ fl oz) Thick Cream
Grated Chocolate

Pour Tequila, Cacao, Kahlúa and cream into a cocktail shaker over ice. Shake and strain into a chilled cocktail glass. Sprinkle chocolate on top and serve.

Piper

12.5% ALC/VOL • 2.1 STD DRINKS

60ml (2 fl oz) Tequila
15ml (½ fl oz) Dark Crème De Cacao
120ml (4 fl oz) Black Coffee (chilled)
15ml (½ fl oz) Fresh Lemon Juice

Pour ingredients into a coffee glass filled with crushed ice, stir and serve.
This drink is also known as Finals Night.

Aztec Surfboard

9.9% ALC/VOL • 2 STD DRINKS

45ml (1½ fl oz) Gold Tequila
15ml (½ fl oz) Pisco
5ml (⅙ fl oz) Blue Curaçao
90ml (3 fl oz) Grapefruit Juice
60ml (2 fl oz) Mango Juice
30ml (1 fl oz) Passion-Fruit Juice
5ml (⅙ fl oz) Orgeat Syrup

Pour ingredients into a cocktail shaker over ice and shake. Strain into a collins glass over ice and serve.

Hot Pants

26.8% ALC/VOL • 1.6 STD DRINKS

45ml (1½ fl oz) Tequila
15ml (½ fl oz) Peppermint Schnapps
10ml (⅓ fl oz) Grapefruit Juice
1 teaspoon Sugar Syrup

Prepare an old-fashioned glass with a salt frosted rim. Pour ingredients into a cocktail shaker over cracked ice and shake. Pour into prepared glass and serve.

Wild Thing

14.3% ALC/VOL • 1.4 STD DRINKS

45ml (1½ fl oz) Tequila
30ml (1 fl oz) Cranberry Juice
15ml (½ fl oz) Fresh Lime Juice
30ml (1 fl oz) Soda Water
Slice of Lime

Pour Tequila and juices into an old-fashioned glass over ice then stir. Add soda and stir gently. Garnish with a slice of lime and serve.

Mexican Clover Club

15.1% ALC/VOL • 1.3 STD DRINKS

45ml (1½ fl oz) Tequila
15ml (½ fl oz) Grenadine
23ml (¾ fl oz) Fresh Lemon Juice
15ml (½ fl oz) Thick Cream
½ Egg White

Pour ingredients into a cocktail shaker over ice and shake. Strain into a chilled cocktail glass and serve.

Juan Blue

12.5% ALC/VOL • 1.6 STD DRINKS

45ml (1½ fl oz) Tequila
10ml (⅓ fl oz) Blue Curaçao
Dash Angostura Bitters
60ml (2 fl oz) Fresh Orange Juice
30ml (1 fl oz) Grapefruit Juice
15ml (½ fl oz) Fresh Lemon Juice

Pour Tequila, Bitters and juices into a cocktail shaker over ice. Shake and strain into a highball glass over ice. Layer Curaçao on top and serve.

Tequila Miel

10.5% ALC/VOL • 1.5 STD DRINKS

45ml (1½ fl oz) Tequila
15ml (½ fl oz) Honey Liqueur
120ml (4 fl oz) Grapefruit Juice

Pour ingredients into a cocktail shaker over ice and shake. Strain into a collins glass over ice and serve.

Jubilee

12.3% ALC/VOL • 2.1 STD DRINKS

30ml (1 fl oz) Tequila
15ml (½ fl oz) Blue Curaçao
15ml (½ fl oz) Gin
15ml (½ fl oz) Vodka
15ml (½ fl oz) Fresh Lemon Juice
½ teaspoon Sugar Syrup
120ml (4 fl oz) Soda Water
Maraschino Cherry

Pour Tequila, Curaçao, Gin, Vodka, juice and sugar into a cocktail shaker over ice. Shake and strain into a highball glass over ice. Add soda and stir gently. Garnish with a cherry and serve.

Joumbaba

8.8% ALC/VOL • 1.4 STD DRINKS

45ml (1½ fl oz) Tequila
60ml (2 fl oz) Grapefruit Juice
90ml (3 fl oz) Tonic Water

Pour Tequila and juice into a highball glass over ice then stir. Add tonic, stir gently and serve.

Last Chance

22.9% ALC/VOL • 1.7 STD DRINKS

53ml (1¾ fl oz) Tequila
8ml (¼ fl oz) Apricot Brandy
30ml (1 fl oz) Fresh Lime Juice
1 teaspoon Honey
Wedge of Lime

Pour Tequila, Brandy, juice and honey into a cocktail shaker over cracked ice. Shake and pour into a chilled old-fashioned glass. Add a wedge of lime and serve.

Alamo Splash

18.4% ALC/VOL • 1.4 STD DRINKS

45ml (1½ fl oz) Tequila
30ml (1 fl oz) Fresh Orange Juice
15ml (½ fl oz) Pineapple Juice
5ml (⅙ fl oz) Lemon-Lime Soda

Pour Tequila and juices into a mixing glass over ice. Stir and strain into a chilled collins glass. Add soda – do not stir, then serve.

Bar Bandit

9.7% ALC/VOL • 1.5 STD DRINKS

30ml (1 fl oz) Gold Tequila
15ml (½ fl oz) Dry Vermouth
15ml (½ fl oz) Raspberry Liqueur
15ml (½ fl oz) Sweet Vermouth
5ml (⅙ fl oz) Fresh Lime Juice
120ml (4 fl oz) Cherry Soda
Maraschino Cherry
Slice of Lime

Pour Tequila, Vermouths, Liqueur and juice into a highball glass over ice then stir. Add soda and stir gently. Garnish with a cherry and slice of lime then serve.

Señor Stinger

32% ALC/VOL • 1.7 STD DRINKS

45ml (1½ fl oz) Tequila
23ml (¾ fl oz) Peppermint Schnapps

Pour ingredients into a cocktail shaker over ice and shake. Strain into a champagne saucer over cracked ice and serve.

Doctor Dawson

10.8% ALC/VOL • 1.8 STD DRINKS

60ml (2 fl oz) Tequila
Dash Angostura Bitters
15ml (½ fl oz) Fresh Lemon Juice
1 teaspoon Sugar Syrup
1 Fresh Egg
90ml (3 fl oz) Soda Water

Pour Tequila, Bitters, juice, sugar and egg into a cocktail shaker over ice. Shake and strain into a highball glass over ice. Add soda, stir gently and serve.

Olé

30.4% ALC/VOL • 1.5 STD DRINKS

30ml (1 fl oz) Tequila
30ml (1 fl oz) Banana Liqueur
Dash Blue Curaçao

Pour Tequila and Liqueur into a cocktail shaker over ice. Shake and strain into a chilled liqueur glass. Add Curaçao – do not stir, then serve.

Chapala

23% ALC/VOL • 1.4 STD DRINKS

45ml (1½ fl oz) Tequila

Dash Cointreau
10ml (⅓ fl oz) Grenadine
10ml (⅓ fl oz) Fresh
Lemon Juice
10ml (⅓ fl oz) Fresh
Orange Juice
Slice of Orange

Pour Tequila, Cointreau, Grenadine and juices into a cocktail shaker over ice. Shake and strain into an old-fashioned glass over ice. Add a slice of orange and serve.

Flower Cocktail

13.8% ALC/VOL • 1.5 STD DRINKS

30ml (1 fl oz) Tequila
15ml (½ fl oz) Mango Liqueur
15ml (½ fl oz) White Curaçao
75ml (2½ fl oz) Fresh
Orange Juice

Pour ingredients into a blender without ice and blend briefly. Pour into a highball glass over ice and serve.

Tequila Fresa

27% ALC/VOL • 1.8 STD DRINKS

45ml (1½ fl oz) Tequila
23ml (¾ fl oz) Strawberry
Liqueur
Dash Orange Bitters
15ml (½ fl oz) Fresh
Lime Juice
Slice of Lime
Strawberry

Pour Tequila, Liqueur, Bitters and juice into a cocktail shaker over ice. Shake and strain into an old-fashioned glass over ice. Add a slice of lime and a strawberry then serve.

Moonraker

11.6% ALC/VOL • 1.6 STD DRINKS

45ml (1½ fl oz) Tequila
15ml (½ fl oz) Blue Curaçao
120ml (4 fl oz) Pineapple Juice

Pour Tequila and juice into a highball glass over ice then stir. Add Curaçao by pouring into centre of drink – do not stir, then serve.

Traffic Light Cooler

15.4% ALC/VOL • 1.6 STD DRINKS

30ml (1 fl oz) Gold Tequila
23ml (¾ fl oz) Midori
15ml (½ fl oz) Sloe Gin
60ml (2 fl oz) Fresh
Orange Juice
5ml (⅙ fl oz) Sweet and Sour
Mix
Cherry
Slice of Lemon
Slice of Lime

Pour Midori into a collins glass over ice and layer Tequila on top. Add sour mix and juice by pouring into glass slowly – do not stir. Add more ice to fill glass and layer Gin on top. Garnish with a cherry, slice of lemon and lime then serve.

Tequila Stinger

35% ALC/VOL • 2.1 STD DRINKS

60ml (2 fl oz) Tequila
15ml (½ fl oz) White Crème De
Menthe

Pour ingredients into a mixing glass over ice and stir. Strain into a chilled cocktail glass and serve.

Juliet

16.4% ALC/VOL • 1.4 STD DRINKS

30ml (1 fl oz) Gold Tequila
30ml (1 fl oz) Pisang Ambon
3 dashes Grenadine
45ml (1½ fl oz) Pineapple Juice
Maraschino Cherry
Slice of Pineapple

Pour Tequila, Pisang Ambon, Grenadine and juice into a cocktail shaker over ice. Shake and strain into a chilled cocktail glass. Garnish with a cherry and slice of pineapple then serve.

Frozen Blackberry Tequila

25.7% ALC/VOL • 1.8 STD DRINKS

45ml (1½ fl oz) Tequila
30ml (1 fl oz) Blackberry
Liqueur
15ml (½ fl oz) Fresh
Lemon Juice
Slice of Lemon

Pour Tequila, Liqueur and juice into a blender over small amount of crushed ice. Blend and pour into an old-fashioned glass over crushed ice. Garnish with a slice of lemon and serve.

Doralto

9.5% ALC/VOL • 1.4 STD DRINKS

45ml (1½ fl oz) Tequila
Dash Angostura Bitters
15ml (½ fl oz) Fresh
Lemon Juice
½ teaspoon Sugar Syrup
120ml (4 fl oz) Tonic Water
Wedge of Lime

Pour Tequila, Bitters, juice and sugar into a cocktail shaker over ice. Shake and strain into a highball glass over ice. Add tonic and stir gently. Garnish with a wedge of lime and serve.

Sloe Tequila

27.8% ALC/VOL • 1.2 STD DRINKS

30ml (1 fl oz) Tequila
15ml (½ fl oz) Sloe Gin
10ml (⅓ fl oz) Fresh
Lime Juice
Twist of Cucumber Peel

Pour Tequila, Gin and juice into a blender over crushed ice. Blend and pour into a chilled old-fashioned glass then add ice to fill glass. Add cucumber peel and serve.

Monkey Tree

14.1% ALC/VOL • 1.4 STD DRINKS

30ml (1 fl oz) Gold Tequila
15ml (½ fl oz) Banana Liqueur
15ml (½ fl oz) Rum Tree
60ml (2 fl oz) Mango Juice
10ml (⅓ fl oz) Fresh Lime Juice

Prepare a cocktail glass with a sugar frosted rim – moistened with Grenadine. Pour ingredients into a cocktail shaker over ice and shake. Strain into prepared glass and serve.

Rosita

26.5% ALC/VOL • 1.9 STD DRINKS

30ml (1 fl oz) Tequila
30ml (1 fl oz) Campari
15ml (½ fl oz) Dry Vermouth
15ml (½ fl oz) Sweet Vermouth
Twist of Lemon Peel

Pour Tequila, Campari and Vermouths into an old-fashioned glass over cracked ice then stir. Add lemon peel and serve with 2 short straws.

Hairy Sunrise

15.1% ALC/VOL • 1.8 STD DRINKS

23ml (¾ fl oz) Tequila
23ml (¾ fl oz) Vodka
15ml (½ fl oz) Cointreau
3 dashes Grenadine
90ml (3 fl oz) Fresh Orange Juice
Slice of Lime

Pour Tequila, Vodka, Cointreau and juice into a blender over cracked ice. Blend and strain into a chilled collins glass. Layer Grenadine on top and garnish with a slice of lime then serve.

Tequila Dubonnet

27% ALC/VOL • 1.3 STD DRINKS

30ml (1 fl oz) Tequila
30ml (1 fl oz) Dubonnet
Slice of Lemon

Pour Tequila and Dubonnet into an old-fashioned glass over ice then stir. Garnish with a slice of lemon and serve.

Mexican Madras

8.4% ALC/VOL • 0.9 STD DRINKS

30ml (1 fl oz) Gold Tequila
90ml (3 fl oz) Cranberry Juice
15ml (½ fl oz) Fresh Orange Juice
Dash Fresh Lime Juice
Slice of Orange

Pour Tequila and juices into a cocktail shaker over ice. Shake and strain into a chilled old-fashioned glass. Garnish with a slice of orange and serve.

Campbell F. Craig

10.9% ALC/VOL • 1.5 STD DRINKS

45ml (1½ fl oz) Tequila
15ml (½ fl oz) Chambord
60ml (2 fl oz) Fresh Orange Juice
60ml (2 fl oz) Pineapple Juice

Pour Tequila and juices into a highball glass over ice then stir. Add Chambord by pouring into centre of drink – do not stir, then serve.
This drink is also known as Tequila Razz.

Tequila Frost

7.1% ALC/VOL • 1.1 STD DRINKS

38ml (1¼ fl oz) Tequila
15ml (½ fl oz) Grenadine
60ml (2 fl oz) Vanilla Milk (chilled)
38ml (1¼ fl oz) Grapefruit Juice
38ml (1¼ fl oz) Pineapple Juice
15ml (½ fl oz) Honey
Maraschino Cherry
Slice of Orange

Pour Tequila, Grenadine, milk, juices and honey into a blender without ice. Blend and pour into a frosted parfait glass. Garnish with a cherry and slice of orange then serve.

Massacre

13% ALC/VOL • 1.9 STD DRINKS

60ml (2 fl oz) Tequila
5ml (⅙ fl oz) Campari
120ml (4 fl oz) Dry Ginger Ale

Pour Tequila and Campari into a highball glass over ice then stir. Add Ginger Ale, stir gently and serve.

Citrus Cactus

22% ALC/VOL • 2 STD DRINKS

60ml (2 fl oz) White Tequila
5ml (⅙ fl oz) Pernod
5ml (⅙ fl oz) Grenadine
15ml (½ fl oz) Fresh Lemon Juice
15ml (½ fl oz) Fresh Lime Juice
1½ teaspoons Sugar Syrup
1 teaspoon Egg White

Pour ingredients into a cocktail shaker over ice and shake. Strain into a cocktail glass over crushed ice and serve.

Gull's Wing

29.1% ALC/VOL • 2.1 STD DRINKS

60ml (2 fl oz) Tequila

15ml (½ fl oz) Banana Liqueur
15ml (½ fl oz) Fresh
Lemon Juice

Pour ingredients into a cocktail shaker over ice and shake. Strain into an old-fashioned glass over crushed ice and serve.

Acapulcoco

26.1% ALC/VOL • 2 STD DRINKS

30ml (1 fl oz) Gold Tequila
30ml (1 fl oz) Kahlúa
20ml (⅔ fl oz) Dark Rum
15ml (½ fl oz) Coconut Cream
Maraschino Cherry
Slice of Orange

Pour Tequila, Kahlúa, Rum and cream into a cocktail shaker over ice. Shake and strain into a chilled cocktail glass. Garnish with a cherry and slice of orange then serve.

California Dream

28.6% ALC/VOL • 2.4 STD DRINKS

60ml (2 fl oz) Tequila
30ml (1 fl oz) Sweet Vermouth
15ml (½ fl oz) Dry Sherry
Maraschino Cherry

Pour Tequila, Vermouth and Sherry into a mixing glass over ice. Stir and strain into a chilled cocktail glass. Garnish with a cherry and serve.

Tequila Canyon

10.1% ALC/VOL • 1.5 STD DRINKS

45ml (1½ fl oz) Tequila
4 dashes Cointreau
120ml (4 fl oz) Cranberry Juice
8ml (¼ fl oz) Fresh
Orange Juice
8ml (¼ fl oz) Pineapple Juice
Slice of Lime

Pour Tequila, Cointreau and cranberry juice into a collins glass over ice then stir. Add orange and pineapple juices - do not stir. Garnish with a slice of lime and serve with a straw.

Norteamericano

33% ALC/VOL • 1.6 STD DRINKS

45ml (1½ fl oz) Tequila
15ml (½ fl oz) Dry Sherry
Twist of Lemon Peel

Pour Tequila and Sherry into a mixing glass over ice. Stir and strain into a chilled cocktail glass. Twist lemon peel above drink and place remainder of peel into drink then serve.

Pacific Sunshine

21.2% ALC/VOL • 2.3 STD DRINKS

45ml (1½ fl oz) Tequila
45ml (1½ fl oz) Blue Curaçao
Dash Angostura Bitters
45ml (1½ fl oz) Sweet and
Sour Mix
Slice of Lemon

Prepare a hurricane glass with a salt frosted rim. Pour Tequila, Curaçao, Bitters and sour mix into a mixing glass over cracked ice. Stir and pour into prepared glass. Garnish with a slice of lemon and serve.

Purple Cactus

17.9% ALC/VOL • 1.6 STD DRINKS

45ml (1½ fl oz) Gold Tequila
15ml (½ fl oz) Sweet Sherry
5ml (⅙ fl oz) Grenadine
45ml (1½ fl oz) Passion-
Fruit Juice
Maraschino Cherry

Pour Tequila, Sherry, Grenadine and juice into a cocktail shaker over ice. Shake and strain into an old-fashioned glass over cracked ice. Garnish with a cherry and serve.

Chico

12.9% ALC/VOL • 1.7 STD DRINKS

30ml (1 fl oz) Tequila
30ml (1 fl oz) Blackberry
Brandy
15ml (½ fl oz) Fresh
Lemon Juice
1 teaspoon Sugar Syrup
90ml (3 fl oz) Soda Water
Slice of Lemon

Pour Tequila, Brandy, juice and sugar into a cocktail shaker over ice. Shake and strain into a collins glass over ice. Add soda and stir gently. Garnish with a slice of lemon and serve.

Viva Villa

21.4% ALC/VOL • 1.4 STD DRINKS

45ml (1½ fl oz) Tequila
30ml (1 fl oz) Fresh Lime Juice
1 teaspoon Sugar Syrup

Prepare an old-fashioned glass with a salt frosted rim. Pour ingredients into a cocktail shaker over ice and shake. Strain into prepared glass and serve.

Cuernavaca Collins

11.8% ALC/VOL • 1.8 STD DRINKS

30ml (1 fl oz) Tequila
30ml (1 fl oz) Gin
30ml (1 fl oz) Fresh Lime Juice
2 teaspoons Sugar Syrup
90ml (3 fl oz) Soda Water
Slice of Lime

Pour Tequila, Gin, juice and sugar into a cocktail shaker over ice. Shake and strain into a collins glass over ice. Add soda and stir gently. Garnish with a slice of lime and serve.

Mint Tequila

26.3% ALC/VOL • 1.3 STD DRINKS

45ml (1½ fl oz) Tequila
15ml (½ fl oz) Fresh Lemon Juice
1 teaspoon Sugar Syrup
6 Fresh Mint Leaves

Pour Tequila, juice and sugar into a blender over crushed ice then add mint leaves. Blend and pour into a chilled old-fashioned glass then serve.

Tequila Rickey

13.8% ALC/VOL • 1.8 STD DRINKS

60ml (2 fl oz) Tequila
15ml (½ fl oz) Fresh Lime Juice
90ml (3 fl oz) Soda Water
Slice of Orange
Twist of Lime Peel
Salt

Pour Tequila and juice into a collins glass over ice then stir. Add soda and stir gently. Add lime peel and sprinkle salt on top. Garnish with a slice of orange and serve.

Cavalier

12.3% ALC/VOL • 1.3 STD DRINKS

30ml (1 fl oz) Gold Tequila
15ml (½ fl oz) Galliano
60ml (2 fl oz) Mandarin Juice
30ml (1 fl oz) Fresh Cream

Pour ingredients into a cocktail shaker over ice and shake. Strain into a chilled cocktail glass and serve.

Tijuana Taxi

14.9% ALC/VOL • 2.8 STD DRINKS

60ml (2 fl oz) Gold Tequila
30ml (1 fl oz) Blue Curaçao
30ml (1 fl oz) Tropical Fruit Schnapps
120ml (4 fl oz) Lemon-Lime Soda
Cherry
Slice of Orange

Pour Tequila, Curaçao and Schnapps into a highball glass over ice then stir. Add soda and stir gently. Garnish with a cherry and slice of orange then serve.

Tequila Flip

20.7% ALC/VOL • 1.8 STD DRINKS

60ml (2 fl oz) Gold Tequila
1 teaspoon Sugar Syrup
1 Fresh Egg
Nutmeg

Pour Tequila, sugar and egg into a cocktail shaker over ice. Shake and strain into a chilled goblet. Sprinkle nutmeg on top and serve.

Downsider

26% ALC/VOL • 2.1 STD DRINKS

45ml (1½ fl oz) Tequila
15ml (½ fl oz) Banana Liqueur
15ml (½ fl oz) Galliano
Dash Angostura Bitters
5ml (1/6 fl oz) Grenadine
15ml (½ fl oz) Fresh Cream
5ml (1/6 fl oz) Fresh Lemon Juice

Pour ingredients into a cocktail shaker over ice and shake. Strain into a chilled cocktail glass and serve.

Leapfrog

33.5% ALC/VOL • 1.7 STD DRINKS

45ml (1½ fl oz) Tequila
15ml (½ fl oz) Sloe Gin
5ml (1/6 fl oz) Sweet Vermouth
Wedge of Lime

Pour Tequila, Gin and Vermouth into an old-fashioned glass over ice then stir. Garnish with a wedge of lime and serve.

Cactus Berry

11.7% ALC/VOL • 2.4 STD DRINKS

38ml (1¼ fl oz) Tequila
38ml (1¼ fl oz) Claret
30ml (1 fl oz) Cointreau
150ml (5 fl oz) Sweet and Sour Mix
Dash Fresh Lime Juice
5ml (1/6 fl oz) Lemon-Lime Soda

Prepare a margarita glass with a salt frosted rim. Pour Tequila, Claret, Cointreau, sour mix and juice into a cocktail shaker over ice. Shake and strain into prepared glass. Add soda – do not stir, then serve.

Sunrise Anise

11.6% ALC/VOL • 1.7 STD DRINKS

45ml (1½ fl oz) Tequila
15ml (½ fl oz) Anise
5ml (1/6 fl oz) Grenadine
120ml (4 fl oz) Fresh Orange Juice

Pour Tequila, Anise and juice into an old-fashioned glass over ice then stir. Layer Grenadine on top and serve with a swizzle stick.

Bunny Bonanza

30.4% ALC/VOL • 2.4 STD DRINKS

45ml (1½ fl oz) Tequila
30ml (1 fl oz) Apple Brandy
3 dashes Curaçao
15ml (½ fl oz) Fresh Lemon Juice
1 teaspoon Sugar Syrup
Slice of Lemon

Pour Tequila, Brandy, Curaçao, juice and sugar into a cocktail shaker over ice. Shake and strain into an old-fashioned glass over ice. Garnish with a slice of lemon and serve.

Tequila Sour

28.5% ALC/VOL • 1.8 STD DRINKS

60ml (2 fl oz) Gold Tequila
15ml (½ fl oz) Fresh Lemon Juice
1 teaspoon Sugar Syrup
Twist of Lemon Peel

Pour Tequila, juice and sugar into a cocktail shaker over ice. Shake and strain into a chilled sour glass. Add lemon peel and serve.

Buttock Clencher

12.9% ALC/VOL • 1.9 STD DRINKS

30ml (1 fl oz) Tequila
30ml (1 fl oz) Dry Gin
8ml (¼ fl oz) Midori
60ml (2 fl oz) Pineapple Juice
60ml (2 fl oz) Lemonade
Maraschino Cherry
Slice of Pineapple

Pour Tequila, Gin, Midori and juice into a cocktail shaker over ice. Shake and strain into a highball glass over ice. Add lemonade and stir gently. Garnish with a cherry and slice of pineapple then serve.

Tequila Colada

8.8% ALC/VOL • 1.4 STD DRINKS

45ml (1½ fl oz) Tequila
120ml (4 fl oz) Pineapple Juice
30ml (1 fl oz) Coconut Cream

Pour ingredients into a blender over crushed ice and blend. Pour into a chilled hurricane glass and serve.

Tachyon

38.4% ALC/VOL • 1.8 STD DRINKS

30ml (1 fl oz) Tequila
30ml (1 fl oz) Pernod
Dash Fresh Lemon Juice
Twist of Lemon Peel

Pour Tequila, Pernod and juice into a mixing glass over ice. Stir and strain into a chilled cocktail glass. Garnish with lemon peel and serve.

This drink may also be served in a highball glass over ice if desired.

Gates of Hell

20.3% ALC/VOL • 1.4 STD DRINKS

45ml (1½ fl oz) Tequila
5ml (1/6 fl oz) Cherry Brandy
20ml (⅔ fl oz) Fresh Lemon Juice
20ml (⅔ fl oz) Fresh Lime Juice

Pour Tequila and juices into a cocktail shaker over ice. Shake and strain into an old-fashioned glass over crushed ice. Add Brandy by pouring gently on top – do not stir, then serve.

Ridley

37.4% ALC/VOL • 1.9 STD DRINKS

30ml (1 fl oz) Gold Tequila
30ml (1 fl oz) Gin
5ml (1/6 fl oz) Galliano
Maraschino Cherry
Slice of Orange

Pour Tequila and Gin into a mixing glass over ice. Stir and strain into a cocktail glass filled with crushed ice then layer Galliano on top. Garnish with a cherry and slice of orange then serve.

Tequila Manhattan

30% ALC/VOL • 2.2 STD DRINKS

60ml (2 fl oz) Tequila
30ml (1 fl oz) Sweet Vermouth
Dash Fresh Lime Juice
Cherry
Slice of Orange

Pour Tequila, Vermouth and juice into a cocktail shaker over ice. Shake and strain into an old-fashioned glass over ice. Add a cherry and slice of orange then serve.

Tequila Suave

26.3% ALC/VOL • 1.5 STD DRINKS

45ml (1½ fl oz) Tequila
5ml (1/6 fl oz) White Crème De Cacao
Dash Angostura Bitters
5ml (1/6 fl oz) Grenadine
15ml (½ fl oz) Fresh Lemon Juice
Maraschino Cherry
Slice of Orange

Pour Tequila, Cacao, Bitters, Grenadine and juice into a cocktail shaker over ice. Shake and strain into a chilled cocktail glass. Garnish with a cherry and slice of orange then serve.

Tequila Frozen Screwdriver

12.7% ALC/VOL • 1.4 STD DRINKS

45ml (1½ fl oz) Tequila
90ml (3 fl oz) Fresh Orange Juice
Slice of Orange

Pour Tequila and juice into a blender over small amount of crushed ice. Blend and pour into a chilled old-fashioned glass. Add a slice of orange and serve.

Purple Gecko

16.4% ALC/VOL • 1.9 STD DRINKS

45ml (1½ fl oz) Tequila
15ml (½ fl oz) Blue Curaçao
15ml (½ fl oz) Red Curaçao
30ml (1 fl oz) Cranberry Juice
30ml (1 fl oz) Sweet and Sour Mix
15ml (½ fl oz) Fresh Lime Juice
Slice of Lime

Prepare a margarita glass with a salt frosted rim. Pour Tequila, Curaçaos, juices and sour mix into a cocktail shaker over cracked ice. Shake and pour into prepared glass. Garnish with a slice of lime and serve.

Daring Dylan

13.8% ALC/VOL • 2.3 STD DRINKS

60ml (2 fl oz) Tequila
30ml (1 fl oz) Kahlúa
120ml (4 fl oz) Hot Chocolate (chilled)

Pour ingredients into a coffee glass filled with crushed ice, stir and serve.

Tequila Sunrise

13.8% ALC/VOL • 1.8 STD DRINKS

60ml (2 fl oz) Tequila
15ml (½ fl oz) Grenadine
90ml (3 fl oz) Fresh Orange Juice
Maraschino Cherry
Slice of Orange

Pour Tequila and juice into a collins glass over ice then stir. Layer Grenadine on top, garnish with a cherry and slice of orange then serve.

Sangrita

18.7% ALC/VOL • 0.9 STD DRINKS

30ml (1 fl oz) Tequila
30ml (1 fl oz) Tomato Juice (chilled)
Dash Fresh Lemon Juice
Pinch of Pepper

Pour Tequila into a shot glass then pour juices into a mixing glass over ice and add pepper. Stir and strain into a chilled shot glass then serve, to be sipped slowly separately.

When a recipe requires Sangrita as an ingredient only use these non-alcohol ingredients.

Corcovado

20.1% ALC/VOL • 2.1 STD DRINKS

30ml (1 fl oz) Tequila
30ml (1 fl oz) Drambuie
15ml (½ fl oz) Blue Curaçao
60ml (2 fl oz) Lemonade
Slice of Orange

Pour Tequila, Drambuie and Curaçao into a cocktail shaker over ice. Shake and strain into an old-fashioned glass over crushed ice. Add lemonade and stir gently. Garnish with a slice of orange and serve with a straw.
This drink is also known as Blue Monday Mexican.

Mexican Mule

6.3% ALC/VOL • 1.3 STD DRINKS

45ml (1½ fl oz) Tequila
210ml (7 fl oz) Ginger Beer
½ Fresh Lime

Pour Tequila into a chilled collins glass over a few ice cubes and add ginger beer then stir gently. Twist ½ lime above drink to release juice – do not stir, then add spent shell and serve.

Silk Stockings

19.8% ALC/VOL • 1.9 STD DRINKS

45ml (1½ fl oz) Tequila
30ml (1 fl oz) White Crème De Cacao
Dash Grenadine
45ml (1½ fl oz) Fresh Cream
Maraschino Cherry
Cinnamon

Pour Tequila, Cacao, Grenadine and cream into a cocktail shaker over ice. Shake and strain into a chilled cocktail glass. Sprinkle cinnamon on top and garnish with a cherry then serve.

Vampiro

7.1% ALC/VOL • 1.4 STD DRINKS

45ml (1½ fl oz) Tequila
90ml (3 fl oz) Sangrita
105ml (3½ fl oz) Grapefruit Juice
Dash Fresh Lime Juice

Pour ingredients into a cocktail shaker over ice and shake. Strain into a collins glass over ice and serve.

Carabinieri

18.5% ALC/VOL • 2.7 STD DRINKS

45ml (1½ fl oz) Tequila
30ml (1 fl oz) Cointreau
15ml (½ fl oz) Galliano
75ml (2½ fl oz) Fresh Orange Juice
5ml (1/6 fl oz) Fresh Lime Juice
Yolk of 1 Egg

Pour ingredients into a cocktail shaker over ice and shake. Strain into a highball glass over crushed ice and serve with a straw.

Gentle Ben

14.5% ALC/VOL • 2.2 STD DRINKS

45ml (1½ fl oz) Tequila
15ml (½ fl oz) Dry Gin
15ml (½ fl oz) Vodka
120ml (4 fl oz) Fresh Orange Juice

Pour ingredients into a highball glass over ice, stir and serve.
This drink is also known as Orange Flux.

Diablo

12.5% ALC/VOL • 1.7 STD DRINKS

45ml (1½ fl oz) Tequila
20ml (⅔ fl oz) Crème De Cassis
15ml (½ fl oz) Fresh Lime Juice
90ml (3 fl oz) Dry Ginger Ale
Slice of Lime

Pour Tequila, Cassis and juice into a highball glass over ice then stir. Add Ginger Ale and stir gently. Garnish with a slice of lime and serve.

Stella's Stinger

36.8% ALC/VOL • 1.6 STD DRINKS

45ml (1½ fl oz) Tequila
5ml (1/6 fl oz) Pernod
5ml (1/6 fl oz) White Crème De Menthe
Wedge of Lemon

Pour Tequila, Pernod and Crème De Menthe into a mixing glass over ice. Stir and strain into a chilled cocktail glass. Garnish with a wedge of lemon and serve.

Tequila Old-Fashioned

31% ALC/VOL • 1.4 STD DRINKS

45ml (1½ fl oz) Tequila
2 dashes Angostura Bitters
5ml (1/6 fl oz) Spring Water
½ teaspoon Sugar Syrup
5ml (1/6 fl oz) Soda Water

Pour Bitters, water and sugar into an old-fashioned glass over ice then stir. Add Tequila and more ice to fill glass then stir. Add soda – do not stir, then serve.

Tequini

33.1% ALC/VOL • 1.6 STD DRINKS

45ml (1½ fl oz) Tequila
15ml (½ fl oz) Dry Vermouth
Dash Angostura Bitters
Twist of Lemon Peel

Pour Tequila, Vermouth and Bitters into a mixing glass over ice. Stir and strain into a chilled martini glass. Twist lemon peel above drink and place remainder of peel into drink then serve.

Hot Mary

14.3% ALC/VOL • 1.8 STD DRINKS

60ml (2 fl oz) Tequila
90ml (3 fl oz) Tomato Juice (chilled)
8ml (¼ fl oz) Fresh Lemon or Lime Juice
Dash Worcestershire Sauce
2 drops Tabasco Sauce
Pinch of Pepper
Pinch of Salt
Slice of Lemon

Prepare a sour glass with a salt frosted rim. Pour Tequila, juices and sauces into a cocktail shaker over ice. Add pepper and salt. Shake and strain into prepared glass. Garnish with a slice of lemon and serve.

Poker in the Lounge

12.8% ALC/VOL • 1.8 STD DRINKS

This drink is also known as Poker Face, p 297.

Tall Sunrise

11.2% ALC/VOL • 2.2 STD DRINKS

60ml (2 fl oz) Tequila
15ml (½ fl oz) Curaçao
5ml (1/6 fl oz) Crème De Cassis
15ml (½ fl oz) Fresh Lime Juice
150ml (5 fl oz) Soda Water
Slice of Lime

Pour Tequila, Curaçao, Cassis and juice into a tall glass over ice then stir. Add soda and stir gently. Garnish with a slice of lime and serve.

Mexican Clover

27.5% ALC/VOL • 1.3 STD DRINKS

30ml (1 fl oz) Tequila
30ml (1 fl oz) Bailey's Irish Cream
Strawberry

Pour Tequila and Bailey's into an old-fashioned glass over ice then stir. Garnish with a strawberry and serve.
This drink is also known as Spanish Joe.

Poker Face

12.8% ALC/VOL • 1.8 STD DRINKS

45ml (1½ fl oz) Tequila
15ml (½ fl oz) Cointreau
120ml (4 fl oz) Pineapple Juice
Wedge of Lime

Pour Tequila, Cointreau and juice into a highball glass over ice then stir. Garnish with a wedge of lime and serve.
This drink is also known as Poker in the Lounge.

Freddie Fudpucker

10.9% ALC/VOL • 1.5 STD DRINKS

30ml (1 fl oz) White Tequila
15ml (½ fl oz) Galliano
15ml (½ fl oz) Kahlúa
120ml (4 fl oz) Fresh Orange Juice

Pour ingredients into a cocktail shaker over cracked ice and shake. Pour into a chilled highball glass and serve.

Prado

20.4% ALC/VOL • 1.7 STD DRINKS

45ml (1½ fl oz) Tequila

15ml (½ fl oz) Maraschino Liqueur
5ml (⅙ fl oz) Grenadine
23ml (¾ fl oz) Fresh Lime Juice
½ Egg White
Maraschino Cherry
Slice of Lemon

Pour Tequila, Liqueur, Grenadine, juice and egg white into a cocktail shaker over ice. Shake and strain into a chilled sour glass. Garnish with a cherry and slice of lemon then serve.

Tequila Sol Nuevo

21% ALC/VOL • 5 STD DRINKS

100ml (3⅓ fl oz) Tequila
100ml (3⅓ fl oz) Red Curaçao
100ml (3⅓ fl oz) Cola

Pour Tequila and Curaçao into a mixing glass over ice. Stir and strain into a chilled highball glass. Add cola, stir gently and serve.

Despertador

8.7% ALC/VOL • 1.1 STD DRINKS

30ml (1 fl oz) White Tequila
10ml (⅓ fl oz) Triple Sec
10ml (⅓ fl oz) Grenadine
100ml (3⅓ fl oz) Grapefruit Juice
2 teaspoons Honey

Pour Tequila, Triple Sec, Grenadine and honey into a cocktail shaker over ice. Shake and strain into a highball glass over ice. Add juice, stir and serve with a straw.

Banana Slide

25.8% ALC/VOL • 2 STD DRINKS

45ml (1½ fl oz) Tequila
15ml (½ fl oz) Banana Liqueur
15ml (½ fl oz) Galliano
10ml (⅓ fl oz) Grenadine
15ml (½ fl oz) Fresh Cream

Pour ingredients into a cocktail shaker over ice and shake. Strain into a chilled cocktail glass and serve.

Berta's Special

10.2% ALC/VOL • 1.8 STD DRINKS

60ml (2 fl oz) White Tequila
2 dashes Orange Bitters
30ml (1 fl oz) Fresh Lime Juice
15ml (½ fl oz) Honey
White of 1 Egg
90ml (3 fl oz) Mineral Water

Pour Tequila, Bitters, juice, honey and egg white into a cocktail shaker over ice. Shake and strain into a highball glass over ice. Add mineral water, stir gently and serve.

Jarana

10.9% ALC/VOL • 1.8 STD DRINKS

60ml (2 fl oz) Tequila
90ml (3 fl oz) Pineapple Juice
¼ Cup Caster Sugar

Pour Tequila into a collins glass over ice and add sugar then stir well. Add juice, stir and serve.

White Bull

19.2% ALC/VOL • 1.3 STD DRINKS

30ml (1 fl oz) Tequila
23ml (¾ fl oz) Kahlúa
30ml (1 fl oz) Fresh Cream

Pour ingredients into an old-fashioned glass filled with ice, stir well and serve.

Deceiver

37% ALC/VOL • 1.3 STD DRINKS

30ml (1 fl oz) Tequila
15ml (½ fl oz) Galliano

Pour Galliano into an old-fashioned glass over ice and add Tequila – do not stir, then serve with a swizzle stick.

Tequila Razz

10.9% ALC/VOL • 1.5 STD DRINKS

This drink is also known as Campbell F. Craig, p 292.

Tesary

15.9% ALC/VOL • 1.5 STD DRINKS

30ml (1 fl oz) White Tequila
15ml (½ fl oz) Kahlúa
15ml (½ fl oz) Licor 43
60ml (2 fl oz) Tomato Juice (chilled)
Slice of Cucumber
Sprig of Fresh Mint

Pour Tequila, Kahlúa, Licor and juice into a cocktail shaker over ice. Shake and strain into a chilled cocktail glass. Garnish with a slice of cucumber and sprig of mint then serve.

Oklahoma Bulldog

7.3% ALC/VOL • 1.4 STD DRINKS

30ml (1 fl oz) Tequila
30ml (1 fl oz) Kahlúa
90ml (3 fl oz) Fresh Cream
90ml (3 fl oz) Cola

Pour Tequila, Kahlúa and cream into a cocktail shaker over ice. Shake and strain into a highball glass over ice. Add cola, stir gently and serve.

Blue Sunset

8.6% ALC/VOL • 1.5 STD DRINKS

30ml (1 fl oz) Tequila
30ml (1 fl oz) Blue Curaçao
80ml (2⅔ fl oz) Fresh Orange Juice
40ml (1⅓ fl oz) Sweet and Sour Mix
40ml (1⅓ fl oz) Lemonade

Pour Tequila, Curaçao, juice and sour mix into a highball glass over ice then stir. Add lemonade, stir gently and serve.

Pepe Ramon

11.9% ALC/VOL • 1.6 STD DRINKS

30ml (1 fl oz) Gold Tequila
20ml (⅔ fl oz) Banana Liqueur
20ml (⅔ fl oz) Midori
10ml (⅓ fl oz) Grenadine
90ml (3 fl oz) Fresh Orange Juice

Pour ingredients into a cocktail shaker over cracked ice and shake. Pour into a chilled highball glass and serve.

Tenedor del Diablo

9.5% ALC/VOL • 1 STD DRINK

20ml (⅔ fl oz) Gold Tequila
10ml (⅓ fl oz) Blue Curaçao
10ml (⅓ fl oz) Triple Sec
83ml (2¾ fl oz) Pineapple Juice
10ml (⅓ fl oz) Fresh Lime Juice

Pour ingredients into a cocktail shaker over ice and shake. Strain into a highball glass filled with crushed ice and serve with a straw.

Rattler

15.6% ALC/VOL • 1.5 STD DRINKS

45ml (1½ fl oz) Tequila
5ml (⅙ fl oz) Triple Sec
60ml (2 fl oz) Grapefruit Juice
8ml (¼ fl oz) Fresh Lime Juice
Wedge of Lime

Pour Tequila, Triple Sec and juices into a tall glass filled with ice then stir. Add a wedge of lime and serve.

Slowly does it

9.7% ALC/VOL • 1.5 STD DRINKS

30ml (1 fl oz) Tequila
20ml (⅔ fl oz) Dark Rum
2 dashes Tia Maria
60ml (2 fl oz) Pineapple Juice
30ml (1 fl oz) Coconut Cream
1 Banana (diced)

Pour Tequila, Tia, juice and cream into a blender over crushed ice then add diced banana. Blend until smooth and pour into a chilled collins glass. Layer Rum on top and serve.

Dorado

18.5% ALC/VOL • 1.8 STD DRINKS

60ml (2 fl oz) Tequila
45ml (1½ fl oz) Fresh Lemon Juice
1 tablespoon Honey

Pour ingredients into a cocktail shaker over ice and shake well. Strain into an old-fashioned glass over ice and serve.

Johan's Scream

26.8% ALC/VOL • 1.8 STD DRINKS

60ml (2 fl oz) Gold Tequila
2 teaspoons Brown Sugar
5 Fresh Mint Leaves
2 Slices of Orange
2 Wedges of Lime

Place sugar, mint leaves, slices of orange and wedges of lime into a mixing glass. Muddle well and add crushed ice. Add Tequila and stir well. Pour into a chilled old-fashioned glass and serve.

Maraca

10.7% ALC/VOL • 1.4 STD DRINKS

45ml (1½ fl oz) Tequila
10ml (⅓ fl oz) Grenadine
90ml (3 fl oz) Pineapple Juice
15ml (½ fl oz) Fresh Lemon Juice

Pour ingredients into a cocktail shaker over ice and shake. Strain into a chilled champagne saucer and serve.

Praying Mantis

9.5% ALC/VOL • 1.3 STD DRINKS

45ml (1½ fl oz) Tequila
10ml (⅓ fl oz) Fresh Lime Juice
5ml (⅙ fl oz) Fresh Lemon Juice
120ml (4 fl oz) Cola
Wedge of Lime

Pour Tequila and juices into a cocktail shaker over ice. Shake and strain into a highball glass half filled with ice. Add cola and stir gently. Garnish with a wedge of lime and serve.

Piñata

19.9% ALC/VOL • 1.2 STD DRINKS

30ml (1 fl oz) Tequila
18ml (⅗ fl oz) Banana Liqueur
30ml (1 fl oz) Fresh Lime Juice

Pour ingredients into a cocktail shaker over ice and shake. Strain into a highball glass filled with ice and serve.

The Clamato Cocktail

17.4% ALC/VOL • 1.3 STD DRINKS

38ml (1¼ fl oz) Tequila
8ml (¼ fl oz) Crème De Cassis
30ml (1 fl oz) Apple Juice
8ml (¼ fl oz) Fresh Lemon Juice
Wedge of Apple

Pour Tequila, Cassis and juices into an old-fashioned glass half filled with ice then stir. Garnish with a wedge of apple and serve.

Parked Car

23.8% ALC/VOL • 2 STD DRINKS

30ml (1 fl oz) Tequila
30ml (1 fl oz) Campari
15ml (½ fl oz) Cointreau
White of 1 Egg

Pour ingredients into a cocktail shaker over ice and shake. Strain into a chilled cocktail glass and serve.

Neon Tequila Monster

15% ALC/VOL • 1.8 STD DRINKS

30ml (1 fl oz) Tequila
30ml (1 fl oz) Vodka
90ml (3 fl oz) Fresh Orange Juice

Pour ingredients into a highball glass over ice, stir and serve.

El Toro

32% ALC/VOL • 2.3 STD DRINKS

60ml (2 fl oz) Tequila
30ml (1 fl oz) Kahlúa

Pour ingredients into a cocktail shaker over ice and shake. Strain into a chilled cocktail glass and serve.

Finals Night

12.5% ALC/VOL • 2.1 STD DRINKS

This drink is also known as *Piper, p 289.*

Passionate Rita

25.7% ALC/VOL • 1.8 STD DRINKS

45ml (1½ fl oz) Tequila
30ml (1 fl oz) Passion-Fruit Liqueur
15ml (½ fl oz) Fresh Lime Juice

Pour ingredients into a cocktail shaker over ice and shake. Strain into a chilled cocktail glass and serve.

Platina Blonde

25.3% ALC/VOL • 1.2 STD DRINKS

40ml (1⅓ fl oz) Tequila
20ml (⅔ fl oz) Fresh Cream

Pour ingredients into a chilled cocktail glass, stir and serve.

Orange Flux

14.5% ALC/VOL • 2.2 STD DRINKS

This drink is also known as *Gentle Ben, p 296.*

Black Matrix

12.2% ALC/VOL • 3.2 STD DRINKS

60ml (2 fl oz) Tequila
60ml (2 fl oz) White Wine
30ml (1 fl oz) Vodka
1 teaspoon Sugar Syrup
180ml (6 fl oz) Root Beer

Pour Tequila, Wine, Vodka and sugar into a mixing glass over ice. Stir and strain into a chilled tall glass. Add root beer, stir gently and serve.

Fuzzy Rita

21.8% ALC/VOL • 2.1 STD DRINKS

45ml (1½ fl oz) Tequila
15ml (½ fl oz) Cointreau
15ml (½ fl oz) Peach Schnapps
45ml (1½ fl oz) Fresh Lime Juice

Pour ingredients into a mixing glass over ice and stir. Strain into an old-fashioned glass over ice and serve.

Rosalita

28.2% ALC/VOL • 2.3 STD DRINKS

45ml (1½ fl oz) Tequila
30ml (1 fl oz) Campari
15ml (½ fl oz) Dry Vermouth
15ml (½ fl oz) Sweet Vermouth
Wedge of Lemon

Pour Tequila, Campari and Vermouths into a cocktail shaker over cracked ice. Shake and pour into a chilled highball glass. Garnish with a wedge of lemon and serve.

Extremely Drunk

28.6% ALC/VOL • 1.6 STD DRINKS

30ml (1 fl oz) Tequila
15ml (½ fl oz) Vodka
8ml (¼ fl oz) Jägermeister
8ml (¼ fl oz) Grenadine
8ml (¼ fl oz) Cranberry Juice

Pour ingredients into a mixing glass over ice and stir. Strain into a chilled cocktail glass and serve.

Tequila Twister

12.7% ALC/VOL • 1.8 STD DRINKS

60ml (2 fl oz) Tequila
30ml (1 fl oz) Fresh Lemon Juice
90ml (3 fl oz) Lemon-Lime Soda

Pour Tequila and juice into a highball glass over ice then stir. Add soda, stir gently and serve.

Spanish Fly

33% ALC/VOL • 1.6 STD DRINKS

45ml (1½ fl oz) Gold Tequila
15ml (½ fl oz) Sweet Sherry

Pour ingredients into an old-fashioned glass over ice, stir and serve.

Spanish Joe

27.5% ALC/VOL • 1.3 STD DRINKS

This drink is also known as *Mexican Clover, p 297.*

Ride in the Desert

8.4% ALC/VOL • 2 STD DRINKS

40ml (1⅓ fl oz) White Tequila
20ml (⅔ fl oz) Red Curaçao
20ml (⅔ fl oz) Triple Sec
200ml (6⅔ fl oz) Fresh Orange Juice
20ml (⅔ fl oz) Grapefruit Juice
Slice of Grapefruit

Pour Tequila, Curaçao, Triple Sec and grapefruit juice into a cocktail shaker over ice. Shake and strain into a tall glass over ice. Add orange juice and stir. Garnish with a slice of grapefruit and serve.

Angry Parakeet

43.6% ALC/VOL • 4.6 STD DRINKS

90ml (3 fl oz) Tequila
45ml (1½ fl oz) Green Chartreuse
Slice of Lemon

Pour Tequila and Chartreuse into a cocktail shaker over crushed ice. Shake and pour into a chilled old-fashioned glass. Garnish with a slice of lemon and serve.

Wet Snatch

12.7% ALC/VOL • 1.8 STD DRINKS

60ml (2 fl oz) Tequila
40ml (1⅓ fl oz) Pineapple Juice
40ml (1⅓ fl oz) Coconut Milk (chilled)
20ml (⅔ fl oz) Raspberry Juice
20ml (⅔ fl oz) Vanilla Syrup
Fresh Whipped Cream

Pour juices, milk and syrup into a blender over cracked ice. Blend well and add Tequila then blend again. Pour into a chilled highball glass, float cream on top and serve.

Lazy Sunday

11.4% ALC/VOL • 1.3 STD DRINKS

45ml (1½ fl oz) Tequila
75ml (2½ fl oz) Cranberry Juice
30ml (1 fl oz) Dry Ginger Ale

Pour Tequila and juice into a mixing glass over ice. Stir and strain into a highball glass over ice. Add Ginger Ale, stir gently and serve.

Smeraldo 86

28.7% ALC/VOL • 1.6 STD DRINKS

30ml (1 fl oz) White Tequila
15ml (½ fl oz) Dry Vermouth
15ml (½ fl oz) Triple Sec
10ml (⅓ fl oz) Blue Curaçao
Dash Fresh Lemon Juice

Pour ingredients into a cocktail shaker over ice and shake. Strain into a chilled cocktail glass and serve.

Frozen Matador

13.9% ALC/VOL • 1.3 STD DRINKS

45ml (1½ fl oz) Tequila
60ml (2 fl oz) Pineapple Juice
18ml (3/5 fl oz) Fresh Lime Juice
Stick of Pineapple

Pour Tequila and juices into a blender over crushed ice. Blend and pour into a chilled old-fashioned glass. Add a stick of pineapple and serve.

Mexican Iceberg

39.4% ALC/VOL • 3.4 STD DRINKS

45ml (1½ fl oz) Tequila
45ml (1½ fl oz) Yukon Jack
15ml (½ fl oz) Triple Sec
5ml (⅙ fl oz) Fresh Lime Juice
Slice of Lime

Pour Tequila, Yukon Jack, Triple Sec and juice into an old-fashioned glass over ice then stir. Garnish with a slice of lime and serve.

Venus Flytrap

24.4% ALC/VOL • 2.9 STD DRINKS

60ml (2 fl oz) Tequila
30ml (1 fl oz) Midori
30ml (1 fl oz) Triple Sec
30ml (1 fl oz) Fresh Lime Juice

Prepare a margarita glass with a salt frosted rim. Pour ingredients into a cocktail shaker over ice and shake. Strain into prepared glass and serve.

Apocalypse No.2

10.6% ALC/VOL • 1.4 STD DRINKS

38ml (1¼ fl oz) Gold Tequila
15ml (½ fl oz) Triple Sec
60ml (2 fl oz) Cranberry Juice
60ml (2 fl oz) Sweet and Sour Mix
Wedge of Lime

Pour Tequila, Triple Sec, juice and sour mix into a cocktail shaker over ice. Shake and strain into a chilled champagne saucer. Add a wedge of lime and serve.

Poolside Tropical

14.8% ALC/VOL • 1.6 STD DRINKS

40ml (1⅓ fl oz) Gold Tequila
10ml (⅓ fl oz) Blue Curaçao
10ml (⅓ fl oz) Coconut Liqueur
75ml (2½ fl oz) Fresh Orange Juice

Pour ingredients into a cocktail shaker over ice and shake. Strain into an old-fashioned glass over ice and serve with a straw.

Valley Xperience

17.9% ALC/VOL • 0.9 STD DRINKS

10ml (⅓ fl oz) White Tequila
10ml (⅓ fl oz) Jägermeister
8ml (¼ fl oz) Orange Curaçao
5ml (⅙ fl oz) Goldschläger
30ml (1 fl oz) White Grape Juice
Dash Tabasco Sauce

Pour ingredients into a cocktail shaker over ice and shake. Strain into a chilled cocktail glass and serve.

The Alamo

26.2% ALC/VOL • 1.3 STD DRINKS

30ml (1 fl oz) Tequila
23ml (¾ fl oz) Kahlúa
8ml (¼ fl oz) Fresh Lime Juice
Slice of Lime

Pour Tequila, Kahlúa and juice into a cocktail shaker over ice. Shake and strain into a chilled sour glass. Garnish with a slice of lime and serve.

Burning Embers

9.1% ALC/VOL • 2 STD DRINKS

40ml (1⅓ fl oz) White Tequila
30ml (1 fl oz) Spiced Rum
180ml (6 fl oz) Tomato Juice (chilled)
20ml (⅔ fl oz) Worcestershire Sauce
2 teaspoons Wasabi
Slice of Avocado

Prepare a tall glass with a salt frosted rim and add ice. Pour Tequila, Rum, juice and sauce into a cocktail shaker over ice then add wasabi. Shake and strain into prepared glass. Garnish with a slice of avocado and serve.

Mexican Mockingbird

12.4% ALC/VOL • 1.6 STD DRINKS

40ml (1⅓ fl oz) White Tequila
20ml (⅔ fl oz) Green Crème De Menthe
100ml (3⅓ fl oz) Mineral Water

Pour Tequila and Crème De Menthe into a cocktail shaker over ice. Shake and strain into a highball glass over ice. Add mineral water – do not stir, then serve with a swizzle stick and straw.

43 Amigos

31.5% ALC/VOL • 3.4 STD DRINKS

90ml (3 fl oz) Gold Tequila
15ml (½ fl oz) Licor 43
15ml (½ fl oz) Triple Sec
15ml (½ fl oz) Fresh Lime Juice
Wedge of Lime

Pour Tequila, Licor, Triple Sec and juice into a cocktail shaker over ice. Shake and strain into a chilled cocktail glass. Garnish with a wedge of lime and serve.

Acalpulco Blue

12.2% ALC/VOL • 1.6 STD DRINKS

38ml (1¼ fl oz) White Tequila
23ml (¾ fl oz) Blue Curaçao
2 teaspoons Sugar Syrup
90ml (3 fl oz) Lemonade

Pour Tequila, Curaçao and sugar into a cocktail shaker over ice. Shake and strain into a highball glass over ice. Add lemonade, stir gently and serve.

La Conga

18.1% ALC/VOL • 1.9 STD DRINKS

60ml (2 fl oz) White Tequila
3 dashes Angostura Bitters
10ml (⅓ fl oz) Pineapple Juice
60ml (2 fl oz) Soda Water
Slice of Lemon

Pour Tequila, Bitters and juice into an old-fashioned glass over ice then stir. Add soda, stir gently and garnish with a slice of lemon then serve.

Mexican Mountie

44% ALC/VOL • 3.1 STD DRINKS

45ml (1½ fl oz) Tequila
45ml (1½ fl oz) Yukon Jack
Wedge of Lime

Pour Tequila and Yukon Jack into an old-fashioned glass over ice then stir. Add a wedge of lime and serve.

Laker

30.5% ALC/VOL • 1 STD DRINK

23ml (¾ fl oz) White Tequila
15ml (½ fl oz) Blue Curaçao
Dash Grenadine
Dash Cranberry Juice
Dash Sweet and Sour Mix

Pour ingredients into a cocktail shaker over ice and shake. Strain into a chilled cocktail glass and serve.

Tequila Mirage

9.1% ALC/VOL • 1.3 STD DRINKS

30ml (1 fl oz) Tequila
30ml (1 fl oz) Chambord
60ml (2 fl oz) Fresh Orange Juice
60ml (2 fl oz) Lemonade

Pour Tequila, Chambord and juice into a cocktail shaker over ice. Shake and strain into a highball glass over ice. Add lemonade, stir gently and serve.

Rude Cosmopolitan

27.5% ALC/VOL • 1.8 STD DRINKS

45ml (1½ fl oz) White Tequila
23ml (¾ fl oz) Triple Sec
2 drops Orange Bitters
15ml (½ fl oz) Fresh Lime Juice
Twist of Orange Peel

Pour Tequila, Triple Sec, Bitters and juice into a cocktail shaker over ice. Shake and strain into a chilled cocktail glass. Garnish with orange peel and serve.

Cholla Bay

14.3% ALC/VOL • 0.9 STD DRINKS

30ml (1 fl oz) Tequila
15ml (½ fl oz) Grenadine
30ml (1 fl oz) Sweet and Sour Mix
1 teaspoon Sugar Syrup

Pour ingredients into a mixing glass without ice and stir. Pour into a margarita glass over ice and serve.

Bobo's Basher

21.8% ALC/VOL • 2.2 STD DRINKS

60ml (2 fl oz) Tequila
30ml (1 fl oz) Hard Cider
15ml (½ fl oz) Beer
15ml (½ fl oz) Blackberry Schnapps
8ml (¼ fl oz) Grenadine

Pour Tequila, Schnapps and Grenadine into a cocktail shaker over ice. Shake and strain into a chilled highball glass. Add Cider and Beer, stir gently then serve.

Bird of Paradise Cocktail No.2

16.6% ALC/VOL • 1.8 STD DRINKS

30ml (1 fl oz) White Tequila
30ml (1 fl oz) White Crème De Cacao
15ml (½ fl oz) Amaretto
60ml (2 fl oz) Fresh Cream

Pour ingredients into a cocktail shaker over ice and shake. Strain into a chilled cocktail glass and serve.

Corazon del Gortez

10.2% ALC/VOL • 1.1 STD DRINKS

20ml (⅔ fl oz) Gold Tequila
10ml (⅓ fl oz) Mandarine Napoleon
10ml (⅓ fl oz) Triple Sec
Dash Blue Curaçao
100ml (3⅓ fl oz) Pineapple Juice

Pour Tequila, Mandarine Napoleon, Triple Sec and juice into a cocktail shaker over ice. Shake and strain into a highball glass over ice. Add Curaçao – do not stir, then serve.

Tequila Ghost

33.1% ALC/VOL • 2.7 STD DRINKS

60ml (2 fl oz) Tequila
30ml (1 fl oz) Pernod
15ml (½ fl oz) Fresh Lemon Juice

Pour ingredients into a cocktail shaker over ice and shake. Strain into an old-fashioned glass half filled with ice and serve.

Triple Sunrise

14.1% ALC/VOL • 1.3 STD DRINKS

30ml (1 fl oz) Tequila
20ml (⅔ fl oz) Triple Sec
Dash Grenadine
20ml (⅔ fl oz) Fresh Lime Juice
½ Mango (diced)

Pour Tequila, Triple Sec, Grenadine and juice into a blender over cracked ice then add diced mango. Blend well and pour into a chilled old-fashioned glass then serve.

Cactus Prick

21.1% ALC/VOL • 2.4 STD DRINKS

60ml (2 fl oz) Tequila
15ml (½ fl oz) Triple Sec
10ml (⅓ fl oz) Drambuie
60ml (2 fl oz) Fresh Lemon Juice

Pour ingredients into a cocktail shaker over ice and shake. Strain into a chilled cocktail glass and serve.

Daisy

21.7% ALC/VOL • 1.8 STD DRINKS

60ml (2 fl oz) Tequila
10ml (⅓ fl oz) Grenadine
30ml (1 fl oz) Fresh Lemon Juice
5ml (⅙ fl oz) Soda Water

Pour Tequila, Grenadine and juice into a cocktail shaker over ice. Shake and strain into an old-fashioned glass over ice. Add soda – do not stir, then serve.

Back Burner

14.4% ALC/VOL • 2.2 STD DRINKS

60ml (2 fl oz) Tequila
15ml (½ fl oz) Galliano
120ml (4 fl oz) Cola

Pour Tequila and Galliano into a cocktail shaker over ice. Shake and strain into a coffee glass over crushed ice. Add cola and add more crushed ice to fill glass, stir gently then serve.

White Cactus

10.9% ALC/VOL • 0.9 STD DRINKS

30ml (1 fl oz) White Tequila
15ml (½ fl oz) Lime Syrup
60ml (2 fl oz) Soda Water

Pour Tequila and syrup into an old-fashioned glass over ice then stir. Add soda, stir gently and serve.

Freddie Fudputter

10.1% ALC/VOL • 1.3 STD DRINKS

30ml (1 fl oz) Tequila
15ml (½ fl oz) Galliano
120ml (4 fl oz) Fresh Orange Juice

Pour ingredients into a collins glass over ice, stir and serve.

Blue Monday Mexican

20.1% ALC/VOL • 2.1 STD DRINKS

This drink is also known as Corcovado, p 296.

Tequila Fever

12.7% ALC/VOL • 1.4 STD DRINKS

40ml (1⅓ fl oz) Gold Tequila
10ml (⅓ fl oz) Orange Curaçao
60ml (2 fl oz) Passion-Fruit Juice
30ml (1 fl oz) Mango Juice

Pour ingredients into a cocktail shaker over ice and shake. Strain into a highball glass over ice then serve with a swizzle stick and straw.

Mexico Orange Blossom

20.6% ALC/VOL • 2.1 STD DRINKS

45ml (1½ fl oz) Tequila
23ml (¾ fl oz) Bénédictine
60ml (2 fl oz) Fresh Orange Juice

Pour ingredients into a blender over cracked ice and blend. Strain into a chilled cocktail glass and serve.

Jackalope

25.5% ALC/VOL • 2.1 STD DRINKS

45ml (1½ fl oz) Tequila
23ml (¾ fl oz) Grand Marnier
30ml (1 fl oz) Fresh Lime Juice
1 teaspoon Sugar Syrup

Prepare a cocktail glass with a salt frosted rim. Pour ingredients into a cocktail shaker over ice and shake. Strain into prepared glass and serve.

Cactus Venom

29.8% ALC/VOL • 1.4 STD DRINKS

30ml (1 fl oz) Tequila
15ml (½ fl oz) Dark Crème De Cacao
15ml (½ fl oz) Kahlúa

Pour ingredients into a cocktail shaker over ice and shake. Strain into a chilled cocktail glass and serve.

Mexican Rose

8.7% ALC/VOL • 1.4 STD DRINKS

30ml (1 fl oz) Tequila
30ml (1 fl oz) Strawberry Liqueur
120ml (4 fl oz) Fresh Milk (chilled)
30ml (1 fl oz) Cherry Juice

Pour ingredients into a cocktail shaker over ice and shake. Strain into a highball glass over ice and serve.

Tequila Slammer

38% ALC/VOL • 1.3 STD DRINKS

45ml (1½ fl oz) Tequila
Salt
Wedge of Lemon

Pour Tequila into a shot glass and sprinkle salt on side of hand. Lick the salt, drink the Tequila in one swallow and then bite into the lemon.

Strawberry Margarita

20.3% ALC/VOL • 2 STD DRINKS

45ml (1½ fl oz) Tequila
15ml (½ fl oz) Cointreau
8ml (¼ fl oz) Strawberry Liqueur
15ml (½ fl oz) Fresh Lemon Juice
4 Strawberries (diced)
Strawberry

Prepare a margarita glass with a sugar frosted rim. Pour Tequila, Cointreau, Liqueur and juice into a blender over cracked ice then add diced strawberries. Blend and strain into prepared glass. Garnish with a strawberry and serve.

Green Iguana Margarita

13.9% ALC/VOL • 1.2 STD DRINKS

30ml (1 fl oz) Tequila
15ml (½ fl oz) Midori
60ml (2 fl oz) Sweet and Sour Mix

Prepare a margarita glass with a salt frosted rim. Pour ingredients into a blender over cracked ice and blend. Pour into prepared glass and serve.

Banana Margarita

20.3% ALC/VOL • 1.9 STD DRINKS

30ml (1 fl oz) Gold Tequila
30ml (1 fl oz) Banana Liqueur
15ml (½ fl oz) Cointreau
30ml (1 fl oz) Fresh Lemon Juice
¼ Banana (diced)
Slice of Banana

Prepare a margarita glass with a sugar frosted rim – moistened with lemon juice. Pour Tequila, Liqueur, Cointreau and juice into a blender over crushed ice then add diced banana. Blend and pour into prepared glass. Garnish with a slice of banana and serve.

Blue Margarita

23.3% ALC/VOL • 1.8 STD DRINKS

45ml (1½ fl oz) Tequila
23ml (¾ fl oz) Blue Curaçao
30ml (1 fl oz) Fresh Lime Juice

Prepare a margarita glass with a salt frosted rim. Pour ingredients into a cocktail shaker over ice and shake. Strain into prepared glass and serve.

Kiwi Margarita

17.5% ALC/VOL • 2.1 STD DRINKS

45ml (1½ fl oz) Tequila
15ml (½ fl oz) Cointreau
15ml (½ fl oz) Midori
15ml (½ fl oz) Fresh Lemon Juice
1 Kiwi Fruit (diced)
Slice of Kiwi Fruit
Slice of Orange

Prepare a margarita glass with a sugar frosted rim. Pour Tequila, Cointreau, Midori and juice into a blender over crushed ice then add diced kiwi fruit. Blend and pour into prepared glass. Garnish with a slice of kiwi fruit and orange then serve.

Apple Margarita

19.5% ALC/VOL • 1.8 STD DRINKS

30ml (1 fl oz) Tequila
30ml (1 fl oz) Cointreau
60ml (2 fl oz) Apple Juice

Pour ingredients into a cocktail shaker over ice and shake. Strain into a chilled margarita glass and serve.

Blackberry Margarita

16.4% ALC/VOL • 1.8 STD DRINKS

53ml (1¾ fl oz) Tequila
15ml (½ fl oz) Blackberry Schnapps
23ml (¾ fl oz) Fresh Lime Juice
10 Blackberries (diced)
2 Blackberries

Prepare a margarita glass with a sugar frosted rim. Pour Tequila, Schnapps and juice into a blender over crushed ice then add diced blackberries. Blend and pour into prepared glass. Garnish with blackberries and serve.

Catalina Margarita

13.5% ALC/VOL • 2.4 STD DRINKS

45ml (1½ fl oz) Tequila
30ml (1 fl oz) Blue Curaçao
30ml (1 fl oz) Peach Schnapps
120ml (4 fl oz) Sweet and Sour Mix

Pour ingredients into a cocktail shaker over ice and shake. Strain into a chilled margarita glass and serve.

Golden Margarita

27.7% ALC/VOL • 2.3 STD DRINKS

45ml (1½ fl oz) Gold Tequila
15ml (½ fl oz) Cointreau
15ml (½ fl oz) Grand Marnier
30ml (1 fl oz) Fresh Lemon Juice
Slice of Lemon

Prepare a margarita glass with a salt frosted rim and add crushed ice. Pour Tequila, Cointreau, Grand Marnier and juice into a cocktail shaker over ice. Shake and strain into prepared glass. Garnish with a slice of lemon and serve.

Margarita

25.7% ALC/VOL • 1.8 STD DRINKS

45ml (1½ fl oz) Tequila
15ml (½ fl oz) Cointreau
30ml (1 fl oz) Fresh Lemon or Lime Juice
Slice of Lemon

Prepare a margarita glass with a salt frosted rim. Pour Tequila, Cointreau and juice into a cocktail shaker over ice. Shake and strain into prepared glass. Garnish with a slice of lemon and serve.

Mandarin Margarita

28.2% ALC/VOL • 2.4 STD DRINKS

45ml (1½ fl oz) Gold Tequila
20ml (⅔ fl oz) Mandarine Napoleon
15ml (½ fl oz) Cointreau
30ml (1 fl oz) Fresh Lemon Juice
Slice of Orange

Prepare a margarita glass with a salt frosted rim. Pour Tequila, Mandarine Napoleon, Cointreau and juice into a blender over cracked ice. Blend and strain into prepared glass. Garnish with a slice of orange and serve.

Peach Margarita

13.5% ALC/VOL • 1 STD DRINK

30ml (1 fl oz) Tequila
8ml (¼ fl oz) Peach Liqueur
15ml (½ fl oz) Fresh Lemon Juice
½ Peach (diced)

Prepare a margarita glass with a sugar frosted rim. Pour Tequila, Liqueur and juice into a blender over crushed ice then add diced peach. Blend and pour into prepared glass then serve.

Pink Margarita

21.2% ALC/VOL • 1.6 STD DRINKS

45ml (1½ fl oz) Tequila
15ml (½ fl oz) Raspberry Liqueur
5ml (1/6 fl oz) Grenadine
15ml (½ fl oz) Fresh Lemon or Lime Juice
½ Egg White

Prepare a margarita glass with a salt frosted rim. Pour ingredients into a cocktail shaker over ice and shake. Strain into prepared glass and serve.

Cadalac Margarita

25.4% ALC/VOL • 2.5 STD DRINKS

60ml (2 fl oz) Tequila
23ml (¾ fl oz) Grand Marnier

38ml (1¼ fl oz) Sweet and Sour Mix
Wedge of Lime

Prepare a margarita glass with a salt frosted rim. Pour Tequila, Grand Marnier and sour mix into a cocktail shaker over ice. Shake and strain into prepared glass. Garnish with a wedge of lime and serve.

Pink Cadillac Margarita

17.9% ALC/VOL • 2.8 STD DRINKS

60ml (2 fl oz) Tequila
30ml (1 fl oz) Cointreau
60ml (2 fl oz) Fresh Lime Juice
30ml (1 fl oz) Cranberry Juice
1 teaspoon Sugar Syrup

Pour ingredients into a cocktail shaker over cracked ice and shake. Pour into a chilled margarita glass and serve.

Electric Margarita

27.8% ALC/VOL • 1.6 STD DRINKS

45ml (1½ fl oz) Tequila
15ml (½ fl oz) Blue Curaçao
15ml (½ fl oz) Rose's Lime Juice
Wedge of Lime

Prepare a margarita glass with a salt frosted rim. Pour Tequila, Curaçao and juice into a cocktail shaker over ice. Shake and strain into prepared glass. Garnish with a wedge of lime and serve.

Tall Margarita

11.4% ALC/VOL • 1.8 STD DRINKS

45ml (1½ fl oz) Tequila
15ml (½ fl oz) Cointreau
23ml (¾ fl oz) Fresh Lemon Juice
120ml (4 fl oz) Bitter-Lemon Soda
Slice of Lemon

Pour Tequila, Cointreau and juice into a cocktail shaker over ice. Shake and strain into a tall glass over ice. Add soda and stir gently. Garnish with a slice of lemon and serve.

Midori Margarita

16.1% ALC/VOL • 1.4 STD DRINKS

30ml (1 fl oz) Tequila
30ml (1 fl oz) Midori
45ml (1½ fl oz) Fresh Lemon Juice
1 teaspoon Sugar Syrup
Slice of Lime

Pour Tequila, Midori, juice and sugar into a cocktail shaker over ice. Shake and strain into a chilled margarita glass. Garnish with a slice of lime and serve.

Blackjack Margarita

13.2% ALC/VOL • 2 STD DRINKS

45ml (1½ fl oz) Tequila
15ml (½ fl oz) Chambord
15ml (½ fl oz) Cointreau
120ml (4 fl oz) Fresh Lime Juice
Wedge of Lime

Prepare a margarita glass with a salt frosted rim. Pour Tequila, Chambord, Cointreau and juice into a cocktail shaker over ice. Shake and strain into prepared glass. Garnish with a wedge of lime and serve.

Apricot Margarita

16.7% ALC/VOL • 1.4 STD DRINKS

30ml (1 fl oz) Tequila
30ml (1 fl oz) Apricot Brandy
45ml (1½ fl oz) Fresh Lemon Juice
1 teaspoon Sugar Syrup
Slice of Apricot

Pour Tequila, Brandy, juice and sugar into a cocktail shaker over ice. Shake and strain into a chilled margarita glass. Garnish with a slice of apricot and serve.

Southern Tradition Margarita

11% ALC/VOL • 2 STD DRINKS

45ml (1½ fl oz) Tequila
23ml (¾ fl oz) Southern Comfort
15ml (½ fl oz) Fresh Lime Juice
150ml (5 fl oz) Sweet and Sour Mix
Wedge of Lime

Pour Tequila, Southern Comfort, juice and sour mix into a cocktail shaker over ice. Shake and strain into a tall glass over ice. Add a wedge of lime and serve.

Baja Margarita

17.7% ALC/VOL • 2.5 STD DRINKS

60ml (2 fl oz) Tequila
30ml (1 fl oz) Damiana Liqueur
90ml (3 fl oz) Fresh Lime Juice

Prepare a margarita glass with a salt frosted rim. Pour ingredients into a cocktail shaker over cracked ice and shake. Pour into prepared glass and serve.

Frozen Margarita

13% ALC/VOL • 1.8 STD DRINKS

This drink is a Margarita (p 305) that is blended with crushed ice.

Apéritifs

Apéritif is derived from the Latin word aperire – meaning 'to open'.

Apéritifs are generally considered to be aromatized Wines.

In short, an apéritif is a drink that is enjoyed before a meal to enhance one's appetite.

Five main apéritifs are:

Byrrh

Byrrh is a French Vermouth apéritif which is a Fortified Brandy with a slight taste of orange.

Campari

A well known Italian apéritif that is spirit-based and very dry. Campari is red in colour with a bitter-sweet taste due to being infused with aromatic and bitter herbs as well as orange peel.

Dubonnet

Dubonnet is a well known French Vermouth apéritif which is a Fortified Wine with quinine for a unique sweet taste.

Sherry

True Sherry originates from Jerez in Spain. There are five main types of Sherry: cream, dry, extra dry, medium and sweet. The drier the Sherry, the cooler it should be served.

Vermouth

Vermouth is a Fortified Wine that originated in France and Italy and is flavoured from dozens of various herbs including wormwood (wurmuth in German). There are four types of Vermouth: Amaro (brown and bitter), dry (clear), sweet (red) and Bianco (golden and very sweet).

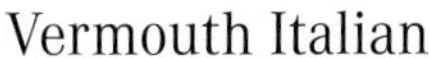

Vermouth Italian

16.8% ALC/VOL • 0.8 STD DRINKS

30ml (1 fl oz) Dry Vermouth
30ml (1 fl oz) Sweet Vermouth
Dash Angostura Bitters
Dash Maraschino Liqueur
Dash Orange Syrup
Wedge of Lemon

Pour Vermouths, Bitters, Liqueur and syrup into a mixing glass over ice. Stir and strain into a chilled cocktail glass. Garnish with a wedge of lemon and serve.

Boswellian Booster

20.4% ALC/VOL • 1.8 STD DRINKS

60ml (2 fl oz) Dry Vermouth
30ml (1 fl oz) Brandy
2 dashes Orange Bitters
15ml (½ fl oz) Fresh Lemon Juice
½ teaspoon Sugar Syrup
Maraschino Cherry

Pour Vermouth, Brandy, Bitters, juice and sugar into a cocktail shaker over ice. Shake and strain into an old-fashioned glass over ice. Garnish with a cherry and serve.

Boyd of the Loch

26.8% ALC/VOL • 1.6 STD DRINKS

45ml (1½ fl oz) Dry Vermouth
30ml (1 fl oz) Scotch Whisky
Wedge of Lemon

Pour Vermouth and Whisky into a mixing glass over ice. Stir and strain into a chilled cocktail glass. Garnish with a wedge of lemon and serve.

Punt e Mes Negroni

21.7% ALC/VOL • 1.2 STD DRINKS

23ml (¾ fl oz) Gin
23ml (¾ fl oz) Punt e Mes
23ml (¾ fl oz) Sweet Vermouth
5ml (⅙ fl oz) Soda Water
Wedge of Lemon

Pour Gin, Punt e Mes and Vermouth into a mixing glass over ice. Stir and strain into a chilled cocktail glass then add soda – do not stir. Add a wedge of lemon and serve.

Campari Cocktail

6.7% ALC/VOL • 1 STD DRINK

30ml (1 fl oz) Campari
30ml (1 fl oz) Sweet Vermouth
120ml (4 fl oz) Soda Water
2 Cherries
2 Slices of Lemon

Pour Campari and Vermouth into a collins glass over ice then stir. Add soda and stir gently. Garnish with cherries and slices of lemon then serve.

Rum Apéritif

22.1% ALC/VOL • 1.5 STD DRINKS

30ml (1 fl oz) Dry Vermouth
30ml (1 fl oz) Light Rum
5ml (⅙ fl oz) Jamaica Rum
15ml (½ fl oz) Fresh Lemon Juice
1 teaspoon Raspberry Syrup
Twist of Lemon Peel

Pour Vermouth, Rums, juice and syrup into a cocktail shaker over ice. Shake and strain into a chilled cocktail glass. Twist lemon peel above drink and place remainder of peel into drink then serve.

Wedding Belle

21.4% ALC/VOL • 1.5 STD DRINKS

30ml (1 fl oz) Dubonnet
30ml (1 fl oz) Gin
15ml (½ fl oz) Cherry Brandy
15ml (½ fl oz) Fresh Orange Juice

Pour ingredients into a cocktail shaker over ice and shake. Strain into a chilled cocktail glass and serve.

Goldfinger

16.7% ALC/VOL • 1.7 STD DRINKS

60ml (2 fl oz) Rosso Antico
30ml (1 fl oz) Vodka
30ml (1 fl oz) Fresh Orange Juice
8ml (¼ fl oz) Fresh Lemon Juice
Slice of Orange
Wedge of Lemon

Pour Rosso Antico, Vodka and juices into a mixing glass over ice. Stir and strain into a chilled champagne saucer. Garnish with a slice of orange and wedge of lemon then serve.

Agincourt

17.7% ALC/VOL • 1.1 STD DRINKS

30ml (1 fl oz) Dry Vermouth
30ml (1 fl oz) Sweet Vermouth
15ml (½ fl oz) Amaretto
5ml (⅙ fl oz) Fresh Lemon Juice

Pour ingredients into a cocktail shaker over ice and shake. Strain into a chilled cocktail glass and serve.

Plum Apéritif

25.4% ALC/VOL • 1.4 STD DRINKS

45ml (1½ fl oz) Dry Vermouth
15ml (½ fl oz) Cognac
8ml (¼ fl oz) Prunelle
Slice of Lemon

Pour Vermouth, Cognac and Prunelle into a mixing glass over ice. Stir and strain into an old-fashioned glass over ice. Add a slice of lemon and serve.

Californian

13.4% ALC/VOL • 1.5 STD DRINKS

45ml (1½ fl oz) Sweet Vermouth
30ml (1 fl oz) Blended Whiskey
60ml (2 fl oz) Fresh Orange Juice
1 teaspoon Orgeat Syrup

Pour ingredients into a cocktail shaker over ice and shake. Strain into a chilled old-fashioned glass over 2 ice cubes and serve.

Triplet Cocktail

23.4% ALC/VOL • 1.8 STD DRINKS

30ml (1 fl oz) Dry Vermouth
30ml (1 fl oz) Gin
30ml (1 fl oz) Peach Brandy
10ml (⅓ fl oz) Fresh Lemon Juice
Maraschino Cherry

Pour Vermouth, Gin, Brandy and juice into a cocktail shaker over ice. Shake and strain into a chilled cocktail glass. Garnish with a cherry and serve.

Fino

16.5% ALC/VOL • 1.1 STD DRINKS

45ml (1½ fl oz) Sweet Vermouth
38ml (1¼ fl oz) Fino Sherry
Slice of Lemon

Pour Vermouth and Sherry into a mixing glass over ice. Stir and strain into an old-fashioned glass over ice. Garnish with a slice of lemon and serve.

Warrior

22.1% ALC/VOL • 1.4 STD DRINKS

30ml (1 fl oz) Dry Vermouth
30ml (1 fl oz) Sweet Vermouth
15ml (½ fl oz) Brandy
3 dashes Cointreau
3 dashes Pernod

Pour ingredients into a mixing glass over ice and stir. Strain into a chilled cocktail glass and serve.

Rose Water

1.3% ALC/VOL • 0.2 STD DRINKS

10ml (⅓ fl oz) Campari
5ml (⅙ fl oz) Grenadine
180ml (6 fl oz) Lemonade

Pour Campari and Grenadine into a highball glass filled with ice then stir. Add lemonade, stir gently and serve.

Graceland

21.5% ALC/VOL • 1.3 STD DRINKS

30ml (1 fl oz) Dry Vermouth
30ml (1 fl oz) Sweet Vermouth
15ml (½ fl oz) Scotch Whisky
Dash Angostura Bitters
Wedge of Lemon

Pour Vermouths, Whisky and Bitters into a mixing glass over ice. Stir and strain into a chilled cocktail glass. Garnish with a wedge of lemon and serve.

Evens Rescues the Damsel of Garstang Tower

23.3% ALC/VOL • 2 STD DRINKS

30ml (1 fl oz) Dry Vermouth
30ml (1 fl oz) Gin
30ml (1 fl oz) Sweet Vermouth
15ml (½ fl oz) Strawberry Liqueur
2 dashes Orange Bitters

Pour ingredients into a mixing glass over ice and stir. Strain into a chilled cocktail glass and serve.

English Highball

14.8% ALC/VOL • 2.1 STD DRINKS

30ml (1 fl oz) Brandy
30ml (1 fl oz) Dry Gin
30ml (1 fl oz) Sweet Vermouth
90ml (3 fl oz) Dry Ginger Ale or Soda Water
Twist of Lemon Peel

Pour Brandy, Gin and Vermouth into a mixing glass over ice. Stir and strain into a highball glass over ice. Add Ginger Ale or soda as desired and stir gently. Garnish with lemon peel and serve.

Phoebe Snow

25.6% ALC/VOL • 2.2 STD DRINKS

60ml (2 fl oz) Dubonnet
45ml (1½ fl oz) Brandy
5ml (⅙ fl oz) Pernod

Pour ingredients into a mixing glass over ice and stir. Strain into a chilled cocktail glass and serve.

Mr. Whippy

8.9% ALC/VOL • 1.4 STD DRINKS

30ml (1 fl oz) Dry Vermouth
30ml (1 fl oz) Grand Marnier
Dash Orange Curaçao
Dash Grenadine
120ml (4 fl oz) Orange Mineral Water Soda
15ml (½ fl oz) Fresh Cream

Pour Vermouth and Grand Marnier into a collins glass filled with ice then stir. Add soda and stir gently then float cream on top. Add Curaçao and Grenadine by pouring over cream then serve.

Campari Cooler

5.4% ALC/VOL • 0.9 STD DRINKS

45ml (1½ fl oz) Campari
60ml (2 fl oz) Fresh Orange Juice
15ml (½ fl oz) Raspberry Syrup
90ml (3 fl oz) Soda Water

Pour Campari, juice and syrup into a cocktail shaker over ice. Shake and strain into a collins glass over ice. Add soda, stir gently and serve.

Picon Punch

27% ALC/VOL • 1.4 STD DRINKS

45ml (1½ fl oz) Amer Picon
15ml (½ fl oz) Cognac
Dash Grenadine
5ml (⅙ fl oz) Soda Water
Twist of Lemon Peel

Pour Amer Picon and Grenadine into an old-fashioned glass over ice then stir. Add soda and stir gently. Layer Cognac on top and twist lemon peel above drink. Place remainder of peel into drink and serve.

Black Power

5% ALC/VOL • 0.7 STD DRINKS

60ml (2 fl oz) Marsala
120ml (4 fl oz) Cola
Slice of Lemon

Pour Marsala into a chilled old-fashioned glass over a few ice cubes and add cola then stir gently. Add a slice of lemon and serve.

Bastardo

20.5% ALC/VOL • 1.3 STD DRINKS

30ml (1 fl oz) Dry Vermouth
30ml (1 fl oz) Sweet Vermouth
15ml (½ fl oz) California Brandy
2 dashes Angostura Bitters
5ml (1/6 fl oz) Soda Water
Slice of Lemon

Pour Vermouths, Brandy and Bitters into an old-fashioned glass over ice then stir. Add soda – do not stir, then add a slice of lemon and serve.

Italian Cooler

4.2% ALC/VOL • 0.6 STD DRINKS

40ml (1⅓ fl oz) Dry Vermouth
10ml (⅓ fl oz) Grenadine
120ml (4 fl oz) Mineral Water

Pour Vermouth and Grenadine into a mixing glass over ice. Stir and strain into a collins glass over ice. Add mineral water – do not stir, then serve with a swizzle stick and straw.

Ferandina

7.6% ALC/VOL • 1.4 STD DRINKS

60ml (2 fl oz) Bianco Vermouth
30ml (1 fl oz) Pimm's No.1
150ml (5 fl oz) Lemonade
Slice of Orange

Pour Vermouth and Pimm's into a collins glass over ice then stir. Add lemonade and stir gently. Garnish with a slice of orange and serve.

Butterfly

13.1% ALC/VOL • 0.8 STD DRINKS

23ml (¾ fl oz) Dry Vermouth
23ml (¾ fl oz) Sweet Vermouth
15ml (½ fl oz) Dubonnet
15ml (½ fl oz) Fresh Orange Juice

Pour ingredients into a cocktail shaker over ice and shake. Strain into an old-fashioned glass over ice and serve.

King Kenneth

6.5% ALC/VOL • 1.1 STD DRINKS

45ml (1½ fl oz) Campari
15ml (½ fl oz) Peach Schnapps
30ml (1 fl oz) Fresh Orange Juice
10ml (⅓ fl oz) Fresh Lemon Juice
120ml (4 fl oz) Tonic Water
Wedge of Lemon

Pour Campari, Schnapps and juices into a cocktail shaker over ice. Shake and strain into a collins glass over ice. Add tonic and stir gently. Garnish with a wedge of lemon and serve.

Ante

29.5% ALC/VOL • 1.6 STD DRINKS

30ml (1 fl oz) Dubonnet
23ml (¾ fl oz) Applejack
15ml (½ fl oz) Cointreau

Pour ingredients into a mixing glass over ice and stir. Strain into a chilled cocktail glass and serve.

Sanctuary

19.4% ALC/VOL • 1.1 STD DRINKS

30ml (1 fl oz) Dubonnet
15ml (½ fl oz) Amer Picon
15ml (½ fl oz) Cointreau
15ml (½ fl oz) Fresh Lemon Juice
Slice of Lemon

Pour Dubonnet, Amer Picon, Cointreau and juice into a cocktail shaker over ice. Shake and strain into an old-fashioned glass over ice. Add a slice of lemon and serve.

Radio City

15.6% ALC/VOL • 1.3 STD DRINKS

30ml (1 fl oz) Dry Sherry
30ml (1 fl oz) Sweet Sherry
15ml (½ fl oz) Gin
30ml (1 fl oz) Lemonade

Pour Sherries and Gin into an old-fashioned glass over cracked ice then stir. Add lemonade, stir gently and serve.

Floridian

13.3% ALC/VOL • 1.3 STD DRINKS

45ml (1½ fl oz) Dry Vermouth
5ml (1/6 fl oz) Falernum
2 dashes Orange Bitters
15ml (½ fl oz) Forbidden Fruit
60ml (2 fl oz) Grapefruit Juice
Slice of Lime

Pour Vermouth, Falernum, Bitters, Forbidden Fruit and juice into a cocktail shaker over ice. Shake and strain into a chilled old-fashioned glass over 2 ice cubes. Garnish with a slice of lime and serve.

Seething Jealousy

18.6% ALC/VOL • 1.1 STD DRINKS

30ml (1 fl oz) Sweet Vermouth
15ml (½ fl oz) Cherry Brandy
15ml (½ fl oz) Scotch Whisky

15ml (½ fl oz) Fresh
Orange Juice

Pour ingredients into a cocktail shaker over ice and shake. Strain into a chilled cocktail glass and serve.

Gladys Delight

6.1% ALC/VOL • 0.9 STD DRINKS

60ml (2 fl oz) Dry Vermouth
5ml (1/6 fl oz) Sweet Vermouth
5ml (1/6 fl oz) Grenadine
120ml (4 fl oz) Dry Ginger Ale
Wedge of Lemon

Pour Vermouths and Grenadine into a collins glass over ice then stir. Add Ginger Ale and stir gently. Garnish with a wedge of lemon and serve.
This drink is also known as Vermouth Sparkle.

Joyce of the Hillhouse

25.3% ALC/VOL • 1.5 STD DRINKS

45ml (1½ fl oz) Sweet
Vermouth
30ml (1 fl oz) Scotch Whisky
Dash Angostura Bitters
Wedge of Lemon

Pour Vermouth, Whisky and Bitters into a mixing glass over ice. Stir and strain into a chilled cocktail glass. Garnish with a wedge of lemon and serve.

Pammy Kay

21.8% ALC/VOL • 1.1 STD DRINKS

30ml (1 fl oz) Dry Vermouth
15ml (½ fl oz) Apricot Brandy
15ml (½ fl oz) Gin
3 dashes Fresh Lemon Juice
3 dashes Fresh Lime Juice

Pour ingredients into a cocktail shaker over ice and shake. Strain into a chilled cocktail glass and serve.

Lillet Noyaux

25.1% ALC/VOL • 1.5 STD DRINKS

45ml (1½ fl oz) Lillet
30ml (1 fl oz) Gin
Dash Crème De Noyaux
Twist of Orange Peel

Pour Lillet, Gin and Noyaux into a mixing glass over ice. Stir and strain into a chilled cocktail glass. Twist orange peel above drink and place remainder of peel into drink then serve.

Westerman Sings the Blues

25.9% ALC/VOL • 1 STD DRINK

30ml (1 fl oz) Dry Vermouth
15ml (½ fl oz) Gin
5ml (1/6 fl oz) Pernod
Slice of Orange

Pour Vermouth, Gin and Pernod into a mixing glass over ice. Stir and strain into a chilled cocktail glass. Garnish with a slice of orange and serve.

Go-for-Broke Cocktail

27.3% ALC/VOL • 1.2 STD DRINKS

30ml (1 fl oz) Dry Vermouth
23ml (¾ fl oz) Gin
3 dashes Cointreau
Dash Angostura Bitters

Pour ingredients into a mixing glass over ice and stir. Strain into a chilled cocktail glass and serve.

Beansy's Battleground

24% ALC/VOL • 1.8 STD DRINKS

45ml (1½ fl oz) Sweet
Vermouth
30ml (1 fl oz) Brandy
15ml (½ fl oz) Peppermint
Schnapps
3 dashes Pernod
Dash Angostura Bitters

Pour ingredients into a mixing glass over ice and stir. Strain into an old-fashioned glass filled with ice and serve.

Combo

19.2% ALC/VOL • 1.3 STD DRINKS

75ml (2½ fl oz) Dry Vermouth
5ml (1/6 fl oz) Cognac
Dash Angostura Bitters
½ teaspoon Sugar Syrup

Pour ingredients into a cocktail shaker over ice and shake. Strain into an old-fashioned glass over ice and serve.

Ceasefire

6.3% ALC/VOL • 1 STD DRINK

15ml (½ fl oz) Cherry Brandy
15ml (½ fl oz) Dry Vermouth
15ml (½ fl oz) Scotch Whisky
150ml (5 fl oz) Lemonade
Cherry
Slice of Lemon

Pour Brandy, Vermouth and Whisky into a highball glass over ice then stir. Add lemonade and stir gently. Garnish with a cherry and slice of lemon then serve with 2 straws.

Claridge Cocktail

28.8% ALC/VOL • 2 STD DRINKS

30ml (1 fl oz) Dry Vermouth
30ml (1 fl oz) Gin
15ml (½ fl oz) Apricot Brandy

15ml (½ fl oz) Cointreau

Pour ingredients into a cocktail shaker over ice and shake. Strain into a chilled cocktail glass and serve.

Camp Grenada

4.7% ALC/VOL • 0.9 STD DRINKS

45ml (1½ fl oz) Campari
15ml (½ fl oz) Grenadine
60ml (2 fl oz) Grapefruit Juice
30ml (1 fl oz) Pineapple Juice
90ml (3 fl oz) Lemonade
Slice of Orange
Slice of Pineapple

Pour Campari, Grenadine and juices into a cocktail shaker over ice. Shake and strain into a collins glass over ice. Add lemonade and stir gently. Garnish with a slice of orange and pineapple then serve.

Wilfred's Weather

27.6% ALC/VOL • 1.2 STD DRINKS

30ml (1 fl oz) Dry Vermouth
23ml (¾ fl oz) Gin
3 dashes Ricard
Dash Angostura Bitters

Pour ingredients into a mixing glass over ice and stir. Strain into a chilled cocktail glass and serve.

Vermouth Maraschino

16.5% ALC/VOL • 1.2 STD DRINKS

60ml (2 fl oz) Dry Vermouth
15ml (½ fl oz) Maraschino Liqueur
2 dashes Orange Bitters
15ml (½ fl oz) Fresh Lemon Juice
Maraschino Cherry

Pour Vermouth, Liqueur, Bitters and juice into a cocktail shaker over ice. Shake and strain into a chilled old-fashioned glass over 2 ice cubes. Garnish with a cherry and serve.

Cinzia

7.5% ALC/VOL • 1.2 STD DRINKS

20ml (⅔ fl oz) Campari
20ml (⅔ fl oz) Vodka
10ml (⅓ fl oz) Triple Sec
150ml (5 fl oz) Tonic Water

Pour Campari, Vodka and Triple Sec into a highball glass over ice then stir. Add tonic, stir gently and serve.

Key Punch

18.5% ALC/VOL • 1.8 STD DRINKS

60ml (2 fl oz) Dark Rum
30ml (1 fl oz) Fresh Lime Juice
30ml (1 fl oz) Sugar Syrup
Cherry
Slice of Lime

Pour Rum, juice and sugar into an old-fashioned glass over ice then stir. Garnish with a cherry and slice of lime then serve.

Southern Tango

10.4% ALC/VOL • 0.9 STD DRINKS

30ml (1 fl oz) Dry Vermouth
15ml (½ fl oz) Southern Comfort
60ml (2 fl oz) Lemonade
Wedge of Lemon

Pour Vermouth and Southern Comfort into a highball glass over cracked ice then stir. Add lemonade and stir gently. Add a wedge of lemon and serve.

Canadian and Campari

27.4% ALC/VOL • 1.6 STD DRINKS

30ml (1 fl oz) Canadian Whisky
30ml (1 fl oz) Dry Vermouth
15ml (½ fl oz) Campari
Twist of Lemon Peel

Pour Whisky, Vermouth and Campari into a mixing glass over ice. Stir and strain into a chilled cocktail glass. Twist lemon peel above drink and place remainder of peel into drink then serve.

Cherry Napoli

5.7% ALC/VOL • 0.9 STD DRINKS

30ml (1 fl oz) Campari
15ml (½ fl oz) Cherry Brandy
150ml (5 fl oz) Tonic Water
2 Cherries

Pour Campari and Brandy into a collins glass over ice then stir. Add tonic and stir gently. Garnish with cherries and serve.

Apple Byrrh

27.3% ALC/VOL • 1.4 STD DRINKS

30ml (1 fl oz) Calvados
15ml (½ fl oz) Byrrh
15ml (½ fl oz) Dry Vermouth
3 dashes Fresh Lemon Juice
Twist of Lemon Peel

Pour Calvados, Byrrh, Vermouth and juice into a cocktail shaker over ice. Shake and strain into a chilled cocktail glass. Twist lemon peel above drink and place remainder of peel into drink then serve.

Victor Bravo

29.7% ALC/VOL • 2.1 STD DRINKS

30ml (1 fl oz) Brandy
30ml (1 fl oz) Dry Gin

30ml (1 fl oz) Sweet Vermouth
Green Olive

Pour Brandy, Gin and Vermouth into a mixing glass over ice. Stir and strain into a chilled cocktail glass. Garnish with an olive and serve.

Orange Kiwi Cream

8.5% ALC/VOL • 1.1 STD DRINKS

45ml (1½ fl oz) Dry Vermouth
15ml (½ fl oz) Drambuie
45ml (1½ fl oz) Fresh Orange Juice
45ml (1½ fl oz) Pineapple Juice
15ml (½ fl oz) Fresh Cream
Slice of Kiwi Fruit
Slice of Orange
Slice of Pineapple

Pour Vermouth, Drambuie, juices and cream into a blender over cracked ice. Blend and strain into a chilled old-fashioned glass. Garnish with a slice of kiwi fruit, orange and pineapple then serve.

Duchess

24.3% ALC/VOL • 1.7 STD DRINKS

30ml (1 fl oz) Dry Vermouth
30ml (1 fl oz) Pernod
30ml (1 fl oz) Sweet Vermouth

Pour ingredients into a cocktail shaker over ice and shake. Strain into a chilled cocktail glass and serve.

Bloody Mary

11% ALC/VOL • 1.8 STD DRINKS

60ml (2 fl oz) Vodka
120ml (4 fl oz) Tomato Juice (chilled)
15ml (½ fl oz) Fresh Lemon Juice
1 teaspoon Worcestershire Sauce
2 drops Tabasco Sauce
Pinch of Pepper
Pinch of Salt
Slice of Lemon
Stick of Celery

Pour lemon juice and sauces into a highball glass over ice then stir. Add pepper and salt. Add more ice and Vodka. Add tomato juice and stir. Garnish with a slice of lemon and stick of celery then serve.

Concrete Coffin

40% ALC/VOL • 2.8 STD DRINKS

60ml (2 fl oz) Drambuie
30ml (1 fl oz) Pernod

Pour ingredients into an old-fashioned glass filled with ice, stir and serve.

Burfentailor

23.1% ALC/VOL • 1.5 STD DRINKS

30ml (1 fl oz) Sweet Vermouth
15ml (½ fl oz) Brandy
15ml (½ fl oz) Gin
10ml (⅓ fl oz) Pernod
5ml (⅙ fl oz) Grenadine
10ml (⅓ fl oz) Fresh Lemon Juice
Maraschino Cherry

Pour Vermouth, Brandy, Gin, Pernod, Grenadine and juice into a cocktail shaker over ice. Shake and strain into an old-fashioned glass over ice. Garnish with a cherry and serve.

Dubonnet Cocktail

26.5% ALC/VOL • 1.3 STD DRINKS

30ml (1 fl oz) Dubonnet
30ml (1 fl oz) Gin
Wedge of Lemon

Pour Dubonnet and Gin into a mixing glass over ice. Stir and strain into a chilled cocktail glass. Garnish with a wedge of lemon and serve.

Sparkling Apéritif

7.6% ALC/VOL • 1.1 STD DRINKS

15ml (½ fl oz) Dry Sherry
15ml (½ fl oz) Dry Vermouth
15ml (½ fl oz) Dubonnet
15ml (½ fl oz) Gin
Dash Grand Marnier
120ml (4 fl oz) Tonic Water
Slice of Orange

Pour Sherry, Vermouth, Dubonnet, Gin and Grand Marnier into a collins glass over ice then stir. Add tonic and stir gently. Garnish with a slice of orange and serve.

Bresnan

13.9% ALC/VOL • 0.9 STD DRINKS

45ml (1½ fl oz) Sweet Vermouth
30ml (1 fl oz) Dry Vermouth
5ml (⅙ fl oz) Crème De Cassis
15ml (½ fl oz) Fresh Lemon Juice

Pour ingredients into a cocktail shaker over ice and shake. Strain into a chilled cocktail glass and serve.

Belle of Ellis Island

22.2% ALC/VOL • 1.5 STD DRINKS

60ml (2 fl oz) Dry Vermouth
15ml (½ fl oz) Brandy
5ml (⅙ fl oz) Cointreau
2 dashes Orange Bitters
½ teaspoon Sugar Syrup
Wedge of Lemon

Pour Vermouth, Brandy, Cointreau, Bitters and sugar into a cocktail shaker over ice. Shake and strain into a chilled cocktail glass. Garnish with a wedge of lemon and serve.

Ferrari

21.1% ALC/VOL • 1.4 STD DRINKS

60ml (2 fl oz) Dry Vermouth
23ml (¾ fl oz) Amaretto
Dash Angostura Bitters

Wedge of Lemon

Pour Vermouth, Amaretto and Bitters into an old-fashioned glass over ice then stir. Garnish with a wedge of lemon and serve.

Old Time Appetizer

27.6% ALC/VOL • 1.1 STD DRINKS

23ml (¾ fl oz) Dubonnet
23ml (¾ fl oz) Rye Whiskey
2 dashes Curaçao
2 dashes Pernod
Dash Peychaud's Bitters
Slice of Orange
Slice of Pineapple
Twist of Lemon Peel

Pour Dubonnet, Whiskey, Curaçao, Pernod and Bitters into an old-fashioned glass over ice then stir. Add lemon peel, garnish with a slice of orange and pineapple then serve.

Allies

27.7% ALC/VOL • 2 STD DRINKS

45ml (1½ fl oz) Dry Vermouth
45ml (1½ fl oz) Gin
2 dashes Kümmel

Pour ingredients into a mixing glass over ice and stir. Strain into a chilled cocktail glass and serve.

Chelsea

24.7% ALC/VOL • 1.4 STD DRINKS

30ml (1 fl oz) Dry Vermouth
23ml (¾ fl oz) Bourbon
5ml (1⁄6 fl oz) Blackberry Brandy
3 dashes Cointreau
10ml (⅓ fl oz) Fresh Lemon Juice
Wedge of Lemon

Pour Vermouth, Bourbon, Brandy, Cointreau and juice into a cocktail shaker over ice. Shake and strain into a chilled cocktail glass. Garnish with a wedge of lemon and serve.

Picon on the Rocks

17.9% ALC/VOL • 0.9 STD DRINKS

45ml (1½ fl oz) Amer Picon
15ml (½ fl oz) Fresh Lemon Juice
5ml (1⁄6 fl oz) Soda Water
Slice of Lemon

Pour Amer Picon and juice into an old-fashioned glass over ice then stir. Add soda – do not stir, then garnish with a slice of lemon and serve.

Moi?

7.9% ALC/VOL • 1.5 STD DRINKS

60ml (2 fl oz) Dry Vermouth
15ml (½ fl oz) Gin
10ml (⅓ fl oz) Crème De Cassis
30ml (1 fl oz) Fresh Lemon Juice
120ml (4 fl oz) Tonic Water
Wedge of Lemon

Pour Vermouth, Gin, Cassis and juice into a cocktail shaker over ice. Shake and strain into a collins glass over ice. Add tonic and stir gently. Garnish with a wedge of lemon and serve.

Soft Rock

11.9% ALC/VOL • 1.7 STD DRINKS

60ml (2 fl oz) Lillet
30ml (1 fl oz) California Brandy
90ml (3 fl oz) Fresh Orange Juice
Slice of Orange (dipped in sugar syrup)

Pour Lillet, Brandy and juice into a cocktail shaker over ice. Shake and strain into an old-fashioned glass over ice. Add a slice of orange and serve.

Bon Appetit

18.3% ALC/VOL • 2 STD DRINKS

45ml (1½ fl oz) Dry Gin
45ml (1½ fl oz) Dubonnet
3 dashes Angostura Bitters
45ml (1½ fl oz) Fresh Orange Juice
Slice of Orange

Pour Gin, Dubonnet, Bitters and juice into a cocktail shaker over ice. Shake and strain into a chilled cocktail glass. Garnish with a slice of orange and serve.

Sacred Mountain of the Pekingese Cloud Gods

11.7% ALC/VOL • 1.1 STD DRINKS

30ml (1 fl oz) Dry Vermouth
15ml (½ fl oz) Southern Comfort
10ml (⅓ fl oz) Blue Curaçao
60ml (2 fl oz) Fresh Orange Juice

Pour Vermouth and Southern Comfort into an old-fashioned glass over ice then stir. Add juice – do not stir. Add Curaçao by pouring into centre of drink – do not stir, then serve with a straw.

Campari Russian

16.5% ALC/VOL • 2.2 STD DRINKS

120ml (4 fl oz) Champagne
30ml (1 fl oz) Campari
15ml (½ fl oz) Vodka
Dash Orange Syrup
Slice of Orange

Pour Campari, Vodka and syrup into a cocktail shaker over ice. Shake and strain into a chilled champagne flute. Add Champagne and stir gently. Garnish with a slice of orange and serve.

Cardinal Cocktail

26.6% ALC/VOL • 1.4 STD DRINKS

23ml (¾ fl oz) Campari
23ml (¾ fl oz) Dry Vermouth
23ml (¾ fl oz) Gin
Twist of Lemon Peel

Pour Campari, Vermouth and Gin into a mixing glass over ice. Stir and strain into a chilled cocktail glass. Twist lemon peel above drink and place remainder of peel into drink then serve.

Shooing Away the Tribes of the Night

27.4% ALC/VOL • 1.3 STD DRINKS

30ml (1 fl oz) Dry Vermouth
23ml (¾ fl oz) Brandy
3 dashes Cointreau
Dash Angostura Bitters
Dash Cherry Brandy
Dash Ricard
Maraschino Cherry
Slice of Orange

Pour Vermouth, Brandies, Cointreau, Bitters and Ricard into an old-fashioned glass over ice then stir. Garnish with a cherry and slice of orange then serve.

Southwest One

20.6% ALC/VOL • 1.1 STD DRINKS

23ml (¾ fl oz) Campari
23ml (¾ fl oz) Vodka
23ml (¾ fl oz) Fresh Orange Juice

Pour ingredients into a cocktail shaker over ice and shake. Strain into a chilled cocktail glass and serve.

Bittersweet

17.1% ALC/VOL • 0.8 STD DRINKS

30ml (1 fl oz) Dry Vermouth
30ml (1 fl oz) Sweet Vermouth
Dash Angostura Bitters
Dash Orange Bitters
Twist of Orange Peel

Pour Vermouths and Bitters into a mixing glass over ice. Stir and strain into a chilled cocktail glass. Twist orange peel above drink and place remainder of peel into drink then serve.

Diabolo

17.8% ALC/VOL • 1.1 STD DRINKS

45ml (1½ fl oz) Dry White Port
30ml (1 fl oz) Dry Vermouth
Dash Fresh Lemon Juice
Twist of Lemon Peel

Pour Port, Vermouth and juice into a cocktail shaker over ice. Shake and strain into a chilled cocktail glass. Twist lemon peel above drink and place remainder of peel into drink then serve.

Firenze Appetizer

33.7% ALC/VOL • 2.7 STD DRINKS

40ml (1⅓ fl oz) Brandy
30ml (1 fl oz) Fernet Branca
30ml (1 fl oz) Green Crème De Menthe

Pour ingredients into a mixing glass over ice and stir. Strain into a chilled cocktail glass and serve.

Sherry Cocktail

18% ALC/VOL • 1.3 STD DRINKS

60ml (2 fl oz) Dry Sherry
30ml (1 fl oz) Dry Vermouth

Pour ingredients into a mixing glass over ice and stir. Strain into a chilled cocktail glass and serve.

Trio

23.3% ALC/VOL • 1.7 STD DRINKS

This drink is also known as Trinity, p 318.

Inca

23.8% ALC/VOL • 1.8 STD DRINKS

30ml (1 fl oz) Dry Gin
30ml (1 fl oz) Dry Sherry
30ml (1 fl oz) Dry Vermouth
2 dashes Orange Bitters
2 dashes Sugar Syrup
Twist of Orange Peel

Pour Gin, Sherry, Vermouth, Bitters and sugar into a mixing glass over ice. Stir and strain into a chilled cocktail glass. Twist orange peel above drink and place remainder of peel into drink then serve.

French Kiss Apéritif

16.5% ALC/VOL • 1.2 STD DRINKS

45ml (1½ fl oz) Dry Vermouth
45ml (1½ fl oz) Sweet Vermouth
Wedge of Lemon

Pour Vermouths into an old-fashioned glass over ice and stir. Garnish with a wedge of lemon and serve.

Vermouth Triple Sec

24.5% ALC/VOL • 1.2 STD DRINKS

30ml (1 fl oz) Dry Vermouth
15ml (½ fl oz) Gin
15ml (½ fl oz) Triple Sec
2 dashes Orange Bitters
Twist of Lemon Peel

Pour Vermouth, Gin, Triple Sec and Bitters into a cocktail shaker over ice. Shake and strain into a chilled cocktail glass. Twist lemon peel above drink and place remainder of peel into drink then serve.

Byrrh Cassis

13.7% ALC/VOL • 0.7 STD DRINKS

45ml (1½ fl oz) Byrrh
8ml (¼ fl oz) Crème De Cassis
15ml (½ fl oz) Fresh Lemon Juice
Slice of Lemon

Pour Byrrh, Cassis and juice into a cocktail shaker over ice. Shake and strain into an old-fashioned glass over ice. Add a splash of soda water if desired and add a slice of lemon then serve.

Tokyo Bloody Mary

5.3% ALC/VOL • 0.8 STD DRINKS

60ml (2 fl oz) Sake
5ml (1/6 fl oz) Dry Sherry
120ml (4 fl oz) Tomato Juice (chilled)
1 teaspoon Tabasco Sauce
½ teaspoon Worcestershire Sauce
Pinch of Celery Salt
Pinch of Pepper
Stick of Celery

Pour sauces into a highball glass over ice then add salt and pepper. Add more ice and stir. Add Sake, Sherry and juice then stir well. Garnish with a stick of celery and serve.

Mary's Delight

23.8% ALC/VOL • 1.4 STD DRINKS

45ml (1½ fl oz) Sweet Vermouth
30ml (1 fl oz) Brandy
Dash Orange Bitters

Pour ingredients into a mixing glass over ice and stir. Strain into a chilled cocktail glass and serve.

Zanzibar

19.7% ALC/VOL • 2 STD DRINKS

75ml (2½ fl oz) Dry Vermouth
30ml (1 fl oz) Dry Gin
Dash Orange Bitters
15ml (½ fl oz) Fresh Lemon Juice
1 teaspoon Sugar Syrup

Pour ingredients into a cocktail shaker over ice and shake. Strain into a chilled cocktail glass and serve.

This drink may also be served in an old-fashioned glass over ice if desired.

Major Billy

18.4% ALC/VOL • 1.1 STD DRINKS

23ml (¾ fl oz) Dry Vermouth
23ml (¾ fl oz) Sweet Vermouth
15ml (½ fl oz) Gin
2 dashes Orange Bitters
10ml (⅓ fl oz) Fresh Orange Juice

Pour ingredients into a cocktail shaker over ice and shake. Strain into a chilled cocktail glass and serve.

Dubonnet Fizz

5.3% ALC/VOL • 0.8 STD DRINKS

60ml (2 fl oz) Dubonnet
15ml (½ fl oz) Fresh Lemon Juice
15ml (½ fl oz) Fresh Orange Juice
90ml (3 fl oz) Soda Water
Slice of Lemon
Slice of Orange

Pour Dubonnet and juices into a cocktail shaker over ice. Shake and strain into a highball glass over ice. Add soda and stir gently. Garnish with a slice of lemon and orange then serve.

Byrrh Cocktail

27% ALC/VOL • 1.6 STD DRINKS

38ml (1¼ fl oz) Byrrh
38ml (1¼ fl oz) Gin
Twist of Lemon Peel

Pour Byrrh and Gin into a mixing glass over ice. Stir and strain into an old-fashioned glass over ice. Twist lemon peel above drink and place remainder of peel into drink then serve.

Earl of Sardinia

7.7% ALC/VOL • 1.1 STD DRINKS

45ml (1½ fl oz) Campari
15ml (½ fl oz) Crème De Cassis
5ml (1/6 fl oz) Grenadine
90ml (3 fl oz) Grapefruit Juice
30ml (1 fl oz) Pineapple Juice

Pour ingredients into a cocktail shaker over ice and shake. Strain into an old-fashioned glass over crushed ice and serve.

Americano

9.2% ALC/VOL • 1.3 STD DRINKS

60ml (2 fl oz) Sweet Vermouth
30ml (1 fl oz) Campari
90ml (3 fl oz) Soda Water
Twist of Lemon Peel

Pour Vermouth and Campari into a highball glass over ice. Add lemon peel and stir. Add soda, stir gently and serve.

Same Old Song

16.4% ALC/VOL • 1.4 STD DRINKS

30ml (1 fl oz) Gin
30ml (1 fl oz) Sweet Vermouth
15ml (½ fl oz) Dry Vermouth
Dash Orange Bitters
30ml (1 fl oz) Fresh Orange Juice
5ml (1/6 fl oz) Fresh Lemon Juice
Slice of Orange

Pour Gin, Vermouths, Bitters and juices into a cocktail shaker over ice. Shake and strain into a chilled cocktail glass. Garnish with a slice of orange and serve.

True Trixie

26.8% ALC/VOL • 2.2 STD DRINKS

60ml (2 fl oz) Campari
23ml (¾ fl oz) Cointreau
23ml (¾ fl oz) Dry Vermouth

Pour ingredients into a mixing glass over ice and stir. Strain into an old-fashioned glass over ice and serve.

Atomic Powered

27.4% ALC/VOL • 1.4 STD DRINKS

30ml (1 fl oz) Dry Vermouth
30ml (1 fl oz) Dry Gin
4 dashes Cherry Brandy
4 drops Pernod
Twist of Lemon Peel

Pour Vermouth, Gin, Brandy and Pernod into a cocktail shaker over ice. Shake and strain into a chilled cocktail glass. Garnish with lemon peel and serve.

Appetizer

12% ALC/VOL • 0.6 STD DRINKS

45ml (1½ fl oz) Dubonnet
15ml (½ fl oz) Fresh Orange Juice
Slice of Orange

Pour Dubonnet and juice into a cocktail shaker over ice. Shake and strain into a chilled cocktail glass. Garnish with a slice of orange and serve.

Downhill Cocktail

24.3% ALC/VOL • 1.5 STD DRINKS

30ml (1 fl oz) Sweet Sherry
15ml (½ fl oz) Dry Vermouth
15ml (½ fl oz) Gin
15ml (½ fl oz) Orange Curaçao
5ml (1/6 fl oz) Cognac
Cherry
Slice of Orange

Pour Sherry, Vermouth, Gin, Curaçao and Cognac into a mixing glass over ice. Stir and strain into an old-fashioned glass over cracked ice. Garnish with a cherry and slice of orange then serve with 2 straws.

Bloody Brit

31% ALC/VOL • 1.5 STD DRINKS

30ml (1 fl oz) Campari
30ml (1 fl oz) Dry Gin

Pour ingredients into a mixing glass over ice and stir. Strain into a chilled old-fashioned glass and serve with a swizzle stick.

Gadzooks

24.5% ALC/VOL • 2 STD DRINKS

30ml (1 fl oz) Apricot Brandy
30ml (1 fl oz) Dry Vermouth
30ml (1 fl oz) Gin
15ml (½ fl oz) Cherry Brandy
5ml (1/6 fl oz) Fresh Lime Juice

Pour ingredients into a cocktail shaker over ice and shake. Strain into a chilled old-fashioned glass and serve.

Coronation

23.6% ALC/VOL • 1.7 STD DRINKS

30ml (1 fl oz) Dry Gin
30ml (1 fl oz) Dry Vermouth
30ml (1 fl oz) Dubonnet

Pour ingredients into a mixing glass over ice and stir. Strain into a chilled cocktail glass and serve.
This drink is also known as Salomé.

Piggot's Preference

26.6% ALC/VOL • 1.7 STD DRINKS

45ml (1½ fl oz) Dry Vermouth
15ml (½ fl oz) Southern Comfort
10ml (⅓ fl oz) Cointreau
10ml (⅓ fl oz) Light Rum
Dash Orange Bitters
Maraschino Cherry

Pour Vermouth, Southern Comfort, Cointreau, Rum and Bitters into a mixing glass over ice. Stir and strain into a chilled cocktail glass. Garnish with a cherry and serve.

Ti-Punch

18.5% ALC/VOL • 1.8 STD DRINKS

60ml (2 fl oz) Light Rum
30ml (1 fl oz) Sugar Syrup
1 Fresh Lime (sliced thinly into ½ rings)

Place slices of lime into a chilled old-fashioned glass and muddle to release juice. Add ice and Rum. Add sugar and stir well then serve with 2 short straws.

Green Gables Cocktail

27.5% ALC/VOL • 1.8 STD DRINKS

45ml (1½ fl oz) Sweet Vermouth
30ml (1 fl oz) Gin

10ml (⅓ fl oz) Green
Chartreuse

Pour ingredients into a mixing glass over ice and stir. Strain into a chilled cocktail glass and serve.

Addington

16.5% ALC/VOL • 0.8 STD DRINKS

30ml (1 fl oz) Dry Vermouth
30ml (1 fl oz) Sweet Vermouth

Pour ingredients into a mixing glass over ice and stir. Strain into a chilled cocktail glass and serve.

Salomé

23.6% ALC/VOL • 1.7 STD DRINKS

This drink is also known as Coronation, p 317.

Jeff Tracy

25.5% ALC/VOL • 1.9 STD DRINKS

30ml (1 fl oz) Cherry Brandy
30ml (1 fl oz) Dry Vermouth
30ml (1 fl oz) Gin
5ml (1/6 fl oz) Sweet Vermouth
Maraschino Cherry

Pour Brandy, Vermouths and Gin into a mixing glass over ice. Stir and strain into a chilled cocktail glass. Garnish with a cherry and serve.

Head-for-the-Hills

10.8% ALC/VOL • 1.2 STD DRINKS

60ml (2 fl oz) Dry Vermouth
15ml (½ fl oz) White Curaçao
60ml (2 fl oz) Soda Water
Wedge of Lemon

Pour Vermouth and Curaçao into an old-fashioned glass over ice then stir. Add soda and stir gently. Garnish with a wedge of lemon and serve.

Bloody Coochie

10.6% ALC/VOL • 3.5 STD DRINKS

90ml (3 fl oz) Vodka
45ml (1½ fl oz) Triple Sec
120ml (4 fl oz) Fruit Punch
120ml (4 fl oz) Fresh
Orange Juice
45ml (1½ fl oz) Sweet and
Sour Mix

Pour ingredients into a hurricane glass filled with ice, stir and serve.

Trinity

23.3% ALC/VOL • 1.7 STD DRINKS

30ml (1 fl oz) Dry Gin
30ml (1 fl oz) Dry Vermouth
30ml (1 fl oz) Sweet Vermouth

Pour ingredients into a mixing glass over ice and stir. Strain into a chilled cocktail glass and serve.
This drink is also known as Trio, p 315.

Thanksgiving Cocktail

23.9% ALC/VOL • 1.5 STD DRINKS

30ml (1 fl oz) Dry Vermouth
23ml (¾ fl oz) Apricot Brandy
23ml (¾ fl oz) Gin
3 dashes Crème De Cassis
3 dashes Fresh Lemon Juice

Pour ingredients into a cocktail shaker over ice and shake. Strain into a chilled cocktail glass and serve.

Lying with the Tigress

25.6% ALC/VOL • 1.6 STD DRINKS

45ml (1½ fl oz) Dry Vermouth
30ml (1 fl oz) Light Rum
Dash Orange Bitters
Dash Rose's Lime Juice

Pour ingredients into a mixing glass over ice and stir. Strain into a chilled cocktail glass and serve.

Hilgert Cocktail

24.3% ALC/VOL • 1.2 STD DRINKS

30ml (1 fl oz) Dry Vermouth
23ml (¾ fl oz) Gin
3 dashes Maraschino Liqueur
Dash Angostura Bitters
5ml (1/6 fl oz) Grapefruit Juice

Pour ingredients into a cocktail shaker over ice and shake. Strain into a chilled cocktail glass and serve.

Mr. New Yorker

21.7% ALC/VOL • 1.4 STD DRINKS

53ml (1¾ fl oz) Dry Vermouth
15ml (½ fl oz) Dry Sherry
15ml (½ fl oz) Dry Gin
Dash Cointreau

Pour ingredients into a mixing glass over ice and stir. Strain into a chilled cocktail glass and serve.

Blonde Jenny

18.3% ALC/VOL • 1.1 STD DRINKS

45ml (1½ fl oz) Dry Vermouth
15ml (½ fl oz) Gin
Dash Orange Bitters
15ml (½ fl oz) Fresh
Orange Juice
Slice of Orange

Pour Vermouth, Gin, Bitters and juice into a cocktail shaker over ice. Shake and strain into a chilled cocktail glass. Garnish with a slice of orange and serve.

Matinée Apéritif

21.8% ALC/VOL • 1.7 STD DRINKS

30ml (1 fl oz) Sweet Vermouth
23ml (¾ fl oz) Gin

15ml (½ fl oz) Green Chartreuse
Dash Orange Bitters
30ml (1 fl oz) Fresh Orange Juice

Pour ingredients into a cocktail shaker over ice and shake. Strain into a chilled cocktail glass and serve.

Hanky Panky Cocktail

28.3% ALC/VOL • 0.7 STD DRINKS

15ml (½ fl oz) Dry Vermouth
15ml (½ fl oz) Gin
2 dashes Fernet Branca
Twist of Orange Peel

Pour Vermouth, Gin, and Fernet Branca into a cocktail shaker over ice. Shake and strain into a chilled cocktail glass. Twist orange peel above drink and discard remainder of peel then serve.

Allies Requirements

26.5% ALC/VOL • 1.7 STD DRINKS

45ml (1½ fl oz) Dry Vermouth
30ml (1 fl oz) Gin
3 dashes Pernod
Dash Angostura Bitters

Pour ingredients into a mixing glass over ice and stir. Strain into a chilled cocktail glass and serve.

Strong-Armed Chris Returns to the Den

21.5% ALC/VOL • 1.4 STD DRINKS

30ml (1 fl oz) Dry Vermouth
23ml (¾ fl oz) Maraschino Liqueur
23ml (¾ fl oz) White Crème De Cacao
5ml (1/6 fl oz) Sweet Vermouth
Maraschino Cherry

Pour Vermouths, Liqueur and Cacao into a mixing glass over ice. Stir and strain into a chilled cocktail glass. Garnish with a cherry and serve.

Vermouth Cocktail

15.9% ALC/VOL • 0.8 STD DRINKS

60ml (2 fl oz) Sweet Vermouth
2 dashes Angostura Bitters
Slice of Lemon

Pour Vermouth and Bitters into a mixing glass over ice. Stir and strain into a chilled cocktail glass. Garnish with a slice of lemon and serve.

Adonis

17.2% ALC/VOL • 0.6 STD DRINKS

30ml (1 fl oz) Dry Sherry
15ml (½ fl oz) Sweet Vermouth
Dash Orange Bitters
Slice of Orange

Pour Sherry, Vermouth and Bitters into a mixing glass over ice. Stir and strain into a chilled cocktail glass. Garnish with a slice of orange and serve.

Martunia

31.9% ALC/VOL • 3 STD DRINKS

90ml (3 fl oz) Gin
15ml (½ fl oz) Dry Vermouth
15ml (½ fl oz) Sweet Vermouth
Pansy Flower

Pour Gin and Vermouths into a mixing glass over ice. Stir and strain into a chilled cocktail glass. Float a flower on top and serve.

One Exciting Night

21.9% ALC/VOL • 1.7 STD DRINKS

30ml (1 fl oz) Dry Vermouth
30ml (1 fl oz) Gin
30ml (1 fl oz) Sweet Vermouth
Dash Grenadine
5ml (1/6 fl oz) Fresh Orange Juice
Twist of Orange Peel

Prepare a cocktail glass with a sugar frosted rim. Pour Vermouths, Gin, Grenadine and juice into a cocktail shaker over ice. Shake and strain into prepared glass. Garnish with orange peel and serve.

Burn's Night Special

26.7% ALC/VOL • 1.8 STD DRINKS

45ml (1½ fl oz) Sweet Vermouth
30ml (1 fl oz) Scotch Whisky
10ml (⅓ fl oz) Bénédictine

Pour ingredients into a mixing glass over ice and stir. Strain into a chilled cocktail glass and serve.

Much Fuss for the Conquering Hero

22.1% ALC/VOL • 1.3 STD DRINKS

30ml (1 fl oz) Sweet Vermouth
23ml (¾ fl oz) Applejack
10ml (⅓ fl oz) Apricot Brandy
2 dashes Orange Bitters
5ml (1/6 fl oz) Fresh Lemon Juice
5ml (1/6 fl oz) Pineapple Juice

Pour ingredients into a cocktail shaker over ice and shake. Strain into a chilled cocktail glass and serve.

Negroni – Zimbabwe Style

11.4% ALC/VOL • 0.9 STD DRINKS

20ml (⅔ fl oz) Gin
10ml (⅓ fl oz) Campari
10ml (⅓ fl oz) Sweet Vermouth
60ml (2 fl oz) Fresh Orange Juice

Prepare an old-fashioned glass with a sugar frosted rim and add ice. Pour ingredients into a cocktail shaker over ice and shake. Strain into prepared glass and serve.

Mayflower Cocktail

22.2% ALC/VOL • 1.5 STD DRINKS

45ml (1½ fl oz) Sweet Vermouth
15ml (½ fl oz) Brandy
15ml (½ fl oz) Dry Vermouth
5ml (1/6 fl oz) Cointreau
5ml (1/6 fl oz) Pernod
2 dashes Orange Bitters

Pour ingredients into a mixing glass over ice and stir. Strain into a chilled cocktail glass and serve.

Arena

17.1% ALC/VOL • 0.8 STD DRINKS

20ml (⅔ fl oz) Dry Vermouth
20ml (⅔ fl oz) Sweet Vermouth
20ml (⅔ fl oz) Sherry
Dash Orange Bitters

Pour ingredients into a mixing glass over ice and stir. Strain into a chilled cocktail glass and serve.

Bloody Caesar

7.3% ALC/VOL • 1.3 STD DRINKS

45ml (1½ fl oz) Vodka
180ml (6 fl oz) Clamato Juice
Dash Tabasco Sauce
Dash Worcestershire Sauce
Pinch of Pepper
Pinch of Salt
Stick of Celery
Wedge of Lime

Pour Vodka into a highball glass over ice and add sauces. Add juice and stir. Sprinkle pepper and salt on top. Garnish with a stick of celery and wedge of lime then serve.

Dutch Apéritif

31.9% ALC/VOL • 2.3 STD DRINKS

60ml (2 fl oz) Hollands Gin
15ml (½ fl oz) Dry Vermouth
15ml (½ fl oz) Orange Curaçao

Pour ingredients into a mixing glass over ice and stir. Strain into a chilled cocktail glass and serve.

Big Red

18.6% ALC/VOL • 1 STD DRINK

30ml (1 fl oz) Sweet Vermouth
23ml (¾ fl oz) Dry Vermouth
15ml (½ fl oz) Sloe Gin
2 dashes Orange Bitters
Slice of Orange

Pour Vermouths, Gin and Bitters into an old-fashioned glass over ice then stir. Garnish with a slice of orange and serve.

Leo the Lion

21.9% ALC/VOL • 1.4 STD DRINKS

60ml (2 fl oz) Dry Vermouth
15ml (½ fl oz) Brandy
5ml (1/6 fl oz) White Crème De Menthe

Pour ingredients into a mixing glass over ice and stir. Strain into a chilled cocktail glass and serve.

Za Za

26.5% ALC/VOL • 1.9 STD DRINKS

45ml (1½ fl oz) Dubonnet
45ml (1½ fl oz) Gin
Dash Campari
Twist of Lemon Peel

Pour Dubonnet, Gin and Campari into a cocktail shaker over ice. Shake and strain into a chilled cocktail glass. Twist lemon peel above drink and place remainder of peel into drink then serve.

Grapefruit Apéritif

12.8% ALC/VOL • 0.6 STD DRINKS

30ml (1 fl oz) Dry Vermouth
15ml (½ fl oz) Sweet Vermouth
15ml (½ fl oz) Grapefruit Juice
Slice of Grapefruit

Pour Vermouths and juice into an old-fashioned glass over ice then stir. Garnish with a slice of grapefruit and serve.

Knock-Out Cocktail

27.7% ALC/VOL • 1.4 STD DRINKS

23ml (¾ fl oz) Dry Vermouth
23ml (¾ fl oz) Gin
15ml (½ fl oz) Anisette
5ml (1/6 fl oz) White Crème De Menthe
Maraschino Cherry

Pour Vermouth, Gin, Anisette and Crème De Menthe into a mixing glass over ice. Stir and strain into a chilled cocktail glass. Garnish with a cherry and serve.

Greenbrier

18.2% ALC/VOL • 1.3 STD DRINKS

60ml (2 fl oz) Dry Sherry
30ml (1 fl oz) Dry Vermouth
2 dashes Campari
Sprig of Fresh Mint

Pour Sherry, Vermouth and Campari into a mixing glass over ice. Stir and strain into a chilled cocktail glass. Garnish with a sprig of mint and serve.

Bloody Marie

12% ALC/VOL • 1.4 STD DRINKS

45ml (1½ fl oz) Vodka
5 drops Pernod
90ml (3 fl oz) Tomato Juice (chilled)
3 dashes Fresh Lemon Juice
8 drops Tabasco Sauce
5 drops Worcestershire Sauce

Pour ingredients into a cocktail shaker over ice and shake. Strain into a highball glass over ice and serve.

Maurice

21.7% ALC/VOL • 1.3 STD DRINKS

30ml (1 fl oz) Gin
15ml (½ fl oz) Dry Vermouth
15ml (½ fl oz) Sweet Vermouth
Dash Angostura Bitters
15ml (½ fl oz) Fresh Orange Juice

Pour ingredients into a cocktail shaker over ice and shake. Strain into a chilled cocktail glass and serve.

Vermouth Sparkle

6.1% ALC/VOL • 0.9 STD DRINKS

60ml (2 fl oz) Dry Vermouth
5ml (1/6 fl oz) Sweet Vermouth
5ml (1/6 fl oz) Grenadine
150ml (5 fl oz) Dry Ginger Ale

Pour Vermouths and Grenadine into a cocktail shaker over ice. Shake and strain into a collins glass half filled with ice. Add Ginger Ale, stir gently and serve.
This drink is also known as Gladys Delight.

Kaytee

18.8% ALC/VOL • 1.2 STD DRINKS

45ml (1½ fl oz) Dry Vermouth
30ml (1 fl oz) Dry Sherry
3 dashes Pernod

Pour ingredients into a mixing glass over ice and stir. Strain into a chilled cocktail glass and serve.

Bloody Mariana

9.1% ALC/VOL • 1.8 STD DRINKS

60ml (2 fl oz) Vodka
180ml (6 fl oz) Tomato Juice (chilled)
5ml (1/6 fl oz) Fresh Lime Juice
Dash Tabasco Sauce
Dash Worcestershire Sauce
Pinch of Celery Salt
Pinch of Oregano
Pinch of Pepper

Pour Vodka, juices and sauces into a cocktail shaker over ice then add remaining ingredients. Shake and strain into a highball glass over ice then serve.

Mary Garden Cocktail

16.7% ALC/VOL • 0.9 STD DRINKS

45ml (1½ fl oz) Dubonnet
23ml (¾ fl oz) Dry Vermouth

Pour ingredients into a mixing glass over ice and stir. Strain into a chilled cocktail glass and serve.

Napoli

26.1% ALC/VOL • 1.9 STD DRINKS

30ml (1 fl oz) Campari
30ml (1 fl oz) Vodka
15ml (½ fl oz) Dry Vermouth
15ml (½ fl oz) Sweet Vermouth
Twist of Orange Peel

Pour Campari, Vodka and Vermouths into a mixing glass over ice. Stir and strain into an old-fashioned glass over ice. Top up with soda water if desired and stir gently. Garnish with orange peel and serve.

Apertivo Cocktail

36.9% ALC/VOL • 2.3 STD DRINKS

45ml (1½ fl oz) Gin
30ml (1 fl oz) Sambuca
3 dashes Orange Bitters

Pour ingredients into a cocktail shaker over ice and shake. Strain into a chilled cocktail glass and serve.

Negroni

28.6% ALC/VOL • 2.7 STD DRINKS

60ml (2 fl oz) Gin
30ml (1 fl oz) Campari
30ml (1 fl oz) Sweet Vermouth
Slice of Orange

Pour Gin, Campari and Vermouth into a mixing glass over ice. Stir and strain into a chilled brandy balloon over a few ice cubes. Top up with soda water if desired and stir gently. Garnish with a slice of orange and serve.

Magique

25% ALC/VOL • 1.7 STD DRINKS

45ml (1½ fl oz) Dry Vermouth
30ml (1 fl oz) Gin
10ml (⅓ fl oz) Crème De Cassis

Pour ingredients into a mixing glass over ice and stir. Strain into a chilled cocktail glass and serve.

Alfa Romeo

18.9% ALC/VOL • 1.8 STD DRINKS

60ml (2 fl oz) Sweet Vermouth
38ml (1¼ fl oz) Gin
Dash Campari
24ml (4/5 fl oz) Grenadine
Cherry

Pour Vermouth, Gin, Campari and Grenadine into a cocktail shaker over ice. Shake and strain into a chilled cocktail glass. Garnish with a cherry and serve.

Dancin' Bones

21.7% ALC/VOL • 1.1 STD DRINKS

45ml (1½ fl oz) Dry Vermouth
10ml (⅓ fl oz) Cherry Brandy
10ml (⅓ fl oz) Gin

Pour ingredients into a mixing glass over ice and stir. Strain into a chilled cocktail glass and serve.

Diplomat

17.2% ALC/VOL • 1.2 STD DRINKS

60ml (2 fl oz) Dry Vermouth
30ml (1 fl oz) Sweet Vermouth
Dash Maraschino Liqueur
Maraschino Cherry
Twist of Lemon Peel

Pour Vermouths and Liqueur into a mixing glass over ice. Stir and strain into a chilled cocktail glass. Twist lemon peel above drink and place remainder of peel into drink. Garnish with a cherry and serve.

Sweet Nan

28% ALC/VOL • 1.5 STD DRINKS

30ml (1 fl oz) Brandy
30ml (1 fl oz) Sweet Vermouth
10ml (⅓ fl oz) Bénédictine

Pour ingredients into an old-fashioned glass over ice, stir and serve.

Lone Tree

25.3% ALC/VOL • 2.1 STD DRINKS

45ml (1½ fl oz) Dry Gin
30ml (1 fl oz) Dry Vermouth
30ml (1 fl oz) Sweet Vermouth
2 dashes Orange Bitters
Maraschino Cherry

Pour Gin, Vermouths and Bitters into a cocktail shaker over ice. Shake and strain into a chilled cocktail glass. Garnish with a cherry and serve.

Mercenary

22.4% ALC/VOL • 1.4 STD DRINKS

60ml (2 fl oz) Dry Vermouth
15ml (½ fl oz) Armagnac
5ml (⅙ fl oz) Green Crème De Menthe

Pour ingredients into a mixing glass over ice and stir. Strain into a chilled cocktail glass and serve.

Estrella Dorado

28.5% ALC/VOL • 1.4 STD DRINKS

30ml (1 fl oz) Dry Gin
10ml (⅓ fl oz) Campari
10ml (⅓ fl oz) Cherry Brandy
10ml (⅓ fl oz) Dry Vermouth
2 dashes Fresh Lemon Juice

Pour ingredients into a cocktail shaker over ice and shake. Strain into a chilled cocktail glass and serve.

Pink Pussy

12.1% ALC/VOL • 1.7 STD DRINKS

60ml (2 fl oz) Campari
30ml (1 fl oz) Peach Brandy
Dash Egg White
90ml (3 fl oz) Bitter-Lemon Soda

Pour Campari, Brandy and egg white into a cocktail shaker over ice. Shake and strain into a highball glass over ice. Add soda, stir gently and serve.

Negroni Cooler

12.1% ALC/VOL • 1.9 STD DRINKS

45ml (1½ fl oz) Campari
45ml (1½ fl oz) Sweet Vermouth
15ml (½ fl oz) Gin
90ml (3 fl oz) Soda Water

Pour Campari, Vermouth and Gin into a cocktail shaker over ice. Shake and strain into a collins glass filled with ice. Add soda, stir gently and serve.

Merry Widow

17% ALC/VOL • 0.8 STD DRINKS

30ml (1 fl oz) Dry Vermouth
30ml (1 fl oz) Dubonnet
Twist of Lemon Peel

Pour Vermouth and Dubonnet into a mixing glass over ice. Stir and strain into a chilled cocktail glass. Garnish with lemon peel and serve.

Byrrh Cassis Cooler

5.8% ALC/VOL • 1 STD DRINK

60ml (2 fl oz) Byrrh
15ml (½ fl oz) Crème De Cassis
150ml (5 fl oz) Soda Water
Slice of Lemon

Pour Byrrh and Cassis into a collins glass over ice then stir. Add soda and stir gently. Garnish with a slice of lemon and serve.

Wysoosler

33.6% ALC/VOL • 2.1 STD DRINKS

30ml (1 fl oz) Sweet Vermouth
23ml (¾ fl oz) Gin
23ml (¾ fl oz) Green Chartreuse
2 dashes Orange Bitters

Pour ingredients into a mixing glass over ice and stir. Strain into a chilled cocktail glass and serve.

Soul Kiss No.2

12.3% ALC/VOL • 1.2 STD DRINKS

30ml (1 fl oz) Dubonnet
30ml (1 fl oz) Dry Vermouth
30ml (1 fl oz) Sweet Vermouth
30ml (1 fl oz) Fresh Orange Juice

Pour ingredients into a cocktail shaker over ice and shake. Strain into a cocktail glass over cracked ice and serve.

Shooters

Shooters originated in America where liquors such as Scotch Whisky or Bourbon were served in shot glasses, with other liqueurs added to metamorphosis.

The ingredients of each drink are required to be layered in order given to create a layered effect. Pour ingredients slowly over the back of a spoon that touches the inside rim of glass, allowing the liquid to flow slowly down the inside of glass. The heavier ingredients are usually poured first to create the greatest visual effect. The ingredients for some shooters are shaken or stirred over ice and then poured into selected glass to be served as a shooter or shot.

Shooters can be served in shot glasses, cocktail glasses, liqueur glasses, cordial glasses or test tubes and should be swallowed in one gulp.

Angel Bliss

44.2% ALC/VOL • 1.4 STD DRINKS

8ml (¼ fl oz) 151-Proof Bacardi
8ml (¼ fl oz) Blue Curaçao
23ml (¾ fl oz) Bourbon

Layer ingredients in order given into a shot glass and serve.

International Incident

24% ALC/VOL • 0.9 STD DRINKS

15ml (½ fl oz) Bailey's Irish Cream
8ml (¼ fl oz) Amaretto
8ml (¼ fl oz) Frangelico
8ml (¼ fl oz) Kahlúa
8ml (¼ fl oz) Vodka

Pour ingredients into a cocktail shaker over ice and shake. Strain into a chilled shot glass and serve.

Banana Split Shooter

18% ALC/VOL • 0.8 STD DRINKS

15ml (½ fl oz) Kahlúa
15ml (½ fl oz) Banana Liqueur
10ml (⅓ fl oz) Strawberry Liqueur
Fresh Whipped Cream

Layer ingredients in order given into a tall Dutch cordial glass, float cream on top and serve.

Honolulu Shooter

19.2% ALC/VOL • 0.6 STD DRINKS

20ml (⅔ fl oz) Gin
Dash Angostura Bitters
5ml (1/6 fl oz) Fresh Orange Juice
5ml (1/6 fl oz) Fresh Lemon Juice
5ml (1/6 fl oz) Pineapple Juice
5ml (1/6 fl oz) Pineapple Syrup

Pour ingredients into a cocktail shaker over ice and shake. Strain into a chilled cordial Lexington glass and serve.

After Eight

19.4% ALC/VOL • 0.6 STD DRINKS

12ml (⅖ fl oz) Kahlúa
10ml (⅓ fl oz) Green Crème De Menthe
18ml (⅗ fl oz) Bailey's Irish Cream

Layer ingredients in order given into a cordial Embassy glass and serve.

Screaming Death Shooter

34.6% ALC/VOL • 1.2 STD DRINKS

15ml (½ fl oz) Kahlúa
10ml (⅓ fl oz) Bourbon
10ml (⅓ fl oz) Bénédictine
5ml (1/6 fl oz) Tennessee Whiskey
5ml (1/6 fl oz) Over-Proof Golden Rum

Layer ingredients in order given into a tall Dutch cordial glass, ignite and shoot while flaming.

Margarita Shooter

26% ALC/VOL • 0.9 STD DRINKS

15ml (½ fl oz) Cointreau
15ml (½ fl oz) Tequila
10ml (⅓ fl oz) Fresh Lemon Juice
5ml (1/6 fl oz) Fresh Lime Juice

Layer ingredients in order given into a shot glass and serve.

The Day After

43.2% ALC/VOL • 1.1 STD DRINKS

10ml (⅓ fl oz) Cointreau
10ml (⅓ fl oz) Tequila
5 drops Blue Curaçao
10ml (⅓ fl oz) Green Chartreuse

Pour Cointreau into a tall Dutch cordial glass and layer Tequila on top. Add Curaçao by drops and layer Chartreuse on top. Ignite, extinguish flame and shoot.

Stalactite

31.9% ALC/VOL • 1.3 STD DRINKS

35ml (1 1/6 fl oz) Sambuca
8ml (¼ fl oz) Bailey's Irish Cream
8ml (¼ fl oz) Black Raspberry Liqueur

Pour Sambuca into a cordial Lexington glass and layer Bailey's on top. Add Liqueur by drops and serve.

Landslider

28.3% ALC/VOL • 0.7 STD DRINKS

10ml (⅓ fl oz) Amaretto
10ml (⅓ fl oz) Bailey's Irish Cream
10ml (⅓ fl oz) Grand Marnier

Layer ingredients in order given into a cordial Embassy glass and serve.

Cherry Ripe Shooter

17.7% ALC/VOL • 0.4 STD DRINKS

10ml (⅓ fl oz) Kahlúa
10ml (⅓ fl oz) Cherry Advocaat
10ml (⅓ fl oz) Sweet Vermouth

Layer ingredients in order given into a cordial Embassy glass and serve.

Sidecar Shooter

28.2% ALC/VOL • 0.8 STD DRINKS

12ml (⅖ fl oz) Brandy
15ml (½ fl oz) Cointreau
10ml (⅓ fl oz) Fresh Lemon Juice

Layer ingredients in order given into a cordial Embassy glass and serve.

Peppermint Pattie

13.3% ALC/VOL • 0.5 STD DRINKS

15ml (½ fl oz) Kahlúa
15ml (½ fl oz) Peppermint Schnapps
15ml (½ fl oz) Fresh Cream

Pour ingredients into a cocktail shaker over ice and shake. Strain into a chilled shot glass and serve.

Fifth Avenue

15.3% ALC/VOL • 0.5 STD DRINKS

15ml (½ fl oz) Dark Crème De Cacao
15ml (½ fl oz) Apricot Brandy
15ml (½ fl oz) Fresh Cream

Layer ingredients in order given into a cordial Lexington glass and serve.

Atomic Bomb

24.1% ALC/VOL • 0.9 STD DRINKS

20ml (⅔ fl oz) Tia Maria
15ml (½ fl oz) Gin
10ml (⅓ fl oz) Fresh Cream

Layer ingredients in order given into a tall Dutch cordial glass and serve.

Mexican Flag

20.4% ALC/VOL • 0.7 STD DRINKS

15ml (½ fl oz) Grenadine
15ml (½ fl oz) Green Crème De Menthe
15ml (½ fl oz) Tequila

Layer ingredients in order given into a cordial Embassy glass and serve.

Flapjack Shooter

19.3% ALC/VOL • 0.7 STD DRINKS

15ml (½ fl oz) Bourbon
15ml (½ fl oz) Sweet Sherry
15ml (½ fl oz) Fresh Cream

Pour ingredients into a cocktail shaker over ice and shake. Strain into a chilled liqueur glass and serve.

Brain Damage

21.1% ALC/VOL • 0.6 STD DRINKS

23ml (¾ fl oz) Malibu
10ml (⅓ fl oz) Parfait Amour
5ml (1/6 fl oz) Advocaat

Layer ingredients in order given into a cordial Lexington glass and serve.

Model 'T'

23.2% ALC/VOL • 0.8 STD DRINKS

15ml (½ fl oz) Kahlúa
15ml (½ fl oz) Banana Liqueur
15ml (½ fl oz) Tia Maria

Layer ingredients in order given into a tall Dutch cordial glass and serve.

Altered State

20.1% ALC/VOL • 0.7 STD DRINKS

15ml (½ fl oz) Kahlúa
15ml (½ fl oz) Peach Liqueur

15ml (½ fl oz) Bailey's Irish Cream

Layer ingredients in order given into a tall Dutch cordial glass and serve.

Towering Inferno

38.9% ALC/VOL • 0.9 STD DRINKS

10ml (⅓ fl oz) Gin
10ml (⅓ fl oz) Triple Sec
10ml (⅓ fl oz) Green Chartreuse

Layer ingredients in order given into a cordial Embassy glass, ignite and shoot while flaming.

Japanese Slipper Shooter

22.6% ALC/VOL • 0.8 STD DRINKS

20ml (⅔ fl oz) Midori
15ml (½ fl oz) Cointreau
10ml (⅓ fl oz) Fresh Lemon Juice

Layer ingredients in order given into a tall Dutch cordial glass and serve.

Buzzard's Breath

22.7% ALC/VOL • 0.8 STD DRINKS

15ml (½ fl oz) Amaretto
15ml (½ fl oz) Kahlúa
15ml (½ fl oz) Peppermint Schnapps

Pour ingredients into a mixing glass over ice and stir. Strain into a chilled shot glass and serve.

A.B.C. Shooter

29.2% ALC/VOL • 0.7 STD DRINKS

8ml (¼ fl oz) Amaretto
10ml (⅓ fl oz) Bailey's Irish Cream
12ml (⅖ fl oz) Cointreau

Layer ingredients in order given into a cordial Embassy glass and serve.

Sex in the Snow

28% ALC/VOL • 0.8 STD DRINKS

12ml (⅖ fl oz) Triple Sec
12ml (⅖ fl oz) Malibu
12ml (⅖ fl oz) Ouzo

Layer ingredients in order given into a cordial Lexington glass, stir gently and shoot through a straw.

Harbor Lights

37.7% ALC/VOL • 1.1 STD DRINKS

12ml (⅖ fl oz) Kahlúa
12ml (⅖ fl oz) Sambuca
12ml (⅖ fl oz) Green Chartreuse

Layer ingredients in order given into a cordial Lexington glass and shoot through a straw.

Calypso

26.8% ALC/VOL • 1 STD DRINK

15ml (½ fl oz) Bailey's Irish Cream
10ml (⅓ fl oz) Malibu
20ml (⅔ fl oz) Jamaica Rum

Layer ingredients in order given into a tall Dutch cordial glass and serve.

Cough Syrup

28.3% ALC/VOL • 0.7 STD DRINKS

10ml (⅓ fl oz) Blue Curaçao
10ml (⅓ fl oz) Green Crème De Menthe
10ml (⅓ fl oz) Vodka

Pour ingredients into a shot glass, stir and serve.

Grand Slam Shooter

26.7% ALC/VOL • 0.6 STD DRINKS

10ml (⅓ fl oz) Banana Liqueur
10ml (⅓ fl oz) Bailey's Irish Cream
10ml (⅓ fl oz) Grand Marnier

Layer ingredients in order given into a cordial Embassy glass and serve.

Martian Hard On

20.4% ALC/VOL • 0.7 STD DRINKS

15ml (½ fl oz) Dark Crème De Cacao
15ml (½ fl oz) Midori
15ml (½ fl oz) Bailey's Irish Cream

Layer ingredients in order given into a tall Dutch cordial glass and serve.

Shamrock Shooter

21% ALC/VOL • 0.5 STD DRINKS

10ml (⅓ fl oz) Dark Crème De Cacao
10ml (⅓ fl oz) Green Crème De Menthe
10ml (⅓ fl oz) Bailey's Irish Cream

Layer ingredients in order given into a cordial Embassy glass and serve.

Suitor

25.5% ALC/VOL • 0.8 STD DRINKS

10ml (⅓ fl oz) Drambuie
10ml (⅓ fl oz) Grand Marnier
10ml (⅓ fl oz) Bailey's Irish Cream
8ml (¼ fl oz) Fresh Milk (chilled)

Layer ingredients in order given into a cordial Lexington glass and serve.

Italian Stallion Shooter

15.2% ALC/VOL • 0.5 STD DRINKS

10ml (⅓ fl oz) Banana Liqueur
10ml (⅓ fl oz) Galliano

18ml (3/5 fl oz) Fresh Cream

Layer ingredients in order given into a cordial Lexington glass and serve.

Coathanger

30% ALC/VOL • 0.9 STD DRINKS

15ml (½ fl oz) Cointreau
15ml (½ fl oz) Tequila
8ml (¼ fl oz) Grenadine
Dash Fresh Milk (chilled)

Layer ingredients in order given into a cordial Lexington glass and serve.

Black Russian Shooter

28.5% ALC/VOL • 0.7 STD DRINKS

15ml (½ fl oz) Kahlúa
15ml (½ fl oz) Vodka

Layer ingredients in order given into a cordial Embassy glass and serve.

Blow Job

15.7% ALC/VOL • 0.6 STD DRINKS

15ml (½ fl oz) Kahlúa
10ml (⅓ fl oz) Banana Liqueur
15ml (½ fl oz) Bailey's Irish Cream
Fresh Whipped Cream

Layer ingredients in order given into a tall Dutch cordial glass, float cream on top and serve.

Slippery Nipple

31% ALC/VOL • 1.1 STD DRINKS

30ml (1 fl oz) Sambuca
15ml (½ fl oz) Bailey's Irish Cream

Layer ingredients in order given into a tall Dutch cordial glass and serve.

Melon Splice Shooter

26.4% ALC/VOL • 0.9 STD DRINKS

15ml (½ fl oz) Midori
15ml (½ fl oz) Galliano
15ml (½ fl oz) Coconut Liqueur

Layer ingredients in order given into a tall Dutch cordial glass and serve.

Angel Kiss

27.2% ALC/VOL • 1 STD DRINK

20ml (⅔ fl oz) Kahlúa
5ml (1/6 fl oz) Bailey's Irish Cream
20ml (⅔ fl oz) Gin

Layer ingredients in order given into a tall Dutch cordial glass and serve.

Icy After Eight

22.5% ALC/VOL • 0.8 STD DRINKS

23ml (¾ fl oz) Vodka
8ml (¼ fl oz) Green Crème De Menthe
15ml (½ fl oz) Chocolate Syrup

Pour ingredients into a cocktail shaker over a crushed ice cube and shake well. Pour into a chilled shot glass and serve.

Bee Sting

38.6% ALC/VOL • 0.9 STD DRINKS

20ml (⅔ fl oz) Tequila
10ml (⅓ fl oz) Yellow Chartreuse

Layer ingredients in order given into a cordial Embassy glass and serve.

Eh Bomb

30% ALC/VOL • 1.1 STD DRINKS

10ml (⅓ fl oz) Green Crème De Menthe
10ml (⅓ fl oz) Bailey's Irish Cream
10ml (⅓ fl oz) Ouzo
15ml (½ fl oz) Tequila

Layer ingredients in order given into a shot glass and serve.

Port and Starboard

11.5% ALC/VOL • 0.3 STD DRINKS

15ml (½ fl oz) Grenadine
15ml (½ fl oz) Green Crème De Menthe

Layer ingredients in order given into a cordial Embassy glass and serve.

Flaming Lamborghini Shooter

36.7% ALC/VOL • 0.9 STD DRINKS

10ml (⅓ fl oz) Kahlúa
10ml (⅓ fl oz) Galliano
10ml (⅓ fl oz) Green Chartreuse

Layer ingredients in order given into a cordial Embassy glass, ignite and shoot while flaming.

White Death

37.7% ALC/VOL • 1.3 STD DRINKS

15ml (½ fl oz) Dry Gin
15ml (½ fl oz) White Tequila
15ml (½ fl oz) Sambuca

Layer ingredients in order given into a shot glass, ignite and shoot while flaming.

Freddie and Pucker

34.5% ALC/VOL • 1 STD DRINK

23ml (¾ fl oz) Galliano
10ml (⅓ fl oz) Tequila
5ml (1/6 fl oz) Orange Curaçao

Pour Galliano into a cordial Lexington glass and layer Tequila on top. Add Curaçao by pouring over Tequila – do not stir, then serve.

Galliano Hot Shot

11.7% ALC/VOL • 0.4 STD DRINKS

15ml (½ fl oz) Galliano
23ml (¾ fl oz) Hot Black Coffee
5ml (1/6 fl oz) Fresh Cream

Layer ingredients in order given into a shot glass and serve.

Penalty Shot

28.8% ALC/VOL • 1 STD DRINK

15ml (½ fl oz) Green Crème De Menthe
15ml (½ fl oz) Tia Maria
15ml (½ fl oz) Vodka

Layer ingredients in order given into a shot glass and serve.

Mint Slice

20% ALC/VOL • 0.7 STD DRINKS

30ml (1 fl oz) Peppermint Schnapps
15ml (½ fl oz) Kahlúa

Layer ingredients in order given into a shot glass and serve.

Agent 99

25.7% ALC/VOL • 0.9 STD DRINKS

15ml (½ fl oz) Parfait Amour
15ml (½ fl oz) Bailey's Irish Cream
15ml (½ fl oz) Ouzo

Layer ingredients in order given into a tall Dutch cordial glass and serve.

Flaming Lover

31.5% ALC/VOL • 0.7 STD DRINKS

15ml (½ fl oz) Sambuca
15ml (½ fl oz) Triple Sec

Pour Sambuca into a cordial Embassy glass and ignite then add Triple Sec while drinking through a straw.

Midori Illusion Shaker

13.4% ALC/VOL • 1.9 STD DRINKS

60ml (2 fl oz) Midori
15ml (½ fl oz) Cointreau
15ml (½ fl oz) Vodka
60ml (2 fl oz) Pineapple Juice
30ml (1 fl oz) Fresh Lemon Juice

Pour ingredients into a cocktail shaker over ice and shake. Strain into four chilled cocktail glasses and serve.

Waffle

19% ALC/VOL • 0.7 STD DRINKS

15ml (½ fl oz) Butterscotch Schnapps
15ml (½ fl oz) Vodka
15ml (½ fl oz) Fresh Orange Juice

Pour ingredients into a cocktail shaker over ice and shake. Strain into a chilled shot glass and serve.

Traffic Light

43.5% ALC/VOL • 1.5 STD DRINKS

10ml (⅓ fl oz) Strawberry Liqueur
10ml (⅓ fl oz) Galliano
23ml (¾ fl oz) Green Chartreuse

Layer ingredients in order given into a tall Dutch cordial glass and serve.

Screwdriver Shooter

33% ALC/VOL • 1.2 STD DRINKS

15ml (½ fl oz) Orange Curaçao
30ml (1 fl oz) Vodka

Layer ingredients in order given into a shot glass and serve.

Avalanche Shoot

27.6% ALC/VOL • 0.7 STD DRINKS

10ml (⅓ fl oz) Kahlúa
8ml (¼ fl oz) Dark Crème De Cacao
12ml (⅖ fl oz) Southern Comfort

Layer ingredients in order given into a cordial Embassy glass and serve.

Light House

33.3% ALC/VOL • 1.2 STD DRINKS

15ml (½ fl oz) Kahlúa
15ml (½ fl oz) Grand Marnier
15ml (½ fl oz) Tequila

Layer ingredients in order given into a tall Dutch cordial glass and serve.

Orgasm Shooter

28.5% ALC/VOL • 1 STD DRINK

23ml (¾ fl oz) Cointreau
23ml (¾ fl oz) Bailey's Irish Cream

Layer ingredients in order given into a shot glass and serve.

T.K.O.

31.7% ALC/VOL • 0.8 STD DRINKS

10ml (⅓ fl oz) Kahlúa
10ml (⅓ fl oz) Tequila
10ml (⅓ fl oz) Ouzo

Layer ingredients in order given into a cordial Embassy glass and serve.

Spanish Fly Shooter

34.5% ALC/VOL • 1.2 STD DRINKS

10ml (⅓ fl oz) Dry Vermouth
15ml (½ fl oz) Tequila
20ml (⅔ fl oz) Scotch Whisky

Layer ingredients in order given into a shot glass and serve.

Dirty Orgasm

30.7% ALC/VOL • 1.1 STD DRINKS

15ml (½ fl oz) Cointreau
15ml (½ fl oz) Galliano
15ml (½ fl oz) Bailey's Irish Cream

Layer ingredients in order given into a tall Dutch cordial glass and serve.

Mexican Berry

27.1% ALC/VOL • 0.6 STD DRINKS

10ml (⅓ fl oz) Kahlúa
10ml (⅓ fl oz) Strawberry Liqueur
10ml (⅓ fl oz) Tequila

Layer ingredients in order given into a cordial Embassy glass and serve.

Flaming Orgy

25.8% ALC/VOL • 0.9 STD DRINKS

10ml (⅓ fl oz) Grenadine
10ml (⅓ fl oz) Green Crème De Menthe
15ml (½ fl oz) Brandy
10ml (⅓ fl oz) Tequila

Layer ingredients in order given into a tall Dutch cordial glass and serve.

Red Indian

29.1% ALC/VOL • 0.8 STD DRINKS

10ml (⅓ fl oz) Dark Crème De Cacao
12ml (⅖ fl oz) Peachtree
15ml (½ fl oz) Canadian Whisky

Layer ingredients in order given into a cordial Lexington glass and serve.

Seduction Shooter

21.4% ALC/VOL • 0.6 STD DRINKS

12ml (⅖ fl oz) Banana Liqueur
12ml (⅖ fl oz) Frangelico
12ml (⅖ fl oz) Bailey's Irish Cream

Layer ingredients in order given into a cordial Lexington glass and serve.

Ghetto Blaster

34.4% ALC/VOL • 1.2 STD DRINKS

10ml (⅓ fl oz) Kahlúa
25ml (⅚ fl oz) Tequila
10ml (⅓ fl oz) Rye Whiskey

Layer ingredients in order given into a shot glass and serve.

Face Off

19% ALC/VOL • 0.7 STD DRINKS

10ml (⅓ fl oz) Grenadine
15ml (½ fl oz) Green Crème De Menthe
10ml (⅓ fl oz) Parfait Amour
10ml (⅓ fl oz) Sambuca

Layer ingredients in order given into a tall Dutch cordial glass and serve.

Leg Spreader

32.3% ALC/VOL • 1.2 STD DRINKS

23ml (¾ fl oz) Sambuca
23ml (¾ fl oz) Tia Maria

Layer ingredients in order given into a shot glass and serve.

Ready, Set, Go!

22.3% ALC/VOL • 0.8 STD DRINKS

15ml (½ fl oz) Strawberry Liqueur
15ml (½ fl oz) Banana Liqueur
15ml (½ fl oz) Midori

Layer ingredients in order given into a tall Dutch cordial glass and serve.

Dark Sunset

22% ALC/VOL • 0.8 STD DRINKS

23ml (¾ fl oz) Dark Crème De Cacao
23ml (¾ fl oz) Malibu

Layer ingredients in order given into a tall Dutch cordial glass and serve.

Bad Sting

27% ALC/VOL • 0.7 STD DRINKS

8ml (¼ fl oz) Grenadine
8ml (¼ fl oz) Anisette
8ml (¼ fl oz) Grand Marnier
8ml (¼ fl oz) Tequila

Layer ingredients in order given into a cordial Lexington glass and serve.

Three Wisemen

41.1% ALC/VOL • 1 STD DRINK

10ml (⅓ fl oz) Jägermeister
10ml (⅓ fl oz) Rumplemintz
10ml (⅓ fl oz) Tequila

Pour ingredients into a mixing glass over ice and stir. Strain into a chilled shot glass and serve.

Spy Catcher

38% ALC/VOL • 1.3 STD DRINKS

30ml (1 fl oz) Canadian Whisky
15ml (½ fl oz) Sambuca

Layer ingredients in order given into a shot glass and serve.

Sex on the Beach Shooter

12.5% ALC/VOL • 0.3 STD DRINKS

10ml (⅓ fl oz) Chambord

10ml (⅓ fl oz) Midori
10ml (⅓ fl oz) Pineapple Juice

Pour ingredients into a cocktail shaker over ice and shake. Strain into a chilled shot glass and serve.

Greek God

39% ALC/VOL • 1.4 STD DRINKS

23ml (¾ fl oz) Ouzo
23ml (¾ fl oz) Pernod

Layer ingredients in order given into a shot glass and serve.

Hurricane Shooter

27.6% ALC/VOL • 0.7 STD DRINKS

8ml (¼ fl oz) Blue Curaçao
8ml (¼ fl oz) Bailey's Irish Cream
8ml (¼ fl oz) Anisette
8ml (¼ fl oz) Tequila

Layer ingredients in order given into a cordial Lexington glass and serve.

Black Jack Shooter

29.5% ALC/VOL • 1 STD DRINK

20ml (⅔ fl oz) Kahlúa
25ml (⅚ fl oz) Ouzo

Layer ingredients in order given into a shot glass and serve.

Dead Green Frog

29.4% ALC/VOL • 0.7 STD DRINKS

6ml (⅕ fl oz) Bailey's Irish Cream
6ml (⅕ fl oz) Green Crème De Menthe
6ml (⅕ fl oz) Kahlúa
6ml (⅕ fl oz) Rumplemintz
6ml (⅕ fl oz) Vodka

Pour ingredients into a mixing glass over ice and stir briefly. Strain into a chilled shot glass and serve.

Jawbreaker

22% ALC/VOL • 0.8 STD DRINKS

45ml (1½ fl oz) Apricot Brandy
5 drops Tabasco Sauce

Pour Brandy into a shot glass and add sauce by drops – do not stir, then serve.

Old Glory

13.3% ALC/VOL • 0.5 STD DRINKS

15ml (½ fl oz) Grenadine
15ml (½ fl oz) Fresh Cream
15ml (½ fl oz) Crème Yvette

Layer ingredients in order given into a tall Dutch cordial glass and serve.

Screaming Lizard Shooter

45.5% ALC/VOL • 1.6 STD DRINKS

25ml (⅚ fl oz) Tequila
20ml (⅔ fl oz) Green Chartreuse

Layer ingredients in order given into a tall Dutch cordial glass and serve.

Night Flight Shooter

22.6% ALC/VOL • 0.8 STD DRINKS

15ml (½ fl oz) Amaretto
15ml (½ fl oz) Blackberry Schnapps
15ml (½ fl oz) Peach Schnapps

Pour ingredients into a cocktail shaker over ice and shake. Strain into a chilled shot glass and serve.

Barman's Breakfast

19.3% ALC/VOL • 0.7 STD DRINKS

30ml (1 fl oz) Peach Schnapps
15ml (½ fl oz) Advocaat

Layer ingredients in order given into a shot glass and serve.

Cherry Blow Pop

21.6% ALC/VOL • 0.5 STD DRINKS

10ml (⅓ fl oz) Amaretto
10ml (⅓ fl oz) Southern Comfort
10ml (⅓ fl oz) Grenadine

Pour ingredients into a cocktail shaker over ice and shake. Strain into a chilled shot glass and serve.

Shooting Star

19% ALC/VOL • 0.7 STD DRINKS

30ml (1 fl oz) Butterscotch Schnapps
15ml (½ fl oz) Bailey's Irish Cream

Layer ingredients in order given into a shot glass and serve.

Tropical Passion

25.5% ALC/VOL • 0.9 STD DRINKS

10ml (⅓ fl oz) Light Rum
10ml (⅓ fl oz) Peach Schnapps
10ml (⅓ fl oz) Sloe Gin
10ml (⅓ fl oz) Triple Sec
3 dashes Fresh Orange Juice

Pour ingredients into a cocktail shaker over ice and shake. Strain into a chilled shot glass and serve.

Peach Picnic

20% ALC/VOL • 0.7 STD DRINKS

23ml (¾ fl oz) Peach Schnapps
23ml (¾ fl oz) Apple Schnapps

Layer ingredients in order given into a shot glass and serve.

Jane's Touch

20.4% ALC/VOL • 0.5 STD DRINKS

10ml (⅓ fl oz) Kahlúa
10ml (⅓ fl oz) Frangelico
10ml (⅓ fl oz) Bailey's Irish Cream

Layer ingredients in order given into a cordial Embassy glass and serve.

Brave Bull Shooter

29% ALC/VOL • 0.9 STD DRINKS

20ml (⅔ fl oz) Kahlúa
20ml (⅔ fl oz) Tequila

Layer ingredients in order given into a shot glass and serve.

Suction Cup

30.3% ALC/VOL • 0.9 STD DRINKS

20ml (⅔ fl oz) Vodka
10ml (⅓ fl oz) Midori
8ml (¼ fl oz) Blue Curaçao

Pour Vodka into a cordial Lexington glass and layer Midori on top. Add Curaçao by pouring over Midori – do not stir, then shoot through a straw.

Tetanus Shot

20% ALC/VOL • 0.5 STD DRINKS

15ml (½ fl oz) Bailey's Irish Cream
15ml (½ fl oz) Cherry Brandy

Pour ingredients into a shot glass, stir and serve.

Candy Cane

20% ALC/VOL • 0.7 STD DRINKS

15ml (½ fl oz) Grenadine
15ml (½ fl oz) Green Crème De Menthe
15ml (½ fl oz) Vodka

Layer ingredients in order given into a tall Dutch cordial glass and serve.

Death Row

57.8% ALC/VOL • 1.4 STD DRINKS

15ml (½ fl oz) 151-Proof Bacardi
15ml (½ fl oz) Tennessee Whiskey

Pour ingredients into a shot glass, stir and serve.

Green Slime

24.4% ALC/VOL • 0.8 STD DRINKS

20ml (⅔ fl oz) Midori
15ml (½ fl oz) Vodka
1 teaspoon Egg White

Pour ingredients in order given into a shot glass, stir gently and serve.

Laser Beam

36.4% ALC/VOL • 1.3 STD DRINKS

25ml (⅚ fl oz) Galliano
20ml (⅔ fl oz) Tequila

Layer ingredients in order given into a tall Dutch cordial glass and serve.

Angel's Kiss

24.3% ALC/VOL • 0.8 STD DRINKS

10ml (⅓ fl oz) Dark Crème De Cacao
10ml (⅓ fl oz) Fresh Cream
10ml (⅓ fl oz) Dry Gin
10ml (⅓ fl oz) Brandy

Layer ingredients in order given into a tall Dutch cordial glass and serve.

Double Date

28% ALC/VOL • 1 STD DRINK

15ml (½ fl oz) Midori
15ml (½ fl oz) White Crème De Menthe
15ml (½ fl oz) Bénédictine

Layer ingredients in order given into a tall Dutch cordial glass and serve.

B-54

27.4% ALC/VOL • 1 STD DRINK

10ml (⅓ fl oz) Kahlúa
15ml (½ fl oz) Bailey's Irish Cream
10ml (⅓ fl oz) Grand Marnier
10ml (⅓ fl oz) Tequila

Layer ingredients in order given into a shot glass and serve.

Leather and Lace

24.7% ALC/VOL • 0.6 STD DRINKS

10ml (⅓ fl oz) Kahlúa
10ml (⅓ fl oz) Vodka
10ml (⅓ fl oz) Bailey's Irish Cream

Layer ingredients in order given into a cordial Embassy glass and serve.

Midori Sour Shooter

14% ALC/VOL • 0.5 STD DRINKS

30ml (1 fl oz) Midori
5ml (⅙ fl oz) Grenadine
10ml (⅓ fl oz) Fresh Lemon Juice

Pour Midori into a tall Dutch cordial glass and add Grenadine – do not stir. Layer juice on top and serve.

Pipsqueak

22.3% ALC/VOL • 0.7 STD DRINKS

20ml (⅔ fl oz) Frangelico
10ml (⅓ fl oz) Vodka
8ml (¼ fl oz) Fresh Lime Juice

Pour ingredients in order given into a cordial Lexington glass, stir gently and serve.

Popsicle

28.1% ALC/VOL • 0.9 STD DRINKS

15ml (½ fl oz) Tia Maria
10ml (⅓ fl oz) Bailey's Irish Cream
15ml (½ fl oz) Vodka

Layer ingredients in order given into a cordial Lexington glass and serve.

B.B.G.

32.4% ALC/VOL • 1.2 STD DRINKS

15ml (½ fl oz) Bénédictine
15ml (½ fl oz) Bailey's Irish Cream
15ml (½ fl oz) Grand Marnier

Layer ingredients in order given into a tall Dutch cordial glass and serve.

Deep Throat

24% ALC/VOL • 0.9 STD DRINKS

20ml (⅔ fl oz) Kahlúa
20ml (⅔ fl oz) Grand Marnier
Fresh Whipped Cream

Layer ingredients in order given into a tall Dutch cordial glass, float cream on top and serve.

Lady Throat Killer

21.2% ALC/VOL • 0.8 STD DRINKS

20ml (⅔ fl oz) Kahlúa
15ml (½ fl oz) Midori
10ml (⅓ fl oz) Frangelico

Layer ingredients in order given into a tall Dutch cordial glass and serve.

Peach Tree Bay

23.6% ALC/VOL • 0.8 STD DRINKS

25ml (⅚ fl oz) Peachtree
15ml (½ fl oz) Pimm's No.1
5ml (⅙ fl oz) Green Crème De Menthe

Pour Peachtree into a tall Dutch cordial glass and layer Pimm's on top. Add Crème De Menthe by pouring over Pimm's – do not stir, then serve.

Bull Shoot

32.1% ALC/VOL • 0.8 STD DRINKS

10ml (⅓ fl oz) Kahlúa
10ml (⅓ fl oz) Light Rum
10ml (⅓ fl oz) Tequila

Layer ingredients in order given into a cordial Embassy glass and serve.

Angry Fijian

20.4% ALC/VOL • 0.5 STD DRINKS

10ml (⅓ fl oz) Banana Liqueur
10ml (⅓ fl oz) Bailey's Irish Cream
10ml (⅓ fl oz) Malibu

Layer ingredients in order given into a test tube and serve.
This drink is also known as Zowie.

Mexican Pumper

19.4% ALC/VOL • 0.6 STD DRINKS

12ml (⅖ fl oz) Grenadine
12ml (⅖ fl oz) Kahlúa
12ml (⅖ fl oz) Tequila

Layer ingredients in order given into a cordial Lexington glass and serve.

Sukiyaki

22.3% ALC/VOL • 0.5 STD DRINKS

10ml (⅓ fl oz) Mango Liqueur
10ml (⅓ fl oz) Apricot Brandy
10ml (⅓ fl oz) Malibu

Layer ingredients in order given into a cordial Embassy glass and serve.

Channel 64

19.4% ALC/VOL • 0.5 STD DRINKS

10ml (⅓ fl oz) Advocaat
10ml (⅓ fl oz) Banana Liqueur
10ml (⅓ fl oz) Bailey's Irish Cream

Layer ingredients in order given into a cordial Embassy glass and serve.

Jelly Bean Shooter

25.3% ALC/VOL • 0.6 STD DRINKS

10ml (⅓ fl oz) Grenadine
10ml (⅓ fl oz) Ouzo
10ml (⅓ fl oz) Tequila

Layer ingredients in order given into a cordial Embassy glass and serve.

Violet Slumber

16% ALC/VOL • 0.5 STD DRINKS

15ml (½ fl oz) Malibu
12ml (⅖ fl oz) Parfait Amour
10ml (⅓ fl oz) Fresh Orange Juice

Layer ingredients in order given into a cordial Lexington glass and serve.

Kamikaze Shooter

29.7% ALC/VOL • 1.1 STD DRINKS

20ml (⅔ fl oz) Vodka
15ml (½ fl oz) Cointreau
10ml (⅓ fl oz) Fresh Lemon Juice

Layer ingredients in order given into a shot glass and serve.

Neutron Bomb

31.7% ALC/VOL • 1.1 STD DRINKS

15ml (½ fl oz) Kahlúa
15ml (½ fl oz) Golden Rum
15ml (½ fl oz) Tequila

Layer ingredients in order given into a shot glass and serve.

Pousse Café

27.6% ALC/VOL • 0.7 STD DRINKS

8ml (¼ fl oz) Grenadine
8ml (¼ fl oz) Maraschino Liqueur
8ml (¼ fl oz) Green Crème De Menthe
8ml (¼ fl oz) Crème Yvette
8ml (¼ fl oz) Yellow Chartreuse
8ml (¼ fl oz) Brandy

Layer ingredients in order given into a pousse café glass and serve.

B & B Shooter

40% ALC/VOL • 1.1 STD DRINKS

18ml (3/5 fl oz) Cognac
18ml (3/5 fl oz) Bénédictine

Layer ingredients in order given into a cordial Lexington glass and serve.

Horney Bull

37.4% ALC/VOL • 0.9 STD DRINKS

10ml (⅓ fl oz) Vodka
10ml (⅓ fl oz) Rum
10ml (⅓ fl oz) Tequila

Layer ingredients in order given into a cordial Embassy glass and serve.

Jumping Jack Flash

34.4% ALC/VOL • 1.2 STD DRINKS

15ml (½ fl oz) Tia Maria
15ml (½ fl oz) Jamaica Rum
15ml (½ fl oz) Bourbon

Layer ingredients in order given into a shot glass and serve.

G.A.S.

33.7% ALC/VOL • 0.8 STD DRINKS

10ml (⅓ fl oz) Galliano
10ml (⅓ fl oz) Amaretto
10ml (⅓ fl oz) Sambuca

Pour Sambuca into a cordial Embassy glass and layer Galliano on top. Add Amaretto – do not stir, then serve.

B-53

25.1% ALC/VOL • 0.6 STD DRINKS

10ml (⅓ fl oz) Kahlúa
10ml (⅓ fl oz) Bailey's Irish Cream
10ml (⅓ fl oz) Tequila

Layer ingredients in order given into a cordial Embassy glass and serve.

Golden Cadillac Shooter

23.2% ALC/VOL • 0.8 STD DRINKS

15ml (½ fl oz) White Crème De Cacao
20ml (⅔ fl oz) Galliano
10ml (⅓ fl oz) Fresh Cream

Layer ingredients in order given into a tall Dutch cordial glass and serve.

Rusty Nail Shooter

40% ALC/VOL • 0.9 STD DRINKS

15ml (½ fl oz) Scotch Whisky
15ml (½ fl oz) Drambuie

Layer ingredients in order given into a cordial Embassy glass and serve.

Quicksilver

32.7% ALC/VOL • 0.8 STD DRINKS

10ml (⅓ fl oz) Banana Liqueur
10ml (⅓ fl oz) Tequila
10ml (⅓ fl oz) Vodka

Layer ingredients in order given into a cordial Embassy glass and serve.

B.B.C.

32.4% ALC/VOL • 1.2 STD DRINKS

15ml (½ fl oz) Bénédictine
15ml (½ fl oz) Bailey's Irish Cream
15ml (½ fl oz) Cointreau

Layer ingredients in order given into a shot glass and serve.

Chocolate Chip

23.4% ALC/VOL • 0.8 STD DRINKS

15ml (½ fl oz) Vandermint
15ml (½ fl oz) Green Crème De Menthe
15ml (½ fl oz) Bailey's Irish Cream

Layer ingredients in order given into a tall Dutch cordial glass and serve.

Irish Flag

26.7% ALC/VOL • 0.6 STD DRINKS

10ml (⅓ fl oz) Green Crème De Menthe
10ml (⅓ fl oz) Bailey's Irish Cream
10ml (⅓ fl oz) Mandarine Napoleon

Layer ingredients in order given into a cordial Lexington glass and serve.

Fruit Tingle Shooter

15.7% ALC/VOL • 0.4 STD DRINKS

10ml (⅓ fl oz) Blue Curaçao
15ml (½ fl oz) Mango Liqueur
5ml (⅙ fl oz) Fresh Lemon Juice

Layer ingredients in order given into a cordial Embassy glass and serve.

K.G.B. Shooter

25.7% ALC/VOL • 0.7 STD DRINKS

12ml (2/5 fl oz) Kahlúa
12ml (2/5 fl oz) Grand Marnier
12ml (2/5 fl oz) Bailey's Irish Cream

Layer ingredients in order given into a cordial Lexington glass and serve.

Alabama Slammer

25.5% ALC/VOL • 0.8 STD DRINKS

10ml (⅓ fl oz) Dry Gin
10ml (⅓ fl oz) Amaretto
10ml (⅓ fl oz) Fresh Orange Juice
10ml (⅓ fl oz) Southern Comfort

Layer ingredients in order given into a shot glass and serve.

Half Nelson

30.6% ALC/VOL • 1.1 STD DRINKS

15ml (½ fl oz) Green Crème De Menthe
10ml (⅓ fl oz) Strawberry Liqueur
20ml (⅔ fl oz) Grand Marnier

Layer ingredients in order given into a shot glass and serve.

Inkahluarable

28.3% ALC/VOL • 0.7 STD DRINKS

10ml (⅓ fl oz) Kahlúa
10ml (⅓ fl oz) Triple Sec
10ml (⅓ fl oz) Grand Marnier

Layer ingredients in order given into a cordial Embassy glass and serve.

Warm Blonde

32.5% ALC/VOL • 0.8 STD DRINKS

15ml (½ fl oz) Southern Comfort
15ml (½ fl oz) Amaretto

Layer ingredients in order given into a cordial Embassy glass and serve.

Break

26.7% ALC/VOL • 0.6 STD DRINKS

10ml (⅓ fl oz) Kahlúa
10ml (⅓ fl oz) Banana Liqueur
10ml (⅓ fl oz) Ouzo

Layer ingredients in order given into a cordial Embassy glass and serve.

Zipper Shooter

31.7% ALC/VOL • 1.1 STD DRINKS

15ml (½ fl oz) Tequila
15ml (½ fl oz) Bailey's Irish Cream
15ml (½ fl oz) Grand Marnier

Layer ingredients in order given into a shot glass and serve.

Silver Spider

34.6% ALC/VOL • 1.1 STD DRINKS

10ml (⅓ fl oz) Vodka
10ml (⅓ fl oz) Light Rum
10ml (⅓ fl oz) Cointreau
10ml (⅓ fl oz) White Crème De Menthe

Layer ingredients in order given into a tall Dutch cordial glass and serve.

69er

26.1% ALC/VOL • 0.9 STD DRINKS

15ml (½ fl oz) Banana Liqueur
15ml (½ fl oz) Bailey's Irish Cream
15ml (½ fl oz) Ouzo

Layer ingredients in order given into a shot glass and serve.

Passion Juice

16.2% ALC/VOL • 0.6 STD DRINKS

20ml (⅔ fl oz) Orange Curaçao
10ml (⅓ fl oz) Cherry Brandy
15ml (½ fl oz) Fresh Orange Juice

Layer ingredients in order given into a shot glass and serve.

Strawberry Cream Shooter

15.3% ALC/VOL • 0.4 STD DRINKS

20ml (⅔ fl oz) Strawberry Liqueur
10ml (⅓ fl oz) Fresh Cream

Layer ingredients in order given into a cordial Embassy glass and serve.

Raider

32.4% ALC/VOL • 0.8 STD DRINKS

15ml (½ fl oz) Bailey's Irish Cream
15ml (½ fl oz) Grand Marnier
15ml (½ fl oz) Cointreau

Layer ingredients in order given into a shot glass and serve.

Vibrator

30.4% ALC/VOL • 0.7 STD DRINKS

10ml (⅓ fl oz) Bailey's Irish Cream
20ml (⅔ fl oz) Southern Comfort

Layer ingredients in order given into a cordial Embassy glass and serve.

Kool Aid

29% ALC/VOL • 0.8 STD DRINKS

10ml (⅓ fl oz) Midori
15ml (½ fl oz) Amaretto
12ml (⅖ fl oz) Vodka

Layer ingredients in order given into a cordial Lexington glass and serve.

Lone Star

25.5% ALC/VOL • 0.6 STD DRINKS

15ml (½ fl oz) Cherry Brandy
10ml (⅓ fl oz) Parfait Amour
5ml (⅙ fl oz) Bacardi

Layer ingredients in order given into a cordial Embassy glass and serve.

Nude Bomb

23.7% ALC/VOL • 0.6 STD DRINKS

10ml (⅓ fl oz) Kahlúa
10ml (⅓ fl oz) Banana Liqueur
10ml (⅓ fl oz) Amaretto

Layer ingredients in order given into a cordial Embassy glass and serve.

Flaming Diamond

33.3% ALC/VOL • 0.8 STD DRINKS

10ml (⅓ fl oz) Strawberry Liqueur
10ml (⅓ fl oz) Grand Marnier
10ml (⅓ fl oz) Vodka

Layer ingredients in order given into a cordial Embassy glass and serve.

Nutty Professor

27% ALC/VOL • 1 STD DRINK

15ml (½ fl oz) Bailey's Irish Cream
15ml (½ fl oz) Frangelico
15ml (½ fl oz) Grand Marnier

Pour ingredients into a cocktail shaker over ice and shake. Strain into a chilled shot glass and serve.

Twain's Orgasm

21% ALC/VOL • 0.5 STD DRINKS

20ml (⅔ fl oz) Peachtree
10ml (⅓ fl oz) Bailey's Irish Cream

Layer ingredients in order given into a cordial Embassy glass and serve.

Great White North

24.7% ALC/VOL • 0.9 STD DRINKS

15ml (½ fl oz) Kahlúa
15ml (½ fl oz) Bailey's Irish Cream
15ml (½ fl oz) Ouzo

Layer ingredients in order given into a tall Dutch cordial glass and serve.

Panty Dropper

28.3% ALC/VOL • 0.7 STD DRINKS

20ml (⅔ fl oz) Frangelico
10ml (⅓ fl oz) Gin

Layer ingredients in order given into a cordial Embassy glass and serve.

Smartie

13% ALC/VOL • 0.3 STD DRINKS

15ml (½ fl oz) Grenadine
10ml (⅓ fl oz) Kahlúa
5ml (⅙ fl oz) Tequila

Layer ingredients in order given into a cordial Embassy glass and serve.

Chocolate Nougat

27% ALC/VOL • 0.6 STD DRINKS

10ml (⅓ fl oz) Frangelico
10ml (⅓ fl oz) Bailey's Irish Cream
10ml (⅓ fl oz) Yellow Chartreuse

Layer ingredients in order given into a cordial Embassy glass and serve.

Lambada

33% ALC/VOL • 1.2 STD DRINKS

15ml (½ fl oz) Mango Liqueur
15ml (½ fl oz) Opal Nera
15ml (½ fl oz) Tequila

Layer ingredients in order given into a shot glass and serve.

Flaming Sambuca

38% ALC/VOL • 0.9 STD DRINKS

30ml (1 fl oz) Sambuca
3 Coffee Beans

Place coffee beans into a cordial Embassy glass and add Sambuca then ignite. Extinguish flame and serve.

Paintbox

20.3% ALC/VOL • 0.5 STD DRINKS

10ml (⅓ fl oz) Cherry Advocaat
10ml (⅓ fl oz) Advocaat
10ml (⅓ fl oz) Blue Curaçao

Layer ingredients in order given into a test tube and serve.

Fire and Ice Shooter

33% ALC/VOL • 0.8 STD DRINKS

20ml (⅔ fl oz) Tequila
10ml (⅓ fl oz) Green Crème De Menthe

Layer ingredients in order given into a cordial Embassy glass and serve.

Black Widow Shooter

20.4% ALC/VOL • 0.5 STD DRINKS

10ml (⅓ fl oz) Strawberry Liqueur
10ml (⅓ fl oz) Black Sambuca
10ml (⅓ fl oz) Fresh Cream

Layer ingredients in order given into a cordial Embassy glass and serve.

Hard On

16% ALC/VOL • 0.4 STD DRINKS

10ml (⅓ fl oz) Kahlúa
10ml (⅓ fl oz) Amaretto
10ml (⅓ fl oz) Fresh Cream

Layer ingredients in order given into a cordial Lexington glass and serve.

Lady Killer

21% ALC/VOL • 0.6 STD DRINKS

15ml (½ fl oz) Kahlúa
15ml (½ fl oz) Midori
5ml (⅙ fl oz) Frangelico

Layer ingredients in order given into a cordial Embassy glass and serve.

Grand Bailey's

24.6% ALC/VOL • 0.6 STD DRINKS

20ml (⅔ fl oz) Bailey's Irish Cream
10ml (⅓ fl oz) Grand Marnier

Layer ingredients in order given into a cordial Embassy glass and serve.

B-52

25.7% ALC/VOL • 0.6 STD DRINKS

10ml (⅓ fl oz) Kahlúa
10ml (⅓ fl oz) Bailey's Irish Cream
10ml (⅓ fl oz) Grand Marnier

Layer ingredients in order given into a test tube and serve.

Godfather Shooter

34% ALC/VOL • 0.8 STD DRINKS

15ml (½ fl oz) Amaretto
15ml (½ fl oz) Scotch Whisky

Layer ingredients in order given into a cordial Embassy glass and serve.

Chastity Belt

20.2% ALC/VOL • 0.6 STD DRINKS

15ml (½ fl oz) Tia Maria
10ml (⅓ fl oz) Frangelico
10ml (⅓ fl oz) Bailey's Irish Cream
5ml (⅙ fl oz) Fresh Cream

Layer ingredients in order given into a tall Dutch cordial glass and serve.

Angel Dew

28.5% ALC/VOL • 0.7 STD DRINKS

15ml (½ fl oz) Bénédictine
15ml (½ fl oz) Bailey's Irish Cream

Layer ingredients in order given into a cordial Embassy glass and serve.

Water-Bubba

20.3% ALC/VOL • 0.6 STD DRINKS

15ml (½ fl oz) Cherry Advocaat
10ml (⅓ fl oz) Advocaat
12ml (⅖ fl oz) Blue Curaçao

Layer ingredients in order given into a cordial Lexington glass and serve.

Perfect Match

22% ALC/VOL • 0.6 STD DRINKS

18ml (⅗ fl oz) Parfait Amour
18ml (⅗ fl oz) Malibu

Layer ingredients in order given into a cordial Lexington glass and serve.

Anabolic Steroids

30.4% ALC/VOL • 0.7 STD DRINKS

15ml (½ fl oz) Midori
15ml (½ fl oz) Cointreau
Dash Blue Curaçao

Layer ingredients in order given into a test tube and serve.

Snake Bite

18.2% ALC/VOL • 0.4 STD DRINKS

15ml (½ fl oz) Kahlúa
15ml (½ fl oz) Green Crème De Menthe

Layer ingredients in order given into a cordial Embassy glass and serve.

401

23.9% ALC/VOL • 0.6 STD DRINKS

10ml (⅓ fl oz) Kahlúa
10ml (⅓ fl oz) Banana Liqueur
5ml (⅙ fl oz) Bailey's Irish Cream
5ml (⅙ fl oz) Tennessee Whiskey

Layer ingredients in order given into a cordial Embassy glass and serve.

Q.F.

19.7% ALC/VOL • 0.5 STD DRINKS

12ml (⅖ fl oz) Kahlúa
12ml (⅖ fl oz) Midori
8ml (¼ fl oz) Bailey's Irish Cream

Layer ingredients in order given into a cordial Embassy glass and serve.

Lamborghini

29% ALC/VOL • 0.7 STD DRINKS

8ml (¼ fl oz) Galliano
15ml (½ fl oz) Kahlúa
8ml (¼ fl oz) Yellow Chartreuse

Layer ingredients in order given into a cordial Embassy glass and serve.

Hell Raiser

27.4% ALC/VOL • 0.6 STD DRINKS

10ml (⅓ fl oz) Strawberry Liqueur
10ml (⅓ fl oz) Midori
10ml (⅓ fl oz) Black Sambuca

Layer ingredients in order given into a shot glass and serve.

Japanese Traffic Lights

22.3% ALC/VOL • 0.5 STD DRINKS

10ml (⅓ fl oz) Banana Liqueur
10ml (⅓ fl oz) Strawberry Liqueur
10ml (⅓ fl oz) Midori

Layer ingredients in order given into a tall Dutch cordial glass and serve.

Angel's Tip

15% ALC/VOL • 0.5 STD DRINKS

15ml (½ fl oz) Dark Crème De Cacao
15ml (½ fl oz) Bailey's Irish Cream
10ml (⅓ fl oz) Fresh Cream

Layer ingredients in order given into a cordial Embassy glass and serve.

Silver Thread

24.1% ALC/VOL • 0.9 STD DRINKS

15ml (½ fl oz) Green Crème De Menthe
15ml (½ fl oz) Banana Liqueur
15ml (½ fl oz) Tia Maria

Layer ingredients in order given into a tall Dutch cordial glass and serve.

Miles of Smiles

29.7% ALC/VOL • 1.1 STD DRINKS

15ml (½ fl oz) Green Crème De Menthe
15ml (½ fl oz) Amaretto
15ml (½ fl oz) Rye Whiskey

Layer ingredients in order given into a tall Dutch cordial glass and serve.

Devil's Handbrake

21.3% ALC/VOL • 0.5 STD DRINKS

10ml (⅓ fl oz) Banana Liqueur
10ml (⅓ fl oz) Mango Liqueur
10ml (⅓ fl oz) Cherry Advocaat

Layer ingredients in order given into a tall Dutch cordial glass and serve.

Stars and Stripes

8.3% ALC/VOL • 0.2 STD DRINKS

10ml (⅓ fl oz) Grenadine
10ml (⅓ fl oz) Thick Cream
10ml (⅓ fl oz) Blue Curaçao

Layer ingredients in order given into a tall Dutch cordial glass and serve.

Monkey's Punch

20% ALC/VOL • 0.6 STD DRINKS

10ml (⅓ fl oz) Kahlúa
15ml (½ fl oz) Green Crème De Menthe
15ml (½ fl oz) Bailey's Irish Cream

Layer ingredients in order given into a cordial Lexington glass and serve.

Test-Tube Baby

38.3% ALC/VOL • 0.9 STD DRINKS

15ml (½ fl oz) Grand Marnier
15ml (½ fl oz) Tequila
Dash Bailey's Irish Cream

Layer ingredients in order given into a test tube and serve.

Fuzzy Irishman

19% ALC/VOL • 0.4 STD DRINKS

10ml (⅓ fl oz) Raspberry Liqueur
10ml (⅓ fl oz) Butterscotch Schnapps
10ml (⅓ fl oz) Bailey's Irish Cream

Pour ingredients in order given into a cordial Embassy glass – do not stir, then serve.

Cough Drop

21% ALC/VOL • 0.7 STD DRINKS

30ml (1 fl oz) Butterscotch Schnapps
15ml (½ fl oz) Green Crème De Menthe

Layer ingredients in order given into a shot glass and serve.

Chocolate Almond

22.7% ALC/VOL • 0.5 STD DRINKS

10ml (⅓ fl oz) Amaretto
10ml (⅓ fl oz) Bailey's Irish Cream
10ml (⅓ fl oz) Dark Crème De Cacao

Layer ingredients in order given into a cordial Embassy glass and serve.

Bloodbath

30.5% ALC/VOL • 0.7 STD DRINKS

15ml (½ fl oz) Strawberry Liqueur
15ml (½ fl oz) Tequila

Layer ingredients in order given into a test tube and serve.

Passed Out Naked on the Bathroom Floor

49.7% ALC/VOL • 1.3 STD DRINKS

8ml (¼ fl oz) Rumplemintz
8ml (¼ fl oz) Jägermeister
8ml (¼ fl oz) Gold Tequila
8ml (¼ fl oz) 151-Proof Bacardi

Pour ingredients in order given into a shot glass – do not stir, then serve.

Tickled Pink

20.4% ALC/VOL • 0.7 STD DRINKS

40ml (1⅓ fl oz) White Crème De Menthe
5ml (⅙ fl oz) Grenadine

Layer ingredients in order given into a shot glass and serve.

Little Bitch

24.4% ALC/VOL • 0.8 STD DRINKS

15ml (½ fl oz) Amaretto
15ml (½ fl oz) Southern Comfort

5ml (1/6 fl oz) Cranberry Juice
5ml (1/6 fl oz) Fresh Orange Juice

Pour ingredients into a cocktail shaker over ice and shake. Strain into a chilled shot glass and serve.

Braindead

25.6% ALC/VOL • 0.9 STD DRINKS

15ml (½ fl oz) Cointreau
15ml (½ fl oz) Vodka
15ml (½ fl oz) Sweet and Sour Mix

Pour ingredients into a cocktail shaker over ice and shake. Strain into a chilled shot glass and serve.

Springbok

18.5% ALC/VOL • 0.5 STD DRINKS

23ml (¾ fl oz) Green Crème De Menthe
8ml (¼ fl oz) Amarula Cream
5ml (1/6 fl oz) Fresh Cream

Layer ingredients in order given into a cordial Embassy glass and serve.

Marajuana Milkshake

14.7% ALC/VOL • 0.5 STD DRINKS

15ml (½ fl oz) White Crème De Cacao
15ml (½ fl oz) Midori
15ml (½ fl oz) Fresh Milk (chilled)

Pour ingredients in order given gently into a shot glass and serve.

Golden Comfort

38.5% ALC/VOL • 1.4 STD DRINKS

15ml (½ fl oz) Goldschläger
15ml (½ fl oz) Jägermeister
15ml (½ fl oz) Southern Comfort

Pour ingredients into a cocktail shaker over ice and shake. Strain into a chilled shot glass and serve.

Flaming Armadillo

37.7% ALC/VOL • 1.3 STD DRINKS

20ml (⅔ fl oz) Tequila
20ml (⅔ fl oz) Amaretto
5ml (1/6 fl oz) 151-Proof Rum

Layer ingredients in order given into a shot glass, ignite and shoot while flaming.

Ironlung

38.4% ALC/VOL • 1.2 STD DRINKS

30ml (1 fl oz) Yukon Jack
3 drops 151-Proof Bacardi
Fresh Whipped Cream

Pour Yukon Jack into a shot glass and add Bacardi by drops – do not stir. Float cream on top and serve.

Brass Balls

20% ALC/VOL • 0.5 STD DRINKS

10ml (⅓ fl oz) Grand Marnier
10ml (⅓ fl oz) Peach Schnapps
10ml (⅓ fl oz) Pineapple Juice

Pour ingredients into a mixing glass over ice and stir. Strain into a chilled shot glass and serve.

Kilted Black Leprechaun

26% ALC/VOL • 0.6 STD DRINKS

10ml (⅓ fl oz) Bailey's Irish Cream
10ml (⅓ fl oz) Malibu
10ml (⅓ fl oz) Drambuie

Pour ingredients gently in order given into a cordial Embassy glass – do not stir, then serve.

Shot of Respect

55.3% ALC/VOL • 1.8 STD DRINKS

20ml (⅔ fl oz) Tequila
20ml (⅔ fl oz) 151-Proof Rum
Dash Tabasco Sauce

Pour Tequila and Rum into a shot glass – do not stir. Add sauce and serve.

69er in a Pool

54.4% ALC/VOL • 1.3 STD DRINKS

15ml (½ fl oz) Vodka
Dash Fresh Lemon Juice
15ml (½ fl oz) 151-Proof Bacardi
Drop of Tabasco Sauce

Layer ingredients in order given into a shot glass and serve.

Gold Baron

48.3% ALC/VOL • 1.2 STD DRINKS

23ml (¾ fl oz) Rumplemintz
8ml (¼ fl oz) Goldschläger

Layer ingredients in order given into a cordial Embassy glass and serve.

Damn Good!

15.9% ALC/VOL • 0.5 STD DRINKS

15ml (½ fl oz) Butterscotch Schnapps
8ml (¼ fl oz) Green Crème De Menthe
8ml (¼ fl oz) Bailey's Irish Cream
8ml (¼ fl oz) Grenadine

Pour Schnapps into a cordial Lexington glass and layer Crème De Menthe on top then layer Bailey's on top. Add Grenadine by pouring down inside rim of glass and allow to settle on bottom of drink then serve.

Return of the Yeti

30.2% ALC/VOL • 1.1 STD DRINKS

15ml (½ fl oz) Lychee Liqueur
15ml (½ fl oz) Parfait Amour
15ml (½ fl oz) Goldschläger

Layer ingredients in order given into a tall Dutch cordial glass and serve.

Blood Clot

18.5% ALC/VOL • 0.9 STD DRINKS

30ml (1 fl oz) Southern Comfort
15ml (½ fl oz) Grenadine
15ml (½ fl oz) Lemonade

Pour Grenadine into a chilled old-fashioned glass and add lemonade then stir gently. Add Southern Comfort – do not stir, then serve.

Tartan Special

26.7% ALC/VOL • 0.6 STD DRINKS

10ml (⅓ fl oz) Bailey's Irish Cream
10ml (⅓ fl oz) Drambuie
10ml (⅓ fl oz) Peachtree

Pour ingredients into a cocktail shaker over ice and shake. Strain into a chilled shot glass and serve.

Licorice Heart

26.1% ALC/VOL • 0.6 STD DRINKS

10ml (⅓ fl oz) Strawberry Liqueur
10ml (⅓ fl oz) Sambuca
10ml (⅓ fl oz) Bailey's Irish Cream

Layer ingredients in order given into a cordial Embassy glass and serve.

Triple Irish Shooter

32.4% ALC/VOL • 0.8 STD DRINKS

10ml (⅓ fl oz) Irish Whiskey
10ml (⅓ fl oz) Irish Mist
10ml (⅓ fl oz) Bailey's Irish Cream

Layer ingredients in order given into a cordial Embassy glass and serve.

Swedish Color

28.3% ALC/VOL • 0.7 STD DRINKS

10ml (⅓ fl oz) Vodka
10ml (⅓ fl oz) Banana Liqueur
10ml (⅓ fl oz) Blue Curaçao

Layer ingredients in order given into a cordial Embassy glass and serve.

Banshee Berry

22% ALC/VOL • 0.6 STD DRINKS

12ml (⅖ fl oz) Banana Liqueur
12ml (⅖ fl oz) Strawberry Schnapps
12ml (⅖ fl oz) White Crème De Cacao

Pour ingredients into a shot glass, stir and serve.

Green Jolly Rancher

24.9% ALC/VOL • 0.7 STD DRINKS

15ml (½ fl oz) Midori
15ml (½ fl oz) Southern Comfort
5ml (⅙ fl oz) Sweet and Sour Mix

Pour ingredients into a cocktail shaker over ice and shake. Strain into a chilled shot glass and serve.

Wet Kiss

16% ALC/VOL • 0.6 STD DRINKS

15ml (½ fl oz) Amaretto
15ml (½ fl oz) Watermelon Schnapps
15ml (½ fl oz) Sweet and Sour Mix

Layer ingredients in order given into a tall Dutch cordial glass and serve.

Bulgaria Unite

20% ALC/VOL • 0.7 STD DRINKS

15ml (½ fl oz) Vodka
15ml (½ fl oz) Green Crème De Menthe
15ml (½ fl oz) Grenadine

Layer ingredients in order given into a tall Dutch cordial glass and serve.

Flaming Russian

49.8% ALC/VOL • 1.8 STD DRINKS

30ml (1 fl oz) Vodka
15ml (½ fl oz) 151-Proof Bacardi

Layer ingredients in order given into a shot glass, ignite and serve.

Great White Shark

37.8% ALC/VOL • 0.9 STD DRINKS

15ml (½ fl oz) Tennessee Whiskey
15ml (½ fl oz) White Tequila
Dash Tabasco Sauce

Pour ingredients into a cocktail shaker over ice and shake. Strain into a chilled shot glass and serve.

Sweet Shot

31% ALC/VOL • 0.8 STD DRINKS

15ml (½ fl oz) Dark Rum
8ml (¼ fl oz) Coconut Liqueur
8ml (¼ fl oz) Amaretto

Layer ingredients in order given into a cordial Lexington glass and serve.

Spot Shooter

27.9% ALC/VOL • 1 STD DRINK

23ml (¾ fl oz) Vodka
23ml (¾ fl oz) Kahlúa
4 drops Bailey's Irish Cream

Pour Vodka into a tall Dutch cordial glass and layer Kahlúa on top. Add Bailey's by drops and serve.

Easy does it

44% ALC/VOL • 1.6 STD DRINKS

15ml (½ fl oz) Bailey's Irish Cream
15ml (½ fl oz) Kahlúa
15ml (½ fl oz) Everclear

Pour Bailey's into a shot glass and add Kahlúa – do not stir. Layer Everclear on top and serve.

Blood of Satan

39.7% ALC/VOL • 1.3 STD DRINKS

10ml (⅓ fl oz) Jägermeister
10ml (⅓ fl oz) Goldschläger
10ml (⅓ fl oz) Irish Whiskey
10ml (⅓ fl oz) Tennessee Whiskey

Layer ingredients in order given into a tall Dutch cordial glass and serve.
This drink is also known as Red Cross.

King's Cup

22.8% ALC/VOL • 0.4 STD DRINKS

15ml (½ fl oz) Galliano
8ml (¼ fl oz) Fresh Cream

Layer ingredients in order given into a cordial Embassy glass and serve.

The Oh Zone Layer

16.7% ALC/VOL • 0.4 STD DRINKS

10ml (⅓ fl oz) Sweet and Sour Mix
10ml (⅓ fl oz) Triple Sec
10ml (⅓ fl oz) Blue Curaçao

Layer ingredients in order given into a cordial Embassy glass and serve.

Flirting Carries

22.7% ALC/VOL • 0.8 STD DRINKS

15ml (½ fl oz) Peach Schnapps
15ml (½ fl oz) Strawberry Liqueur
15ml (½ fl oz) Triple Sec

Layer ingredients in order given into a tall Dutch cordial glass and serve.

Echo Hemoraging Tumor

17.3% ALC/VOL • 0.4 STD DRINKS

30ml (1 fl oz) Bailey's Irish Cream
6 drops Blue Curaçao
8 drops Strawberry Schnapps

Pour Bailey's into a shot glass and add Curaçao by drops. Add Schnapps by drops and serve.

American Flag Cordial

26.7% ALC/VOL • 0.6 STD DRINKS

10ml (⅓ fl oz) Grenadine
10ml (⅓ fl oz) Maraschino Liqueur
10ml (⅓ fl oz) Crème Yvette

Layer ingredients in order given into a cordial Embassy glass and serve.

Sacrilicious

18.7% ALC/VOL • 0.4 STD DRINKS

10ml (⅓ fl oz) Bacardi Limon
10ml (⅓ fl oz) Midori
10ml (⅓ fl oz) Fresh Lime Juice

Pour ingredients into a mixing glass over ice and stir. Strain into a chilled shot glass and serve.

Twister Shooter

32.4% ALC/VOL • 0.8 STD DRINKS

10ml (⅓ fl oz) Cherry Brandy
10ml (⅓ fl oz) Ouzo
10ml (⅓ fl oz) Vodka

Layer ingredients in order given into a cordial Embassy glass and serve.

Leather Whip

30.8% ALC/VOL • 0.8 STD DRINKS

8ml (¼ fl oz) Peach Schnapps
8ml (¼ fl oz) Tennessee Whiskey
8ml (¼ fl oz) Tequila
8ml (¼ fl oz) Triple Sec

Pour ingredients into a shot glass, stir and serve.

Cunnilingus

9.6% ALC/VOL • 0.2 STD DRINKS

8ml (¼ fl oz) Bailey's Irish Cream
8ml (¼ fl oz) Peach Schnapps
15ml (½ fl oz) Pineapple Juice

Pour ingredients into a mixing glass over ice and stir. Strain into a chilled shot glass and serve.

Sex in the Parking Lot

24.5% ALC/VOL • 0.9 STD DRINKS

15ml (½ fl oz) Apple Schnapps
15ml (½ fl oz) Chambord
15ml (½ fl oz) Vodka

Pour ingredients into a cocktail shaker over ice and shake. Strain into a chilled shot glass and serve.

Beam Me Up Scottie

20.1% ALC/VOL • 0.5 STD DRINKS

10ml (⅓ fl oz) Kahlúa
10ml (⅓ fl oz) Banana Liqueur
10ml (⅓ fl oz) Bailey's Irish Cream

Layer ingredients in order given into a cordial Embassy glass and serve.

Mushroom

12.7% ALC/VOL • 0.5 STD DRINKS

15ml (½ fl oz) Grenadine
15ml (½ fl oz) Midori
15ml (½ fl oz) Bailey's Irish Cream

Pour Grenadine into a shot glass and layer Midori on top. Add Bailey's by pouring into centre of drink – do not stir, then serve.

T.L.A.

28.3% ALC/VOL • 0.8 STD DRINKS

15ml (½ fl oz) Tequila
15ml (½ fl oz) Amaretto
5ml (1/6 fl oz) Fresh Lime Juice

Layer ingredients in order given into a cordial Lexington glass and serve.

Jenifer's Tattoo

26% ALC/VOL • 0.6 STD DRINKS

12ml (2/5 fl oz) Butterscotch Schnapps
6ml (1/5 fl oz) Tequila
12ml (2/5 fl oz) Sloe Gin

Layer ingredients in order given into a cordial Lexington glass and serve.

Mexican Breeze

30.7% ALC/VOL • 0.7 STD DRINKS

10ml (⅓ fl oz) Southern Comfort
10ml (⅓ fl oz) Tequila
10ml (⅓ fl oz) Bailey's Irish Cream

Layer ingredients in order given into a cordial Embassy glass and serve.

Alaskian Oil Slick

22.8% ALC/VOL • 0.7 STD DRINKS

20ml (⅔ fl oz) Blue Curaçao
20ml (⅔ fl oz) Peppermint Schnapps
Dash Jägermeister

Pour Curaçao and Schnapps into a mixing glass over ice. Stir and strain into a chilled shot glass. Add Jägermeister – do not stir, then serve.

Flame Thrower

30.9% ALC/VOL • 0.8 STD DRINKS

8ml (¼ fl oz) Brandy
8ml (¼ fl oz) Bénédictine
15ml (½ fl oz) White Crème De Cacao

Layer ingredients in order given into a shot glass and serve.

Backfire

24.7% ALC/VOL • 0.6 STD DRINKS

10ml (⅓ fl oz) Kahlúa
10ml (⅓ fl oz) Bailey's Irish Cream
10ml (⅓ fl oz) Vodka

Layer ingredients in order given into a cordial Embassy glass and serve.

Three Stages of Friendship

51.1% ALC/VOL • 1.2 STD DRINKS

10ml (⅓ fl oz) 151-Proof Rum
10ml (⅓ fl oz) Tennessee Whiskey
10ml (⅓ fl oz) Tequila

Pour ingredients into a shot glass, stir and serve.

Door County Cherry Cheesecake

9.5% ALC/VOL • 0.7 STD DRINKS

45ml (1½ fl oz) Vanilla Schnapps
30ml (1 fl oz) Maraschino Cherry Juice
15ml (½ fl oz) Cranberry Juice
5ml (1/6 fl oz) Fresh Cream

Pour ingredients into a cocktail shaker over ice and shake. Strain into three chilled shot glasses and serve.

Rhino

25.7% ALC/VOL • 0.9 STD DRINKS

15ml (½ fl oz) Kahlúa
15ml (½ fl oz) Cointreau
15ml (½ fl oz) Amarula Cream

Layer ingredients in order given into a tall Dutch cordial glass and serve.

City Hot Shot

16.7% ALC/VOL • 0.3 STD DRINKS

8ml (¼ fl oz) Triple Sec
8ml (¼ fl oz) Blue Curaçao
8ml (¼ fl oz) Grenadine

Pour ingredients in order given into a cordial Embassy glass – do not stir, then serve.

Arrack Attack

34.8% ALC/VOL • 1.4 STD DRINKS

20ml (⅔ fl oz) Green Crème De Menthe
20ml (⅔ fl oz) Arrack
10ml (⅓ fl oz) Sambuca

Layer ingredients in order given into a liqueur glass, ignite and serve with a straw.

Liberace

31.8% ALC/VOL • 0.8 STD DRINKS

10ml (⅓ fl oz) Kahlúa
10ml (⅓ fl oz) Fresh Milk (chilled)

10ml (⅓ fl oz) 151-Proof Bacardi

Layer ingredients in order given into a cordial Embassy glass and ignite. Extinguish flame and serve.

Chip Shot

12.7% ALC/VOL • 0.5 STD DRINKS

15ml (½ fl oz) Light Rum
15ml (½ fl oz) Cranberry Juice
15ml (½ fl oz) Pineapple Juice

Pour ingredients into a cocktail shaker over ice and shake. Strain into a chilled shot glass and serve.

Afterbirth

12.4% ALC/VOL • 0.4 STD DRINKS

15ml (½ fl oz) Bailey's Irish Cream
15ml (½ fl oz) Raspberry Schnapps
15ml (½ fl oz) Grenadine

Pour Schnapps and Grenadine into a shot glass then stir. Layer Bailey's on top and serve.

Chocolate Chimp

24.1% ALC/VOL • 0.9 STD DRINKS

15ml (½ fl oz) Dark Crème De Cacao
15ml (½ fl oz) Tia Maria
15ml (½ fl oz) Banana Liqueur

Layer ingredients in order given into a tall Dutch cordial glass and serve.

Berlin Wall

42.9% ALC/VOL • 1 STD DRINK

10ml (⅓ fl oz) Jägermeister
10ml (⅓ fl oz) Goldschläger
10ml (⅓ fl oz) Rumplemintz

Layer ingredients in order given into a cordial Embassy glass and serve.

Southern Fruity Passion

20.6% ALC/VOL • 0.6 STD DRINKS

12ml (⅖ fl oz) Southern Comfort
12ml (⅖ fl oz) Triple Sec
12ml (⅖ fl oz) Grenadine

Layer ingredients in order given into a cordial Embassy glass and serve.

Jamboree

24.5% ALC/VOL • 0.7 STD DRINKS

15ml (½ fl oz) Vodka
15ml (½ fl oz) Wilderberry Schnapps
5ml (⅙ fl oz) Cranberry Juice

Pour ingredients into a mixing glass over ice and stir. Strain into a chilled shot glass and serve.

Pleasure Dome

33.3% ALC/VOL • 1.2 STD DRINKS

15ml (½ fl oz) Brandy
15ml (½ fl oz) White Crème De Cacao
15ml (½ fl oz) Bénédictine

Layer ingredients in order given into a tall Dutch cordial glass and serve.

G-Spot

17.8% ALC/VOL • 0.6 STD DRINKS

15ml (½ fl oz) Chambord
15ml (½ fl oz) Southern Comfort
15ml (½ fl oz) Fresh Orange Juice

Pour ingredients into a cocktail shaker over ice and shake. Strain into a chilled shot glass and serve.

Anonymous

17.8% ALC/VOL • 0.6 STD DRINKS

15ml (½ fl oz) Chambord
15ml (½ fl oz) Southern Comfort
15ml (½ fl oz) Sweet and Sour Mix

Pour ingredients into a mixing glass over ice and stir. Strain into a chilled shot glass and serve.

John Doe

20.7% ALC/VOL • 0.7 STD DRINKS

15ml (½ fl oz) Bailey's Irish Cream
15ml (½ fl oz) Raspberry Liqueur
15ml (½ fl oz) Triple Sec

Pour ingredients into a cocktail shaker over ice and shake. Strain into a chilled shot glass and serve.

Blue Moon Shooter

23.3% ALC/VOL • 0.6 STD DRINKS

10ml (⅓ fl oz) Amaretto
10ml (⅓ fl oz) Blue Curaçao
10ml (⅓ fl oz) Bailey's Irish Cream

Layer ingredients in order given into a cordial Embassy glass and serve.

B-51

20.4% ALC/VOL • 0.5 STD DRINKS

10ml (⅓ fl oz) Kahlúa
10ml (⅓ fl oz) Bailey's Irish Cream
10ml (⅓ fl oz) Frangelico

Layer ingredients in order given into a shot glass and serve.
This drink is also known as 747, p 345.

Estonian Forest Fire

34.7% ALC/VOL • 0.9 STD DRINKS

30ml (1 fl oz) Vodka
12 drops Tabasco Sauce
1 Fresh Kiwi Fruit

Pour Vodka and sauce into a shot glass then stir. Serve with a kiwi fruit – to be consumed after shooting.

Doucet Devil

29% ALC/VOL • 0.7 STD DRINKS

15ml (½ fl oz) Amaretto
8ml (¼ fl oz) Southern Comfort
8ml (¼ fl oz) Banana Liqueur

Layer ingredients in order given into a cordial Embassy glass and serve.

Rattlesnake Shooter

20.1% ALC/VOL • 0.5 STD DRINKS

10ml (⅓ fl oz) Kahlúa
10ml (⅓ fl oz) White Crème De Cacao
10ml (⅓ fl oz) Bailey's Irish Cream

Layer ingredients in order given into a test tube and serve.

Louisiana Shooter

35.6% ALC/VOL • 0.9 STD DRINKS

30ml (1 fl oz) Tequila
Dash Tabasco Sauce
¼ teaspoon Horseradish
Piece of Fresh Oyster

Place a piece of oyster into a shot glass, add remaining ingredients and stir well then serve.

Amy Girl

22.4% ALC/VOL • 0.6 STD DRINKS

12ml (⅖ fl oz) Banana Liqueur
12ml (⅖ fl oz) Frangelico
12ml (⅖ fl oz) Butterscotch Schnapps

Layer ingredients in order given into a cordial Lexington glass and serve.

Meloncholy Baby

27.6% ALC/VOL • 0.7 STD DRINKS

10ml (⅓ fl oz) Midori
10ml (⅓ fl oz) Vodka
10ml (⅓ fl oz) Triple Sec

Layer ingredients in order given into a cordial Embassy glass and serve.
This drink is also known as Koala Bear.

Cocaine

17.8% ALC/VOL • 0.6 STD DRINKS

15ml (½ fl oz) Chambord
15ml (½ fl oz) Vodka
15ml (½ fl oz) Grapefruit Juice

Pour ingredients into a cocktail shaker over ice and shake. Strain into a chilled shot glass and serve.

Placenta

21.8% ALC/VOL • 0.5 STD DRINKS

15ml (½ fl oz) Amaretto
15ml (½ fl oz) Bailey's Irish Cream
3 drops Grenadine

Pour Amaretto into a cordial Embassy glass and add Bailey's – do not stir. Add Grenadine by drops and serve.

Innocent Eyes

25.1% ALC/VOL • 0.6 STD DRINKS

10ml (⅓ fl oz) Kahlúa
10ml (⅓ fl oz) Sambuca
10ml (⅓ fl oz) Bailey's Irish Cream

Layer ingredients in order given into a cordial Embassy glass and serve.

Smurf Town

16.5% ALC/VOL • 0.5 STD DRINKS

15ml (½ fl oz) Blue Curaçao
15ml (½ fl oz) Peach Schnapps
5 drops Grenadine
Fresh Whipped Cream

Pour Curaçao and Schnapps into a shot glass then stir. Float cream on top and add Grenadine by drops over cream then serve.

Lick it Real Good

19% ALC/VOL • 0.7 STD DRINKS

23ml (¾ fl oz) Tequila
23ml (¾ fl oz) Fresh Orange Juice

Pour ingredients into a shot glass, stir and serve.

Chocolate Sundae

15.1% ALC/VOL • 0.5 STD DRINKS

10ml (⅓ fl oz) Kahlúa
10ml (⅓ fl oz) Bailey's Irish Cream
10ml (⅓ fl oz) White Crème De Cacao
Fresh Whipped Cream

Layer ingredients in order given into a cordial Lexington glass, float cream on top and serve.

Dancin' Cowboy

20.1% ALC/VOL • 0.5 STD DRINKS

10ml (⅓ fl oz) Banana Liqueur
10ml (⅓ fl oz) Kahlúa
10ml (⅓ fl oz) Bailey's Irish Cream

Layer ingredients in order given into a shot glass and serve.

Jamaica Dust

21.1% ALC/VOL • 0.5 STD DRINKS

10ml (⅓ fl oz) Southern Comfort
10ml (⅓ fl oz) Tia Maria
10ml (⅓ fl oz) Pineapple Juice

Pour ingredients into a cocktail shaker over ice and shake. Strain into a chilled shot glass and serve.

Vanilla Kiss

6.7% ALC/VOL • 0.2 STD DRINKS

15ml (½ fl oz) Vanilla Schnapps
15ml (½ fl oz) Hot Cocoa
15ml (½ fl oz) Fresh Cream

Layer ingredients in order given into a tall Dutch cordial glass and serve.

Bob Marley Shot

42.4% ALC/VOL • 1 STD DRINK

15ml (½ fl oz) 151-Proof Bacardi
8ml (¼ fl oz) White Crème De Menthe
8ml (¼ fl oz) Grenadine

Pour Grenadine and Crème De Menthe into a shot glass - do not stir. Layer Bacardi on top and ignite then serve with a straw.

Fiery Blue Mustang

47.6% ALC/VOL • 1.7 STD DRINKS

15ml (½ fl oz) Banana Liqueur
15ml (½ fl oz) Blue Curaçao
15ml (½ fl oz) Everclear

Pour ingredients into a shot glass and stir. Ignite then extinguish flame and serve.

Mind Eraser

19% ALC/VOL • 1.3 STD DRINKS

30ml (1 fl oz) Vodka
30ml (1 fl oz) Kahlúa
30ml (1 fl oz) Soda Water

Layer ingredients in order given into an old-fashioned glass over cracked ice. Serve with a straw and shoot through straw.

Spice Cake

21.7% ALC/VOL • 0.6 STD DRINKS

12ml (2/5 fl oz) Amaretto
12ml (2/5 fl oz) Bailey's Irish Cream
12ml (2/5 fl oz) Cinnamon Schnapps

Pour ingredients into a cocktail shaker over ice and shake. Strain into a chilled shot glass and serve.

Coffee Grinder

23.5% ALC/VOL • 0.7 STD DRINKS

12ml (2/5 fl oz) Amaretto
12ml (2/5 fl oz) Bailey's Irish Cream
12ml (2/5 fl oz) Kahlúa
4 drops Scotch Whisky

Pour ingredients into a shot glass, stir and serve.

Apple Pie Shot

28.1% ALC/VOL • 1 STD DRINK

30ml (1 fl oz) Vodka
5ml (1/6 fl oz) Cinnamon Schnapps
8ml (¼ fl oz) Apple Juice

Pour ingredients into a mixing glass over ice and stir. Strain into a chilled shot glass and serve.

Camel Driver

27.5% ALC/VOL • 0.9 STD DRINKS

20ml (⅔ fl oz) Sambuca
20ml (⅔ fl oz) Bailey's Irish Cream

Layer ingredients in order given into a cordial Lexington glass and serve.
This drink is also known as Dirty Nipple.

Green Fly Shooter

22% ALC/VOL • 0.5 STD DRINKS

15ml (½ fl oz) Green Crème De Menthe
15ml (½ fl oz) Midori

Layer ingredients in order given into a cordial Embassy glass and serve.

Red Cross

39.7% ALC/VOL • 1.3 STD DRINKS

This drink is also known as Blood of Satan, p 339.

Screamer

35% ALC/VOL • 1.1 STD DRINKS

8ml (¼ fl oz) Gin
8ml (¼ fl oz) Light Rum
8ml (¼ fl oz) Tequila
8ml (¼ fl oz) Triple Sec
8ml (¼ fl oz) Vodka

Pour ingredients into a mixing glass over ice and stir. Strain into a chilled shot glass and serve.

Miami Ice

20.5% ALC/VOL • 0.5 STD DRINKS

15ml (½ fl oz) Kahlúa
15ml (½ fl oz) Malibu

Pour ingredients into a cocktail shaker over ice and shake. Strain into a chilled shot glass and serve.

Bayou Juice

16.8% ALC/VOL • 0.5 STD DRINKS

8ml (¼ fl oz) Amaretto
8ml (¼ fl oz) Malibu
8ml (¼ fl oz) Spiced Rum
8ml (¼ fl oz) Cranberry Juice
8ml (¼ fl oz) Pineapple Juice

Pour ingredients into a cocktail shaker over ice and shake. Strain into a chilled shot glass and serve.

Black Rain

18.7% ALC/VOL • 0.5 STD DRINKS

8ml (¼ fl oz) Black Sambuca
23ml (¾ fl oz) Champagne

Pour ingredients in order given into a shot glass, stir briefly and serve.

Angel's Ride

20% ALC/VOL • 0.7 STD DRINKS

15ml (½ fl oz) Dark Crème De Cacao
15ml (½ fl oz) Brandy
15ml (½ fl oz) Fresh Cream

Layer ingredients in order given into a pousse café glass and serve.

Mexican Leprechaun

30.5% ALC/VOL • 0.7 STD DRINKS

15ml (½ fl oz) Green Crème De Menthe
15ml (½ fl oz) Tequila

Layer ingredients in order given into a cordial Embassy glass and serve.

Flatliner

37.1% ALC/VOL • 1.2 STD DRINKS

20ml (⅔ fl oz) Sambuca
Dash Tabasco Sauce
20ml (⅔ fl oz) White Tequila

Layer ingredients in order given into a cordial Lexington glass and serve.

Red Skittle

10% ALC/VOL • 0.2 STD DRINKS

15ml (½ fl oz) Butterscotch Schnapps
15ml (½ fl oz) Grenadine

Pour ingredients into a shot glass, stir and serve.

Horsemen of the Apocalypse

38.3% ALC/VOL • 1.2 STD DRINKS

10ml (⅓ fl oz) Spiced Rum
10ml (⅓ fl oz) Tennessee Whiskey
10ml (⅓ fl oz) Tequila
10ml (⅓ fl oz) Bourbon

Pour each ingredient into individual shot glasses and shoot one after the other in order given.

Pineapple Bomber

21.6% ALC/VOL • 0.5 STD DRINKS

10ml (⅓ fl oz) Amaretto
10ml (⅓ fl oz) Southern Comfort
10ml (⅓ fl oz) Pineapple Juice

Pour ingredients into a cocktail shaker over ice and shake. Strain into a chilled shot glass and serve.

What Crisis?

10.3% ALC/VOL • 0.3 STD DRINKS

10ml (⅓ fl oz) Midori
10ml (⅓ fl oz) Peach Schnapps
10ml (⅓ fl oz) Cranberry Juice
10ml (⅓ fl oz) Fresh Orange Juice

Pour ingredients into a cocktail shaker over ice and shake. Strain into a chilled shot glass and serve.

Christmas Tree

27.6% ALC/VOL • 1 STD DRINK

15ml (½ fl oz) Vodka
15ml (½ fl oz) Green Crème De Menthe
15ml (½ fl oz) Cherry Brandy

Layer ingredients in order given into a tall Dutch cordial glass and serve.

Chocolate Covered Cherry Shot

22.9% ALC/VOL • 0.6 STD DRINKS

10ml (⅓ fl oz) Amaretto
10ml (⅓ fl oz) Kahlúa
10ml (⅓ fl oz) White Crème De Cacao
Dash Grenadine

Pour Amaretto, Kahlúa and Cacao into a shot glass then stir. Add Grenadine – do not stir, then serve.

Raging Indian

28.8% ALC/VOL • 0.7 STD DRINKS

8ml (¼ fl oz) Everclear
8ml (¼ fl oz) Kahlúa
8ml (¼ fl oz) Fresh Orange Juice
8ml (¼ fl oz) Mango Nectar

Pour ingredients into a cocktail shaker over ice and shake. Strain into a chilled shot glass and serve.

Twin Sisters

34% ALC/VOL • 0.9 STD DRINKS

15ml (½ fl oz) Bacardi
15ml (½ fl oz) Spiced Rum
Dash Rose's Lime Juice
Dash Cola

Pour Bacardi, Rum and juice into a cocktail shaker over ice. Shake and strain into a chilled shot glass. Add cola – do not stir, then serve.

Black Samurai

10.3% ALC/VOL • 0.4 STD DRINKS

30ml (1 fl oz) Sake
15ml (½ fl oz) Soy Sauce

Pour ingredients in order given into a shot glass – do not stir, then serve.

Irish Headlock

30.6% ALC/VOL • 0.8 STD DRINKS

8ml (¼ fl oz) Amaretto
8ml (¼ fl oz) Brandy
8ml (¼ fl oz) Bailey's Irish Cream
8ml (¼ fl oz) Irish Whiskey

Layer ingredients in order given into a cordial Embassy glass and serve.

Smoothie Nipple

20% ALC/VOL • 0.5 STD DRINKS

15ml (½ fl oz) Butterscotch Schnapps
15ml (½ fl oz) Kahlúa

Pour ingredients into a shot glass, stir and serve.

Lava Lamp

21.1% ALC/VOL • 0.5 STD DRINKS

8ml (¼ fl oz) Kahlúa
8ml (¼ fl oz) Strawberry Liqueur
8ml (¼ fl oz) Frangelico
8ml (¼ fl oz) Bailey's Irish Cream
3 drops Advocaat

Pour Kahlúa, Liqueur and Frangelico into a shot glass – do not stir. Layer Bailey's on top and add Advocaat by drops then serve.

Earthquake Shooter

34.3% ALC/VOL • 0.8 STD DRINKS

10ml (⅓ fl oz) Southern Comfort
10ml (⅓ fl oz) Amaretto
10ml (⅓ fl oz) Sambuca

Layer ingredients in order given into a cordial Embassy glass and serve.

B-28

19.9% ALC/VOL • 0.9 STD DRINKS

10ml (⅓ fl oz) Amaretto
10ml (⅓ fl oz) Kahlúa
30ml (1 fl oz) Bailey's Irish Cream
10ml (⅓ fl oz) Butterscotch Schnapps

Layer ingredients in order given into a liqueur glass and serve.

Cock Sucking Cowboy

19.5% ALC/VOL • 0.5 STD DRINKS

30ml (1 fl oz) Butterscotch Schnapps
5ml (⅙ fl oz) Bailey's Irish Cream

Layer ingredients in order given into a shot glass and serve.

Pink Panty

27.6% ALC/VOL • 0.7 STD DRINKS

15ml (½ fl oz) Cinnamon Schnapps
15ml (½ fl oz) Vodka
Dash Cranberry Juice

Pour Schnapps and Vodka into a cocktail shaker over ice. Shake and strain into a chilled shot glass. Add juice – do not stir, then serve.

A Bomb

22.5% ALC/VOL • 0.7 STD DRINKS

15ml (½ fl oz) Vodka
15ml (½ fl oz) Kahlúa
8ml (¼ fl oz) Black Coffee (chilled)

Layer ingredients in order given into a cordial Lexington glass and serve.

Burning Nazi

42.5% ALC/VOL • 1 STD DRINK

15ml (½ fl oz) Jägermeister
15ml (½ fl oz) Rumplemintz

Pour ingredients into a shot glass, stir and serve.

This drink is also known as Screaming Nazi.

Wrinkly Granny

20% ALC/VOL • 0.5 STD DRINKS

15ml (½ fl oz) Green Crème De Menthe
15ml (½ fl oz) Bailey's Irish Cream

Layer ingredients in order given into a cordial Embassy glass and serve.

747

20.4% ALC/VOL • 0.5 STD DRINKS

This drink is also known as B-51, p 341.

Mind Probe

49.5% ALC/VOL • 1.2 STD DRINKS

10ml (⅓ fl oz) Jägermeister
10ml (⅓ fl oz) Sambuca
10ml (⅓ fl oz) 151-Proof Rum

Pour ingredients in order given into a shot glass – do not stir, then serve.

Green Lizard

59.3% ALC/VOL • 1.8 STD DRINKS

30ml (1 fl oz) Green Chartreuse
8ml (¼ fl oz) 151-Proof Bacardi

Layer ingredients in order given into a shot glass, ignite and serve.

Dirty Nipple

27.5% ALC/VOL • 0.9 STD DRINKS

This drink is also known as Camel Driver, p 343.

Blurricane

39.1% ALC/VOL • 1.9 STD DRINKS

10ml (⅓ fl oz) Blue Curaçao
10ml (⅓ fl oz) Jägermeister

10ml (⅓ fl oz) Wild Turkey Bourbon
10ml (⅓ fl oz) Ouzo
10ml (⅓ fl oz) Goldschläger
10ml (⅓ fl oz) Rumplemintz

Layer ingredients in order given into an old-fashioned glass and serve.

German Burrito

36.5% ALC/VOL • 0.9 STD DRINKS

15ml (½ fl oz) Jägermeister
15ml (½ fl oz) Tequila

Pour ingredients into a shot glass, stir and serve.

Stained Blue Dress

31% ALC/VOL • 0.7 STD DRINKS

15ml (½ fl oz) Vodka
15ml (½ fl oz) Blue Curaçao
2 drops Bailey's Irish Cream

Pour Vodka into a cordial Embassy glass and layer Curaçao on top. Add Bailey's by drops and serve.

Canadian Ice

35% ALC/VOL • 0.8 STD DRINKS

15ml (½ fl oz) Peppermint Schnapps
15ml (½ fl oz) Yukon Jack

Pour ingredients into a shot glass, stir and serve.

Koala Bear

27.6% ALC/VOL • 0.7 STD DRINKS

This drink is also known as Meloncholy Baby, p 342.

I.R.A.

32.4% ALC/VOL • 0.8 STD DRINKS

10ml (⅓ fl oz) Bailey's Irish Cream
10ml (⅓ fl oz) Irish Mist
10ml (⅓ fl oz) Irish Whiskey

Pour ingredients into a shot glass, stir and serve.

Demon Drop

47.5% ALC/VOL • 1.1 STD DRINKS

15ml (½ fl oz) Everclear
15ml (½ fl oz) Fresh Orange Juice

Layer ingredients in order given into a shot glass and serve.

Jellyfish

23.2% ALC/VOL • 0.7 STD DRINKS

15ml (½ fl oz) Amaretto
15ml (½ fl oz) Dark Crème De Cacao
8ml (¼ fl oz) Bailey's Irish Cream
3 drops Grenadine

Pour Amaretto and Cacao into a shot glass – do not stir. Layer Bailey's on top and add Grenadine by drops then serve.

Maiden's Prayer Shooter

31.3% ALC/VOL • 1.1 STD DRINKS

15ml (½ fl oz) Dry Gin
15ml (½ fl oz) Apple Brandy
15ml (½ fl oz) Lillet

Pour ingredients into a cocktail shaker over ice and shake. Strain into a chilled shot glass and serve.

Angel's Delight

12.8% ALC/VOL • 0.3 STD DRINKS

8ml (¼ fl oz) Grenadine
8ml (¼ fl oz) Fresh Cream
8ml (¼ fl oz) Triple Sec
8ml (¼ fl oz) Sloe Gin

Layer ingredients in order given into a pousse café glass and serve.

Pussy Foot Shooter

17.7% ALC/VOL • 0.5 STD DRINKS

15ml (½ fl oz) Chambord
10ml (⅓ fl oz) Lemonade
10ml (⅓ fl oz) Vodka

Layer ingredients in order given into a shot glass and serve.

Gingerbread Man

29.5% ALC/VOL • 0.7 STD DRINKS

8ml (¼ fl oz) Bailey's Irish Cream
8ml (¼ fl oz) Butterscotch Schnapps
8ml (¼ fl oz) Goldschläger
8ml (¼ fl oz) Vodka

Pour ingredients into a cocktail shaker over ice and shake. Strain into a chilled shot glass and serve.

After Five

19.1% ALC/VOL • 0.5 STD DRINKS

10ml (⅓ fl oz) Kahlúa
10ml (⅓ fl oz) Peppermint Schnapps
10ml (⅓ fl oz) Bailey's Irish Cream

Layer ingredients in order given into a shot glass and serve.

Electrical Storm

29% ALC/VOL • 0.7 STD DRINKS

8ml (¼ fl oz) Bailey's Irish Cream
8ml (¼ fl oz) Peppermint Schnapps
8ml (¼ fl oz) Goldschläger
8ml (¼ fl oz) Jägermeister

Layer ingredients in order given into a cordial Embassy glass and serve.

Skull

25.7% ALC/VOL • 0.6 STD DRINKS

10ml (⅓ fl oz) Bailey's Irish Cream
10ml (⅓ fl oz) Blended Whiskey
10ml (⅓ fl oz) Kahlúa

Pour ingredients into a mixing glass over ice and stir. Strain into a chilled shot glass and serve.

California Surfer

14.1% ALC/VOL • 0.4 STD DRINKS

10ml (⅓ fl oz) Jägermeister
10ml (⅓ fl oz) Malibu
20ml (⅔ fl oz) Pineapple Juice

Pour ingredients into a cocktail shaker over ice and shake. Strain into a chilled shot glass and serve.

Sour Pussy

40.8% ALC/VOL • 1.1 STD DRINKS

15ml (½ fl oz) Everclear
5ml (⅙ fl oz) Grenadine
15ml (½ fl oz) Fresh Lemon Juice

Pour ingredients into a shot glass, stir and serve.

Brain Teaser

26.9% ALC/VOL • 0.9 STD DRINKS

20ml (⅔ fl oz) Bailey's Irish Cream
20ml (⅔ fl oz) Sambuca
3 dashes Advocaat

Pour Bailey's into a shot glass and layer Sambuca on top. Add Advocaat by drops and serve with a straw.

Mud Slide

24.8% ALC/VOL • 0.9 STD DRINKS

15ml (½ fl oz) Amaretto
15ml (½ fl oz) Peppermint Schnapps
15ml (½ fl oz) Tia Maria

Pour ingredients into a cocktail shaker over ice and shake. Strain into a chilled shot glass and serve.

Special Emotion

24.4% ALC/VOL • 0.5 STD DRINKS

5ml (⅙ fl oz) Vodka
5ml (⅙ fl oz) Fresh Orange Juice
5ml (⅙ fl oz) Dark Rum
5ml (⅙ fl oz) Triple Sec
5ml (⅙ fl oz) Parfait Amour

Layer ingredients in order given into a cordial Embassy glass and serve.

Illicit Affair

13.9% ALC/VOL • 0.4 STD DRINKS

15ml (½ fl oz) Peppermint Schnapps
15ml (½ fl oz) Bailey's Irish Cream
Fresh Whipped Cream

Layer ingredients in order given into a tall Dutch cordial glass, float cream on top and serve.

Eskimo Joe

15% ALC/VOL • 0.4 STD DRINKS

8ml (¼ fl oz) Bailey's Irish Cream
8ml (¼ fl oz) Fresh Milk (chilled)
8ml (¼ fl oz) White Crème De Menthe
8ml (¼ fl oz) Cinnamon Schnapps

Layer ingredients in order given into a shot glass and serve.

Pearl Diver

14% ALC/VOL • 0.5 STD DRINKS

15ml (½ fl oz) Malibu
15ml (½ fl oz) Midori
15ml (½ fl oz) Pineapple Juice

Pour ingredients into a shot glass, stir and serve.

Blaster

27.7% ALC/VOL • 0.7 STD DRINKS

10ml (⅓ fl oz) Banana Liqueur
10ml (⅓ fl oz) Cointreau
10ml (⅓ fl oz) Kahlúa

Layer ingredients in order given into a cordial Embassy glass and serve.

Great Balls of Fire

28.9% ALC/VOL • 1 STD DRINK

15ml (½ fl oz) Goldschläger
15ml (½ fl oz) Cinnamon Schnapps
15ml (½ fl oz) Cherry Brandy

Layer ingredients in order given into a shot glass and serve.

Rock Lobster

22.7% ALC/VOL • 0.5 STD DRINKS

10ml (⅓ fl oz) Amaretto
10ml (⅓ fl oz) Bailey's Irish Cream
10ml (⅓ fl oz) White Crème De Cacao

Layer ingredients in order given into a cordial Embassy glass and serve.

An Offer You Can't Refuse

35.3% ALC/VOL • 1.3 STD DRINKS

15ml (½ fl oz) Amaretto
15ml (½ fl oz) Fernet Branca
15ml (½ fl oz) Sambuca

Pour ingredients into a cocktail shaker over ice and shake. Strain into a chilled shot glass and serve.

Epidural

38.3% ALC/VOL • 1.2 STD DRINKS

10ml (⅓ fl oz) Everclear
10ml (⅓ fl oz) Malibu
10ml (⅓ fl oz) Vodka
10ml (⅓ fl oz) Coconut Cream

Pour ingredients into a mixing glass over ice and stir. Strain into a chilled test tube and serve.

Tired Pussy

18.1% ALC/VOL • 0.6 STD DRINKS

38ml (1¼ fl oz) Malibu
3 dashes Cranberry Juice
3 dashes Pineapple Juice

Pour ingredients into a cocktail shaker over ice and shake. Strain into a chilled shot glass and serve.

Mind Game

18.1% ALC/VOL • 0.4 STD DRINKS

8ml (¼ fl oz) Blue Curaçao
8ml (¼ fl oz) Ricard
15ml (½ fl oz) Fresh Milk (chilled)

Pour ingredients into a cocktail shaker over ice and shake. Strain into a chilled shot glass and serve.

Rocket Fuel

29% ALC/VOL • 0.9 STD DRINKS

20ml (⅔ fl oz) Light Rum
20ml (⅔ fl oz) Peppermint Schnapps

Pour ingredients into a mixing glass over ice and stir. Strain into a chilled shot glass and serve.

Concord

35.2% ALC/VOL • 1.1 STD DRINKS

15ml (½ fl oz) Tia Maria
15ml (½ fl oz) Bailey's Irish Cream
10ml (⅓ fl oz) 151-Proof Bacardi

Layer ingredients in order given into a shot glass, ignite and serve.

Freddy Kruger

36.7% ALC/VOL • 1.3 STD DRINKS

15ml (½ fl oz) Jägermeister
15ml (½ fl oz) Sambuca
15ml (½ fl oz) Vodka

Pour ingredients into a shot glass, stir and serve.

Swell Sex

20.7% ALC/VOL • 0.6 STD DRINKS

10ml (⅓ fl oz) Malibu
10ml (⅓ fl oz) Midori
10ml (⅓ fl oz) Vodka
5ml (⅙ fl oz) Pineapple Juice
½ teaspoon Fresh Cream

Pour ingredients into a cocktail shaker over ice and shake. Strain into a chilled shot glass and serve.

Necrophiliac

21.5% ALC/VOL • 0.5 STD DRINKS

15ml (½ fl oz) Blue Curaçao
15ml (½ fl oz) Advocaat

Layer ingredients in order given into a cordial Embassy glass and serve.

Snapple Shooter

17% ALC/VOL • 0.4 STD DRINKS

12ml (⅖ fl oz) Vodka
4 dashes Triple Sec
8ml (¼ fl oz) Cranberry Juice
8ml (¼ fl oz) Fresh Orange Juice

Pour ingredients into a mixing glass over ice and stir. Strain into a chilled shot glass and serve.

Flaming Gorilla

38.4% ALC/VOL • 1.4 STD DRINKS

15ml (½ fl oz) Peppermint Schnapps
15ml (½ fl oz) Kahlúa
15ml (½ fl oz) 151-Proof Bacardi

Layer ingredients in order given into a shot glass and ignite. Extinguish flame and serve.

Protein Smoothie

13.3% ALC/VOL • 0.3 STD DRINKS

10ml (⅓ fl oz) Scotch Whisky
10ml (⅓ fl oz) Clamato Juice
10ml (⅓ fl oz) Fresh Cream

Pour ingredients into a cocktail shaker over ice and shake. Strain into a chilled shot glass and serve.

Irish Monk

20.4% ALC/VOL • 0.5 STD DRINKS

10ml (⅓ fl oz) Peppermint Schnapps
10ml (⅓ fl oz) Bailey's Irish Cream
10ml (⅓ fl oz) Frangelico

Layer ingredients in order given into a cordial Embassy glass and serve.

German Chocolate Cake

19.5% ALC/VOL • 0.6 STD DRINKS

15ml (½ fl oz) Dark Crème De Cacao
15ml (½ fl oz) Malibu
5ml (⅙ fl oz) Frangelico
5ml (⅙ fl oz) Fresh Cream

Pour ingredients into a cocktail shaker over ice and shake. Strain into a chilled shot glass and serve.

Bad Habit

28.5% ALC/VOL • 0.7 STD DRINKS

15ml (½ fl oz) Vodka
15ml (½ fl oz) Peach Schnapps

Pour ingredients in order given into a shot glass – do not stir, then serve.

Greek Lightning

30.2% ALC/VOL • 0.7 STD DRINKS

10ml (⅓ fl oz) Chambord
10ml (⅓ fl oz) Ouzo
10ml (⅓ fl oz) Vodka

Pour ingredients into a mixing glass over ice and stir. Strain into a chilled shot glass and serve.

Hard Rocka

25% ALC/VOL • 0.6 STD DRINKS

10ml (⅓ fl oz) Midori
10ml (⅓ fl oz) Vodka
10ml (⅓ fl oz) Bailey's Irish Cream

Layer ingredients in order given into a cordial Lexington glass and serve.

Bonfire

21.6% ALC/VOL • 0.8 STD DRINKS

38ml (1¼ fl oz) Bailey's Irish Cream
8ml (¼ fl oz) Goldschläger
Cinnamon

Pour Bailey's into a shot glass and layer Goldschläger on top. Sprinkle cinnamon on top and serve.

Death by Fire

13.3% ALC/VOL • 0.3 STD DRINKS

10ml (⅓ fl oz) Cinnamon Schnapps
10ml (⅓ fl oz) Peppermint Schnapps
10ml (⅓ fl oz) Tabasco Sauce

Pour ingredients into a shot glass, stir and serve.

Power Drill

17.5% ALC/VOL • 0.9 STD DRINKS

30ml (1 fl oz) Vodka
5ml (⅙ fl oz) Beer
30ml (1 fl oz) Fresh Orange Juice

Pour Vodka and juice into an old-fashioned glass – do not stir. Add Beer by pouring on top and serve.

Liquid Cocaine Shooter

51.3% ALC/VOL • 1.8 STD DRINKS

15ml (½ fl oz) Jägermeister
15ml (½ fl oz) 151-Proof Rum
15ml (½ fl oz) Goldschläger

Layer ingredients in order given into a tall Dutch cordial glass and serve.

Galactic Ale

22% ALC/VOL • 2.1 STD DRINKS

38ml (1¼ fl oz) Vodka
38ml (1¼ fl oz) Blue Curaçao
15ml (½ fl oz) Blackberry Schnapps
30ml (1 fl oz) Fresh Lime Juice

Pour ingredients into a mixing glass over ice and stir. Strain into three chilled shot glasses and serve.

Arizona Antifreeze

19.3% ALC/VOL • 0.5 STD DRINKS

10ml (⅓ fl oz) Vodka
10ml (⅓ fl oz) Midori
10ml (⅓ fl oz) Sweet and Sour Mix

Pour ingredients in order given into a shot glass – do not stir, then serve.

Grandma in a Wheelchair

26.2% ALC/VOL • 0.9 STD DRINKS

20ml (⅔ fl oz) Grand Marnier
10ml (⅓ fl oz) Tequila
5ml (⅙ fl oz) Fresh Lime Juice
10ml (⅓ fl oz) Lemon-Lime Soda

Pour Grand Marnier, Tequila and juice into a cocktail shaker over ice. Shake and strain into a chilled shot glass. Add soda, stir gently and serve.

Mocha Shot

14.4% ALC/VOL • 0.5 STD DRINKS

15ml (½ fl oz) Kahlúa
15ml (½ fl oz) Dark Crème De Cacao
15ml (½ fl oz) Fresh Milk (chilled)

Layer ingredients in order given into a shot glass and serve.

Black Forest Cake

20.1% ALC/VOL • 0.7 STD DRINKS

15ml (½ fl oz) Bailey's Irish Cream
15ml (½ fl oz) Cherry Brandy
15ml (½ fl oz) Kahlúa

Pour Brandy and Kahlúa into a cocktail shaker over ice. Shake and strain into a chilled tall Dutch cordial glass. Layer Bailey's on top and serve.

Fourth of July

8.3% ALC/VOL • 0.3 STD DRINKS

15ml (½ fl oz) Grenadine
15ml (½ fl oz) Fresh Cream
15ml (½ fl oz) Blue Curaçao

Layer ingredients in order given into a tall Dutch cordial glass and serve.

Southern Comfort

Southern Comfort originated in the late nineteenth century in the south of America where peaches were marinated in Bourbon, this drink was known as Cuffs and Buttons. The sweet fruit juice of the peaches made the Bourbon more tolerable to drink for those who could not manage drinking straight Bourbon.

It is believed that a bar tender changed the name of this drink from Cuffs and Buttons to Southern Comfort.

The drink became quite popular that a distiller named M.W. Heron perfected Southern Comfort, creating a sweet smooth Bourbon-based peach liqueur as we know it today. This liqueur was distilled in New Orleans on the banks of the Mississippi and began marketing under the trademarked name of Southern Comfort.

Created from a combination of Bourbon, Peach Liqueur, herbs and other ingredients, the recipe for Southern Comfort remains a closely guarded family secret. Southern Comfort is enjoyed neat, over ice and in selected cocktails.

Southern Raspberry

19% ALC/VOL • 1 STD DRINK

23ml (¾ fl oz) Southern Comfort
23ml (¾ fl oz) Framboise
15ml (½ fl oz) Fresh Lemon Juice
1 teaspoon Sugar Syrup
5ml (⅙ fl oz) Soda Water
Slice of Lemon

Pour Southern Comfort, Framboise, juice and sugar into a cocktail shaker over ice. Shake and strain into a collins glass over ice. Add soda and stir gently. Add a slice of lemon and serve.

Comfortable Milk Punch

8.1% ALC/VOL • 1.8 STD DRINKS

60ml (2 fl oz) Southern Comfort
210ml (7 fl oz) Fresh Milk (chilled)
1 teaspoon Sugar Syrup
Nutmeg

Pour Southern Comfort, milk and sugar into a cocktail shaker over ice. Shake and strain into a chilled highball glass. Sprinkle nutmeg on top and serve.

Preservation Tipple

13.9% ALC/VOL • 1.2 STD DRINKS

30ml (1 fl oz) Southern Comfort
8ml (¼ fl oz) Pastis
15ml (½ fl oz) Fresh Orange Juice
1½ teaspoons Egg White
½ Peach (diced)

Pour Southern Comfort, Pastis, juice and egg white into a blender over small amount of crushed ice then add diced peach. Blend until smooth and pour into a chilled champagne flute then serve.

Kentucky Cobbler

23.8% ALC/VOL • 1.8 STD DRINKS

45ml (1½ fl oz) Southern Comfort
30ml (1 fl oz) Peppermint Schnapps
15ml (½ fl oz) Fresh Lemon Juice
1 teaspoon Sugar Syrup
Sprig of Fresh Mint

Pour Southern Comfort, Schnapps, juice and sugar into a highball glass over cracked ice then stir. Add a sprig of mint and serve.

Comfort Zone

10.5% ALC/VOL • 1.3 STD DRINKS

30ml (1 fl oz) Southern Comfort
30ml (1 fl oz) Bailey's Irish Cream
60ml (2 fl oz) Fresh Milk (chilled)
1 teaspoon Sugar Syrup
3 Strawberries (diced)
Strawberry

Pour Southern Comfort, Bailey's, milk and sugar into a blender over crushed ice then add diced strawberries. Blend until smooth and pour into a chilled highball glass. Garnish with a strawberry and serve. *This drink is also known as Kelly's Comfort.*

Birthday Cocktail

13.9% ALC/VOL • 1.2 STD DRINKS

30ml (1 fl oz) Southern Comfort
15ml (½ fl oz) Dark Crème De Cacao
60ml (2 fl oz) Fresh Cream

Pour ingredients into a cocktail shaker over ice and shake. Strain into a chilled cocktail glass and serve.

South Seas

13.9% ALC/VOL • 1.6 STD DRINKS

30ml (1 fl oz) Southern Comfort
15ml (½ fl oz) Blue Curaçao
15ml (½ fl oz) Pernod
60ml (2 fl oz) Orange-Mango Juice
30ml (1 fl oz) Fresh Cream
Slice of Mango

Pour Southern Comfort, Pernod, juice and cream into a cocktail shaker over ice. Shake and strain into a chilled highball glass then add Curaçao by pouring into centre of drink – do not stir. Garnish with a slice of mango and serve.

British Comfort

21.1% ALC/VOL • 1.7 STD DRINKS

45ml (1½ fl oz) Southern Comfort
15ml (½ fl oz) Gin
30ml (1 fl oz) Fresh Orange Juice
15ml (½ fl oz) Fresh Lemon Juice

Pour ingredients into a cocktail shaker over ice and shake. Strain into a chilled cocktail glass and serve.

Marimba

15.6% ALC/VOL • 1.5 STD DRINKS

30ml (1 fl oz) Southern Comfort
15ml (½ fl oz) Gin
8ml (¼ fl oz) Amaretto
30ml (1 fl oz) Mango Juice
30ml (1 fl oz) Pineapple Juice
8ml (¼ fl oz) Fresh Lime Juice
Slice of Orange
Slice of Pineapple

Pour Southern Comfort, Gin, Amaretto and juices into a cocktail shaker over ice. Shake and strain into a chilled cocktail glass. Garnish with a slice of orange and pineapple then serve.

Southern Comfort Manhattan

32.4% ALC/VOL • 1.6 STD DRINKS

45ml (1½ fl oz) Southern Comfort
15ml (½ fl oz) Dry Vermouth
Dash Angostura Bitters

Pour ingredients into a cocktail shaker over ice and shake. Strain into a chilled cocktail glass and serve.

Tobacco Road

10.2% ALC/VOL • 1.3 STD DRINKS

45ml (1½ fl oz) Southern Comfort
5ml (1/6 fl oz) Grenadine
90ml (3 fl oz) Fresh Orange Juice
23ml (¾ fl oz) Fresh Lemon Juice
Slice of Orange

Pour Southern Comfort, Grenadine and juices into a cocktail shaker over ice. Shake and strain into a highball glass over ice. Add a slice of orange and serve.

Long Suit

9.6% ALC/VOL • 1.8 STD DRINKS

60ml (2 fl oz) Southern Comfort
2 dashes Angostura Bitters
90ml (3 fl oz) Grapefruit Juice
90ml (3 fl oz) Tonic Water
Slice of Lime

Pour Southern Comfort, Bitters and juice into a collins glass over ice then stir. Add tonic and stir gently. Add a slice of lime and serve.

Tennessee Sour No.2

14.2% ALC/VOL • 2.4 STD DRINKS

60ml (2 fl oz) Southern Comfort
30ml (1 fl oz) Orange Curaçao
15ml (½ fl oz) Fresh Lemon Juice
15ml (½ fl oz) Fresh Lime Juice
90ml (3 fl oz) Soda Water
Slice of Orange
Twist of Lime Peel

Pour Southern Comfort, Curaçao and juices into a cocktail shaker over ice. Shake and strain into a sour glass over ice. Add soda and stir gently. Garnish with a slice of orange and lime peel then serve.

Wagon Wheel

29.1% ALC/VOL • 3.4 STD DRINKS

90ml (3 fl oz) Southern Comfort
23ml (¾ fl oz) Cognac
10ml (⅓ fl oz) Grenadine
23ml (¾ fl oz) Fresh Lemon Juice

Pour ingredients into a cocktail shaker over ice and shake. Strain into a chilled cocktail glass and serve.

Comfortable Screw Up Against a Fuzzy Wall

13.2% ALC/VOL • 1.6 STD DRINKS

23ml (¾ fl oz) Southern Comfort
15ml (½ fl oz) Peach Schnapps
15ml (½ fl oz) Vodka
8ml (¼ fl oz) Galliano
90ml (3 fl oz) Fresh Orange Juice

Pour ingredients into a cocktail shaker over ice and shake. Strain into a highball glass half filled with ice and serve.

Frozen Southern Comfort

27.6% ALC/VOL • 1.9 STD DRINKS

60ml (2 fl oz) Southern Comfort
5ml (⅙ fl oz) Maraschino Liqueur
15ml (½ fl oz) Fresh Lime Juice
½ teaspoon Sugar Syrup

Pour ingredients into a blender over crushed ice and blend. Pour into a chilled champagne saucer and serve with 2 short straws.

The America's Cup

12.3% ALC/VOL • 1.7 STD DRINKS

30ml (1 fl oz) Southern Comfort
15ml (½ fl oz) Bacardi
15ml (½ fl oz) Galliano
60ml (2 fl oz) Fresh Cream
30ml (1 fl oz) Fresh Orange Juice
30ml (1 fl oz) Pineapple Juice
Sprig of Fresh Mint
Wedge of Pineapple

Pour Southern Comfort, Bacardi, Galliano, cream and juices into a cocktail shaker over ice. Shake and strain into a chilled champagne saucer. Garnish with a sprig of mint and wedge of pineapple then serve.

Hacienda Shock

13.4% ALC/VOL • 1.6 STD DRINKS

45ml (1½ fl oz) Southern Comfort
15ml (½ fl oz) White Crème De Cacao
90ml (3 fl oz) Fresh Milk (chilled)

Pour ingredients into an old-fashioned glass over ice, stir and serve.

Southern Love

24.7% ALC/VOL • 1.8 STD DRINKS

30ml (1 fl oz) Southern Comfort
30ml (1 fl oz) Brandy
30ml (1 fl oz) Fresh Cream
Sprig of Fresh Mint
Strawberry

Pour Southern Comfort, Brandy and cream into a cocktail shaker over ice. Shake and strain into a chilled champagne flute. Garnish with a sprig of mint and a strawberry then serve.

Corvette

12.8% ALC/VOL • 2 STD DRINKS

45ml (1½ fl oz) Southern Comfort
30ml (1 fl oz) Sloe Gin
5ml (⅙ fl oz) Campari
120ml (4 fl oz) Lemonade

Pour Southern Comfort, Gin and Campari into a highball glass over ice then stir. Add lemonade, stir gently and serve.

Southern Comfort Cocktail

22.5% ALC/VOL • 3 STD DRINKS

30ml (1 fl oz) Southern Comfort
60ml (2 fl oz) Bourbon
15ml (½ fl oz) Dry Vermouth

30ml (1 fl oz) Fresh Orange Juice
10ml (⅓ fl oz) Fresh Lemon Juice
¼ Fresh Peach (diced)
Slice of Orange
Slice of Peach
Slice of Tamarillo

Pour Southern Comfort, Bourbon, Vermouth and juices and into a blender over cracked ice then add diced peach. Blend and strain into a chilled collins glass. Garnish with a slice of orange, peach and tamarillo then serve.

Kelly's Comfort

10.5% ALC/VOL • 1.3 STD DRINKS

This drink is also known as Comfort Zone, p 351.

Davenport

14.2% ALC/VOL • 2.2 STD DRINKS

45ml (1½ fl oz) Southern Comfort
30ml (1 fl oz) Port
15ml (½ fl oz) Dark Rum
5ml (⅙ fl oz) Grenadine
10ml (⅓ fl oz) Fresh Lemon Juice
90ml (3 fl oz) Cola
Cherry
Slice of Lemon

Pour Southern Comfort, Port, Rum, Grenadine and juice into a cocktail shaker over ice. Shake and strain into a highball glass over ice. Add cola and stir gently. Garnish with a cherry and slice of lemon then serve.

Comfortable Stinger

37% ALC/VOL • 3.1 STD DRINKS

45ml (1½ fl oz) Southern Comfort
60ml (2 fl oz) Brandy

Pour ingredients into a cocktail shaker over ice and shake. Strain into a chilled cocktail glass and serve.

Dawn Chorus

12.4% ALC/VOL • 1.4 STD DRINKS

30ml (1 fl oz) Southern Comfort
23ml (¾ fl oz) Port
15ml (½ fl oz) Punt e Mes
5ml (⅙ fl oz) Grenadine
10ml (⅓ fl oz) Fresh Lemon Juice
60ml (2 fl oz) Cola

Pour Southern Comfort, Port, Punt e Mes, Grenadine and juice into a cocktail shaker over ice. Shake and strain into an old-fashioned glass over cracked ice. Add cola, stir gently and serve.

Orange Comfort

10.1% ALC/VOL • 1.3 STD DRINKS

45ml (1½ fl oz) Southern Comfort
120ml (4 fl oz) Fresh Orange Juice
Slice of Orange

Pour Southern Comfort and juice into a highball glass over ice then stir. Garnish with a slice of orange and serve.

Bazooka

19.9% ALC/VOL • 1.1 STD DRINKS

30ml (1 fl oz) Southern Comfort
15ml (½ fl oz) Banana Liqueur
5ml (⅙ fl oz) Grenadine
23ml (¾ fl oz) Whipping Cream
2 Cherry Halves

Pour Southern Comfort, Liqueur, Grenadine and cream into a cocktail shaker over ice. Shake and strain into a chilled liqueur glass. Garnish with cherry halves and serve.

Sicilian Kiss

34% ALC/VOL • 2.4 STD DRINKS

60ml (2 fl oz) Southern Comfort
30ml (1 fl oz) Amaretto
Green Cherry
Red Cherry

Pour Southern Comfort and Amaretto into an old-fashioned glass over ice then stir. Garnish with cherries and serve.

Lazy Lover

17.7% ALC/VOL • 1.8 STD DRINKS

45ml (1½ fl oz) Southern Comfort
15ml (½ fl oz) Armagnac
30ml (1 fl oz) Pineapple Juice
23ml (¾ fl oz) Fresh Lime Juice
15ml (½ fl oz) Passion-Fruit Syrup
Cherry

Pour Southern Comfort, Armagnac, juices and syrup into a cocktail shaker over ice. Shake and strain into a chilled cocktail glass. Garnish with a cherry and serve.

Southern Mint Julep

36.5% ALC/VOL • 2.7 STD DRINKS

45ml (1½ fl oz) Southern Comfort
45ml (1½ fl oz) Bourbon
1 teaspoon Sugar Syrup
4 Sprigs of Fresh Mint

Pour Southern Comfort, Bourbon and sugar into a collins glass over crushed ice then stir. Add sprigs of mint and muddle well then serve.

Winning Horse

10.5% ALC/VOL • 1.5 STD DRINKS

30ml (1 fl oz) Southern Comfort
15ml (½ fl oz) Dark Rum
15ml (½ fl oz) Sweet Vermouth
120ml (4 fl oz) Cola
Cherry
Slice of Orange

Pour Southern Comfort, Rum and Vermouth into a goblet over ice then stir. Add cola and stir gently. Garnish with a cherry and slice of orange then serve.

Comfortable Flip

20.2% ALC/VOL • 1.8 STD DRINKS

60ml (2 fl oz) Southern Comfort
1 teaspoon Sugar Syrup
1 Fresh Egg
Nutmeg

Pour Southern Comfort, sugar and egg into a cocktail shaker over ice. Shake and strain into a chilled goblet. Sprinkle nutmeg on top and serve.

Big Easy Martini

16.4% ALC/VOL • 1.6 STD DRINKS

45ml (1½ fl oz) Southern Comfort
15ml (½ fl oz) Raspberry Liqueur
30ml (1 fl oz) Sweet and Sour Mix
30ml (1 fl oz) Lemon-Lime Soda
Twist of Lime Peel

Prepare a cocktail glass with a sugar frosted rim. Pour Southern Comfort, Liqueur and sour mix into a cocktail shaker over ice. Shake and strain into prepared glass. Add soda and stir gently. Garnish with lime peel and serve.

Memphis Belle

37% ALC/VOL • 2.6 STD DRINKS

90ml (3 fl oz) Southern Comfort
½ Fresh Peach
Maraschino Cherry

Place ½ peach into a chilled champagne saucer and place a cherry on top. Add crushed ice to fill glass then add Southern Comfort. Serve with 2 short straws and a teaspoon.

Yellow Fingers

14.1% ALC/VOL • 2.2 STD DRINKS

30ml (1 fl oz) Southern Comfort
30ml (1 fl oz) Vodka
15ml (½ fl oz) Galliano
30ml (1 fl oz) Fresh Orange Juice
90ml (3 fl oz) Lemonade

Pour Southern Comfort, Vodka, Galliano and juice into a cocktail shaker over ice. Shake and strain into a highball glass over ice. Add lemonade, stir gently and serve.

Southern Comfort Strawberry Frappé

30% ALC/VOL • 1.1 STD DRINKS

23ml (¾ fl oz) Southern Comfort
23ml (¾ fl oz) Strawberry Liqueur
Slice of Lemon
Twist of Orange Peel

Pour Southern Comfort and Liqueur into a mixing glass without ice. Stir and pour into a champagne saucer filled with crushed ice. Twist orange peel above drink and place remainder of peel into drink. Add a slice of lemon and serve with 2 short straws.

Mississippi Mud

17.1% ALC/VOL • 2 STD DRINKS

45ml (1½ fl oz) Southern Comfort
45ml (1½ fl oz) Kahlúa
2 scoops Vanilla Ice Cream
Grated Chocolate

Pour Southern Comfort and Kahlúa into a blender without ice then add ice cream. Blend until smooth and pour into a chilled cocktail glass. Sprinkle chocolate on top and serve.

Southern Peach

24% ALC/VOL • 1.4 STD DRINKS

30ml (1 fl oz) Southern Comfort
30ml (1 fl oz) Peach Liqueur
15ml (½ fl oz) Thick Cream
Slice of Peach

Pour Southern Comfort, Liqueur and cream into a cocktail shaker over ice. Shake and strain into an old-fashioned glass over cracked ice. Add a slice of peach and serve.

Sangaree Comfort

32% ALC/VOL • 1.8 STD DRINKS

30ml (1 fl oz) Southern Comfort
30ml (1 fl oz) Bourbon
5ml (1/6 fl oz) Peach Brandy
5ml (1/6 fl oz) Fresh Lemon Juice
½ teaspoon Sugar Syrup
Nutmeg

Pour Southern Comfort, Bourbon, Brandy, juice and sugar into a mixing glass over ice. Stir and strain into an old-fashioned glass over ice. Sprinkle nutmeg on top and serve.

Climax

21.6% ALC/VOL • 1.8 STD DRINKS

45ml (1½ fl oz) Southern Comfort
30ml (1 fl oz) Kahlúa
30ml (1 fl oz) Whipping Cream

Pour ingredients into a cocktail shaker over cracked ice and shake. Pour into a chilled old-fashioned glass and serve.

Gummy Bear

5.3% ALC/VOL • 1 STD DRINK

15ml (½ fl oz) Southern Comfort
15ml (½ fl oz) Amaretto
15ml (½ fl oz) Midori
15ml (½ fl oz) Grenadine
90ml (3 fl oz) Fresh Orange Juice
90ml (3 fl oz) Pineapple Juice
5ml (1/6 fl oz) Lemon-Lime Soda

Pour Southern Comfort, Amaretto, Midori, Grenadine and juices into a cocktail shaker over ice. Shake and strain into a highball glass over ice. Add soda – do not stir, then serve.

Redneck Blitzkreig

14.4% ALC/VOL • 2.6 STD DRINKS

45ml (1½ fl oz) Southern Comfort
45ml (1½ fl oz) Jägermeister
135ml (4½ fl oz) Soda Water

Pour Southern Comfort and Jägermeister into a cocktail shaker over cracked ice. Shake and pour into a chilled highball glass. Add soda, stir gently and serve.

Border Thrill

7.2% ALC/VOL • 1.5 STD DRINKS

30ml (1 fl oz) Southern Comfort
15ml (½ fl oz) Tequila
8ml (¼ fl oz) Triple Sec
Dash Grenadine
180ml (6 fl oz) Fresh Orange Juice
30ml (1 fl oz) Sweet and Sour Mix

Pour ingredients into a blender over crushed ice and blend until smooth. Pour into a chilled collins glass and serve.

Riverboat Queen

35.5% ALC/VOL • 3.8 STD DRINKS

120ml (4 fl oz) Southern Comfort
15ml (½ fl oz) Apricot Brandy
Maraschino Cherry
Slice of Apricot

Pour Southern Comfort and Brandy into a champagne saucer over crushed ice then stir gently. Garnish with a cherry and slice of apricot then serve.

Slow Comfortable Flip

17.2% ALC/VOL • 1.5 STD DRINKS

30ml (1 fl oz) Southern Comfort
30ml (1 fl oz) Sloe Gin
1 teaspoon Sugar Syrup
1 Fresh Egg
Nutmeg

Pour Southern Comfort, Gin, sugar and egg into a cocktail shaker over ice. Shake and strain into a chilled goblet. Sprinkle nutmeg on top and serve.

Southern Slide

18.2% ALC/VOL • 3 STD DRINKS

60ml (2 fl oz) Southern Comfort
60ml (2 fl oz) Tia Maria
3 scoops Vanilla Ice Cream
Grated Chocolate

Pour Southern Comfort and Tia into a blender over small amount of crushed ice then add ice cream. Blend until smooth and pour into a chilled parfait glass. Sprinkle chocolate on top and serve.

Brain Blender

13.4% ALC/VOL • 2 STD DRINKS

30ml (1 fl oz) Southern Comfort
15ml (½ fl oz) Banana Liqueur
15ml (½ fl oz) Light Rum
15ml (½ fl oz) Peach Brandy
5ml (1/6 fl oz) Bénédictine
5ml (1/6 fl oz) Grenadine
30ml (1 fl oz) Fresh Orange Juice

30ml (1 fl oz) Guava Juice
30ml (1 fl oz) Mango Juice
15ml (½ fl oz) Fresh Lime Juice
Slice of Mango
Slice of Orange
Slice of Peach

Pour Southern Comfort, Liqueur, Rum, Brandy, Bénédictine, Grenadine and juices into a blender over crushed ice. Blend and pour into a chilled goblet. Garnish with a slice of mango, orange and peach then serve.

Southern Banana Comfort

20.2% ALC/VOL • 1.8 STD DRINKS

30ml (1 fl oz) Southern Comfort
30ml (1 fl oz) Golden Rum
15ml (½ fl oz) Fresh Lime Juice
1 teaspoon Sugar Syrup
½ Banana (diced)

Pour Southern Comfort, Rum, juice and sugar into a blender over crushed ice then add diced banana. Blend and pour into a chilled champagne saucer then serve.

Comfortable Screw

10.1% ALC/VOL • 1.3 STD DRINKS

30ml (1 fl oz) Southern Comfort
15ml (½ fl oz) Vodka
120ml (4 fl oz) Fresh Orange Juice
Slice of Orange

Pour Southern Comfort and Vodka into an old-fashioned glass over ice then stir. Add juice and stir well. Garnish with a slice of orange and serve.

Southern Cuba Libre

18.5% ALC/VOL • 3.1 STD DRINKS

45ml (1½ fl oz) Southern Comfort
60ml (2 fl oz) Dark Rum
15ml (½ fl oz) Fresh Lime Juice
90ml (3 fl oz) Cola
Slice of Lime

Pour Southern Comfort, Rum and juice into a collins glass over ice then stir. Add cola and stir gently. Garnish with a slice of lime and serve.

Southern Malted

15.1% ALC/VOL • 2.9 STD DRINKS

60ml (2 fl oz) Southern Comfort
60ml (2 fl oz) Dark Crème De Cacao
120ml (4 fl oz) Malted Milk (chilled)

Pour ingredients into a blender over small amount of crushed ice and blend until smooth. Pour into a chilled collins glass and serve.

Eight Inch Tongue

22.8% ALC/VOL • 1.9 STD DRINKS

15ml (½ fl oz) Southern Comfort
15ml (½ fl oz) Amaretto
15ml (½ fl oz) Brandy
15ml (½ fl oz) Peach Schnapps
15ml (½ fl oz) Vodka
30ml (1 fl oz) Cranberry Juice

Pour ingredients into a mixing glass over ice and stir. Strain into a chilled highball glass and serve.

Comfort Colada

12.3% ALC/VOL • 1.3 STD DRINKS

45ml (1½ fl oz) Southern Comfort
60ml (2 fl oz) Pineapple Juice
30ml (1 fl oz) Coconut Cream

Pour ingredients into a blender over crushed ice and blend. Pour into a chilled collins glass and serve with a straw.

Southern Man

20.9% ALC/VOL • 0.7 STD DRINKS

8ml (¼ fl oz) Southern Comfort
8ml (¼ fl oz) Amaretto
8ml (¼ fl oz) Peach Schnapps
8ml (¼ fl oz) Triple Sec
5ml (⅙ fl oz) Cranberry Juice
5ml (⅙ fl oz) Sweet and Sour Mix

Pour ingredients into a cocktail shaker over ice and shake. Strain into a chilled cocktail glass and serve.

Dixie Delight

30.1% ALC/VOL • 2.3 STD DRINKS

30ml (1 fl oz) Southern Comfort
30ml (1 fl oz) Dry Vermouth
30ml (1 fl oz) Gin
3 dashes Pernod
½ teaspoon Sugar Syrup

Pour ingredients into a mixing glass over ice and stir. Strain into a chilled cocktail glass and serve.

Othello

7% ALC/VOL • 1.5 STD DRINKS

30ml (1 fl oz) Southern Comfort
20ml (⅔ fl oz) Parfait Amour
10ml (⅓ fl oz) Banana Liqueur
Dash Orange Curaçao
Dash Fresh Lemon Juice
Dash Pineapple Juice
210ml (7 fl oz) Lemonade

Pour Southern Comfort, Parfait Amour, Liqueur, Curaçao and juices into a mixing glass over ice. Stir and strain into a chilled highball glass. Add lemonade, stir gently and serve.

Cold Comfort Coffee

10.9% ALC/VOL • 1.5 STD DRINKS

23ml (¾ fl oz) Southern Comfort
23ml (¾ fl oz) Dark Rum
8ml (¼ fl oz) Dark Crème De Cacao
120ml (4 fl oz) Black Coffee (chilled)

Pour ingredients into a cocktail shaker over ice and shake. Strain into a goblet over crushed ice and serve.

Geneva Summit

23.2% ALC/VOL • 1.8 STD DRINKS

30ml (1 fl oz) Southern Comfort
30ml (1 fl oz) Vodka
5ml (1/6 fl oz) Peppermint Schnapps
15ml (½ fl oz) Fresh Lime Juice
15ml (½ fl oz) Fresh Orange Juice
5ml (1/6 fl oz) Lemon-Lime Soda

Pour Southern Comfort, Vodka, Schnapps and juices into a cocktail shaker over ice. Shake and strain into a cocktail glass over ice. Add soda, stir gently and serve. *This drink is also known as Hoo Doo.*

American Sweetheart

18.5% ALC/VOL • 0.9 STD DRINKS

30ml (1 fl oz) Southern Comfort
Dash Dry Vermouth
30ml (1 fl oz) Sweet and Sour Mix

Pour ingredients into a cocktail shaker over ice and shake. Strain into a chilled old-fashioned glass over a few ice cubes and serve.

Mount Vesuvius

42.1% ALC/VOL • 6.3 STD DRINKS

45ml (1½ fl oz) Southern Comfort
45ml (1½ fl oz) Applejack
45ml (1½ fl oz) 151-Proof Dark Rum
30ml (1 fl oz) Light Rum
15ml (½ fl oz) Fresh Lemon or Lime Juice
2 teaspoons Sugar Syrup
Twist of Lemon or Lime Peel

Pour Southern Comfort, Applejack, Light Rum, juice and sugar into a blender over cracked ice. Blend and pour into a chilled highball glass. Twist lemon or lime peel above drink and discard remainder of peel. Layer Dark Rum on top and ignite then serve with a straw.

Southern Rusty Nail

38.5% ALC/VOL • 1.8 STD DRINKS

30ml (1 fl oz) Southern Comfort
30ml (1 fl oz) Bourbon

Pour ingredients into an old-fashioned glass over ice, stir and serve.

Slow and Comfortable Screw

18.5% ALC/VOL • 2.6 STD DRINKS

30ml (1 fl oz) Southern Comfort
30ml (1 fl oz) Dry Gin
30ml (1 fl oz) Vodka
90ml (3 fl oz) Fresh Orange Juice
Slice of Orange

Pour Southern Comfort, Gin and Vodka into a mixing glass over ice. Stir and strain into a highball glass over ice. Add juice and stir. Garnish with a slice of orange and serve.

Maria's Delight

6.7% ALC/VOL • 1.2 STD DRINKS

20ml (⅔ fl oz) Southern Comfort
10ml (⅓ fl oz) Safari
10ml (⅓ fl oz) Vodka
5ml (1/6 fl oz) Cointreau
180ml (6 fl oz) Dry Ginger Ale

Pour Southern Comfort, Safari, Vodka and Cointreau into a mixing glass over ice. Stir and strain into a chilled highball glass. Add Ginger Ale, stir gently and serve.

Jufu Cocktail

7% ALC/VOL • 1.7 STD DRINKS

30ml (1 fl oz) Southern Comfort
15ml (½ fl oz) Amaretto
15ml (½ fl oz) Vodka
15ml (½ fl oz) Grenadine
15ml (½ fl oz) Fresh Lime Juice
210ml (7 fl oz) Lemon-Lime Soda

Pour Southern Comfort, Amaretto, Vodka, Grenadine and juice into a cocktail shaker over ice. Shake and strain into a hurricane glass over ice. Add soda, stir gently and serve.

Comfortable Fizz

10.3% ALC/VOL • 1.7 STD DRINKS

60ml (2 fl oz) Southern Comfort
30ml (1 fl oz) Fresh Lemon Juice

1 teaspoon Caster Sugar
120ml (4 fl oz) Soda Water

Pour Southern Comfort and juice into a cocktail shaker over ice then add sugar. Shake and strain into a highball glass over ice. Add soda, stir gently and serve.

Frozen Southern Hurricane

12.3% ALC/VOL • 1.7 STD DRINKS

60ml (2 fl oz) Southern Comfort
15ml (½ fl oz) Grenadine
60ml (2 fl oz) Strawberry Daiquiri Mix
30ml (1 fl oz) Fresh Orange Juice
15ml (½ fl oz) Lemon-Lime Soda
Cherry
Wedge of Orange

Pour Southern Comfort, Grenadine, daiquiri mix and juice into a blender over crushed ice. Blend and pour into a chilled hurricane glass then add soda – do not stir. Garnish with a cherry and wedge of orange then serve.

Hoo Doo

23.2% ALC/VOL • 1.8 STD DRINKS

This drink is also known as *Geneva Summit, p 357.*

Southern Suicide

23.1% ALC/VOL • 1.4 STD DRINKS

23ml (¾ fl oz) Southern Comfort
23ml (¾ fl oz) Tennessee Whiskey
8ml (¼ fl oz) Grenadine
15ml (½ fl oz) Fresh Orange Juice
8ml (¼ fl oz) Lemonade

Pour Southern Comfort, Whiskey, Grenadine and juice into a cocktail shaker over cracked ice. Shake and pour into a chilled highball glass. Add lemonade, stir gently and serve.

Alabama Riot

10% ALC/VOL • 3.1 STD DRINKS

60ml (2 fl oz) Southern Comfort
30ml (1 fl oz) Peppermint Schnapps
30ml (1 fl oz) Vodka
240ml (8 fl oz) Fruit Punch
30ml (1 fl oz) Fresh Lime Juice

Pour fruit punch into a hurricane glass over ice then add Southern Comfort. Add Schnapps and Vodka then stir. Add juice – do not stir, then serve with a swizzle stick.

Cubins Cracker

6.1% ALC/VOL • 1.2 STD DRINKS

15ml (½ fl oz) Southern Comfort
15ml (½ fl oz) Blue Curaçao
15ml (½ fl oz) Peach Schnapps
15ml (½ fl oz) Raspberry Liqueur
195ml (6½ fl oz) Fresh Orange Juice

Pour Southern Comfort, Schnapps and juice into a cocktail shaker over cracked ice. Shake and pour into a chilled collins glass. Add Curaçao by pouring down inside rim of glass and allow to settle on bottom of drink. Layer Liqueur on top and serve.

Paddlesteamer

10.6% ALC/VOL • 1.8 STD DRINKS

30ml (1 fl oz) Southern Comfort
30ml (1 fl oz) Vodka
60ml (2 fl oz) Fresh Orange Juice
90ml (3 fl oz) Dry Ginger Ale

Pour Southern Comfort, Vodka and juice into a cocktail shaker over ice. Shake and strain into a highball glass over ice. Add Ginger Ale, stir gently and serve.

Slow Comfortable Screw – Mexican Style

9.6% ALC/VOL • 1.6 STD DRINKS

15ml (½ fl oz) Southern Comfort
15ml (½ fl oz) Sloe Gin
15ml (½ fl oz) Galliano
15ml (½ fl oz) Tequila
150ml (5 fl oz) Fresh Orange Juice

Build ingredients into a collins glass over ice then serve with a swizzle stick and straw.

Pineapple Plantation

8.3% ALC/VOL • 1.2 STD DRINKS

23ml (¾ fl oz) Southern Comfort
23ml (¾ fl oz) Amaretto
90ml (3 fl oz) Pineapple Juice
45ml (1½ fl oz) Sweet and Sour Mix

Pour Southern Comfort, Amaretto and juice into a cocktail shaker over ice. Shake and strain into a highball glass over ice. Add sour mix, stir and serve.

Southern Stirrup

7.4% ALC/VOL • 1.3 STD DRINKS

45ml (1½ fl oz) Southern Comfort
60ml (2 fl oz) Grapefruit Juice
45ml (1½ fl oz) Cranberry Juice

15ml (½ fl oz) Fresh Lemon Juice
60ml (2 fl oz) Soda Water

Pour Southern Comfort and juices into a highball glass over ice then stir. Add soda, stir gently and serve.

Comfortable Screw Up Against a Wall

13.8% ALC/VOL • 1.6 STD DRINKS

23ml (¾ fl oz) Southern Comfort
23ml (¾ fl oz) Vodka
8ml (¼ fl oz) Galliano
90ml (3 fl oz) Fresh Orange Juice

Pour ingredients into a cocktail shaker over ice and shake. Strain into a highball glass half filled with ice and serve.

Southern Banana

5.5% ALC/VOL • 1.4 STD DRINKS

30ml (1 fl oz) Southern Comfort
30ml (1 fl oz) Banana Liqueur
30ml (1 fl oz) Fresh Cream
240ml (8 fl oz) Cola

Pour Southern Comfort, Liqueur and cream into a mixing glass over ice. Stir well and strain into a chilled tall glass. Add cola, stir gently and serve.

The American Way of Pleasure

12.8% ALC/VOL • 1.7 STD DRINKS

60ml (2 fl oz) Southern Comfort
83ml (2¾ fl oz) Pineapple Juice
20ml (⅔ fl oz) Fresh Lime Juice
2 teaspoons Sugar Syrup

Pour ingredients into a cocktail shaker over cracked ice and shake. Pour into a chilled highball glass and serve.

Millennium Eclipse

16.1% ALC/VOL • 1.3 STD DRINKS

30ml (1 fl oz) Southern Comfort
20ml (⅔ fl oz) Blue Curaçao
30ml (1 fl oz) Pineapple Juice
20ml (⅔ fl oz) Fresh Lemon Juice
Slice of Lemon

Pour Southern Comfort, Curaçao and juices into a blender over crushed ice. Blend until smooth and pour into a chilled parfait glass. Garnish with a slice of lemon and serve.

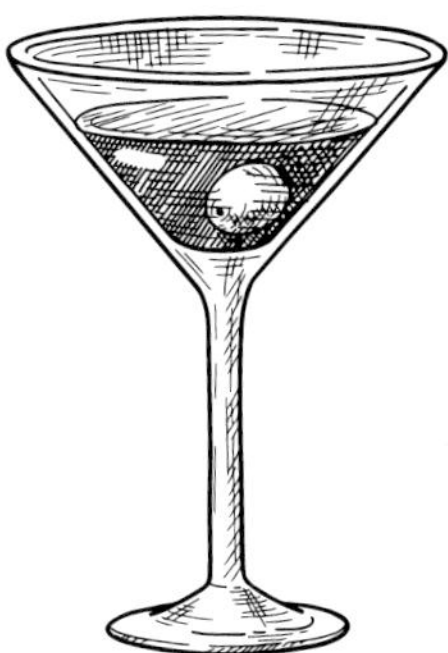

Southern Comfort Pink

24.8% ALC/VOL • 1.2 STD DRINKS

20ml (⅔ fl oz) Southern Comfort
20ml (⅔ fl oz) Bacardi
10ml (⅓ fl oz) Grenadine
10ml (⅓ fl oz) Grapefruit Juice

Pour ingredients into a cocktail shaker over ice and shake. Strain into a chilled cocktail glass and serve.

Magic's Tornado

21.1% ALC/VOL • 2.3 STD DRINKS

40ml (1⅓ fl oz) Southern Comfort
40ml (1⅓ fl oz) Vodka
30ml (1 fl oz) Fresh Lime Juice
30ml (1 fl oz) Almond Extract
Slice of Lemon

Pour Southern Comfort, Vodka, juice and extract into a cocktail shaker over cracked ice. Shake and pour into a chilled old-fashioned glass. Garnish with a slice of lemon and serve.

Grand Canard

11.1% ALC/VOL • 2 STD DRINKS

30ml (1 fl oz) Southern Comfort
30ml (1 fl oz) Tia Maria
15ml (½ fl oz) Grand Marnier
150ml (5 fl oz) Fresh Milk (chilled)

Pour ingredients into a cocktail shaker over ice and shake. Strain into a chilled zombie glass and serve.

Comfortable Squirrel

12.7% ALC/VOL • 1.5 STD DRINKS

30ml (1 fl oz) Southern Comfort
15ml (½ fl oz) Crème De Noyaux
15ml (½ fl oz) White Crème De Cacao
90ml (3 fl oz) Thick Cream
Nutmeg

Pour Southern Comfort, Noyaux, Cacao and cream into a cocktail shaker over ice. Shake and strain into an old-fashioned glass over ice. Sprinkle nutmeg on top and serve.

Slow Comfortable Screw in Between the Sheets

9.8% ALC/VOL • 1.6 STD DRINKS

15ml (½ fl oz) Southern Comfort
15ml (½ fl oz) Vodka
15ml (½ fl oz) Cointreau
15ml (½ fl oz) Sloe Gin
150ml (5 fl oz) Fresh Orange Juice

Build ingredients into a collins glass over ice then serve with a swizzle stick and straw.

Comfortable Fuzzy Screw

16.6% ALC/VOL • 3.3 STD DRINKS

45ml (1½ fl oz) Southern Comfort
45ml (1½ fl oz) Peach Schnapps
45ml (1½ fl oz) Vodka
120ml (4 fl oz) Fresh Orange Juice
Slice of Orange

Pour Southern Comfort, Schnapps and Vodka into a mixing glass over ice. Stir and strain into a highball glass over ice. Add juice and stir. Garnish with a slice of orange and serve.

Hawaiian Comfort

10.9% ALC/VOL • 1.5 STD DRINKS

30ml (1 fl oz) Southern Comfort
30ml (1 fl oz) Amaretto
30ml (1 fl oz) Grenadine
60ml (2 fl oz) Sweet and Sour Mix
30ml (1 fl oz) Pineapple Juice

Pour ingredients into a cocktail shaker over ice and shake. Strain into a margarita glass over ice and serve.

Slow Comfortable Screw on a Dogbox

17.8% ALC/VOL • 3.7 STD DRINKS

45ml (1½ fl oz) Southern Comfort
45ml (1½ fl oz) Sloe Gin
45ml (1½ fl oz) Tennessee Whiskey
5ml (1/6 fl oz) Grenadine
120ml (4 fl oz) Fresh Orange Juice

Pour ingredients into a cocktail shaker over ice and shake. Strain into a collins glass over ice and serve.

Rhubarb Syrup

21.4% ALC/VOL • 2 STD DRINKS

45ml (1½ fl oz) Southern Comfort
45ml (1½ fl oz) Kahlúa
1 scoop Vanilla Ice Cream
Grated Chocolate

Pour Southern Comfort and Kahlúa into a blender without ice then add ice cream. Blend until smooth and pour into a chilled cocktail glass. Sprinkle chocolate on top and serve.

One Exciting Night No.2

7.7% ALC/VOL • 1.5 STD DRINKS

30ml (1 fl oz) Southern Comfort
23ml (¾ fl oz) Peach Schnapps
8ml (¼ fl oz) Galliano
Dash Grenadine
180ml (6 fl oz) Fresh Orange Juice
2 Strawberries
Slice of Orange

Prepare a collins glass with a sugar frosted rim. Pour Southern Comfort, Schnapps, Galliano, Grenadine and juice into a blender over crushed ice. Blend until smooth and pour into prepared glass. Garnish with a slice of orange and strawberries then serve.

Blended Comfort

10.8% ALC/VOL • 1.1 STD DRINKS

30ml (1 fl oz) Southern Comfort
15ml (½ fl oz) Dry Vermouth
30ml (1 fl oz) Fresh Lemon Juice
30ml (1 fl oz) Fresh Orange Juice
¼ Fresh Peach (diced)
Slice of Orange
Slice of Peach

Pour Southern Comfort, Vermouth and juices into a blender without ice then add diced peach. Blend until smooth and pour into a collins glass over crushed ice then stir. Garnish with a slice of orange and peach then serve with a straw.

Malibu

Malibu was first produced in 1980 and originates from Barbados where Rum has been produced since the mid-seventeenth century.

The production of Malibu begins with mixing molasses from the island's sugar cane crops with spring water and yeast which then converts the sugar into alcohol. On completion of the fermentation process this mixture known as 'wash' is transferred into a continuous still. After distillation the Rum is stored in oak barrels to mature over one to two years. The final stage for the production of Malibu is blending the Light Rum with coconut and sugar resulting in a Light Rum-based sweet coconut-flavour Rum liqueur.

Ram

11.6% ALC/VOL • 0.9 STD DRINKS

30ml (1 fl oz) Malibu
15ml (½ fl oz) Galliano
45ml (1½ fl oz) Fresh Orange Juice
Fresh Whipped Cream

Pour Malibu, Galliano and juice into a cocktail shaker over ice. Shake and strain into a chilled champagne saucer. Float cream on top and serve.

Heat Wave

4.4% ALC/VOL • 0.9 STD DRINKS

38ml (1¼ fl oz) Malibu
15ml (½ fl oz) Peach Schnapps
15ml (½ fl oz) Grenadine
90ml (3 fl oz) Fresh Orange Juice
90ml (3 fl oz) Pineapple Juice
Slice of Peach

Pour Malibu, Schnapps and juices into a hurricane glass over ice then stir. Layer Grenadine on top and garnish with a slice of peach then serve.

Fresh Coconut

3.6% ALC/VOL • 0.6 STD DRINKS

38ml (1¼ fl oz) Malibu
3 dashes Grenadine
180ml (6 fl oz) Grapefruit Juice
3 dashes Lemon-Lime Soda

Pour Malibu and juice into a collins glass over ice then stir. Add Grenadine and soda, stir gently then serve with a straw.

Malibu Magic

7.3% ALC/VOL • 1 STD DRINK

30ml (1 fl oz) Malibu
30ml (1 fl oz) Strawberry Liqueur
60ml (2 fl oz) Fresh Cream
30ml (1 fl oz) Fresh Orange Juice
3 Strawberries (diced)
Strawberry
Twist of Orange Peel

Pour Malibu, Liqueur, cream and juice into a blender over crushed ice then add diced strawberries. Blend and pour into a chilled hurricane glass. Garnish with a strawberry and orange peel then serve.

Malibu Beach

9.7% ALC/VOL • 1.4 STD DRINKS

30ml (1 fl oz) Malibu
30ml (1 fl oz) Vodka
60ml (2 fl oz) Fresh Orange Juice
60ml (2 fl oz) Pineapple Juice

Pour ingredients into a cocktail shaker over ice and shake. Strain into a highball glass over ice and serve.

Mini Cooper

12.6% ALC/VOL • 0.7 STD DRINKS

45ml (1½ fl oz) Malibu
15ml (½ fl oz) Fresh Lemon Juice
15ml (½ fl oz) Coconut Cream

Pour ingredients into a cocktail shaker over ice and shake. Strain into a chilled cocktail glass and serve.

Eye of the Tiger

11.7% ALC/VOL • 1.8 STD DRINKS

30ml (1 fl oz) Malibu
30ml (1 fl oz) Golden Rum
15ml (½ fl oz) Dark Rum

30ml (1 fl oz) Fresh
Lemon Juice
30ml (1 fl oz) Cranberry Juice
30ml (1 fl oz) Fresh
Orange Juice
30ml (1 fl oz) Sugar Syrup
Slice of Orange

Pour Malibu, Golden Rum, juices and sugar into a cocktail shaker over ice. Shake and strain into a highball glass over ice. Layer Dark Rum on top and garnish with a slice of orange then serve.

Coconut Grove

11.9% ALC/VOL • 2.2 STD DRINKS

45ml (1½ fl oz) Malibu
30ml (1 fl oz) Banana Liqueur
30ml (1 fl oz) Light Rum
120ml (4 fl oz) Pineapple Juice
5ml (1/6 fl oz) Fresh
Lemon Juice
Maraschino Cherry
Slice of Lemon
Slice of Pineapple

Pour Malibu, Liqueur, Rum and juices into a cocktail shaker over ice. Shake and strain into a chilled collins glass. Garnish with a cherry, slice of lemon and pineapple then serve.

Storm Trooper

11.6% ALC/VOL • 2.7 STD DRINKS

60ml (2 fl oz) Malibu
60ml (2 fl oz) Vodka
180ml (6 fl oz) Fresh Milk
(chilled)

Pour ingredients into a cocktail shaker over ice and shake. Strain into a chilled tall glass and serve.

Malibu Blush

17.4% ALC/VOL • 1.4 STD DRINKS

30ml (1 fl oz) Malibu
30ml (1 fl oz) Dry Gin
Dash Banana Liqueur
Dash Campari
30ml (1 fl oz) Apple Juice
10ml (⅓ fl oz) Pineapple Juice
Dash Egg White
Maraschino Cherry

Pour Malibu, Gin, Liqueur, Campari, juices and egg white into a cocktail shaker over ice. Shake and strain into a chilled champagne flute. Garnish with a cherry and serve.

Copacabana

11.2% ALC/VOL • 1.3 STD DRINKS

20ml (⅔ fl oz) Malibu
20ml (⅔ fl oz) Banana Liqueur
20ml (⅔ fl oz) Grand Marnier
60ml (2 fl oz) Pineapple Juice
30ml (1 fl oz) Coconut Cream
Raspberry
Slice of Lemon

Pour Malibu, Liqueur, Grand Marnier, juice and cream into a cocktail shaker over ice. Shake and strain into a chilled champagne saucer. Garnish with a raspberry and slice of lemon then serve.

Sweet Dreams No.2

4.4% ALC/VOL • 1 STD DRINK

60ml (2 fl oz) Malibu
75ml (2½ fl oz) Banana Juice
75ml (2½ fl oz) Fresh
Orange Juice
75ml (2½ fl oz)
Strawberry Juice

Pour ingredients into a mixing glass over ice and stir. Strain into a chilled highball glass and serve.

Maria Mia

14.5% ALC/VOL • 1.6 STD DRINKS

45ml (1½ fl oz) Malibu
45ml (1½ fl oz) Pisang Ambon
5ml (1/6 fl oz) Amaretto
45ml (1½ fl oz) Thick Cream
Maraschino Cherry
Slice of Banana
Wedge of Lemon

Pour Malibu, Pisang Ambon, Amaretto and cream into a cocktail shaker over ice. Shake and strain into a chilled cocktail glass. Garnish with a cherry, slice of banana and wedge of lemon then serve.

Malibu Dreams

7.7% ALC/VOL • 1.5 STD DRINKS

90ml (3 fl oz) Malibu
5ml (1/6 fl oz) Grenadine
150ml (5 fl oz) Lemon-Lime
Soda

Pour Malibu and Grenadine into a mixing glass over ice. Stir and strain into a highball glass over ice. Add soda, stir gently and serve.

Bad Girl Cocktail

10.8% ALC/VOL • 1 STD DRINK

15ml (½ fl oz) Malibu
15ml (½ fl oz) Advocaat
15ml (½ fl oz) Banana Liqueur
8ml (¼ fl oz) Galliano
30ml (1 fl oz) Fresh Cream
½ Banana (diced)

Pour Malibu, Advocaat, Liqueur, Galliano and cream into a blender over crushed ice then add diced banana. Blend until smooth and pour into a chilled champagne saucer then serve.

Malibu Pop

19.7% ALC/VOL • 1.1 STD DRINKS

30ml (1 fl oz) Malibu
30ml (1 fl oz) Blue Curaçao
5ml (1/6 fl oz) Cranberry Juice
5ml (1/6 fl oz) Pineapple Juice

Pour Malibu and Curaçao into a cocktail shaker over ice. Shake and strain into a highball glass over ice. Add juices, stir and serve.

Illusion

17.2% ALC/VOL • 1.2 STD DRINKS

30ml (1 fl oz) Malibu
15ml (½ fl oz) Cointreau
15ml (½ fl oz) Midori
30ml (1 fl oz) Fresh Cream
Sprig of Fresh Mint
Wedge of Kiwi Fruit

Pour Malibu, Cointreau, Midori and cream into a cocktail shaker over ice. Shake and strain into a chilled champagne saucer. Garnish with a sprig of mint and wedge of kiwi fruit then serve.

Red Jobber

21.7% ALC/VOL • 1 STD DRINK

30ml (1 fl oz) Malibu
8ml (¼ fl oz) Banana Liqueur
8ml (¼ fl oz) Jägermeister
8ml (¼ fl oz) Strawberry Liqueur
5ml (1/6 fl oz) Grenadine

Pour ingredients into a cocktail shaker over ice and shake. Strain into a chilled cocktail glass and serve.

Happy Days

6% ALC/VOL • 1.2 STD DRINKS

30ml (1 fl oz) Malibu
30ml (1 fl oz) Peach Schnapps
15ml (½ fl oz) Advocaat
60ml (2 fl oz) Fresh Orange Juice
60ml (2 fl oz) Pineapple Juice
60ml (2 fl oz) Fresh Cream
Raspberry

Pour Malibu, Schnapps, Advocaat, juices and cream into a cocktail shaker over ice. Shake and strain into a chilled goblet. Garnish with a raspberry and serve.

Baby Aspirin

12.6% ALC/VOL • 1 STD DRINK

45ml (1½ fl oz) Malibu
15ml (½ fl oz) Triple Sec
15ml (½ fl oz) Grenadine
15ml (½ fl oz) Fresh Orange Juice
15ml (½ fl oz) Pineapple Juice

Pour ingredients into a cocktail shaker over ice and shake. Strain into a chilled cocktail glass and serve.

Malibu Massage

6.3% ALC/VOL • 0.7 STD DRINKS

15ml (½ fl oz) Malibu
15ml (½ fl oz) White Crème De Cacao
8ml (¼ fl oz) Triple Sec
30ml (1 fl oz) Fresh Milk (chilled)
2 teaspoons Coconut Syrup
60ml (2 fl oz) Lemon-Lime Soda
Cherry
Slice of Orange

Pour Malibu, Cacao, Triple Sec, milk and syrup into a cocktail shaker over cracked ice. Shake and pour into a chilled old-fashioned glass. Add soda and stir gently. Garnish with a cherry and slice of orange then serve.

A Day at the Beach

17.5% ALC/VOL • 0.8 STD DRINKS

30ml (1 fl oz) Malibu
15ml (½ fl oz) Amaretto
15ml (½ fl oz) Grenadine
Strawberry
Wedge of Pineapple

Pour Malibu and Amaretto into a cocktail shaker over cracked ice. Shake and pour into a highball glass over ice then add Grenadine – do not stir. Garnish with a strawberry and wedge of pineapple then serve.

Explorer's Reward

14.3% ALC/VOL • 1.5 STD DRINKS

40ml (1⅓ fl oz) Malibu
40ml (1⅓ fl oz) Midori
10ml (⅓ fl oz) Dry Sherry
40ml (1⅓ fl oz) Fresh Cream
Maraschino Cherry

Pour Malibu, Midori, Sherry and cream into a cocktail shaker over ice. Shake and strain into a chilled champagne saucer. Garnish with a cherry and serve.

Pink Paradise

8.5% ALC/VOL • 1.4 STD DRINKS

45ml (1½ fl oz) Malibu
30ml (1 fl oz) Amaretto
90ml (3 fl oz) Cranberry Juice
45ml (1½ fl oz) Pineapple Juice
Maraschino Cherry
Wedge of Pineapple

Pour Malibu, Amaretto and juices into a hurricane glass over ice then stir. Garnish with a cherry and wedge of pineapple then serve.

Malibu Tropicale

9.3% ALC/VOL • 1.5 STD DRINKS

30ml (1 fl oz) Malibu
30ml (1 fl oz) Banana Liqueur
30ml (1 fl oz) Midori
60ml (2 fl oz) Papaya Juice
60ml (2 fl oz) Pineapple Juice

Pour ingredients into a cocktail shaker over ice and shake. Strain into a highball glass over ice and serve.

Alien Surprise

7% ALC/VOL • 1 STD DRINK

30ml (1 fl oz) Malibu
15ml (½ fl oz) Midori
15ml (½ fl oz) Peach Schnapps
60ml (2 fl oz) Fresh Orange Juice
60ml (2 fl oz) Sweet and Sour Mix
2 Cherries

Pour Malibu, Midori, Schnapps, juice and sour mix into a cocktail shaker over ice. Shake and strain into a collins glass over ice. Garnish with cherries and serve.

Hawaii Orgasm

15.6% ALC/VOL • 1.6 STD DRINKS

30ml (1 fl oz) Malibu
18ml (3/5 fl oz) Brandy
18ml (3/5 fl oz) Vodka
30ml (1 fl oz) Cranberry Juice
30ml (1 fl oz) Pineapple Juice

Pour ingredients into a cocktail shaker over ice and shake. Strain into a chilled cocktail glass and serve.

Malibu Wipeout

14.5% ALC/VOL • 1.4 STD DRINKS

30ml (1 fl oz) Malibu
30ml (1 fl oz) Citrus Vodka
30ml (1 fl oz) Cranberry Juice
30ml (1 fl oz) Pineapple Juice
Cherry
Piece of Pineapple

Pour Malibu, Vodka and juices into a mixing glass over ice. Stir and strain into a chilled parfait glass. Garnish with a cherry and piece of pineapple then serve.

Bunny Killer

11.4% ALC/VOL • 1.9 STD DRINKS

60ml (2 fl oz) Malibu
30ml (1 fl oz) Light Rum
60ml (2 fl oz) Fresh Orange Juice
60ml (2 fl oz) Pineapple Juice
Slice of Orange

Pour Malibu, Rum and juices into a tall glass over ice then stir well. Add a slice of orange and serve.

Cool Breeze

10.1% ALC/VOL • 1.2 STD DRINKS

45ml (1½ fl oz) Malibu
15ml (½ fl oz) Light Rum
60ml (2 fl oz) Pineapple Juice
30ml (1 fl oz) Cranberry Juice
Slice of Pineapple

Pour Malibu, Rum and juices into a cocktail shaker over cracked ice. Shake and pour into a chilled highball glass. Garnish with a slice of pineapple and serve.

Light of Havana

4.7% ALC/VOL • 1 STD DRINK

30ml (1 fl oz) Malibu
30ml (1 fl oz) Midori
60ml (2 fl oz) Fresh Orange Juice
60ml (2 fl oz) Pineapple Juice
90ml (3 fl oz) Soda Water

Pour Malibu, Midori and juices into a cocktail shaker over ice. Shake and strain into a chilled highball glass. Add soda, stir gently and serve.

No Problem!

6.7% ALC/VOL • 0.9 STD DRINKS

30ml (1 fl oz) Malibu
23ml (¾ fl oz) Banana Liqueur
30ml (1 fl oz) Grapefruit Juice
30ml (1 fl oz) Fresh Orange Juice
30ml (1 fl oz) Pineapple Juice
15ml (½ fl oz) Fruit Juice
15ml (½ fl oz) Fresh Lime Juice

Pour ingredients into a cocktail shaker over cracked ice and shake. Pour into a chilled highball glass and serve.

Malibu Mocha Milkshake

12.9% ALC/VOL • 2.5 STD DRINKS

120ml (4 fl oz) Malibu
30ml (1 fl oz) Dark Crème De Cacao
90ml (3 fl oz) Fresh Milk (chilled)
2 teaspoons Sugar Syrup

Pour Malibu, milk and sugar into a blender over small amount of crushed ice. Blend until smooth and pour into a chilled highball glass over a few ice cubes. Add Cacao, stir and serve.

Caribbean Screwdriver

5.8% ALC/VOL • 1.5 STD DRINKS

30ml (1 fl oz) Malibu
30ml (1 fl oz) Banana Liqueur
30ml (1 fl oz) Peach Schnapps
120ml (4 fl oz) Fresh Orange Juice
60ml (2 fl oz) Pineapple Juice
60ml (2 fl oz) Fresh Cream
Cherry

Pour Malibu, Liqueur, Schnapps, juices and cream into a cocktail shaker over ice. Shake and strain into a chilled tall glass. Garnish with a cherry and serve.

Cointreau

Cointreau is a clear orange-flavour liqueur created in 1849 by Adolphe Cointreau and his brother Edouard-Jean in Angers, France.

Tropical sweet and bitter orange peels are distilled to create Cointreau from a secret recipe that has been passed down through the generations of the Cointreau family.

Sweet and bitter orange peels are shipped to the Cointreau distillery in Angers from the Caribbean and Spain. The peels are then macerated in alcohol for several weeks for the oils to seep from the peels. This spirit is then carefully blended before being transferred into copper stills with pure spring water. The distilling process then begins to create the clear subtle orange-flavour liqueur that is Cointreau.

Cointreau would arguably be the finest Triple Sec Curaçao and can be enjoyed neat, over ice, with mixers or as an additive in cocktails.

Monte Christo

38.5% ALC/VOL • 1.8 STD DRINKS

30ml (1 fl oz) Cointreau
30ml (1 fl oz) Citrus Vodka

Pour ingredients into a mixing glass over ice and stir. Strain into a chilled cocktail glass and serve.

Cointreau Old-Fashioned Way

37% ALC/VOL • 1.8 STD DRINKS

30ml (1 fl oz) Cointreau
30ml (1 fl oz) Brandy
2 dashes Angostura Bitters
1 teaspoon Sugar Syrup
Slice of Orange
Sprig of Fresh Mint
Strawberry

Pour Brandy into an old-fashioned glass over ice and add Bitters. Add sugar and stir then layer Cointreau on top. Garnish with a slice of orange, sprig of mint and a strawberry then serve.

Ethel Duffy Cocktail

28.6% ALC/VOL • 1.6 STD DRINKS

23ml (¾ fl oz) Cointreau
23ml (¾ fl oz) Apricot Brandy
23ml (¾ fl oz) White Crème De Menthe

Pour ingredients into a cocktail shaker over ice and shake. Strain into a chilled cocktail glass and serve.

Burning Desire

17.1% ALC/VOL • 1.4 STD DRINKS

30ml (1 fl oz) Cointreau
15ml (½ fl oz) Galliano
5ml (1/6 fl oz) Grenadine
50ml (1⅔ fl oz) Fresh Orange Juice
Dash Egg White

Pour ingredients into a cocktail shaker over ice and shake. Strain into a chilled champagne saucer and serve.

Dodge Special

37.9% ALC/VOL • 1.8 STD DRINKS

30ml (1 fl oz) Cointreau
30ml (1 fl oz) Gin
Dash Grapefruit Juice
Twist of Orange Peel

Pour Cointreau, Gin and juice into a mixing glass over ice. Stir and strain into a chilled cocktail glass. Garnish with orange peel and serve.

Crooked Sister

33.3% ALC/VOL • 2.4 STD DRINKS

30ml (1 fl oz) Cointreau
30ml (1 fl oz) Gin
30ml (1 fl oz) White Crème De Cacao
Cherry
Slice of Orange

Pour Cointreau, Gin and Cacao into a mixing glass over ice. Stir and strain into an old-fashioned glass over ice. Garnish with a cherry and slice of orange then serve.

Cointreau Sun Riser

12.6% ALC/VOL • 0.9 STD DRINKS

30ml (1 fl oz) Cointreau
5ml (1/6 fl oz) Grenadine
60ml (2 fl oz) Fresh Orange Juice
Cherry
Wedge of Lemon

Pour Cointreau into an old-fashioned glass over ice and add juice then stir. Add Grenadine – do not stir. Garnish with a cherry and wedge of lemon then serve.

Kismet Hardy

12.3% ALC/VOL • 2 STD DRINKS

30ml (1 fl oz) Cointreau
23ml (¾ fl oz) Dark Rum
15ml (½ fl oz) Amaretto
15ml (½ fl oz) Grenadine
90ml (3 fl oz) Pineapple Juice
30ml (1 fl oz) Grapefruit Juice
Cherry
Slice of Orange

Pour Cointreau, Rum, Amaretto, Grenadine and juices into a blender over crushed ice. Blend and pour into a chilled goblet. Garnish with a cherry and slice of orange then serve.

Mainbrace

25.6% ALC/VOL • 1.8 STD DRINKS

30ml (1 fl oz) Cointreau
30ml (1 fl oz) Gin
30ml (1 fl oz) Grapefruit Juice

Pour ingredients into a cocktail shaker over ice and shake. Strain into a chilled cocktail glass and serve.

Life Saver

15.6% ALC/VOL • 1.7 STD DRINKS

30ml (1 fl oz) Cointreau
15ml (½ fl oz) Brandy
15ml (½ fl oz) White Crème De Menthe
15ml (½ fl oz) Grapefruit Juice
60ml (2 fl oz) Tonic Water
Slice of Orange
Sprig of Fresh Mint

Pour Cointreau, Brandy, Crème De Menthe and juice into a cocktail shaker over ice. Shake and strain into a goblet over ice. Add tonic and stir gently. Garnish with a slice of orange and sprig of mint then serve.

Dangerous Liaisons

26.6% ALC/VOL • 1.6 STD DRINKS

30ml (1 fl oz) Cointreau
30ml (1 fl oz) Tia Maria
15ml (½ fl oz) Sweet and Sour Mix

Pour ingredients into a cocktail shaker over ice and shake. Strain into a chilled sherry glass and serve.

Riviera

29.5% ALC/VOL • 2.8 STD DRINKS

60ml (2 fl oz) Cointreau
30ml (1 fl oz) Bacardi
30ml (1 fl oz) Fresh Lemon Juice
Twist of Lemon Peel

Pour Cointreau, Bacardi and juice into an old-fashioned glass over ice then stir. Garnish with lemon peel and serve.

Knee Breaker

29.5% ALC/VOL • 1.8 STD DRINKS

30ml (1 fl oz) Cointreau
30ml (1 fl oz) Parfait Amour
15ml (½ fl oz) Peter Heering Liqueur
Dash Frangelico

Pour ingredients into a cocktail shaker over ice and shake. Strain into a chilled cocktail glass and serve.

Lady Scarlet

31% ALC/VOL • 1.7 STD DRINKS

20ml (⅔ fl oz) Cointreau
20ml (⅔ fl oz) Gin
10ml (⅓ fl oz) Angostura Bitters
10ml (⅓ fl oz) Dry Vermouth
10ml (⅓ fl oz) Fresh Lime Juice
Cherry
Twist of Lemon Peel

Pour Cointreau, Gin, Bitters, Vermouth and juice into a cocktail shaker over ice. Shake and strain into a chilled cocktail glass. Garnish with a cherry and lemon peel then serve.

Broadway Smile

33.4% ALC/VOL • 3.6 STD DRINKS

45ml (1½ fl oz) Cointreau
45ml (1½ fl oz) Crème De Cassis
45ml (1½ fl oz) Swedish Punsch

Pour ingredients in order given into a cocktail glass – do not stir, then serve.

Coffee No.1

25.6% ALC/VOL • 1.8 STD DRINKS

30ml (1 fl oz) Cointreau
30ml (1 fl oz) Brandy
30ml (1 fl oz) Black Coffee (chilled)
Strawberry

Pour Cointreau, Brandy and coffee into a cocktail shaker over ice. Shake and strain into a chilled cocktail glass. Garnish with a strawberry and serve.

Lover's Delight

37.3% ALC/VOL • 4 STD DRINKS

45ml (1½ fl oz) Cointreau
45ml (1½ fl oz) Brandy

45ml (1½ fl oz) Forbidden Fruit

Pour ingredients into a cocktail shaker over ice and shake. Strain into a chilled cocktail glass and serve.

Hot Dream

16.4% ALC/VOL • 1.4 STD DRINKS

30ml (1 fl oz) Cointreau
15ml (½ fl oz) Galliano
30ml (1 fl oz) Pineapple Juice
30ml (1 fl oz) Fresh Cream

Pour ingredients into a cocktail shaker over ice and shake. Strain into a chilled champagne saucer and serve.

Between the Sheets

28.8% ALC/VOL • 1.4 STD DRINKS

15ml (½ fl oz) Cointreau
15ml (½ fl oz) Brandy
15ml (½ fl oz) Light Rum
15ml (½ fl oz) Fresh Lemon Juice

Pour ingredients into a cocktail shaker over ice and shake. Strain into a chilled cocktail glass and serve.

Kamikaze

30.4% ALC/VOL • 1.8 STD DRINKS

30ml (1 fl oz) Cointreau
30ml (1 fl oz) Vodka
15ml (½ fl oz) Fresh Lemon Juice
Dash Lime Syrup
Slice of Lemon
Slice of Orange

Pour Cointreau, Vodka, juice and syrup into a cocktail shaker over ice. Shake and strain into a chilled cocktail glass. Garnish with a slice of lemon and orange then serve.

Duval

39.4% ALC/VOL • 2.8 STD DRINKS

60ml (2 fl oz) Cointreau
30ml (1 fl oz) Sambuca

Pour ingredients into a mixing glass over ice and stir. Strain into a chilled cocktail glass and serve.

Angel Delight

20.8% ALC/VOL • 1.8 STD DRINKS

30ml (1 fl oz) Cointreau
30ml (1 fl oz) Gin
Dash Grenadine
50ml (1⅔ fl oz) Fresh Cream

Pour ingredients into a cocktail shaker over ice and shake. Strain into a chilled champagne saucer and serve.

Per F'amour

17% ALC/VOL • 1.2 STD DRINKS

30ml (1 fl oz) Cointreau
15ml (½ fl oz) Parfait Amour
45ml (1½ fl oz) Fresh Orange Juice
Dash Egg White

Pour ingredients into a cocktail shaker over ice and shake. Strain into a chilled cocktail glass and serve.

Golden Sunset

18.1% ALC/VOL • 2 STD DRINKS

38ml (1¼ fl oz) Cointreau
38ml (1¼ fl oz) White Crème De Cacao
5ml (⅙ fl oz) Galliano
38ml (1¼ fl oz) Thick Cream
23ml (¾ fl oz) Fresh Orange Juice
Cherry
½ Slice of Orange

Pour Cointreau, Cacao, Galliano, cream and juice into a cocktail shaker over ice. Shake and strain into a chilled cocktail glass. Garnish with a cherry and ½ slice of orange then serve.

Crazy Tip

17.2% ALC/VOL • 0.9 STD DRINKS

30ml (1 fl oz) Cointreau
40ml (1⅓ fl oz) Coconut Cream

Pour ingredients into a cocktail shaker over ice and shake. Strain into a chilled cocktail glass and serve.

Harrison Ford

24% ALC/VOL • 2.3 STD DRINKS

48ml (1⅗ fl oz) Cointreau
24ml (⅘ fl oz) Scotch Whisky
48ml (1⅗ fl oz) Grenadine
Olive
Twist of Lemon Peel

Pour Cointreau, Whisky and Grenadine into a cocktail shaker over ice. Shake and strain into a chilled cocktail glass. Twist lemon peel above drink and discard remainder of peel. Garnish with an olive and serve.

Platinum Blonde

31.2% ALC/VOL • 1.8 STD DRINKS

30ml (1 fl oz) Cointreau
30ml (1 fl oz) Light Rum
15ml (½ fl oz) Thick Cream

Pour ingredients into a cocktail shaker over ice and shake. Strain into a chilled cocktail glass and serve.

Petite Fleur

25.2% ALC/VOL • 1.8 STD DRINKS

30ml (1 fl oz) Cointreau
30ml (1 fl oz) Light Rum
30ml (1 fl oz) Grapefruit Juice
½ teaspoon Sugar Syrup
Maraschino Cherry

Pour Cointreau, Rum, juice and sugar into a cocktail shaker over ice. Shake and strain into a chilled cocktail glass. Garnish with a cherry and serve.

Tight Lips

30.8% ALC/VOL • 1.8 STD DRINKS

30ml (1 fl oz) Cointreau
30ml (1 fl oz) Bacardi
15ml (½ fl oz) Grenadine
Dash Egg White

Pour ingredients into a cocktail shaker over ice and shake. Strain into a chilled cocktail glass and serve.

Bush Peak

19.1% ALC/VOL • 2.8 STD DRINKS

23ml (¾ fl oz) Cointreau
23ml (¾ fl oz) Brandy
23ml (¾ fl oz) Galliano
23ml (¾ fl oz) Grand Marnier
Dash Grenadine
90ml (3 fl oz) Fresh Orange Juice

Pour Cointreau, Brandy, Galliano, Grand Marnier and juice into a cocktail shaker over ice. Shake and strain into a highball glass over ice. Add Grenadine – do not stir, then serve.

Deauville Cocktail

31.6% ALC/VOL • 0.9 STD DRINKS

15ml (½ fl oz) Cointreau
15ml (½ fl oz) Apple Brandy
8ml (¼ fl oz) Fresh Lemon Juice

Pour ingredients into a cocktail shaker over ice and shake. Strain into a chilled cocktail glass and serve.

Sunburnt

16.1% ALC/VOL • 1.4 STD DRINKS

30ml (1 fl oz) Cointreau
25ml (5/6 fl oz) Peachtree
5ml (1/6 fl oz) Grenadine
5ml (1/6 fl oz) Fresh Lemon Juice
½ Fresh Peach (diced)

Pour Grenadine into a chilled cocktail glass then pour Cointreau, Peachtree and juice into a blender without ice. Add diced peach and blend until smooth. Add crushed ice and blend briefly. Pour into glass over Grenadine – do not stir, then serve.

Cross Bow

33.3% ALC/VOL • 2.4 STD DRINKS

30ml (1 fl oz) Cointreau
30ml (1 fl oz) Dark Crème De Cacao
30ml (1 fl oz) Gin

Pour ingredients into a mixing glass over ice and stir. Strain into a chilled cocktail glass and serve.

Caribbean Cocktail

35.8% ALC/VOL • 2.1 STD DRINKS

30ml (1 fl oz) Cointreau
30ml (1 fl oz) Brandy
15ml (½ fl oz) Orange Curaçao
Wedge of Orange

Pour Cointreau, Brandy and Curaçao into a mixing glass over ice. Stir and strain into a chilled cocktail glass. Garnish with a wedge of orange and serve.

Deauville

29.3% ALC/VOL • 1.4 STD DRINKS

15ml (½ fl oz) Cointreau
15ml (½ fl oz) Brandy
15ml (½ fl oz) Pernod
15ml (½ fl oz) Fresh Lemon Juice

Pour ingredients into a cocktail shaker over ice and shake. Strain into a chilled cocktail glass and serve.

Top of the Sheets

37.5% ALC/VOL • 2.7 STD DRINKS

30ml (1 fl oz) Cointreau
30ml (1 fl oz) Bacardi
30ml (1 fl oz) Brandy
Dash Fresh Lemon Juice
Dash Egg White
2 Maraschino Cherries

Pour Cointreau, Bacardi, Brandy, juice and egg white into a cocktail shaker over ice. Shake and strain into a chilled cocktail glass. Garnish with cherries and serve.

Silent Third

26.7% ALC/VOL • 1.9 STD DRINKS

30ml (1 fl oz) Cointreau
30ml (1 fl oz) Scotch Whisky
30ml (1 fl oz) Fresh Lemon Juice

Pour ingredients into a cocktail shaker over ice and shake. Strain into a chilled cocktail glass and serve.

Fun-Ski

15.4% ALC/VOL • 1.8 STD DRINKS

30ml (1 fl oz) Cointreau

30ml (1 fl oz) Dry Gin
60ml (2 fl oz) Coconut Cream
30ml (1 fl oz) Thick Cream
Maraschino Cherry
Pineapple Leaf
Slice of Orange

Pour Cointreau, Gin and creams into a blender over crushed ice. Blend and pour into a chilled goblet. Garnish with a cherry, pineapple leaf and slice of orange then serve.

Countdown

34% ALC/VOL • 1.4 STD DRINKS

45ml (1½ fl oz) Cointreau
8ml (¼ fl oz) Fresh Lime Juice

Pour ingredients into a cocktail shaker over ice and shake. Strain into a chilled cocktail glass and serve.

Golden Lilly

38% ALC/VOL • 2.7 STD DRINKS

30ml (1 fl oz) Cointreau
30ml (1 fl oz) Brandy
30ml (1 fl oz) Gin
Dash Pernod

Pour ingredients into a cocktail shaker over ice and shake. Strain into an old-fashioned glass half filled with ice and serve.

Neopolitan

39.5% ALC/VOL • 3.7 STD DRINKS

60ml (2 fl oz) Cointreau
30ml (1 fl oz) Grand Marnier
30ml (1 fl oz) Light Rum

Pour ingredients into a cocktail shaker over ice and shake. Strain into a chilled cocktail glass and serve.

Odd McIntyre

23.6% ALC/VOL • 1.7 STD DRINKS

23ml (¾ fl oz) Cointreau
23ml (¾ fl oz) Brandy
23ml (¾ fl oz) Lillet
23ml (¾ fl oz) Fresh Lemon Juice

Pour ingredients into a mixing glass over ice and stir. Strain into a chilled cocktail glass and serve.
This drink is also known as Hoopla.

Hibernian Special

33.7% ALC/VOL • 2.4 STD DRINKS

30ml (1 fl oz) Cointreau
30ml (1 fl oz) Gin
30ml (1 fl oz) Green Curaçao
Dash Fresh Lemon Juice

Pour ingredients into a cocktail shaker over ice and shake. Strain into a chilled cocktail glass and serve.

The Trip

43.9% ALC/VOL • 2.6 STD DRINKS

25ml (5/6 fl oz) Cointreau
25ml (5/6 fl oz) Green Chartreuse
25ml (5/6 fl oz) Kirsch
Cherry

Place a cherry into a chilled cocktail glass then pour Cointreau, Chartreuse and Kirsch into a mixing glass over ice. Stir and strain into glass over cherry then serve.

Foxi Cocktail

19.3% ALC/VOL • 1.8 STD DRINKS

30ml (1 fl oz) Cointreau
30ml (1 fl oz) Dark Rum
60ml (2 fl oz) Pineapple Juice

Pour ingredients into a blender over cracked ice and blend. Strain into a chilled champagne saucer and serve.

Bubble Yum

14.5% ALC/VOL • 1.5 STD DRINKS

30ml (1 fl oz) Cointreau
30ml (1 fl oz) Banana Liqueur
60ml (2 fl oz) Fresh Cream
2 teaspoons Raspberry Syrup

Pour ingredients into a cocktail shaker over ice and shake. Strain into a chilled champagne saucer and serve.

White Lily Cocktail

37.9% ALC/VOL • 2.1 STD DRINKS

23ml (¾ fl oz) Cointreau
23ml (¾ fl oz) Gin
23ml (¾ fl oz) Light Rum
Dash Anisette

Pour ingredients into a cocktail shaker over ice and shake. Strain into a chilled cocktail glass and serve.

French Kiss No.2

17.2% ALC/VOL • 1.8 STD DRINKS

30ml (1 fl oz) Cointreau
30ml (1 fl oz) Kahlúa
15ml (½ fl oz) Galliano
60ml (2 fl oz) Fresh Cream
Nutmeg

Pour Cointreau, Kahlúa and cream into a cocktail shaker over ice. Shake and strain into a chilled champagne saucer. Layer Galliano on top and ignite. Extinguish flame and sprinkle nutmeg on top then serve.

Beverly's Hills

37.6% ALC/VOL • 2 STD DRINKS

45ml (1½ fl oz) Cointreau
15ml (½ fl oz) Cognac
8ml (¼ fl oz) Kahlúa

Pour ingredients into a blender over cracked ice and blend. Strain into a chilled cocktail glass and serve.

Monkey's Tail

21.8% ALC/VOL • 1.9 STD DRINKS

30ml (1 fl oz) Cointreau

30ml (1 fl oz) Lemon Vodka
30ml (1 fl oz) Fresh Cream
20ml (⅔ fl oz) Apricot Nectar

Pour ingredients into a cocktail shaker over ice and shake. Strain into a chilled cocktail glass and serve.

Wallis Blue Cocktail

25.6% ALC/VOL • 1.8 STD DRINKS

30ml (1 fl oz) Cointreau
30ml (1 fl oz) Dry Gin
30ml (1 fl oz) Fresh Lime Juice

Prepare an old-fashioned glass with a sugar frosted rim – moistened with lime juice. Pour ingredients into a cocktail shaker over ice and shake. Strain into prepared glass and serve.

Strawberry Daze

15.7% ALC/VOL • 1.9 STD DRINKS

30ml (1 fl oz) Cointreau
20ml (⅔ fl oz) Strawberry Liqueur
20ml (⅔ fl oz) Tequila
45ml (1½ fl oz) Fresh Orange Juice
4 Strawberries (diced)
Strawberry

Pour Cointreau, Liqueur, Tequila and juice into a blender over crushed ice then add diced strawberries. Blend and pour into a chilled champagne saucer. Garnish with a strawberry and serve.

Highland Morning

17.2% ALC/VOL • 2.1 STD DRINKS

38ml (1¼ fl oz) Cointreau
30ml (1 fl oz) Scotch Whisky
90ml (3 fl oz) Grapefruit Juice

Pour ingredients into a mixing glass over cracked ice and stir. Pour into a chilled old-fashioned glass and serve.

North Polar

33.9% ALC/VOL • 2.4 STD DRINKS

30ml (1 fl oz) Cointreau
30ml (1 fl oz) Campari
30ml (1 fl oz) Gin
Slice of Orange

Pour Cointreau, Campari and Gin into a mixing glass over ice. Stir and strain into an old-fashioned glass over ice. Garnish with a slice of orange and serve.

Apricot Orange

16.7% ALC/VOL • 1.4 STD DRINKS

40ml (1⅓ fl oz) Cointreau
10ml (⅓ fl oz) Apricot Brandy
30ml (1 fl oz) Apricot Nectar
30ml (1 fl oz) Fresh Orange Juice

Pour ingredients into a cocktail shaker over ice and shake. Strain into a chilled cocktail glass and serve.

Lord Ashley Cocktail

17.4% ALC/VOL • 1.2 STD DRINKS

15ml (½ fl oz) Cointreau
15ml (½ fl oz) Advocaat
15ml (½ fl oz) Banana Liqueur
15ml (½ fl oz) White Crème De Cacao
30ml (1 fl oz) Fresh Cream
Slice of Banana
Slice of Orange

Pour Cointreau, Advocaat, Liqueur, Cacao and cream into a cocktail shaker over ice. Shake and strain into a chilled goblet. Garnish with a slice of banana and orange then serve.

Pacific Pacifier

25.8% ALC/VOL • 1.2 STD DRINKS

30ml (1 fl oz) Cointreau
15ml (½ fl oz) Banana Liqueur
15ml (½ fl oz) Fresh Cream

Pour ingredients into a cocktail shaker over cracked ice and shake. Pour into a chilled old-fashioned glass and serve.

Zadec

25.6% ALC/VOL • 1.8 STD DRINKS

30ml (1 fl oz) Cointreau
30ml (1 fl oz) Vodka
30ml (1 fl oz) Black Coffee (chilled)

Pour ingredients into a cocktail shaker over ice and shake. Strain into a chilled cocktail glass and serve.

Blanche

33% ALC/VOL • 2 STD DRINKS

30ml (1 fl oz) Cointreau
30ml (1 fl oz) Anisette
15ml (½ fl oz) White Curaçao

Pour ingredients into a cocktail shaker over ice and shake. Strain into a chilled cocktail glass and serve.

Hoopla

23.6% ALC/VOL • 1.7 STD DRINKS

This drink is also known as Odd McIntyre, p 370.

V.I.P. No.2

32.7% ALC/VOL • 2.3 STD DRINKS

30ml (1 fl oz) Cointreau
30ml (1 fl oz) Bourbon
30ml (1 fl oz) Dry Vermouth
Slice of Orange

Pour Cointreau, Bourbon and Vermouth into a mixing glass over ice. Stir and strain into a chilled cocktail glass. Garnish with a slice of orange and serve.

Mer du Sud

9.7% ALC/VOL • 1.5 STD DRINKS

40ml (1⅓ fl oz) Cointreau
10ml (⅓ fl oz) Blue Curaçao
40ml (1⅓ fl oz) Pineapple Juice
100ml (3⅓ fl oz) Dry Ginger Ale

Pour Cointreau, Curaçao and juice into a mixing glass over ice. Stir and strain into a highball glass over ice. Add Ginger Ale, stir gently and serve.

London Kamikaze

30.8% ALC/VOL • 1.8 STD DRINKS

30ml (1 fl oz) Cointreau
30ml (1 fl oz) Gin
15ml (½ fl oz) Rose's Lime Juice

Pour ingredients into a cocktail shaker over ice and shake. Strain into a chilled cocktail glass and serve.

Nomad

20.3% ALC/VOL • 1.4 STD DRINKS

30ml (1 fl oz) Cointreau
30ml (1 fl oz) Midori
30ml (1 fl oz) Fresh Lemon Juice

Pour ingredients into a cocktail shaker over ice and shake. Strain into a chilled cocktail glass and serve.

Kiss of Sweetness

20.3% ALC/VOL • 1.8 STD DRINKS

40ml (1⅓ fl oz) Cointreau
30ml (1 fl oz) Midori
40ml (1⅓ fl oz) Fresh Lime Juice

Pour ingredients into a cocktail shaker over ice and shake. Strain into a chilled cocktail glass and serve.

Schnapps

Schnapps is a German word and is the generic term for white (clear) Brandies that are distilled from fruits. Commercial Schnapps produced today are being produced from alcohol that is created from grain or potato mash and flavoured with a variety of fruits and herbs during the distilling process with the majority also adding glycerine and sugar syrup solutions to sweeten their products, thus producing a product that is more of a liqueur than traditional Schnapps. Schnapps is also often referred to as an infused Gin or Vodka.

Traditional Schnapps is served straight in small glasses and are swallowed in one gulp much like a shot.

There are a vast variety of Schnapps produced from very sweet through to dry. The % alc/vol of Schnapps varies significantly between the many varieties available, for the purpose of calculating % alc/vol for Schnapps recipes 20% alc/vol has been used due to the majority of commercial Schnapps that are being sold are in the vicinity of this mark – so only use as a guide.

American Apple Pie

2.1% ALC/VOL • 0.5 STD DRINKS

30ml (1 fl oz) Cinnamon Schnapps
250ml (8⅓ fl oz) Apple Juice

Pour ingredients into a chilled highball glass, stir and serve.

Sweet Tooth

15.7% ALC/VOL • 1.1 STD DRINKS

30ml (1 fl oz) Butterscotch Schnapps
15ml (½ fl oz) Frangelico
15ml (½ fl oz) Vandermint
30ml (1 fl oz) Fresh Cream
Grated Chocolate

Pour Schnapps, Frangelico, Vandermint and cream into a cocktail shaker over ice. Shake and strain into a chilled goblet. Sprinkle chocolate on top and serve.

Silk Stocking

13.5% ALC/VOL • 1 STD DRINK

30ml (1 fl oz) Butterscotch Schnapps
15ml (½ fl oz) Advocaat
15ml (½ fl oz) White Crème De Cacao
30ml (1 fl oz) Fresh Cream
Grated Chocolate

Pour Schnapps, Advocaat, Cacao and cream into a cocktail shaker over ice. Shake and strain into a chilled goblet. Sprinkle chocolate on top and serve.

Strawberry Fetish

6.7% ALC/VOL • 1 STD DRINK

45ml (1½ fl oz) Strawberry Schnapps
15ml (½ fl oz) Frangelico
8ml (¼ fl oz) Grenadine
30ml (1 fl oz) Whipping Cream
60ml (2 fl oz) Lemonade
30ml (1 fl oz) Soda Water
Strawberry

Pour Schnapps, Frangelico, Grenadine and cream into a cocktail shaker over ice. Shake and strain into a collins glass over cracked ice. Add lemonade and soda then stir gently. Garnish with a strawberry and serve.

Blue Glory

7% ALC/VOL • 1.2 STD DRINKS

60ml (2 fl oz) Peppermint Schnapps
15ml (½ fl oz) Blue Curaçao
150ml (5 fl oz) Bitter-Lemon Soda

Pour Schnapps and Curaçao into a highball glass over ice then stir. Add soda, stir gently and serve.

Merlin's Love Potion

25.6% ALC/VOL • 1.7 STD DRINKS

60ml (2 fl oz) Watermelon Schnapps
15ml (½ fl oz) Lemon Vodka
8ml (¼ fl oz) Strawberry Brandy
Slice of Lemon
Strawberry

Pour Schnapps, Vodka and Brandy into a cocktail shaker over ice. Shake and strain into a champagne saucer filled with crushed ice. Garnish with a slice of lemon and a strawberry then serve with 2 short straws.

Peach Tree Climber

17.7% ALC/VOL • 1.3 STD DRINKS

30ml (1 fl oz) Peach Schnapps
30ml (1 fl oz) White Crème De Cacao
15ml (½ fl oz) Peppermint Schnapps
½ scoop Vanilla Ice Cream

Pour Schnapps and Cacao into a blender over small amount of crushed ice then add ice cream. Blend until smooth and pour into a chilled cocktail glass then serve.

Munchausen

8.1% ALC/VOL • 1.7 STD DRINKS

45ml (1½ fl oz) Watermelon Schnapps
30ml (1 fl oz) Lemon Vodka
5ml (⅙ fl oz) Grenadine
60ml (2 fl oz) Mandarin Juice
60ml (2 fl oz) Pineapple Juice
60ml (2 fl oz) Lemonade

Pour Schnapps, Vodka, Grenadine and juices into a cocktail shaker over ice. Shake and strain into a collins glass over cracked ice. Add lemonade, stir gently and serve.

Strawberry Fields Forever

9% ALC/VOL • 1.4 STD DRINKS

60ml (2 fl oz) Strawberry Schnapps
15ml (½ fl oz) Brandy
120ml (4 fl oz) Soda Water
Strawberry

Pour Schnapps and Brandy into a highball glass over ice then stir. Add soda and stir gently. Garnish with a strawberry and serve.

Peppermint Schnapps Fizz

11.3% ALC/VOL • 1.8 STD DRINKS

30ml (1 fl oz) Peppermint Schnapps
45ml (1½ fl oz) Gin
30ml (1 fl oz) Fresh Lemon Juice
1 teaspoon Caster Sugar
90ml (3 fl oz) Soda Water
Slice of Lemon
Sprig of Fresh Mint

Pour Schnapps, Gin and juice into a cocktail shaker over ice then add sugar. Shake and strain into a highball glass over ice. Add soda and stir gently. Garnish with a slice of lemon and sprig of mint then serve.

Allota Something

25.1% ALC/VOL • 2.7 STD DRINKS

45ml (1½ fl oz) Butterscotch Schnapps
45ml (1½ fl oz) Bailey's Irish Cream
45ml (1½ fl oz) Light Rum

Pour ingredients into a mixing glass over ice and stir. Strain into a chilled cocktail glass and serve.

Apple Granny Crisp

10.9% ALC/VOL • 1.1 STD DRINKS

30ml (1 fl oz) Apple Schnapps
15ml (½ fl oz) Bailey's Irish Cream
15ml (½ fl oz) Brandy
2 scoops Vanilla Ice Cream
Fresh Whipped Cream
Cinnamon

Pour Schnapps, Bailey's and Brandy into a blender over cracked ice then add ice cream. Blend and strain into a chilled parfait glass. Float cream on top and sprinkle cinnamon over cream then serve.

German Bight

12.2% ALC/VOL • 1.2 STD DRINKS

30ml (1 fl oz) Apple Schnapps
15ml (½ fl oz) Bärenfang
10ml (⅓ fl oz) Dry Vermouth
10ml (⅓ fl oz) Sweet Vermouth
60ml (2 fl oz) Pineapple Juice

Pour ingredients into a cocktail shaker over ice and shake. Strain into a chilled cocktail glass and serve.

Peach Cicel

10.3% ALC/VOL • 1.4 STD DRINKS

60ml (2 fl oz) Peach Schnapps
30ml (1 fl oz) Vanilla Schnapps
60ml (2 fl oz) Peach Sherbet
15ml (½ fl oz) Fresh Whipped Cream
Slice of Peach (diced)
Maraschino Cherry

Pour Schnapps into a blender over small amount of crushed ice then add sherbet and diced peach. Blend until smooth and pour into a chilled champagne saucer. Float cream on top and garnish with a cherry then serve.

Apocalypse

26.7% ALC/VOL • 1.7 STD DRINKS

30ml (1 fl oz) Peppermint Schnapps
23ml (¾ fl oz) Kahlúa
15ml (½ fl oz) Bourbon
15ml (½ fl oz) Vodka

Pour ingredients into a mixing glass over ice and stir. Strain into a chilled cocktail glass and serve.

Peach Up

8.7% ALC/VOL • 1.3 STD DRINKS

30ml (1 fl oz) Peach Schnapps
30ml (1 fl oz) Dry Vermouth
15ml (½ fl oz) Gin
120ml (4 fl oz) Lemonade

Pour Schnapps, Vermouth and Gin into a highball glass over ice then stir. Add lemonade, stir gently and serve.

Something Different

8% ALC/VOL • 1.1 STD DRINKS

30ml (1 fl oz) Peach Schnapps
30ml (1 fl oz) Amaretto
60ml (2 fl oz) Cranberry Juice
60ml (2 fl oz) Pineapple Juice

Pour ingredients into a cocktail shaker over ice and shake. Strain into a highball glass over ice and serve.

Jug Wobbler

11.5% ALC/VOL • 1.8 STD DRINKS

30ml (1 fl oz) Apple Schnapps
30ml (1 fl oz) Gin
15ml (½ fl oz) Dry Vermouth
8ml (¼ fl oz) Pernod
120ml (4 fl oz) Lemonade

Pour Schnapps, Gin, Vermouth and Pernod into a highball glass over ice then stir. Add lemonade, stir gently and serve.

The Brass Fiddle

10.4% ALC/VOL • 1.7 STD DRINKS

60ml (2 fl oz) Peach Schnapps
23ml (¾ fl oz) Tennessee Whiskey
30ml (1 fl oz) Grenadine
60ml (2 fl oz) Pineapple Juice
30ml (1 fl oz) Fresh Orange Juice
Cherry
Slice of Pineapple

Pour Grenadine into a chilled parfait glass and swirl around glass. Pour Schnapps, Whiskey and juices into a blender over crushed ice. Blend until smooth and pour into prepared glass over Grenadine – do not stir. Garnish with a cherry and slice of pineapple then serve.

Twin Peach

6.7% ALC/VOL • 1 STD DRINK

60ml (2 fl oz) Peach Schnapps
120ml (4 fl oz) Cranberry Juice
Slice of Peach

Pour Schnapps and juice into a highball glass over ice then stir. Garnish with a slice of peach and serve.

Chocolate Mint

7.7% ALC/VOL • 0.9 STD DRINKS

30ml (1 fl oz) Peppermint Schnapps
15ml (½ fl oz) Vodka
45ml (1½ fl oz) Fresh Milk (chilled)
2 scoops Chocolate Ice Cream

Pour Schnapps, Vodka and milk into a blender without ice then add ice cream. Blend until smooth and pour into an old-fashioned glass over ice, stir then serve.

Wolf's Lair

22% ALC/VOL • 1.8 STD DRINKS

30ml (1 fl oz) Peach Schnapps
30ml (1 fl oz) Brandy
15ml (½ fl oz) Bärenfang
30ml (1 fl oz) Fresh Cream

Pour ingredients into a cocktail shaker over ice and shake. Strain into a chilled champagne flute and serve.

Peach Melba

6.7% ALC/VOL • 0.7 STD DRINKS

30ml (1 fl oz) Peach Schnapps
15ml (½ fl oz) Black Raspberry Liqueur
90ml (3 fl oz) Fresh Cream
Slice of Peach

Pour Schnapps, Liqueur and cream into a cocktail shaker over cracked ice. Shake and pour into a chilled old-fashioned glass. Garnish with a slice of peach and serve with 2 short straws.

Apple Pie No.2

20% ALC/VOL • 1.5 STD DRINKS

90ml (3 fl oz) Apple Schnapps
5ml (1/6 fl oz) Cinnamon Schnapps
Slice of Apple
Cinnamon

Pour Schnapps into an old-fashioned glass over ice and stir. Sprinkle cinnamon on top and garnish with a slice of apple then serve.

Orange Blossom Special

1.9% ALC/VOL • 0.5 STD DRINKS

30ml (1 fl oz) Peach Schnapps
90ml (3 fl oz) Orange Sherbet
75ml (2½ fl oz) Fresh Cream
75ml (2½ fl oz) Lemon-Lime Soda
1½ scoops Vanilla Ice Cream
Cherry
Slice of Orange

Pour Schnapps and cream into a blender over small amount of crushed ice. Add sherbet and ice cream. Blend and pour into a chilled tall glass. Add soda and stir gently. Garnish with a cherry and slice of orange then serve.

Peppermint Twist

20.6% ALC/VOL • 1.2 STD DRINKS

30ml (1 fl oz) Peppermint Schnapps
30ml (1 fl oz) Kahlúa
15ml (½ fl oz) Dark Crème De Cacao

Pour ingredients into a cocktail shaker over ice and shake. Strain into a chilled cocktail glass and serve.

Peppermint Stick

14.4% ALC/VOL • 1.5 STD DRINKS

45ml (1½ fl oz) Peppermint Schnapps
45ml (1½ fl oz) White Crème De Cacao
45ml (1½ fl oz) Fresh Cream
Cherry

Pour Schnapps, Cacao and cream into a cocktail shaker over ice. Shake and strain into a chilled champagne flute. Garnish with a cherry and serve.

Peach Flip

10.9% ALC/VOL • 0.9 STD DRINKS

60ml (2 fl oz) Peach Schnapps
1 teaspoon Sugar Syrup
1 Fresh Egg
Nutmeg

Pour Schnapps, sugar and egg into a cocktail shaker over ice. Shake and strain into a chilled goblet. Sprinkle nutmeg on top and serve.

Tennessee Waltz

2.9% ALC/VOL • 0.6 STD DRINKS

38ml (1¼ fl oz) Peach Schnapps
60ml (2 fl oz) Pineapple Juice
30ml (1 fl oz) Passion-Fruit Juice
4 scoops Vanilla Ice Cream
Fresh Whipped Cream
Strawberry

Pour Schnapps and juices into a blender without ice then add ice cream. Blend until smooth and pour into a chilled parfait glass. Float cream on top and garnish with a strawberry then serve.

Strawberry Sunrise

6.2% ALC/VOL • 1 STD DRINK

60ml (2 fl oz) Strawberry Schnapps
15ml (½ fl oz) Grenadine
120ml (4 fl oz) Fresh Orange Juice

Pour ingredients into a cocktail shaker over ice and shake. Strain into a chilled brandy balloon and serve.

Guesswork Cocktail

11.8% ALC/VOL • 1.3 STD DRINKS

30ml (1 fl oz) Peach Schnapps
23ml (¾ fl oz) Gin
10ml (⅓ fl oz) Dry Sherry
30ml (1 fl oz) Passion-Fruit Juice
30ml (1 fl oz) Pineapple Juice
15ml (½ fl oz) Fresh Lime Juice

Pour ingredients into a cocktail shaker over ice and shake. Strain into a chilled cocktail glass and serve.

Spanish Fly No.2

17.5% ALC/VOL • 1.7 STD DRINKS

30ml (1 fl oz) Butterscotch Schnapps
30ml (1 fl oz) Vanilla Schnapps
30ml (1 fl oz) Cherry Liqueur
30ml (1 fl oz) Cola

Pour Schnapps and Liqueur into an old-fashioned glass over ice then stir. Add cola, stir gently and serve.

Shindig

7.5% ALC/VOL • 0.7 STD DRINKS

45ml (1½ fl oz) Peppermint Schnapps
75ml (2½ fl oz) Fresh Orange Juice
Cherry
Slice of Orange

Pour Schnapps and juice into a cocktail shaker over cracked ice. Shake and pour into a chilled old-fashioned glass. Garnish with a cherry and slice of orange then serve.

Simpatico

11.1% ALC/VOL • 1.8 STD DRINKS

60ml (2 fl oz) Peppermint Schnapps
30ml (1 fl oz) Light Rum
120ml (4 fl oz) Bitter-Lemon Soda
Slice of Lemon

Pour Schnapps and Rum into a collins glass over ice then stir. Add soda and stir gently. Garnish with a slice of lemon and serve.

Sex on the Pool Table

15.5% ALC/VOL • 2 STD DRINKS

30ml (1 fl oz) Peach Schnapps
30ml (1 fl oz) Chambord
30ml (1 fl oz) Midori
30ml (1 fl oz) Triple Sec
30ml (1 fl oz) Grapefruit Juice

Pour ingredients into a cocktail shaker over cracked ice and shake. Pour into a chilled highball glass and serve.

Kaiser's Jest

14.4% ALC/VOL • 1 STD DRINK

30ml (1 fl oz) Peppermint Schnapps
30ml (1 fl oz) White Crème De Cacao
1 scoop Vanilla Ice Cream

Pour Schnapps and Cacao into a blender over small amount of crushed ice then add ice cream. Blend until smooth and pour into a chilled champagne saucer then serve with 2 straws.

Wellidian

18.3% ALC/VOL • 4.8 STD DRINKS

120ml (4 fl oz) Apple Schnapps
100ml (3⅓ fl oz) Jamaica Rum
60ml (2 fl oz) Kiwi Juice
53ml (1¾ fl oz) Orange Soda
Slice of Kiwi Fruit
Slice of Orange

Pour Schnapps, Rum and juice into a mixing glass over ice. Stir and strain into a chilled tall glass. Add soda and stir gently. Garnish with a slice of kiwi fruit and orange then serve.

Smurfs Up

4.9% ALC/VOL • 1.2 STD DRINKS

45ml (1½ fl oz) Tropical Schnapps
15ml (½ fl oz) Vodka
240ml (8 fl oz) Pineapple Juice

Pour ingredients into a chilled tall glass over a few ice cubes, stir and serve.

Peach Nehi

16.6% ALC/VOL • 1 STD DRINK

23ml (¾ fl oz) Peach Schnapps
23ml (¾ fl oz) Vodka
23ml (¾ fl oz) Sweet and Sour Mix
5ml (⅙ fl oz) Pineapple Juice
5ml (⅙ fl oz) Lemonade

Pour Schnapps, Vodka, sour mix and juice into a cocktail shaker over ice. Shake and strain into an old-fashioned glass over ice. Add lemonade, stir gently and serve.

Burning Sun

5.5% ALC/VOL • 0.7 STD DRINKS

45ml (1½ fl oz) Strawberry Schnapps
120ml (4 fl oz) Pineapple Juice
Strawberry

Pour Schnapps and juice into a highball glass over ice then stir. Garnish with a strawberry and serve.

Blended Georgia Peach

6.6% ALC/VOL • 1 STD DRINK

23ml (¾ fl oz) Peach Schnapps
23ml (¾ fl oz) Vodka
90ml (3 fl oz) Fresh Orange Juice
60ml (2 fl oz) Peach Nectar
Slice of Peach

Pour Schnapps, Vodka, juice and nectar into a blender over crushed ice. Blend and pour into a chilled highball glass. Garnish with a slice of peach and serve.

Peppermint Lemonade

2.8% ALC/VOL • 0.4 STD DRINKS

23ml (¾ fl oz) Peppermint Schnapps
23ml (¾ fl oz) Fresh Lemon Juice
120ml (4 fl oz) Soda Water

Pour Schnapps and juice into an old-fashioned glass over ice then stir. Add soda, stir gently and serve.

Montana Fire

21.4% ALC/VOL • 2.8 STD DRINKS

60ml (2 fl oz) Cinnamon Schnapps
60ml (2 fl oz) Peppermint Schnapps
30ml (1 fl oz) Tequila
15ml (½ fl oz) Tabasco Sauce

Pour ingredients into a mixing glass over ice and stir. Strain into a chilled highball glass and serve.

Firecracker

21.3% ALC/VOL • 1.5 STD DRINKS

45ml (1½ fl oz) Cinnamon Schnapps
45ml (1½ fl oz) Cherry Brandy
Dash Tabasco Sauce
Cinnamon

Pour Schnapps, Brandy and sauce into a cocktail shaker over ice. Shake and strain into a chilled old-fashioned glass. Sprinkle cinnamon on top and serve.

Elf Tea

3.7% ALC/VOL • 0.4 STD DRINKS

15ml (½ fl oz) Peppermint Schnapps
15ml (½ fl oz) Bailey's Irish Cream
120ml (4 fl oz) Strong Black Tea (chilled)

Pour ingredients into a mixing glass over ice and stir. Strain into an old-fashioned glass over ice and serve.

Thursday Night Juice Break

3.3% ALC/VOL • 0.7 STD DRINKS

45ml (1½ fl oz) Peach Schnapps
90ml (3 fl oz) Fresh Orange Juice
45ml (1½ fl oz) Grapefruit Juice
5ml (1/6 fl oz) Maraschino Cherry Juice
90ml (3 fl oz) Lemonade
Maraschino Cherry

Pour Schnapps and juices into a highball glass over ice then stir. Add lemonade and stir gently. Garnish with a cherry and serve.

Fuzzy Melonberry

5.1% ALC/VOL • 1 STD DRINK

30ml (1 fl oz) Peach Schnapps
30ml (1 fl oz) Midori
180ml (6 fl oz) Cranberry Juice

Pour ingredients into a highball glass over ice, stir and serve.

Summer Peach

9.5% ALC/VOL • 1.3 STD DRINKS

30ml (1 fl oz) Peach Schnapps
30ml (1 fl oz) Vodka
60ml (2 fl oz) Cranberry Juice
60ml (2 fl oz) Fresh Orange Juice

Pour ingredients into a cocktail shaker over ice and shake. Strain into a highball glass over ice and serve. *This drink is also known as Pierced Navel.*

Get Fruity

15.3% ALC/VOL • 1.4 STD DRINKS

30ml (1 fl oz) Lemon Schnapps
30ml (1 fl oz) Midori
30ml (1 fl oz) Tropical Schnapps
30ml (1 fl oz) Lemon-Lime Soda

Pour Schnapps and Midori into a highball glass half filled with ice then stir. Add soda, stir gently and serve.

Orange Climax

8.2% ALC/VOL • 0.9 STD DRINKS

30ml (1 fl oz) Peach Schnapps
15ml (½ fl oz) Tennessee Whiskey
60ml (2 fl oz) Pineapple Juice
30ml (1 fl oz) Fresh Orange Juice
Fresh Whipped Cream

Pour Schnapps, Whiskey and juices into a cocktail shaker over ice. Shake and strain into a chilled old-fashioned glass. Float cream on top and serve.

Kooch

10% ALC/VOL • 0.5 STD DRINKS

30ml (1 fl oz) Peppermint Schnapps
30ml (1 fl oz) Clam Juice
Wedge of Onion

Pour Schnapps and juice into an old-fashioned glass then stir. Garnish with a wedge of onion and serve.

Just Peachy

13.3% ALC/VOL • 1.9 STD DRINKS

120ml (4 fl oz) Peach Schnapps
60ml (2 fl oz) Iced Tea

Pour ingredients into a mixing glass over ice and stir. Strain into a highball glass over ice and serve.

Peachy

13.2% ALC/VOL • 1.9 STD DRINKS

120ml (4 fl oz) Peach Schnapps
60ml (2 fl oz) Grapefruit Juice
2 dashes Fresh Lime Juice
2 Slices of Banana
2 Wedges of Peach

Pour Schnapps and juices into a cocktail shaker over ice. Shake and strain into a hurricane glass half filled with crushed ice then stir. Add slices of banana and wedges of peach then serve with a straw.

Rocky Mountain Cooler

4% ALC/VOL • 0.7 STD DRINKS

45ml (1½ fl oz) Peach Schnapps
120ml (4 fl oz) Pineapple Juice
60ml (2 fl oz) Lemon-Lime Soda

Pour Schnapps and juice into a collins glass over ice then stir. Add soda, stir gently and serve.

A Thumb in the Air

20% ALC/VOL • 2.4 STD DRINKS

30ml (1 fl oz) Blueberry Schnapps
30ml (1 fl oz) Butterscotch Schnapps
30ml (1 fl oz) Cinnamon Schnapps
30ml (1 fl oz) Peach Schnapps
30ml (1 fl oz) Peppermint Schnapps

Pour ingredients into a mixing glass over ice and stir. Strain into a chilled old-fashioned glass and serve.

Peach Beseech

13.1% ALC/VOL • 1.9 STD DRINKS

45ml (1½ fl oz) Peach Schnapps
30ml (1 fl oz) Vodka
15ml (½ fl oz) White Crème De Cacao
90ml (3 fl oz) Fresh Milk (chilled)

Pour ingredients into a cocktail shaker over ice and shake. Strain into a collins glass half filled with ice and serve.

Roadbasher

14.2% ALC/VOL • 1.6 STD DRINKS

60ml (2 fl oz) Peach Schnapps
23ml (¾ fl oz) Vodka
30ml (1 fl oz) Apple Juice
30ml (1 fl oz) Pineapple Juice
Dash Maple Syrup

Pour Schnapps and Vodka into a highball glass over ice then stir. Pour juices into a cocktail shaker over ice and shake. Strain gently into glass over first mixture and add syrup, stir then serve.

Holland Calling

9.5% ALC/VOL • 1.3 STD DRINKS

30ml (1 fl oz) Peach Schnapps
30ml (1 fl oz) Vodka
120ml (4 fl oz) Soda Water

Pour Schnapps and Vodka into a tall glass over ice then stir. Add soda, stir gently and serve.

Apple-Snake Ride

26.3% ALC/VOL • 3 STD DRINKS

30ml (1 fl oz) Apple Schnapps
30ml (1 fl oz) Amaretto
30ml (1 fl oz) Cointreau
30ml (1 fl oz) Vodka
23ml (¾ fl oz) Fresh Lime Juice

Pour ingredients into a mixing glass over ice and stir. Strain into a chilled old-fashioned glass and serve.

Berry Melon

15.3% ALC/VOL • 0.7 STD DRINKS

30ml (1 fl oz) Blackberry Schnapps
15ml (½ fl oz) Midori
15ml (½ fl oz) Fresh Orange Juice

Pour ingredients into a cocktail shaker over ice and shake. Strain into an old-fashioned glass over ice and serve.

Y.M.C.A.

21.1% ALC/VOL • 2 STD DRINKS

60ml (2 fl oz) Peach Schnapps
30ml (1 fl oz) Banana Liqueur
30ml (1 fl oz) Midori

Pour ingredients into a cocktail shaker over ice and shake. Strain into a chilled cocktail glass and serve.

Cinnamon Kiss

15% ALC/VOL • 0.7 STD DRINKS

45ml (1½ fl oz) Cinnamon Schnapps
15ml (½ fl oz) Grenadine

Pour ingredients into a mixing glass over ice and stir. Strain into a cocktail glass over ice and serve.

Pierced Navel

9.5% ALC/VOL • 1.3 STD DRINKS

This drink is also known as Summer Peach, p 377.

Betsy Clear

7.6% ALC/VOL • 1.3 STD DRINKS

30ml (1 fl oz) Peach Schnapps
30ml (1 fl oz) Vodka
165ml (5½ fl oz) Lemonade
Wedge of Orange

Pour Schnapps and Vodka into a highball glass over ice then stir. Add lemonade and stir gently. Garnish with a wedge of orange and serve.

Pee Pee

19% ALC/VOL • 1.3 STD DRINKS

30ml (1 fl oz) Peach Schnapps
30ml (1 fl oz) Vodka
30ml (1 fl oz) Pineapple Juice
Wedge of Lemon

Pour Schnapps, Vodka and juice into a highball glass filled with ice then stir. Garnish with a wedge of lemon and serve.

Herby

5.4% ALC/VOL • 0.8 STD DRINKS

20ml (⅔ fl oz) Blackberry Schnapps
10ml (⅓ fl oz) Dry Gin
10ml (⅓ fl oz) Triple Sec
150ml (5 fl oz) Tonic Water

Pour Schnapps, Gin and Triple Sec into a cocktail shaker over ice. Shake and strain into a highball glass over ice. Add tonic, stir gently and serve.

Mint Ice Cream Soda

1.5% ALC/VOL • 0.4 STD DRINKS

23ml (¾ fl oz) Peppermint Schnapps
105ml (3½ fl oz) Fresh Milk (chilled)
2 scoops Vanilla Ice Cream
120ml (4 fl oz) Soda Water

Pour Schnapps and milk into a chilled collins glass. Add ice cream and stir well to combine ingredients. Add soda, stir gently and serve.

Cat Nip

6.7% ALC/VOL • 0.5 STD DRINKS

30ml (1 fl oz) Apple Schnapps
30ml (1 fl oz) Lemonade
30ml (1 fl oz) Lemon-Lime Soda

Pour Schnapps into an old-fashioned glass over ice and add lemonade. Add soda, stir gently and serve.

Mad Hatter

14.3% ALC/VOL • 1.4 STD DRINKS

30ml (1 fl oz) Peach Schnapps
30ml (1 fl oz) Vodka
30ml (1 fl oz) Cola
30ml (1 fl oz) Lemonade

Pour Schnapps and Vodka into a cocktail shaker over ice. Shake and strain into a chilled old-fashioned glass then add cola. Add lemonade, stir gently and serve.

Golden Star

11% ALC/VOL • 1 STD DRINK

30ml (1 fl oz) Vanilla Schnapps
23ml (¾ fl oz) Amaretto
2 scoops Vanilla Ice Cream

Pour Schnapps and Amaretto into a blender without ice then add ice cream. Blend until smooth and pour into a chilled parfait glass then serve.

Something Peachie

7.5% ALC/VOL • 1.5 STD DRINKS

23ml (¾ fl oz) Peach Schnapps
23ml (¾ fl oz) Triple Sec
23ml (¾ fl oz) Vodka
90ml (3 fl oz) Fresh Orange Juice
90ml (3 fl oz) Pineapple Juice
Cherry
Slice of Orange

Pour Schnapps, Triple Sec, Vodka and juices into a cocktail shaker over ice. Shake and strain into a tall glass over ice. Garnish with a cherry and slice of orange then serve.

Strawberry Stripper

5.8% ALC/VOL • 1.3 STD DRINKS

45ml (1½ fl oz) Strawberry Schnapps
30ml (1 fl oz) Triple Sec
210ml (7 fl oz) Fresh Orange Juice

Pour juice, Schnapps and Triple Sec into a chilled highball glass – do not stir, then serve.

Short Dog Cooler

5% ALC/VOL • 0.9 STD DRINKS

60ml (2 fl oz) Peach Schnapps
120ml (4 fl oz) Pineapple Juice
60ml (2 fl oz) Lemon-Lime Soda
Slice of Pineapple

Pour Schnapps and juice into a cocktail shaker over ice. Shake and strain into a collins glass over ice. Add soda and stir gently. Garnish with a slice of pineapple and serve.

Alpenglühen

9.8% ALC/VOL • 0.3 STD DRINKS

20ml (⅔ fl oz) Blackberry Schnapps
20ml (⅔ fl oz) Fresh Orange Juice
Dash Fresh Cream

Pour Schnapps and juice into a mixing glass over ice. Stir and strain into a chilled cocktail glass. Add cream – do not stir, then serve.

Arctic Sunset

10.9% ALC/VOL • 2.8 STD DRINKS

60ml (2 fl oz) Peppermint Schnapps
60ml (2 fl oz) Rye Whiskey
150ml (5 fl oz) Cranberry Juice
60ml (2 fl oz) Fresh Orange Juice

Pour Schnapps, Whiskey and cranberry juice into a mixing glass over ice. Stir and strain into a chilled tall glass over a few ice cubes. Add orange juice - do not stir, then serve with a swizzle stick.

BCC

20% ALC/VOL • 1.3 STD DRINKS

40ml (1⅓ fl oz) Blackberry Schnapps
10ml (⅓ fl oz) Cognac
10ml (⅓ fl oz) Cointreau
20ml (⅔ fl oz) Grenadine

Pour ingredients into a cocktail shaker over ice and shake. Strain into a chilled cocktail glass and serve.

Andrea's Violent Orgasm

11.7% ALC/VOL • 2.8 STD DRINKS

120ml (4 fl oz) Peach Schnapps
30ml (1 fl oz) Vodka
150ml (5 fl oz) Mango Juice

Pour Schnapps and Vodka into a tall glass over ice then stir. Add juice, stir well and serve.

Breath Freshener

25.6% ALC/VOL • 1.8 STD DRINKS

60ml (2 fl oz) Peppermint Schnapps
30ml (1 fl oz) Vodka
Peppermint Candy Leaf

Place candy leaf into a chilled old-fashioned glass then pour Schnapps and Vodka into a mixing glass over ice. Stir and strain into glass over candy then serve.

Midnight Lemonade

5.3% ALC/VOL • 0.7 STD DRINKS

45ml (1½ fl oz) Raspberry Schnapps
120ml (4 fl oz) Lemonade
5ml (⅙ fl oz) Lemon-Lime Soda
Wedge of Lemon

Pour Schnapps into a collins glass filled with ice and add lemonade then stir gently. Add soda – do not stir, then garnish with a wedge of lemon and serve.

Apple Cola

5.6% ALC/VOL • 1.4 STD DRINKS

40ml (1⅓ fl oz) Apple Schnapps
40ml (1⅓ fl oz) Triple Sec
240ml (8 fl oz) Cola
Wedge of Apple

Pour Schnapps and Triple Sec into a chilled tall glass then stir. Add cola and stir gently. Garnish with a wedge of apple and serve.

Blue Popsicle

16% ALC/VOL • 1.9 STD DRINKS

45ml (1½ fl oz) Blueberry Schnapps
30ml (1 fl oz) Blue Curaçao
30ml (1 fl oz) Triple Sec
45ml (1½ fl oz) Sweet and Sour Mix

Pour ingredients into a blender over large amount of crushed ice and blend. Pour into a chilled tall glass and serve with a straw.

Nokia

10.2% ALC/VOL • 0.8 STD DRINKS

30ml (1 fl oz) Blackberry Schnapps
10ml (⅓ fl oz) Vodka
40ml (1⅓ fl oz) Fresh Milk (chilled)
Yolk of 1 Egg

Pour ingredients into a cocktail shaker over ice and shake. Strain into a chilled champagne flute and serve.

B-Bob

7% ALC/VOL • 1.5 STD DRINKS

40ml (1⅓ fl oz) Peach Schnapps
30ml (1 fl oz) Bacardi
20ml (⅔ fl oz) Grenadine
165ml (5½ fl oz) Fresh Orange Juice
20ml (⅔ fl oz) Fresh Lime Juice

Pour ingredients into a cocktail shaker over ice and shake. Strain into a chilled highball glass and serve.

Peppermint Tonic

2% ALC/VOL • 0.5 STD DRINKS

30ml (1 fl oz) Peppermint Schnapps
23ml (¾ fl oz) Fresh Lemon Juice
240ml (8 fl oz) Tonic Water
Twist of Lemon Peel

Pour Schnapps and juice into a mixing glass over ice. Stir and strain into a chilled highball glass. Add tonic and stir gently. Garnish with lemon peel and serve.

Green Dreams

2.3% ALC/VOL • 0.4 STD DRINKS

23ml (¾ fl oz) Peppermint Schnapps
60ml (2 fl oz) Fresh Orange Juice
60ml (2 fl oz) Pineapple Juice
53ml (1¾ fl oz) Passion-Fruit Juice
Slice of Pineapple

Pour Schnapps and juices into a cocktail shaker over ice. Shake and strain into a chilled highball glass. Garnish with a slice of pineapple and serve.

Carrot Cake

26.9% ALC/VOL • 1 STD DRINK

15ml (½ fl oz) Butterscotch Schnapps
15ml (½ fl oz) Bailey's Irish Cream
15ml (½ fl oz) Goldschläger

Pour ingredients into a mixing glass over ice and stir. Strain into a chilled brandy balloon and serve.

Dick-in-the-Dirt

36.1% ALC/VOL • 2.6 STD DRINKS

30ml (1 fl oz) Peach Schnapps
15ml (½ fl oz) 151-Proof Bacardi
15ml (½ fl oz) Southern Comfort
15ml (½ fl oz) Yukon Jack
5ml (1/6 fl oz) Grand Marnier
5ml (1/6 fl oz) Cranberry Juice
5ml (1/6 fl oz) Pineapple Juice

Pour ingredients into a tall glass over ice, stir well and serve.

Shavetail

8.6% ALC/VOL • 0.7 STD DRINKS

45ml (1½ fl oz) Peppermint Schnapps
30ml (1 fl oz) Pineapple Juice
30ml (1 fl oz) Fresh Cream

Pour ingredients into a cocktail shaker over ice and shake. Strain into a chilled highball glass and serve.

Frozen Fuzzy

10.6% ALC/VOL • 0.7 STD DRINKS

30ml (1 fl oz) Peach Schnapps
15ml (½ fl oz) Triple Sec
15ml (½ fl oz) Grenadine
15ml (½ fl oz) Fresh Lime Juice
5ml (1/6 fl oz) Lemon-Lime Soda
Slice of Lime

Pour Schnapps, Triple Sec, Grenadine and juice into a blender over large amount of crushed ice. Blend until slushy and pour into a chilled cocktail glass. Add soda and stir gently. Garnish with a slice of lime and serve.

C Spot

3% ALC/VOL • 0.8 STD DRINKS

45ml (1½ fl oz) Peach Schnapps
300ml (10 fl oz) Cranberry Juice
Slice of Orange

Pour Schnapps and juice into a chilled tall glass then stir. Garnish with a slice of orange and serve.

Lady Kiss

2.1% ALC/VOL • 0.3 STD DRINKS

20ml (⅔ fl oz) Peach Schnapps
75ml (2½ fl oz) Peach Nectar
60ml (2 fl oz) Fresh Orange Juice
40ml (1⅓ fl oz) Passion-Fruit Juice

Pour ingredients into a cocktail shaker over ice and shake. Strain into a highball glass over ice and serve with a straw.

Misty Sunset

20.5% ALC/VOL • 0.4 STD DRINKS

20ml (⅔ fl oz) Peach Schnapps
Dash Orange Bitters
Dash Red Curaçao

Pour ingredients into an old-fashioned glass filled with ice, stir and serve.

Crypto Nugget

22.5% ALC/VOL • 1 STD DRINK

23ml (¾ fl oz) Apple Schnapps
15ml (½ fl oz) Vodka
8ml (¼ fl oz) Blue Curaçao
8ml (¼ fl oz) Fresh Lime Juice

Pour ingredients into a cocktail shaker over cracked ice and shake. Pour into a chilled sour glass and serve.

Audra's Navel

8% ALC/VOL • 1.9 STD DRINKS

120ml (4 fl oz) Peach Schnapps
180ml (6 fl oz) Mango Juice
Maraschino Cherry

Pour Schnapps and juice into a collins glass over ice then stir. Garnish with a cherry and serve.

Lil Lolita

13.2% ALC/VOL • 1.3 STD DRINKS

23ml (¾ fl oz) Blackberry Schnapps
23ml (¾ fl oz) Blue Curaçao
23ml (¾ fl oz) Red Curaçao
53ml (1¾ fl oz) Fresh Orange Juice

Pour ingredients into a blender over cracked ice and blend. Pour into a chilled old-fashioned glass and serve.

Blues Club

5% ALC/VOL • 0.9 STD DRINKS

60ml (2 fl oz) Blueberry Schnapps
60ml (2 fl oz) Fresh Orange Juice
120ml (4 fl oz) Soda Water

Pour Schnapps and juice into a highball glass over ice then stir. Add soda, stir gently and serve.

Blue Light Special

8.4% ALC/VOL • 0.8 STD DRINKS

23ml (¾ fl oz) Apple Schnapps
8ml (¼ fl oz) Blue Curaçao
8ml (¼ fl oz) Vodka
75ml (2½ fl oz) Pineapple Juice

Pour ingredients into a cocktail shaker over ice and shake. Strain into a chilled cocktail glass and serve.

New Wave

10% ALC/VOL • 0.5 STD DRINKS

30ml (1 fl oz) Peach Schnapps
20ml (⅔ fl oz) Pineapple Juice
10ml (⅓ fl oz) Fresh Cream

Pour ingredients into a cocktail shaker over ice and shake. Strain into a chilled cocktail glass and serve.

Cherry Cheese Cake

5% ALC/VOL • 0.9 STD DRINKS

60ml (2 fl oz) Vanilla Schnapps
150ml (5 fl oz) Cranberry Juice
30ml (1 fl oz) Cherry Juice

Pour ingredients into a cocktail shaker over cracked ice and shake. Pour into a chilled highball glass and serve.

Vanillacream

5% ALC/VOL • 0.3 STD DRINKS

20ml (⅔ fl oz) Vanilla Schnapps
40ml (1⅓ fl oz) Pineapple Juice
20ml (⅔ fl oz) Fresh Cream

Pour ingredients into a cocktail shaker over ice and shake. Strain into a chilled cocktail glass and serve.

Flower Power

19.1% ALC/VOL • 0.7 STD DRINKS

20ml (⅔ fl oz) Peach Schnapps
20ml (⅔ fl oz) Coconut Liqueur
5ml (1/6 fl oz) Soda Water

Pour Schnapps and Liqueur into a mixing glass over ice. Stir and strain into a chilled cocktail glass. Add soda – do not stir, then serve.

Touchdown Tea

4.4% ALC/VOL • 0.9 STD DRINKS

60ml (2 fl oz) Peach Schnapps
180ml (6 fl oz) Iced Tea
30ml (1 fl oz) Fresh Lemon Juice

Pour Schnapps and juice into a mixing glass over ice. Stir and strain into a chilled highball glass. Add tea, stir and serve.

Index

B

D

G

M

N

O

First published in 2022 by New Holland Publishers
Sydney

Level 1, 178 Fox Valley Road, Wahroonga, NSW 2076, Australia

newhollandpublishers.com

A record of this book is held at the National Library of Australia.

ISBN 9781760795245

Group Managing Director: Fiona Schultz
Designer: Andrew Davies
Production Director: Arlene Gippert
Printed in China

10 9 8 7 6 5 4 3 2 1

Keep up with New Holland Publishers:

NewHollandPublishers

@newhollandpublishers